Magus of the Library

Mitsu Izumi

Based on *Kafna of the Wind*
Written by Sophie Schwimm • Translated by Taito Hamada

5

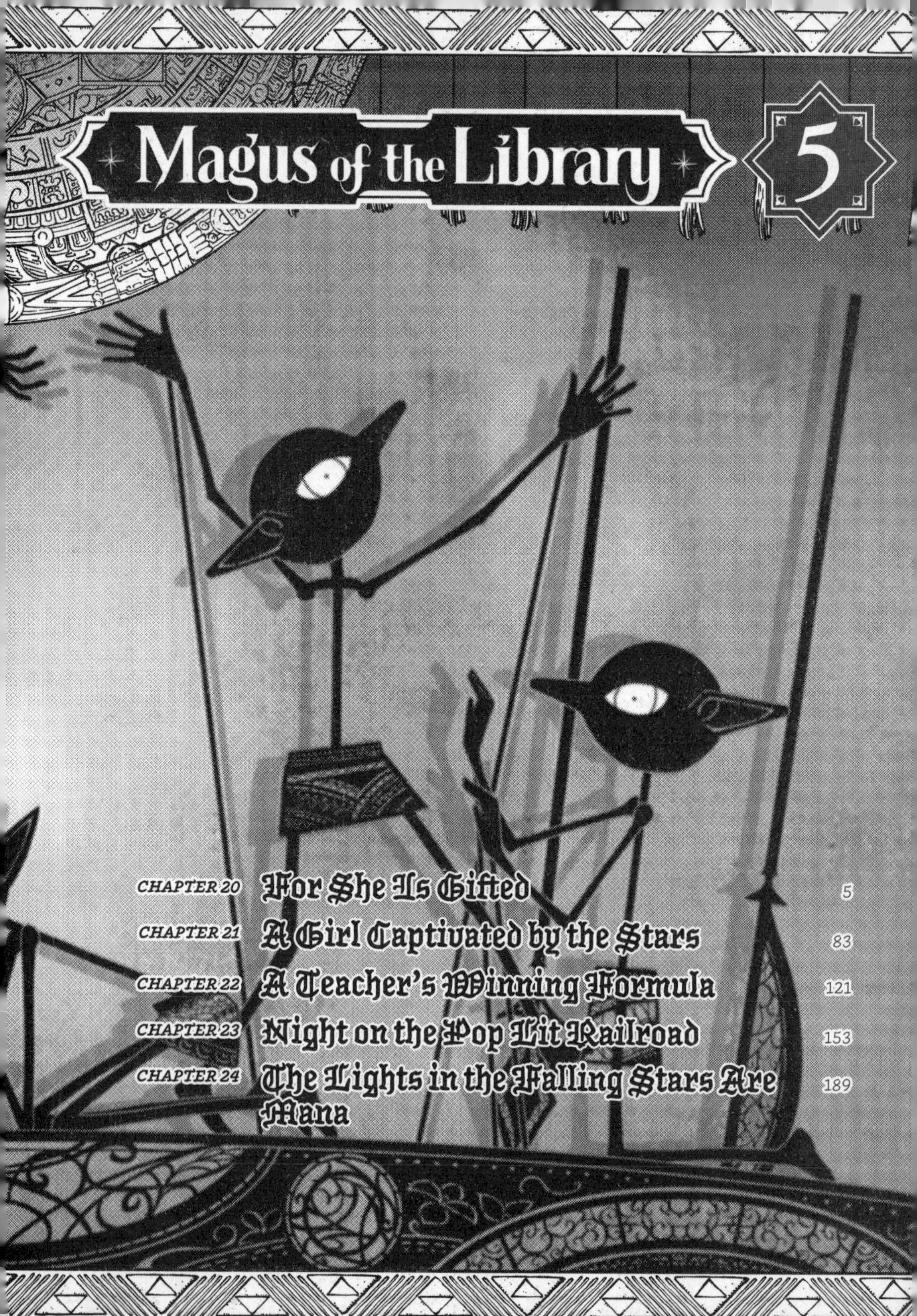

Magus of the Library 5

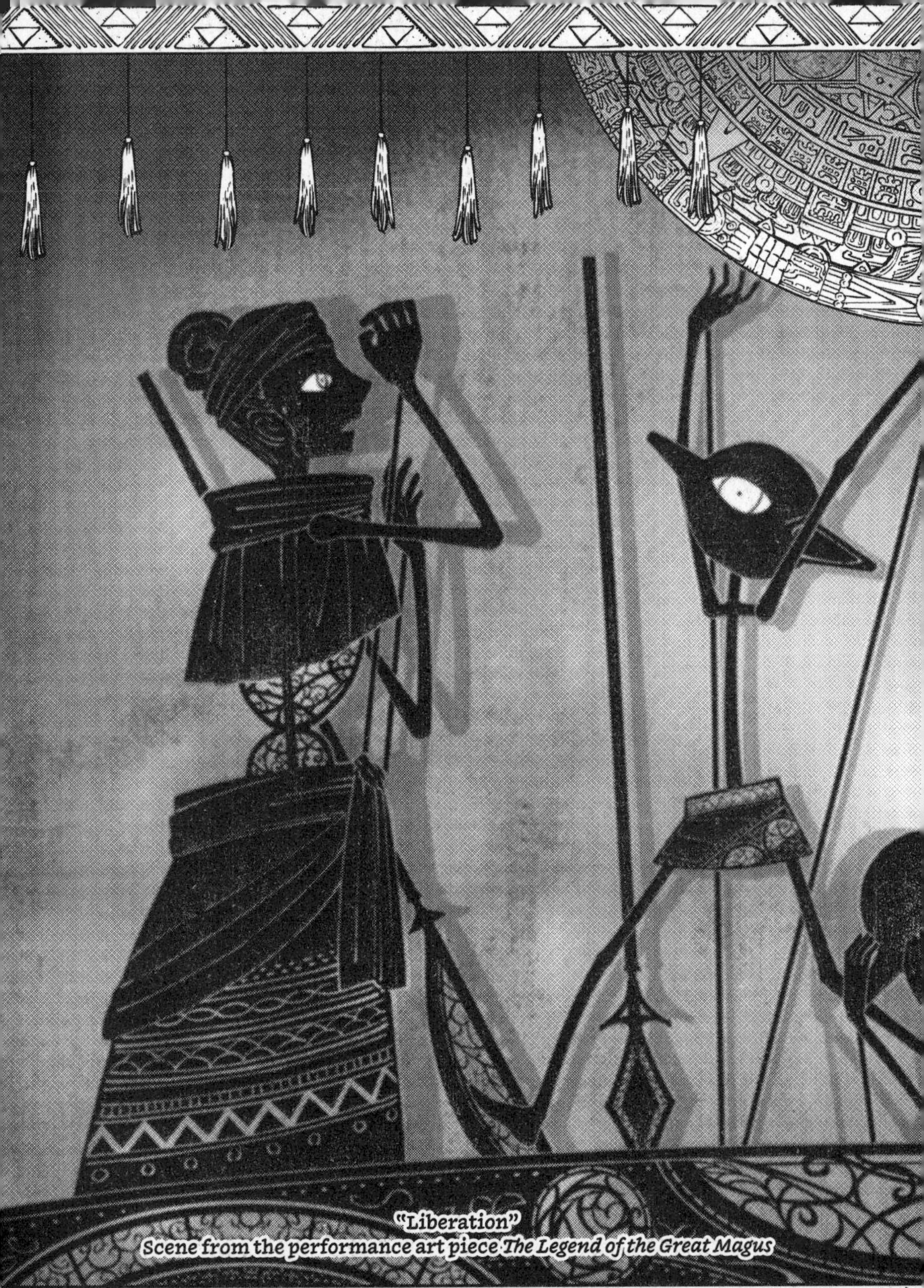

"Liberation"
Scene from the performance art piece *The Legend of the Great Magus*

The "truth" is merely a compilation of events.
It is not always the case that the events
compiled are themselves true.

—Zarud Voynix
The Man Known as the Great Thinker

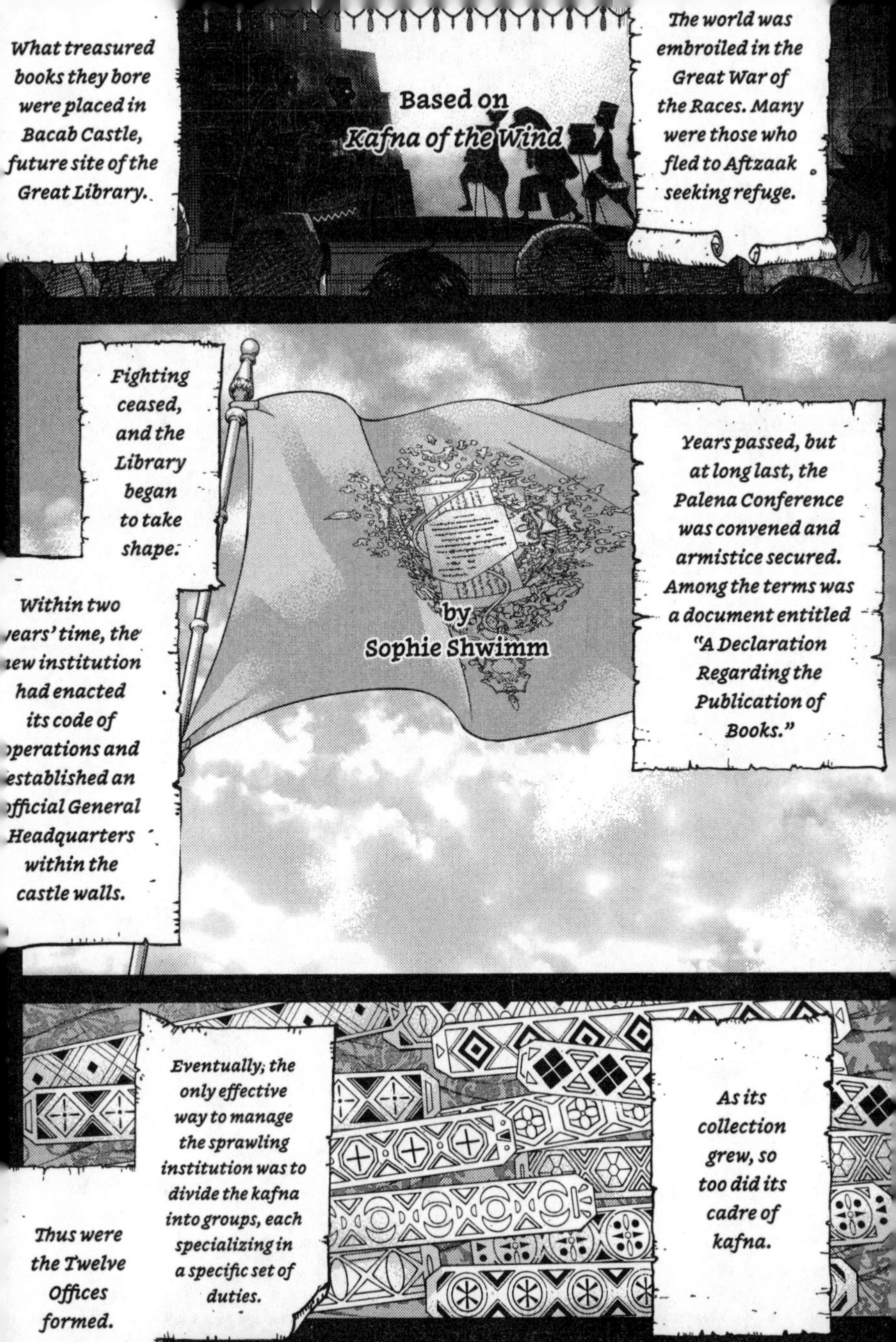
The world was embroiled in the Great War of the Races. Many were those who fled to Aftzaak seeking refuge.
Based on
Kafna of the Wind
What treasured books they bore were placed in Bacab Castle, future site of the Great Library.
Years passed, but at long last, the Palena Conference was convened and armistice secured. Among the terms was a document entitled "A Declaration Regarding the Publication of Books."
by
Sophie Shwimm
Fighting ceased, and the Library began to take shape.
Within two ears' time, the ew institution had enacted its code of perations and established an fficial General Headquarters within the castle walls.
As its collection grew, so too did its cadre of kafna.
Eventually, the only effective way to manage the sprawling institution was to divide the kafna into groups, each specializing in a specific set of duties.
Thus were the Twelve Offices formed.

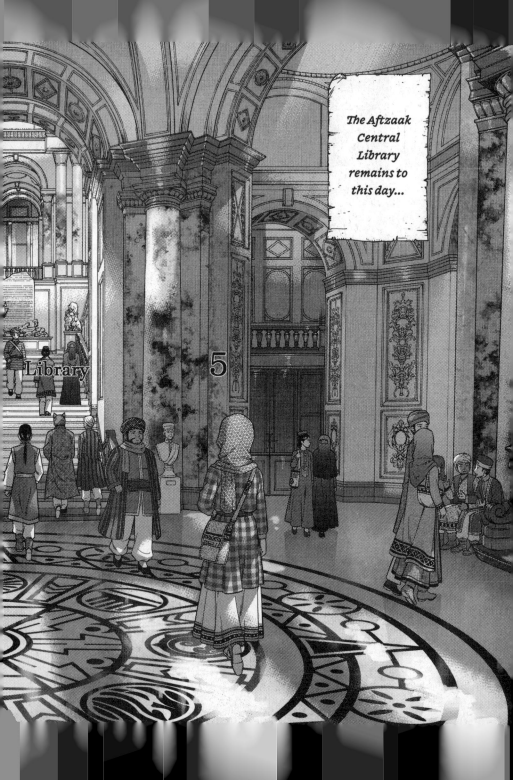

The Aftzaak
Central
Library
remains to
this day...

Library

5

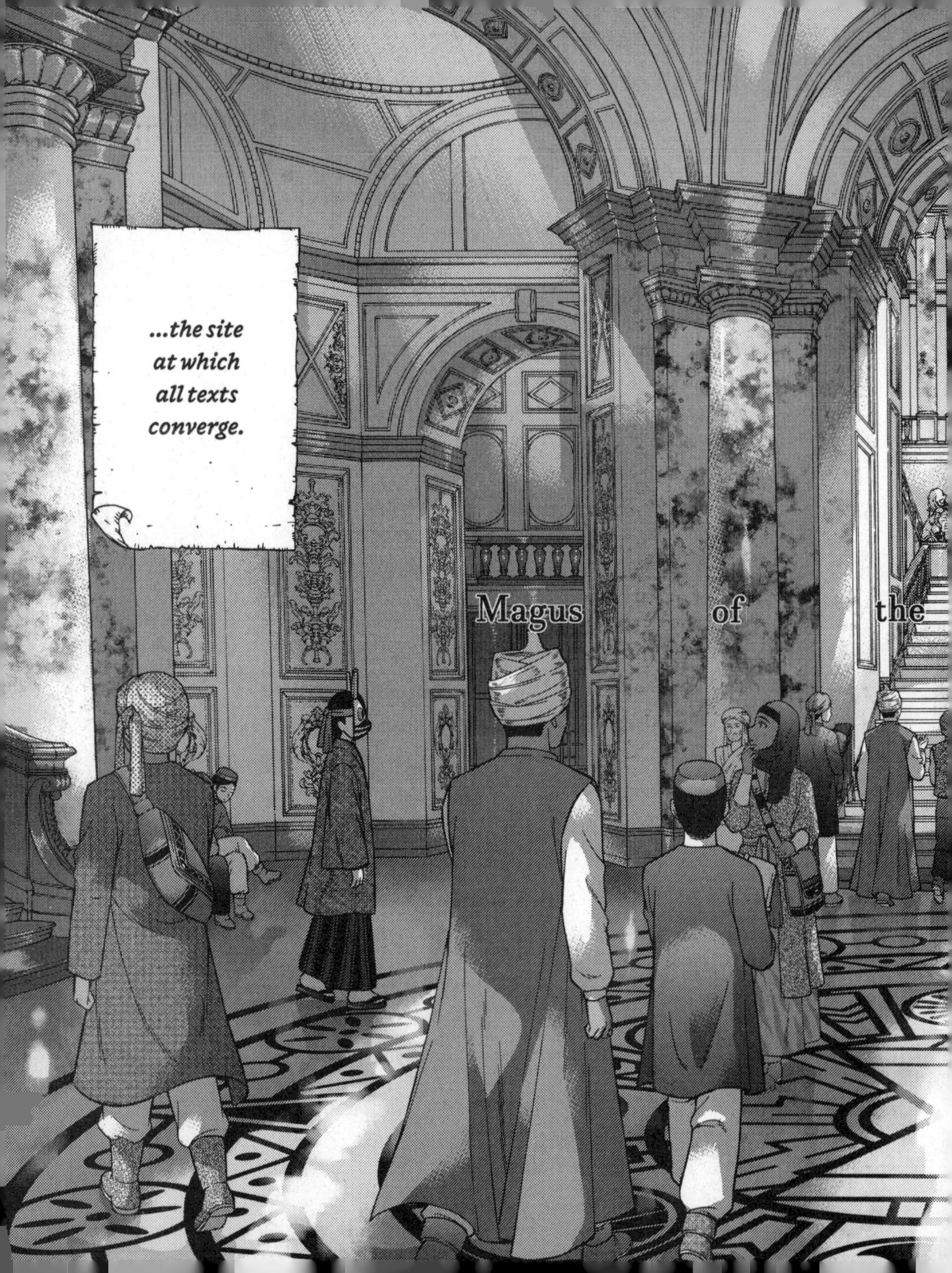
...the site at which all texts converge.
Magus of the

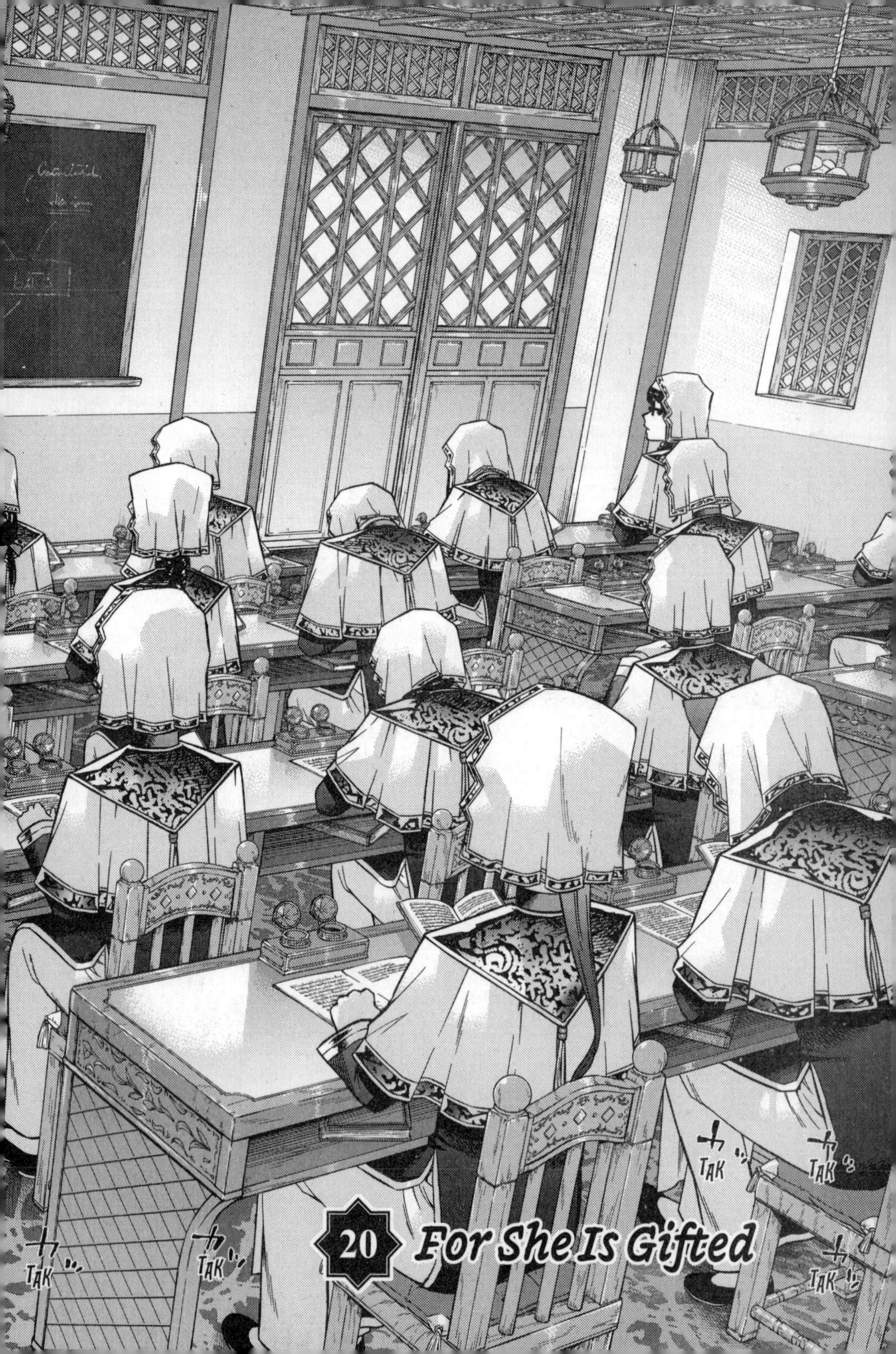

TAK
TAK
20 For She Is Gifted
TAK
TAK
TAK

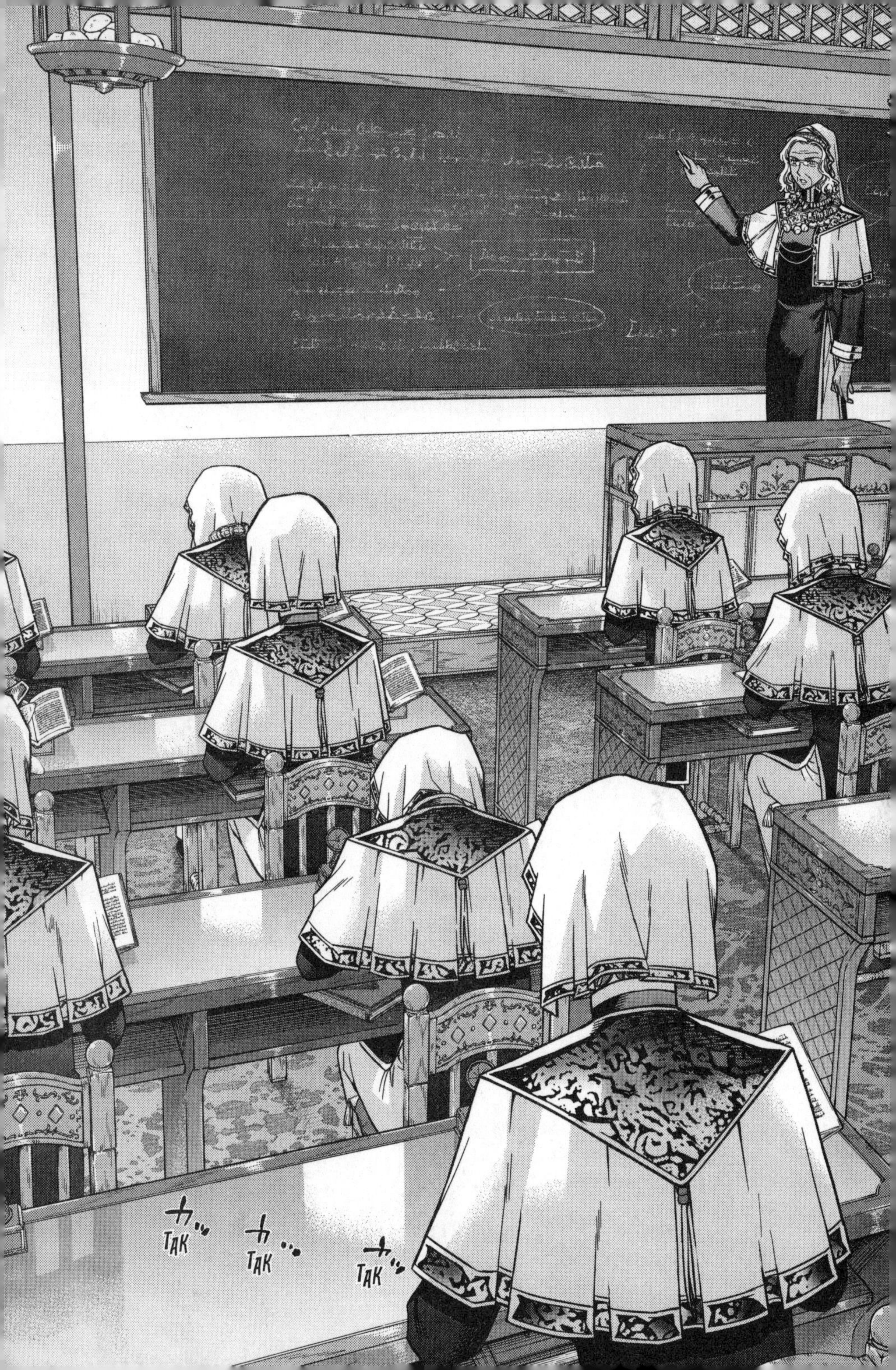
カ TAK
カ TAK
カ TAK

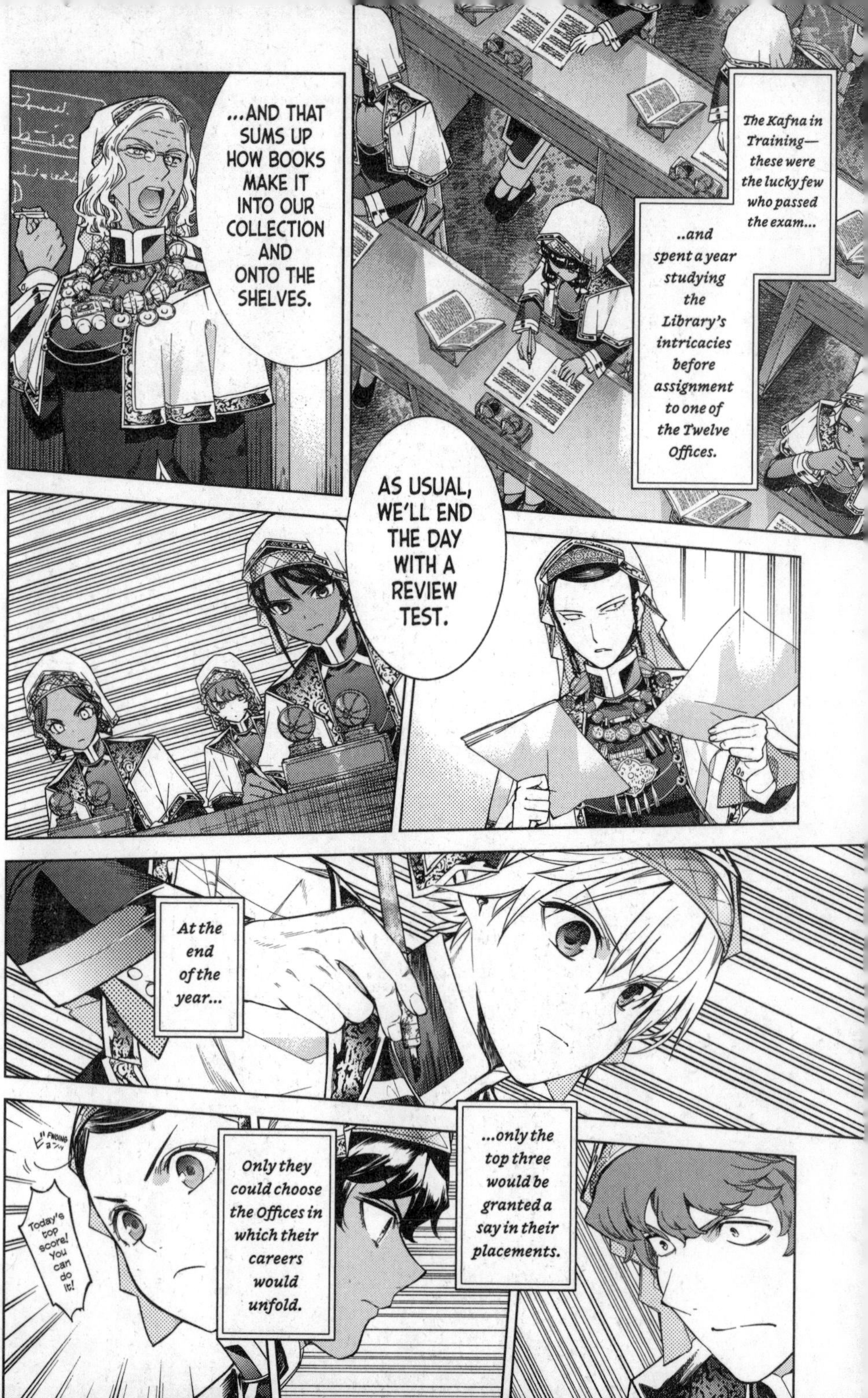
The Kafna in Training—these were the lucky few who passed the exam...
..and spent a year studying the Library's intricacies before assignment to one of the Twelve Offices.
...AND THAT SUMS UP HOW BOOKS MAKE IT INTO OUR COLLECTION AND ONTO THE SHELVES.
AS USUAL, WE'LL END THE DAY WITH A REVIEW TEST.
At the end of the year...
...only the top three would be granted a say in their placements.
Only they could choose the Offices in which their careers would unfold.
FWOING
Today's top score! You can do it!

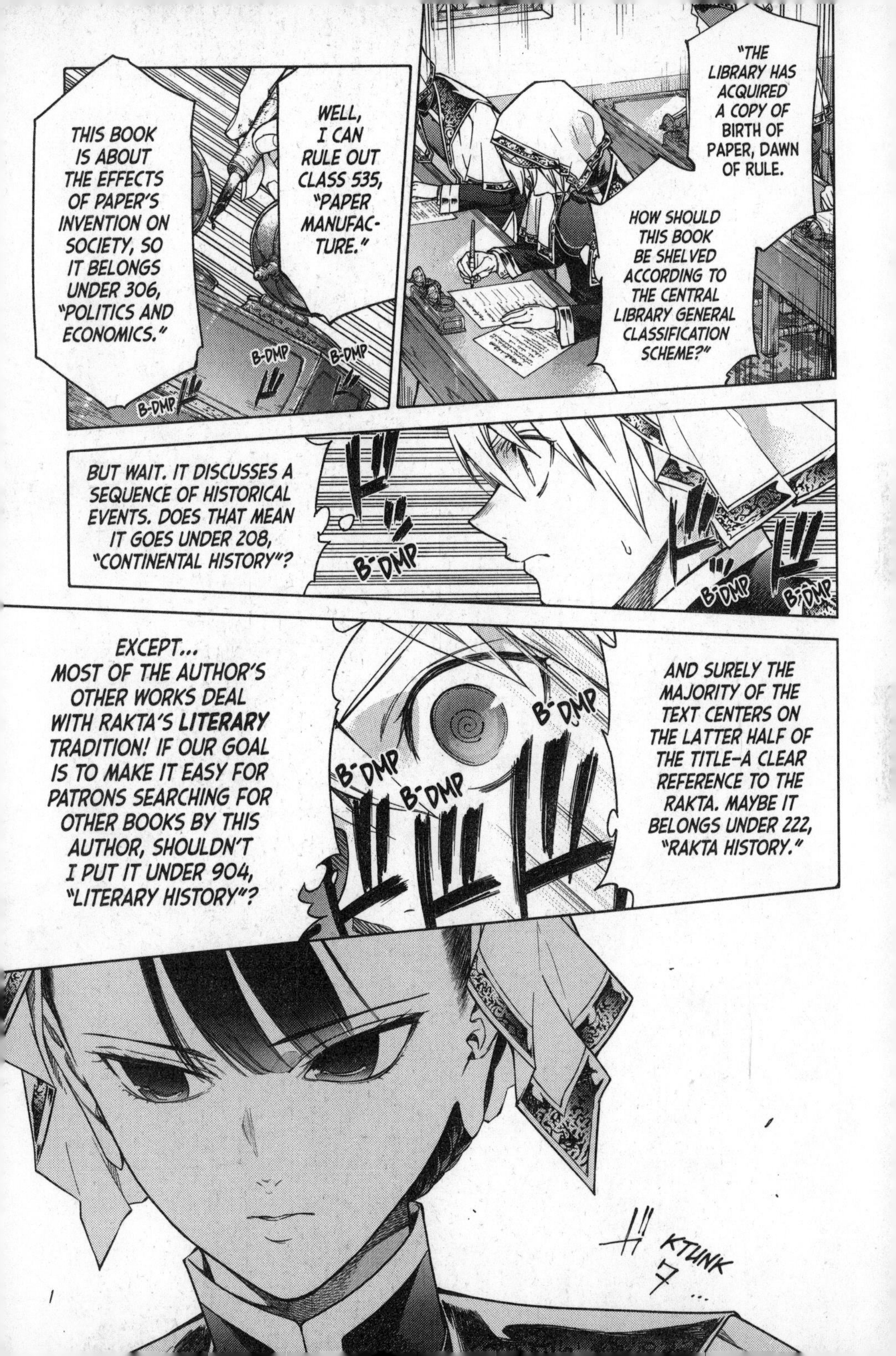
"THE LIBRARY HAS ACQUIRED A COPY OF BIRTH OF PAPER, DAWN OF RULE.
HOW SHOULD THIS BOOK BE SHELVED ACCORDING TO THE CENTRAL LIBRARY GENERAL CLASSIFICATION SCHEME?"
WELL, I CAN RULE OUT CLASS 535, "PAPER MANUFAC-TURE."
THIS BOOK IS ABOUT THE EFFECTS OF PAPER'S INVENTION ON SOCIETY, SO IT BELONGS UNDER 306, "POLITICS AND ECONOMICS."
B-DMP
B-DMP
B-DMP
B-DMP
B-DMP
BUT WAIT. IT DISCUSSES A SEQUENCE OF HISTORICAL EVENTS. DOES THAT MEAN IT GOES UNDER 208, "CONTINENTAL HISTORY"?
B-DMP
AND SURELY THE MAJORITY OF THE TEXT CENTERS ON THE LATTER HALF OF THE TITLE—A CLEAR REFERENCE TO THE RAKTA. MAYBE IT BELONGS UNDER 222, "RAKTA HISTORY."
B-DMP
B-DMP
B-DMP
EXCEPT... MOST OF THE AUTHOR'S OTHER WORKS DEAL WITH RAKTA'S **LITERARY** TRADITION! IF OUR GOAL IS TO MAKE IT EASY FOR PATRONS SEARCHING FOR OTHER BOOKS BY THIS AUTHOR, SHOULDN'T I PUT IT UNDER 904, "LITERARY HISTORY"?
KTUNK

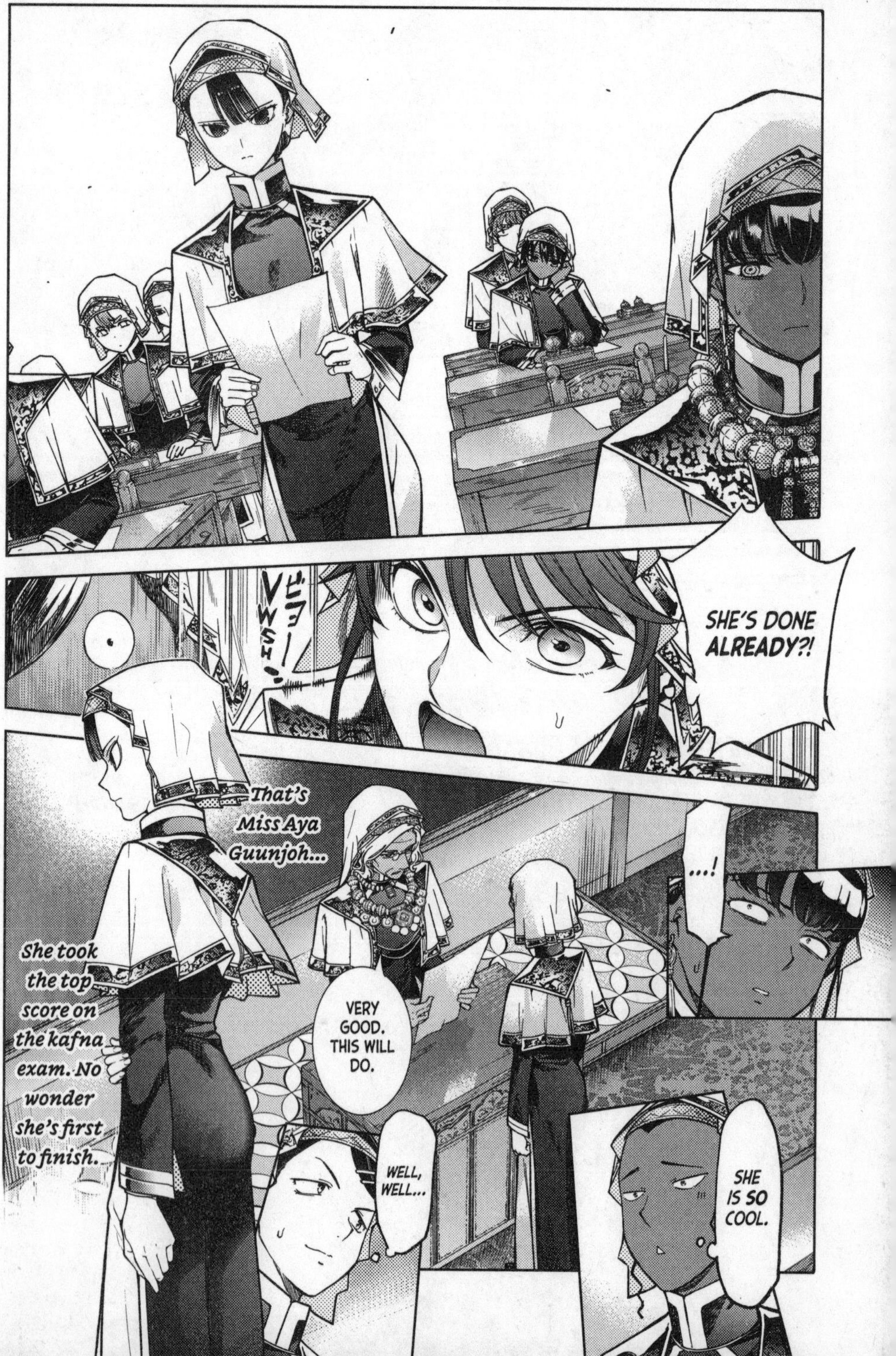
SHE'S DONE ALREADY?!
VWSH!
...!
That's Miss Aya Guunjoh...
VERY GOOD. THIS WILL DO.
She took the top score on the kafna exam. No wonder she's first to finish.
SHE IS SO COOL.
WELL, WELL...

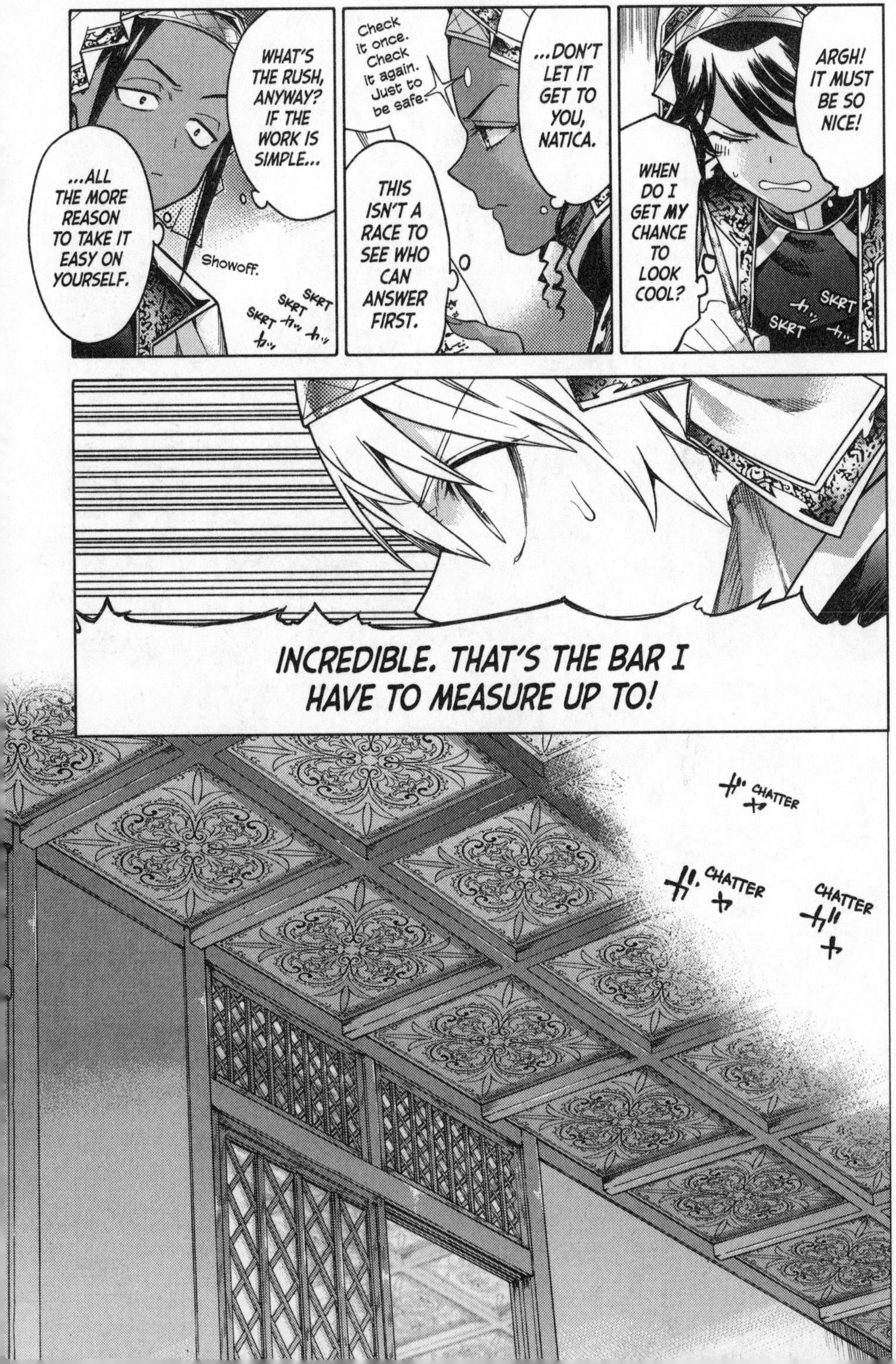
ARGH! IT MUST BE SO NICE!
WHEN DO I GET MY CHANCE TO LOOK COOL?
SKRT
SKRT
...DON'T LET IT GET TO YOU, NATICA.
Check it once. Check it again. Just to be safe.
THIS ISN'T A RACE TO SEE WHO CAN ANSWER FIRST.
WHAT'S THE RUSH, ANYWAY? IF THE WORK IS SIMPLE...
...ALL THE MORE REASON TO TAKE IT EASY ON YOURSELF.
Showoff.
SKRT
SKRT
SKRT
INCREDIBLE. THAT'S THE BAR I HAVE TO MEASURE UP TO!
CHATTER
CHATTER
CHATTER

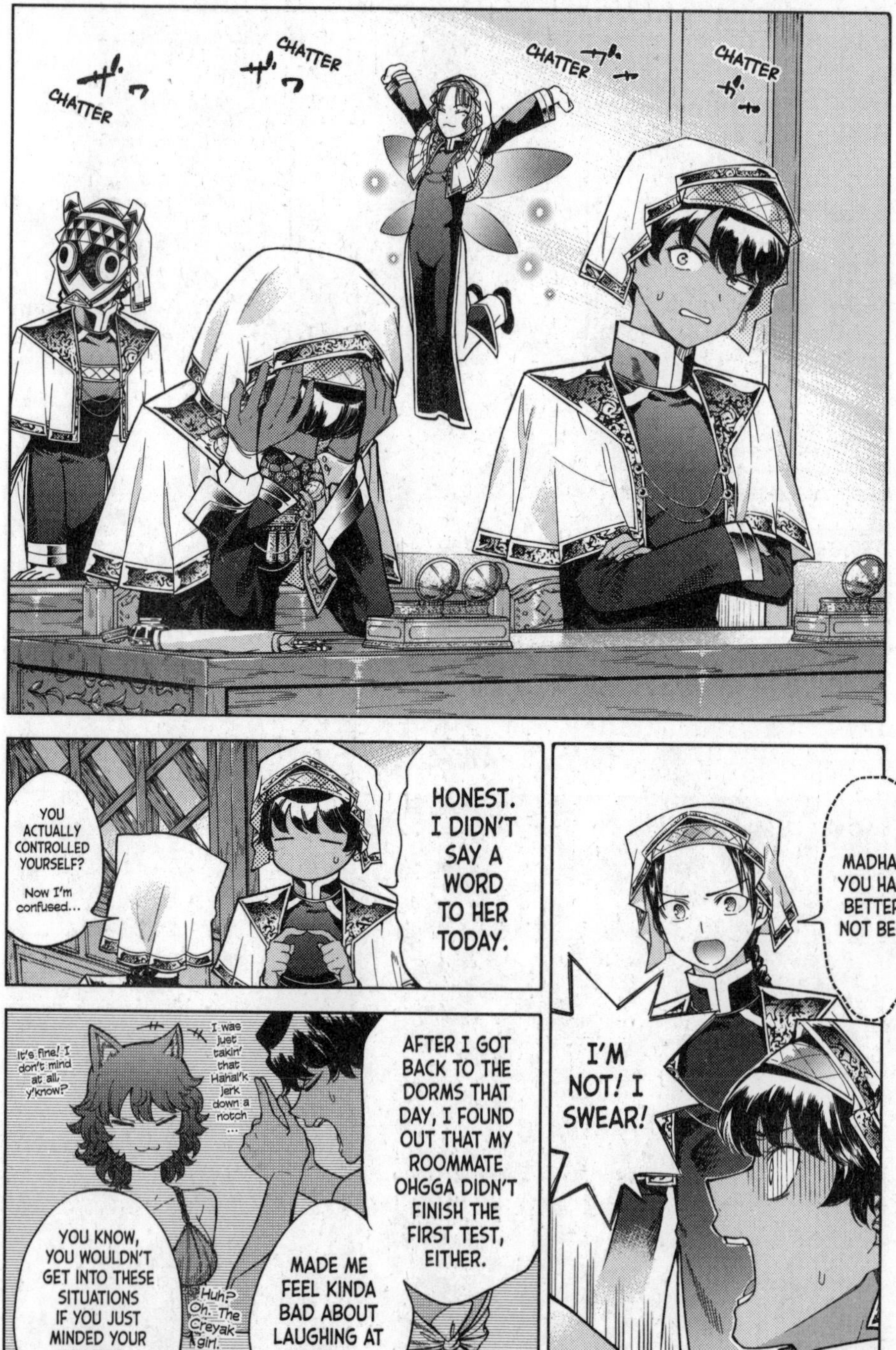
CHATTER
CHATTER
CHATTER
CHATTER
MADHA! YOU HAD BETTER NOT BE–
I'M NOT! I SWEAR!
HONEST. I DIDN'T SAY A WORD TO HER TODAY.
YOU ACTUALLY CONTROLLED YOURSELF? Now I'm confused...
AFTER I GOT BACK TO THE DORMS THAT DAY, I FOUND OUT THAT MY ROOMMATE OHGGA DIDN'T FINISH THE FIRST TEST, EITHER.
MADE ME FEEL KINDA BAD ABOUT LAUGHING AT MEDINA...
I was just takin' that Hahal'k jerk down a notch...
It's fine! I don't mind at all, y'know?
YOU KNOW, YOU WOULDN'T GET INTO THESE SITUATIONS IF YOU JUST MINDED YOUR MANNERS IN THE FIRST PLACE.
Huh? Oh. The Creyak girl.

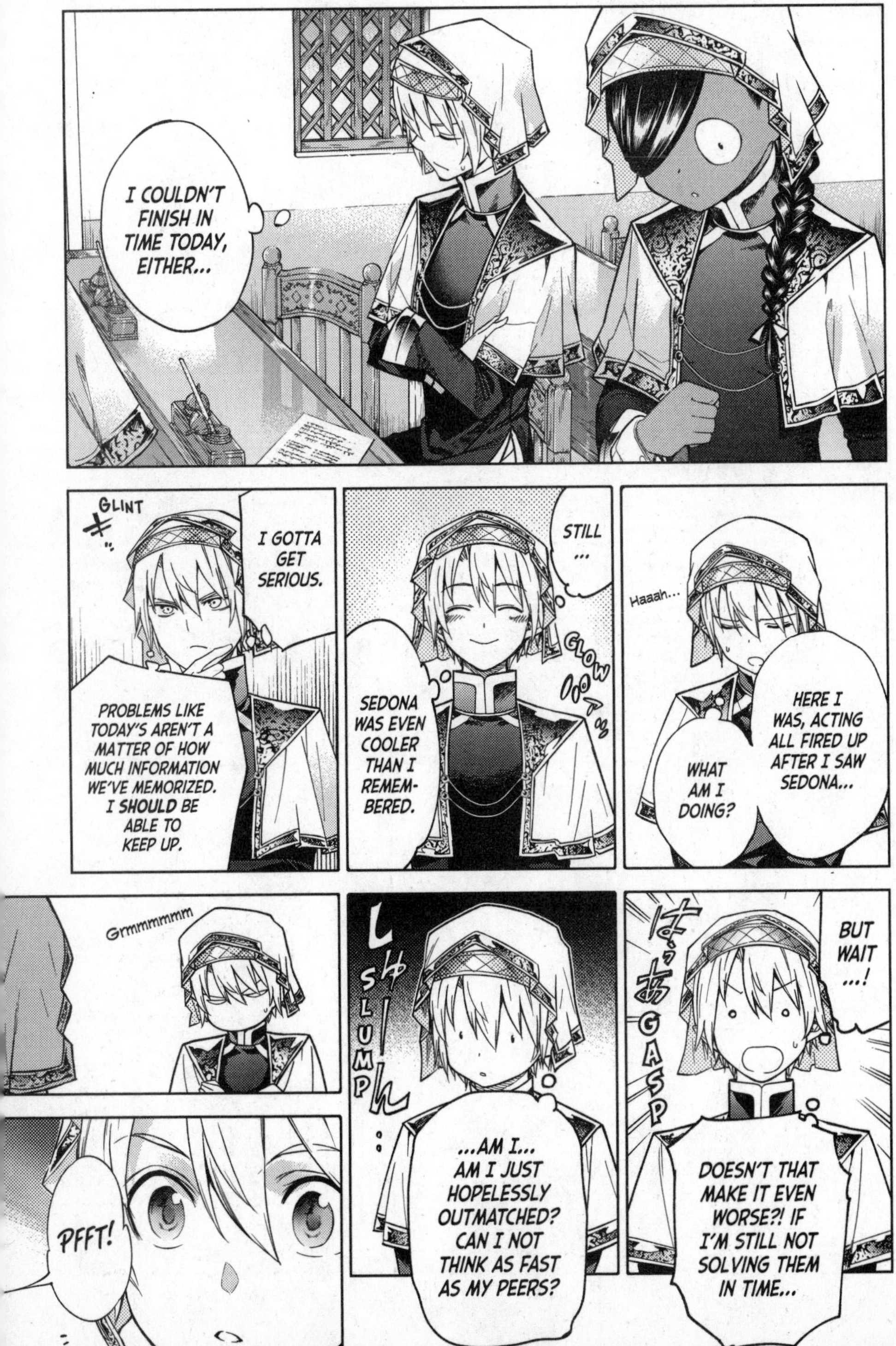
I COULDN'T FINISH IN TIME TODAY, EITHER...
Haaah...
HERE I WAS, ACTING ALL FIRED UP AFTER I SAW SEDONA...
WHAT AM I DOING?
STILL ...
SEDONA WAS EVEN COOLER THAN I REMEMBERED.
GLOW
GLINT
I GOTTA GET SERIOUS.
PROBLEMS LIKE TODAY'S AREN'T A MATTER OF HOW MUCH INFORMATION WE'VE MEMORIZED. I SHOULD BE ABLE TO KEEP UP.
BUT WAIT ...!
GASP
DOESN'T THAT MAKE IT EVEN WORSE?! IF I'M STILL NOT SOLVING THEM IN TIME...
SLUMP
...AM I... AM I JUST HOPELESSLY OUTMATCHED? CAN I NOT THINK AS FAST AS MY PEERS?
Grmmmmmm
PFFT!

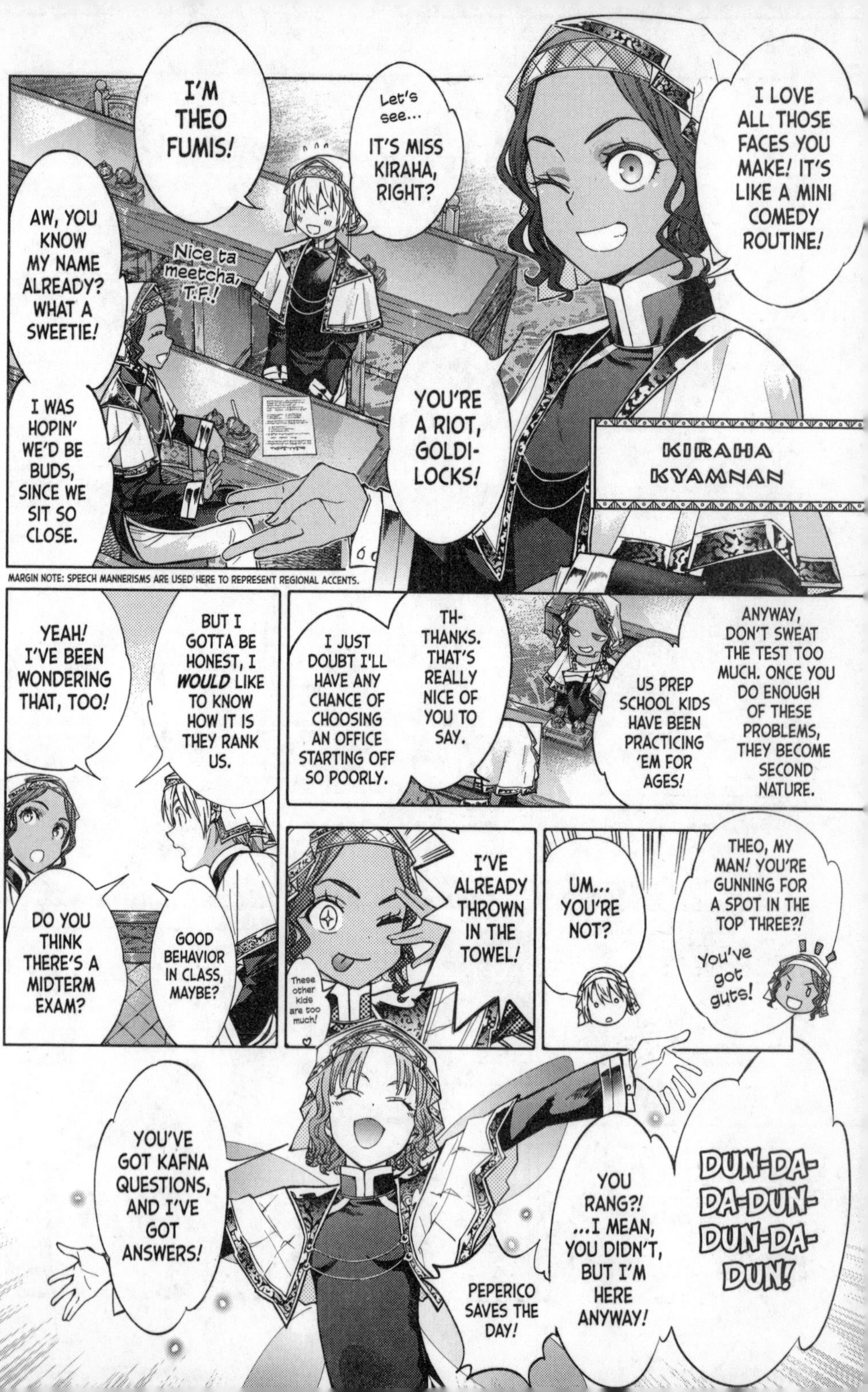
I LOVE ALL THOSE FACES YOU MAKE! IT'S LIKE A MINI COMEDY ROUTINE!
KIRAHA KYAMNAN
YOU'RE A RIOT, GOLDILOCKS!
Let's see... IT'S MISS KIRAHA, RIGHT?
I'M THEO FUMIS!
Nice ta meetcha, T.F.!
AW, YOU KNOW MY NAME ALREADY? WHAT A SWEETIE!
I WAS HOPIN' WE'D BE BUDS, SINCE WE SIT SO CLOSE.
MARGIN NOTE: SPEECH MANNERISMS ARE USED HERE TO REPRESENT REGIONAL ACCENTS.
ANYWAY, DON'T SWEAT THE TEST TOO MUCH. ONCE YOU DO ENOUGH OF THESE PROBLEMS, THEY BECOME SECOND NATURE.
US PREP SCHOOL KIDS HAVE BEEN PRACTICING 'EM FOR AGES!
TH-THANKS. THAT'S REALLY NICE OF YOU TO SAY.
I JUST DOUBT I'LL HAVE ANY CHANCE OF CHOOSING AN OFFICE STARTING OFF SO POORLY.
THEO, MY MAN! YOU'RE GUNNING FOR A SPOT IN THE TOP THREE?!
You've got guts!
UM... YOU'RE NOT?
I'VE ALREADY THROWN IN THE TOWEL!
These other kids are too much!
BUT I GOTTA BE HONEST, I *WOULD* LIKE TO KNOW HOW IT IS THEY RANK US.
YEAH! I'VE BEEN WONDERING THAT, TOO!
GOOD BEHAVIOR IN CLASS, MAYBE?
DO YOU THINK THERE'S A MIDTERM EXAM?
DUN-DA-DA-DUN-DUN-DA-DUN!
YOU RANG?! ...I MEAN, YOU DIDN'T, BUT I'M HERE ANYWAY!
PEPERICO SAVES THE DAY!
YOU'VE GOT KAFNA QUESTIONS, AND I'VE GOT ANSWERS!

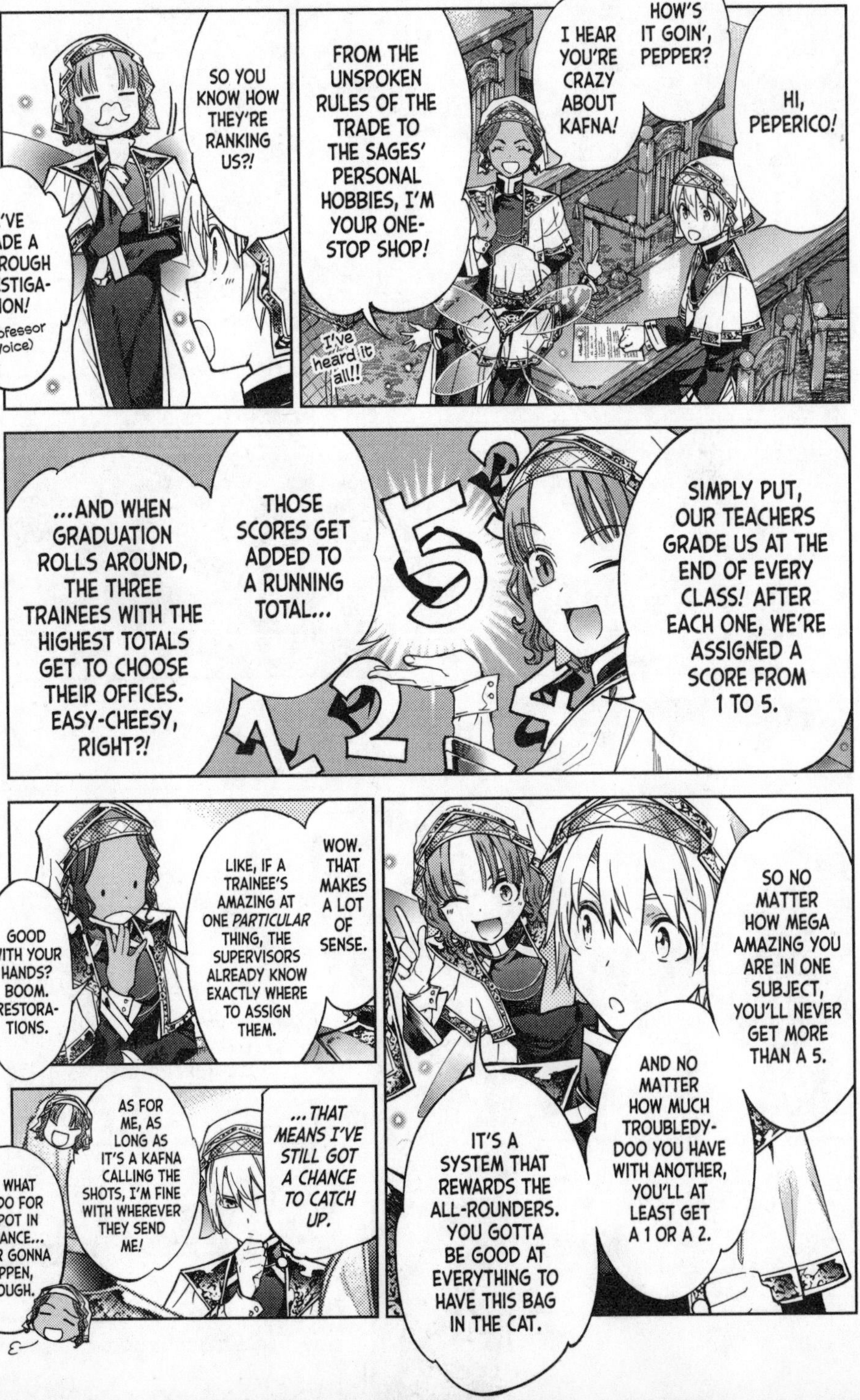
HI, PEPERICO!
HOW'S IT GOIN', PEPPER?
I HEAR YOU'RE CRAZY ABOUT KAFNA!
FROM THE UNSPOKEN RULES OF THE TRADE TO THE SAGES' PERSONAL HOBBIES, I'M YOUR ONE-STOP SHOP!
I've heard it all!!
SO YOU KNOW HOW THEY'RE RANKING US?!
I'VE MADE A THOROUGH INVESTIGATION!
(Professor Voice)
SIMPLY PUT, OUR TEACHERS GRADE US AT THE END OF EVERY CLASS! AFTER EACH ONE, WE'RE ASSIGNED A SCORE FROM 1 TO 5.
THOSE SCORES GET ADDED TO A RUNNING TOTAL...
...AND WHEN GRADUATION ROLLS AROUND, THE THREE TRAINEES WITH THE HIGHEST TOTALS GET TO CHOOSE THEIR OFFICES. EASY-CHEESY, RIGHT?!
SO NO MATTER HOW MEGA AMAZING YOU ARE IN ONE SUBJECT, YOU'LL NEVER GET MORE THAN A 5.
AND NO MATTER HOW MUCH TROUBLEDY-DOO YOU HAVE WITH ANOTHER, YOU'LL AT LEAST GET A 1 OR A 2.
IT'S A SYSTEM THAT REWARDS THE ALL-ROUNDERS. YOU GOTTA BE GOOD AT EVERYTHING TO HAVE THIS BAG IN THE CAT.
WOW. THAT MAKES A LOT OF SENSE.
LIKE, IF A TRAINEE'S AMAZING AT ONE *PARTICULAR* THING, THE SUPERVISORS ALREADY KNOW EXACTLY WHERE TO ASSIGN THEM.
GOOD WITH YOUR HANDS? BOOM. RESTORATIONS.
...THAT MEANS I'VE STILL GOT A CHANCE TO CATCH UP.
AS FOR ME, AS LONG AS IT'S A KAFNA CALLING THE SHOTS, I'M FINE WITH WHEREVER THEY SEND ME!
OH, WHAT I'D DO FOR A SPOT IN GUIDANCE... NEVER GONNA HAPPEN, THOUGH.

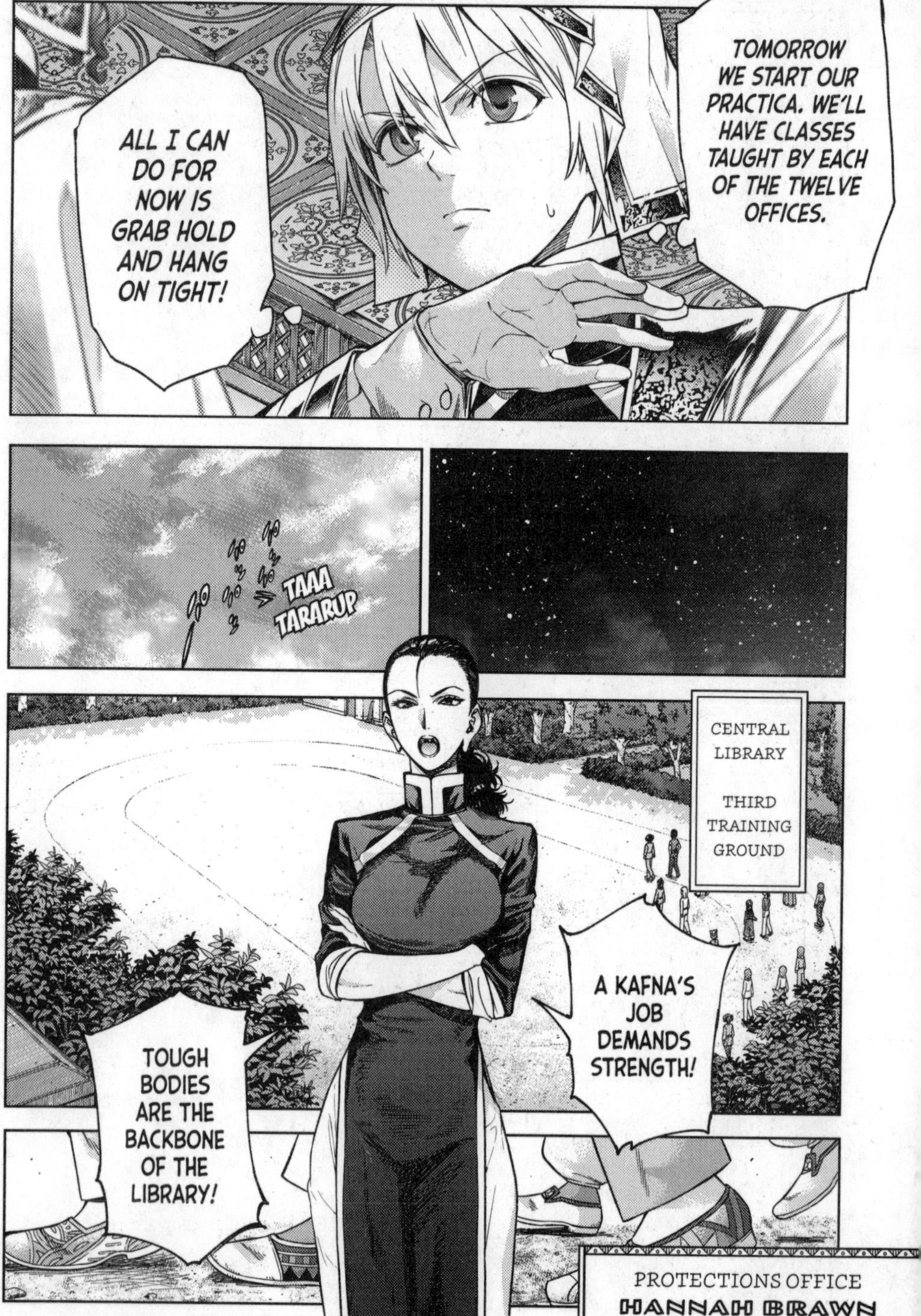
TOMORROW WE START OUR PRACTICA. WE'LL HAVE CLASSES TAUGHT BY EACH OF THE TWELVE OFFICES.
ALL I CAN DO FOR NOW IS GRAB HOLD AND HANG ON TIGHT!
TAAA TARARUP
CENTRAL LIBRARY
THIRD TRAINING GROUND
A KAFNA'S JOB DEMANDS STRENGTH!
TOUGH BODIES ARE THE BACKBONE OF THE LIBRARY!
PROTECTIONS OFFICE
HANNAH BRAWN

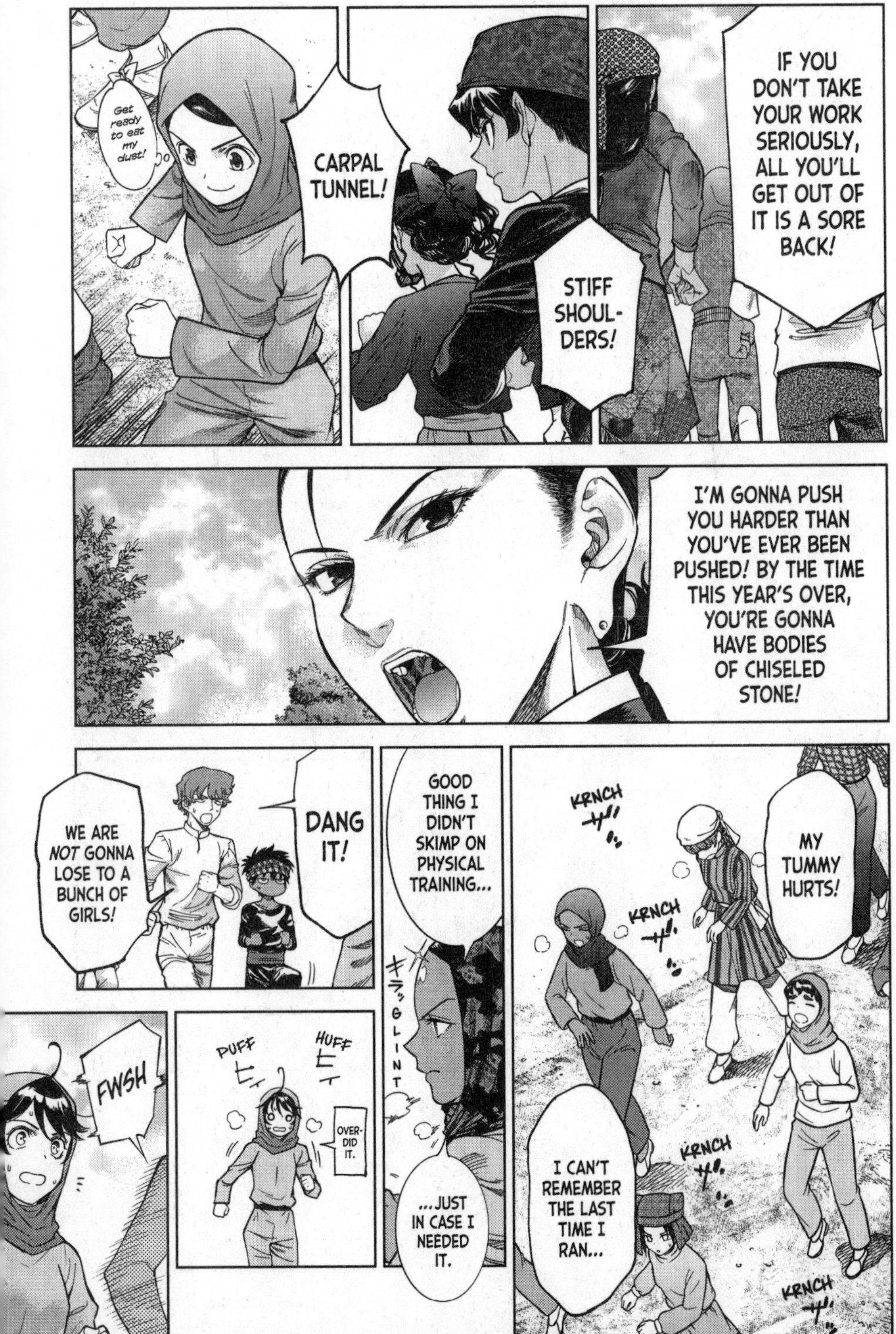

IF YOU DON'T TAKE YOUR WORK SERIOUSLY, ALL YOU'LL GET OUT OF IT IS A SORE BACK!
STIFF SHOUL-DERS!
CARPAL TUNNEL!
Get ready to eat my dust!
I'M GONNA PUSH YOU HARDER THAN YOU'VE EVER BEEN PUSHED! BY THE TIME THIS YEAR'S OVER, YOU'RE GONNA HAVE BODIES OF CHISELED STONE!
MY TUMMY HURTS!
KRNCH
KRNCH
KRNCH
I CAN'T REMEMBER THE LAST TIME I RAN...
KRNCH
GOOD THING I DIDN'T SKIMP ON PHYSICAL TRAINING...
GLINT
...JUST IN CASE I NEEDED IT.
DANG IT!
WE ARE *NOT* GONNA LOSE TO A BUNCH OF GIRLS!
HUFF
PUFF
OVER-DID IT.
FWSH

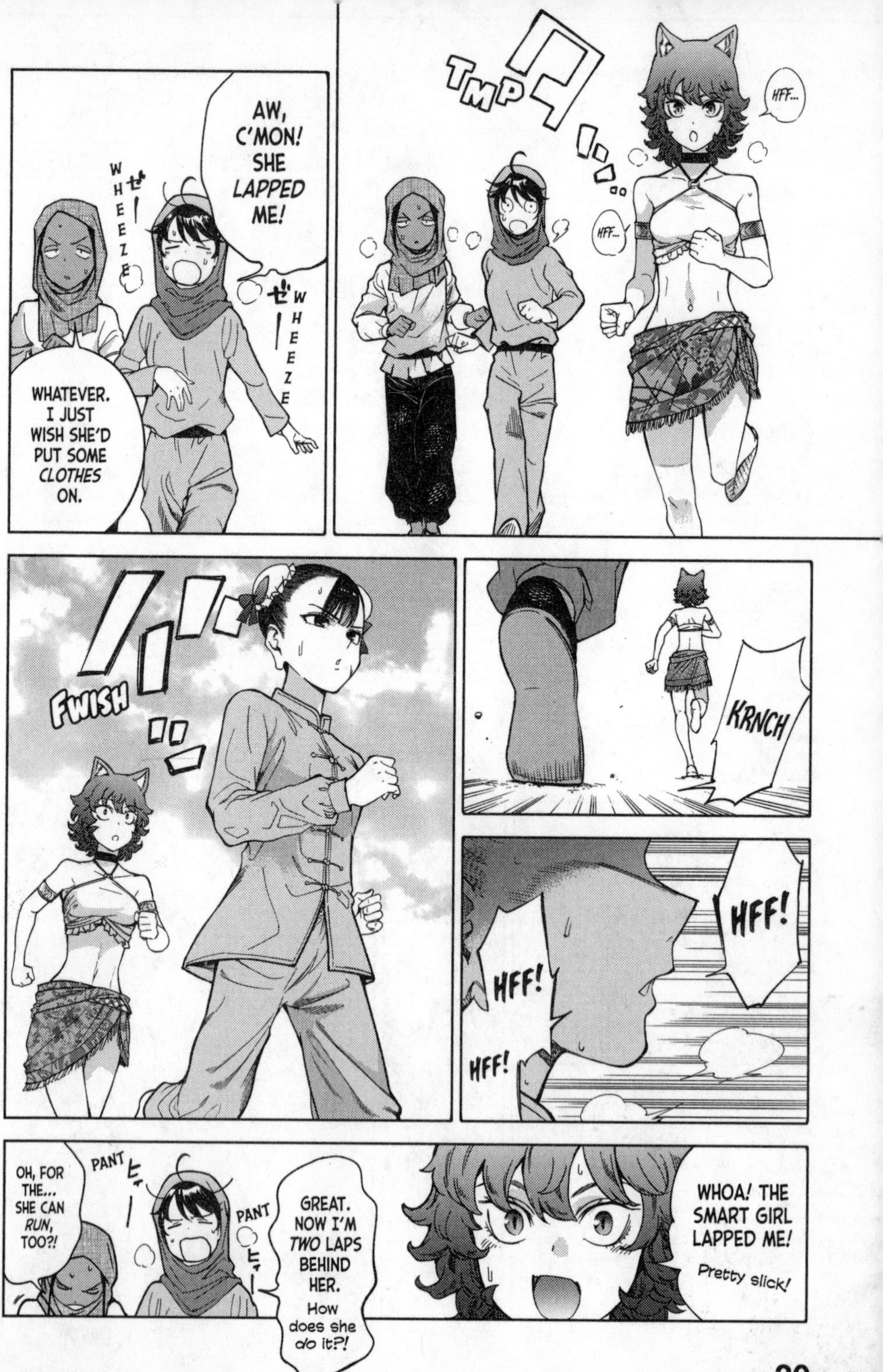

TMP
HFF...
HFF...
AW, C'MON! SHE *LAPPED* ME!
WHEEZE ゼ
WHEEZE ゼ
WHATEVER. I JUST WISH SHE'D PUT SOME *CLOTHES* ON.
KRNCH
HFF!
HFF!
HFF!
FWISH
WHOA! THE SMART GIRL LAPPED ME!
Pretty slick!
PANT
GREAT. NOW I'M *TWO* LAPS BEHIND HER.
How does she *do* it?!
PANT
OH, FOR THE... SHE CAN *RUN*, TOO?!

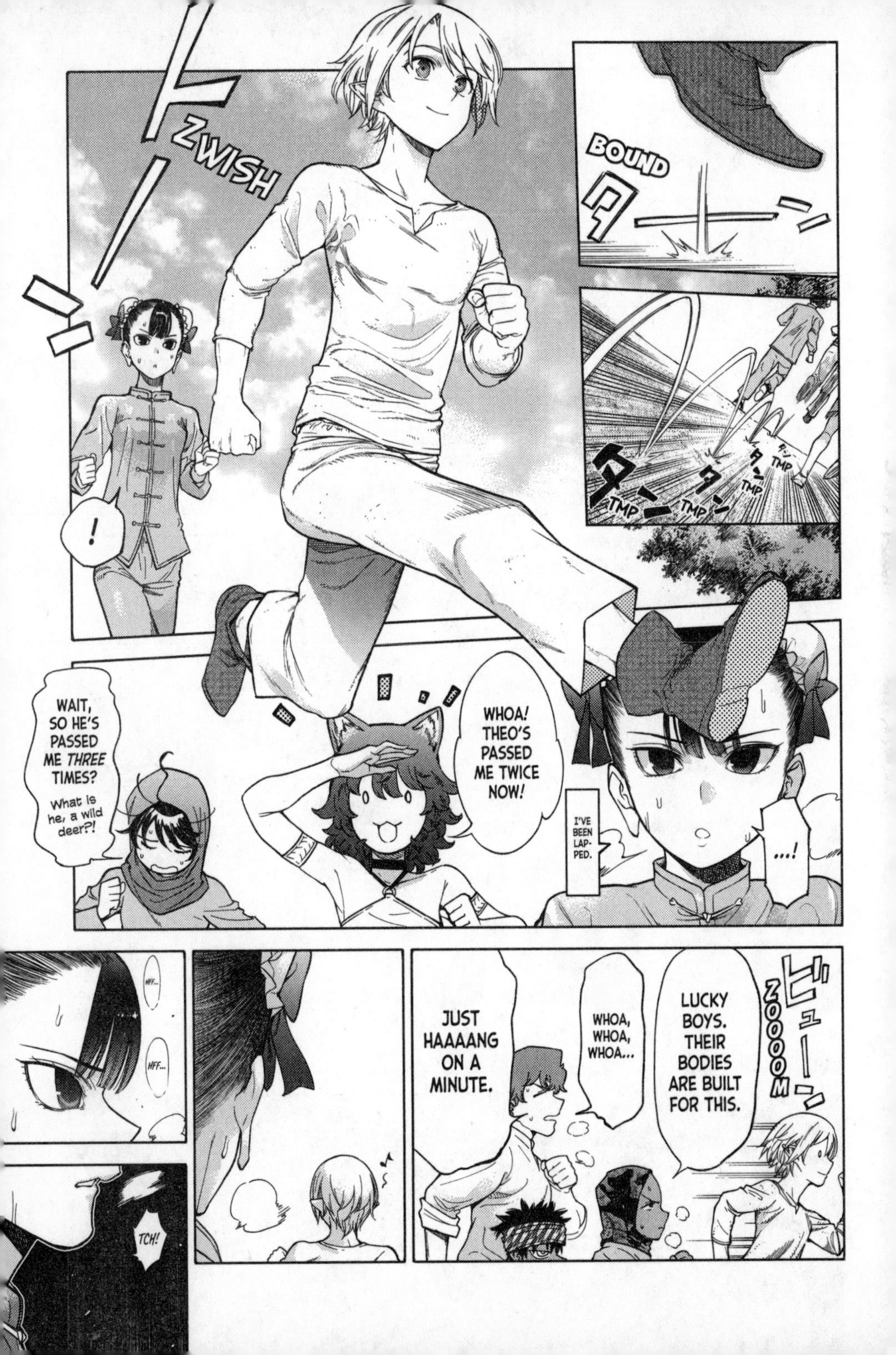
BOUND
TMP TMP TMP TMP
ZWISH
!
...!
I'VE BEEN LAPPED.
WHOA! THEO'S PASSED ME TWICE NOW!
WAIT, SO HE'S PASSED ME *THREE* TIMES?
What is he, a wild deer?!
ZOOOOOM
LUCKY BOYS. THEIR BODIES ARE BUILT FOR THIS.
WHOA, WHOA, WHOA...
JUST HAAAANG ON A MINUTE.
HFF...
HFF...
TCH!

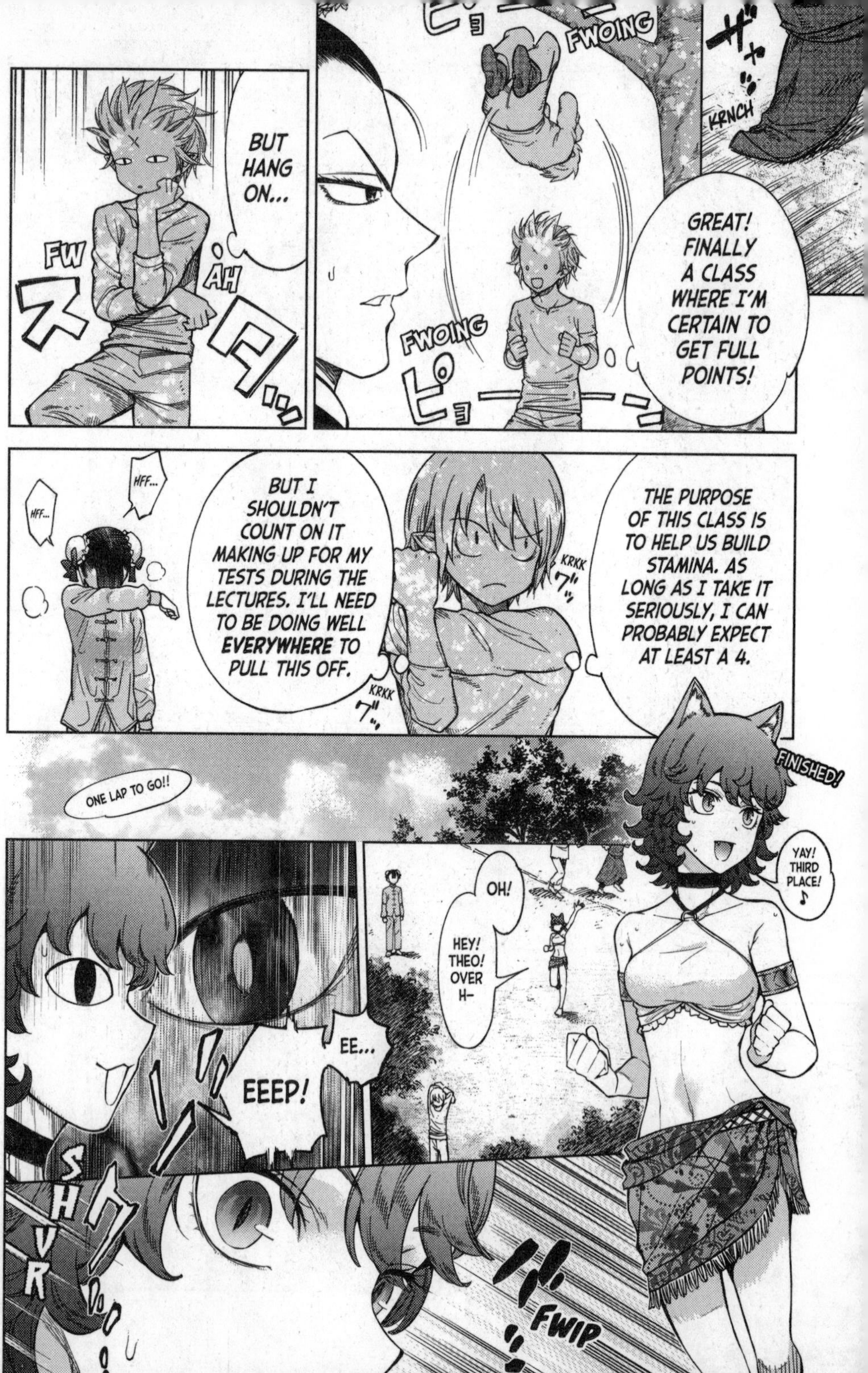

KRNCH
GREAT! FINALLY A CLASS WHERE I'M CERTAIN TO GET FULL POINTS!
FWOING
FWOING
BUT HANG ON...
AH
FW
THE PURPOSE OF THIS CLASS IS TO HELP US BUILD STAMINA. AS LONG AS I TAKE IT SERIOUSLY, I CAN PROBABLY EXPECT AT LEAST A 4.
KRKK
KRKK
BUT I SHOULDN'T COUNT ON IT MAKING UP FOR MY TESTS DURING THE LECTURES. I'LL NEED TO BE DOING WELL **EVERYWHERE** TO PULL THIS OFF.
HFF...
HFF...
FINISHED!
ONE LAP TO GO!!
YAY! THIRD PLACE! ♪
OH!
HEY! THEO! OVER H–
EE...
EEEP!
SHVR
FWIP

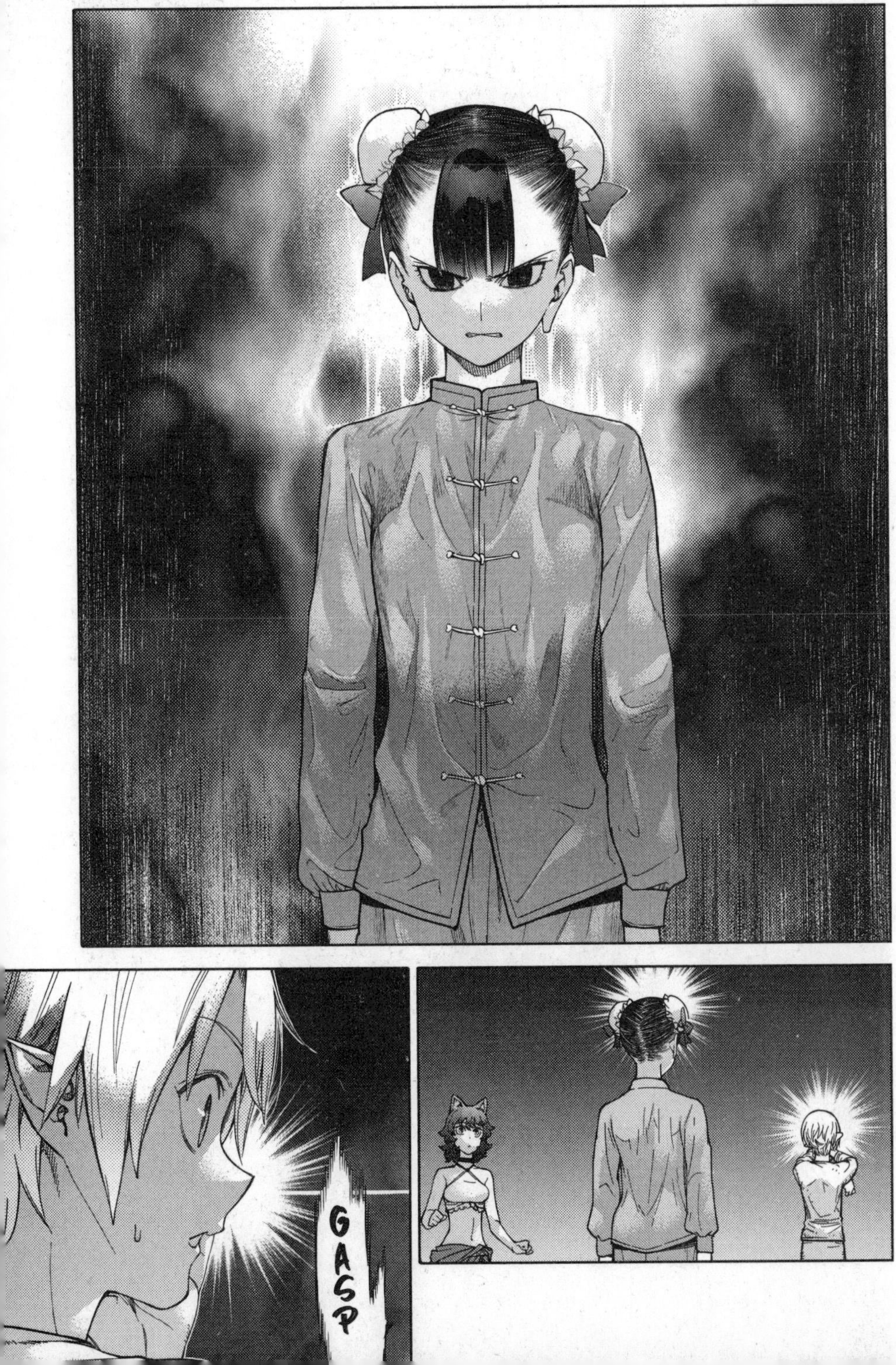
GASP

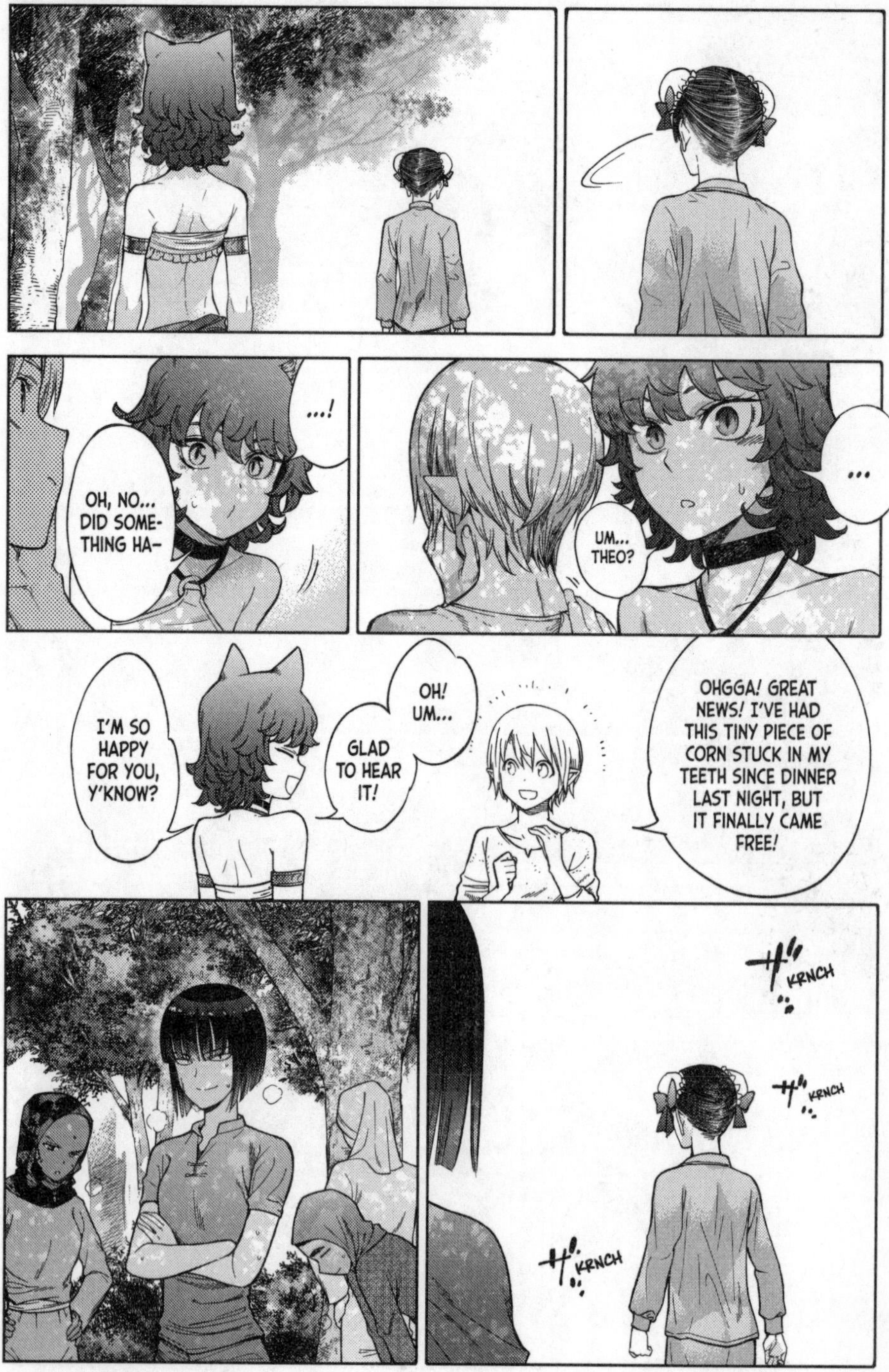
...
UM... THEO?
...!
OH, NO... DID SOME-THING HA-
OHGGA! GREAT NEWS! I'VE HAD THIS TINY PIECE OF CORN STUCK IN MY TEETH SINCE DINNER LAST NIGHT, BUT IT FINALLY CAME FREE!
OH! UM...
GLAD TO HEAR IT!
I'M SO HAPPY FOR YOU, Y'KNOW?
KRNCH
KRNCH
KRNCH

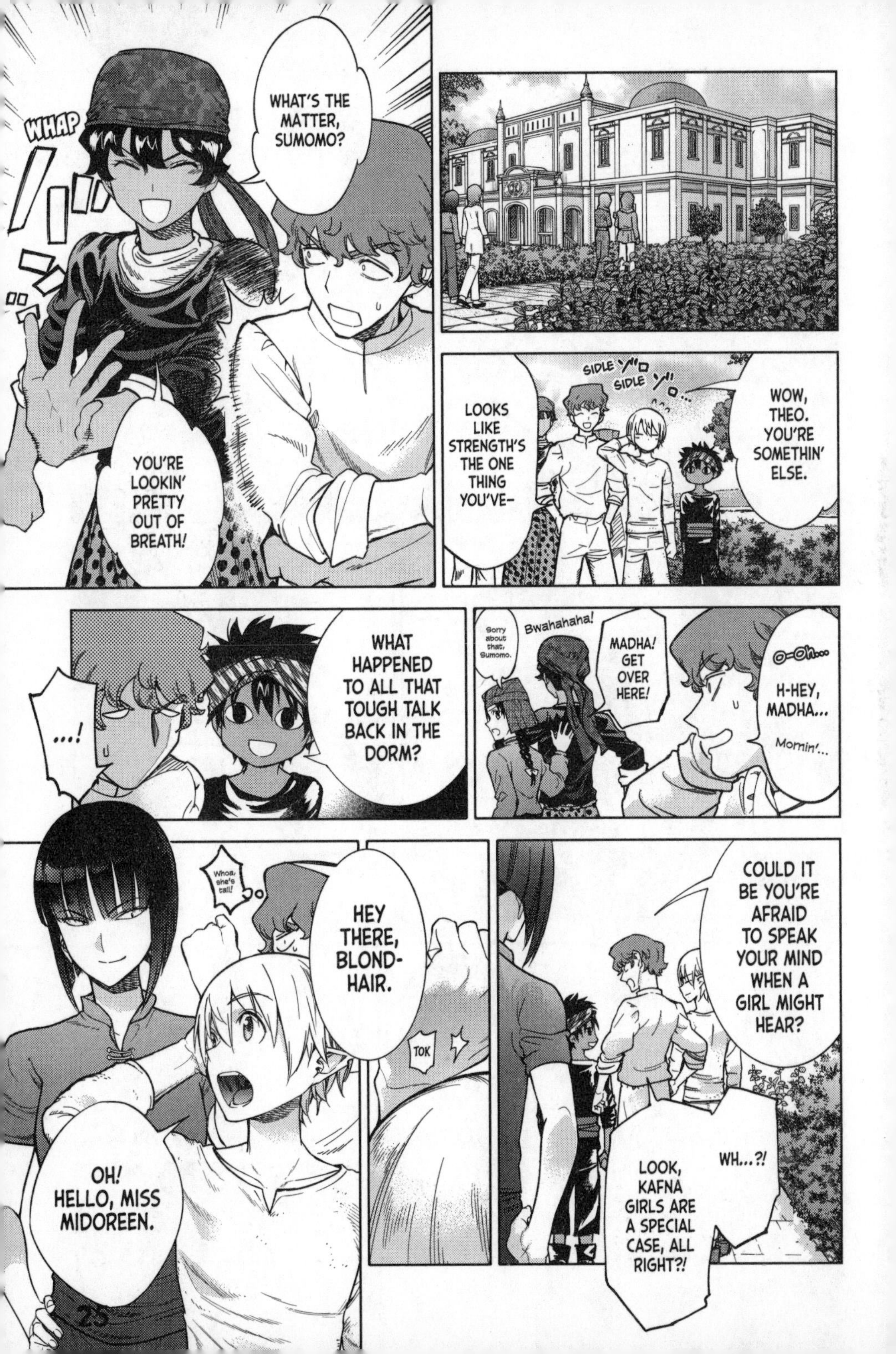

SIDLE
SIDLE
WOW, THEO. YOU'RE SOMETHIN' ELSE.
LOOKS LIKE STRENGTH'S THE ONE THING YOU'VE–
WHAP
WHAT'S THE MATTER, SUMOMO?
YOU'RE LOOKIN' PRETTY OUT OF BREATH!
O-Oh...
H-HEY, MADHA...
Mornin'...
MADHA! GET OVER HERE!
Bwahahaha!
Sorry about that, Sumomo.
WHAT HAPPENED TO ALL THAT TOUGH TALK BACK IN THE DORM?
...!
COULD IT BE YOU'RE AFRAID TO SPEAK YOUR MIND WHEN A GIRL MIGHT HEAR?
WH...?!
LOOK, KAFNA GIRLS ARE A SPECIAL CASE, ALL RIGHT?!
HEY THERE, BLOND-HAIR.
TOK
Whoa, she's tall!
OH! HELLO, MISS MIDOREEN.

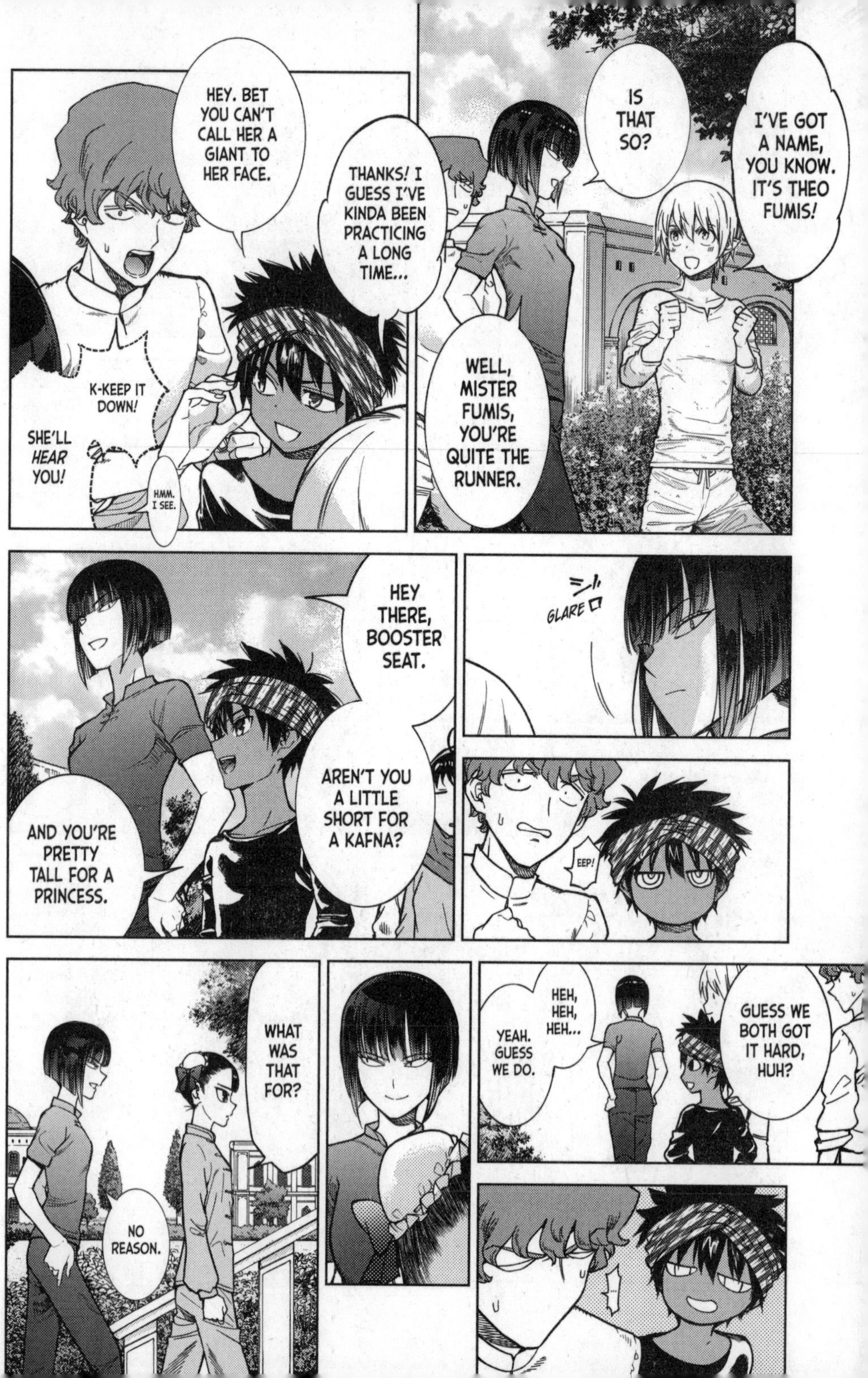
I'VE GOT A NAME, YOU KNOW. IT'S THEO FUMIS!
IS THAT SO?
WELL, MISTER FUMIS, YOU'RE QUITE THE RUNNER.
THANKS! I GUESS I'VE KINDA BEEN PRACTICING A LONG TIME...
HEY. BET YOU CAN'T CALL HER A GIANT TO HER FACE.
K-KEEP IT DOWN!
SHE'LL *HEAR* YOU!
HMM. I SEE.
GLARE
EEP!
HEY THERE, BOOSTER SEAT.
AREN'T YOU A LITTLE SHORT FOR A KAFNA?
AND YOU'RE PRETTY TALL FOR A PRINCESS.
GUESS WE BOTH GOT IT HARD, HUH?
HEH, HEH, HEH...
YEAH. GUESS WE DO.
...
WHAT WAS THAT FOR?
NO REASON.

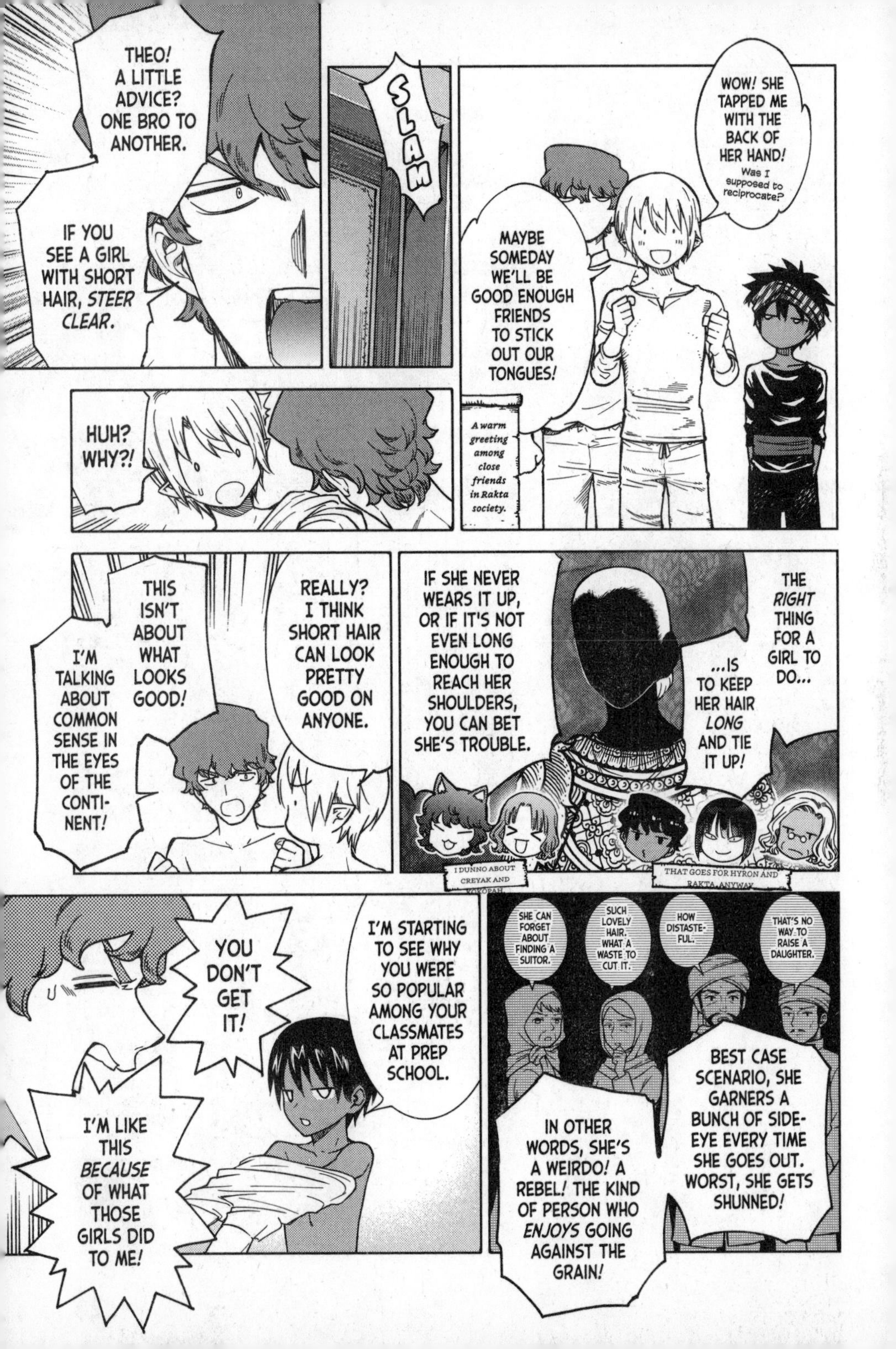
WOW! SHE TAPPED ME WITH THE BACK OF HER HAND! Was I supposed to reciprocate?
MAYBE SOMEDAY WE'LL BE GOOD ENOUGH FRIENDS TO STICK OUT OUR TONGUES!
A warm greeting among close friends in Rakta society.
SLAM
THEO! A LITTLE ADVICE? ONE BRO TO ANOTHER.
IF YOU SEE A GIRL WITH SHORT HAIR, STEER CLEAR.
HUH? WHY?!
THE RIGHT THING FOR A GIRL TO DO...
...IS TO KEEP HER HAIR LONG AND TIE IT UP!
IF SHE NEVER WEARS IT UP, OR IF IT'S NOT EVEN LONG ENOUGH TO REACH HER SHOULDERS, YOU CAN BET SHE'S TROUBLE.
THAT GOES FOR HYRON AND RAKTA, ANYWAY.
I DUNNO ABOUT CREYAK AND KOKOPAH.
REALLY? I THINK SHORT HAIR CAN LOOK PRETTY GOOD ON ANYONE.
THIS ISN'T ABOUT WHAT LOOKS GOOD!
I'M TALKING ABOUT COMMON SENSE IN THE EYES OF THE CONTI-NENT!
THAT'S NO WAY TO RAISE A DAUGHTER.
HOW DISTASTE-FUL.
SUCH LOVELY HAIR. WHAT A WASTE TO CUT IT.
SHE CAN FORGET ABOUT FINDING A SUITOR.
BEST CASE SCENARIO, SHE GARNERS A BUNCH OF SIDE-EYE EVERY TIME SHE GOES OUT. WORST, SHE GETS SHUNNED!
IN OTHER WORDS, SHE'S A WEIRDO! A REBEL! THE KIND OF PERSON WHO ENJOYS GOING AGAINST THE GRAIN!
I'M STARTING TO SEE WHY YOU WERE SO POPULAR AMONG YOUR CLASSMATES AT PREP SCHOOL.
YOU DON'T GET IT!
I'M LIKE THIS BECAUSE OF WHAT THOSE GIRLS DID TO ME!

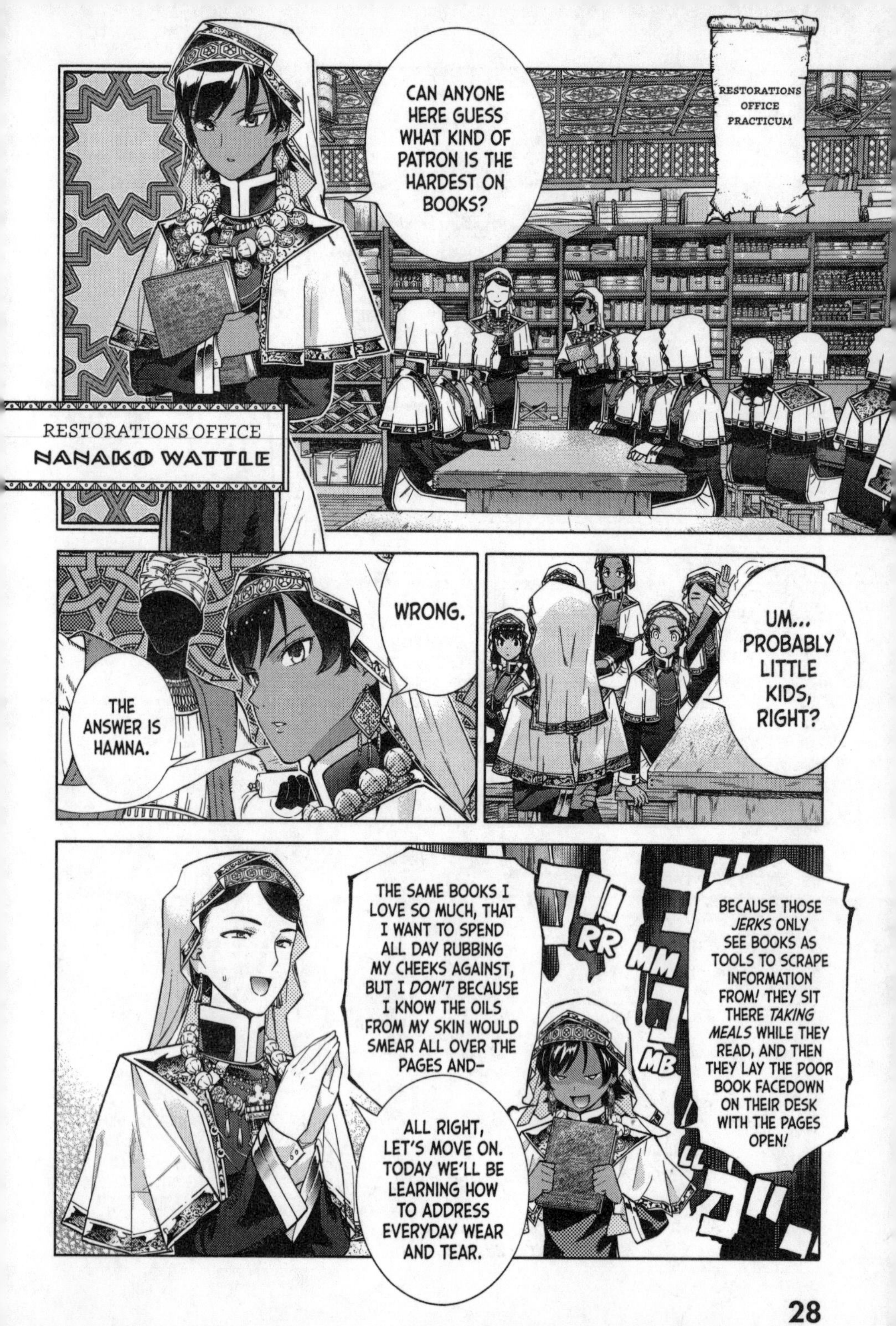
RESTORATIONS OFFICE PRACTICUM
CAN ANYONE HERE GUESS WHAT KIND OF PATRON IS THE HARDEST ON BOOKS?
RESTORATIONS OFFICE
NANAKO WATTLE
UM... PROBABLY LITTLE KIDS, RIGHT?
WRONG.
THE ANSWER IS HAMNA.
BECAUSE THOSE *JERKS* ONLY SEE BOOKS AS TOOLS TO SCRAPE INFORMATION FROM! THEY SIT THERE *TAKING MEALS* WHILE THEY READ, AND THEN THEY LAY THE POOR BOOK FACEDOWN ON THEIR DESK WITH THE PAGES OPEN!
RR
MM
MB
LL
THE SAME BOOKS I LOVE SO MUCH, THAT I WANT TO SPEND ALL DAY RUBBING MY CHEEKS AGAINST, BUT I *DON'T* BECAUSE I KNOW THE OILS FROM MY SKIN WOULD SMEAR ALL OVER THE PAGES AND–
ALL RIGHT, LET'S MOVE ON. TODAY WE'LL BE LEARNING HOW TO ADDRESS EVERYDAY WEAR AND TEAR.

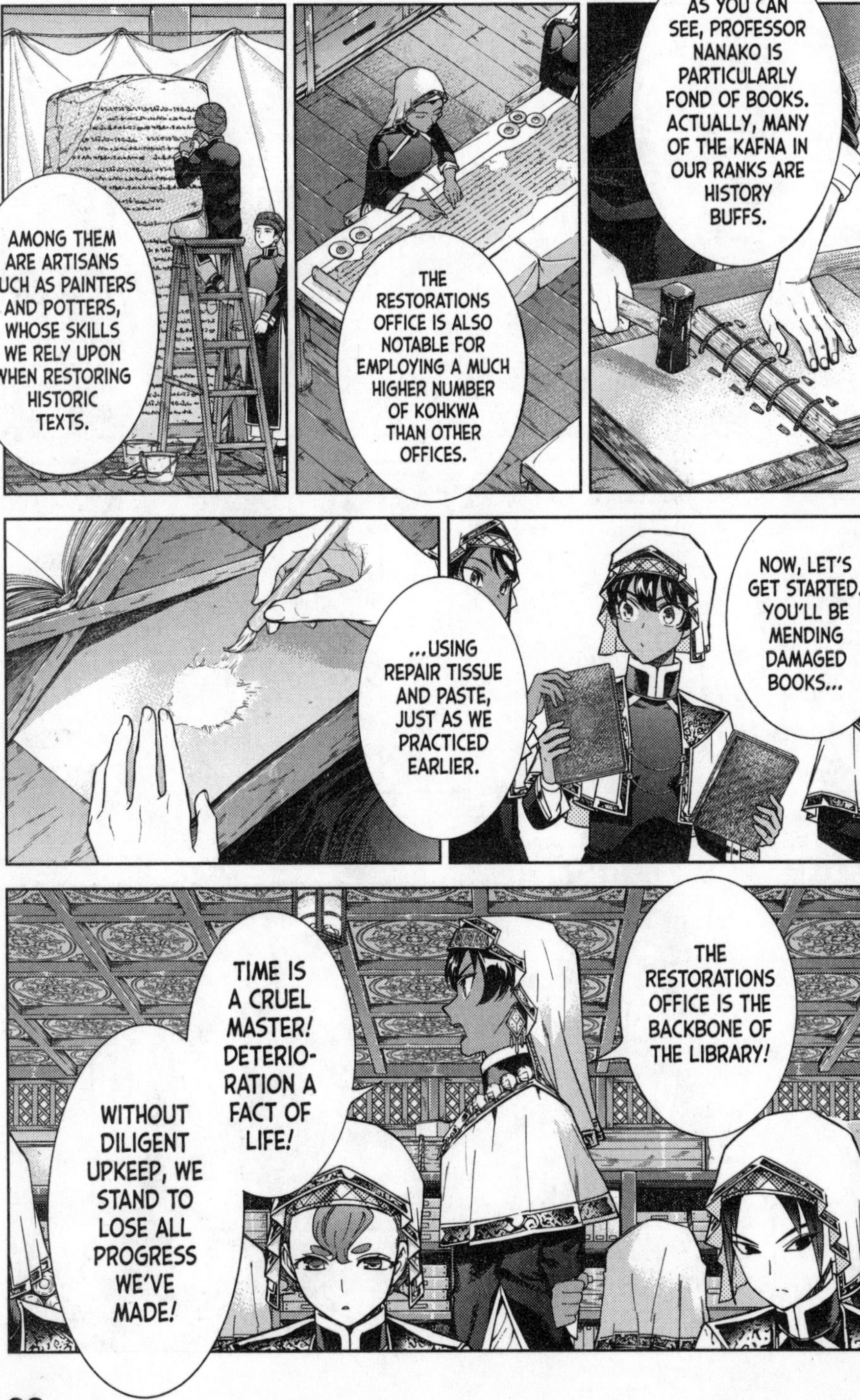
AS YOU CAN SEE, PROFESSOR NANAKO IS PARTICULARLY FOND OF BOOKS. ACTUALLY, MANY OF THE KAFNA IN OUR RANKS ARE HISTORY BUFFS.
THE RESTORATIONS OFFICE IS ALSO NOTABLE FOR EMPLOYING A MUCH HIGHER NUMBER OF KOHKWA THAN OTHER OFFICES.
AMONG THEM ARE ARTISANS SUCH AS PAINTERS AND POTTERS, WHOSE SKILLS WE RELY UPON WHEN RESTORING HISTORIC TEXTS.
NOW, LET'S GET STARTED. YOU'LL BE MENDING DAMAGED BOOKS...
...USING REPAIR TISSUE AND PASTE, JUST AS WE PRACTICED EARLIER.
THE RESTORATIONS OFFICE IS THE BACKBONE OF THE LIBRARY!
TIME IS A CRUEL MASTER! DETERIO-RATION A FACT OF LIFE!
WITHOUT DILIGENT UPKEEP, WE STAND TO LOSE ALL PROGRESS WE'VE MADE!

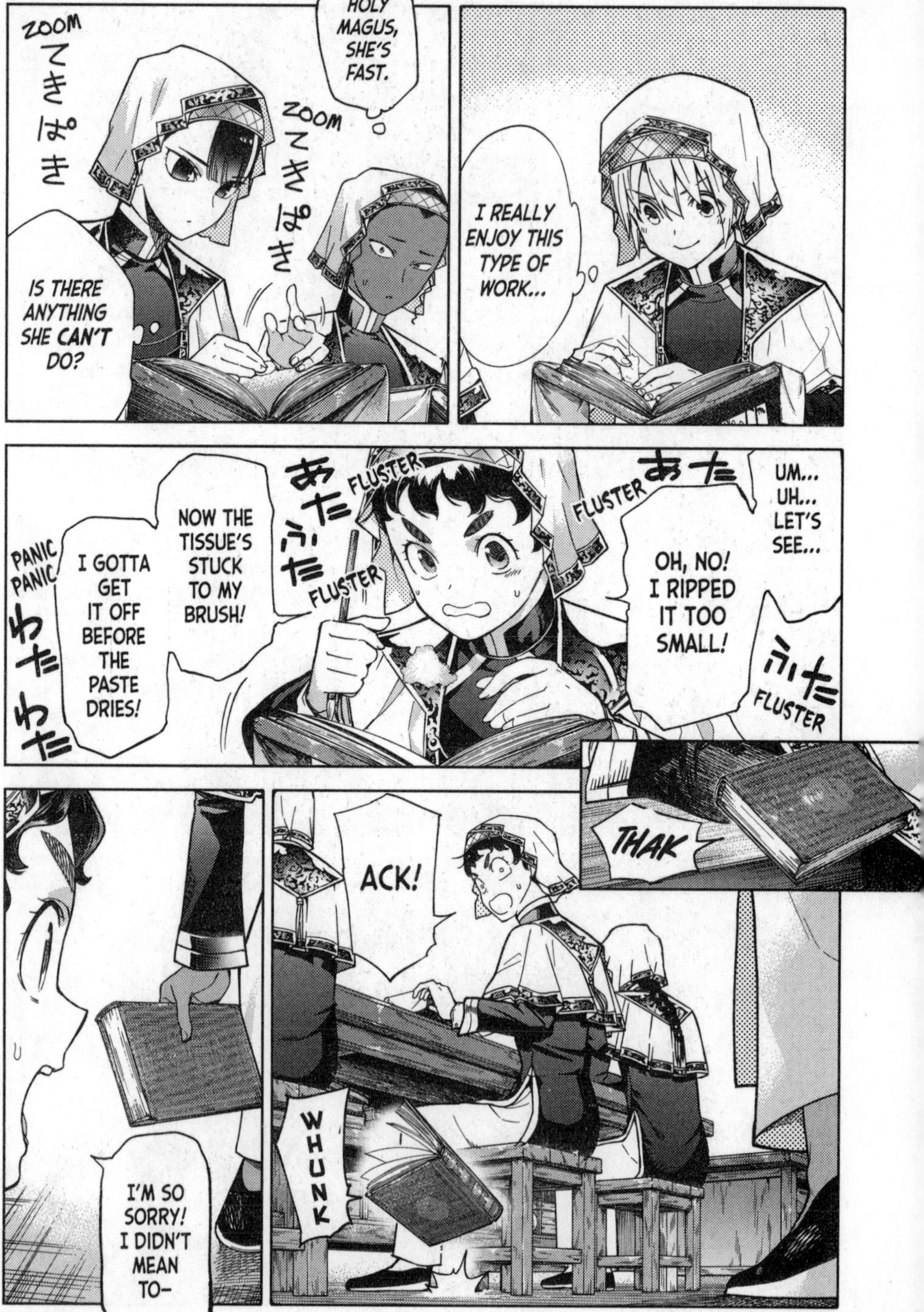
I REALLY ENJOY THIS TYPE OF WORK...
HOLY MAGUS, SHE'S FAST.
ZOOM てきぱき
ZOOM てきぱき
IS THERE ANYTHING SHE CAN'T DO?
UM... UH... LET'S SEE...
FLUSTER あた
OH, NO! I RIPPED IT TOO SMALL!
ふた FLUSTER
あた FLUSTER
ふた FLUSTER
NOW THE TISSUE'S STUCK TO MY BRUSH!
PANIC PANIC わたわた
I GOTTA GET IT OFF BEFORE THE PASTE DRIES!
THAK
ACK!
WHUNK
I'M SO SORRY! I DIDN'T MEAN TO–

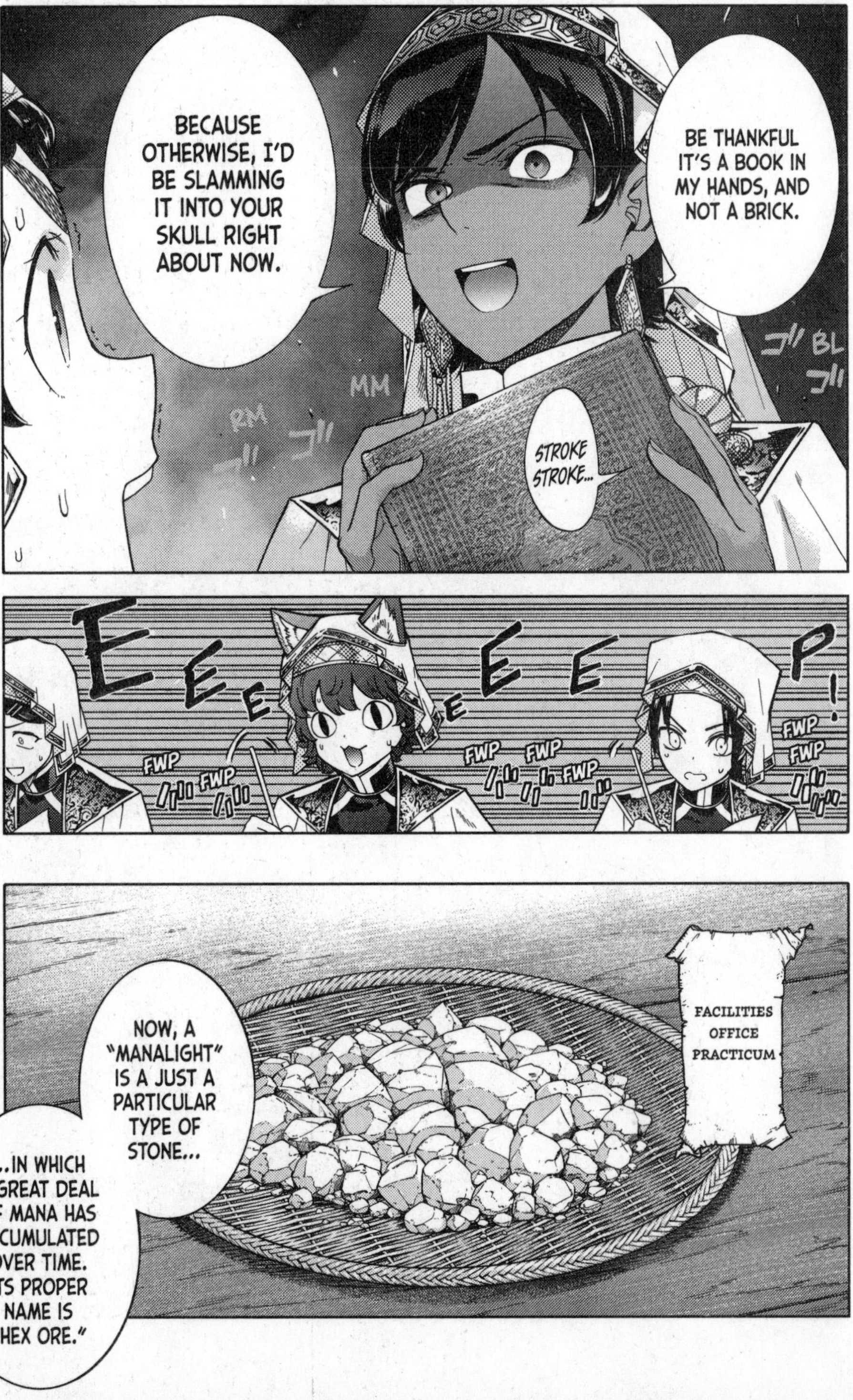
BE THANKFUL IT'S A BOOK IN MY HANDS, AND NOT A BRICK.
BECAUSE OTHERWISE, I'D BE SLAMMING IT INTO YOUR SKULL RIGHT ABOUT NOW.
BL
MM
RM
STROKE STROKE...
EEEEEEEP!
FWP FWP FWP FWP FWP FWP FWP
FACILITIES OFFICE PRACTICUM
NOW, A "MANALIGHT" IS A JUST A PARTICULAR TYPE OF STONE...
...IN WHICH A GREAT DEAL OF MANA HAS ACCUMULATED OVER TIME. ITS PROPER NAME IS "HEX ORE."

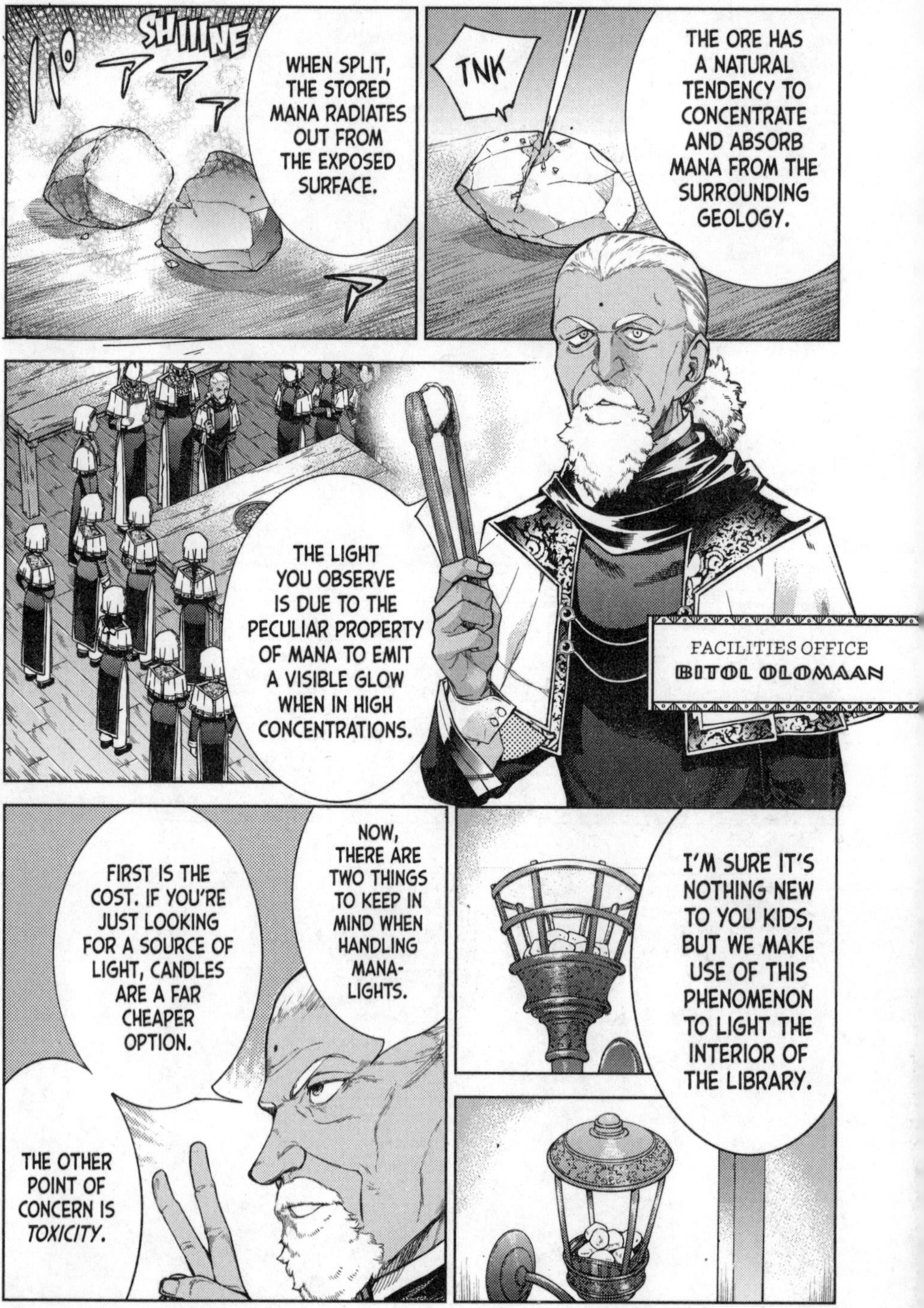
TNK
THE ORE HAS A NATURAL TENDENCY TO CONCENTRATE AND ABSORB MANA FROM THE SURROUNDING GEOLOGY.
SHIIINE
WHEN SPLIT, THE STORED MANA RADIATES OUT FROM THE EXPOSED SURFACE.
THE LIGHT YOU OBSERVE IS DUE TO THE PECULIAR PROPERTY OF MANA TO EMIT A VISIBLE GLOW WHEN IN HIGH CONCENTRATIONS.
FACILITIES OFFICE
BITOL OLOMAAN
I'M SURE IT'S NOTHING NEW TO YOU KIDS, BUT WE MAKE USE OF THIS PHENOMENON TO LIGHT THE INTERIOR OF THE LIBRARY.
NOW, THERE ARE TWO THINGS TO KEEP IN MIND WHEN HANDLING MANA-LIGHTS.
FIRST IS THE COST. IF YOU'RE JUST LOOKING FOR A SOURCE OF LIGHT, CANDLES ARE A FAR CHEAPER OPTION.
THE OTHER POINT OF CONCERN IS *TOXICITY*.

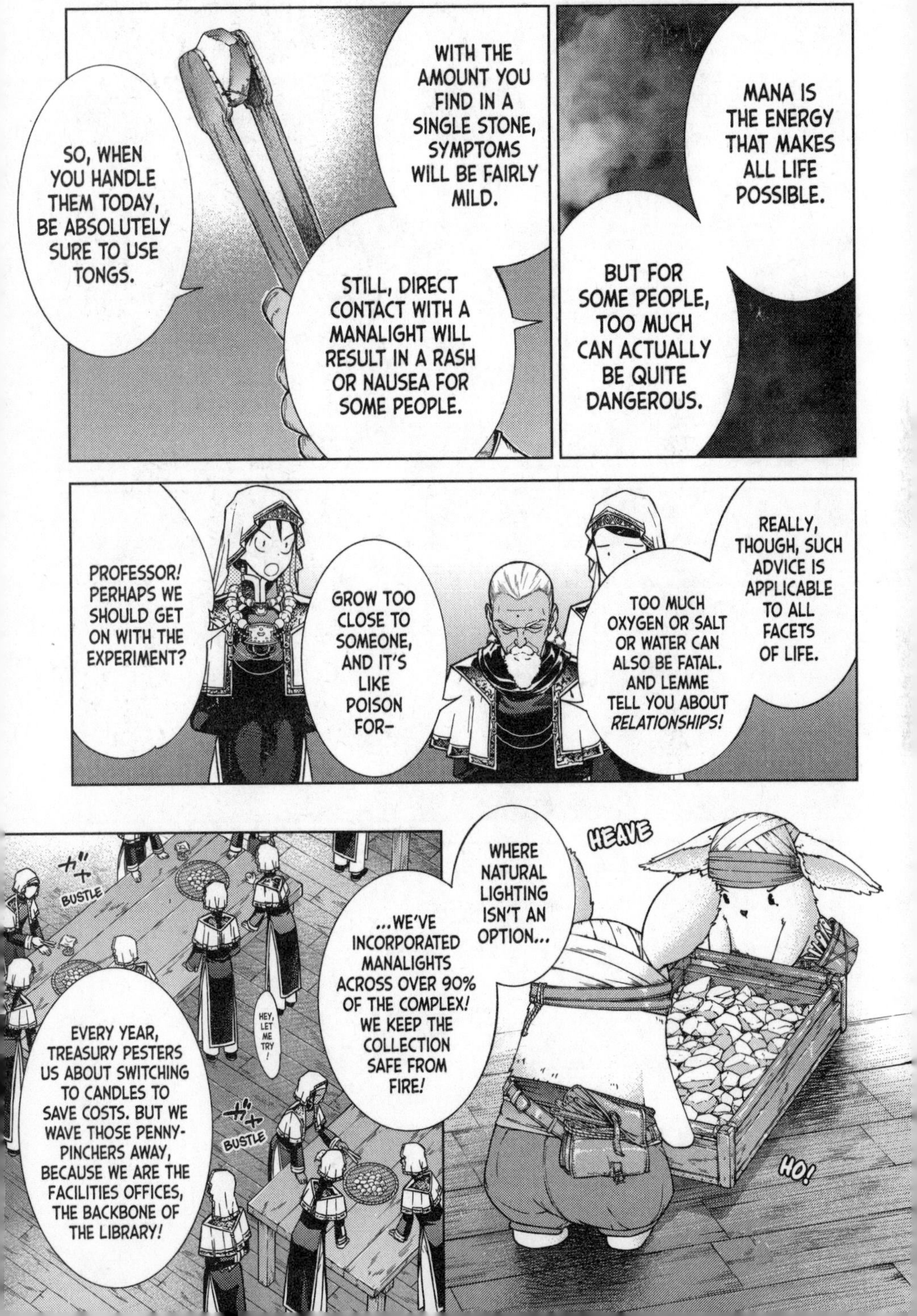
MANA IS THE ENERGY THAT MAKES ALL LIFE POSSIBLE.
BUT FOR SOME PEOPLE, TOO MUCH CAN ACTUALLY BE QUITE DANGEROUS.
WITH THE AMOUNT YOU FIND IN A SINGLE STONE, SYMPTOMS WILL BE FAIRLY MILD.
STILL, DIRECT CONTACT WITH A MANALIGHT WILL RESULT IN A RASH OR NAUSEA FOR SOME PEOPLE.
SO, WHEN YOU HANDLE THEM TODAY, BE ABSOLUTELY SURE TO USE TONGS.
REALLY, THOUGH, SUCH ADVICE IS APPLICABLE TO ALL FACETS OF LIFE.
TOO MUCH OXYGEN OR SALT OR WATER CAN ALSO BE FATAL. AND LEMME TELL YOU ABOUT *RELATIONSHIPS!*
GROW TOO CLOSE TO SOMEONE, AND IT'S LIKE POISON FOR–
PROFESSOR! PERHAPS WE SHOULD GET ON WITH THE EXPERIMENT?
HEAVE
WHERE NATURAL LIGHTING ISN'T AN OPTION...
...WE'VE INCORPORATED MANALIGHTS ACROSS OVER 90% OF THE COMPLEX! WE KEEP THE COLLECTION SAFE FROM FIRE!
HO!
ガヤ
BUSTLE
HEY, LET ME TRY!
ガヤ
BUSTLE
EVERY YEAR, TREASURY PESTERS US ABOUT SWITCHING TO CANDLES TO SAVE COSTS. BUT WE WAVE THOSE PENNY-PINCHERS AWAY, BECAUSE WE ARE THE FACILITIES OFFICES, THE BACKBONE OF THE LIBRARY!

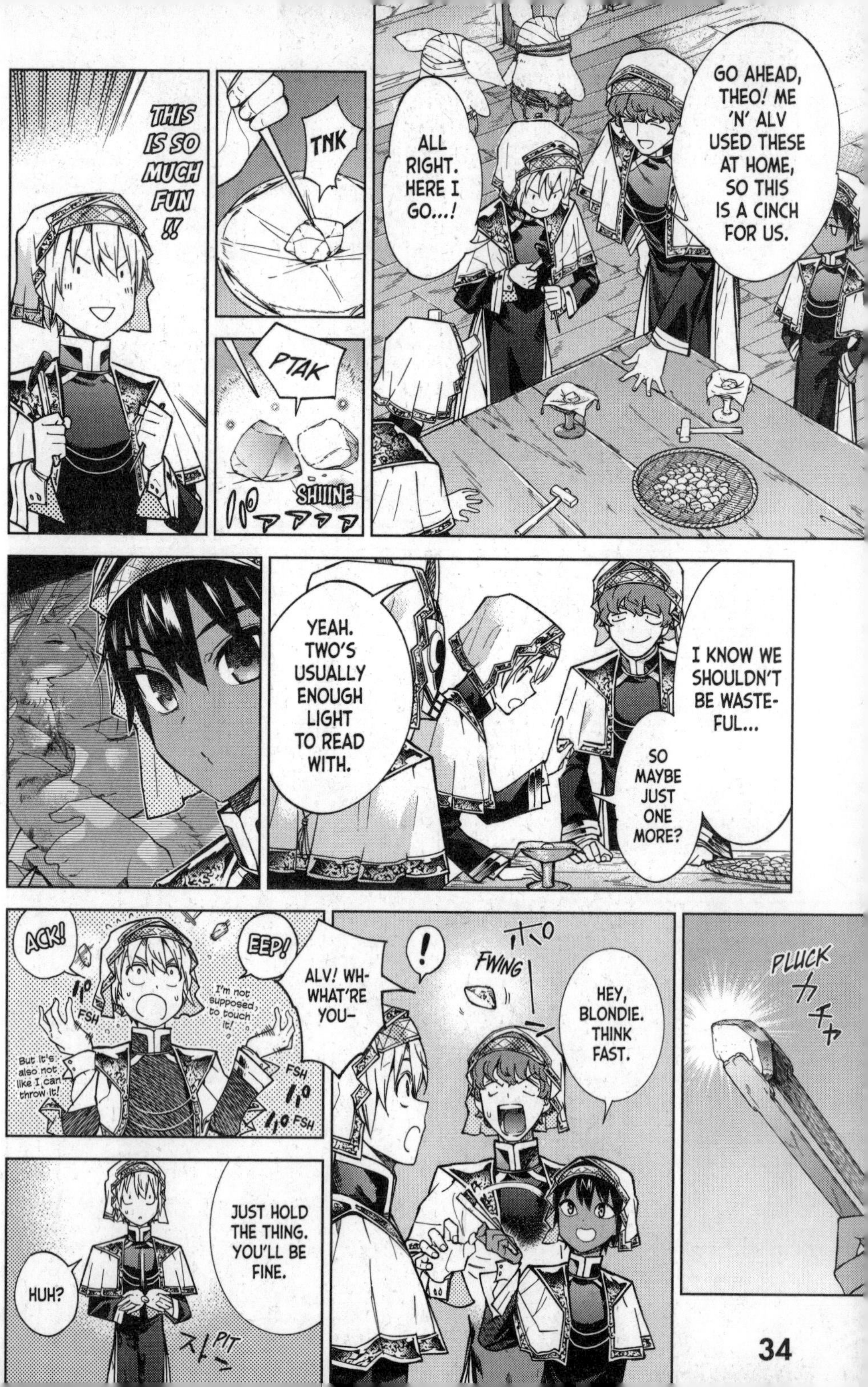
GO AHEAD, THEO! ME 'N' ALV USED THESE AT HOME, SO THIS IS A CINCH FOR US.
ALL RIGHT. HERE I GO...!
TNK
PTAK
SHIIINE
THIS IS SO MUCH FUN!!
I KNOW WE SHOULDN'T BE WASTE-FUL...
SO MAYBE JUST ONE MORE?
YEAH. TWO'S USUALLY ENOUGH LIGHT TO READ WITH.
PLUCK
!
FWING
HEY, BLONDIE. THINK FAST.
ALV! WH-WHAT'RE YOU–
ACK!
EEP!
I'm not supposed to touch it!
But it's also not like I can throw it!
FSH
FSH
FSH
JUST HOLD THE THING. YOU'LL BE FINE.
HUH?
PIT

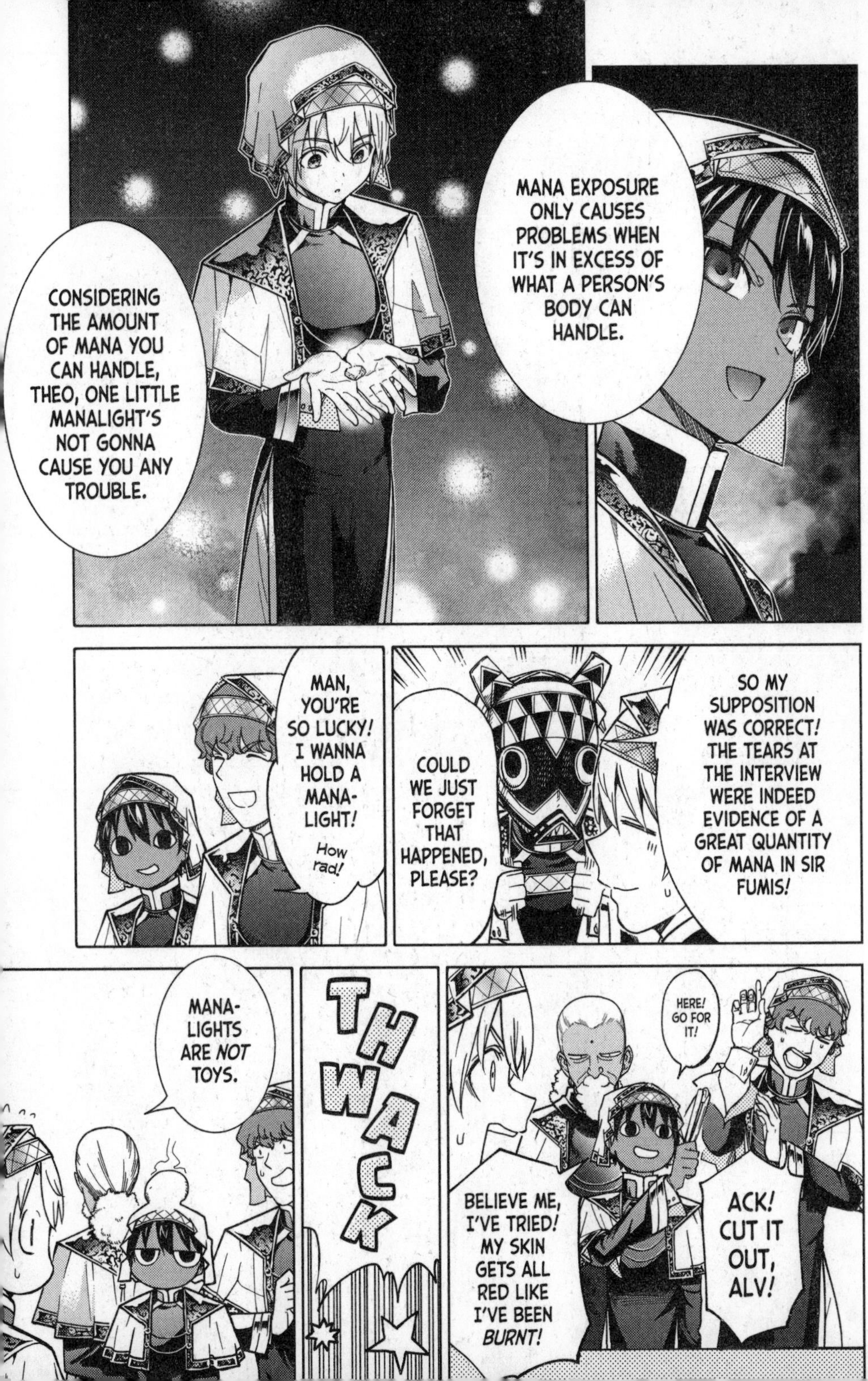
MANA EXPOSURE ONLY CAUSES PROBLEMS WHEN IT'S IN EXCESS OF WHAT A PERSON'S BODY CAN HANDLE.
CONSIDERING THE AMOUNT OF MANA YOU CAN HANDLE, THEO, ONE LITTLE MANALIGHT'S NOT GONNA CAUSE YOU ANY TROUBLE.
SO MY SUPPOSITION WAS CORRECT! THE TEARS AT THE INTERVIEW WERE INDEED EVIDENCE OF A GREAT QUANTITY OF MANA IN SIR FUMIS!
COULD WE JUST FORGET THAT HAPPENED, PLEASE?
MAN, YOU'RE SO LUCKY! I WANNA HOLD A MANA-LIGHT!
How rad!
HERE! GO FOR IT!
ACK! CUT IT OUT, ALV!
BELIEVE ME, I'VE TRIED! MY SKIN GETS ALL RED LIKE I'VE BEEN *BURNT*!
THWACK
MANA-LIGHTS ARE *NOT* TOYS.

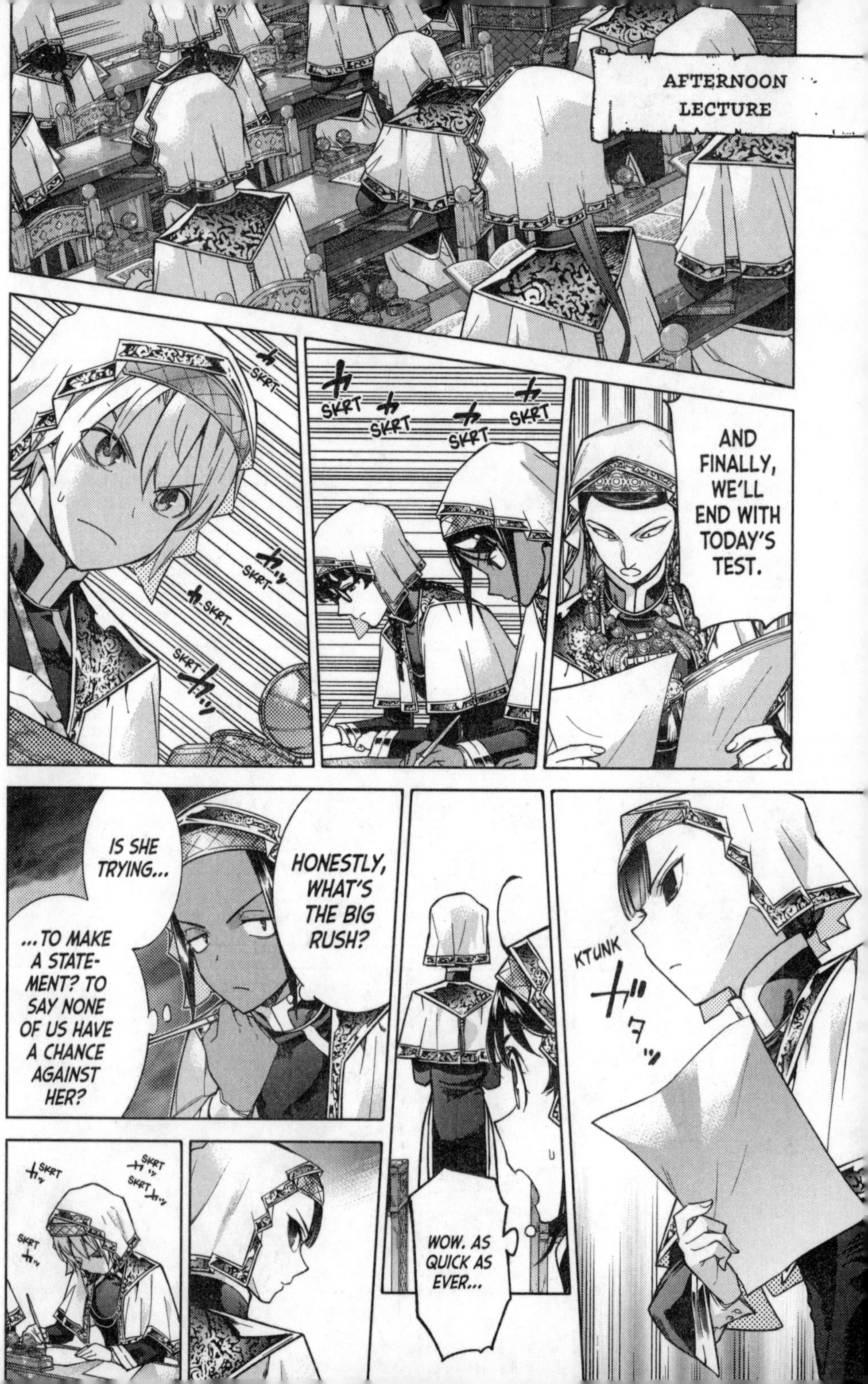
AFTERNOON LECTURE
AND FINALLY, WE'LL END WITH TODAY'S TEST.
SKRT
SKRT
SKRT
SKRT
SKRT
SKRT
SKRT
SKRT
KTUNK
WOW. AS QUICK AS EVER...
HONESTLY, WHAT'S THE BIG RUSH?
IS SHE TRYING...
...TO MAKE A STATEMENT? TO SAY NONE OF US HAVE A CHANCE AGAINST HER?
SKRT
SKRT
SKRT

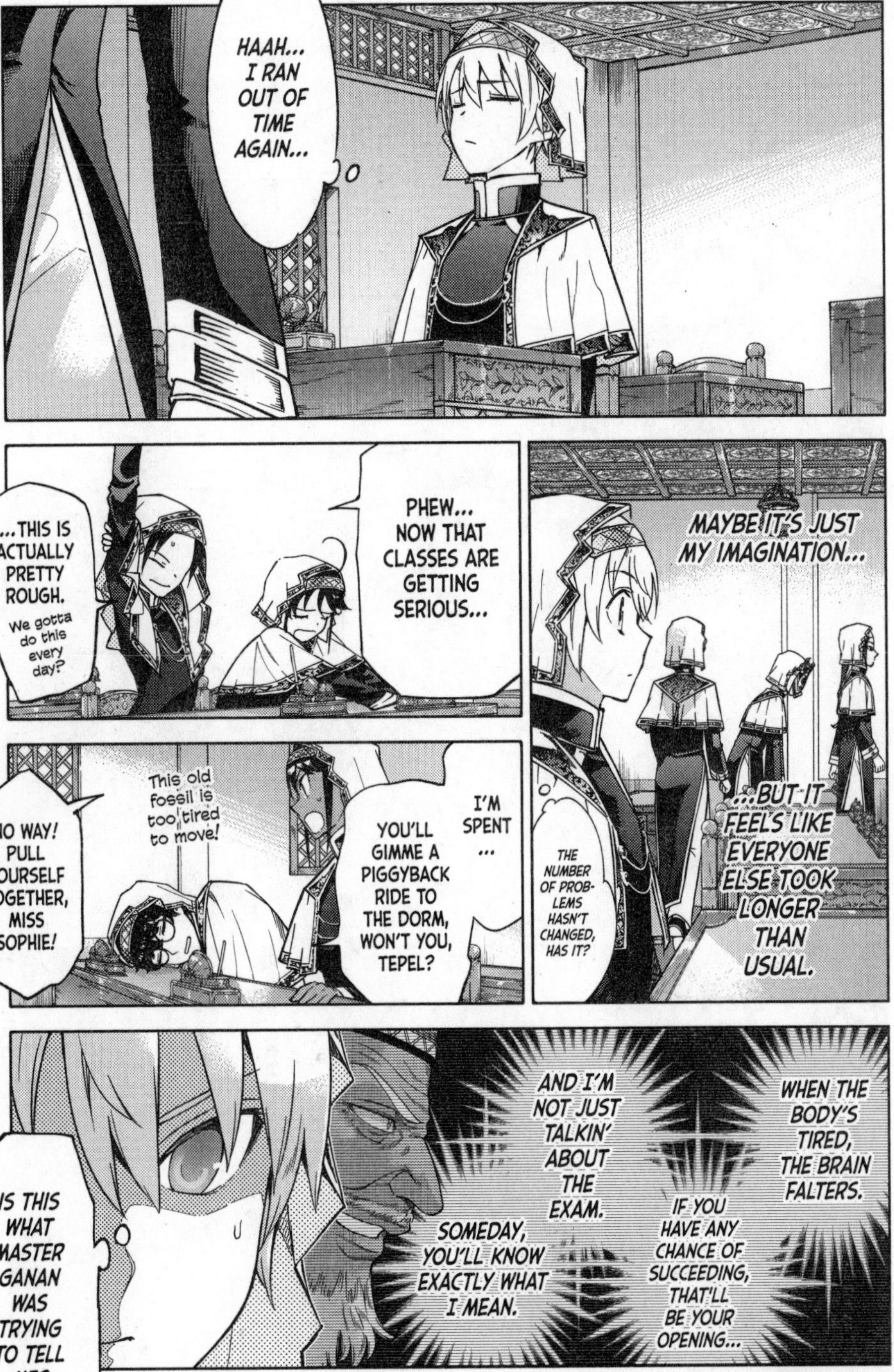
HAAH... I RAN OUT OF TIME AGAIN...
MAYBE IT'S JUST MY IMAGINATION...
...BUT IT FEELS LIKE EVERYONE ELSE TOOK LONGER THAN USUAL.
THE NUMBER OF PROB-LEMS HASN'T CHANGED, HAS IT?
PHEW... NOW THAT CLASSES ARE GETTING SERIOUS...
...THIS IS ACTUALLY PRETTY ROUGH.
We gotta do this every day?
I'M SPENT ...
YOU'LL GIMME A PIGGYBACK RIDE TO THE DORM, WON'T YOU, TEPEL?
This old fossil is too tired to move!
NO WAY! PULL YOURSELF TOGETHER, MISS SOPHIE!
WHEN THE BODY'S TIRED, THE BRAIN FALTERS.
IF YOU HAVE ANY CHANCE OF SUCCEEDING, THAT'LL BE YOUR OPENING...
AND I'M NOT JUST TALKIN' ABOUT THE EXAM.
SOMEDAY, YOU'LL KNOW EXACTLY WHAT I MEAN.
IS THIS WHAT MASTER GANAN WAS TRYING TO TELL ME?

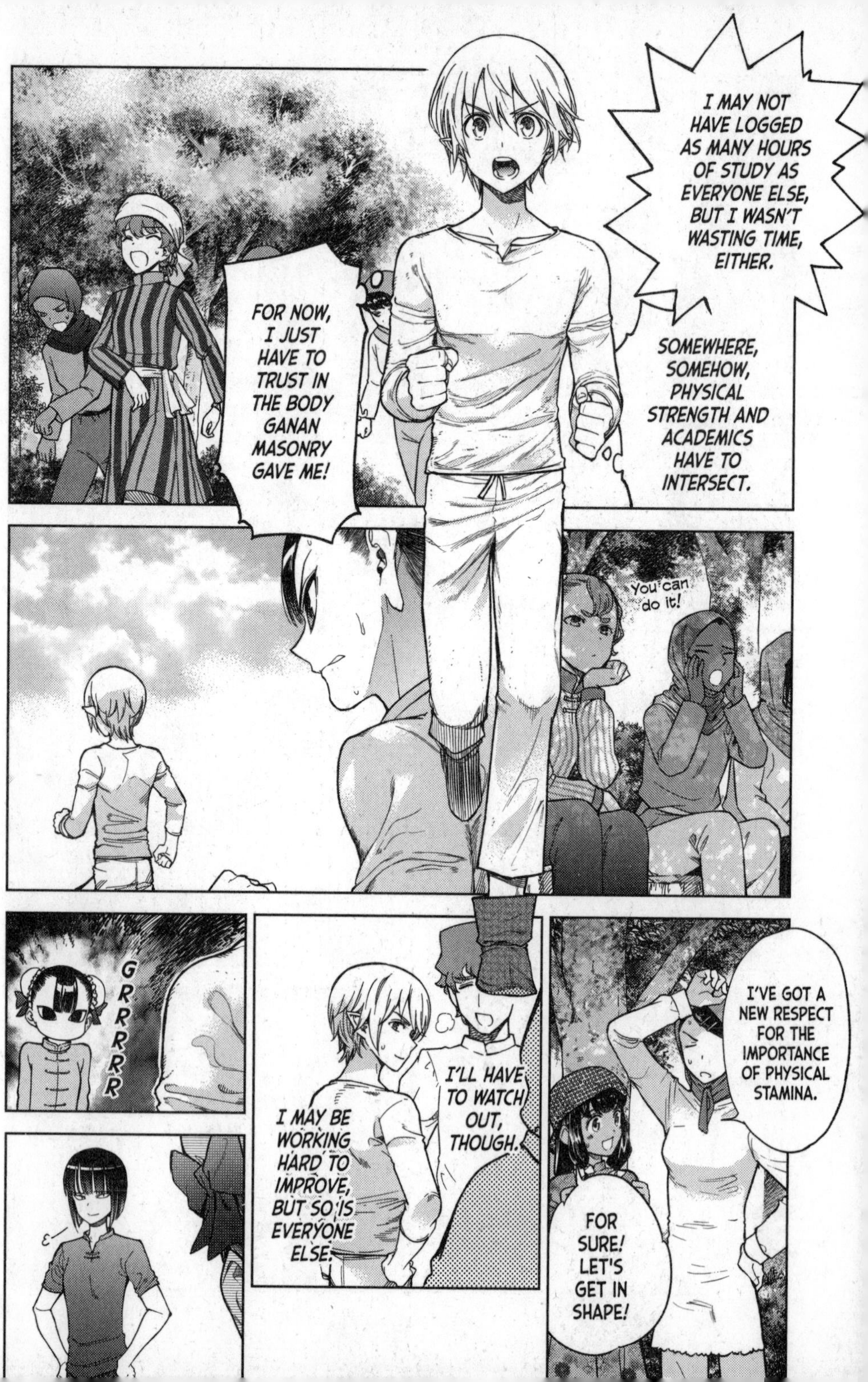
I MAY NOT HAVE LOGGED AS MANY HOURS OF STUDY AS EVERYONE ELSE, BUT I WASN'T WASTING TIME, EITHER.
SOMEWHERE, SOMEHOW, PHYSICAL STRENGTH AND ACADEMICS HAVE TO INTERSECT.
FOR NOW, I JUST HAVE TO TRUST IN THE BODY GANAN MASONRY GAVE ME!
You can do it!
I'VE GOT A NEW RESPECT FOR THE IMPORTANCE OF PHYSICAL STAMINA.
FOR SURE! LET'S GET IN SHAPE!
I'LL HAVE TO WATCH OUT, THOUGH.
I MAY BE WORKING HARD TO IMPROVE, BUT SO IS EVERYONE ELSE.
GRRRRRR

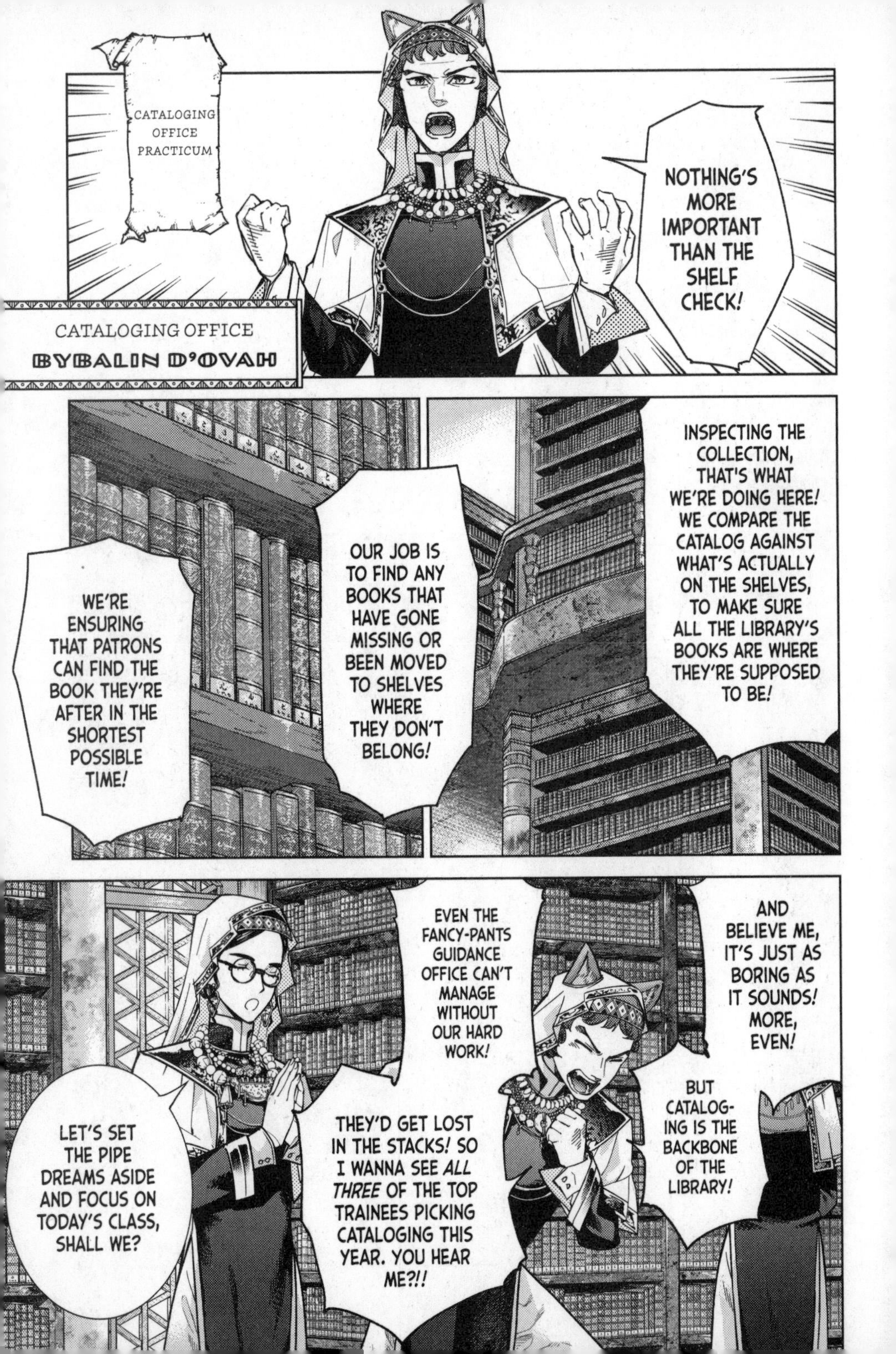
CATALOGING OFFICE PRACTICUM
NOTHING'S MORE IMPORTANT THAN THE SHELF CHECK!
CATALOGING OFFICE
BYBALIN D'OVAH
INSPECTING THE COLLECTION, THAT'S WHAT WE'RE DOING HERE! WE COMPARE THE CATALOG AGAINST WHAT'S ACTUALLY ON THE SHELVES, TO MAKE SURE ALL THE LIBRARY'S BOOKS ARE WHERE THEY'RE SUPPOSED TO BE!
OUR JOB IS TO FIND ANY BOOKS THAT HAVE GONE MISSING OR BEEN MOVED TO SHELVES WHERE THEY DON'T BELONG!
WE'RE ENSURING THAT PATRONS CAN FIND THE BOOK THEY'RE AFTER IN THE SHORTEST POSSIBLE TIME!
AND BELIEVE ME, IT'S JUST AS BORING AS IT SOUNDS! MORE, EVEN!
EVEN THE FANCY-PANTS GUIDANCE OFFICE CAN'T MANAGE WITHOUT OUR HARD WORK!
BUT CATALOG-ING IS THE BACKBONE OF THE LIBRARY!
THEY'D GET LOST IN THE STACKS! SO I WANNA SEE *ALL THREE* OF THE TOP TRAINEES PICKING CATALOGING THIS YEAR. YOU HEAR ME?!!
LET'S SET THE PIPE DREAMS ASIDE AND FOCUS ON TODAY'S CLASS, SHALL WE?

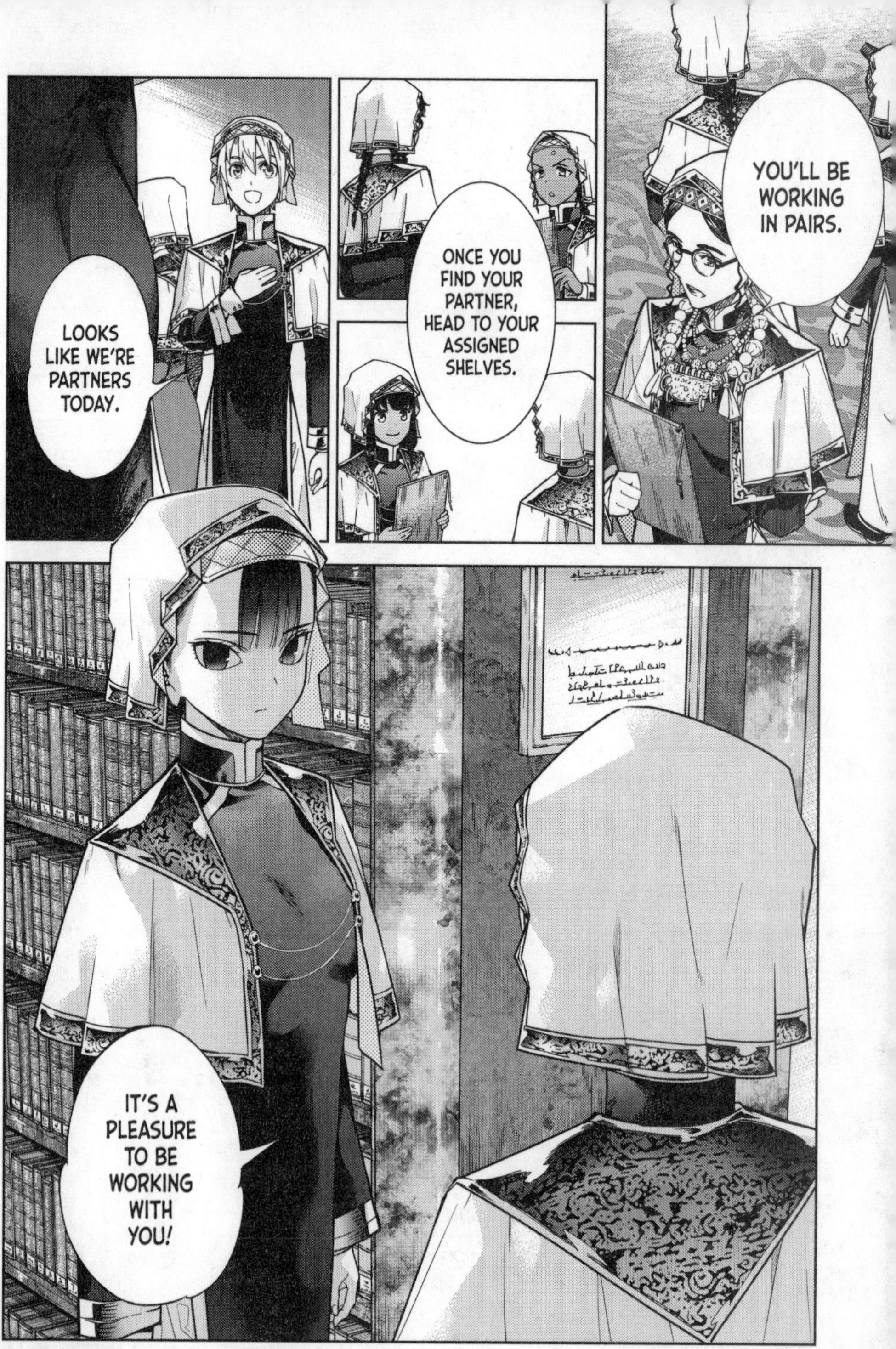
YOU'LL BE WORKING IN PAIRS.
ONCE YOU FIND YOUR PARTNER, HEAD TO YOUR ASSIGNED SHELVES.
LOOKS LIKE WE'RE PARTNERS TODAY.
IT'S A PLEASURE TO BE WORKING WITH YOU!

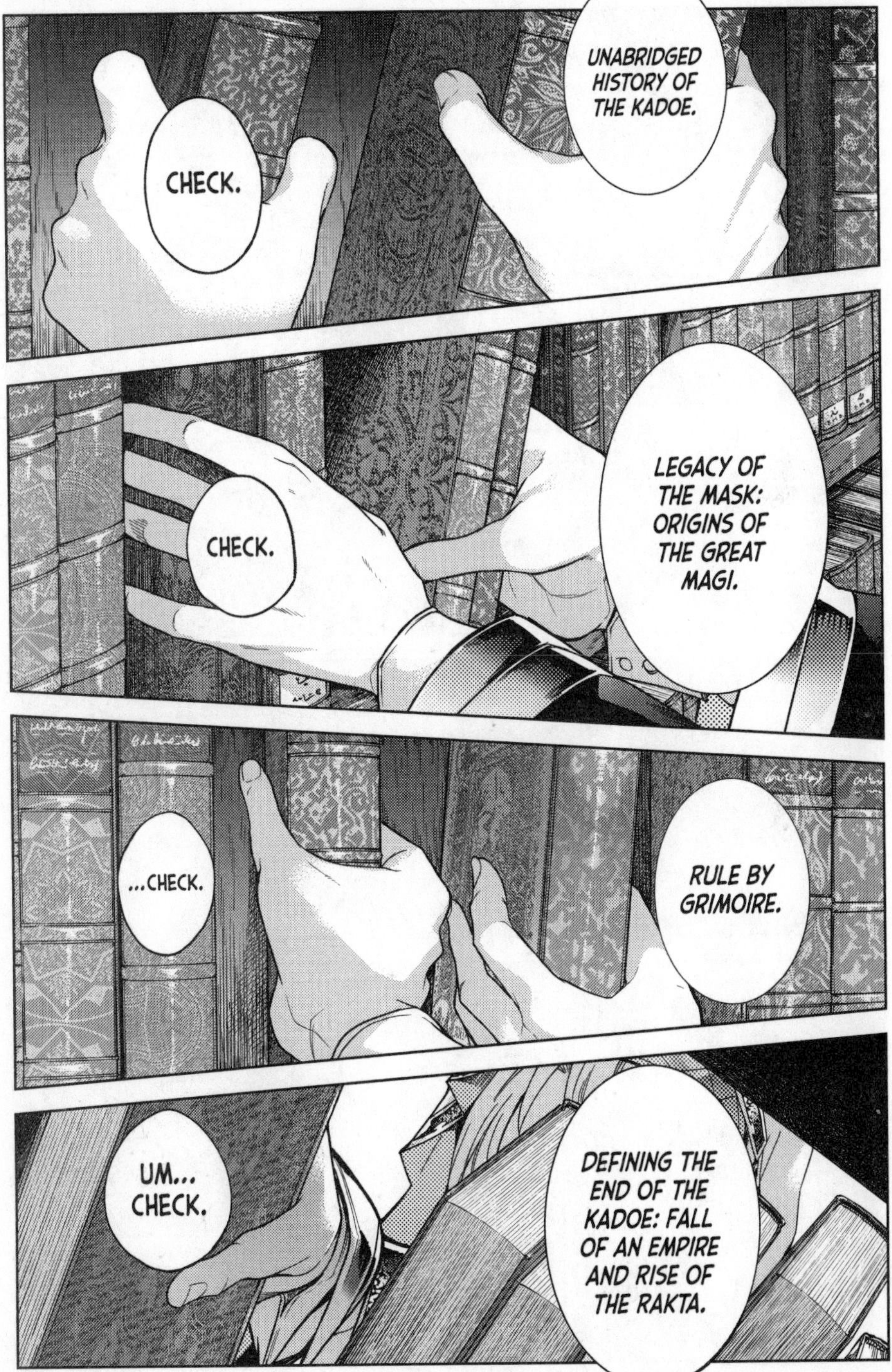
UNABRIDGED HISTORY OF THE KADOE.
CHECK.
LEGACY OF THE MASK: ORIGINS OF THE GREAT MAGI.
CHECK.
RULE BY GRIMOIRE.
...CHECK.
DEFINING THE END OF THE KADOE: FALL OF AN EMPIRE AND RISE OF THE RAKTA.
UM... CHECK.

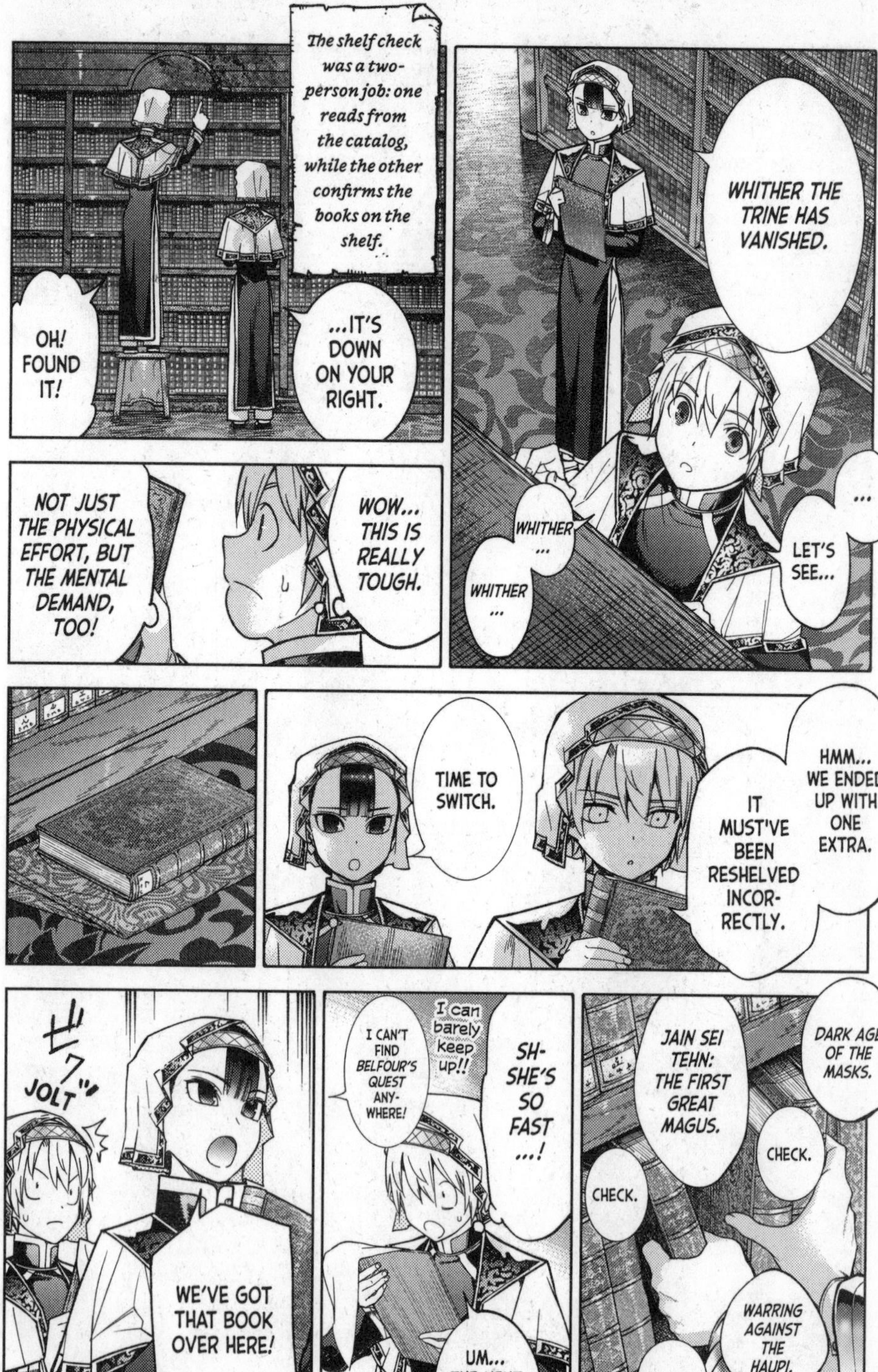
WHITHER THE TRINE HAS VANISHED.
...
LET'S SEE...
WHITHER...
WHITHER...
The shelf check was a two-person job: one reads from the catalog, while the other confirms the books on the shelf.
...IT'S DOWN ON YOUR RIGHT.
OH! FOUND IT!
WOW... THIS IS REALLY TOUGH.
NOT JUST THE PHYSICAL EFFORT, BUT THE MENTAL DEMAND, TOO!
HMM... WE ENDED UP WITH ONE EXTRA.
IT MUST'VE BEEN RESHELVED INCORRECTLY.
TIME TO SWITCH.
DARK AGE OF THE MASKS.
JAIN SEI TEHN: THE FIRST GREAT MAGUS.
CHECK.
CHECK.
WARRING AGAINST THE HAUPI.
CHECK.
SH-SHE'S SO FAST...!
I can barely keep up!!
I CAN'T FIND BELFOUR'S QUEST ANYWHERE!
UM... THE NEXT ONE IS...
JOLT
WE'VE GOT THAT BOOK OVER HERE!

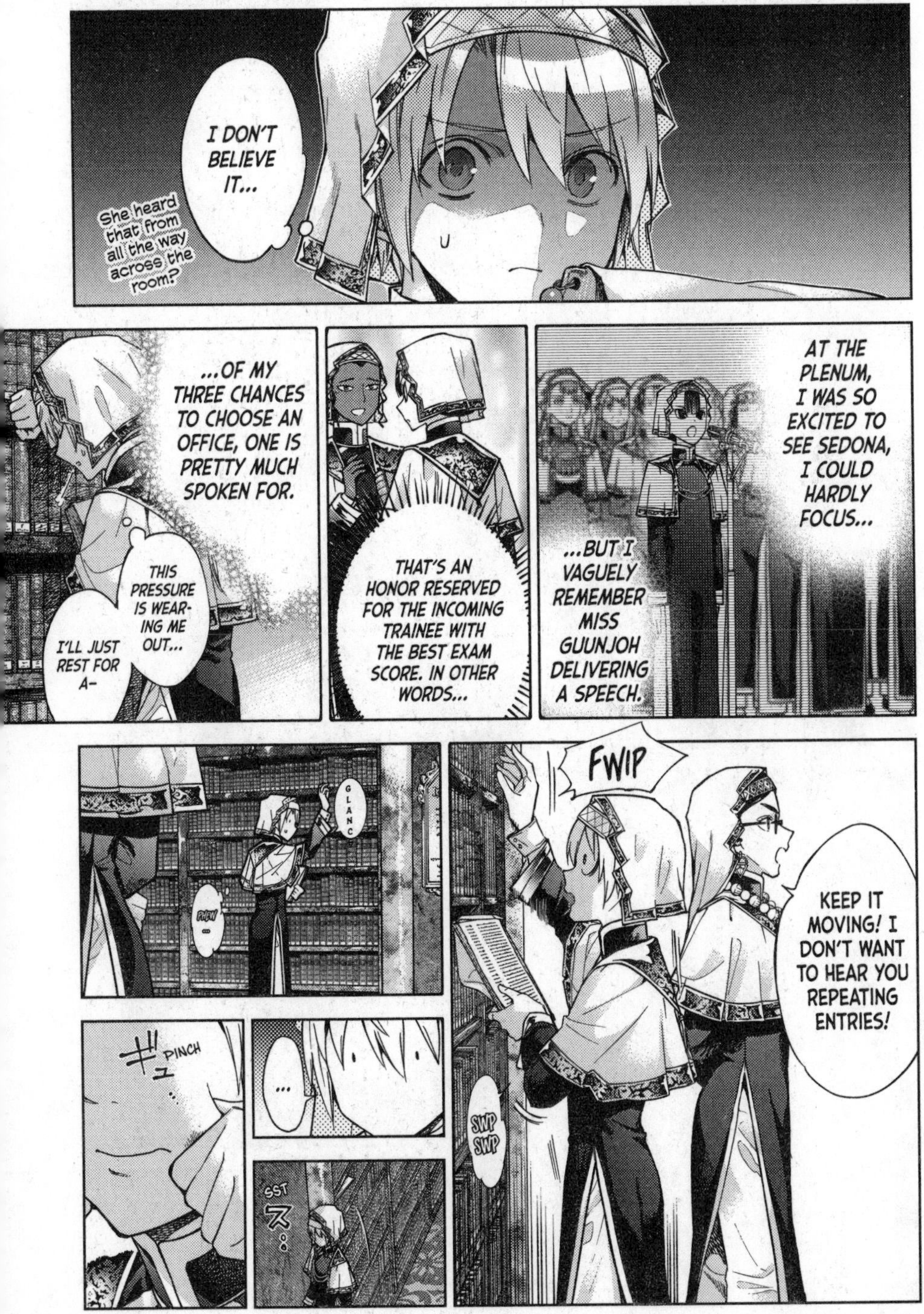
I DON'T BELIEVE IT...
She heard that from all the way across the room?
AT THE PLENUM, I WAS SO EXCITED TO SEE SEDONA, I COULD HARDLY FOCUS...
...BUT I VAGUELY REMEMBER MISS GUUNJOH DELIVERING A SPEECH.
THAT'S AN HONOR RESERVED FOR THE INCOMING TRAINEE WITH THE BEST EXAM SCORE. IN OTHER WORDS...
...OF MY THREE CHANCES TO CHOOSE AN OFFICE, ONE IS PRETTY MUCH SPOKEN FOR.
THIS PRESSURE IS WEARING ME OUT...
I'LL JUST REST FOR A-
FWIP
KEEP IT MOVING! I DON'T WANT TO HEAR YOU REPEATING ENTRIES!
SWP SWP
GLANC
PHEW ...
...
SST
PINCH

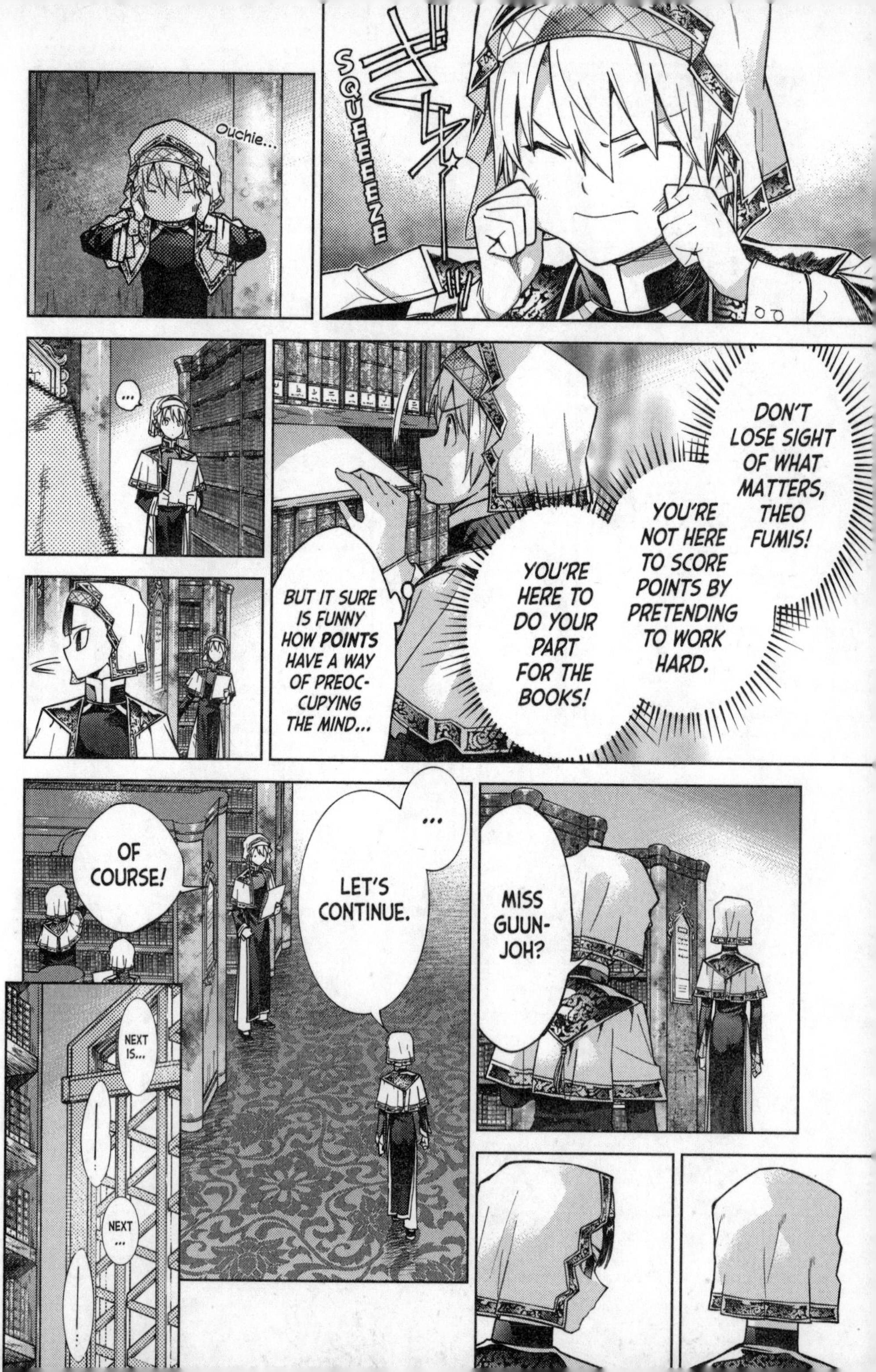
SQUEEEEZE
Ouchie...
DON'T LOSE SIGHT OF WHAT MATTERS, THEO FUMIS!
YOU'RE NOT HERE TO SCORE POINTS BY PRETENDING TO WORK HARD.
YOU'RE HERE TO DO YOUR PART FOR THE BOOKS!
BUT IT SURE IS FUNNY HOW **POINTS** HAVE A WAY OF PREOC-CUPYING THE MIND...
...
MISS GUUN-JOH?
...
LET'S CONTINUE.
OF COURSE!
NEXT IS...
!
NEXT ...
!

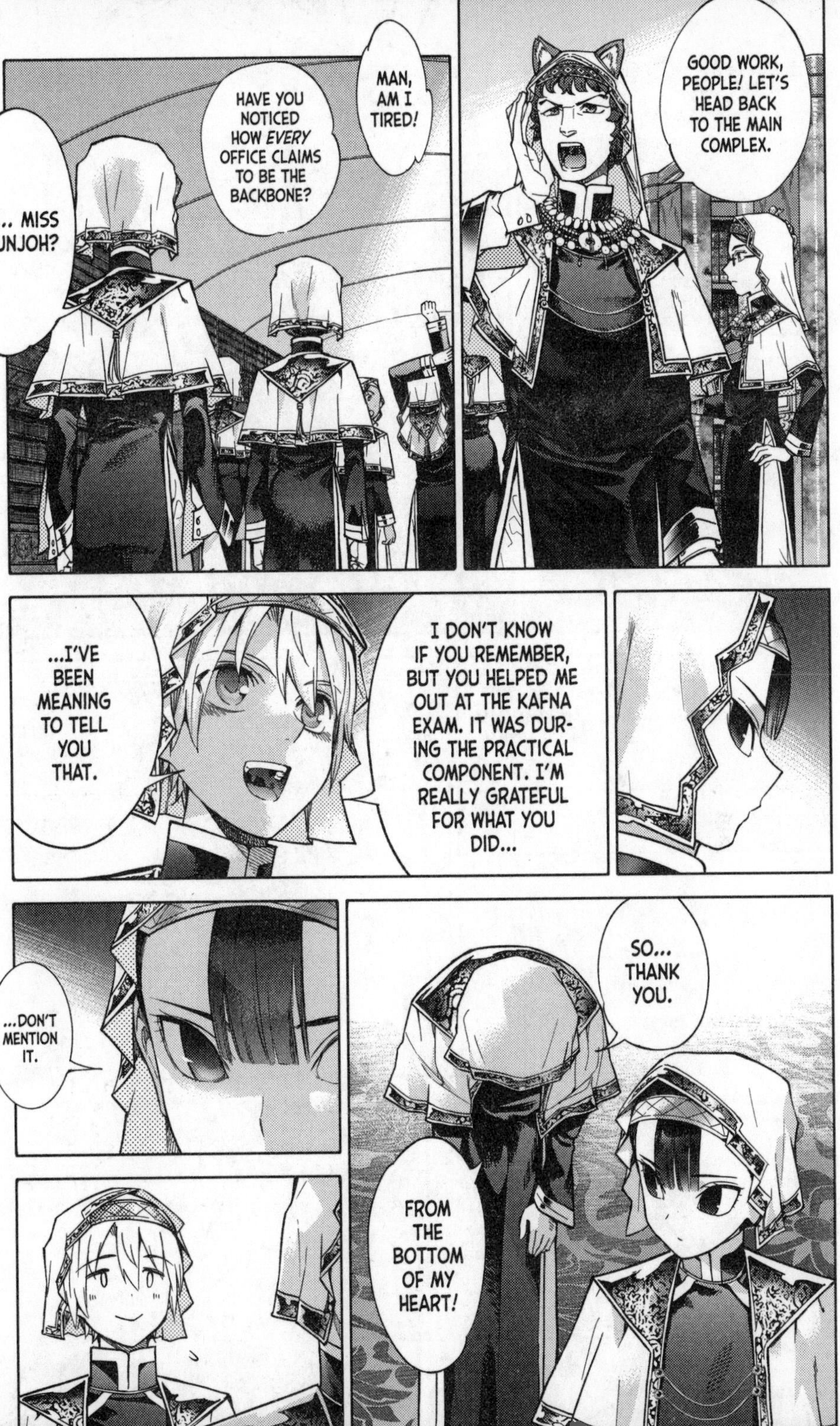
GOOD WORK, PEOPLE! LET'S HEAD BACK TO THE MAIN COMPLEX.
MAN, AM I TIRED!
HAVE YOU NOTICED HOW *EVERY* OFFICE CLAIMS TO BE THE BACKBONE?
UM... MISS GUUNJOH?
I DON'T KNOW IF YOU REMEMBER, BUT YOU HELPED ME OUT AT THE KAFNA EXAM. IT WAS DURING THE PRACTICAL COMPONENT. I'M REALLY GRATEFUL FOR WHAT YOU DID...
...I'VE BEEN MEANING TO TELL YOU THAT.
SO... THANK YOU.
FROM THE BOTTOM OF MY HEART!
...DON'T MENTION IT.

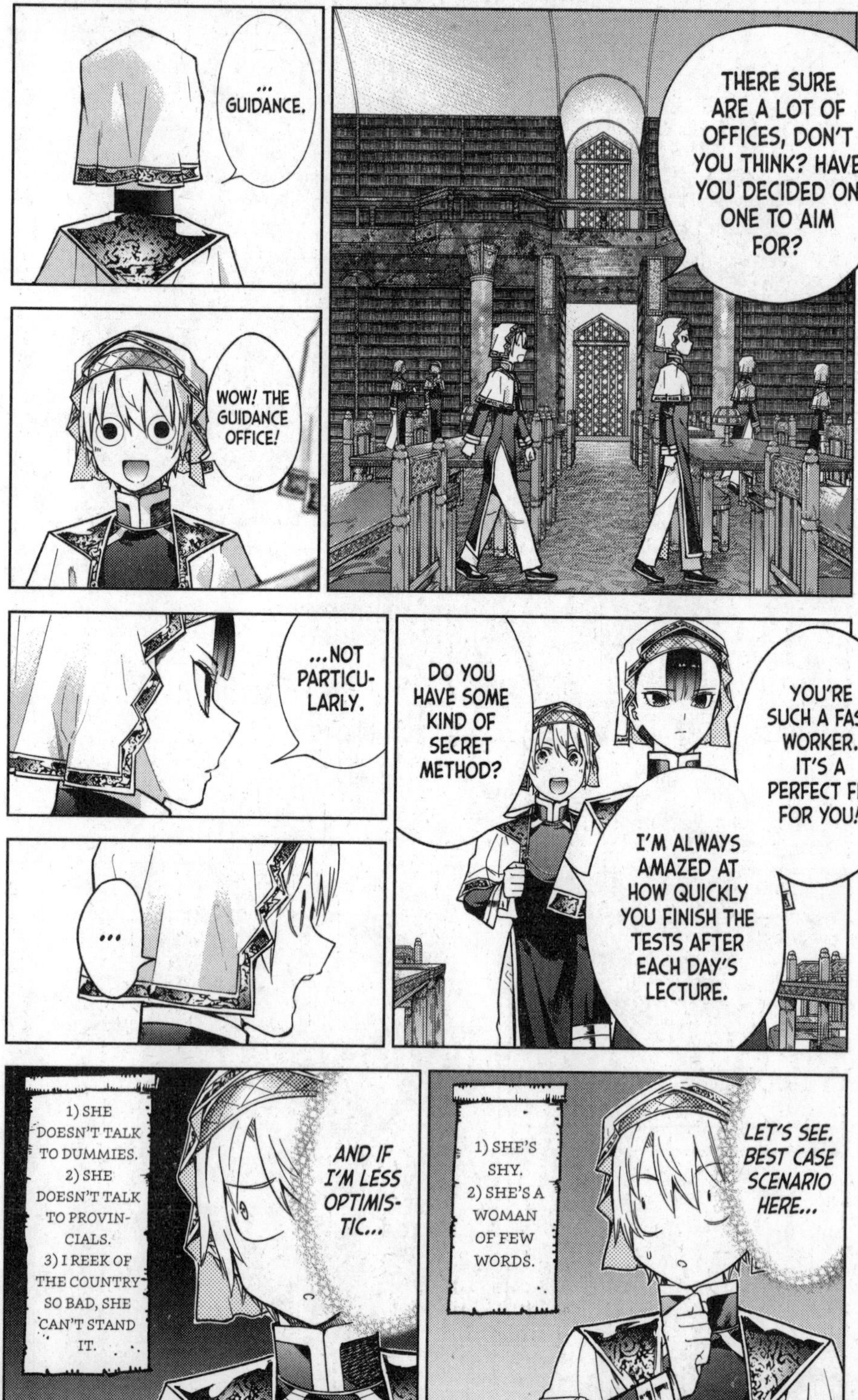
THERE SURE ARE A LOT OF OFFICES, DON'T YOU THINK? HAVE YOU DECIDED ON ONE TO AIM FOR?
... GUIDANCE.
WOW! THE GUIDANCE OFFICE!
YOU'RE SUCH A FAST WORKER. IT'S A PERFECT FIT FOR YOU!
I'M ALWAYS AMAZED AT HOW QUICKLY YOU FINISH THE TESTS AFTER EACH DAY'S LECTURE.
DO YOU HAVE SOME KIND OF SECRET METHOD?
...NOT PARTICU-LARLY.
...
LET'S SEE. BEST CASE SCENARIO HERE...
1) SHE'S SHY. 2) SHE'S A WOMAN OF FEW WORDS.
AND IF I'M LESS OPTIMIS-TIC...
1) SHE DOESN'T TALK TO DUMMIES. 2) SHE DOESN'T TALK TO PROVIN-CIALS. 3) I REEK OF THE COUNTRY SO BAD, SHE CAN'T STAND IT.

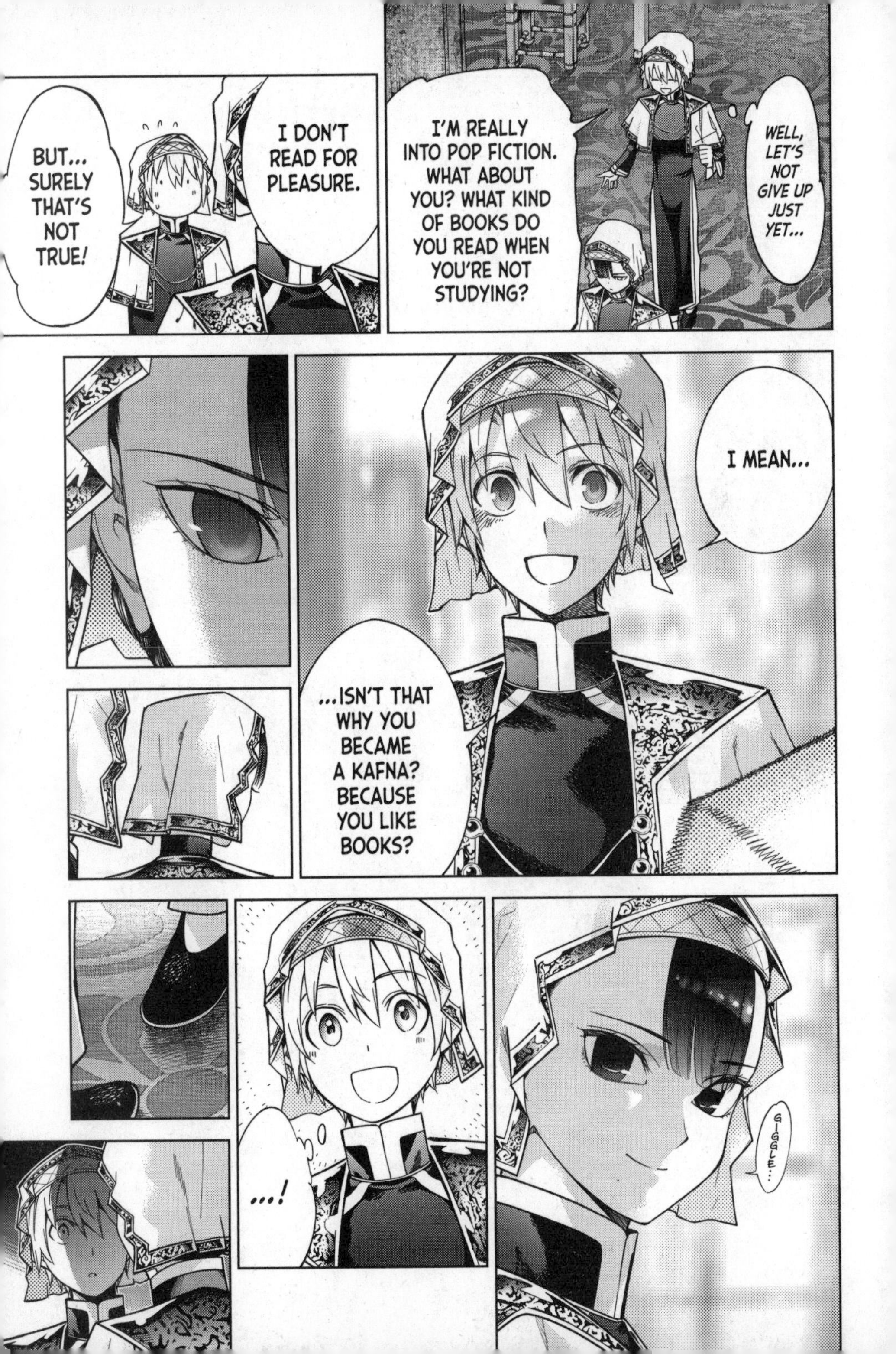
WELL, LET'S NOT GIVE UP JUST YET...
I'M REALLY INTO POP FICTION. WHAT ABOUT YOU? WHAT KIND OF BOOKS DO YOU READ WHEN YOU'RE NOT STUDYING?
I DON'T READ FOR PLEASURE.
BUT... SURELY THAT'S NOT TRUE!
I MEAN...
...ISN'T THAT WHY YOU BECAME A KAFNA? BECAUSE YOU LIKE BOOKS?
GIGGLE...
...!

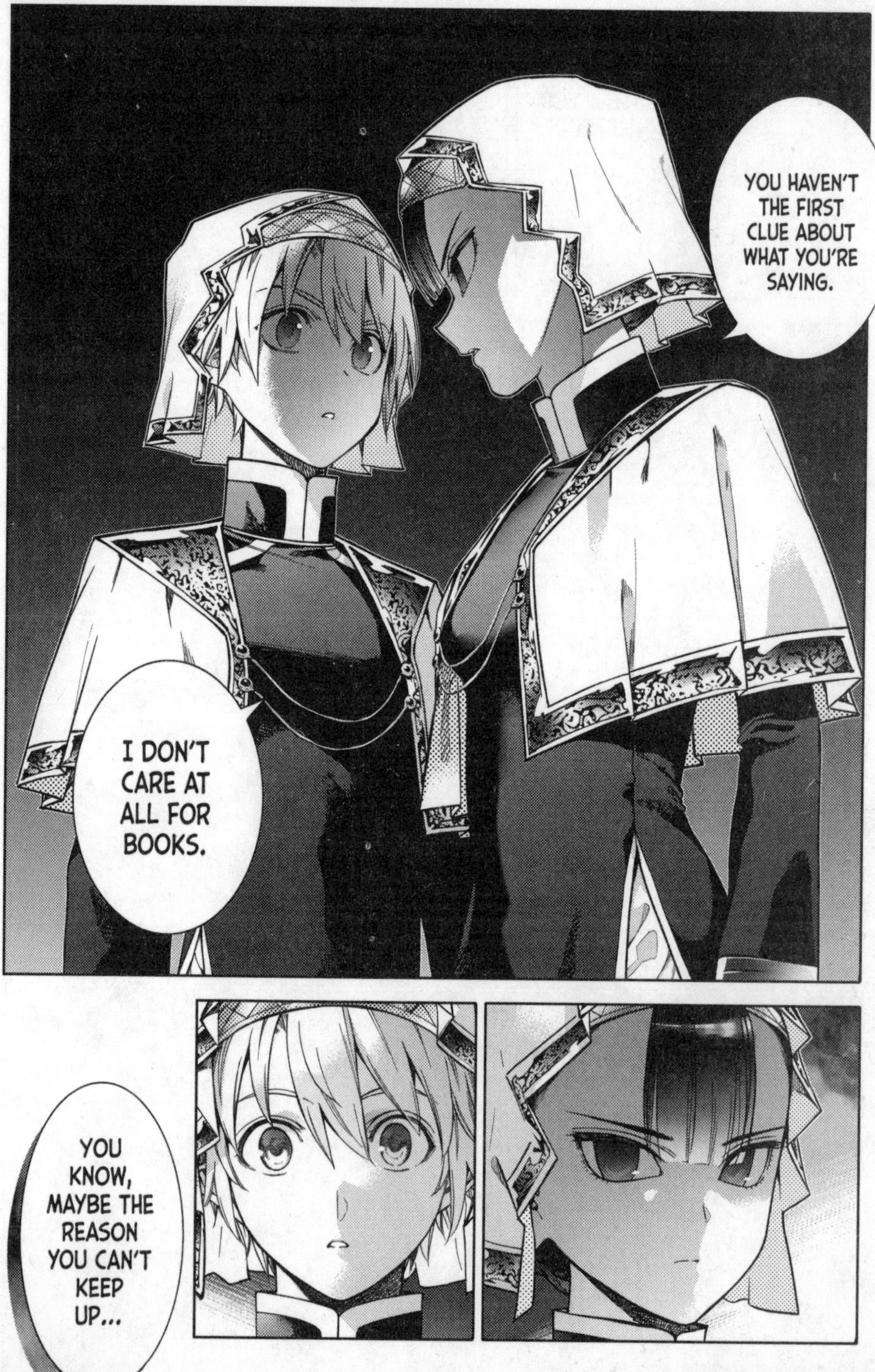

YOU HAVEN'T THE FIRST CLUE ABOUT WHAT YOU'RE SAYING.
I DON'T CARE AT ALL FOR BOOKS.
YOU KNOW, MAYBE THE REASON YOU CAN'T KEEP UP...

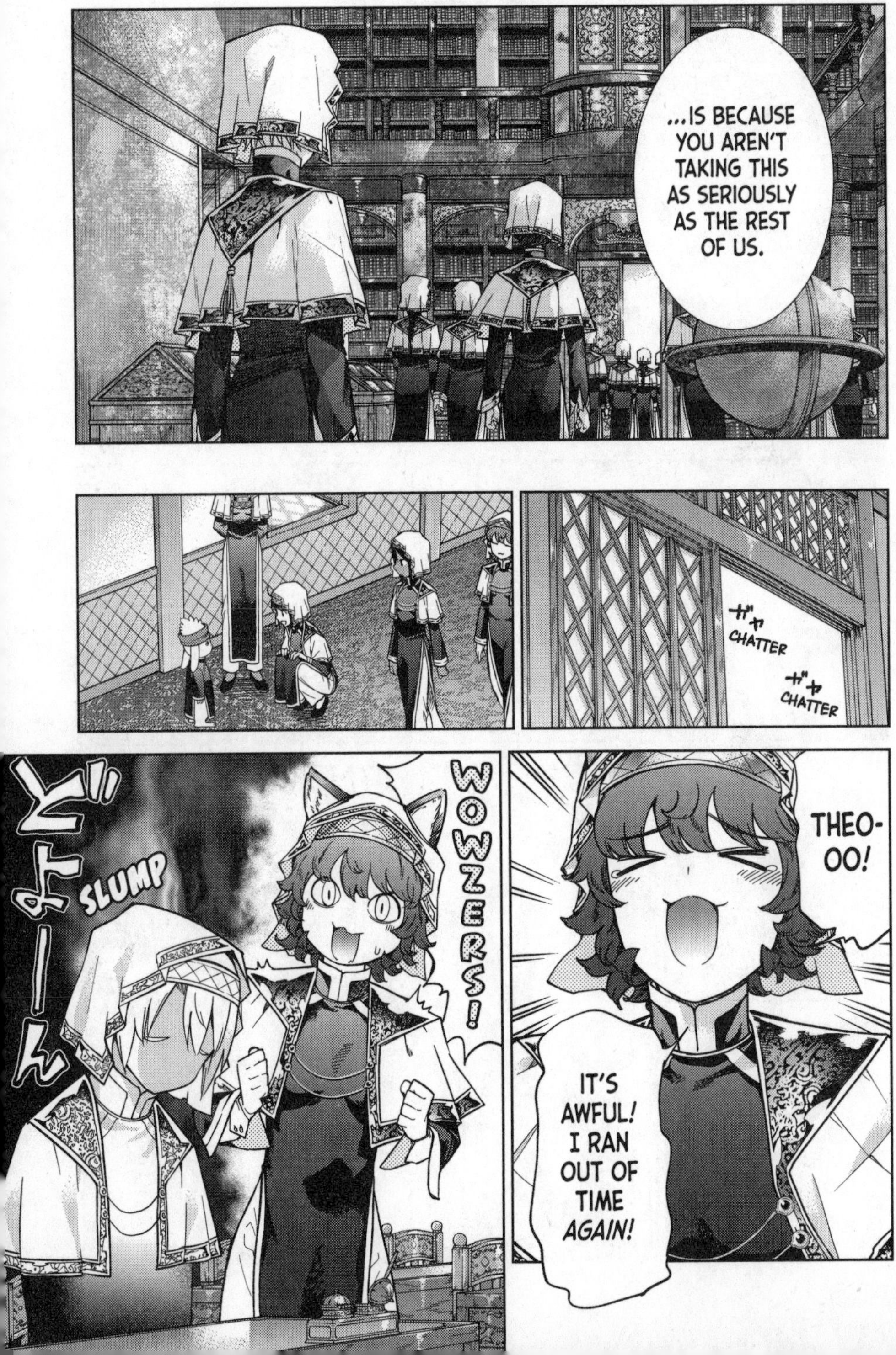
...IS BECAUSE YOU AREN'T TAKING THIS AS SERIOUSLY AS THE REST OF US.
ガヤ
CHATTER
ガヤ
CHATTER
THEO-OO!
IT'S AWFUL! I RAN OUT OF TIME *AGAIN!*
WOWZERS!
SLUMP
どよーん

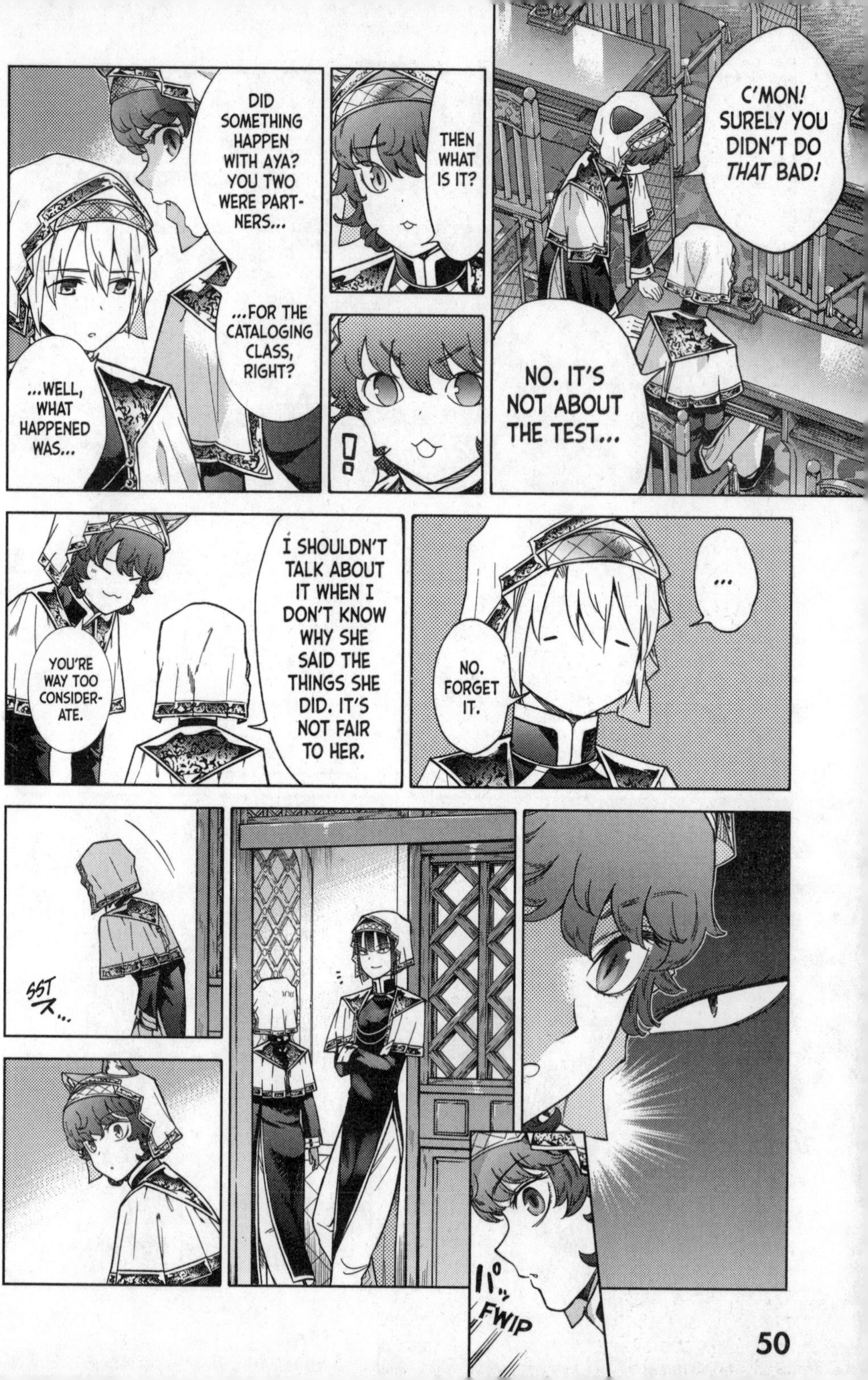
C'MON! SURELY YOU DIDN'T DO *THAT* BAD!
NO. IT'S NOT ABOUT THE TEST...
THEN WHAT IS IT?
!
DID SOMETHING HAPPEN WITH AYA? YOU TWO WERE PART-NERS...
...FOR THE CATALOGING CLASS, RIGHT?
...WELL, WHAT HAPPENED WAS...
...
NO. FORGET IT.
I SHOULDN'T TALK ABOUT IT WHEN I DON'T KNOW WHY SHE SAID THE THINGS SHE DID. IT'S NOT FAIR TO HER.
YOU'RE WAY TOO CONSIDER-ATE.
FWIP
SST...

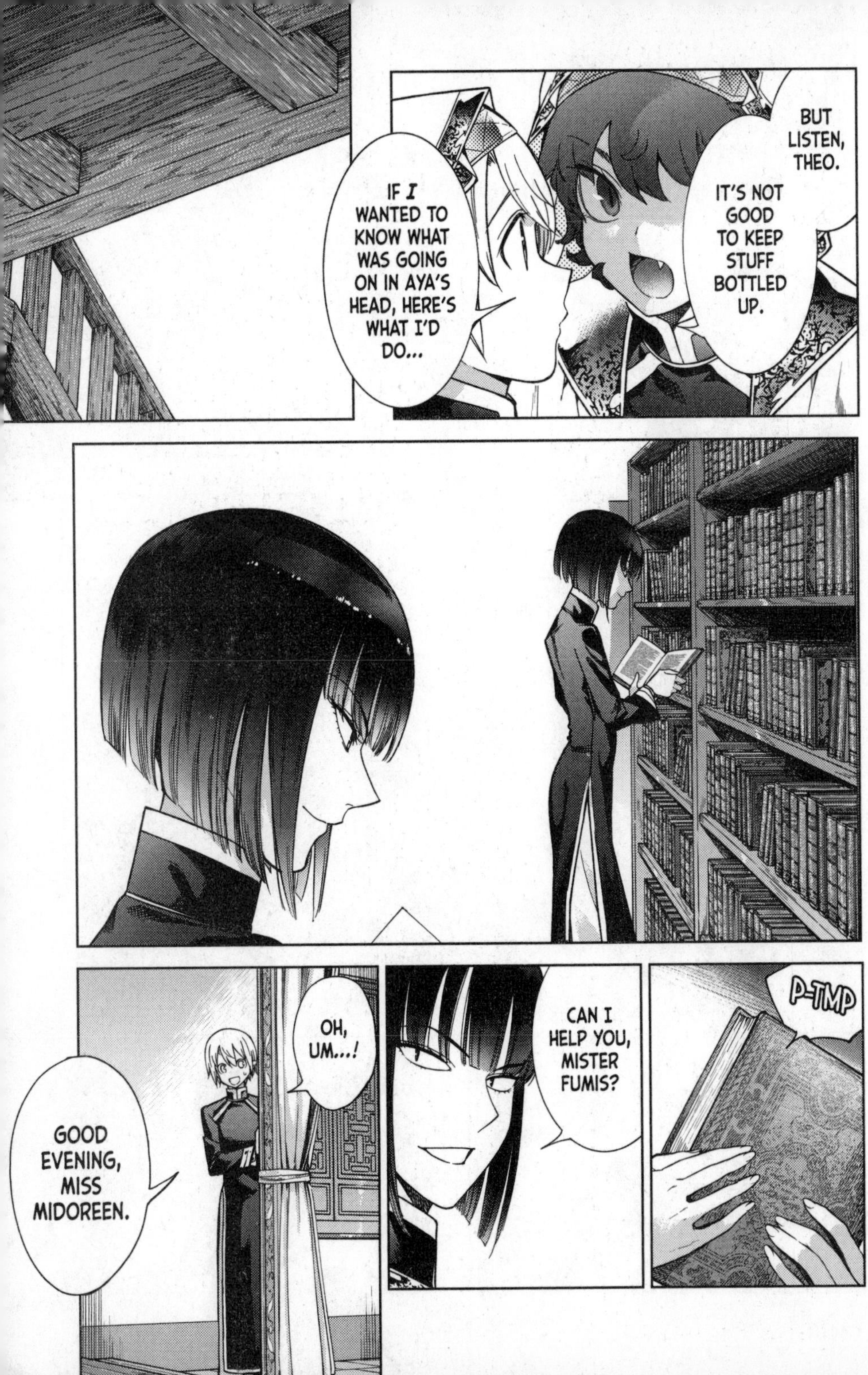
BUT LISTEN, THEO. IT'S NOT GOOD TO KEEP STUFF BOTTLED UP.
IF *I* WANTED TO KNOW WHAT WAS GOING ON IN AYA'S HEAD, HERE'S WHAT I'D DO...
P-TMP
CAN I HELP YOU, MISTER FUMIS?
OH, UM...!
GOOD EVENING, MISS MIDOREEN.

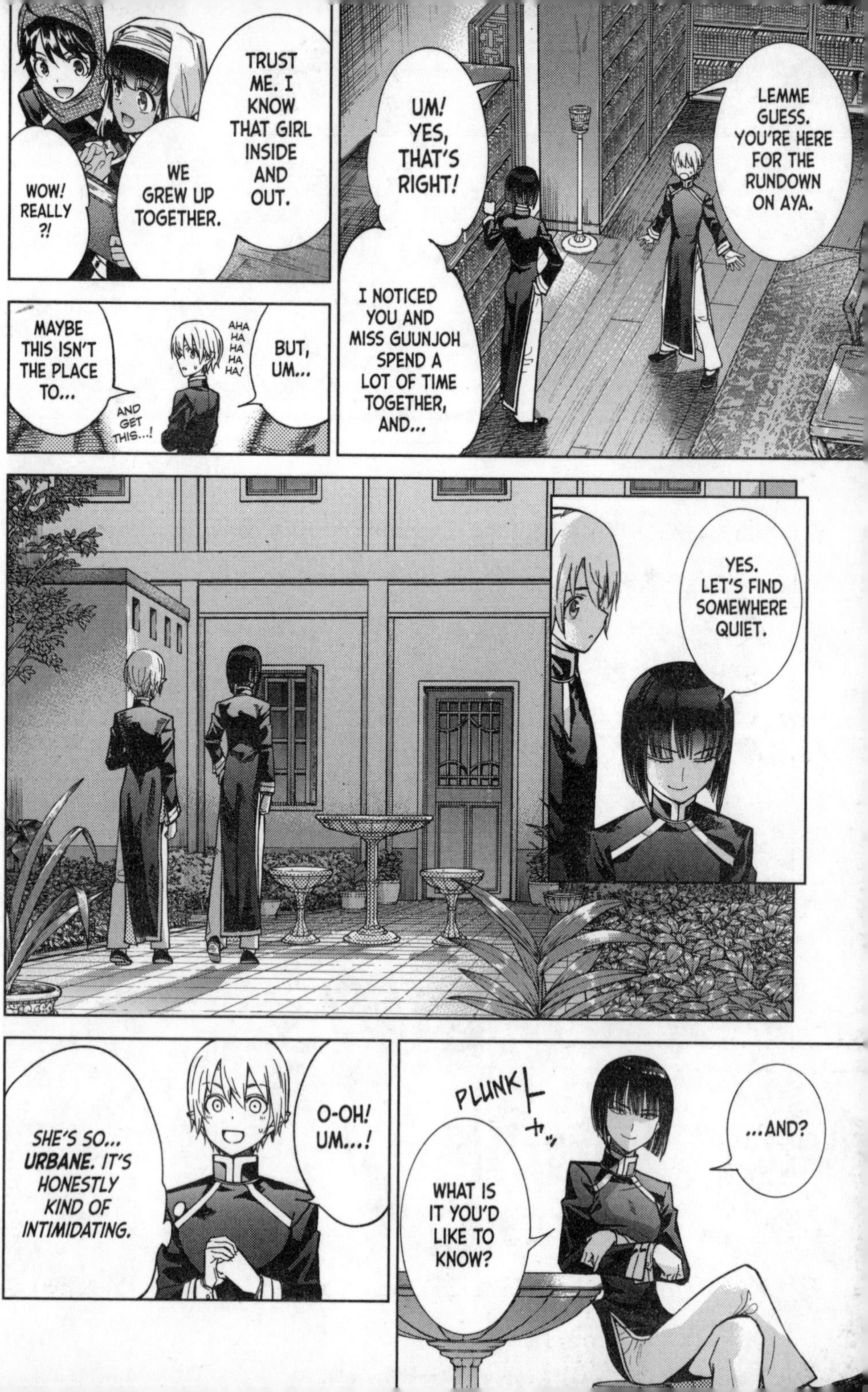
LEMME GUESS. YOU'RE HERE FOR THE RUNDOWN ON AYA.
UM! YES, THAT'S RIGHT!
I NOTICED YOU AND MISS GUUNJOH SPEND A LOT OF TIME TOGETHER, AND...
TRUST ME. I KNOW THAT GIRL INSIDE AND OUT.
WE GREW UP TOGETHER.
WOW! REALLY ?!
BUT, UM...
AHA HA HA HA HA!
MAYBE THIS ISN'T THE PLACE TO...
AND GET THIS...!
YES. LET'S FIND SOMEWHERE QUIET.
...AND?
PLUNK
WHAT IS IT YOU'D LIKE TO KNOW?
O-OH! UM...!
SHE'S SO... URBANE. IT'S HONESTLY KIND OF INTIMIDATING.

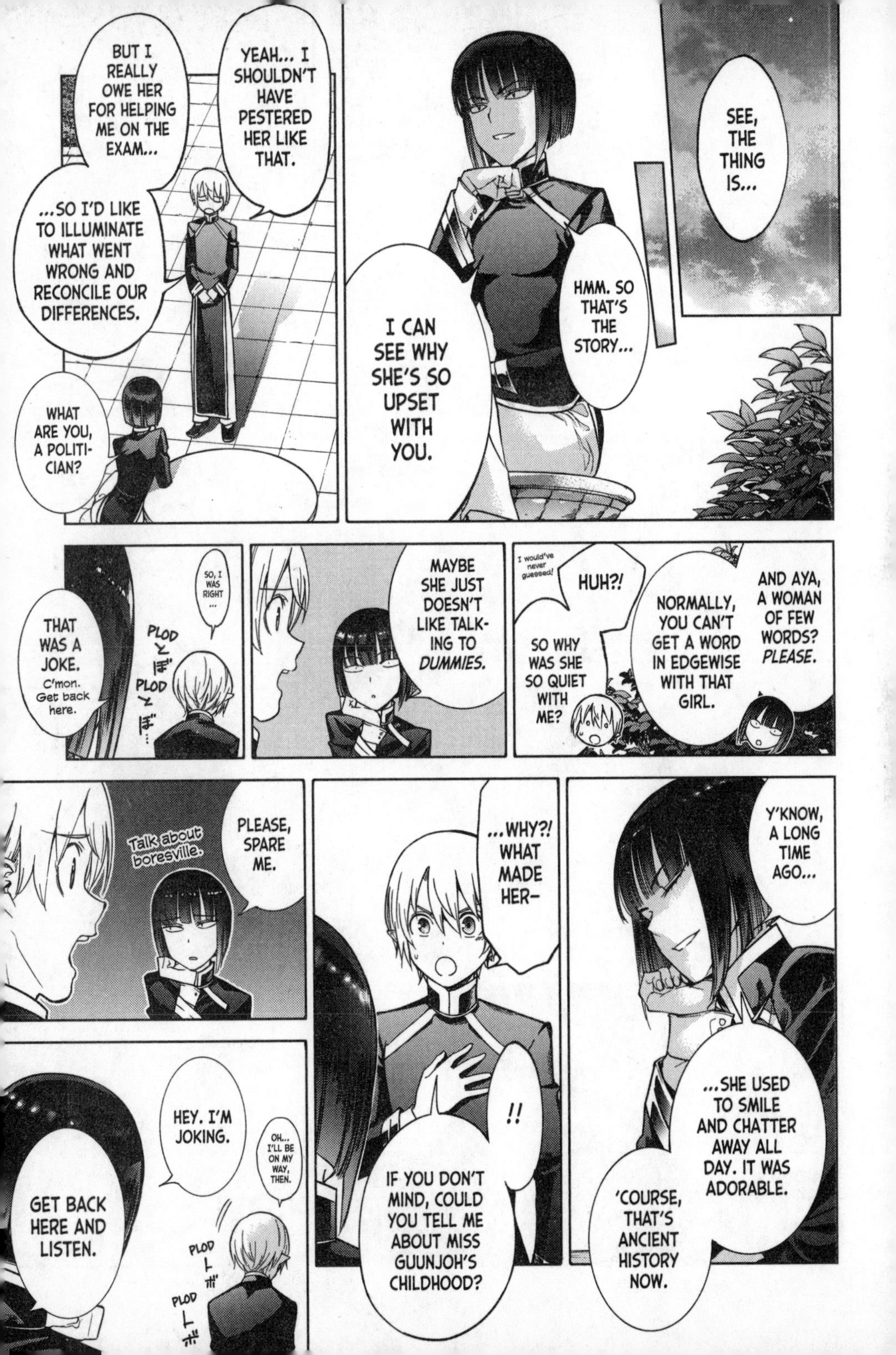
SEE, THE THING IS...
HMM. SO THAT'S THE STORY...
I CAN SEE WHY SHE'S SO UPSET WITH YOU.
YEAH... I SHOULDN'T HAVE PESTERED HER LIKE THAT.
BUT I REALLY OWE HER FOR HELPING ME ON THE EXAM...
...SO I'D LIKE TO ILLUMINATE WHAT WENT WRONG AND RECONCILE OUR DIFFERENCES.
WHAT ARE YOU, A POLITICIAN?
AND AYA, A WOMAN OF FEW WORDS? *PLEASE.*
NORMALLY, YOU CAN'T GET A WORD IN EDGEWISE WITH THAT GIRL.
HUH?!
I would've never guessed!
SO WHY WAS SHE SO QUIET WITH ME?
MAYBE SHE JUST DOESN'T LIKE TALKING TO *DUMMIES.*
SO, I WAS RIGHT...
PLOD とぼ PLOD とぼ...
THAT WAS A JOKE.
C'mon. Get back here.
Y'KNOW, A LONG TIME AGO...
...SHE USED TO SMILE AND CHATTER AWAY ALL DAY. IT WAS ADORABLE.
'COURSE, THAT'S ANCIENT HISTORY NOW.
...WHY?! WHAT MADE HER–
!!
IF YOU DON'T MIND, COULD YOU TELL ME ABOUT MISS GUUNJOH'S CHILDHOOD?
PLEASE, SPARE ME.
Talk about boresville.
HEY. I'M JOKING.
OH... I'LL BE ON MY WAY, THEN.
GET BACK HERE AND LISTEN.
PLOD トボ PLOD トボ

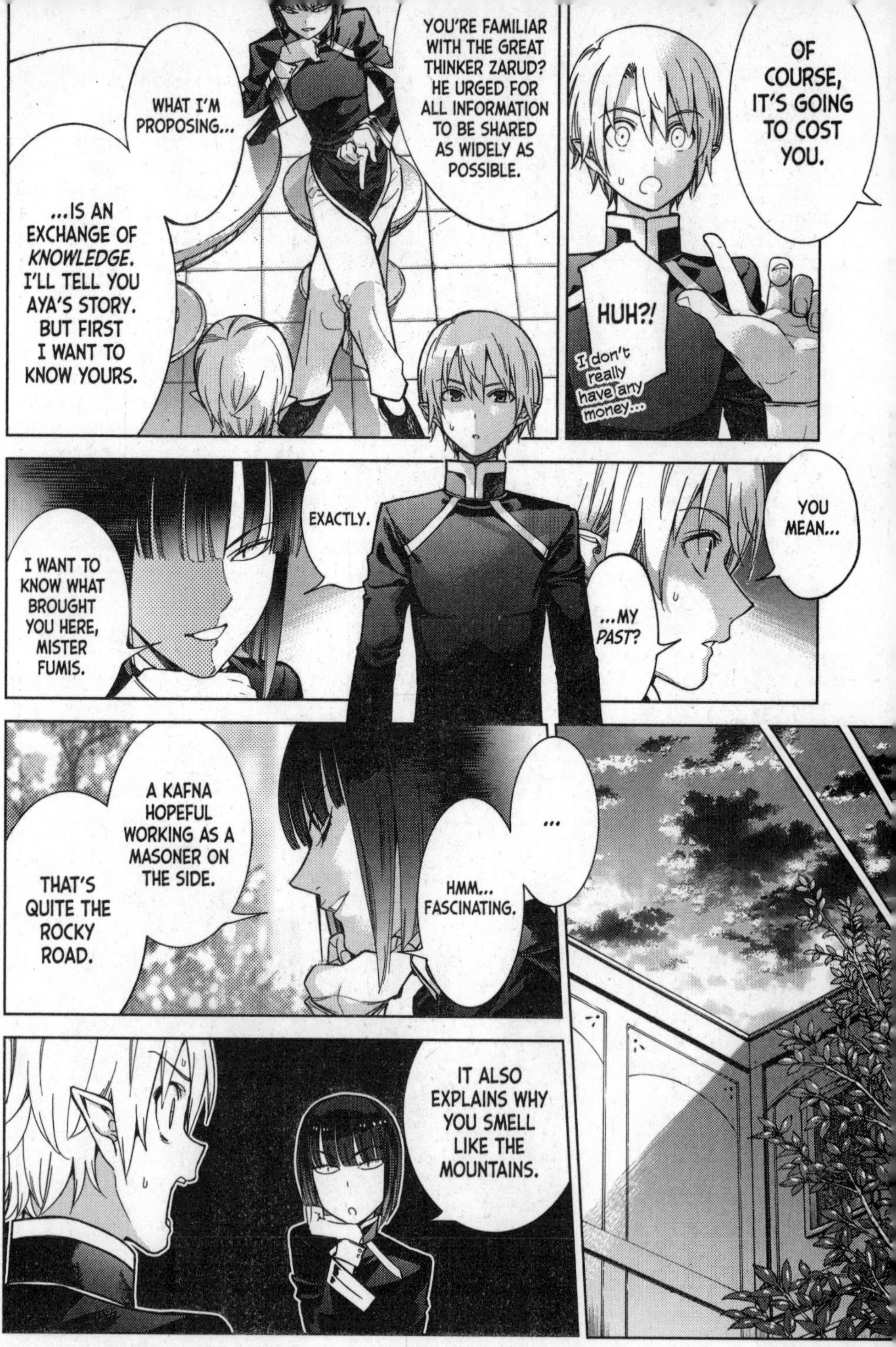
OF COURSE, IT'S GOING TO COST YOU.
HUH?!
I don't really have any money...
YOU'RE FAMILIAR WITH THE GREAT THINKER ZARUD? HE URGED FOR ALL INFORMATION TO BE SHARED AS WIDELY AS POSSIBLE.
WHAT I'M PROPOSING...
...IS AN EXCHANGE OF *KNOWLEDGE*. I'LL TELL YOU AYA'S STORY. BUT FIRST I WANT TO KNOW YOURS.
YOU MEAN...
...MY *PAST*?
EXACTLY.
I WANT TO KNOW WHAT BROUGHT YOU HERE, MISTER FUMIS.
...
HMM... FASCINATING.
A KAFNA HOPEFUL WORKING AS A MASONER ON THE SIDE.
THAT'S QUITE THE ROCKY ROAD.
IT ALSO EXPLAINS WHY YOU SMELL LIKE THE MOUNTAINS.

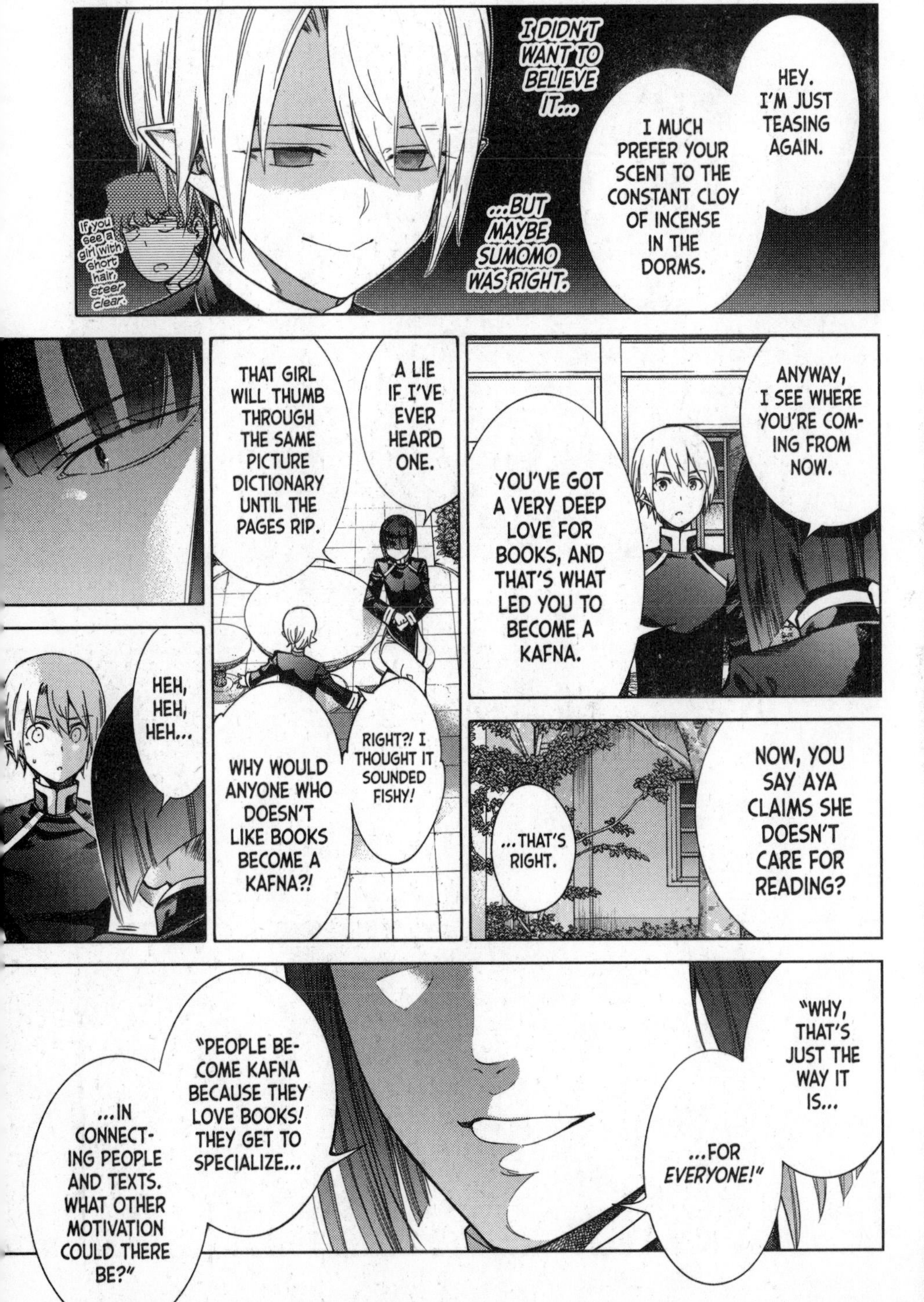
HEY. I'M JUST TEASING AGAIN.
I MUCH PREFER YOUR SCENT TO THE CONSTANT CLOY OF INCENSE IN THE DORMS.
I DIDN'T WANT TO BELIEVE IT...
...BUT MAYBE SUMOMO WAS RIGHT.
If you see a girl with short hair, steer clear.
ANYWAY, I SEE WHERE YOU'RE COM-ING FROM NOW.
YOU'VE GOT A VERY DEEP LOVE FOR BOOKS, AND THAT'S WHAT LED YOU TO BECOME A KAFNA.
NOW, YOU SAY AYA CLAIMS SHE DOESN'T CARE FOR READING?
...THAT'S RIGHT.
A LIE IF I'VE EVER HEARD ONE.
THAT GIRL WILL THUMB THROUGH THE SAME PICTURE DICTIONARY UNTIL THE PAGES RIP.
RIGHT?! I THOUGHT IT SOUNDED FISHY!
WHY WOULD ANYONE WHO DOESN'T LIKE BOOKS BECOME A KAFNA?!
HEH, HEH, HEH...
"WHY, THAT'S JUST THE WAY IT IS...
...FOR *EVERYONE!*"
"PEOPLE BE-COME KAFNA BECAUSE THEY LOVE BOOKS! THEY GET TO SPECIALIZE...
...IN CONNECT-ING PEOPLE AND TEXTS. WHAT OTHER MOTIVATION COULD THERE BE?"

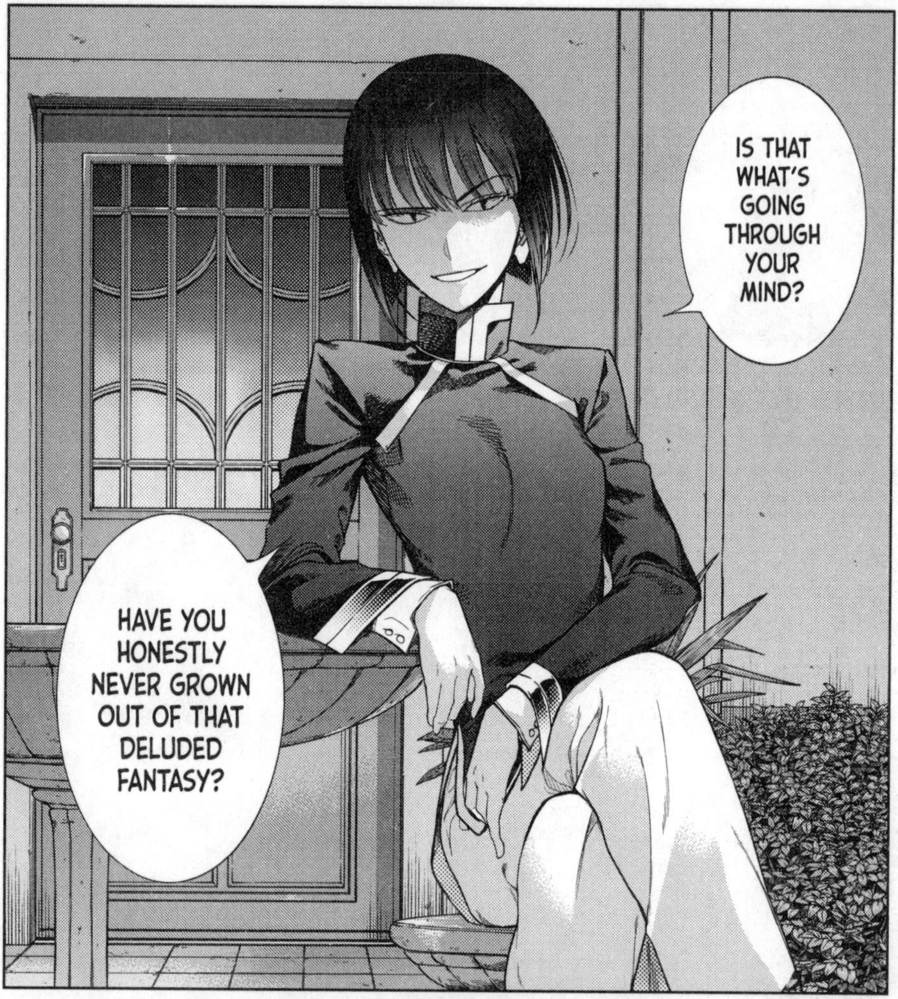
IS THAT WHAT'S GOING THROUGH YOUR MIND?
HAVE YOU HONESTLY NEVER GROWN OUT OF THAT DELUDED FANTASY?

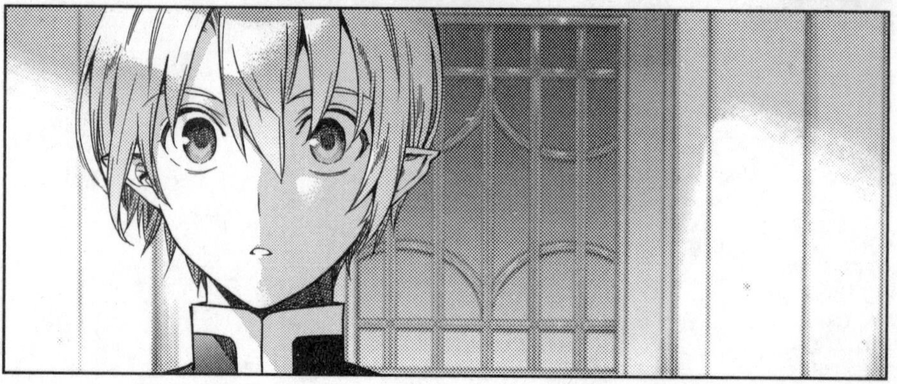

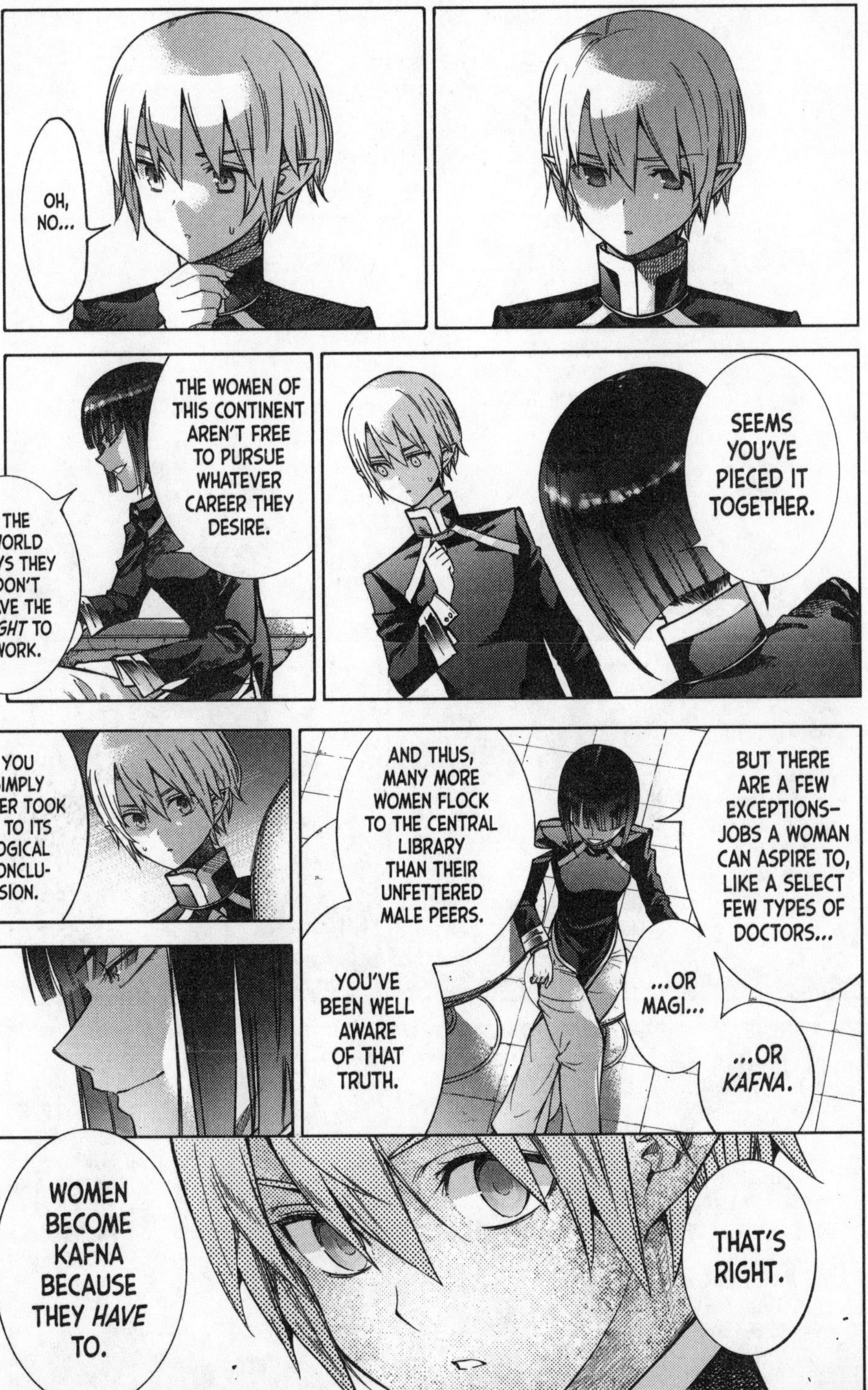
OH, NO...
SEEMS YOU'VE PIECED IT TOGETHER.
THE WOMEN OF THIS CONTINENT AREN'T FREE TO PURSUE WHATEVER CAREER THEY DESIRE.
THE WORLD SAYS THEY DON'T HAVE THE *RIGHT* TO WORK.
BUT THERE ARE A FEW EXCEPTIONS—JOBS A WOMAN CAN ASPIRE TO, LIKE A SELECT FEW TYPES OF DOCTORS...
...OR MAGI...
...OR *KAFNA*.
AND THUS, MANY MORE WOMEN FLOCK TO THE CENTRAL LIBRARY THAN THEIR UNFETTERED MALE PEERS.
YOU'VE BEEN WELL AWARE OF THAT TRUTH.
YOU SIMPLY NEVER TOOK IT TO ITS LOGICAL CONCLUSION.
WOMEN BECOME KAFNA BECAUSE THEY *HAVE* TO.
THAT'S RIGHT.

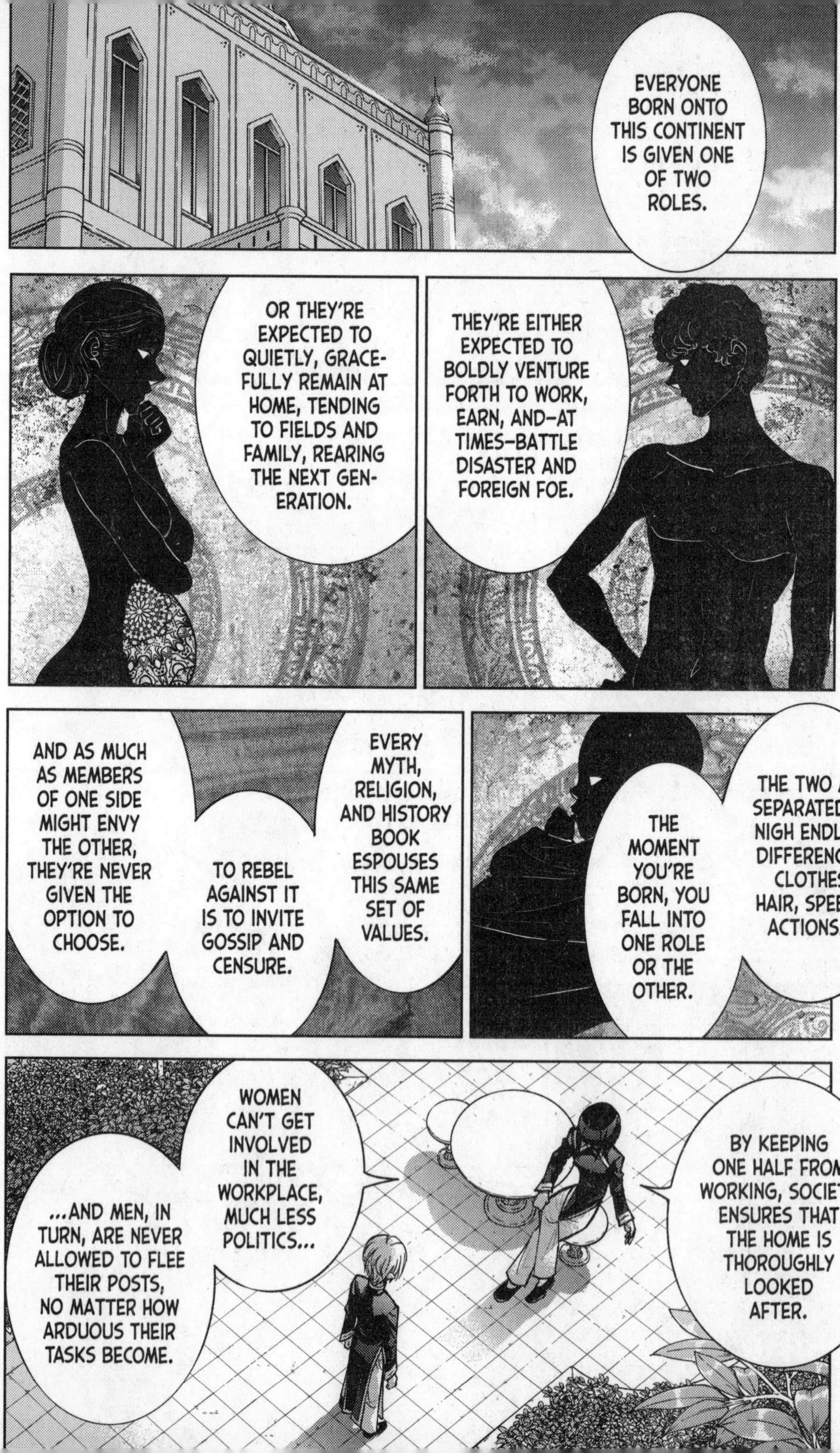
EVERYONE BORN ONTO THIS CONTINENT IS GIVEN ONE OF TWO ROLES.
THEY'RE EITHER EXPECTED TO BOLDLY VENTURE FORTH TO WORK, EARN, AND—AT TIMES—BATTLE DISASTER AND FOREIGN FOE.
OR THEY'RE EXPECTED TO QUIETLY, GRACEFULLY REMAIN AT HOME, TENDING TO FIELDS AND FAMILY, REARING THE NEXT GENERATION.
THE TWO ARE SEPARATED BY NIGH ENDLESS DIFFERENCES. CLOTHES, HAIR, SPEECH, ACTIONS...
THE MOMENT YOU'RE BORN, YOU FALL INTO ONE ROLE OR THE OTHER.
EVERY MYTH, RELIGION, AND HISTORY BOOK ESPOUSES THIS SAME SET OF VALUES.
TO REBEL AGAINST IT IS TO INVITE GOSSIP AND CENSURE.
AND AS MUCH AS MEMBERS OF ONE SIDE MIGHT ENVY THE OTHER, THEY'RE NEVER GIVEN THE OPTION TO CHOOSE.
BY KEEPING ONE HALF FROM WORKING, SOCIETY ENSURES THAT THE HOME IS THOROUGHLY LOOKED AFTER.
WOMEN CAN'T GET INVOLVED IN THE WORKPLACE, MUCH LESS POLITICS...
...AND MEN, IN TURN, ARE NEVER ALLOWED TO FLEE THEIR POSTS, NO MATTER HOW ARDUOUS THEIR TASKS BECOME.

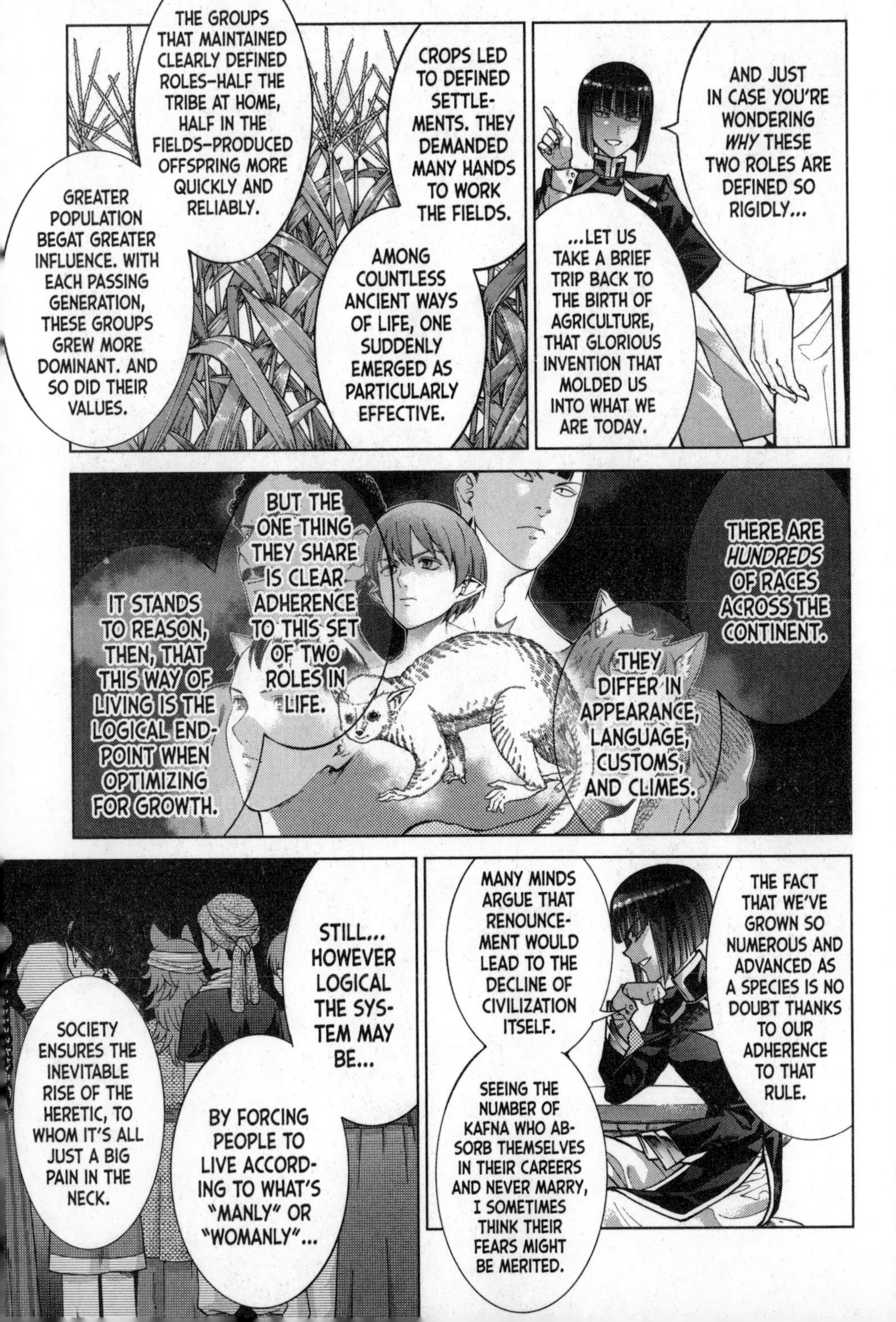
AND JUST IN CASE YOU'RE WONDERING *WHY* THESE TWO ROLES ARE DEFINED SO RIGIDLY...
...LET US TAKE A BRIEF TRIP BACK TO THE BIRTH OF AGRICULTURE, THAT GLORIOUS INVENTION THAT MOLDED US INTO WHAT WE ARE TODAY.
CROPS LED TO DEFINED SETTLE-MENTS. THEY DEMANDED MANY HANDS TO WORK THE FIELDS.
AMONG COUNTLESS ANCIENT WAYS OF LIFE, ONE SUDDENLY EMERGED AS PARTICULARLY EFFECTIVE.
THE GROUPS THAT MAINTAINED CLEARLY DEFINED ROLES—HALF THE TRIBE AT HOME, HALF IN THE FIELDS—PRODUCED OFFSPRING MORE QUICKLY AND RELIABLY.
GREATER POPULATION BEGAT GREATER INFLUENCE. WITH EACH PASSING GENERATION, THESE GROUPS GREW MORE DOMINANT. AND SO DID THEIR VALUES.
THERE ARE *HUNDREDS* OF RACES ACROSS THE CONTINENT.
THEY DIFFER IN APPEARANCE, LANGUAGE, CUSTOMS, AND CLIMES.
BUT THE ONE THING THEY SHARE IS CLEAR ADHERENCE TO THIS SET OF TWO ROLES IN LIFE.
IT STANDS TO REASON, THEN, THAT THIS WAY OF LIVING IS THE LOGICAL END-POINT WHEN OPTIMIZING FOR GROWTH.
THE FACT THAT WE'VE GROWN SO NUMEROUS AND ADVANCED AS A SPECIES IS NO DOUBT THANKS TO OUR ADHERENCE TO THAT RULE.
MANY MINDS ARGUE THAT RENOUNCE-MENT WOULD LEAD TO THE DECLINE OF CIVILIZATION ITSELF.
SEEING THE NUMBER OF KAFNA WHO AB-SORB THEMSELVES IN THEIR CAREERS AND NEVER MARRY, I SOMETIMES THINK THEIR FEARS MIGHT BE MERITED.
STILL... HOWEVER LOGICAL THE SYS-TEM MAY BE...
BY FORCING PEOPLE TO LIVE ACCORD-ING TO WHAT'S "MANLY" OR "WOMANLY"...
SOCIETY ENSURES THE INEVITABLE RISE OF THE HERETIC, TO WHOM IT'S ALL JUST A BIG PAIN IN THE NECK.

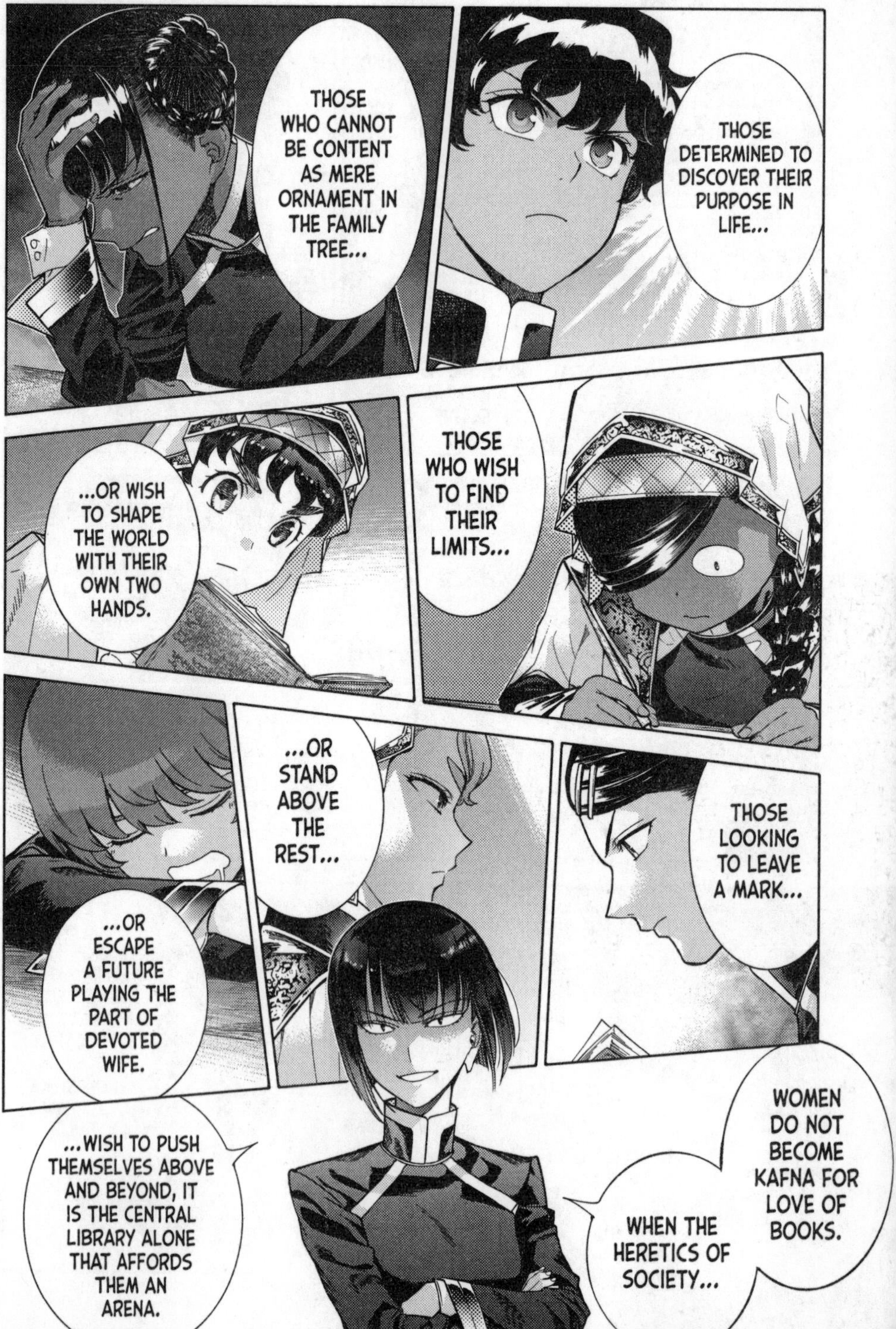
THOSE DETERMINED TO DISCOVER THEIR PURPOSE IN LIFE...
THOSE WHO CANNOT BE CONTENT AS MERE ORNAMENT IN THE FAMILY TREE...
THOSE WHO WISH TO FIND THEIR LIMITS...
...OR WISH TO SHAPE THE WORLD WITH THEIR OWN TWO HANDS.
THOSE LOOKING TO LEAVE A MARK...
...OR STAND ABOVE THE REST...
...OR ESCAPE A FUTURE PLAYING THE PART OF DEVOTED WIFE.
WOMEN DO NOT BECOME KAFNA FOR LOVE OF BOOKS.
WHEN THE HERETICS OF SOCIETY...
...WISH TO PUSH THEMSELVES ABOVE AND BEYOND, IT IS THE CENTRAL LIBRARY ALONE THAT AFFORDS THEM AN ARENA.

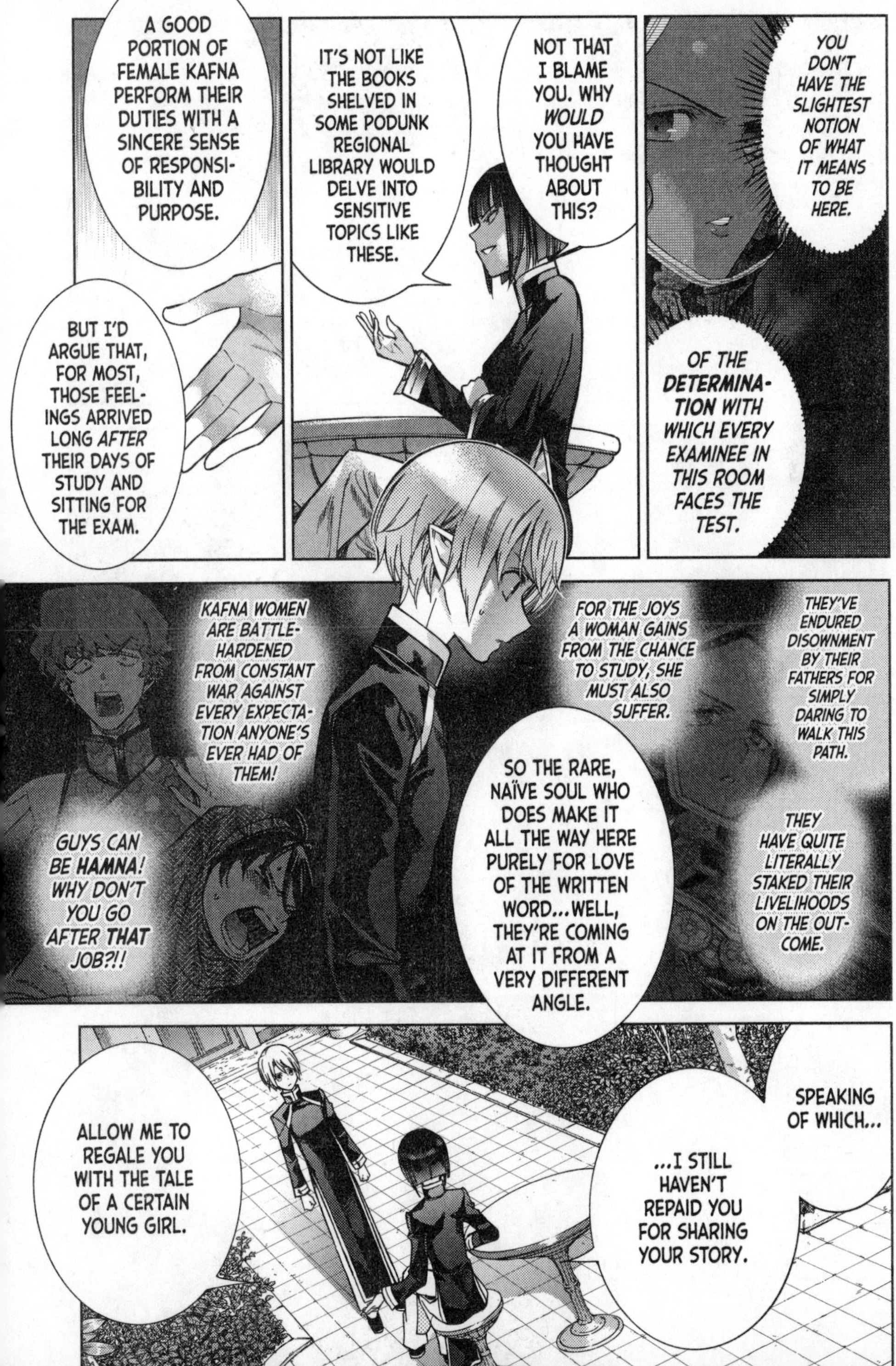
YOU DON'T HAVE THE SLIGHTEST NOTION OF WHAT IT MEANS TO BE HERE.
OF THE DETERMINATION WITH WHICH EVERY EXAMINEE IN THIS ROOM FACES THE TEST.
NOT THAT I BLAME YOU. WHY WOULD YOU HAVE THOUGHT ABOUT THIS?
IT'S NOT LIKE THE BOOKS SHELVED IN SOME PODUNK REGIONAL LIBRARY WOULD DELVE INTO SENSITIVE TOPICS LIKE THESE.
A GOOD PORTION OF FEMALE KAFNA PERFORM THEIR DUTIES WITH A SINCERE SENSE OF RESPONSIBILITY AND PURPOSE.
BUT I'D ARGUE THAT, FOR MOST, THOSE FEELINGS ARRIVED LONG AFTER THEIR DAYS OF STUDY AND SITTING FOR THE EXAM.
THEY'VE ENDURED DISOWNMENT BY THEIR FATHERS FOR SIMPLY DARING TO WALK THIS PATH.
FOR THE JOYS A WOMAN GAINS FROM THE CHANCE TO STUDY, SHE MUST ALSO SUFFER.
THEY HAVE QUITE LITERALLY STAKED THEIR LIVELIHOODS ON THE OUTCOME.
SO THE RARE, NAÏVE SOUL WHO DOES MAKE IT ALL THE WAY HERE PURELY FOR LOVE OF THE WRITTEN WORD...WELL, THEY'RE COMING AT IT FROM A VERY DIFFERENT ANGLE.
KAFNA WOMEN ARE BATTLE-HARDENED FROM CONSTANT WAR AGAINST EVERY EXPECTATION ANYONE'S EVER HAD OF THEM!
GUYS CAN BE HAMNA! WHY DON'T YOU GO AFTER THAT JOB?!!
SPEAKING OF WHICH...
...I STILL HAVEN'T REPAID YOU FOR SHARING YOUR STORY.
ALLOW ME TO REGALE YOU WITH THE TALE OF A CERTAIN YOUNG GIRL.

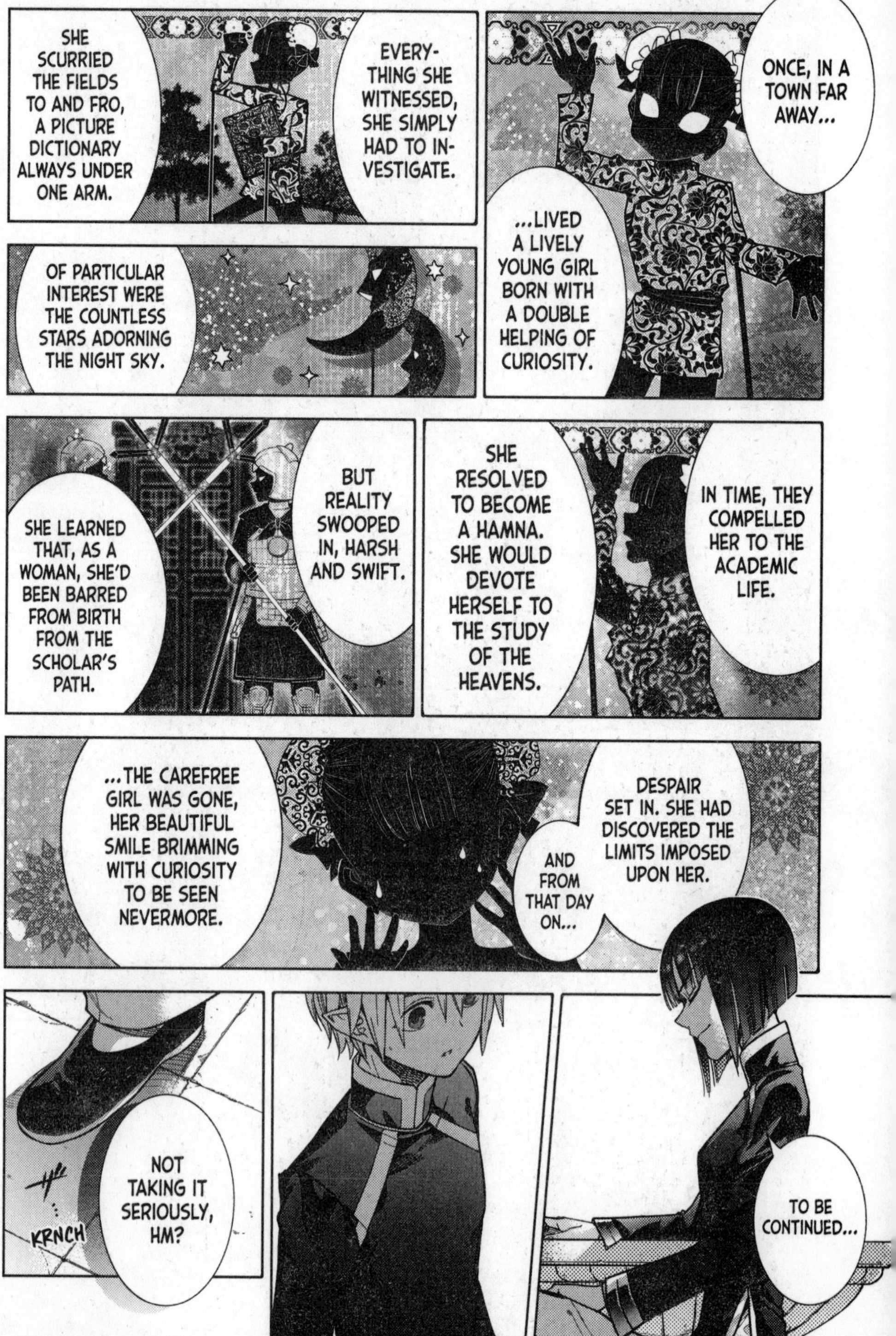
ONCE, IN A TOWN FAR AWAY...
...LIVED A LIVELY YOUNG GIRL BORN WITH A DOUBLE HELPING OF CURIOSITY.
EVERY-THING SHE WITNESSED, SHE SIMPLY HAD TO IN-VESTIGATE.
SHE SCURRIED THE FIELDS TO AND FRO, A PICTURE DICTIONARY ALWAYS UNDER ONE ARM.
OF PARTICULAR INTEREST WERE THE COUNTLESS STARS ADORNING THE NIGHT SKY.
IN TIME, THEY COMPELLED HER TO THE ACADEMIC LIFE.
SHE RESOLVED TO BECOME A HAMNA. SHE WOULD DEVOTE HERSELF TO THE STUDY OF THE HEAVENS.
BUT REALITY SWOOPED IN, HARSH AND SWIFT.
SHE LEARNED THAT, AS A WOMAN, SHE'D BEEN BARRED FROM BIRTH FROM THE SCHOLAR'S PATH.
DESPAIR SET IN. SHE HAD DISCOVERED THE LIMITS IMPOSED UPON HER.
AND FROM THAT DAY ON...
...THE CAREFREE GIRL WAS GONE, HER BEAUTIFUL SMILE BRIMMING WITH CURIOSITY TO BE SEEN NEVERMORE.
TO BE CONTINUED...
NOT TAKING IT SERIOUSLY, HM?
KRNCH

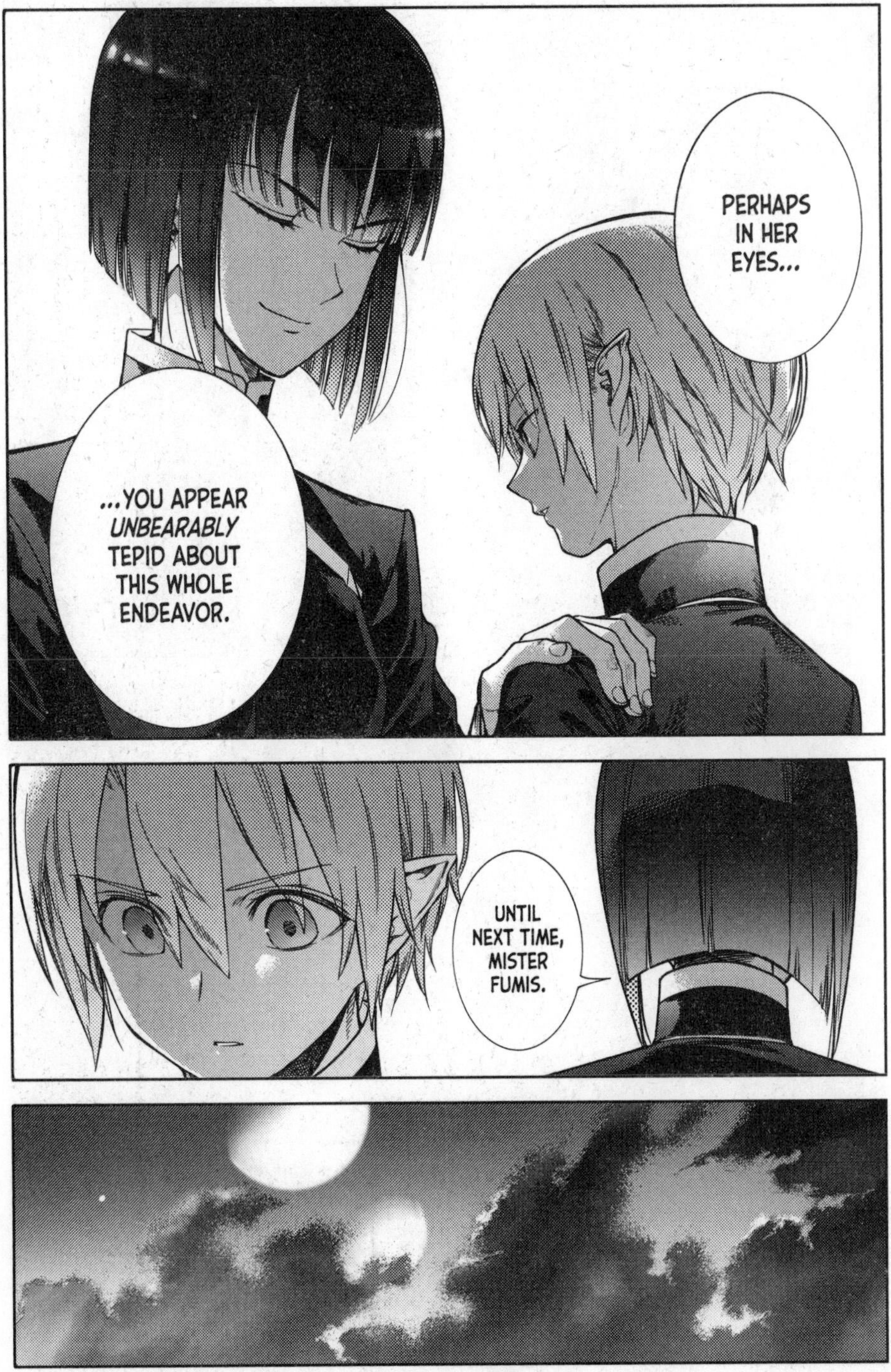
PERHAPS IN HER EYES...
...YOU APPEAR *UNBEARABLY* TEPID ABOUT THIS WHOLE ENDEAVOR.
UNTIL NEXT TIME, MISTER FUMIS.

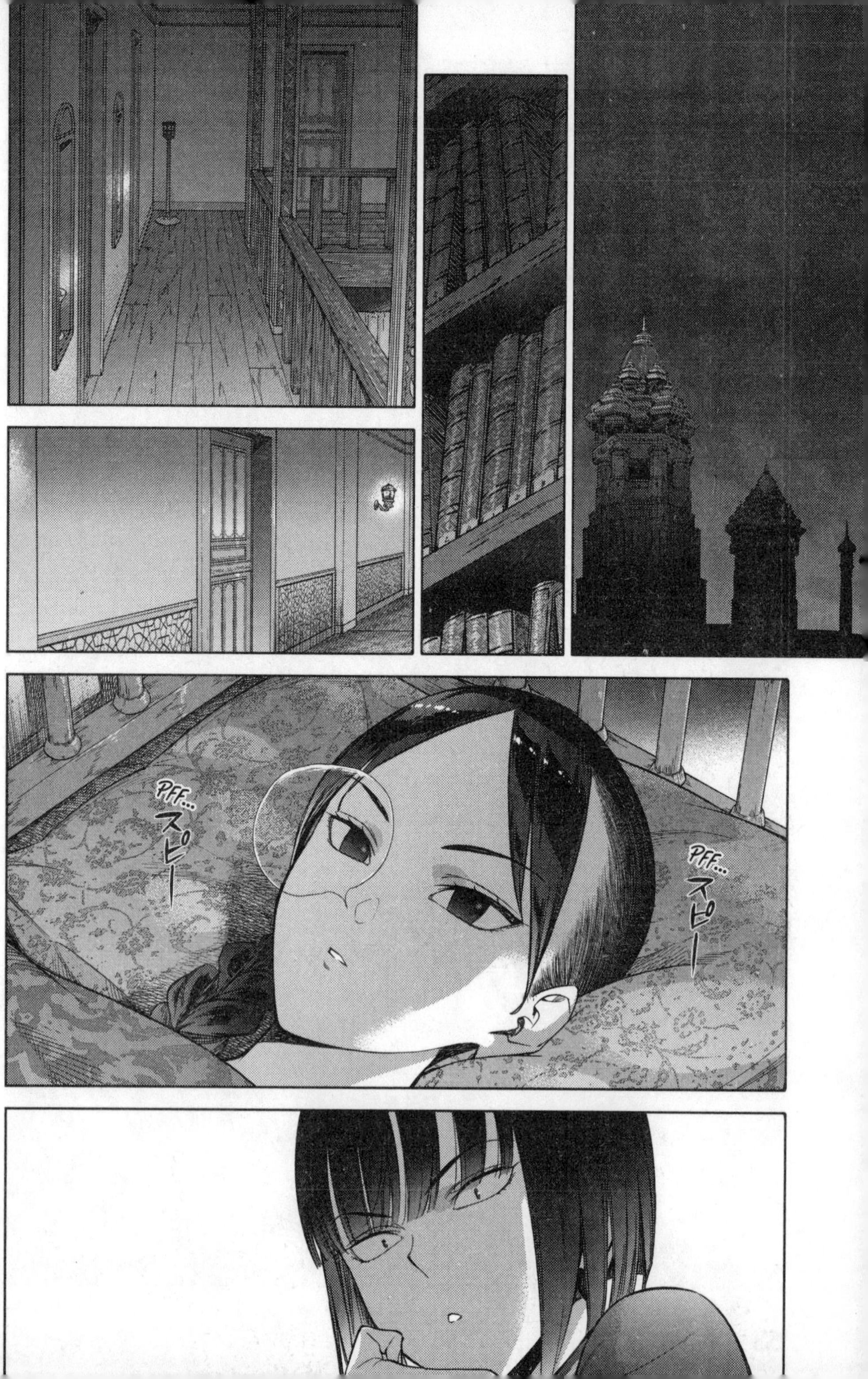
PFF...
スピー
PFF...
スピー

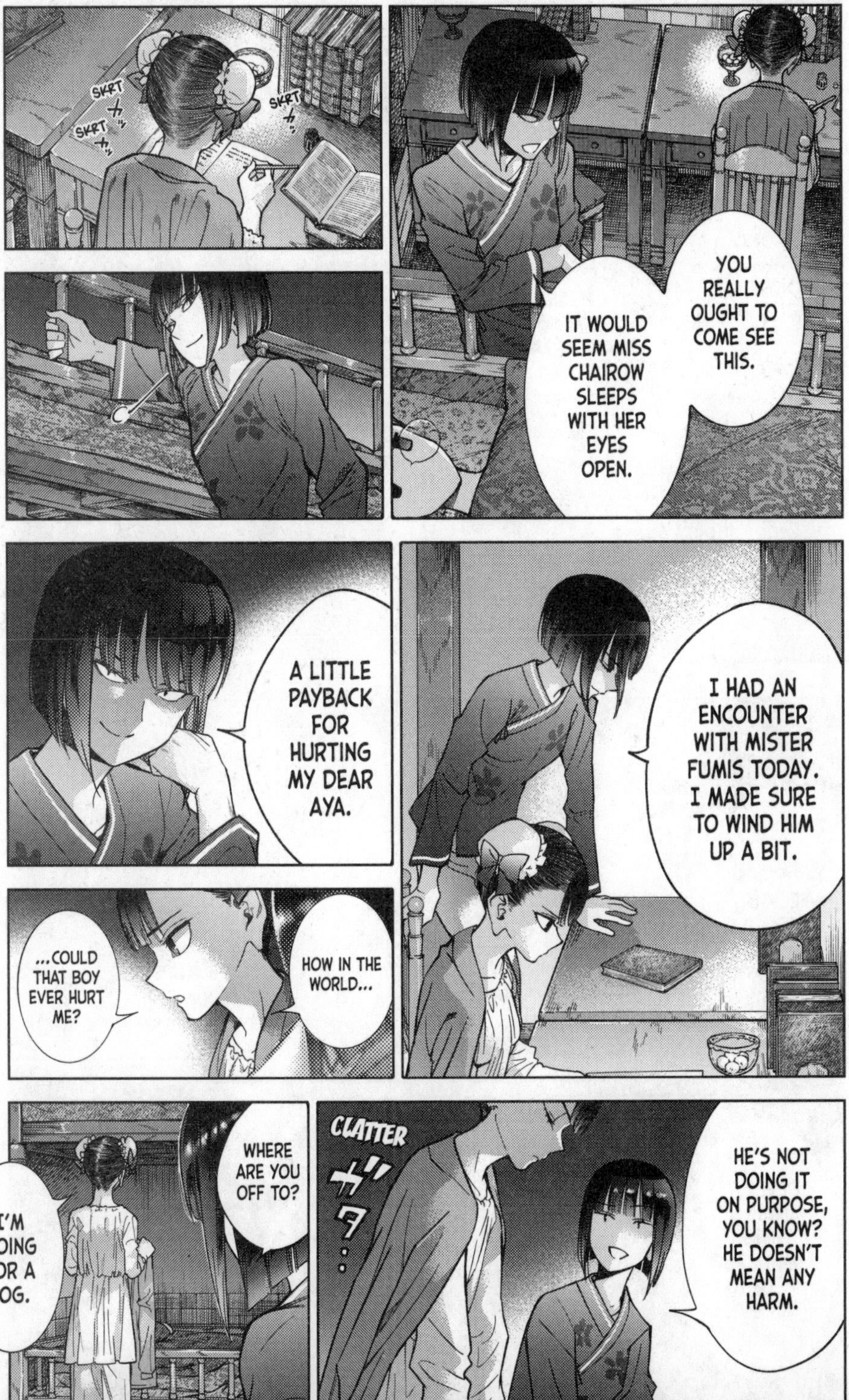
YOU REALLY OUGHT TO COME SEE THIS.
IT WOULD SEEM MISS CHAIROW SLEEPS WITH HER EYES OPEN.
SKRT
SKRT
SKRT
I HAD AN ENCOUNTER WITH MISTER FUMIS TODAY. I MADE SURE TO WIND HIM UP A BIT.
A LITTLE PAYBACK FOR HURTING MY DEAR AYA.
HOW IN THE WORLD...
...COULD THAT BOY EVER HURT ME?
CLATTER
HE'S NOT DOING IT ON PURPOSE, YOU KNOW? HE DOESN'T MEAN ANY HARM.
WHERE ARE YOU OFF TO?
I'M GOING FOR A JOG.

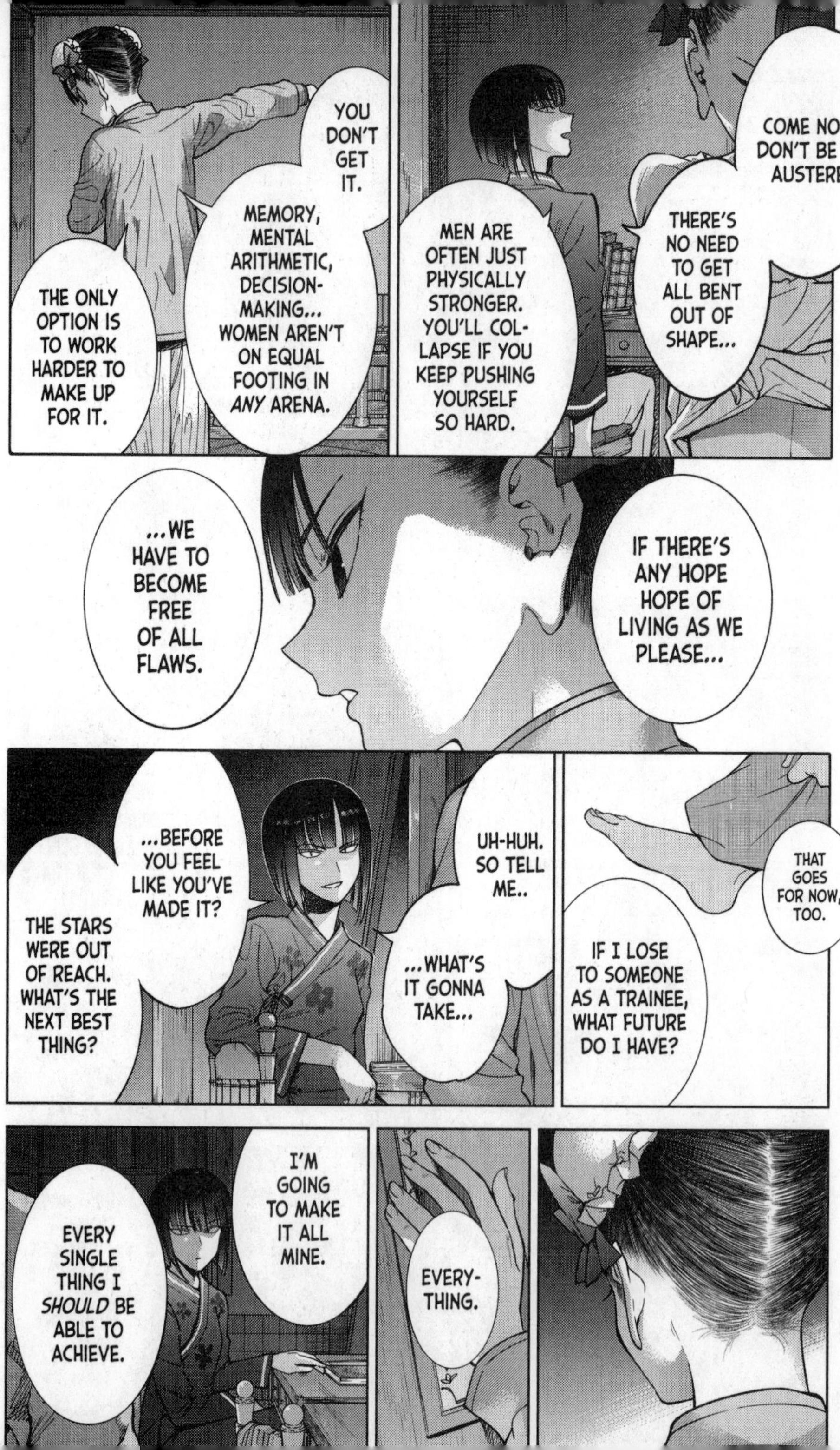
COME NOW. DON'T BE SO AUSTERE.
THERE'S NO NEED TO GET ALL BENT OUT OF SHAPE...
MEN ARE OFTEN JUST PHYSICALLY STRONGER. YOU'LL COL-LAPSE IF YOU KEEP PUSHING YOURSELF SO HARD.
YOU DON'T GET IT.
MEMORY, MENTAL ARITHMETIC, DECISION-MAKING... WOMEN AREN'T ON EQUAL FOOTING IN *ANY* ARENA.
THE ONLY OPTION IS TO WORK HARDER TO MAKE UP FOR IT.
IF THERE'S ANY HOPE HOPE OF LIVING AS WE PLEASE...
...WE HAVE TO BECOME FREE OF ALL FLAWS.
THAT GOES FOR NOW, TOO.
IF I LOSE TO SOMEONE AS A TRAINEE, WHAT FUTURE DO I HAVE?
UH-HUH. SO TELL ME..
...WHAT'S IT GONNA TAKE...
...BEFORE YOU FEEL LIKE YOU'VE MADE IT?
THE STARS WERE OUT OF REACH. WHAT'S THE NEXT BEST THING?
EVERY-THING.
I'M GOING TO MAKE IT ALL MINE.
EVERY SINGLE THING I *SHOULD* BE ABLE TO ACHIEVE.

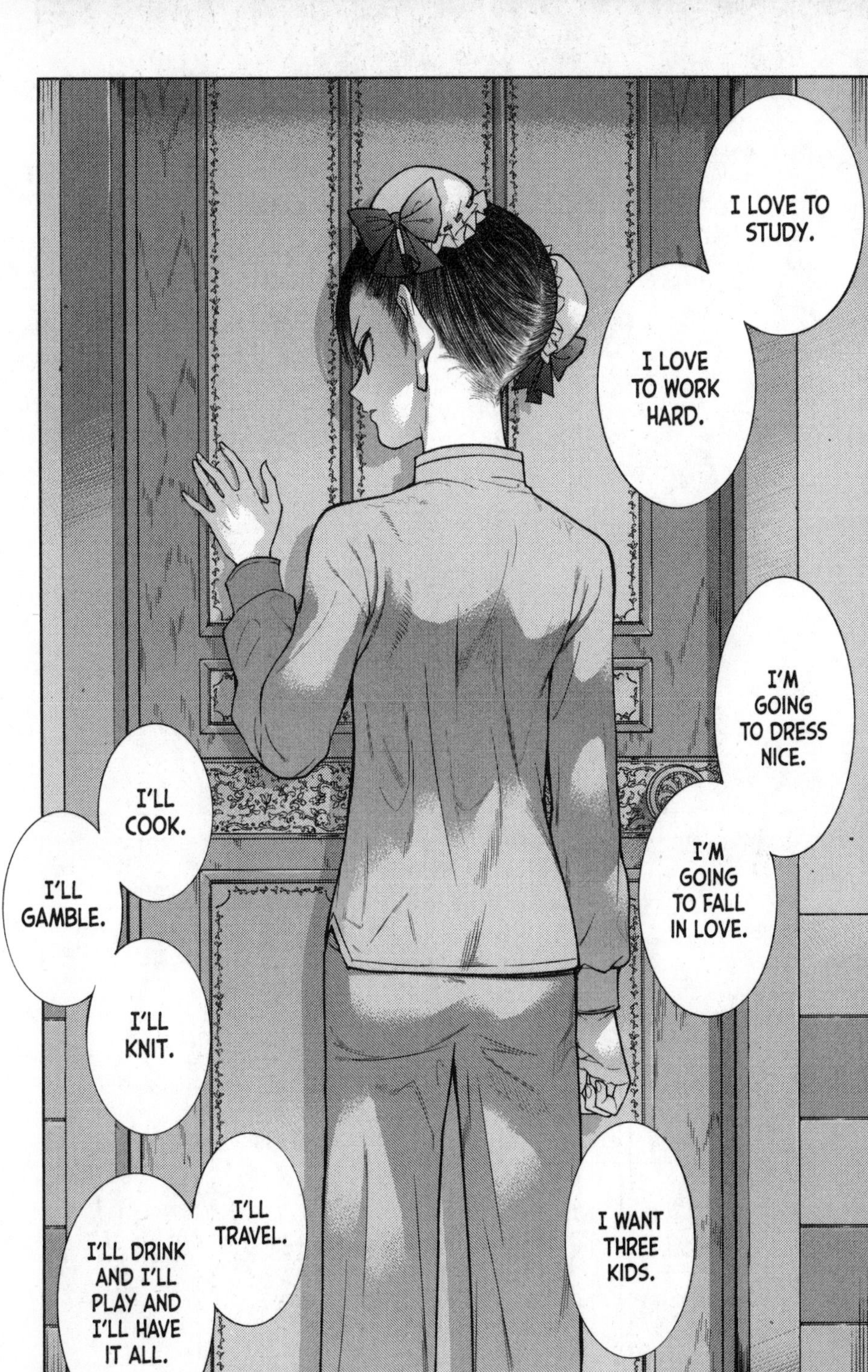

I LOVE TO STUDY.
I LOVE TO WORK HARD.
I'M GOING TO DRESS NICE.
I'M GOING TO FALL IN LOVE.
I'LL COOK.
I'LL GAMBLE.
I'LL KNIT.
I WANT THREE KIDS.
I'LL TRAVEL.
I'LL DRINK AND I'LL PLAY AND I'LL HAVE IT ALL.

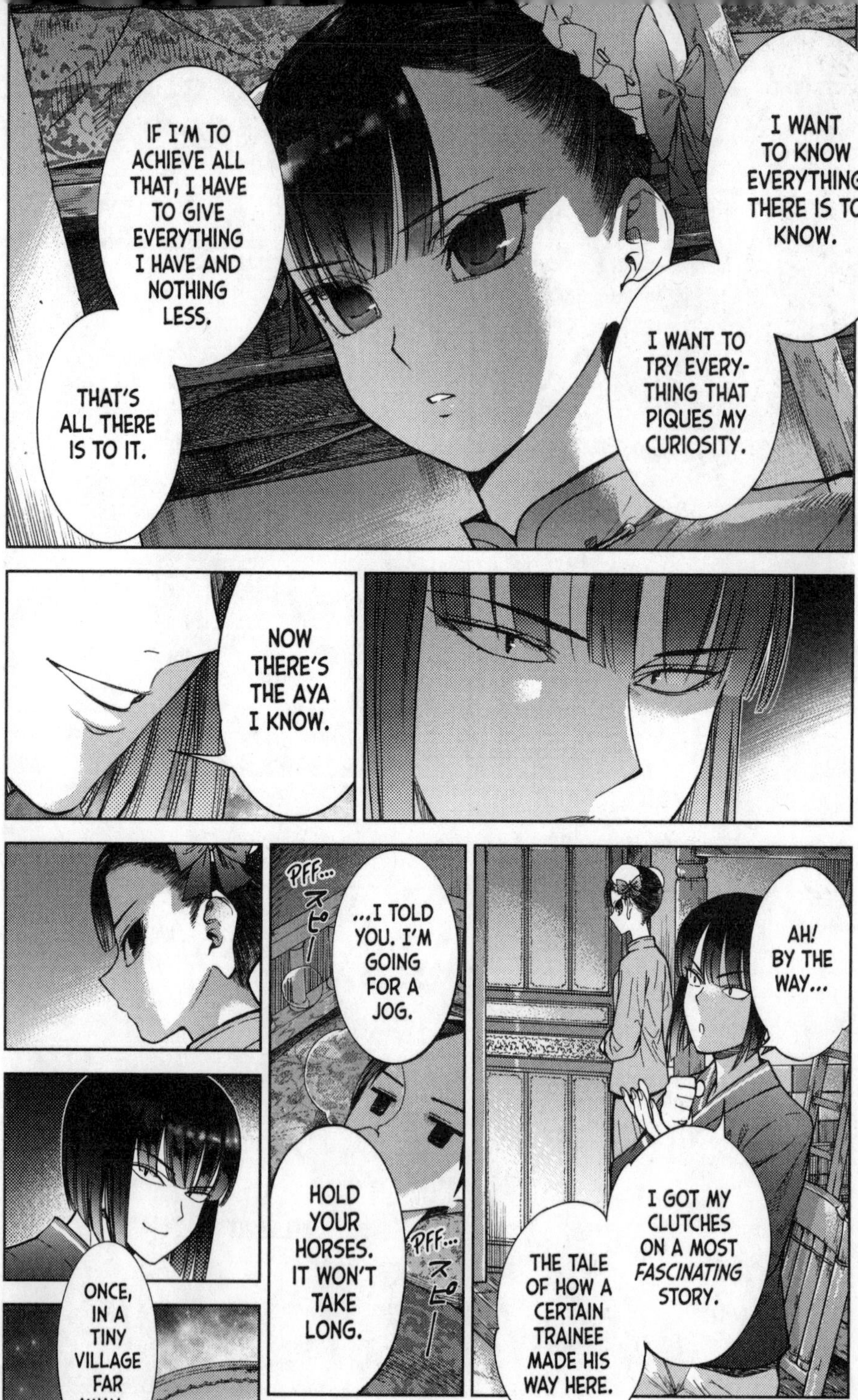
I WANT TO KNOW EVERYTHING THERE IS TO KNOW.
I WANT TO TRY EVERYTHING THAT PIQUES MY CURIOSITY.
IF I'M TO ACHIEVE ALL THAT, I HAVE TO GIVE EVERYTHING I HAVE AND NOTHING LESS.
THAT'S ALL THERE IS TO IT.
NOW THERE'S THE AYA I KNOW.
AH! BY THE WAY...
I GOT MY CLUTCHES ON A MOST *FASCINATING* STORY.
THE TALE OF HOW A CERTAIN TRAINEE MADE HIS WAY HERE.
PFF... スピー
...I TOLD YOU. I'M GOING FOR A JOG.
HOLD YOUR HORSES. IT WON'T TAKE LONG.
PFF... スピー
ONCE, IN A TINY VILLAGE FAR AWAY...

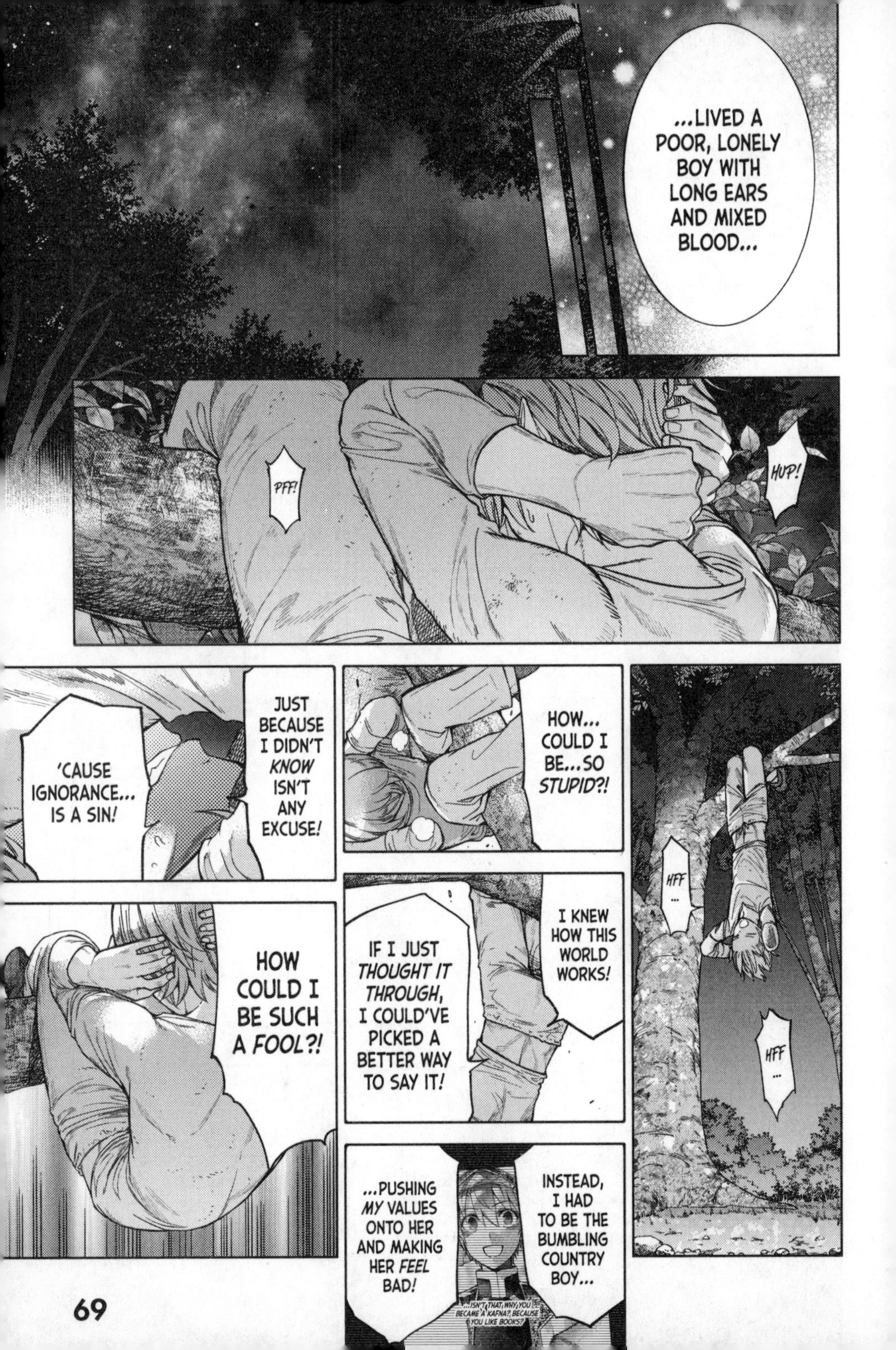
...LIVED A POOR, LONELY BOY WITH LONG EARS AND MIXED BLOOD...
HUP!
PFF!
HFF...
HFF...
HOW... COULD I BE...SO *STUPID*?!
JUST BECAUSE I DIDN'T *KNOW* ISN'T ANY EXCUSE!
'CAUSE IGNORANCE... IS A SIN!
I KNEW HOW THIS WORLD WORKS!
IF I JUST *THOUGHT IT THROUGH*, I COULD'VE PICKED A BETTER WAY TO SAY IT!
HOW COULD I BE SUCH A *FOOL*?!
INSTEAD, I HAD TO BE THE BUMBLING COUNTRY BOY...
...PUSHING *MY* VALUES ONTO HER AND MAKING HER *FEEL* BAD!
...ISN'T THAT WHY YOU BECAME A KAFNA? BECAUSE YOU LIKE BOOKS?

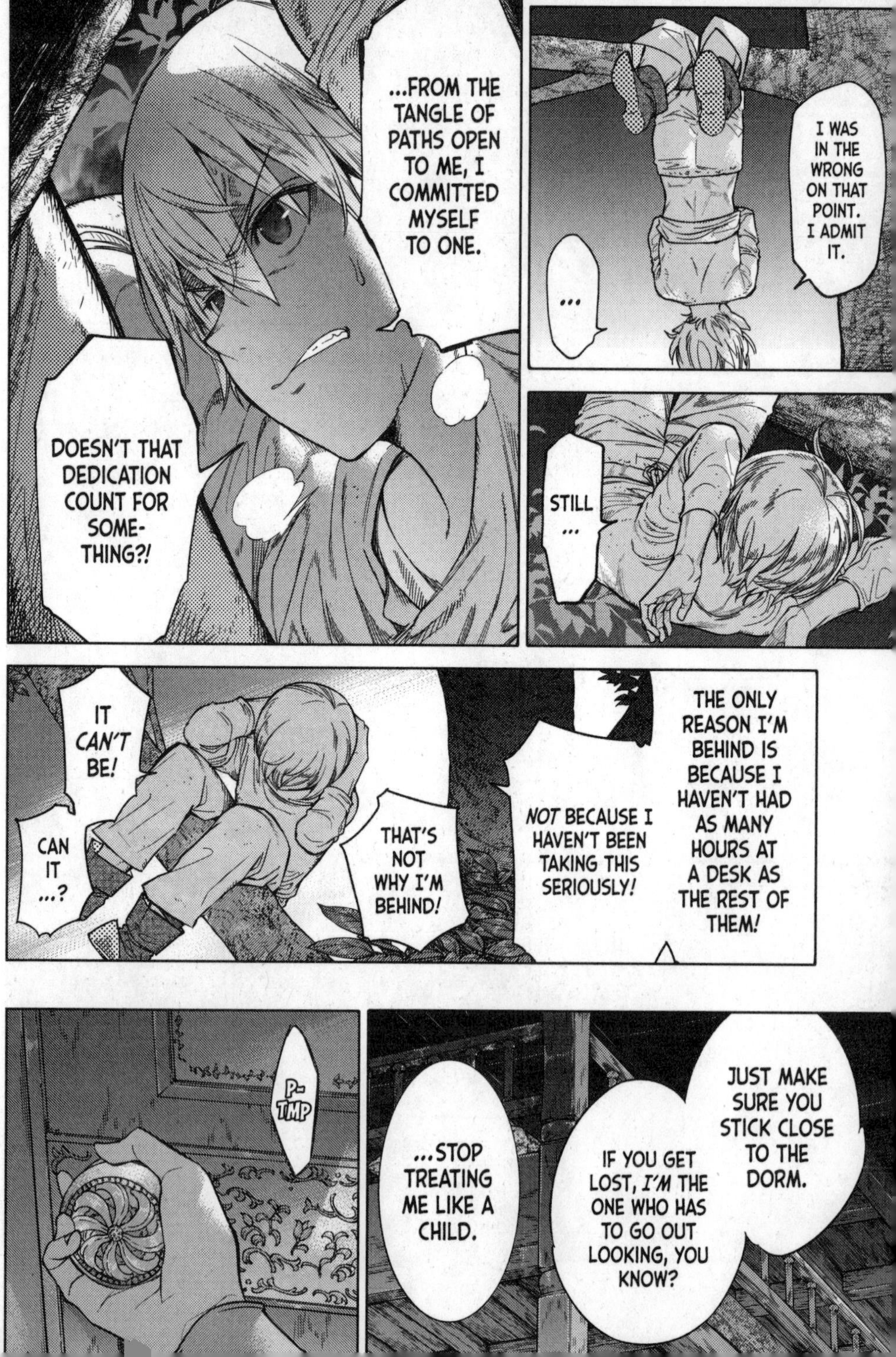
I WAS IN THE WRONG ON THAT POINT. I ADMIT IT.
...
STILL...
...FROM THE TANGLE OF PATHS OPEN TO ME, I COMMITTED MYSELF TO ONE.
DOESN'T THAT DEDICATION COUNT FOR SOME-THING?!
THE ONLY REASON I'M BEHIND IS BECAUSE I HAVEN'T HAD AS MANY HOURS AT A DESK AS THE REST OF THEM!
NOT BECAUSE I HAVEN'T BEEN TAKING THIS SERIOUSLY!
THAT'S NOT WHY I'M BEHIND!
IT *CAN'T* BE!
CAN IT ...?
JUST MAKE SURE YOU STICK CLOSE TO THE DORM.
IF YOU GET LOST, *I'M* THE ONE WHO HAS TO GO OUT LOOKING, YOU KNOW?
...STOP TREATING ME LIKE A CHILD.
P-TMP

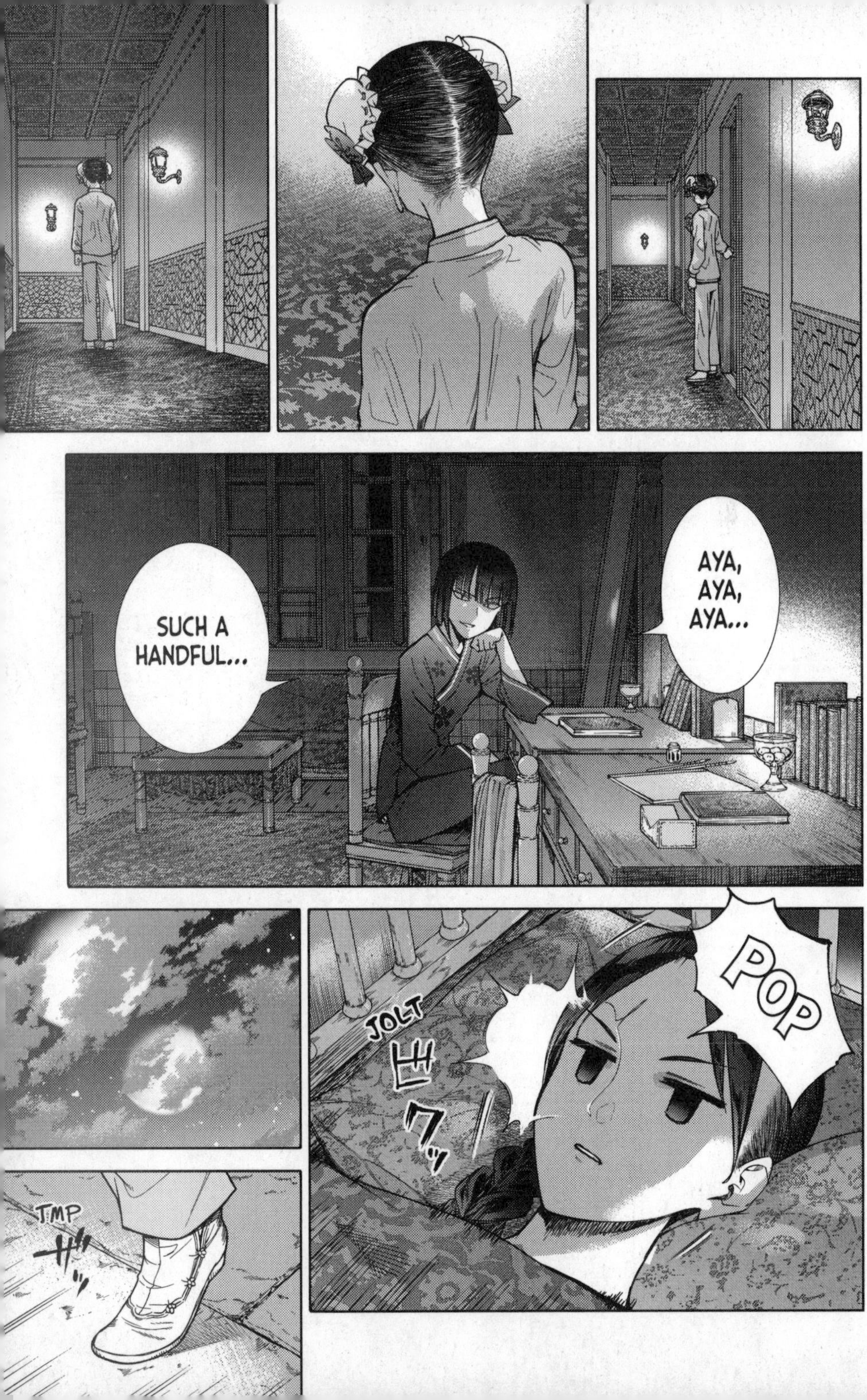
AYA, AYA, AYA...
SUCH A HANDFUL...
POP
JOLT
ビクッ
TMP
ザッ

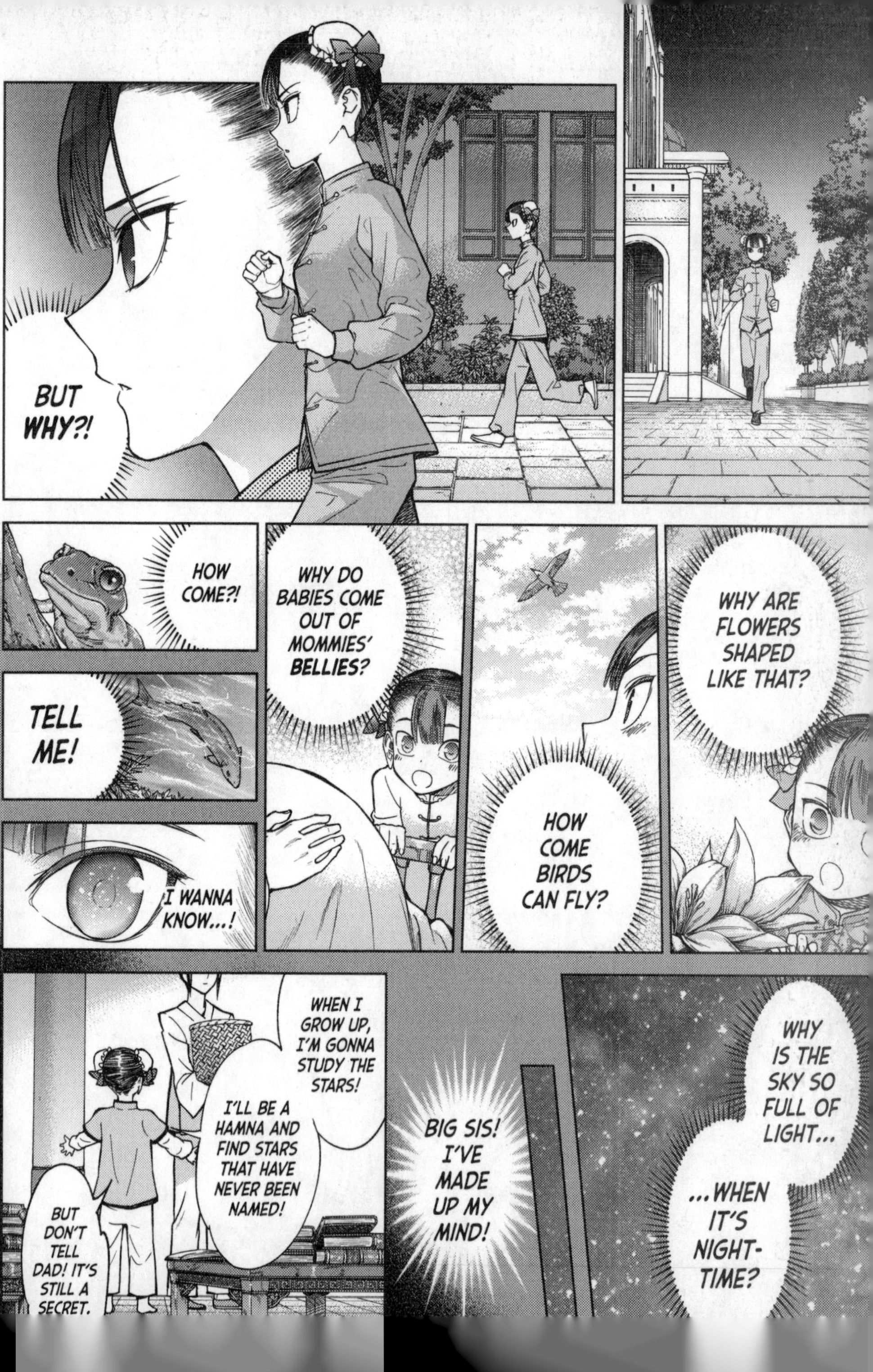
BUT WHY?!
WHY ARE FLOWERS SHAPED LIKE THAT?
HOW COME BIRDS CAN FLY?
WHY DO BABIES COME OUT OF MOMMIES' BELLIES?
HOW COME?!
TELL ME!
I WANNA KNOW...!
WHY IS THE SKY SO FULL OF LIGHT...
...WHEN IT'S NIGHT-TIME?
BIG SIS! I'VE MADE UP MY MIND!
WHEN I GROW UP, I'M GONNA STUDY THE STARS!
I'LL BE A HAMNA AND FIND STARS THAT HAVE NEVER BEEN NAMED!
BUT DON'T TELL DAD! IT'S STILL A SECRET.

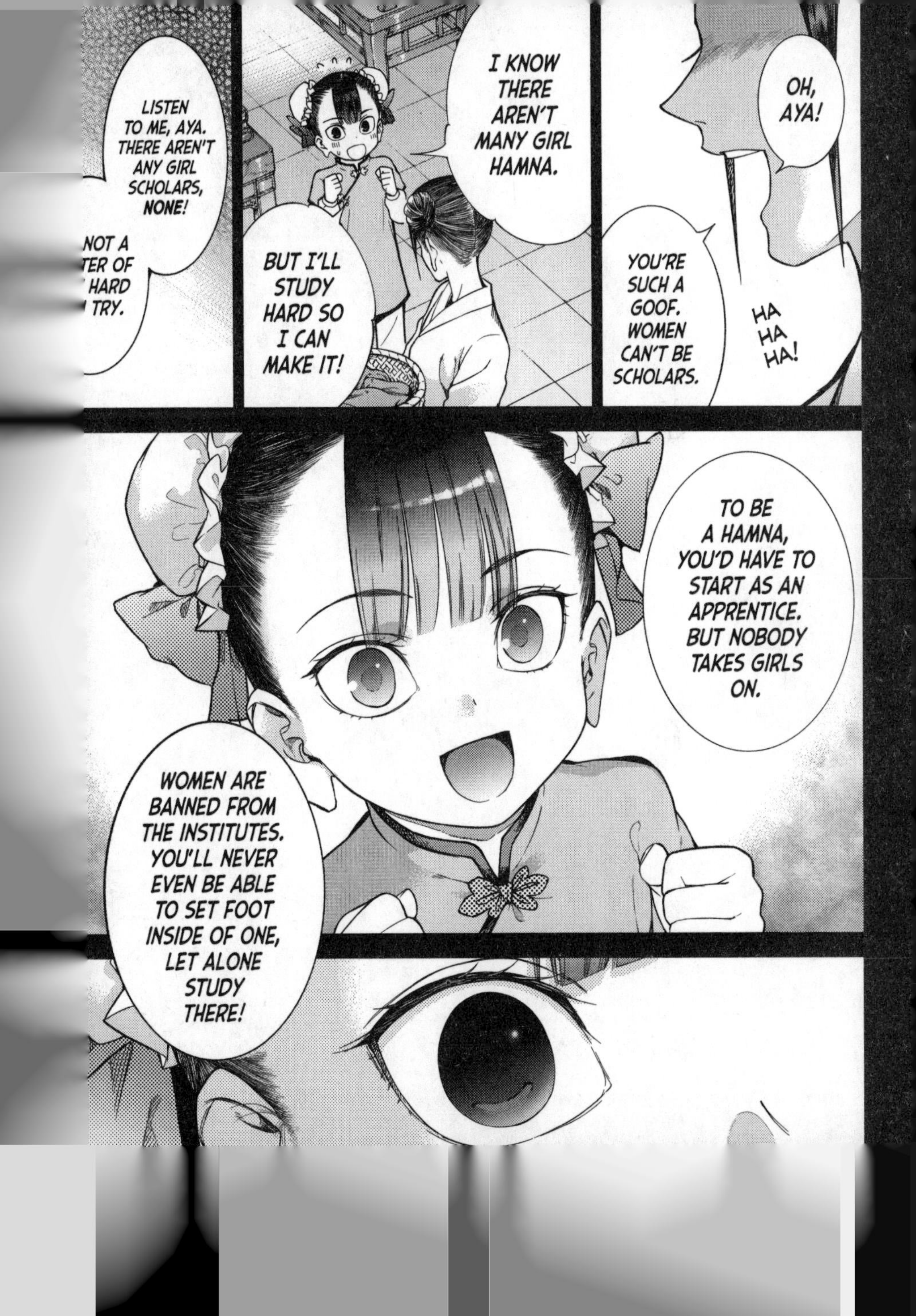
OH, AYA!
HA HA HA!
YOU'RE SUCH A GOOF. WOMEN CAN'T BE SCHOLARS.
I KNOW THERE AREN'T MANY GIRL HAMNA.
BUT I'LL STUDY HARD SO I CAN MAKE IT!
LISTEN TO ME, AYA. THERE AREN'T ANY GIRL SCHOLARS, NONE!
NOT A
TER OF
' HARD
TRY.
TO BE A HAMNA, YOU'D HAVE TO START AS AN APPRENTICE. BUT NOBODY TAKES GIRLS ON.
WOMEN ARE BANNED FROM THE INSTITUTES. YOU'LL NEVER EVEN BE ABLE TO SET FOOT INSIDE OF ONE, LET ALONE STUDY THERE!

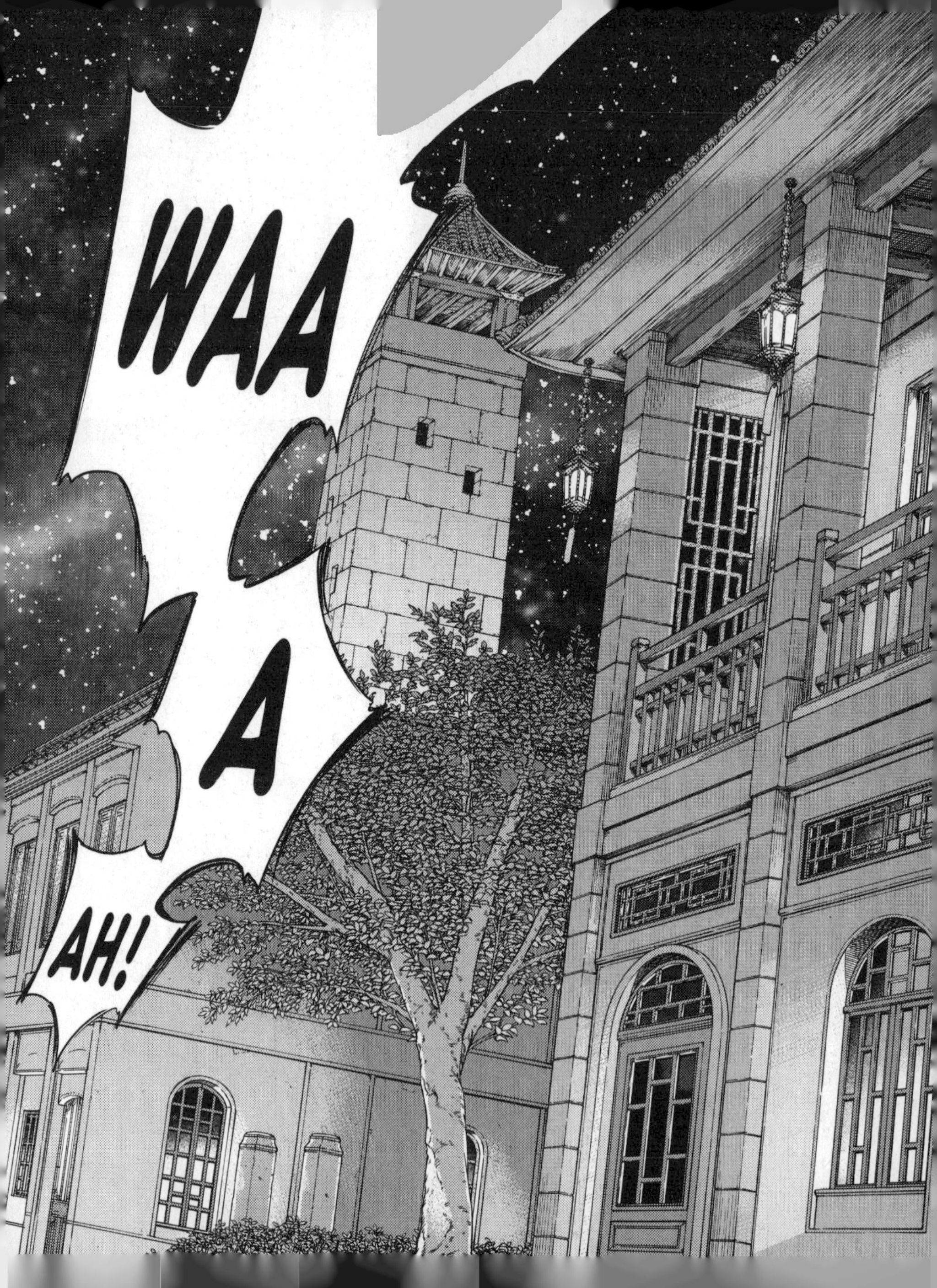
WAA
A
AH!

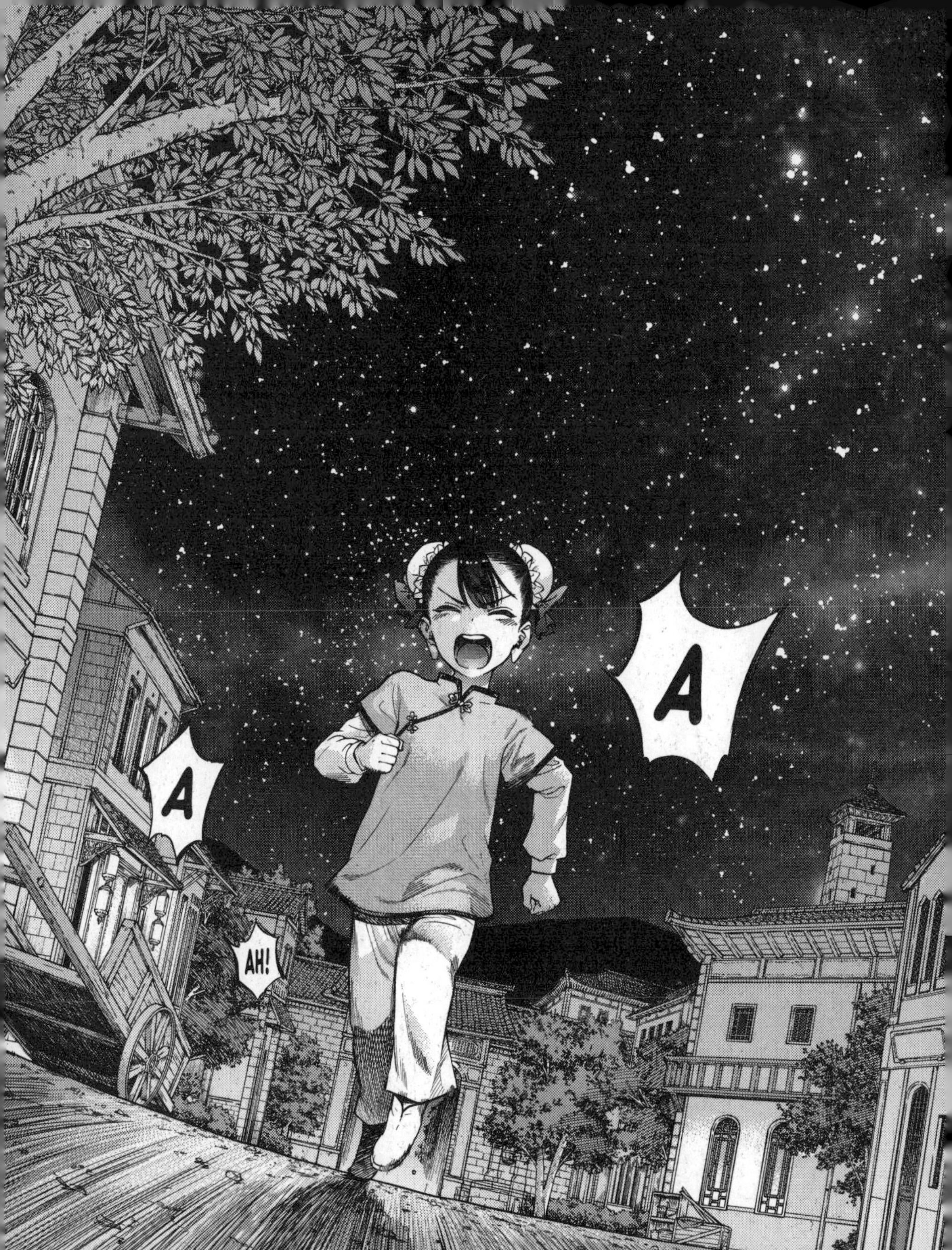
A
A
AH!

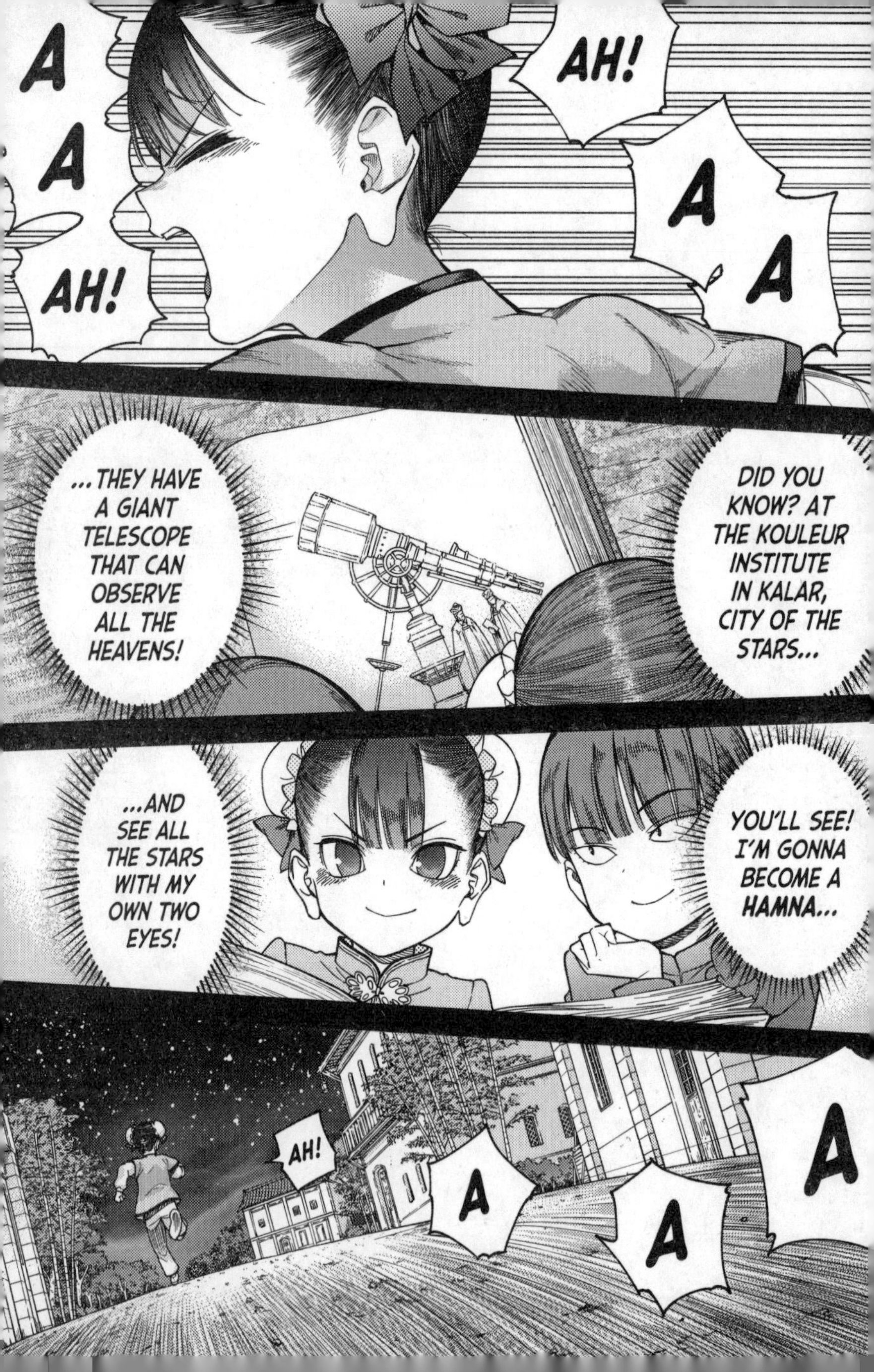
AH!
A
A
A
A
AH!
DID YOU KNOW? AT THE KOULEUR INSTITUTE IN KALAR, CITY OF THE STARS...
...THEY HAVE A GIANT TELESCOPE THAT CAN OBSERVE ALL THE HEAVENS!
YOU'LL SEE! I'M GONNA BECOME A HAMNA...
...AND SEE ALL THE STARS WITH MY OWN TWO EYES!
A
A
A
AH!

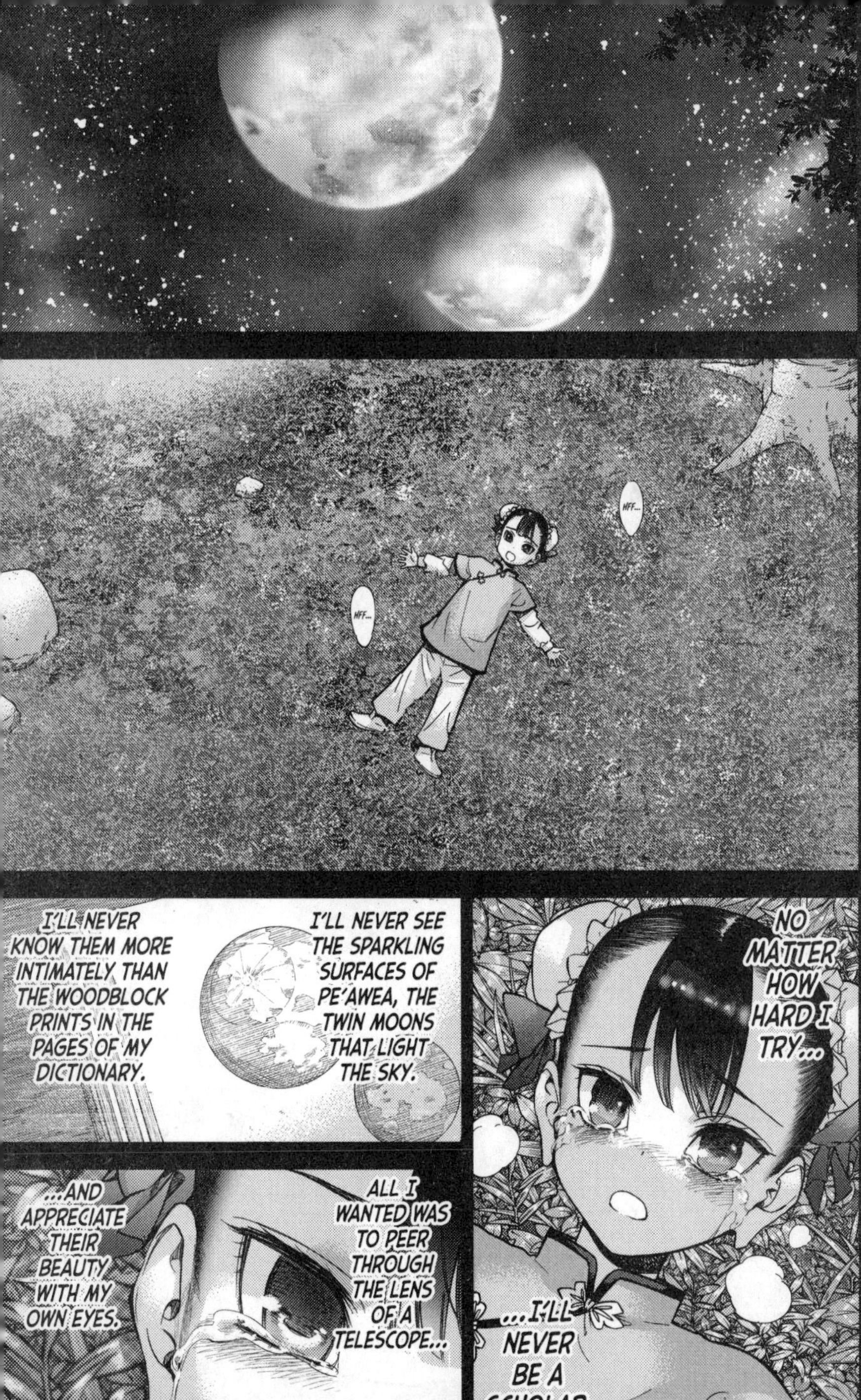

HFF...
HFF...
NO MATTER HOW HARD I TRY...
...I'LL NEVER BE A SCHOLAR.
I'LL NEVER SEE THE SPARKLING SURFACES OF PE'AWEA, THE TWIN MOONS THAT LIGHT THE SKY.
I'LL NEVER KNOW THEM MORE INTIMATELY THAN THE WOODBLOCK PRINTS IN THE PAGES OF MY DICTIONARY.
ALL I WANTED WAS TO PEER THROUGH THE LENS OF A TELESCOPE...
...AND APPRECIATE THEIR BEAUTY WITH MY OWN EYES.

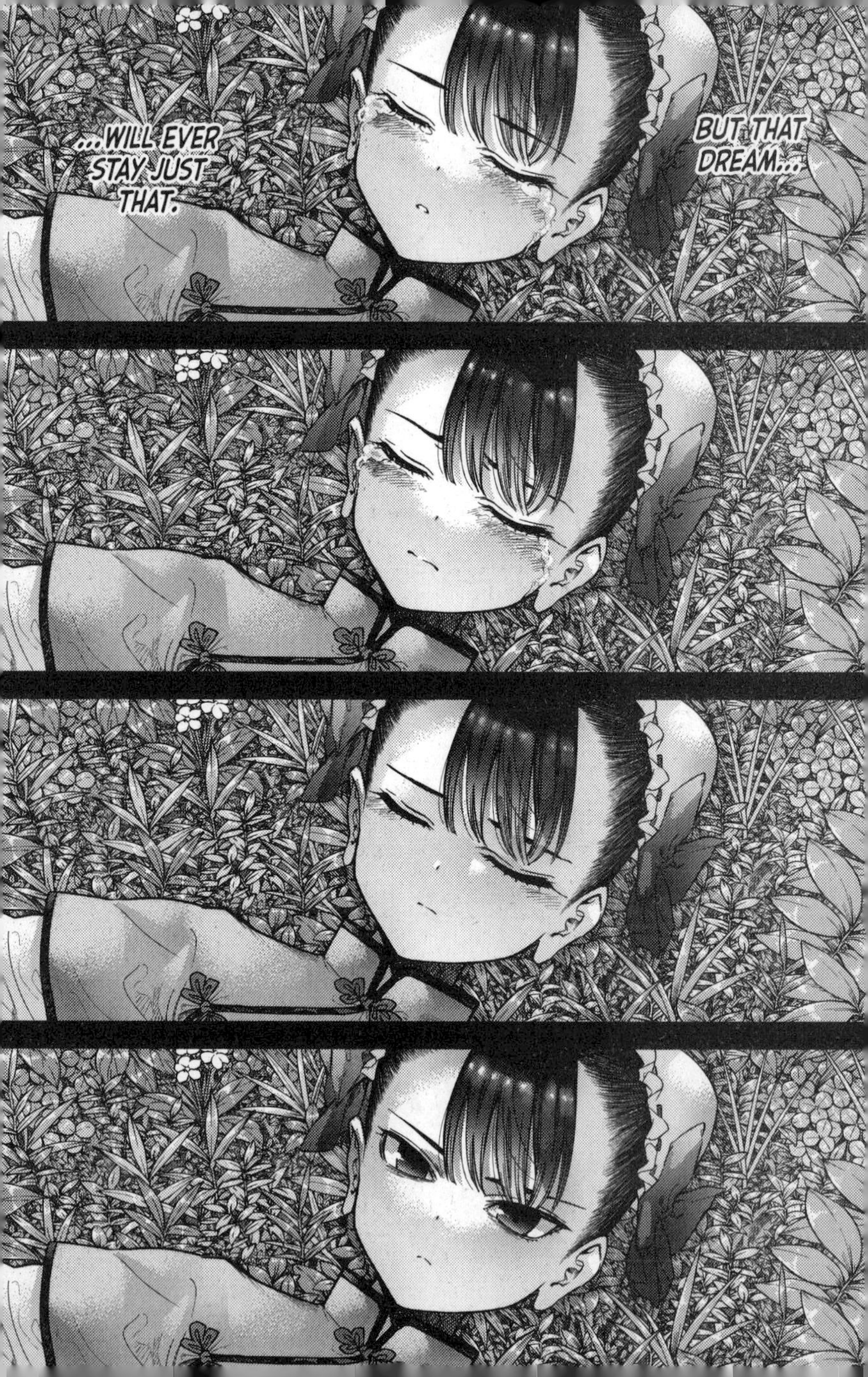
BUT THAT DREAM...
...WILL EVER STAY JUST THAT.

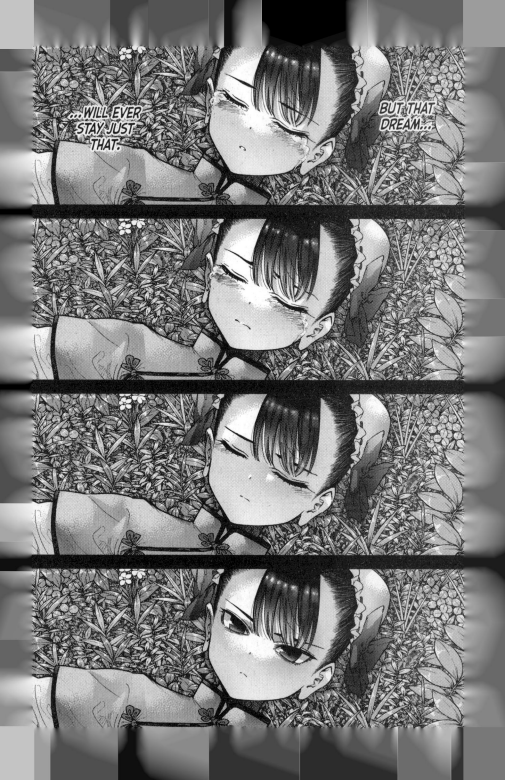

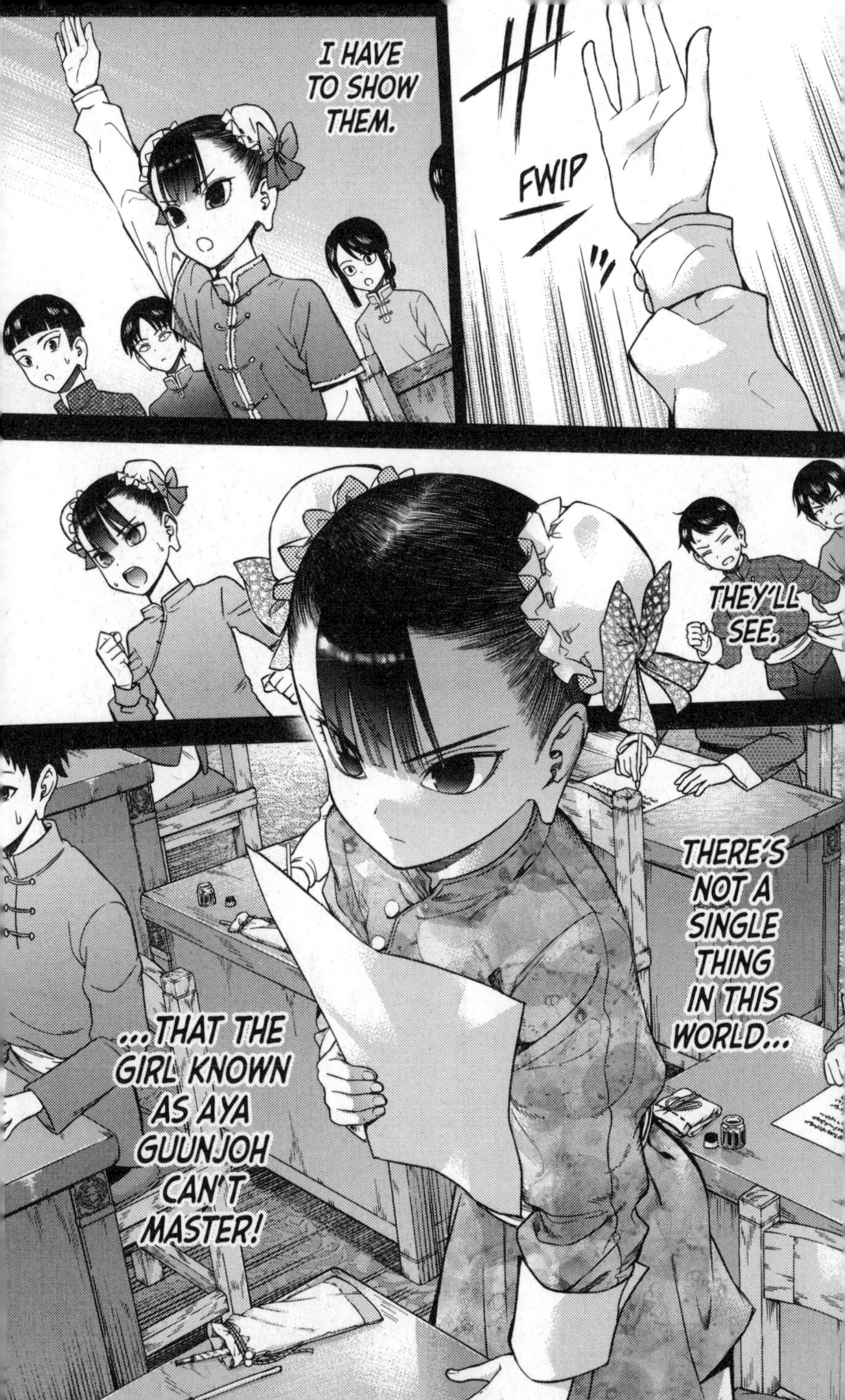
FWIP
I HAVE TO SHOW THEM.
THEY'LL SEE.
THERE'S NOT A SINGLE THING IN THIS WORLD...
...THAT THE GIRL KNOWN AS AYA GUUNJOH CAN'T MASTER!

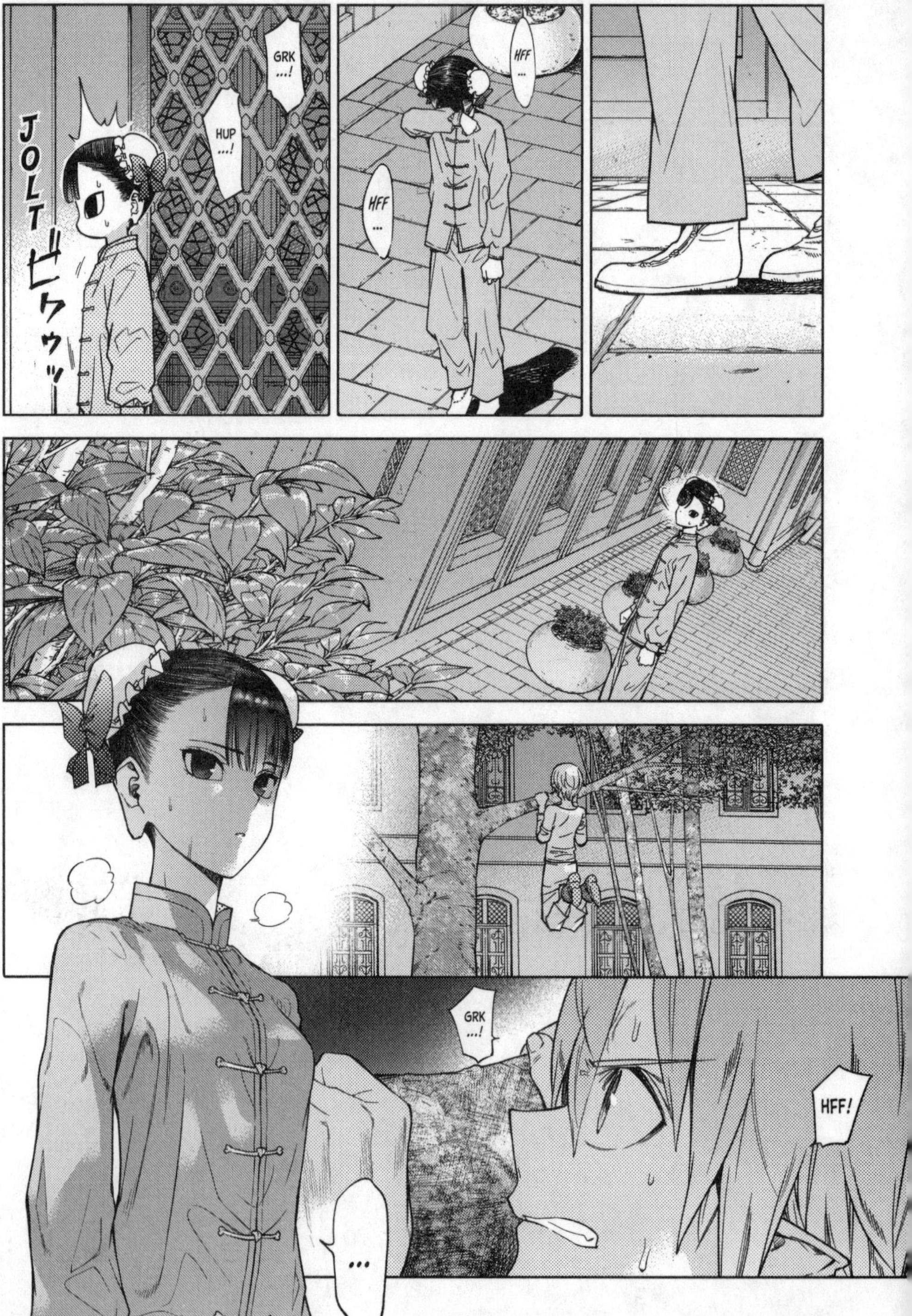
HFF ...
HFF ...
GRK ...!
HUP ...!
JOLT
ビクゥッ
GRK ...!
HFF!
...

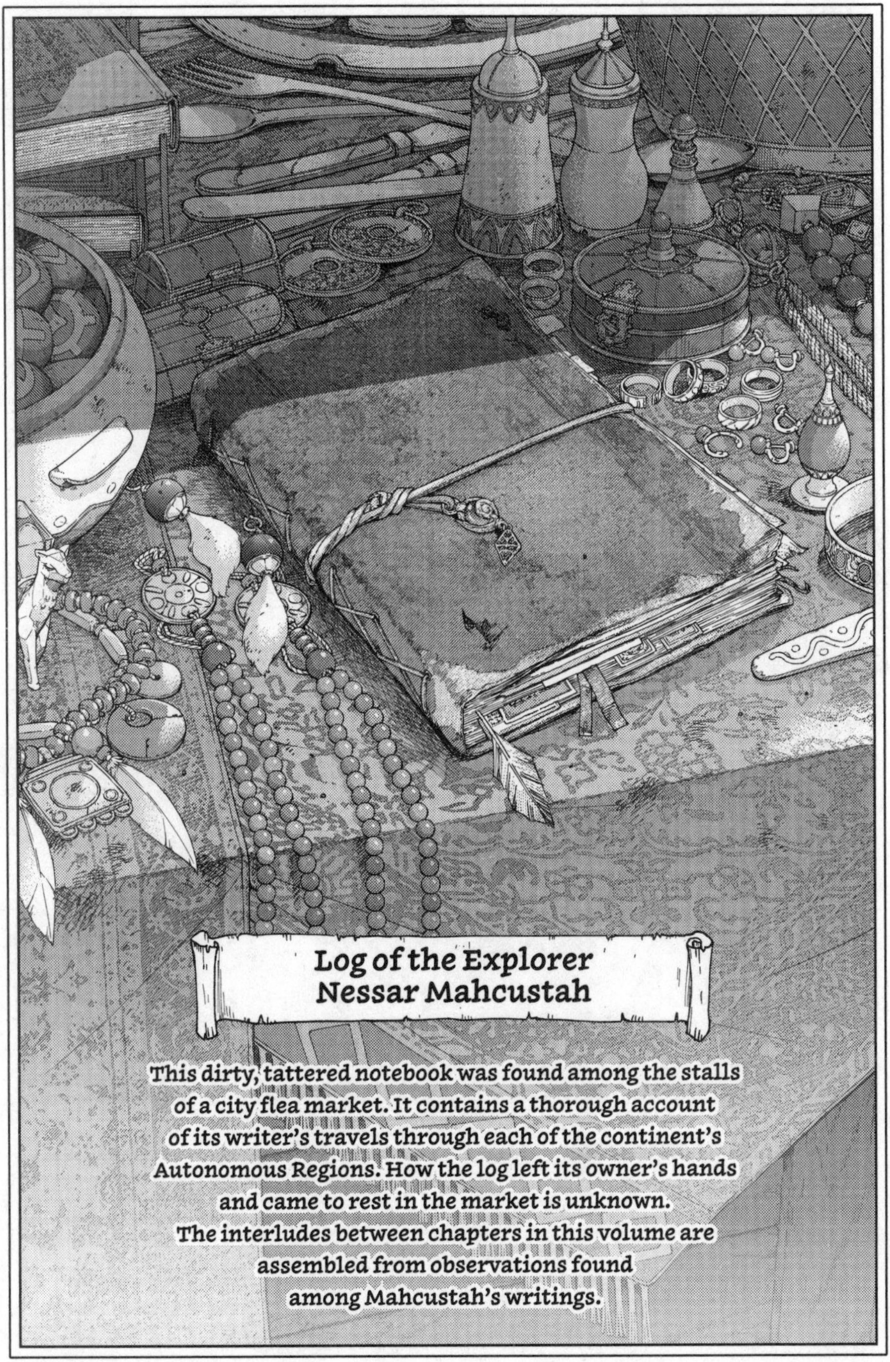
Log of the Explorer
Nessar Mahcustah
This dirty, tattered notebook was found among the stalls of a city flea market. It contains a thorough account of its writer's travels through each of the continent's Autonomous Regions. How the log left its owner's hands and came to rest in the market is unknown.
The interludes between chapters in this volume are assembled from observations found among Mahcustah's writings.

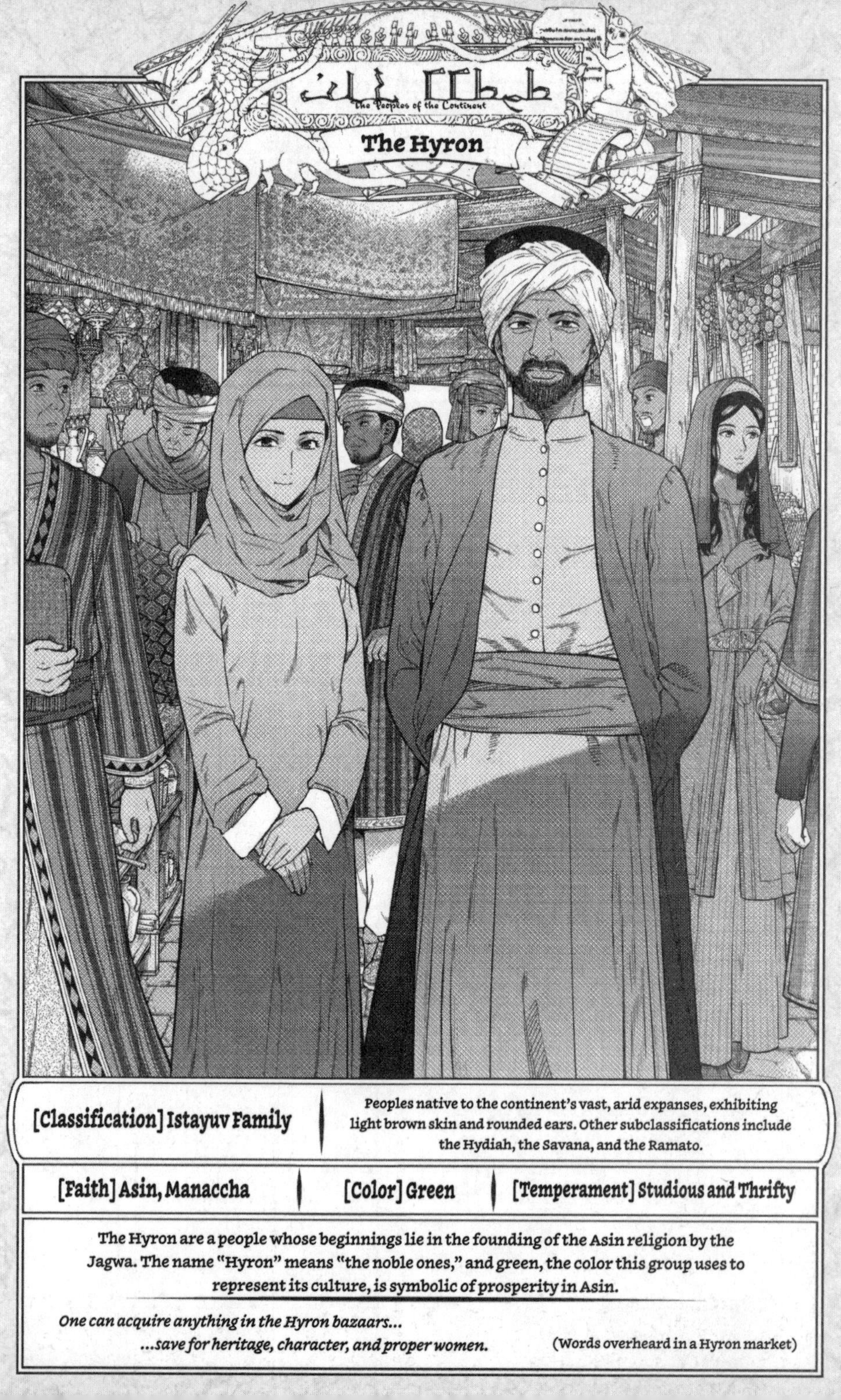
The Peoples of the Continent
The Hyron

[Classification] Istayuv Family

Peoples native to the continent's vast, arid expanses, exhibiting light brown skin and rounded ears. Other subclassifications include the Hydiah, the Savana, and the Ramato.

[Faith] Asin, Manaccha | **[Color] Green** | **[Temperament] Studious and Thrifty**

The Hyron are a people whose beginnings lie in the founding of the Asin religion by the Jagwa. The name "Hyron" means "the noble ones," and green, the color this group uses to represent its culture, is symbolic of prosperity in Asin.

One can acquire anything in the Hyron bazaars...
...save for heritage, character, and proper women.

(Words overheard in a Hyron market)

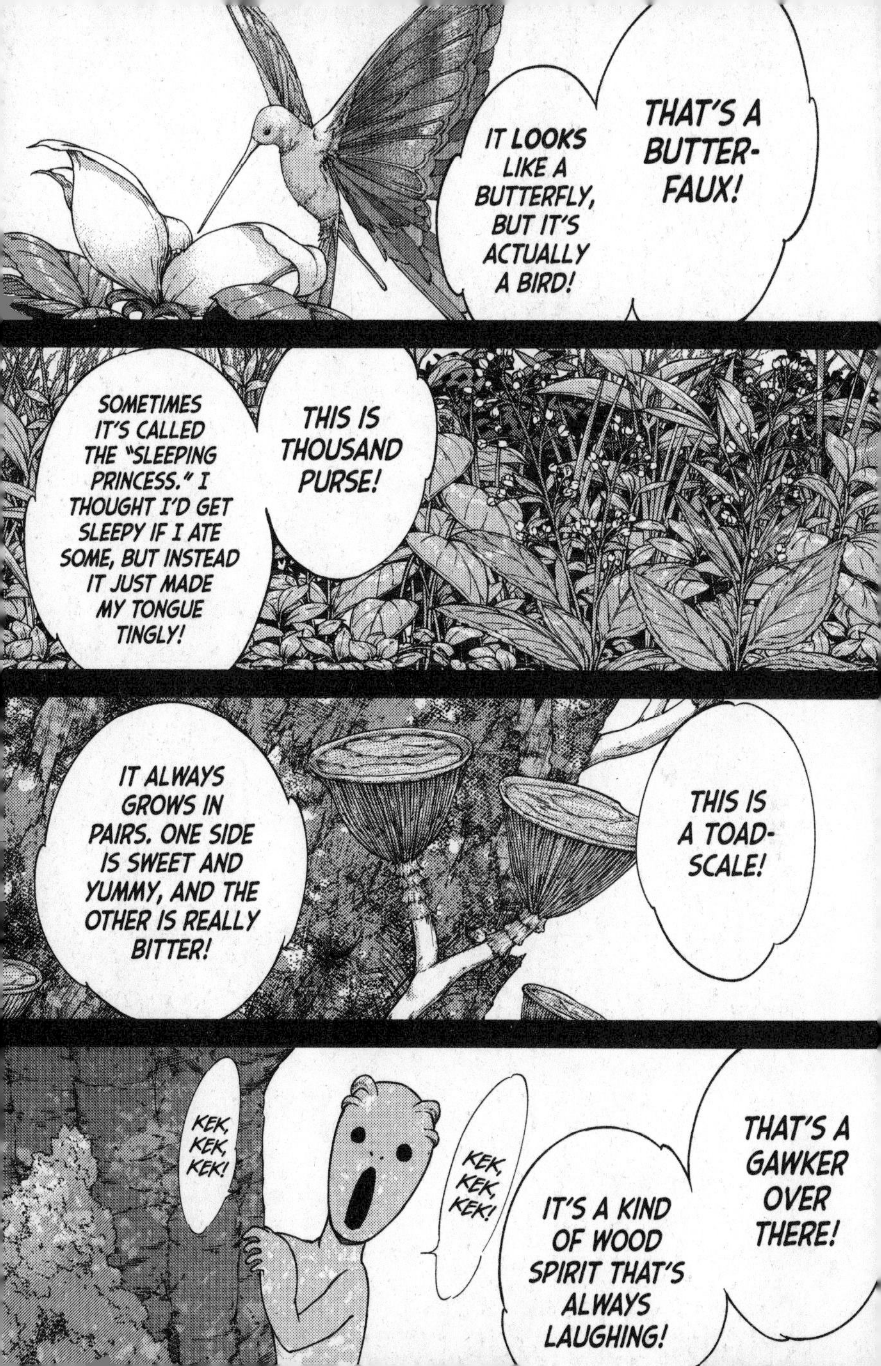
THAT'S A BUTTER-FAUX!
IT LOOKS LIKE A BUTTERFLY, BUT IT'S ACTUALLY A BIRD!
THIS IS THOUSAND PURSE!
SOMETIMES IT'S CALLED THE "SLEEPING PRINCESS." I THOUGHT I'D GET SLEEPY IF I ATE SOME, BUT INSTEAD IT JUST MADE MY TONGUE TINGLY!
THIS IS A TOAD-SCALE!
IT ALWAYS GROWS IN PAIRS. ONE SIDE IS SWEET AND YUMMY, AND THE OTHER IS REALLY BITTER!
THAT'S A GAWKER OVER THERE!
IT'S A KIND OF WOOD SPIRIT THAT'S ALWAYS LAUGHING!
KEK, KEK, KEK!
KEK, KEK, KEK!

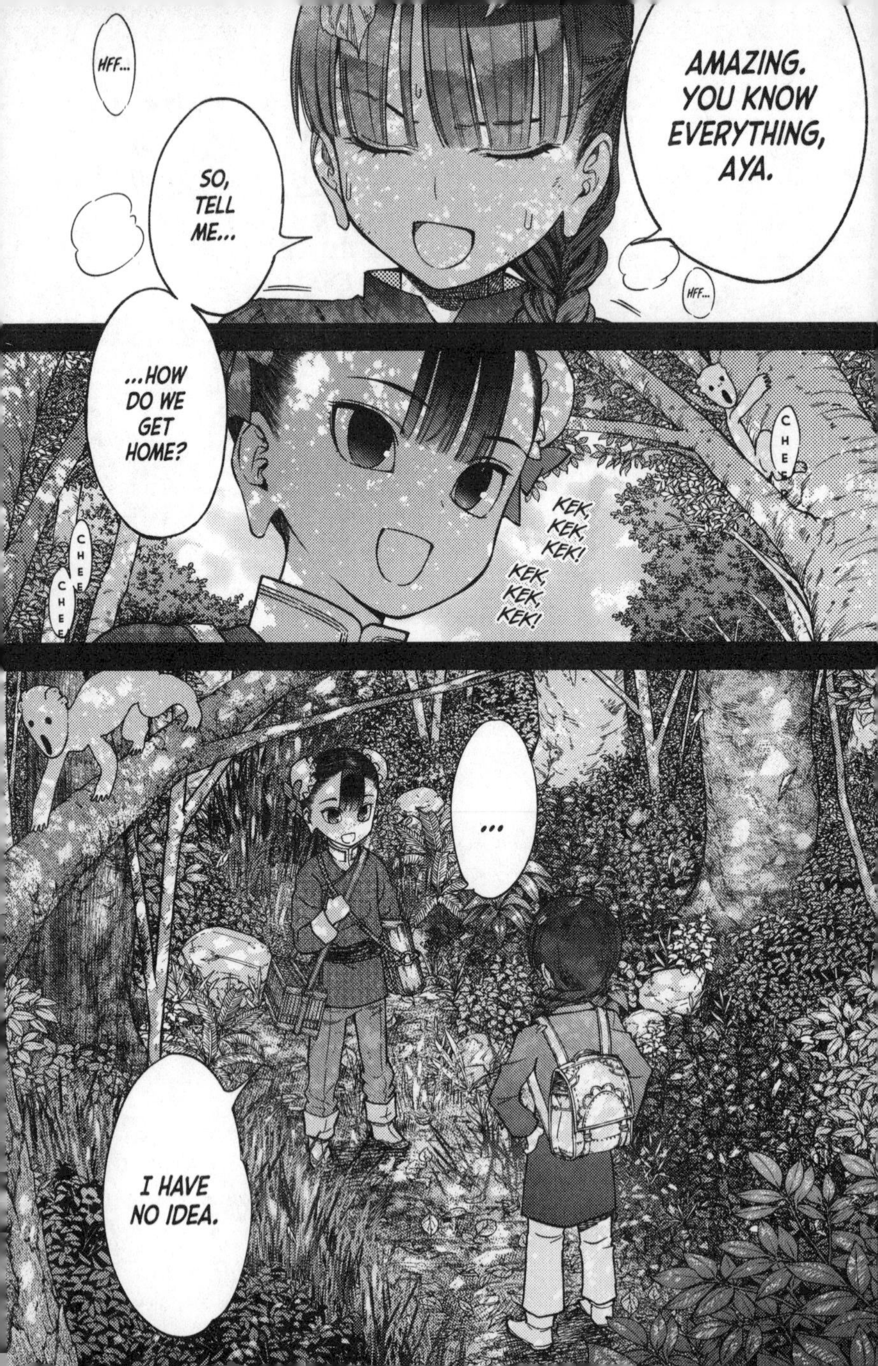
AMAZING. YOU KNOW EVERYTHING, AYA.
HFF...
HFF...
SO, TELL ME...
...HOW DO WE GET HOME?
CHEE
KEK, KEK, KEK!
KEK, KEK, KEK!
CHEE
CHEE
...
I HAVE NO IDEA.

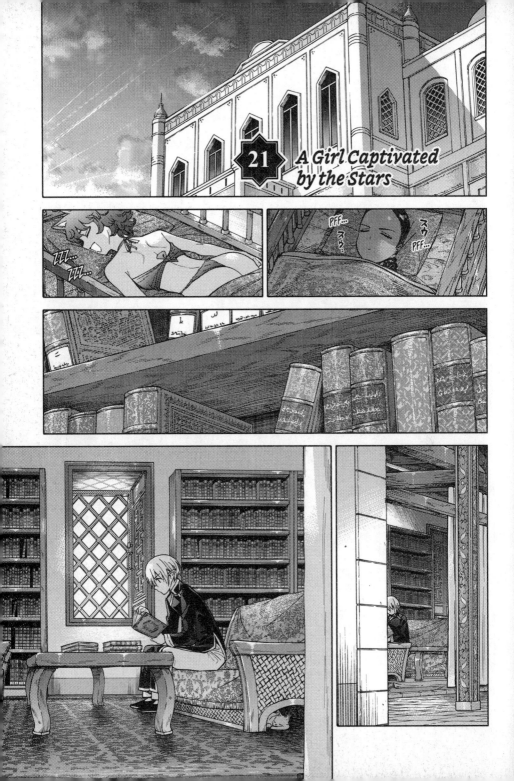

21 *A Girl Captivated by the Stars*

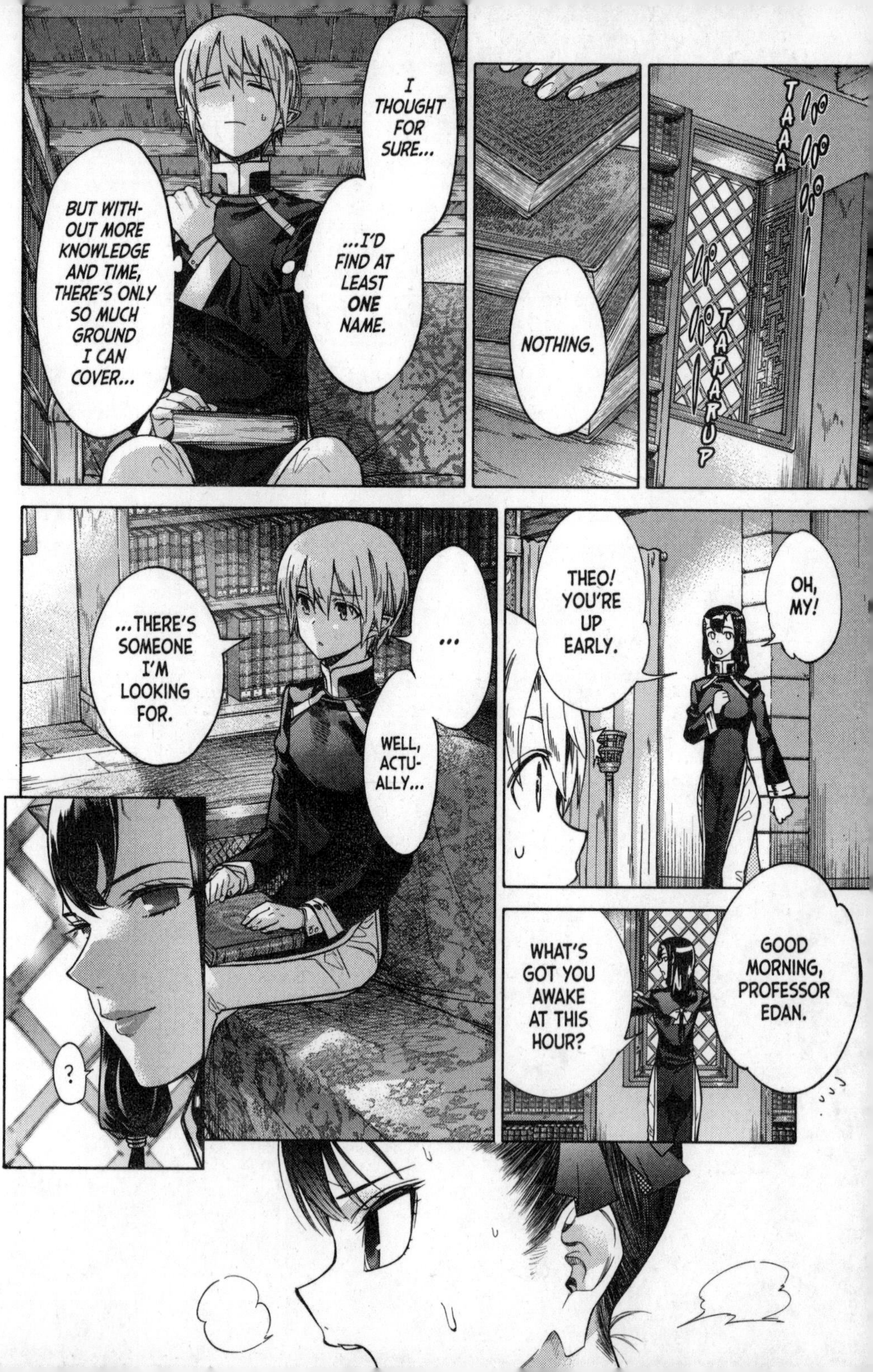
TAAA
TARARUP
NOTHING.
I THOUGHT FOR SURE...
...I'D FIND AT LEAST ONE NAME.
BUT WITH-OUT MORE KNOWLEDGE AND TIME, THERE'S ONLY SO MUCH GROUND I CAN COVER...
OH, MY!
THEO! YOU'RE UP EARLY.
GOOD MORNING, PROFESSOR EDAN.
WHAT'S GOT YOU AWAKE AT THIS HOUR?
...
WELL, ACTU-ALLY...
...THERE'S SOMEONE I'M LOOKING FOR.
?

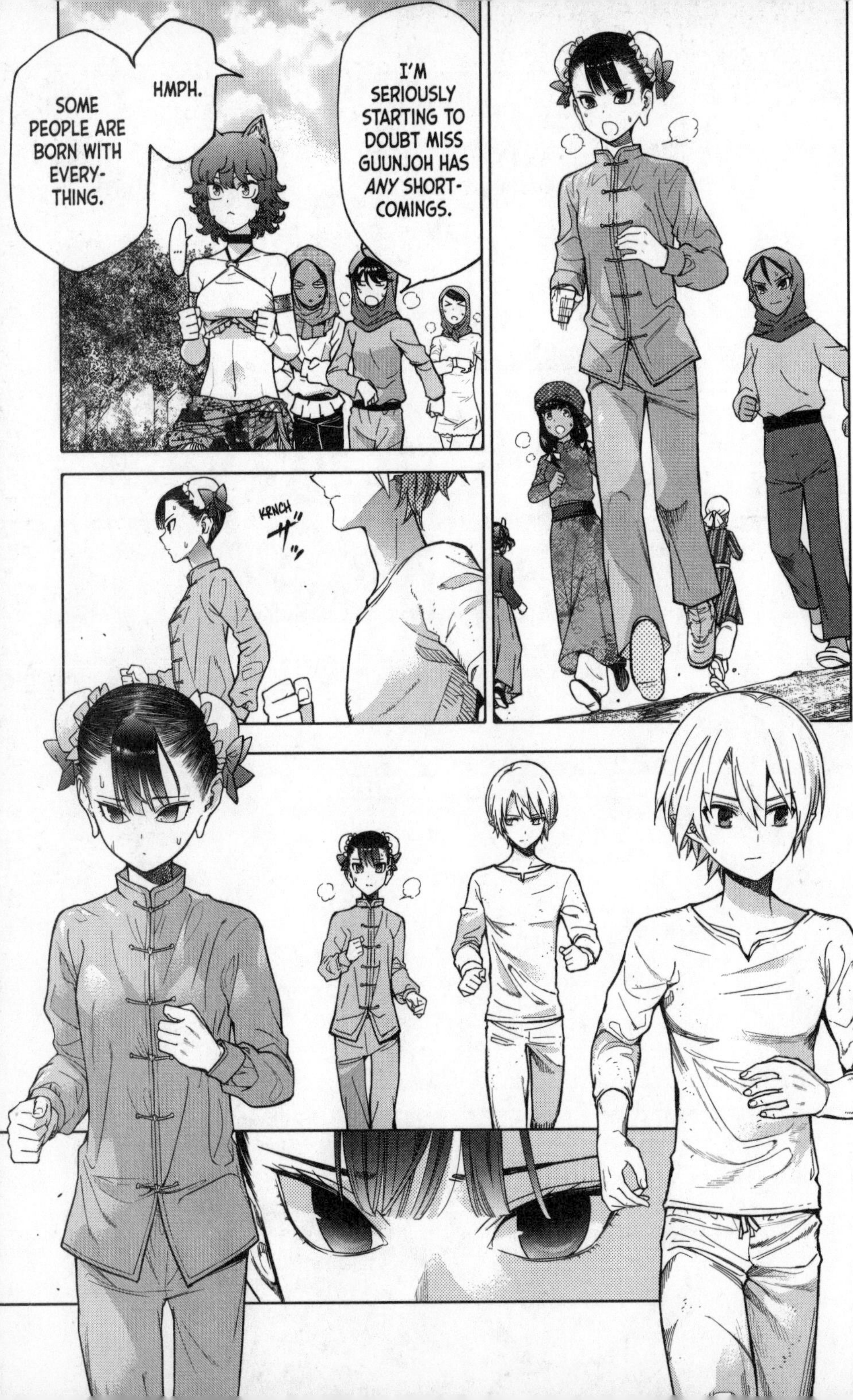
I'M SERIOUSLY STARTING TO DOUBT MISS GUUNJOH HAS *ANY* SHORT-COMINGS.
HMPH.
SOME PEOPLE ARE BORN WITH EVERY-THING.
...
KRNCH

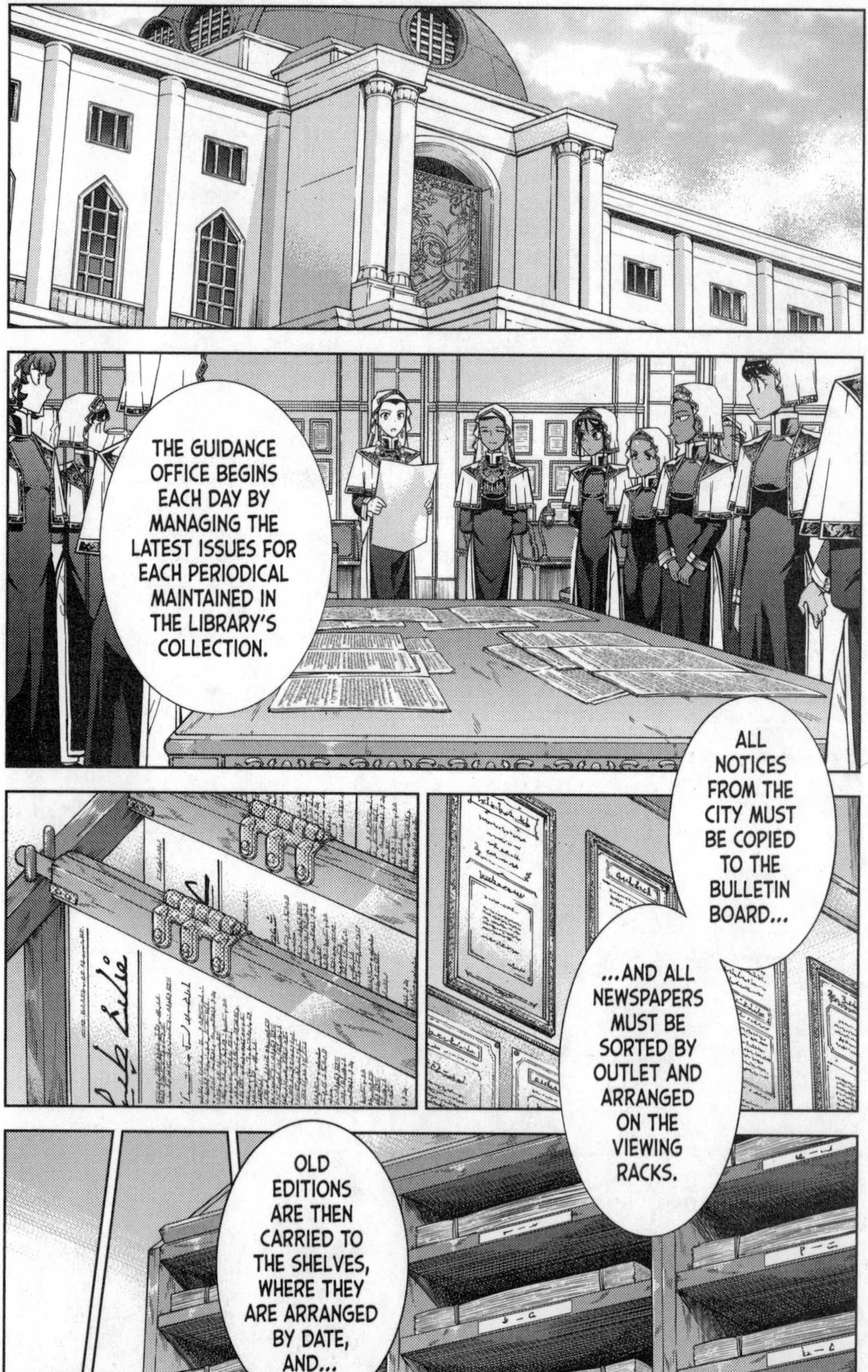
THE GUIDANCE OFFICE BEGINS EACH DAY BY MANAGING THE LATEST ISSUES FOR EACH PERIODICAL MAINTAINED IN THE LIBRARY'S COLLECTION.
ALL NOTICES FROM THE CITY MUST BE COPIED TO THE BULLETIN BOARD...
...AND ALL NEWSPAPERS MUST BE SORTED BY OUTLET AND ARRANGED ON THE VIEWING RACKS.
OLD EDITIONS ARE THEN CARRIED TO THE SHELVES, WHERE THEY ARE ARRANGED BY DATE, AND...

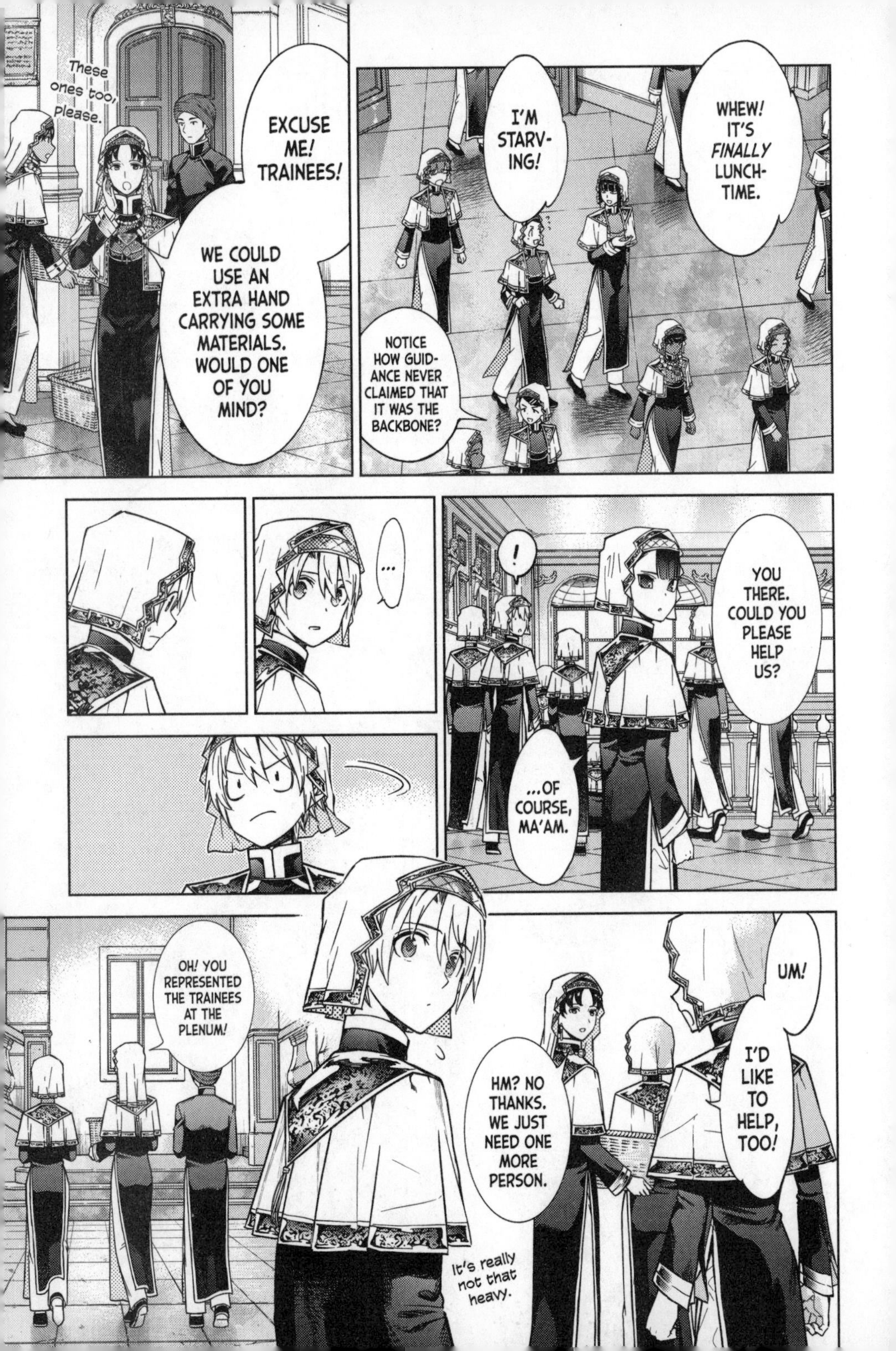
WHEW! IT'S *FINALLY* LUNCH-TIME.
I'M STARVING!
NOTICE HOW GUIDANCE NEVER CLAIMED THAT IT WAS THE BACKBONE?
EXCUSE ME! TRAINEES!
These ones too, please.
WE COULD USE AN EXTRA HAND CARRYING SOME MATERIALS. WOULD ONE OF YOU MIND?
YOU THERE. COULD YOU PLEASE HELP US?
!
...OF COURSE, MA'AM.
...
UM!
I'D LIKE TO HELP, TOO!
HM? NO THANKS. WE JUST NEED ONE MORE PERSON.
It's really not that heavy.
OH! YOU REPRESENTED THE TRAINEES AT THE PLENUM!

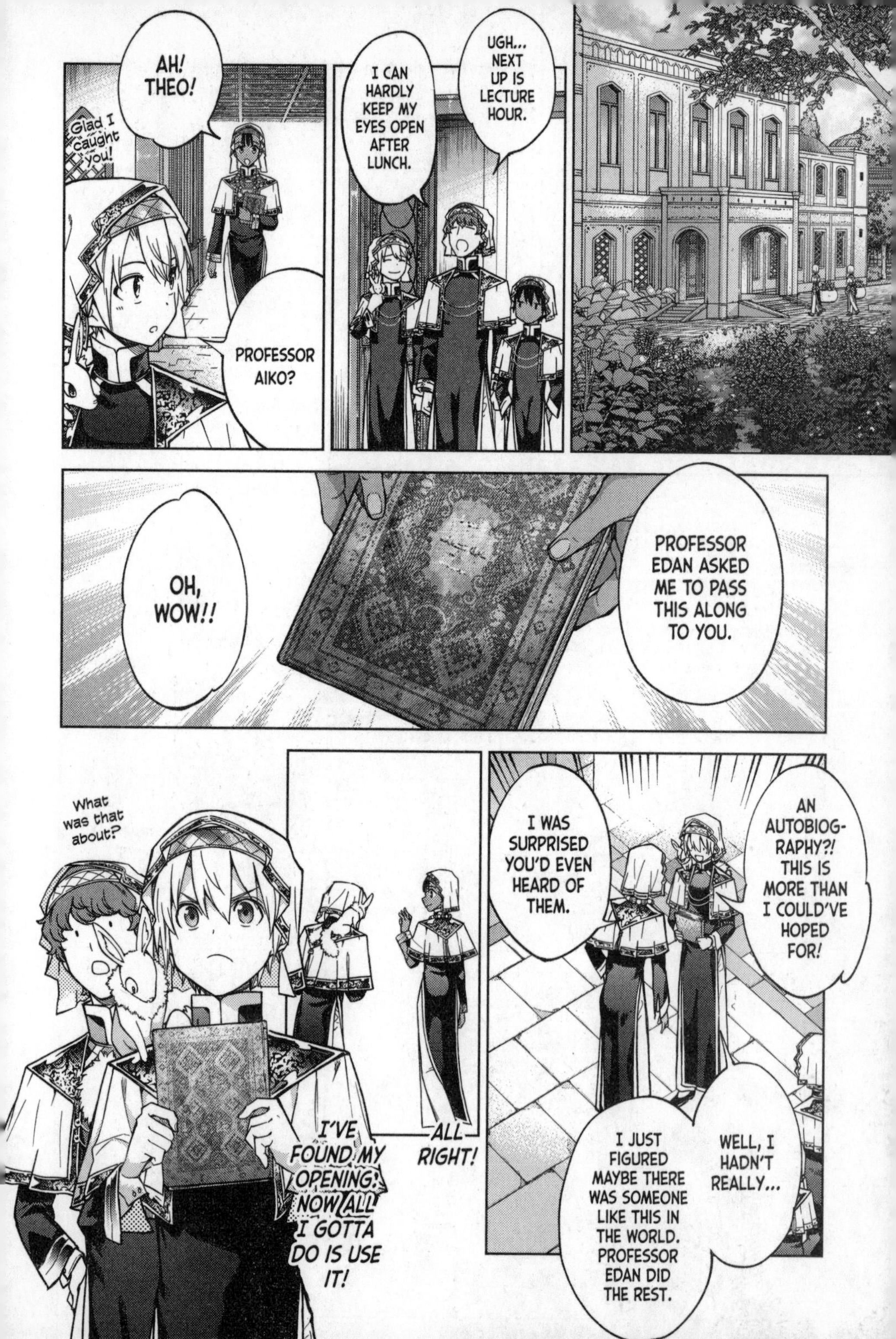
UGH... NEXT UP IS LECTURE HOUR.
I CAN HARDLY KEEP MY EYES OPEN AFTER LUNCH.
AH! THEO!
Glad I caught you!
PROFESSOR AIKO?
PROFESSOR EDAN ASKED ME TO PASS THIS ALONG TO YOU.
OH, WOW!!
AN AUTOBIOGRAPHY?! THIS IS MORE THAN I COULD'VE HOPED FOR!
I WAS SURPRISED YOU'D EVEN HEARD OF THEM.
WELL, I HADN'T REALLY...
I JUST FIGURED MAYBE THERE WAS SOMEONE LIKE THIS IN THE WORLD. PROFESSOR EDAN DID THE REST.
ALL RIGHT!
I'VE FOUND MY OPENING! NOW ALL I GOTTA DO IS USE IT!
What was that about?

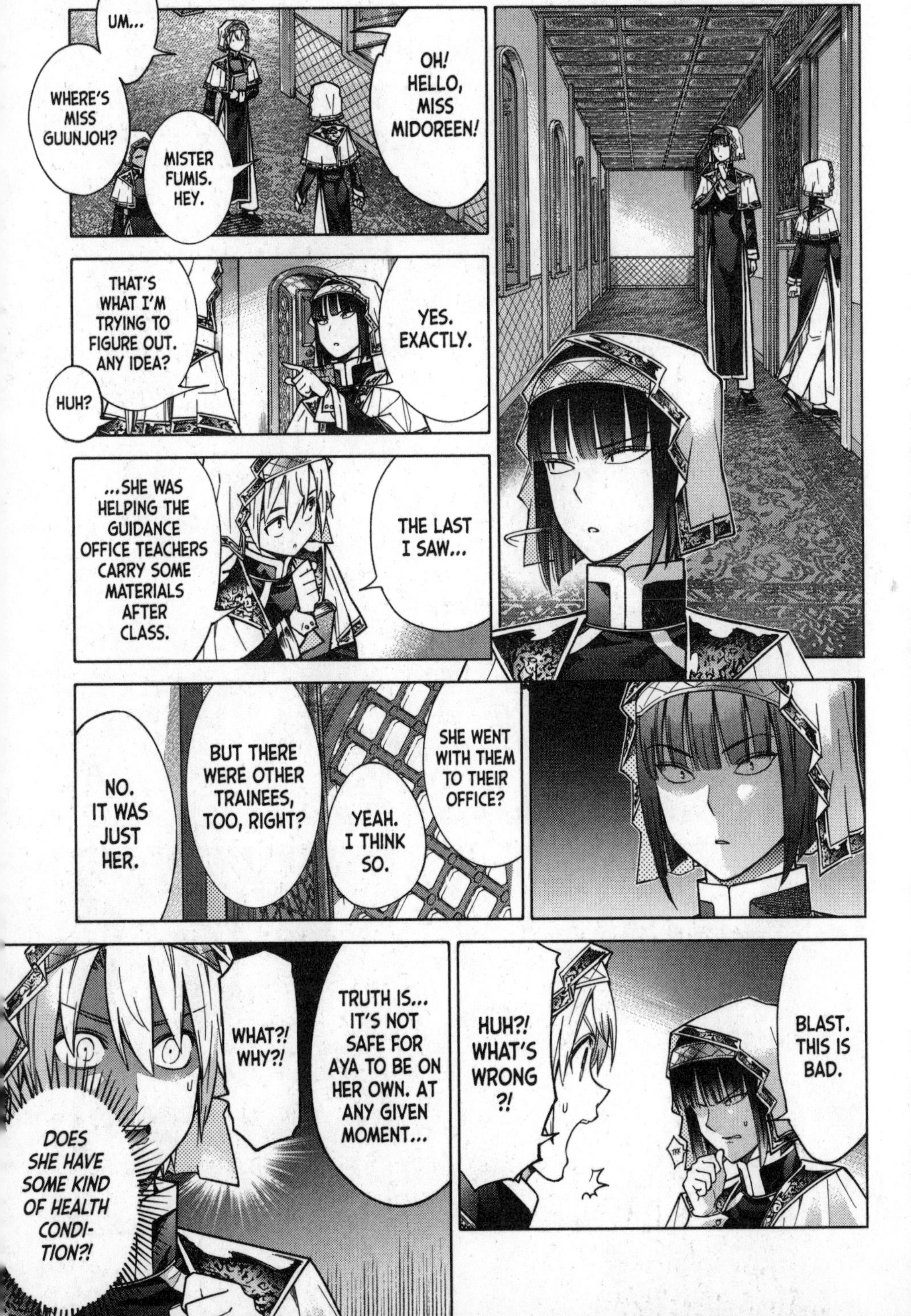
OH! HELLO, MISS MIDOREEN!
MISTER FUMIS. HEY.
UM...
WHERE'S MISS GUUNJOH?
YES. EXACTLY.
THAT'S WHAT I'M TRYING TO FIGURE OUT. ANY IDEA?
HUH?
THE LAST I SAW...
...SHE WAS HELPING THE GUIDANCE OFFICE TEACHERS CARRY SOME MATERIALS AFTER CLASS.
SHE WENT WITH THEM TO THEIR OFFICE?
YEAH. I THINK SO.
BUT THERE WERE OTHER TRAINEES, TOO, RIGHT?
NO. IT WAS JUST HER.
BLAST. THIS IS BAD.
HUH?! WHAT'S WRONG ?!
TRUTH IS... IT'S NOT SAFE FOR AYA TO BE ON HER OWN. AT ANY GIVEN MOMENT...
WHAT?! WHY?!
DOES SHE HAVE SOME KIND OF HEALTH CONDI-TION?!

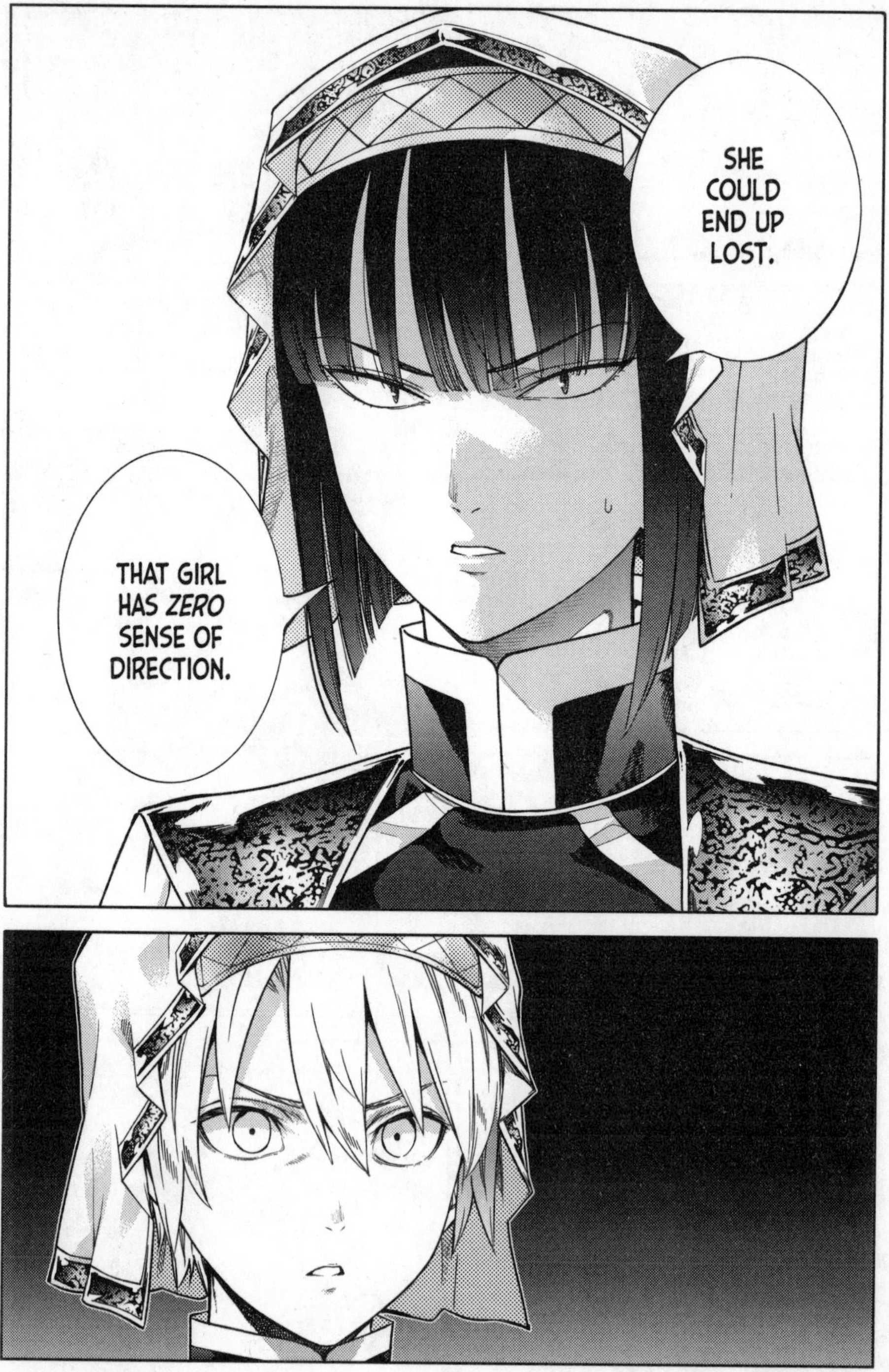
SHE COULD END UP LOST.
THAT GIRL HAS *ZERO* SENSE OF DIRECTION.

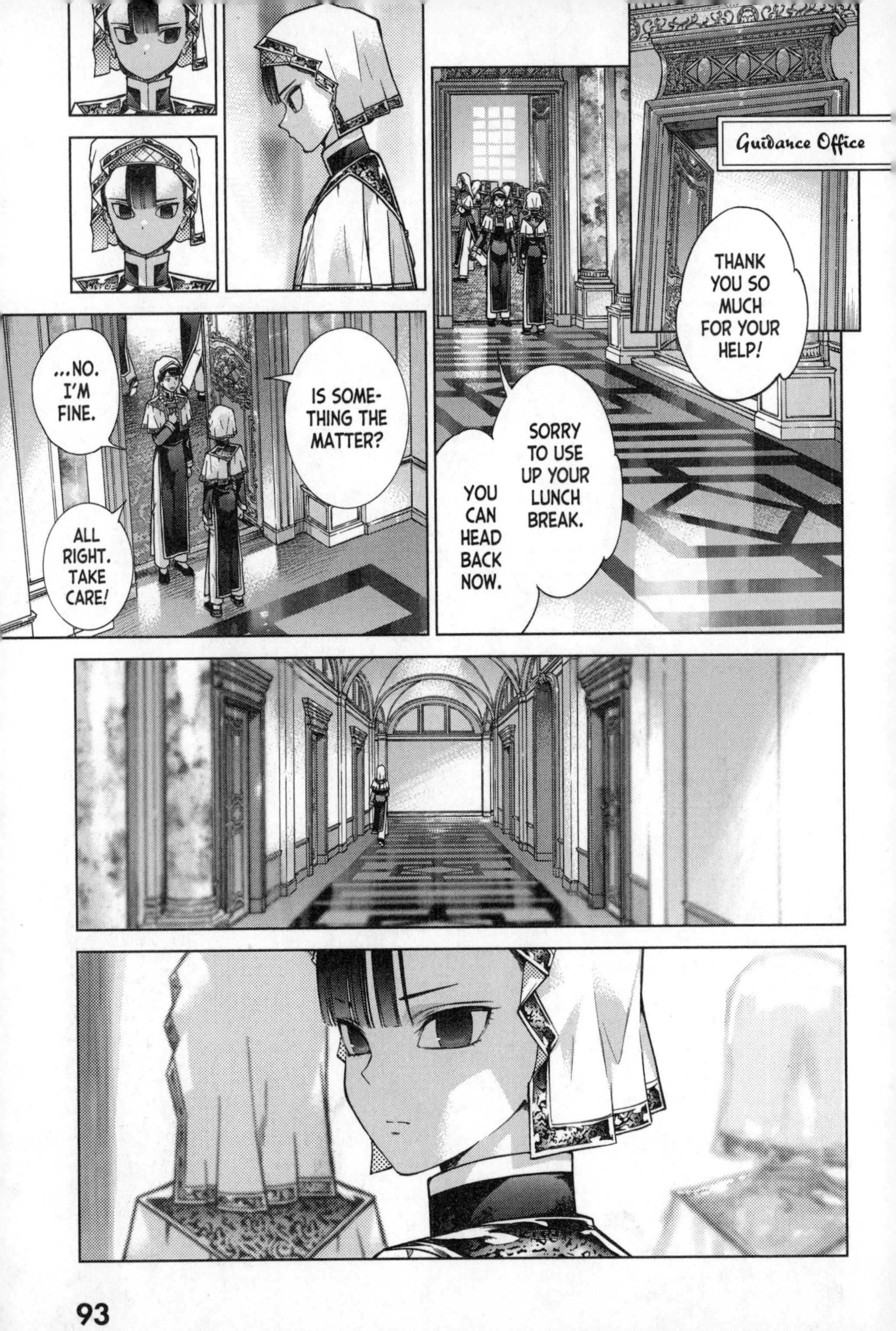
Guidance Office
THANK YOU SO MUCH FOR YOUR HELP!
SORRY TO USE UP YOUR LUNCH BREAK.
YOU CAN HEAD BACK NOW.
IS SOME-THING THE MATTER?
...NO. I'M FINE.
ALL RIGHT. TAKE CARE!

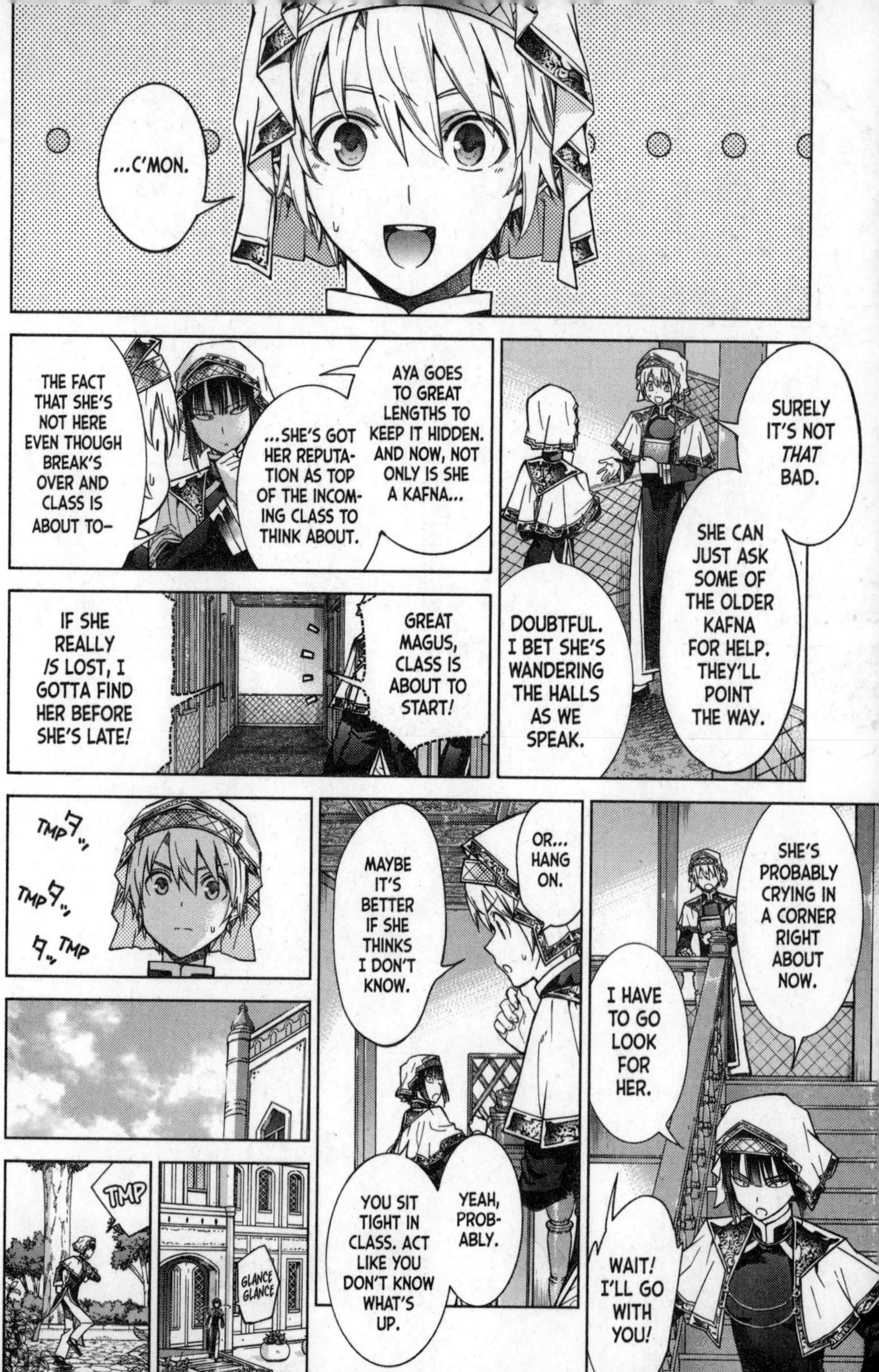
...C'MON.
SURELY IT'S NOT *THAT* BAD.
SHE CAN JUST ASK SOME OF THE OLDER KAFNA FOR HELP. THEY'LL POINT THE WAY.
DOUBTFUL. I BET SHE'S WANDERING THE HALLS AS WE SPEAK.
AYA GOES TO GREAT LENGTHS TO KEEP IT HIDDEN. AND NOW, NOT ONLY IS SHE A KAFNA...
...SHE'S GOT HER REPUTATION AS TOP OF THE INCOMING CLASS TO THINK ABOUT.
THE FACT THAT SHE'S NOT HERE EVEN THOUGH BREAK'S OVER AND CLASS IS ABOUT TO–
GREAT MAGUS, CLASS IS ABOUT TO START!
IF SHE REALLY *IS* LOST, I GOTTA FIND HER BEFORE SHE'S LATE!
SHE'S PROBABLY CRYING IN A CORNER RIGHT ABOUT NOW.
I HAVE TO GO LOOK FOR HER.
WAIT! I'LL GO WITH YOU!
OR... HANG ON.
MAYBE IT'S BETTER IF SHE THINKS I DON'T KNOW.
YEAH, PROBABLY.
YOU SIT TIGHT IN CLASS. ACT LIKE YOU DON'T KNOW WHAT'S UP.
TMP
TMP
TMP
GLANCE GLANCE
TMP

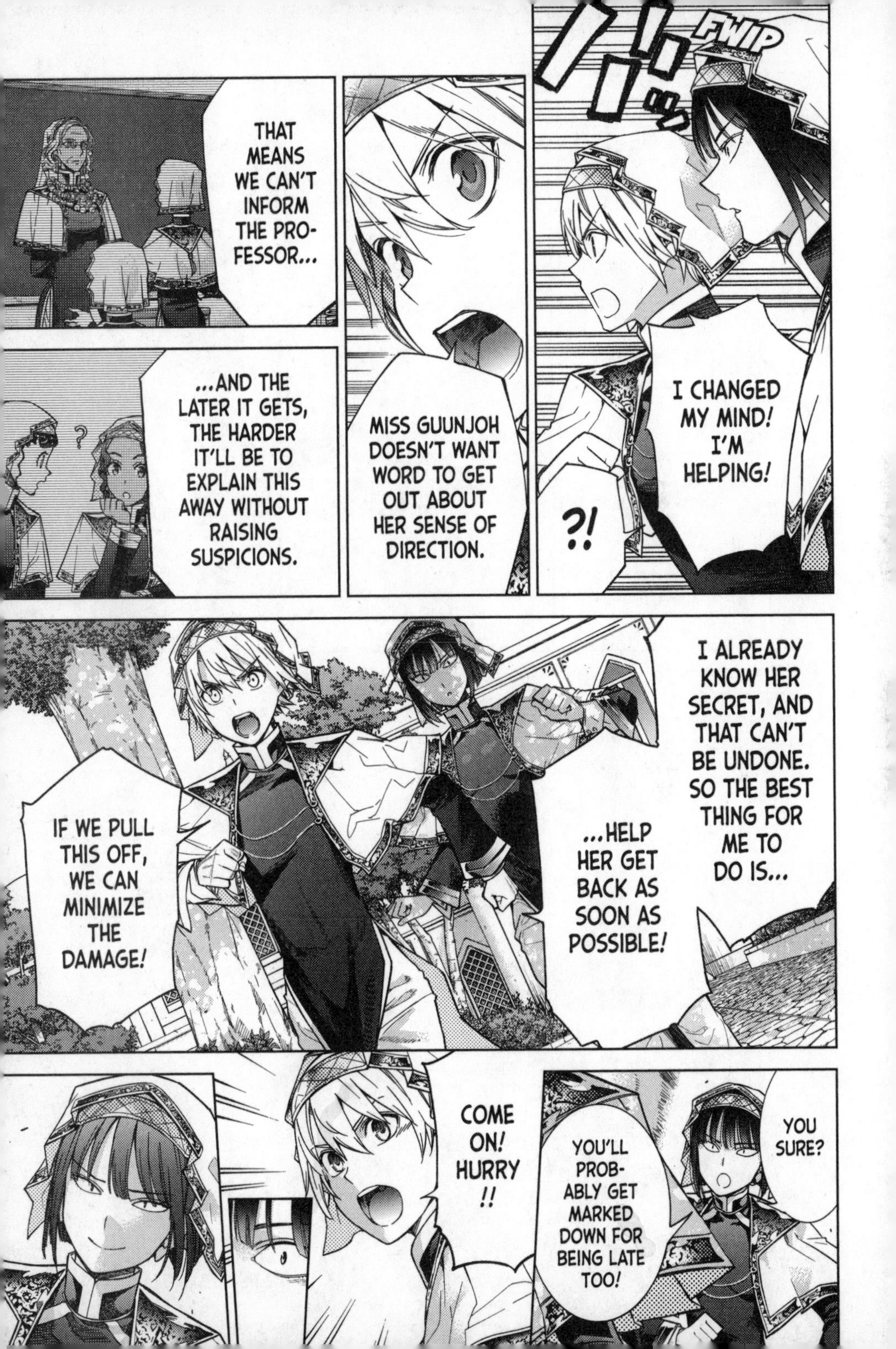
FWIP
?!
I CHANGED MY MIND! I'M HELPING!
MISS GUUNJOH DOESN'T WANT WORD TO GET OUT ABOUT HER SENSE OF DIRECTION.
THAT MEANS WE CAN'T INFORM THE PROFESSOR...
...AND THE LATER IT GETS, THE HARDER IT'LL BE TO EXPLAIN THIS AWAY WITHOUT RAISING SUSPICIONS.
?
I ALREADY KNOW HER SECRET, AND THAT CAN'T BE UNDONE. SO THE BEST THING FOR ME TO DO IS...
...HELP HER GET BACK AS SOON AS POSSIBLE!
IF WE PULL THIS OFF, WE CAN MINIMIZE THE DAMAGE!
YOU SURE?
YOU'LL PROBABLY GET MARKED DOWN FOR BEING LATE TOO!
COME ON! HURRY!!

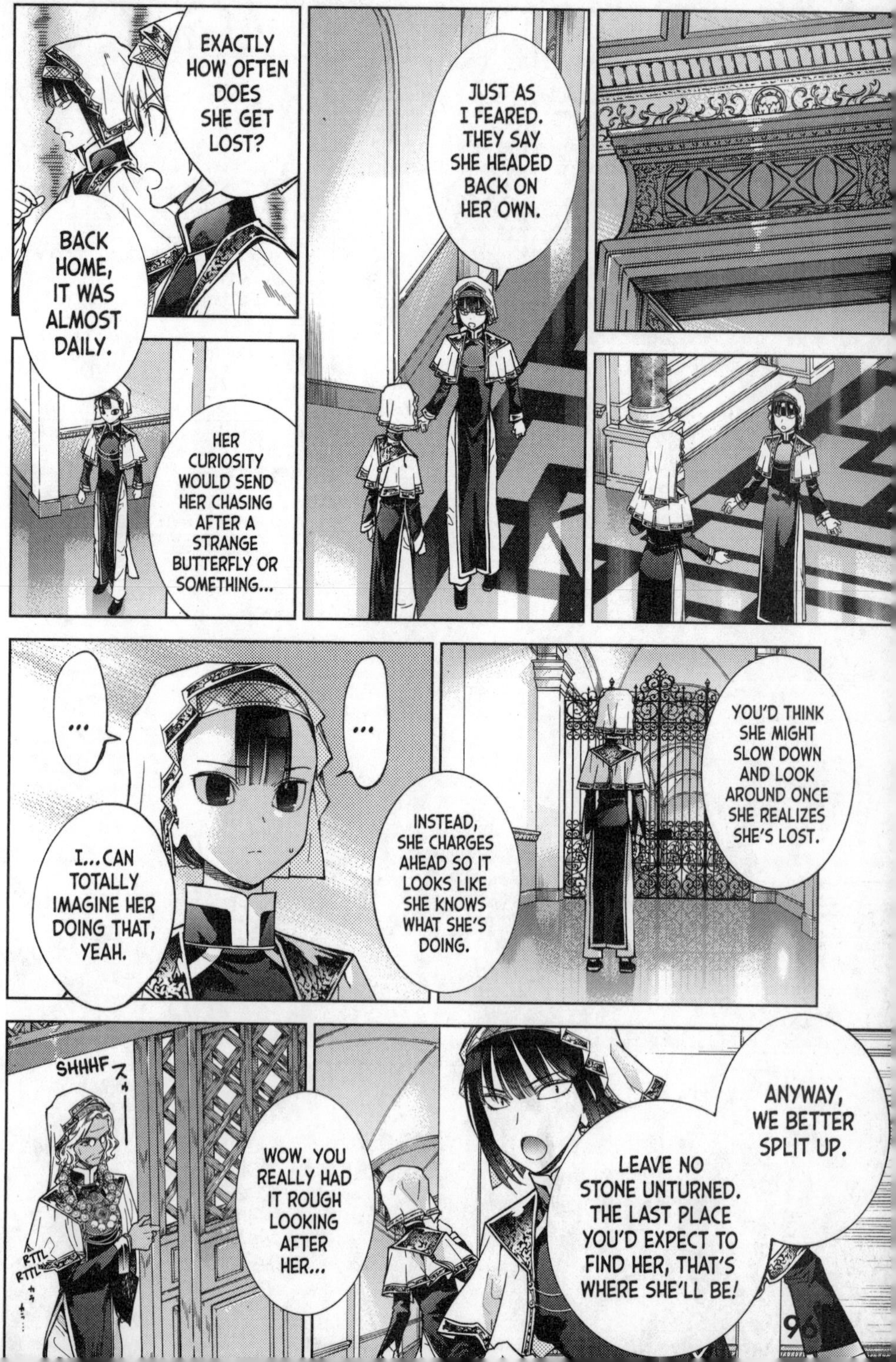
JUST AS I FEARED. THEY SAY SHE HEADED BACK ON HER OWN.
EXACTLY HOW OFTEN DOES SHE GET LOST?
BACK HOME, IT WAS ALMOST DAILY.
HER CURIOSITY WOULD SEND HER CHASING AFTER A STRANGE BUTTERFLY OR SOMETHING...
YOU'D THINK SHE MIGHT SLOW DOWN AND LOOK AROUND ONCE SHE REALIZES SHE'S LOST.
INSTEAD, SHE CHARGES AHEAD SO IT LOOKS LIKE SHE KNOWS WHAT SHE'S DOING.
...
...
I...CAN TOTALLY IMAGINE HER DOING THAT, YEAH.
ANYWAY, WE BETTER SPLIT UP.
LEAVE NO STONE UNTURNED. THE LAST PLACE YOU'D EXPECT TO FIND HER, THAT'S WHERE SHE'LL BE!
WOW. YOU REALLY HAD IT ROUGH LOOKING AFTER HER...
SHHHF
RTTL RTTL

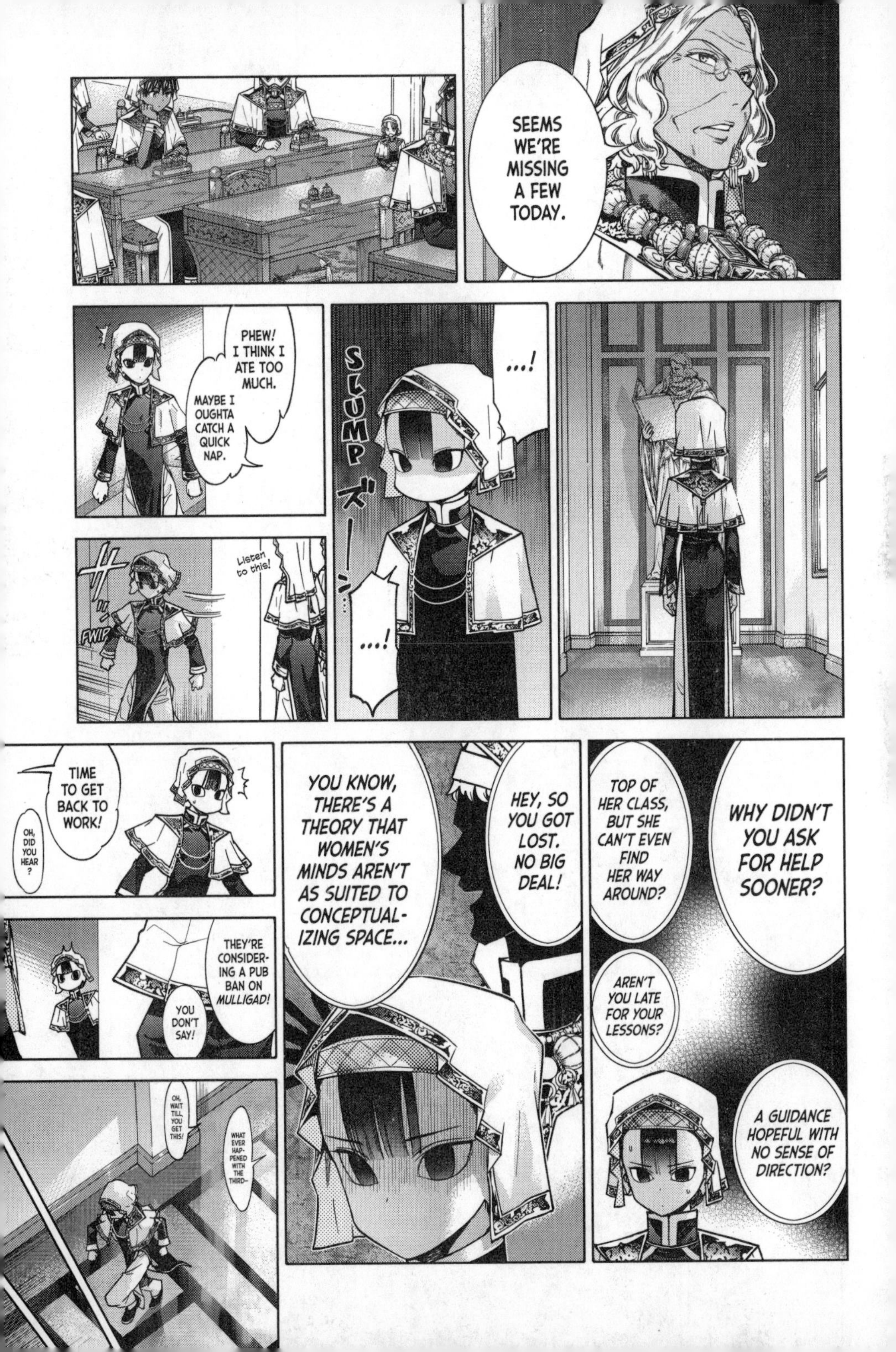
SEEMS WE'RE MISSING A FEW TODAY.
...!
SLUMP
ズー
...!
PHEW! I THINK I ATE TOO MUCH.
MAYBE I OUGHTA CATCH A QUICK NAP.
Listen to this!
FWIP
WHY DIDN'T YOU ASK FOR HELP SOONER?
TOP OF HER CLASS, BUT SHE CAN'T EVEN FIND HER WAY AROUND?
AREN'T YOU LATE FOR YOUR LESSONS?
A GUIDANCE HOPEFUL WITH NO SENSE OF DIRECTION?
HEY, SO YOU GOT LOST. NO BIG DEAL!
YOU KNOW, THERE'S A THEORY THAT WOMEN'S MINDS AREN'T AS SUITED TO CONCEPTUALIZING SPACE...
TIME TO GET BACK TO WORK!
OH, DID YOU HEAR?
THEY'RE CONSIDERING A PUB BAN ON *MULLIGAD*!
YOU DON'T SAY!
OH, WAIT TILL YOU GET THIS!
WHATEVER HAPPENED WITH THE THIRD–

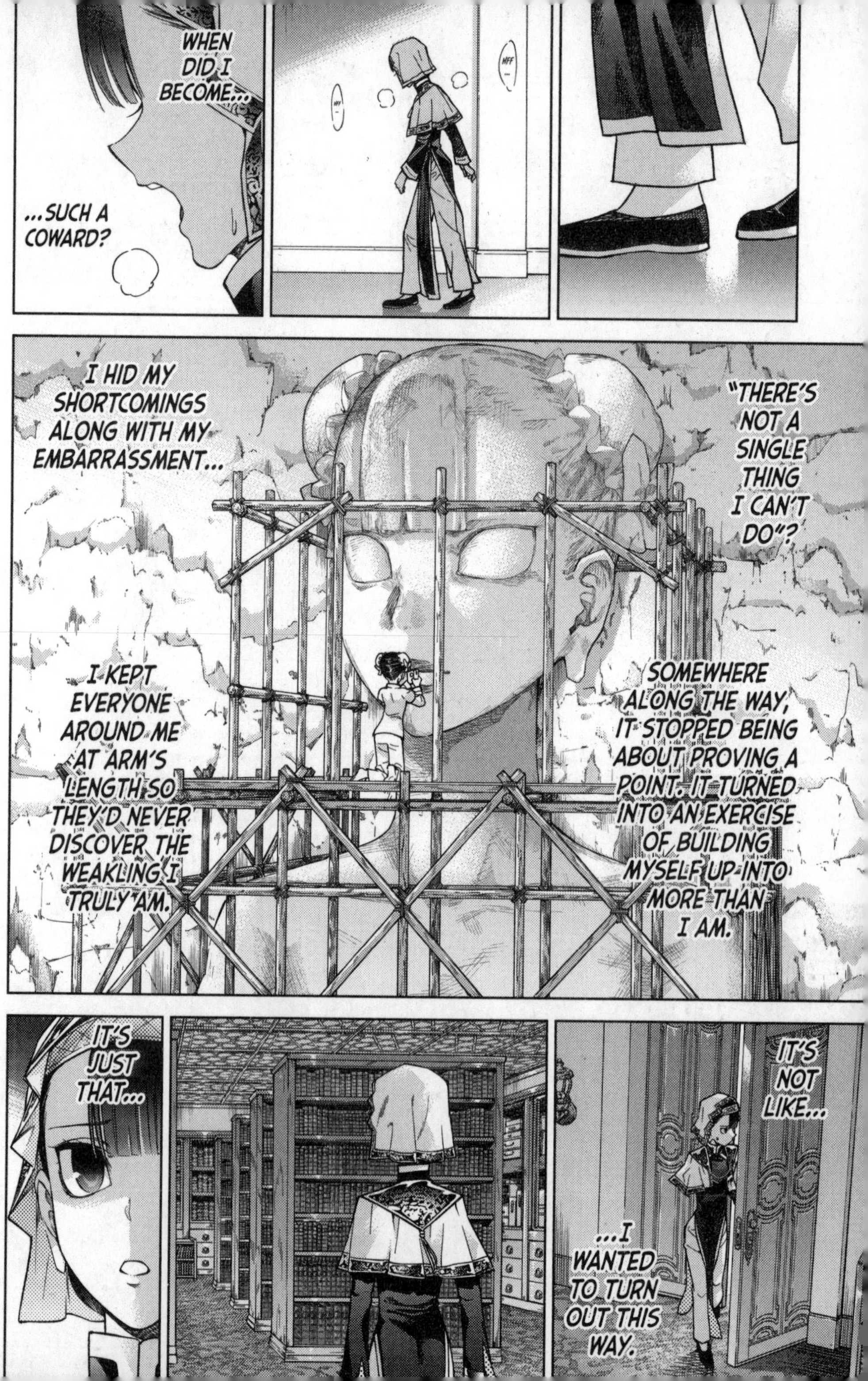
HFF...
HFF...
WHEN DID I BECOME...
...SUCH A COWARD?
"THERE'S NOT A SINGLE THING I CAN'T DO"?
I HID MY SHORTCOMINGS ALONG WITH MY EMBARRASSMENT...
SOMEWHERE ALONG THE WAY, IT STOPPED BEING ABOUT PROVING A POINT. IT TURNED INTO AN EXERCISE OF BUILDING MYSELF UP INTO MORE THAN I AM.
I KEPT EVERYONE AROUND ME AT ARM'S LENGTH SO THEY'D NEVER DISCOVER THE WEAKLING I TRULY AM.
IT'S NOT LIKE...
...I WANTED TO TURN OUT THIS WAY.
IT'S JUST THAT...

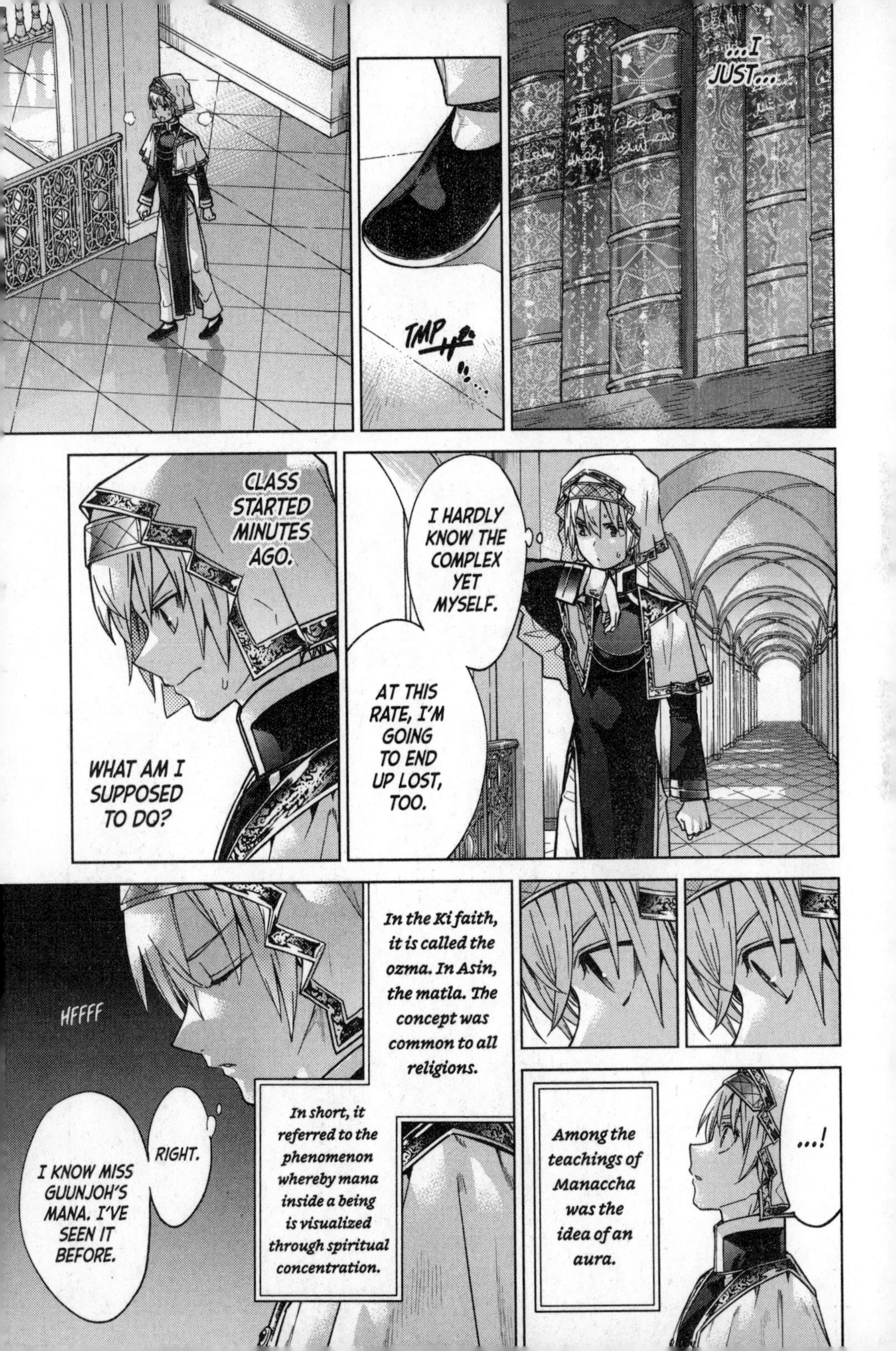
...I JUST...
TMP
...
I HARDLY KNOW THE COMPLEX YET MYSELF.
AT THIS RATE, I'M GOING TO END UP LOST, TOO.
CLASS STARTED MINUTES AGO.
WHAT AM I SUPPOSED TO DO?
...!
Among the teachings of Manaccha was the idea of an aura.
In the Ki faith, it is called the ozma. In Asin, the matla. The concept was common to all religions.
In short, it referred to the phenomenon whereby mana inside a being is visualized through spiritual concentration.
HFFFF
RIGHT.
I KNOW MISS GUUNJOH'S MANA. I'VE SEEN IT BEFORE.

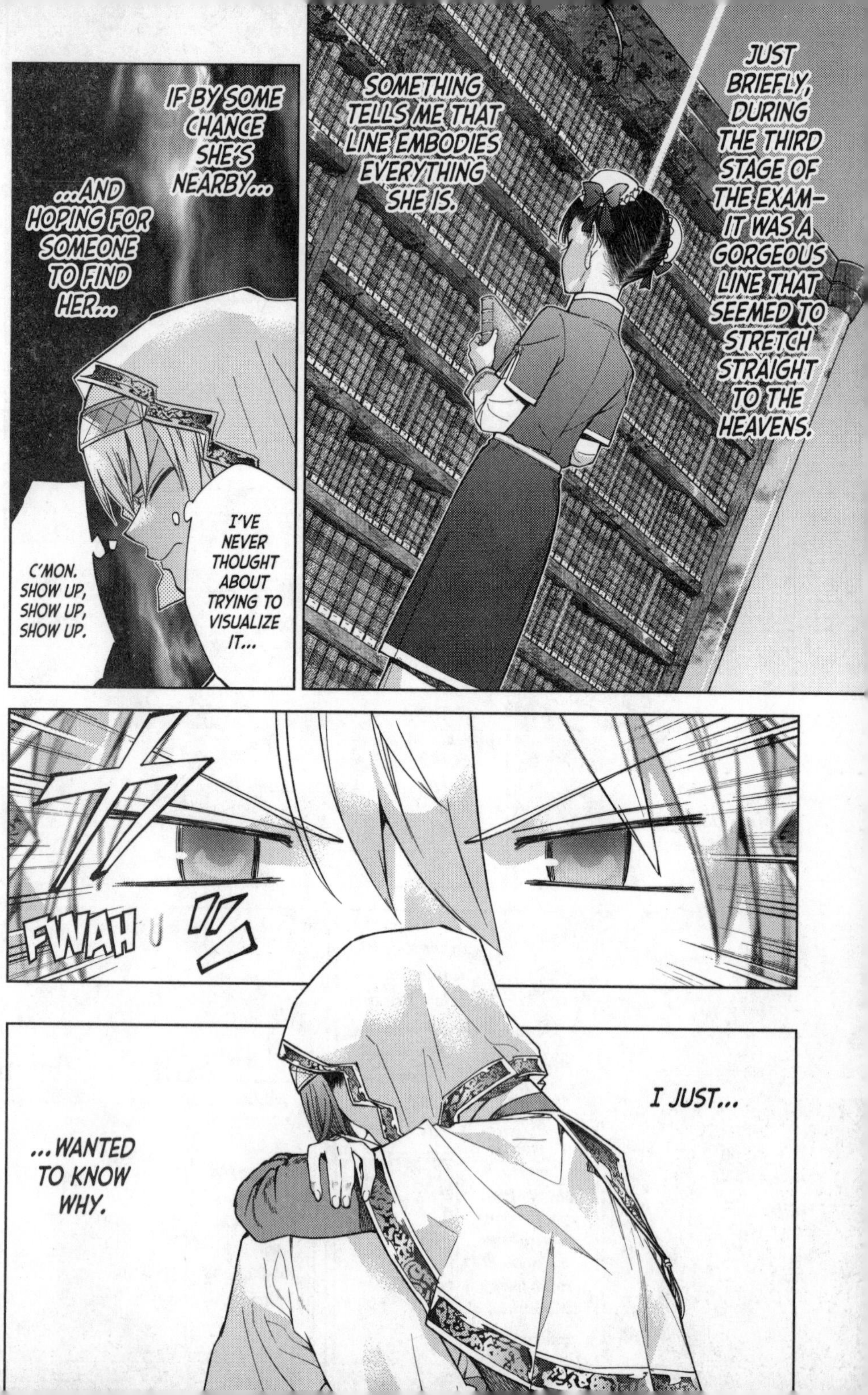
JUST BRIEFLY, DURING THE THIRD STAGE OF THE EXAM–IT WAS A GORGEOUS LINE THAT SEEMED TO STRETCH STRAIGHT TO THE HEAVENS.
SOMETHING TELLS ME THAT LINE EMBODIES EVERYTHING SHE IS.
IF BY SOME CHANCE SHE'S NEARBY...
...AND HOPING FOR SOMEONE TO FIND HER...
I'VE NEVER THOUGHT ABOUT TRYING TO VISUALIZE IT...
C'MON. SHOW UP, SHOW UP, SHOW UP.
FWAH
I JUST...
...WANTED TO KNOW WHY.

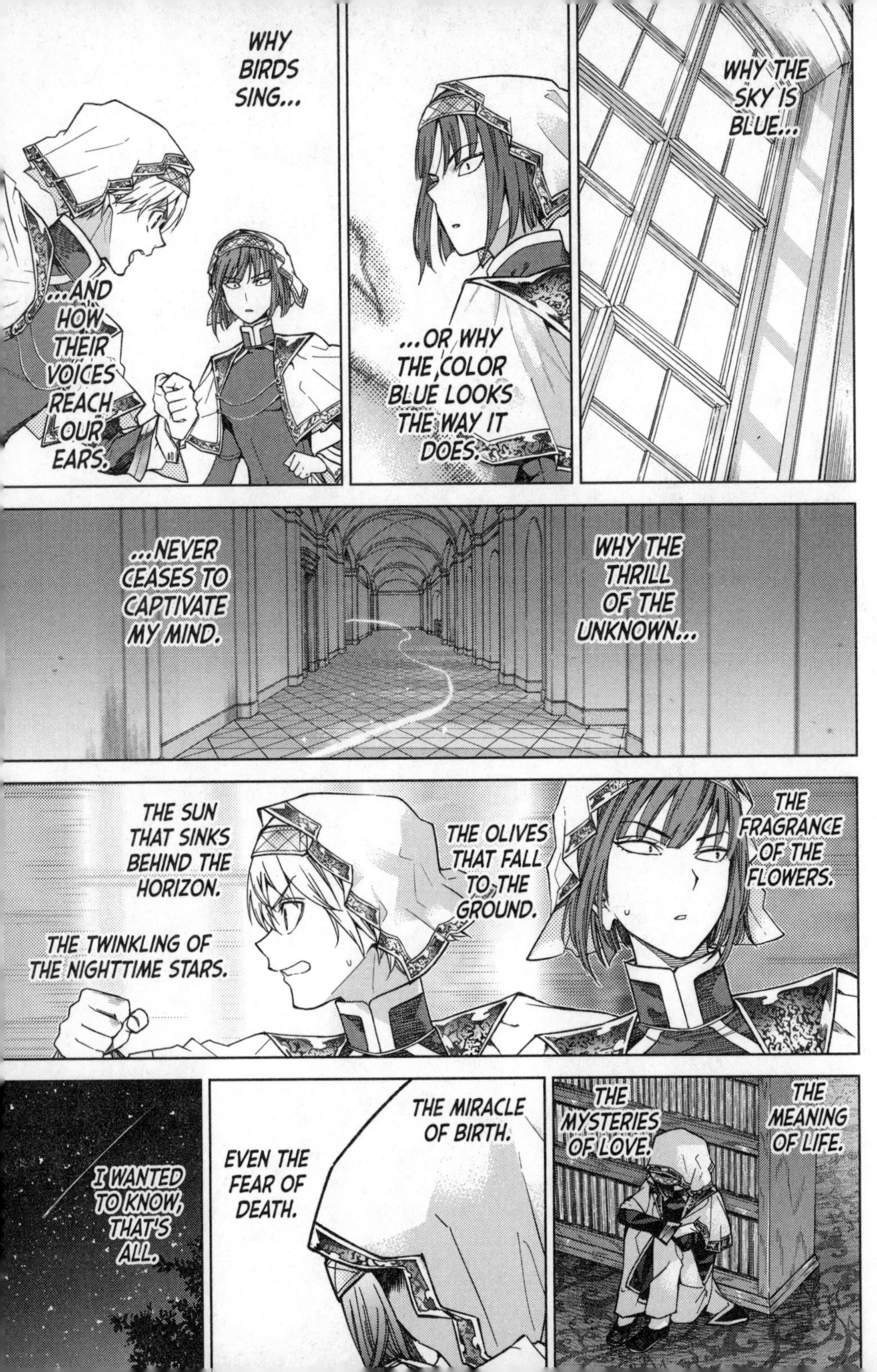
WHY THE SKY IS BLUE...
...OR WHY THE COLOR BLUE LOOKS THE WAY IT DOES.
WHY BIRDS SING...
...AND HOW THEIR VOICES REACH OUR EARS.
WHY THE THRILL OF THE UNKNOWN...
...NEVER CEASES TO CAPTIVATE MY MIND.
THE FRAGRANCE OF THE FLOWERS.
THE OLIVES THAT FALL TO THE GROUND.
THE SUN THAT SINKS BEHIND THE HORIZON.
THE TWINKLING OF THE NIGHTTIME STARS.
THE MEANING OF LIFE.
THE MYSTERIES OF LOVE.
THE MIRACLE OF BIRTH.
EVEN THE FEAR OF DEATH.
I WANTED TO KNOW, THAT'S ALL.

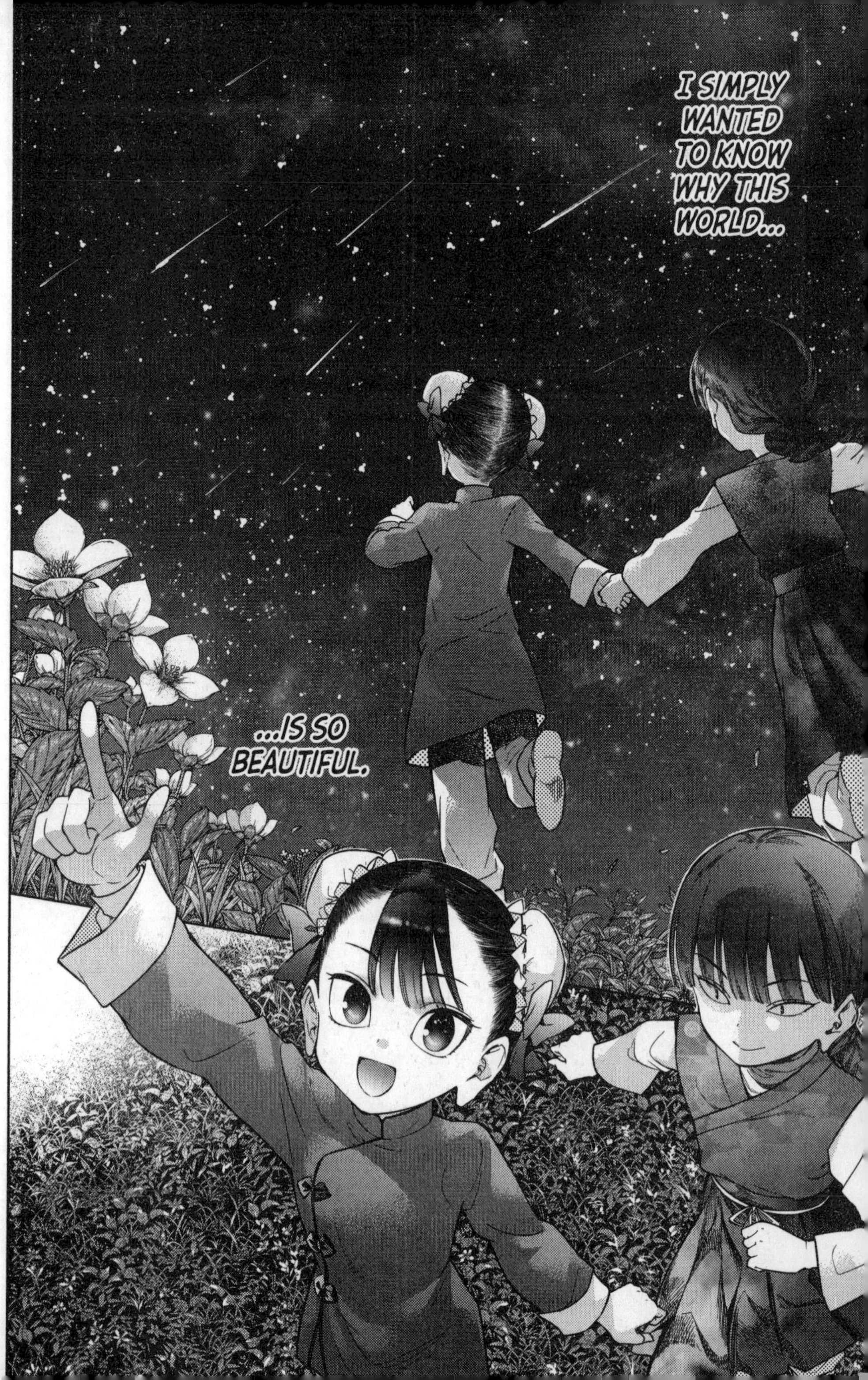
I SIMPLY WANTED TO KNOW WHY THIS WORLD...
...IS SO BEAUTIFUL.

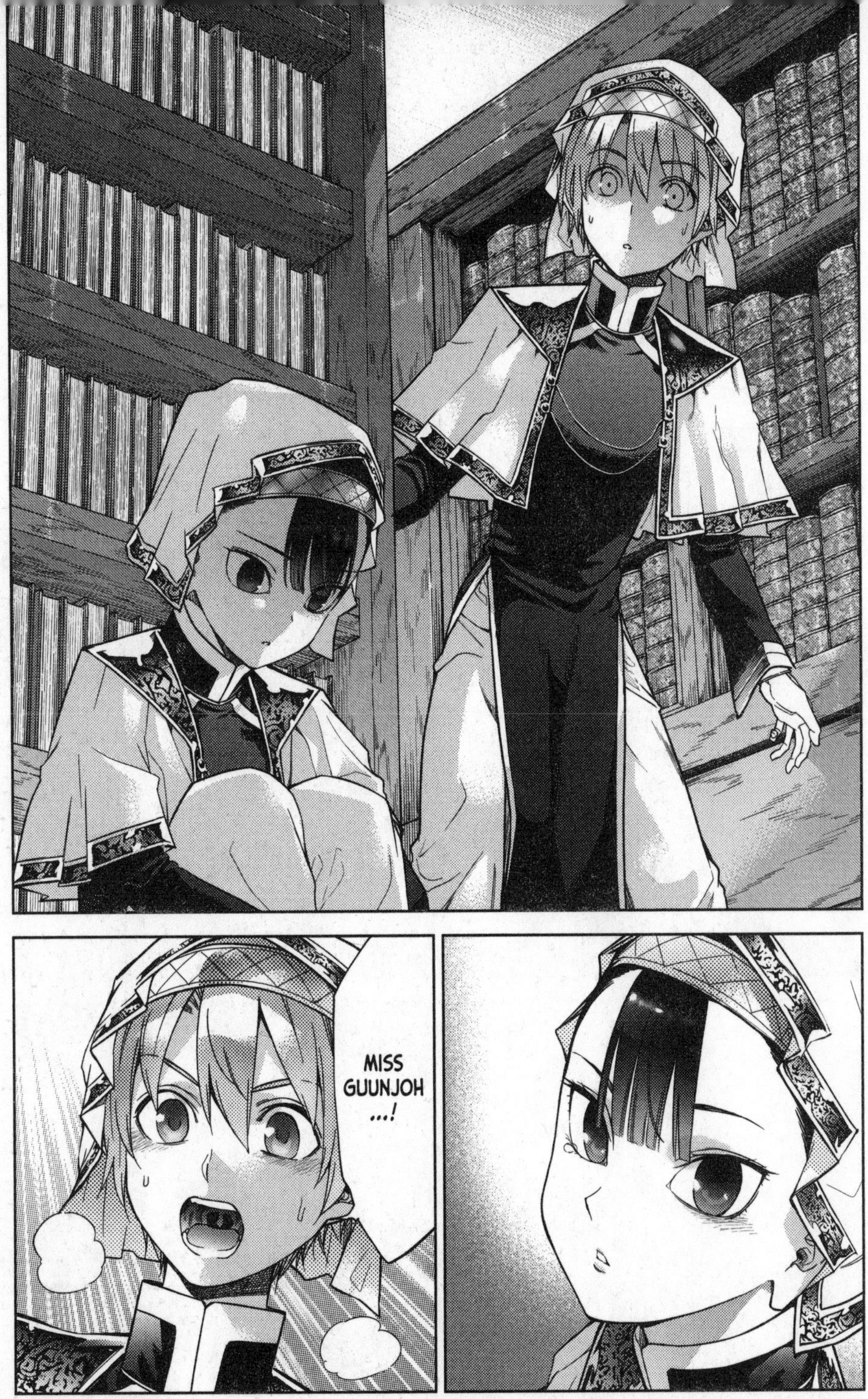
MISS GUUNJOH ...!

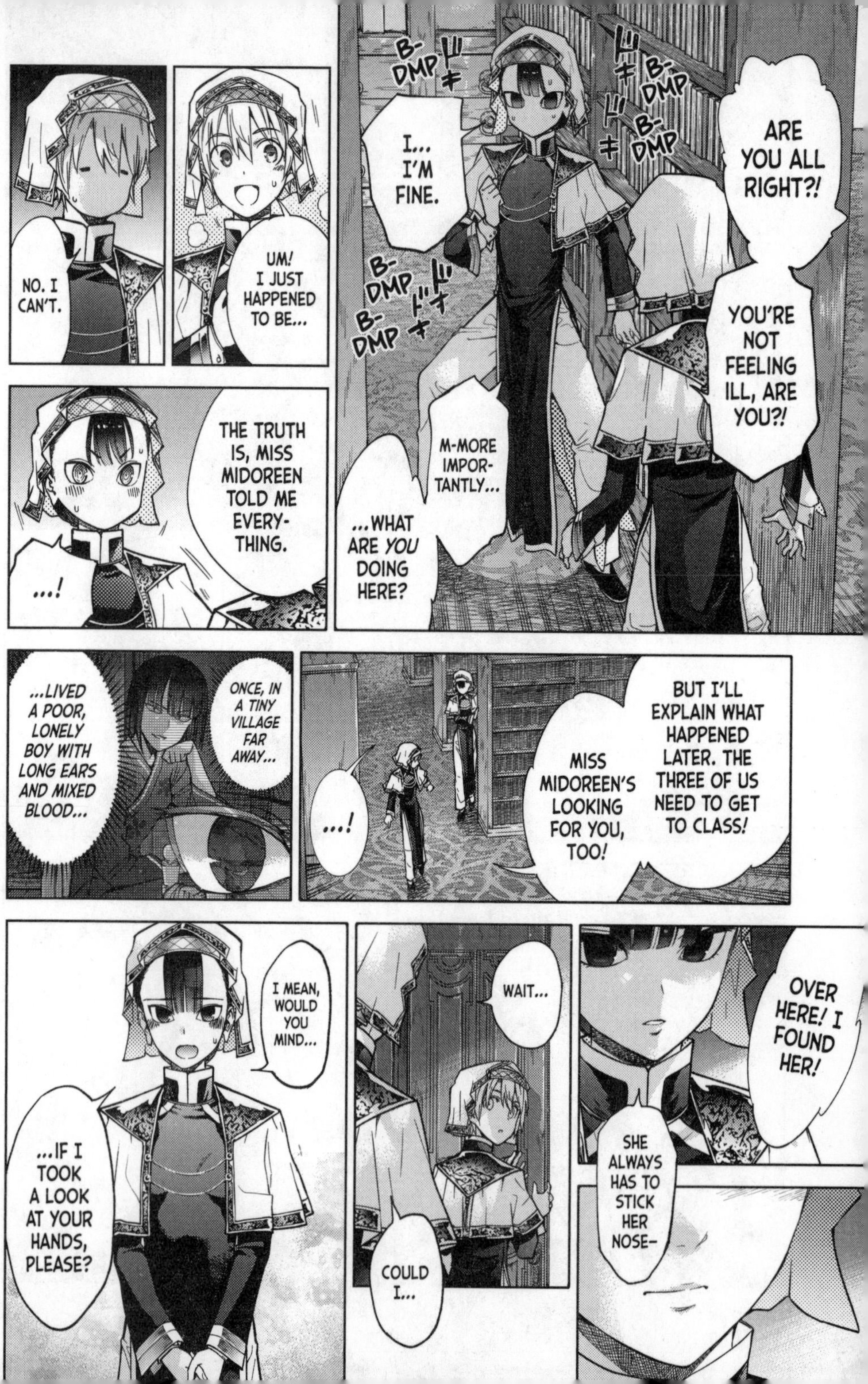
B-DMP
B-DMP
B-DMP
ARE YOU ALL RIGHT?!
YOU'RE NOT FEELING ILL, ARE YOU?!
I... I'M FINE.
B-DMP
B-DMP
M-MORE IMPOR-TANTLY...
...WHAT ARE YOU DOING HERE?
UM! I JUST HAPPENED TO BE...
NO. I CAN'T.
THE TRUTH IS, MISS MIDOREEN TOLD ME EVERY-THING.
...!
BUT I'LL EXPLAIN WHAT HAPPENED LATER. THE THREE OF US NEED TO GET TO CLASS!
MISS MIDOREEN'S LOOKING FOR YOU, TOO!
...!
ONCE, IN A TINY VILLAGE FAR AWAY...
...LIVED A POOR, LONELY BOY WITH LONG EARS AND MIXED BLOOD...
OVER HERE! I FOUND HER!
SHE ALWAYS HAS TO STICK HER NOSE-
WAIT...
COULD I...
I MEAN, WOULD YOU MIND...
...IF I TOOK A LOOK AT YOUR HANDS, PLEASE?

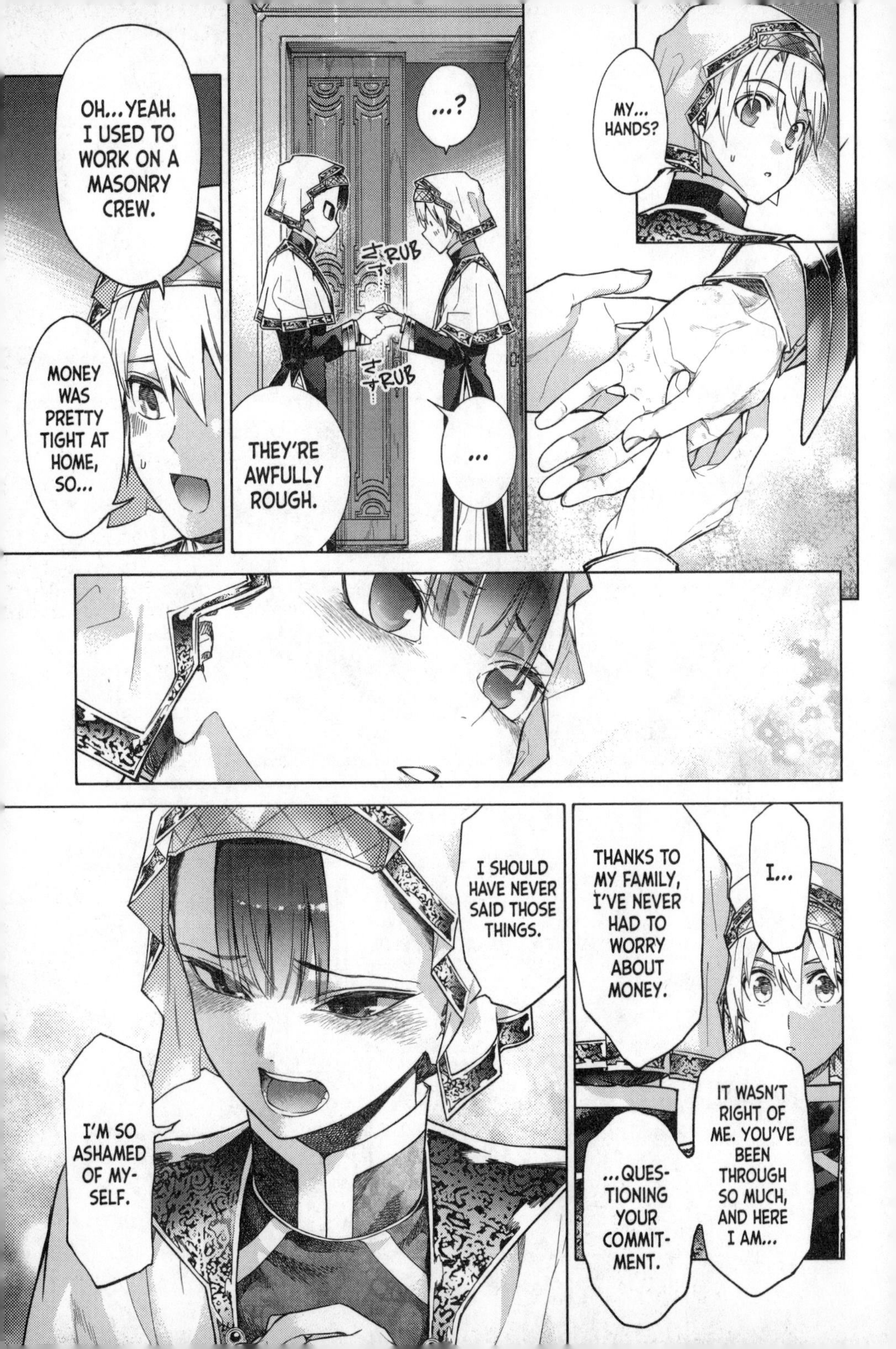
MY... HANDS?
...?
さす RUB
さす RUB
...
THEY'RE AWFULLY ROUGH.
OH...YEAH. I USED TO WORK ON A MASONRY CREW.
MONEY WAS PRETTY TIGHT AT HOME, SO...
I...
THANKS TO MY FAMILY, I'VE NEVER HAD TO WORRY ABOUT MONEY.
IT WASN'T RIGHT OF ME. YOU'VE BEEN THROUGH SO MUCH, AND HERE I AM...
...QUESTIONING YOUR COMMITMENT.
I SHOULD HAVE NEVER SAID THOSE THINGS.
I'M SO ASHAMED OF MYSELF.

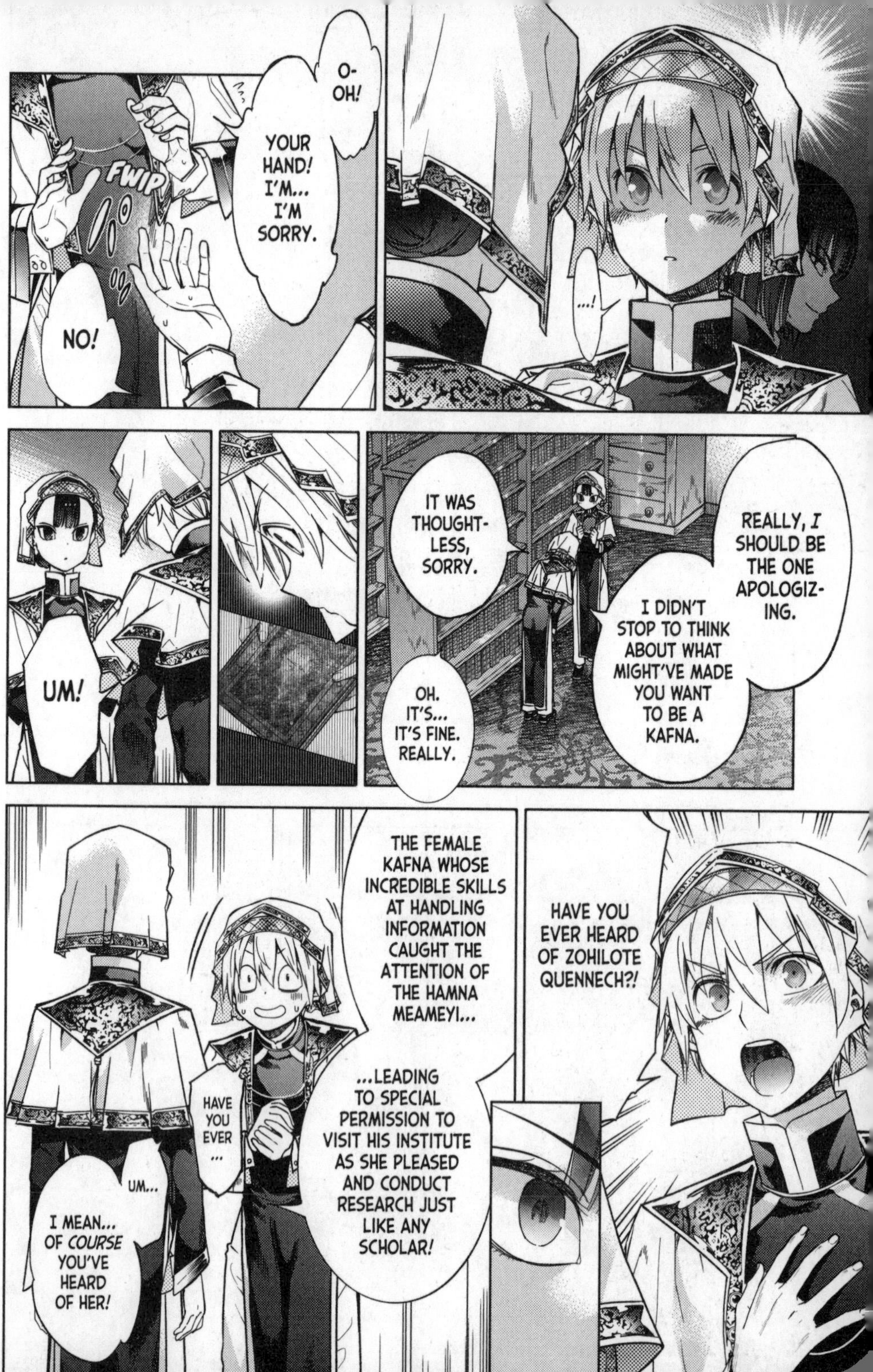

...!
O- OH!
YOUR HAND! I'M... I'M SORRY.
FWIP
NO!
REALLY, *I* SHOULD BE THE ONE APOLOGIZ- ING.
I DIDN'T STOP TO THINK ABOUT WHAT MIGHT'VE MADE YOU WANT TO BE A KAFNA.
IT WAS THOUGHT- LESS, SORRY.
OH. IT'S... IT'S FINE. REALLY.
UM!
HAVE YOU EVER HEARD OF ZOHILOTE QUENNECH?!
THE FEMALE KAFNA WHOSE INCREDIBLE SKILLS AT HANDLING INFORMATION CAUGHT THE ATTENTION OF THE HAMNA MEAMEYI...
...LEADING TO SPECIAL PERMISSION TO VISIT HIS INSTITUTE AS SHE PLEASED AND CONDUCT RESEARCH JUST LIKE ANY SCHOLAR!
HAVE YOU EVER ...
UM...
I MEAN... OF *COURSE* YOU'VE HEARD OF HER!

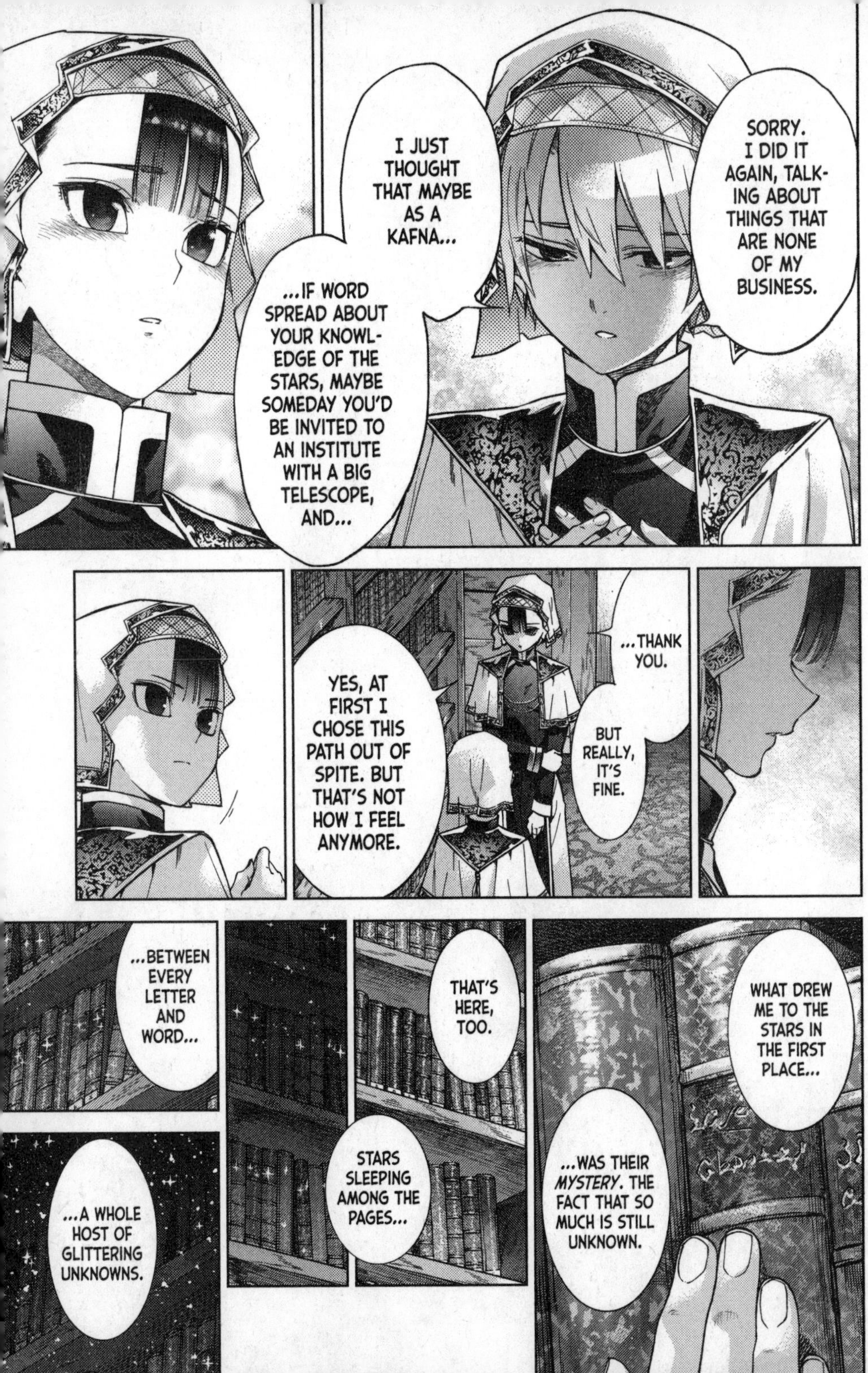
SORRY. I DID IT AGAIN, TALKING ABOUT THINGS THAT ARE NONE OF MY BUSINESS.
I JUST THOUGHT THAT MAYBE AS A KAFNA...
...IF WORD SPREAD ABOUT YOUR KNOWLEDGE OF THE STARS, MAYBE SOMEDAY YOU'D BE INVITED TO AN INSTITUTE WITH A BIG TELESCOPE, AND...
...THANK YOU.
BUT REALLY, IT'S FINE.
YES, AT FIRST I CHOSE THIS PATH OUT OF SPITE. BUT THAT'S NOT HOW I FEEL ANYMORE.
WHAT DREW ME TO THE STARS IN THE FIRST PLACE...
...WAS THEIR *MYSTERY*. THE FACT THAT SO MUCH IS STILL UNKNOWN.
THAT'S HERE, TOO.
STARS SLEEPING AMONG THE PAGES...
...BETWEEN EVERY LETTER AND WORD...
...A WHOLE HOST OF GLITTERING UNKNOWNS.

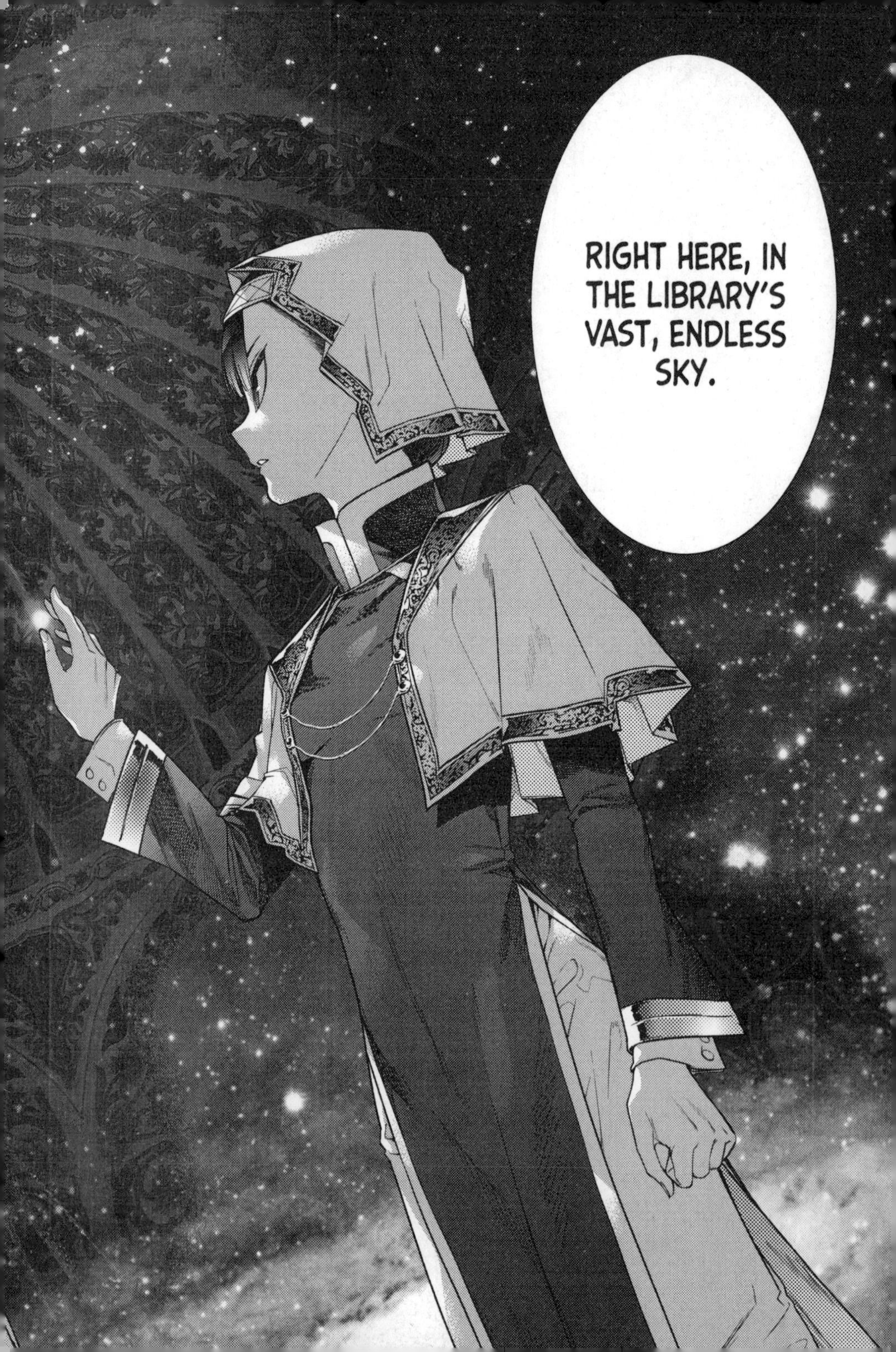
RIGHT HERE, IN THE LIBRARY'S VAST, ENDLESS SKY.

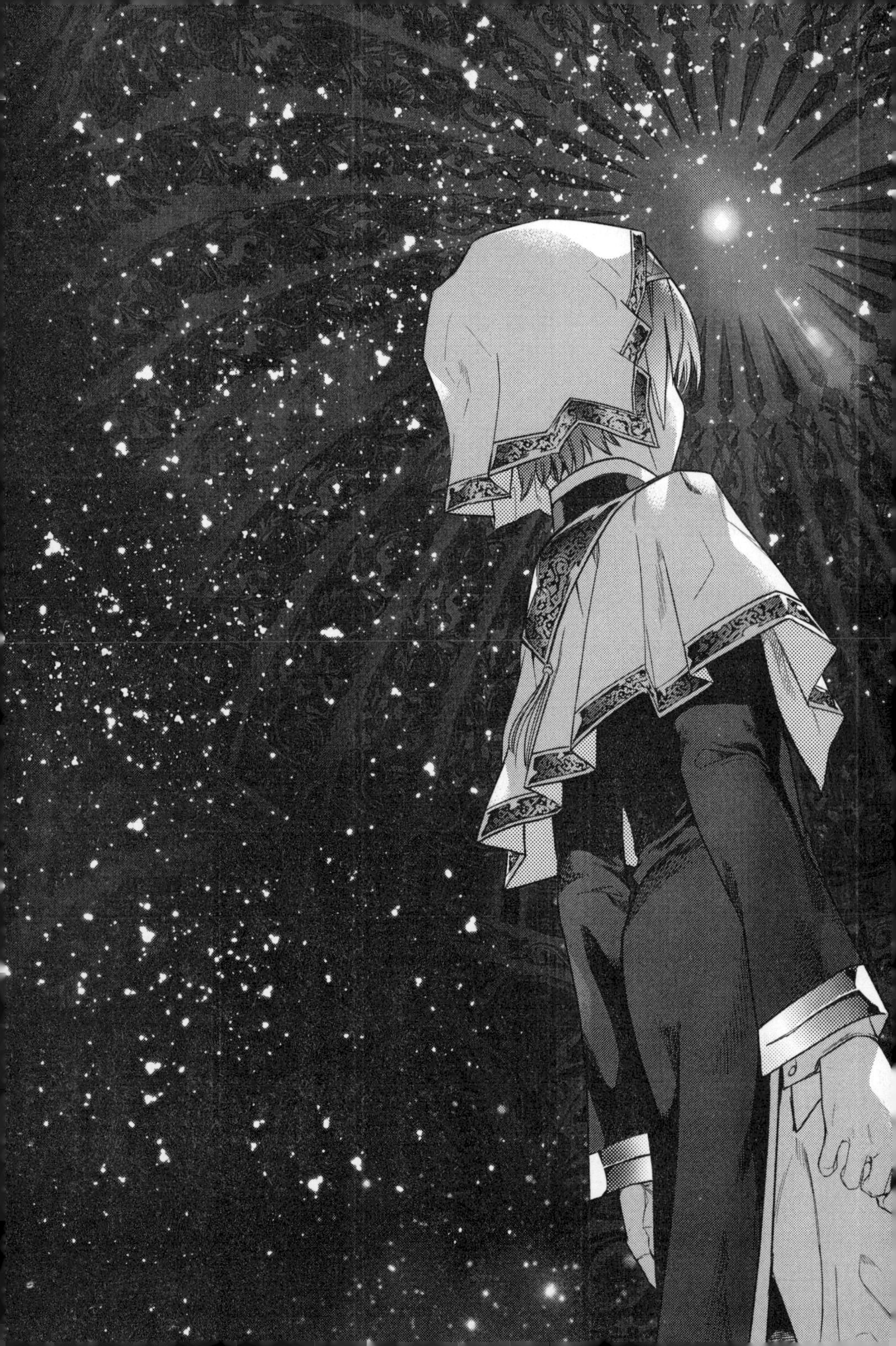

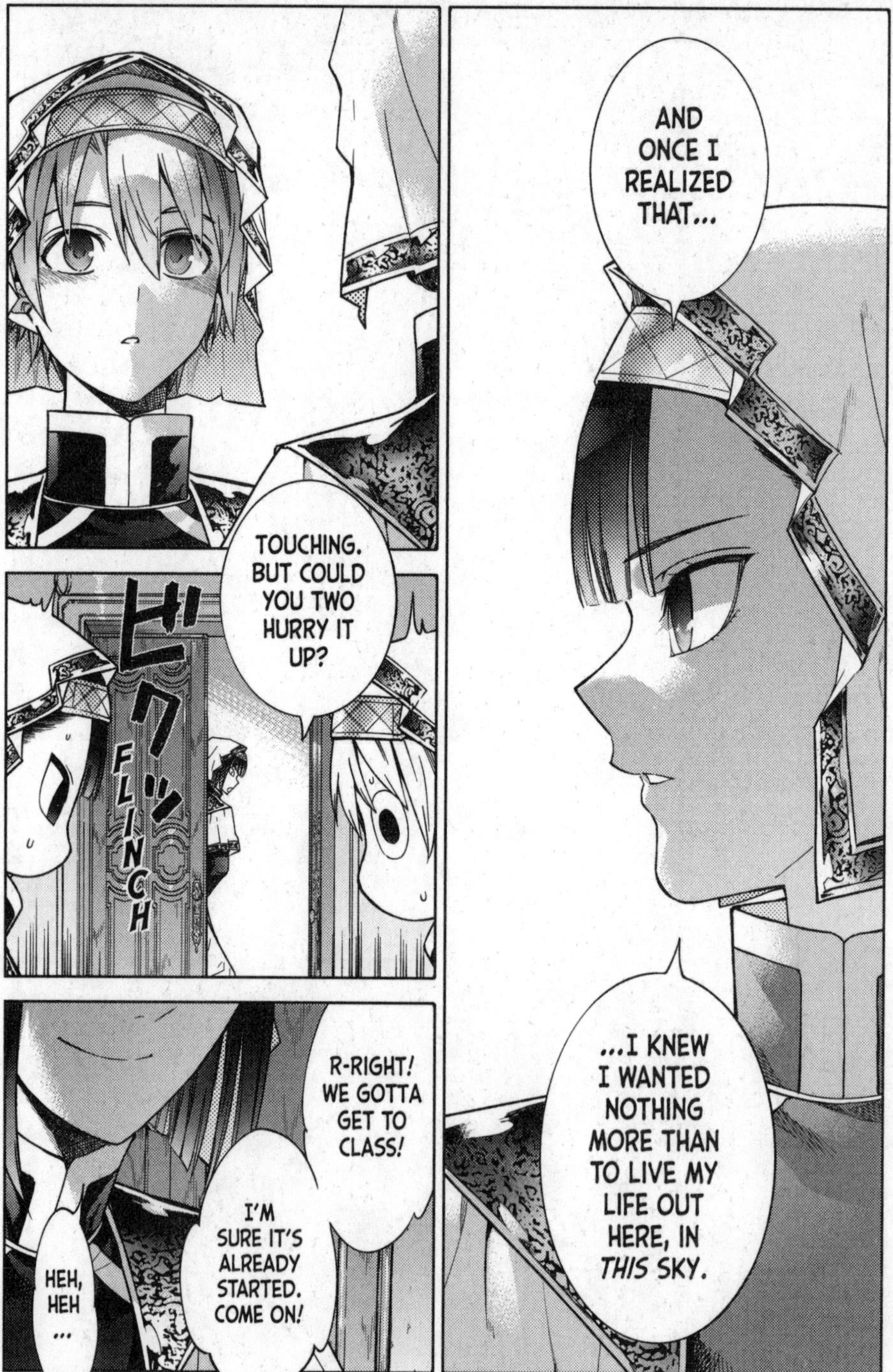
AND ONCE I REALIZED THAT...
...I KNEW I WANTED NOTHING MORE THAN TO LIVE MY LIFE OUT HERE, IN *THIS* SKY.
TOUCHING. BUT COULD YOU TWO HURRY IT UP?
ビクッ
FLINCH
R-RIGHT! WE GOTTA GET TO CLASS!
I'M SURE IT'S ALREADY STARTED. COME ON!
HEH, HEH ...

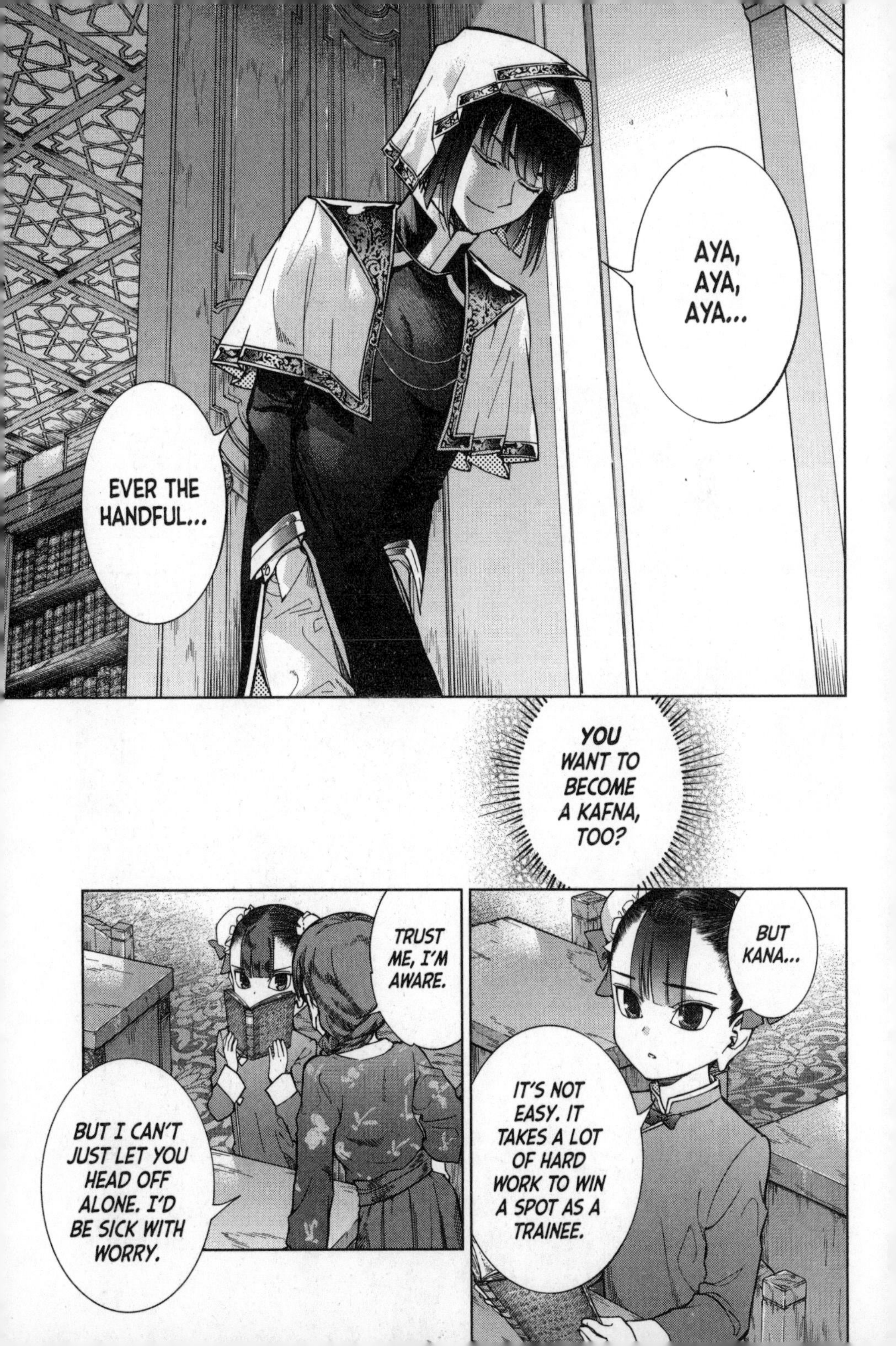
AYA, AYA, AYA...
EVER THE HANDFUL...
YOU WANT TO BECOME A KAFNA, TOO?
BUT KANA...
IT'S NOT EASY. IT TAKES A LOT OF HARD WORK TO WIN A SPOT AS A TRAINEE.
TRUST ME, I'M AWARE.
BUT I CAN'T JUST LET YOU HEAD OFF ALONE. I'D BE SICK WITH WORRY.

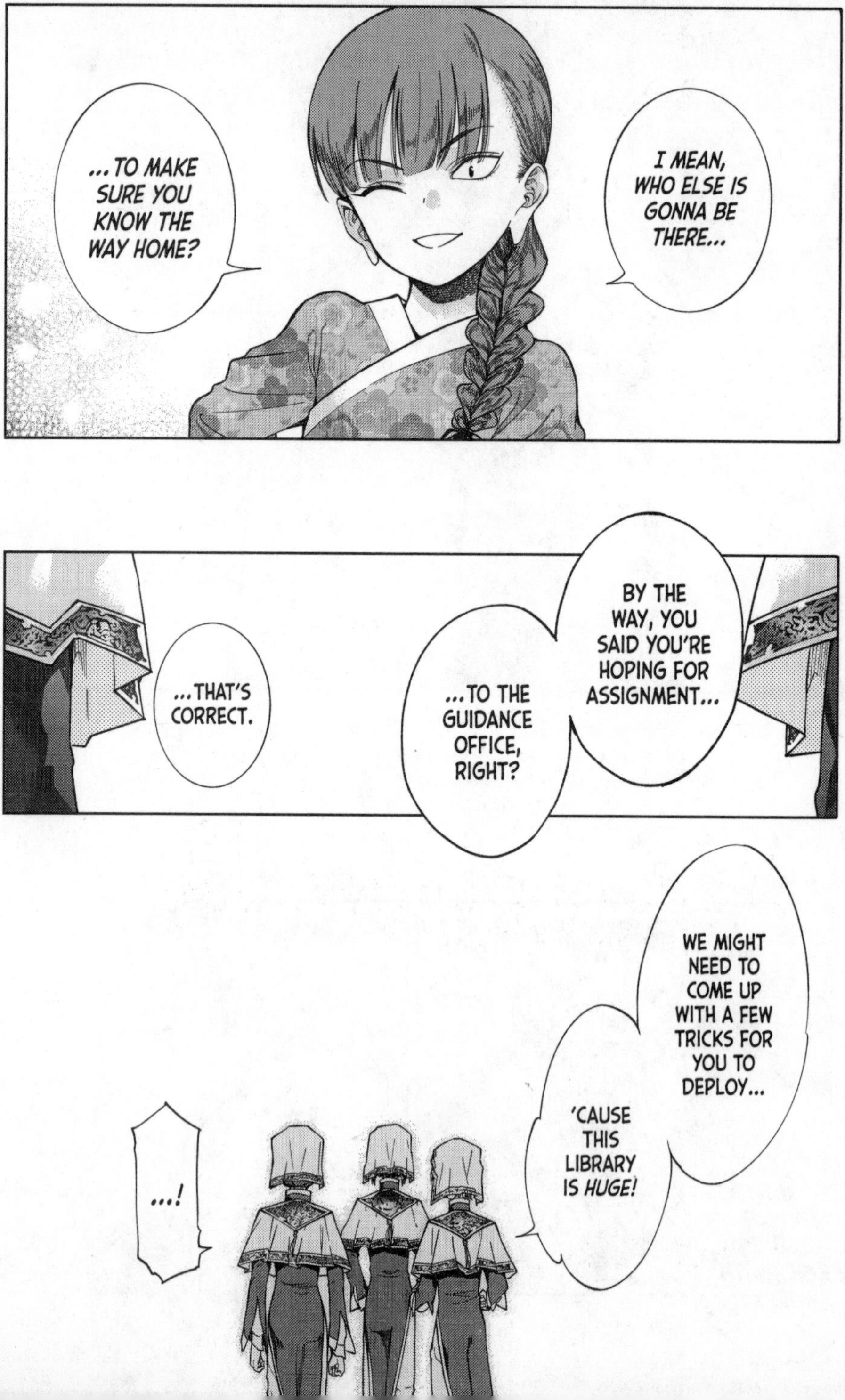
I MEAN, WHO ELSE IS GONNA BE THERE...
...TO MAKE SURE YOU KNOW THE WAY HOME?
BY THE WAY, YOU SAID YOU'RE HOPING FOR ASSIGNMENT...
...TO THE GUIDANCE OFFICE, RIGHT?
...THAT'S CORRECT.
WE MIGHT NEED TO COME UP WITH A FEW TRICKS FOR YOU TO DEPLOY...
'CAUSE THIS LIBRARY IS *HUGE!*
...!

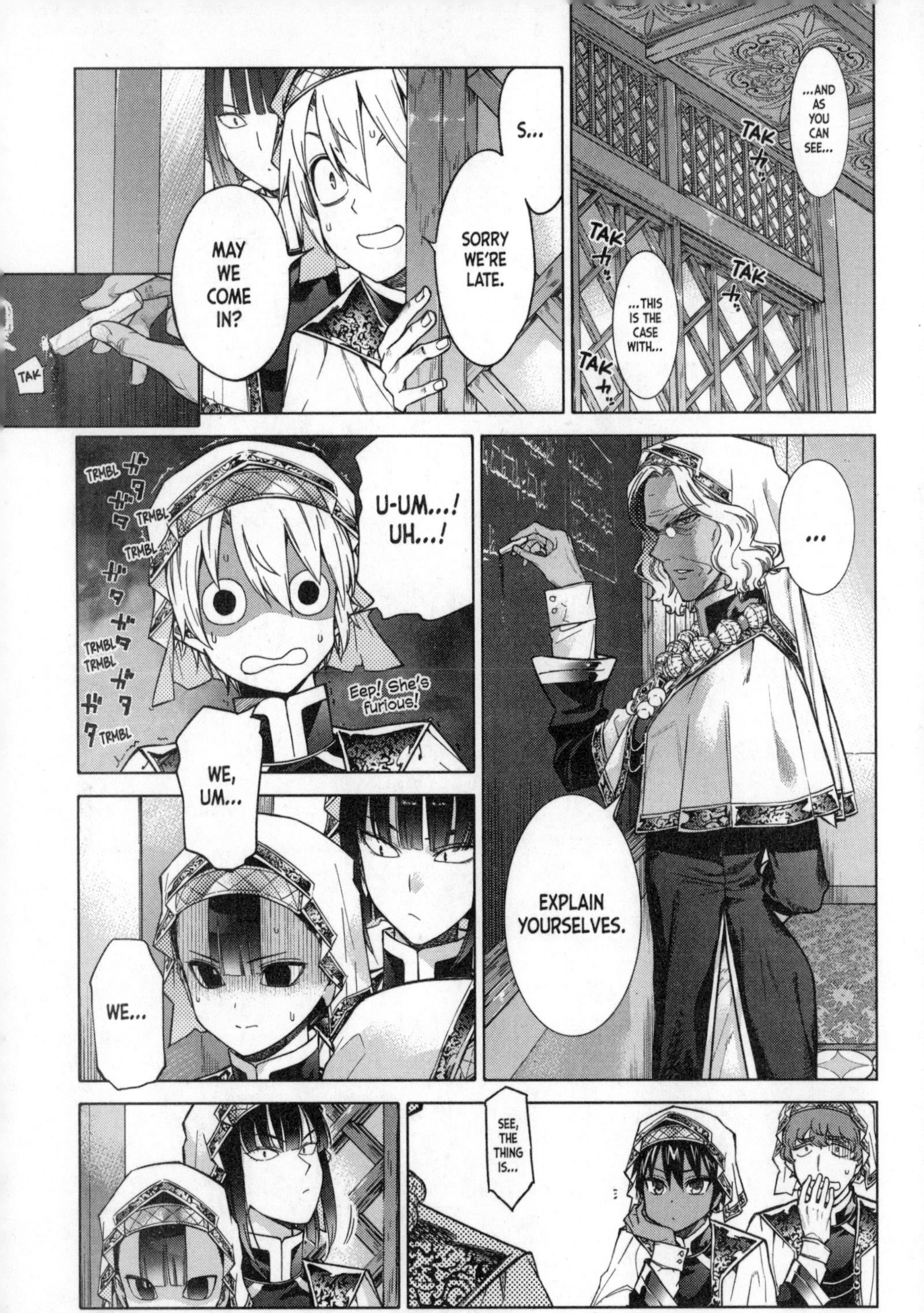
...AND AS YOU CAN SEE...
TAK
TAK
...THIS IS THE CASE WITH...
TAK
TAK
S...
SORRY WE'RE LATE.
MAY WE COME IN?
TAK
...
EXPLAIN YOURSELVES.
U-UM...! UH...!
TRMBL
TRMBL
TRMBL
TRMBL
TRMBL
TRMBL
Eep! She's furious!
WE, UM...
WE...
SEE, THE THING IS...

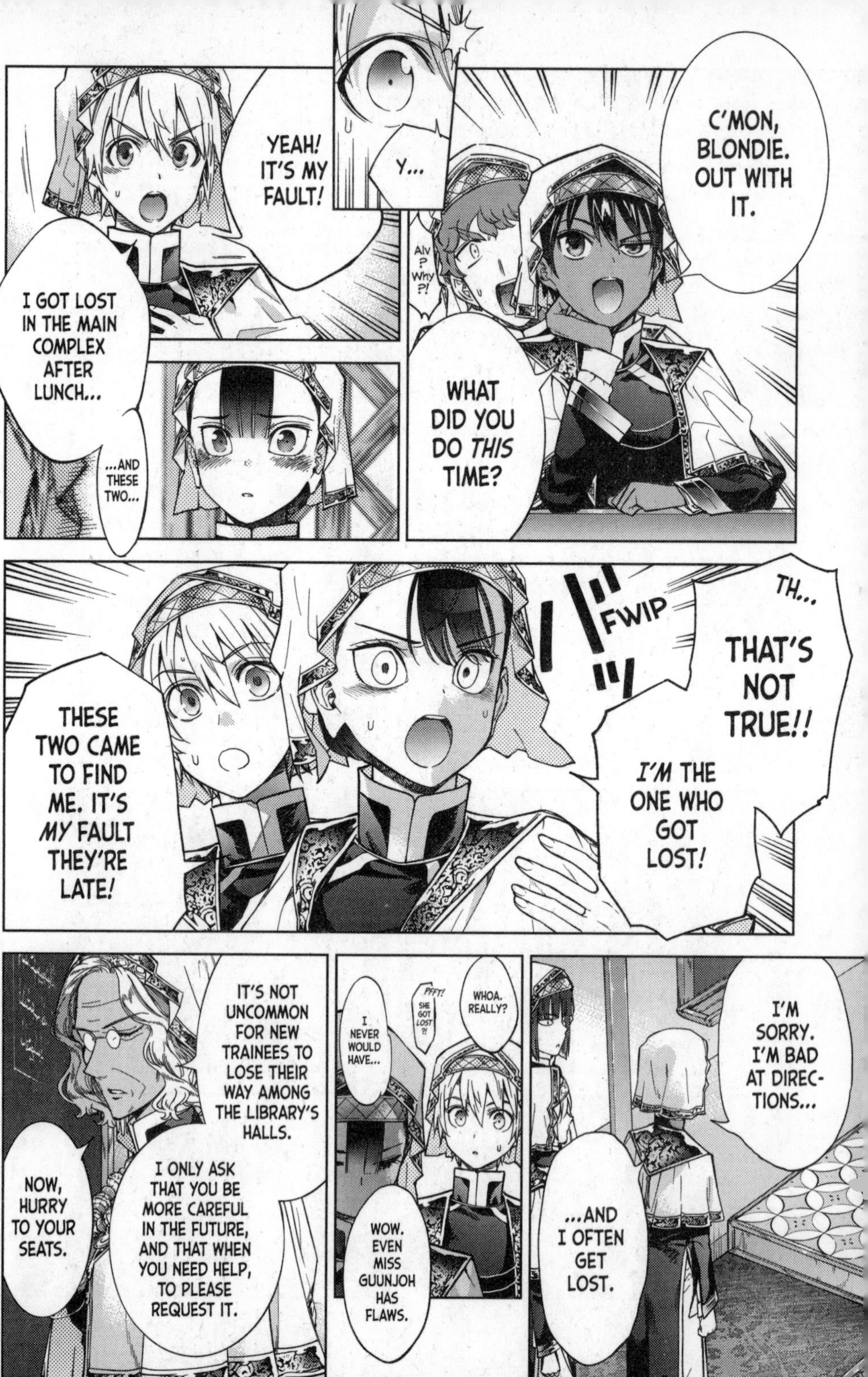
C'MON, BLONDIE. OUT WITH IT.
ALV? WHY?!
WHAT DID YOU DO *THIS* TIME?
Y...
YEAH! IT'S MY FAULT!
I GOT LOST IN THE MAIN COMPLEX AFTER LUNCH...
...AND THESE TWO...
TH...
THAT'S NOT TRUE!!
I'M THE ONE WHO GOT LOST!
FWIP
THESE TWO CAME TO FIND ME. IT'S *MY* FAULT THEY'RE LATE!
I'M SORRY. I'M BAD AT DIREC-TIONS...
...AND I OFTEN GET LOST.
WHOA, REALLY?
PFFT! SHE GOT LOST?!
I NEVER WOULD HAVE...
WOW. EVEN MISS GUUNJOH HAS FLAWS.
IT'S NOT UNCOMMON FOR NEW TRAINEES TO LOSE THEIR WAY AMONG THE LIBRARY'S HALLS.
I ONLY ASK THAT YOU BE MORE CAREFUL IN THE FUTURE, AND THAT WHEN YOU NEED HELP, TO PLEASE REQUEST IT.
NOW, HURRY TO YOUR SEATS.

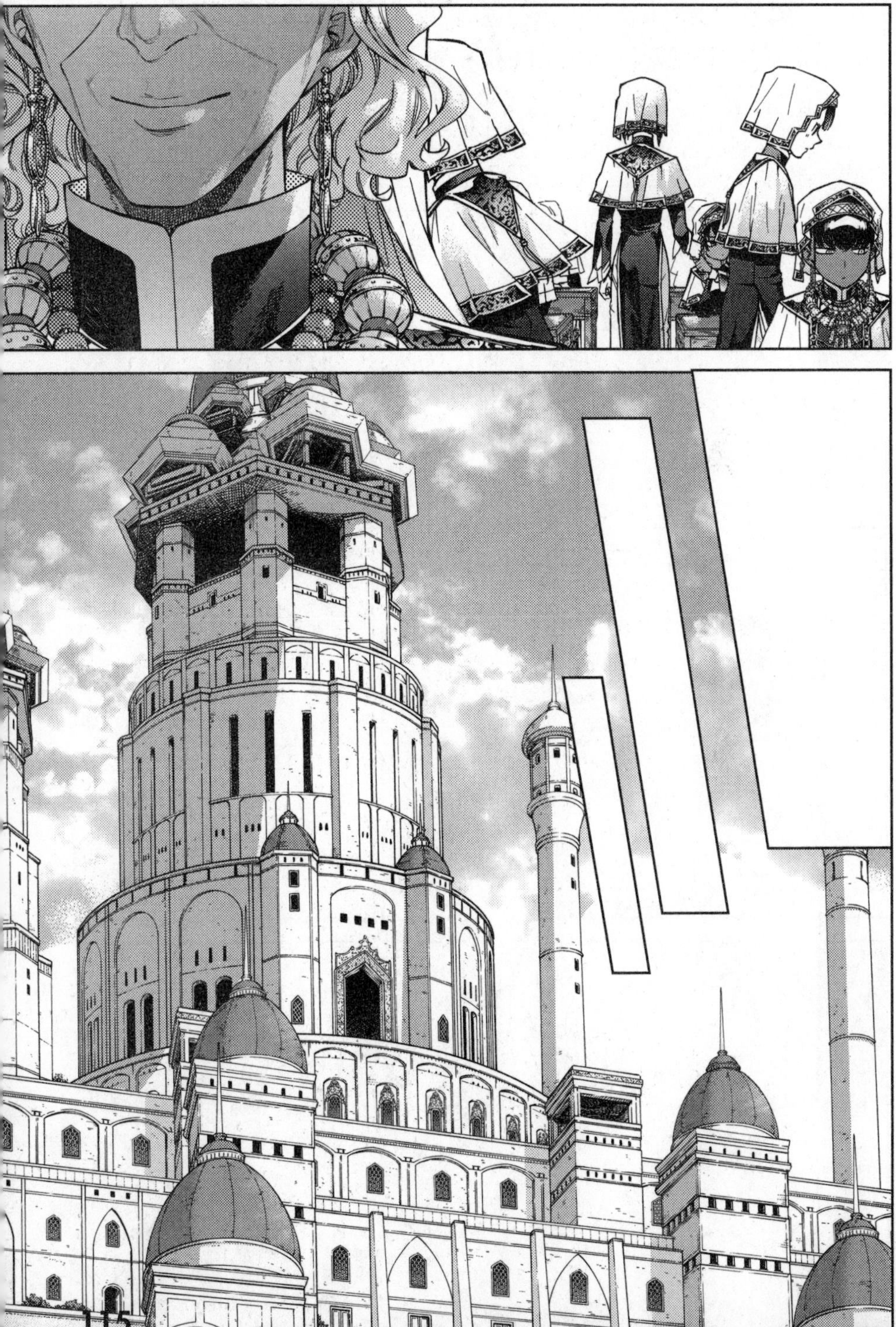

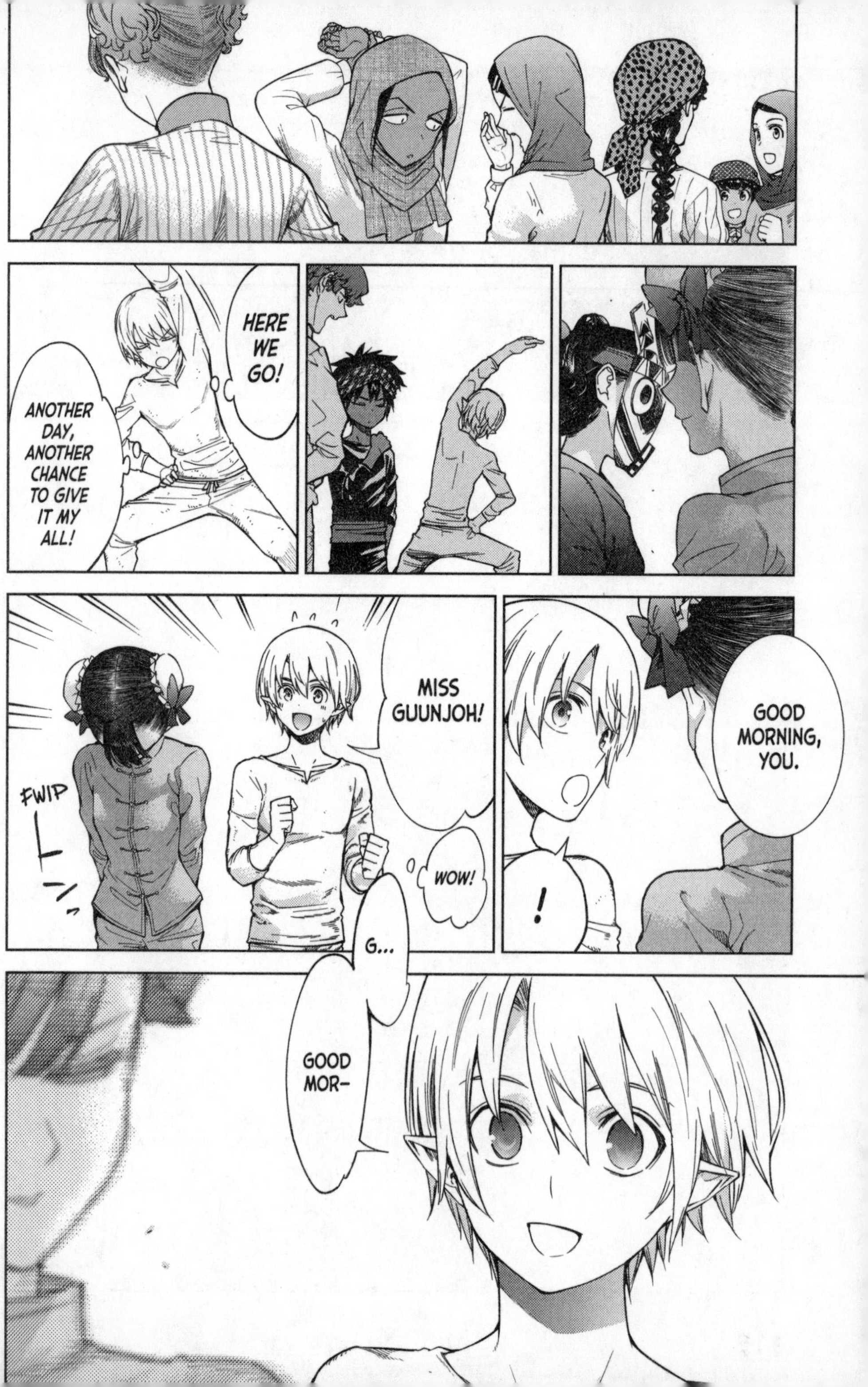
HERE WE GO!
ANOTHER DAY, ANOTHER CHANCE TO GIVE IT MY ALL!
GOOD MORNING, YOU.
!
MISS GUUNJOH!
WOW!
FWIP
G...
GOOD MOR-

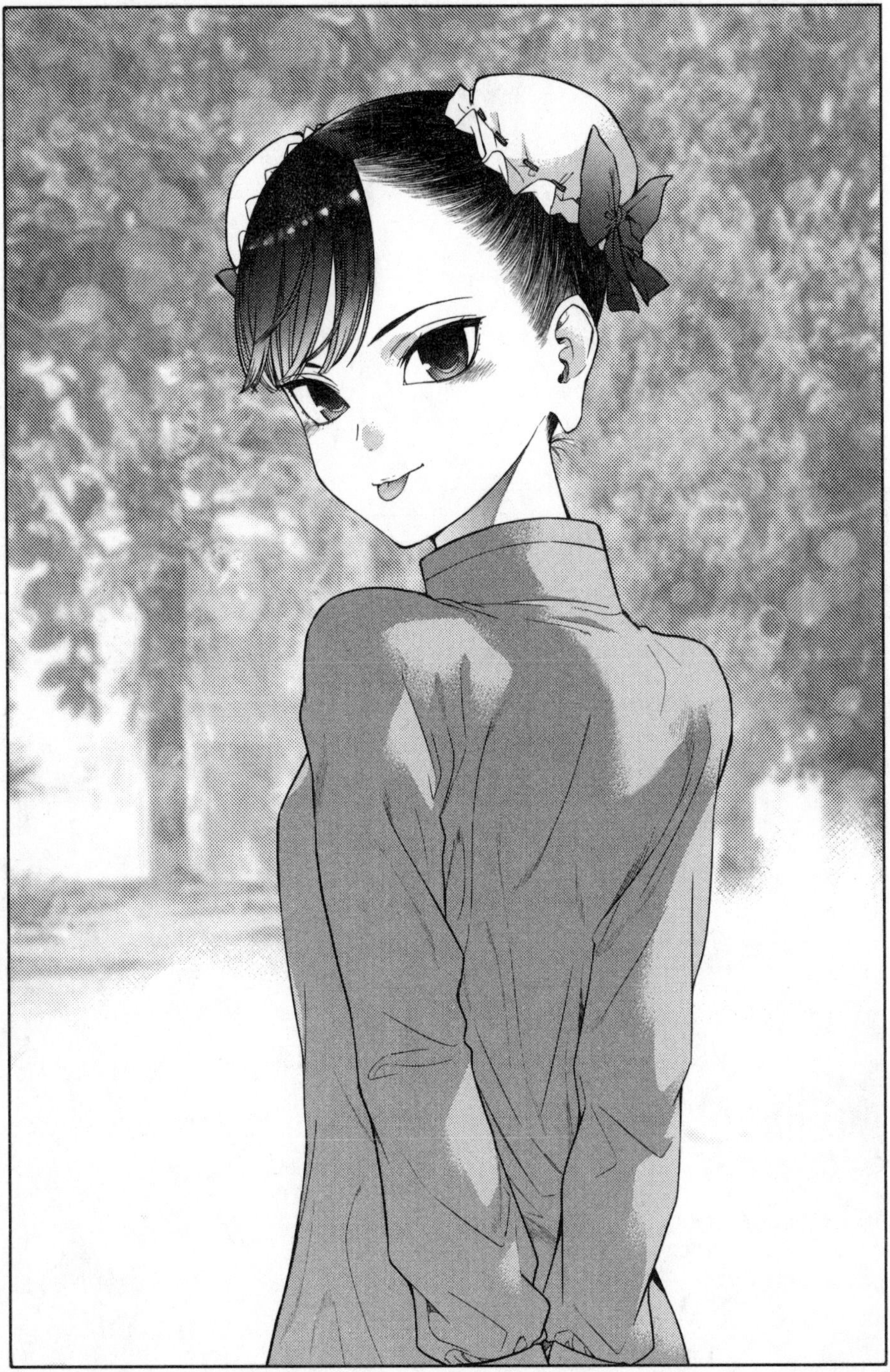

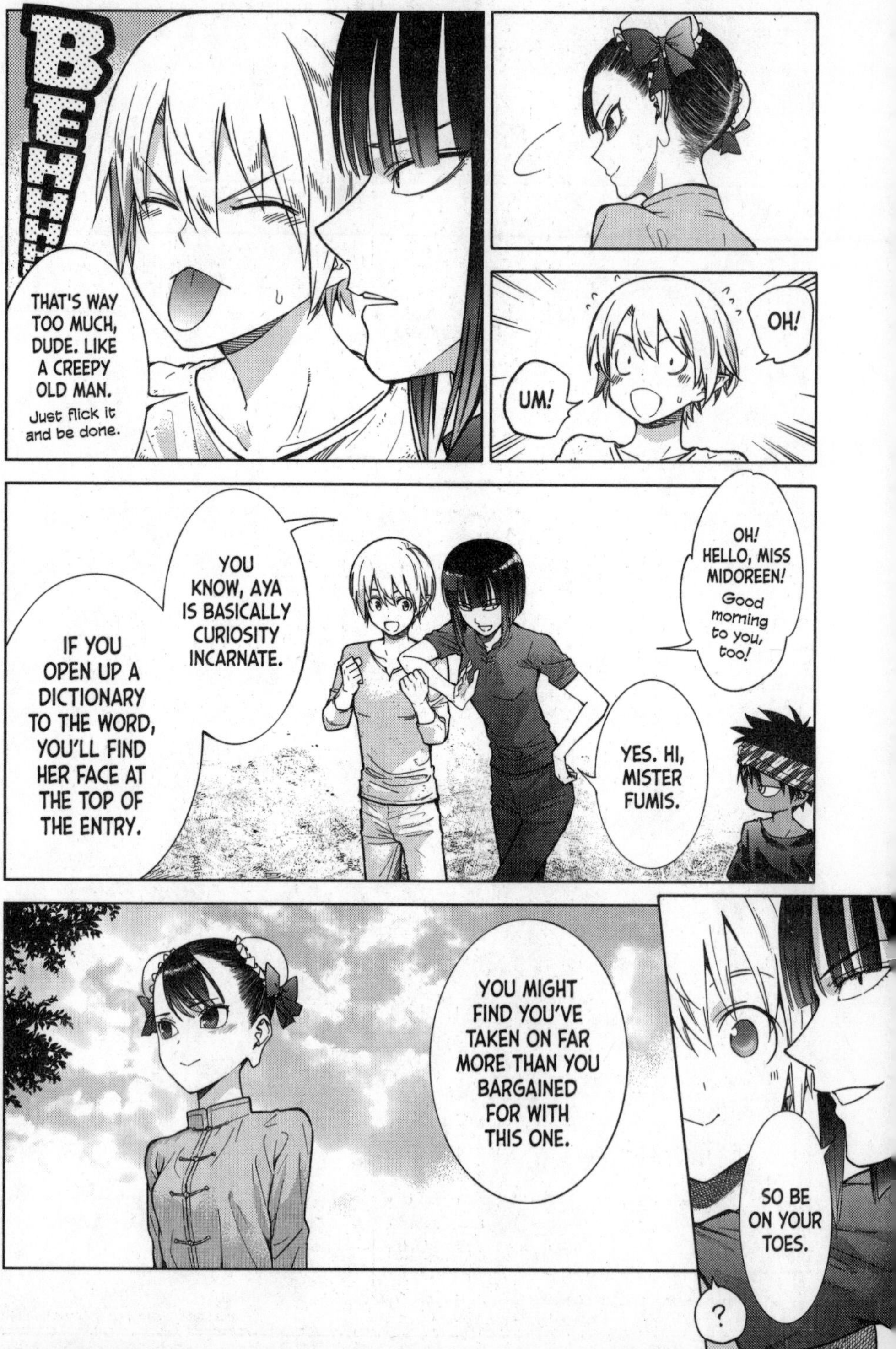
OH!
UM!
BEHHH
THAT'S WAY TOO MUCH, DUDE. LIKE A CREEPY OLD MAN.
Just flick it and be done.
OH! HELLO, MISS MIDOREEN!
Good morning to you, too!
YES. HI, MISTER FUMIS.
YOU KNOW, AYA IS BASICALLY CURIOSITY INCARNATE.
IF YOU OPEN UP A DICTIONARY TO THE WORD, YOU'LL FIND HER FACE AT THE TOP OF THE ENTRY.
YOU MIGHT FIND YOU'VE TAKEN ON FAR MORE THAN YOU BARGAINED FOR WITH THIS ONE.
SO BE ON YOUR TOES.
?

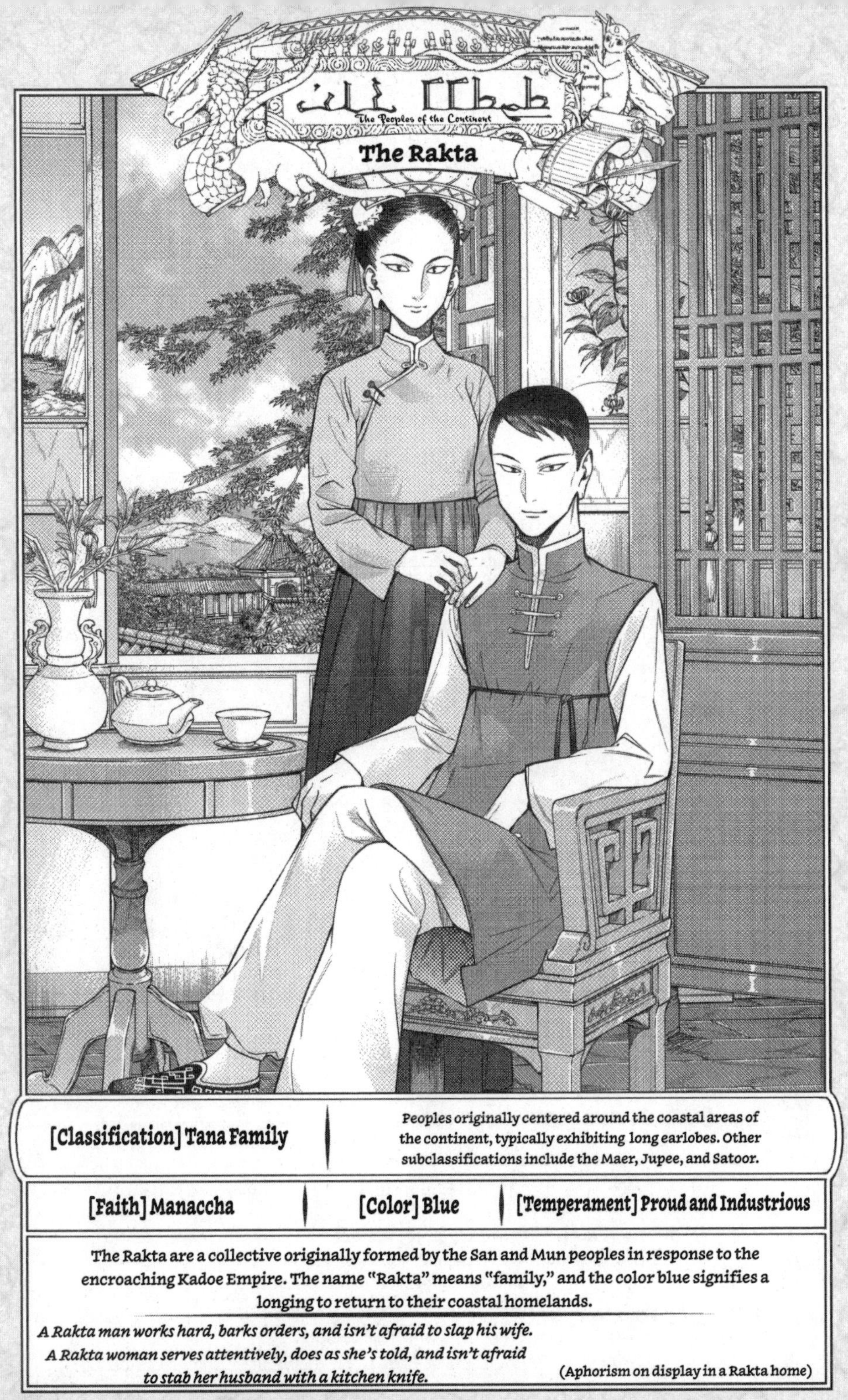
The Peoples of the Continent
The Rakta

[Classification] Tana Family

Peoples originally centered around the coastal areas of the continent, typically exhibiting long earlobes. Other subclassifications include the Maer, Jupee, and Satoor.

[Faith] Manaccha | **[Color] Blue** | **[Temperament] Proud and Industrious**

The Rakta are a collective originally formed by the San and Mun peoples in response to the encroaching Kadoe Empire. The name "Rakta" means "family," and the color blue signifies a longing to return to their coastal homelands.

A Rakta man works hard, barks orders, and isn't afraid to slap his wife.
A Rakta woman serves attentively, does as she's told, and isn't afraid to stab her husband with a kitchen knife.

(Aphorism on display in a Rakta home)

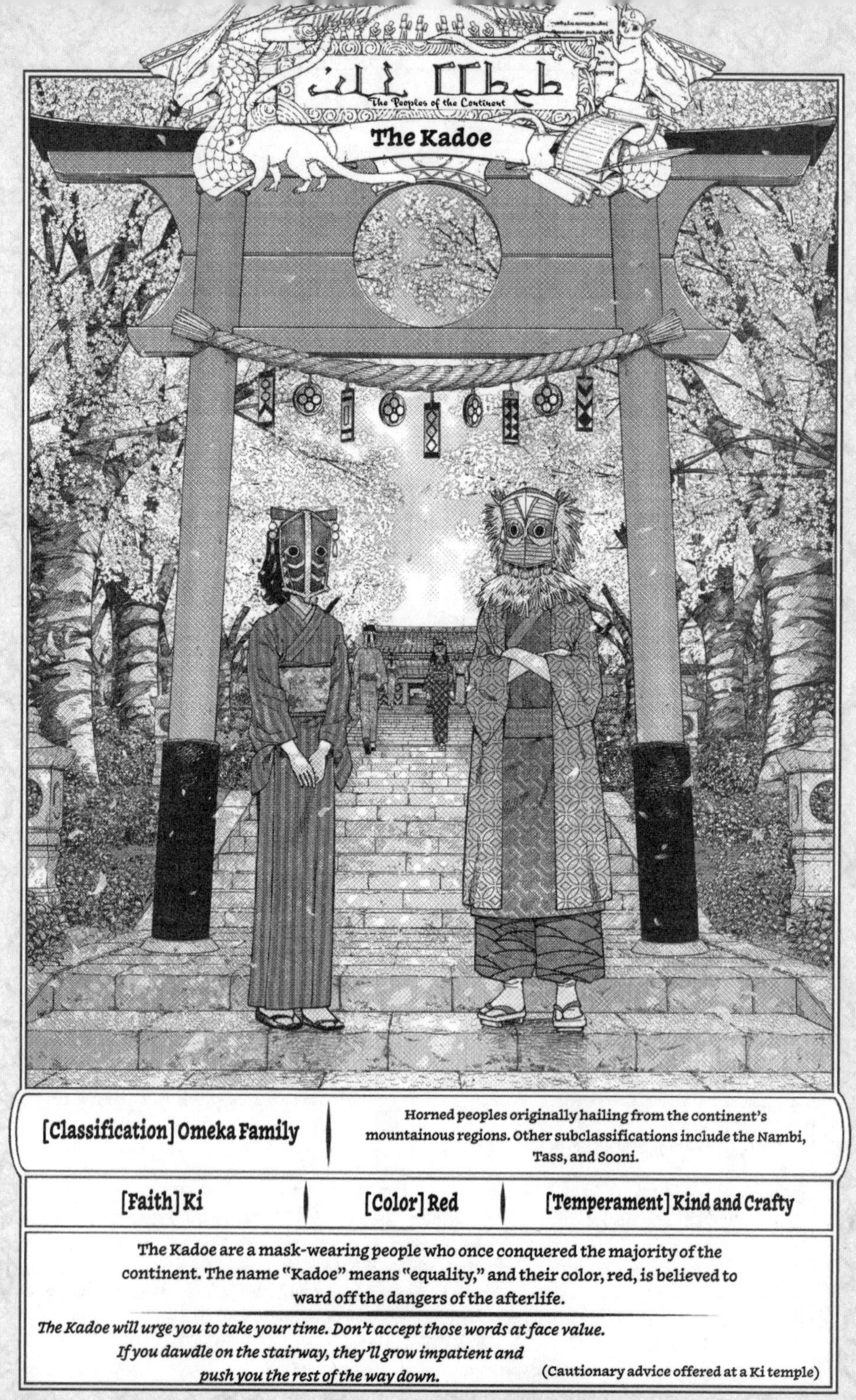
The Peoples of the Continent
The Kadoe

[Classification] Omeka Family

Horned peoples originally hailing from the continent's mountainous regions. Other subclassifications include the Nambi, Tass, and Sooni.

[Faith] Ki | **[Color] Red** | **[Temperament] Kind and Crafty**

The Kadoe are a mask-wearing people who once conquered the majority of the continent. The name "Kadoe" means "equality," and their color, red, is believed to ward off the dangers of the afterlife.

The Kadoe will urge you to take your time. Don't accept those words at face value. If you dawdle on the stairway, they'll grow impatient and push you the rest of the way down.

(Cautionary advice offered at a Ki temple)

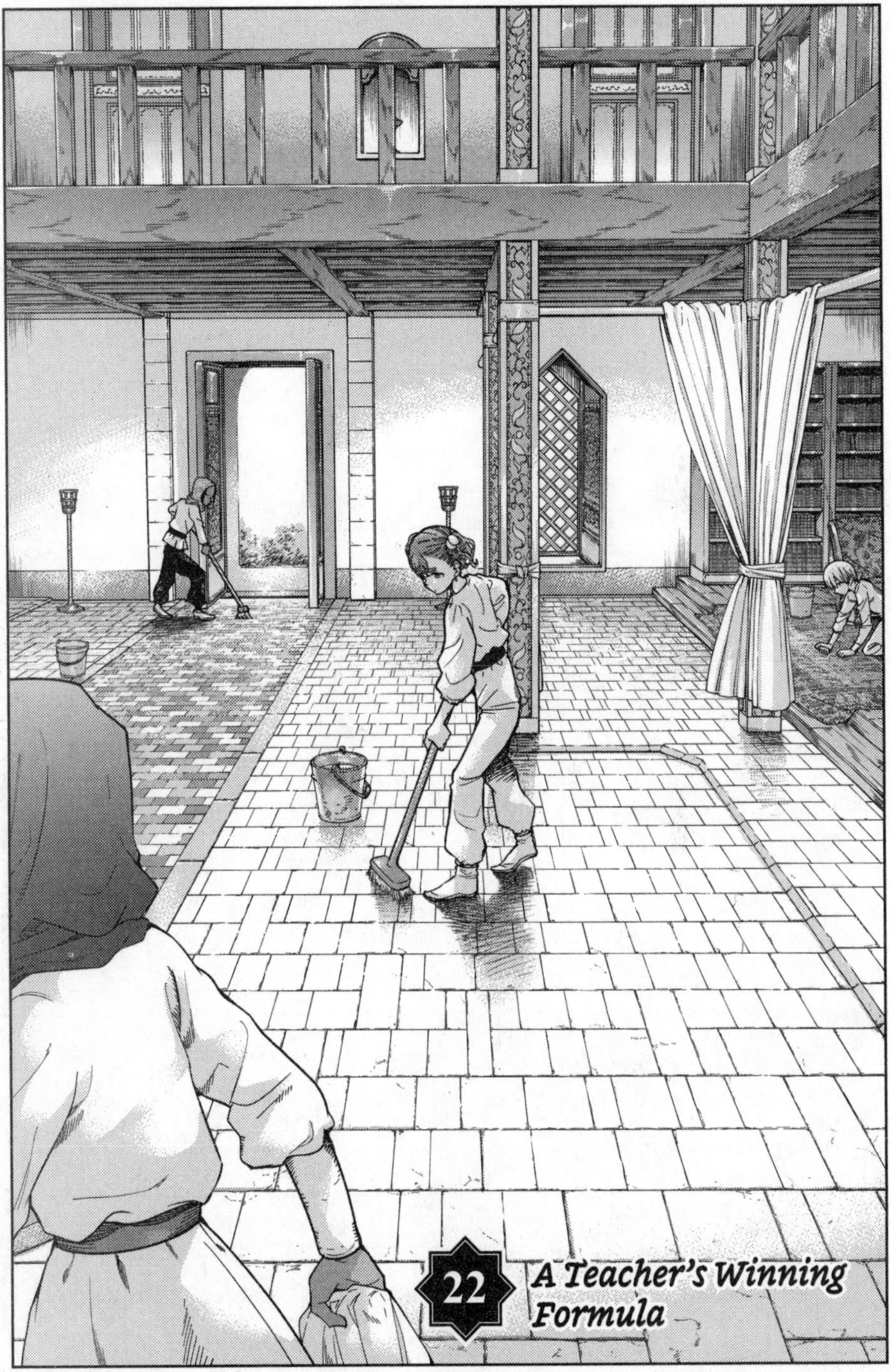
22
A Teacher's Winning Formula

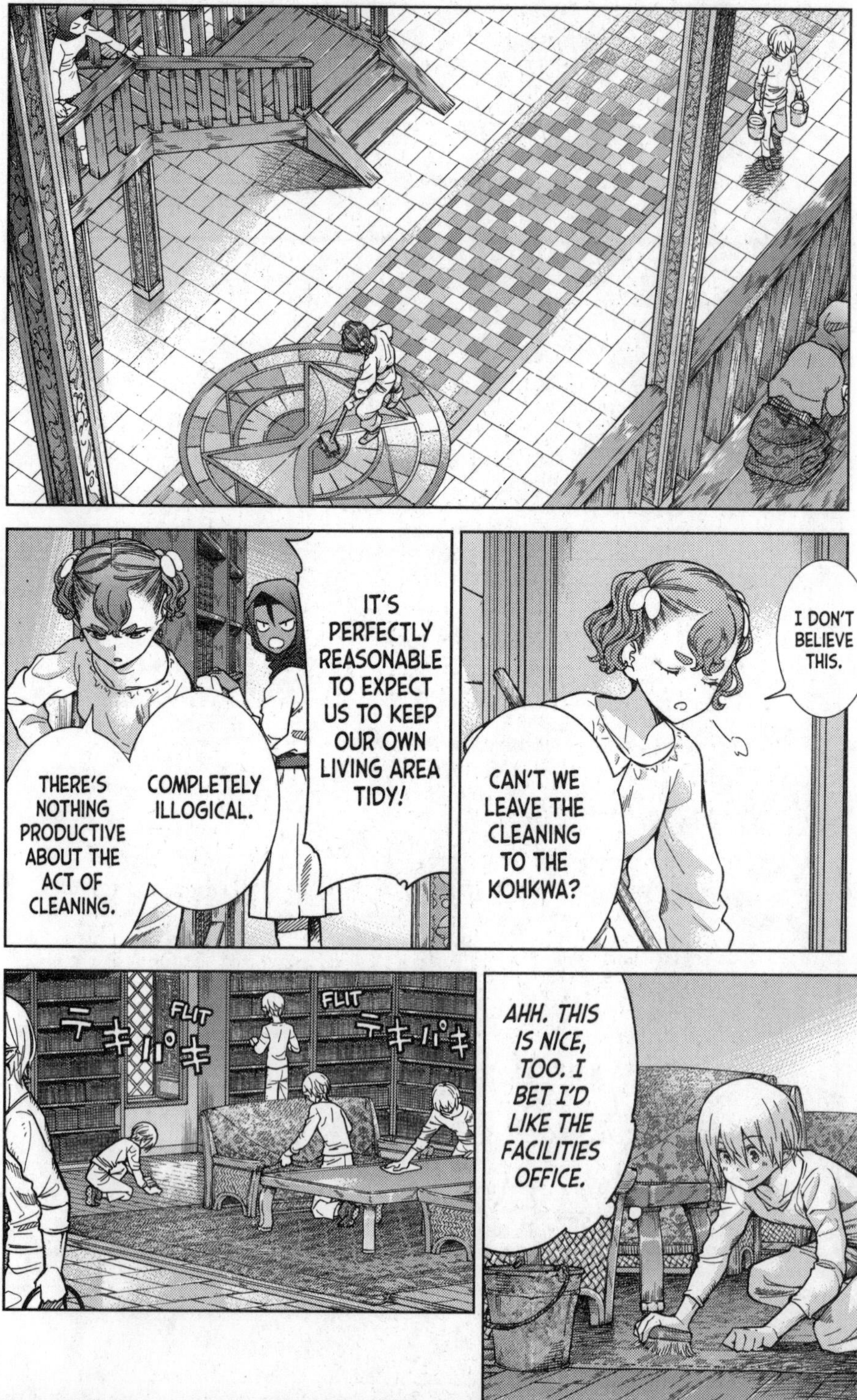
I DON'T BELIEVE THIS.
CAN'T WE LEAVE THE CLEANING TO THE KOHKWA?
IT'S PERFECTLY REASONABLE TO EXPECT US TO KEEP OUR OWN LIVING AREA TIDY!
COMPLETELY ILLOGICAL.
THERE'S NOTHING PRODUCTIVE ABOUT THE ACT OF CLEANING.
AHH. THIS IS NICE, TOO. I BET I'D LIKE THE FACILITIES OFFICE.
FLIT
テキパキ
FLIT
テキパキ

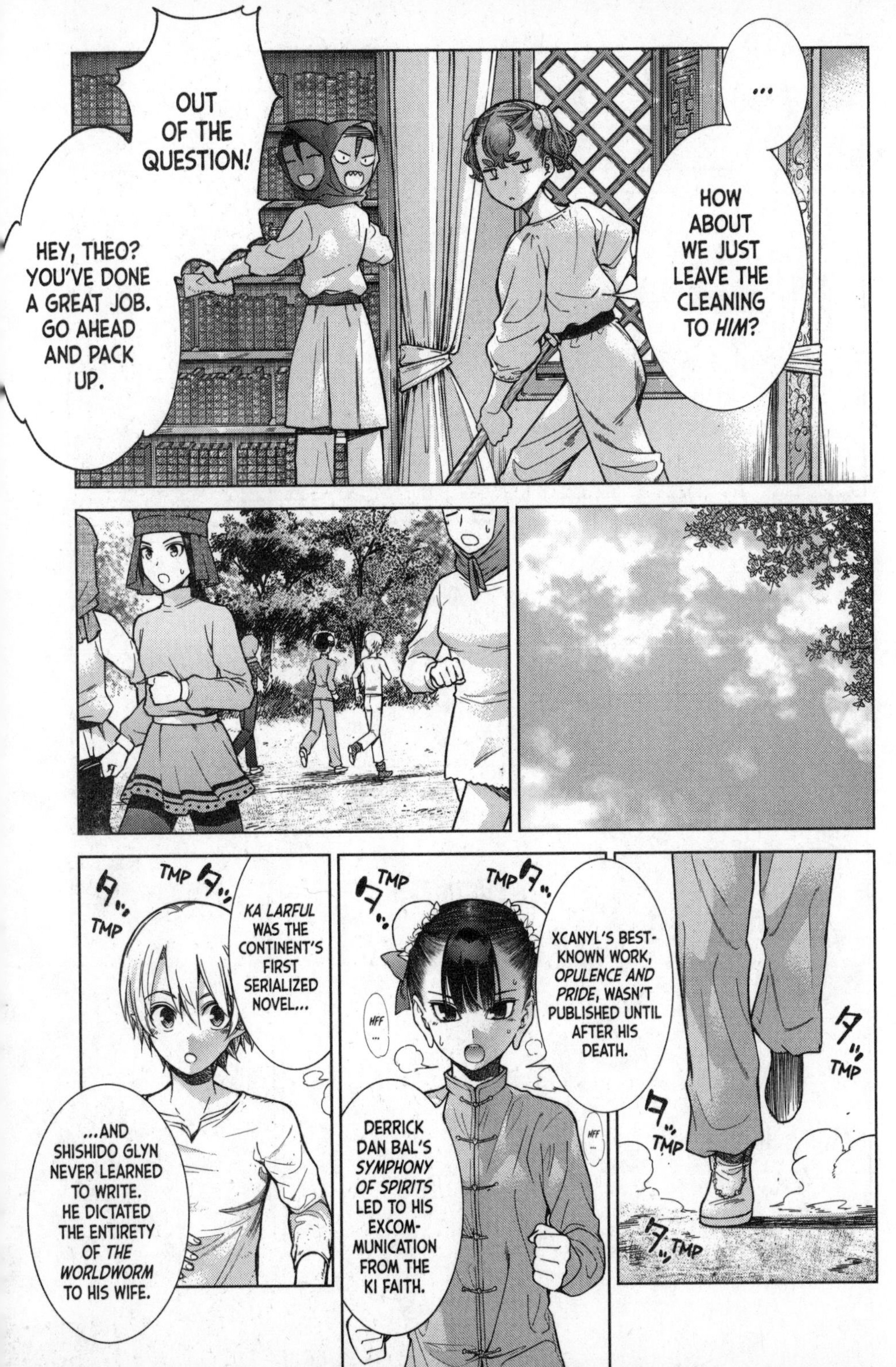
...
HOW ABOUT WE JUST LEAVE THE CLEANING TO *HIM*?
OUT OF THE QUESTION!
HEY, THEO? YOU'VE DONE A GREAT JOB. GO AHEAD AND PACK UP.
タッ TMP
タッ TMP
タッ TMP
タッ TMP
XCANYL'S BEST-KNOWN WORK, *OPULENCE AND PRIDE*, WASN'T PUBLISHED UNTIL AFTER HIS DEATH.
タッ TMP
HFF ...
DERRICK DAN BAL'S *SYMPHONY OF SPIRITS* LED TO HIS EXCOMMUNICATION FROM THE KI FAITH.
HFF ...
TMP タッ
KA LARFUL WAS THE CONTINENT'S FIRST SERIALIZED NOVEL...
タッ TMP
...AND SHISHIDO GLYN NEVER LEARNED TO WRITE. HE DICTATED THE ENTIRETY OF *THE WORLDWORM* TO HIS WIFE.

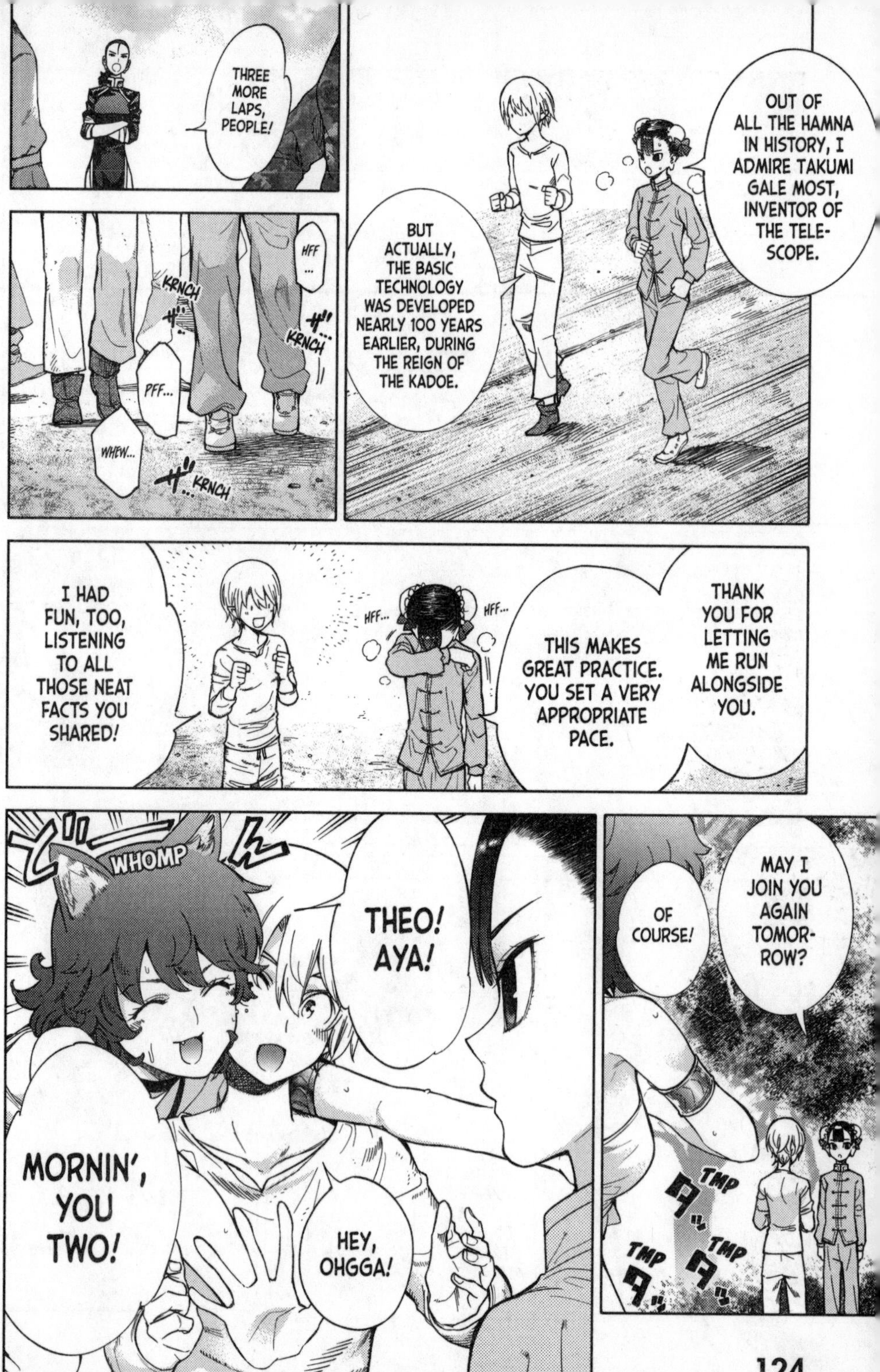
OUT OF ALL THE HAMNA IN HISTORY, I ADMIRE TAKUMI GALE MOST, INVENTOR OF THE TELE-SCOPE.
BUT ACTUALLY, THE BASIC TECHNOLOGY WAS DEVELOPED NEARLY 100 YEARS EARLIER, DURING THE REIGN OF THE KADOE.
THREE MORE LAPS, PEOPLE!
HFF...
KRNCH
KRNCH
PFF...
WHEW...
KRNCH
THANK YOU FOR LETTING ME RUN ALONGSIDE YOU.
THIS MAKES GREAT PRACTICE. YOU SET A VERY APPROPRIATE PACE.
HFF...
HFF...
I HAD FUN, TOO, LISTENING TO ALL THOSE NEAT FACTS YOU SHARED!
MAY I JOIN YOU AGAIN TOMOR-ROW?
OF COURSE!
TMP
TMP
TMP
WHOMP
THEO! AYA!
MORNIN', YOU TWO!
HEY, OHGGA!

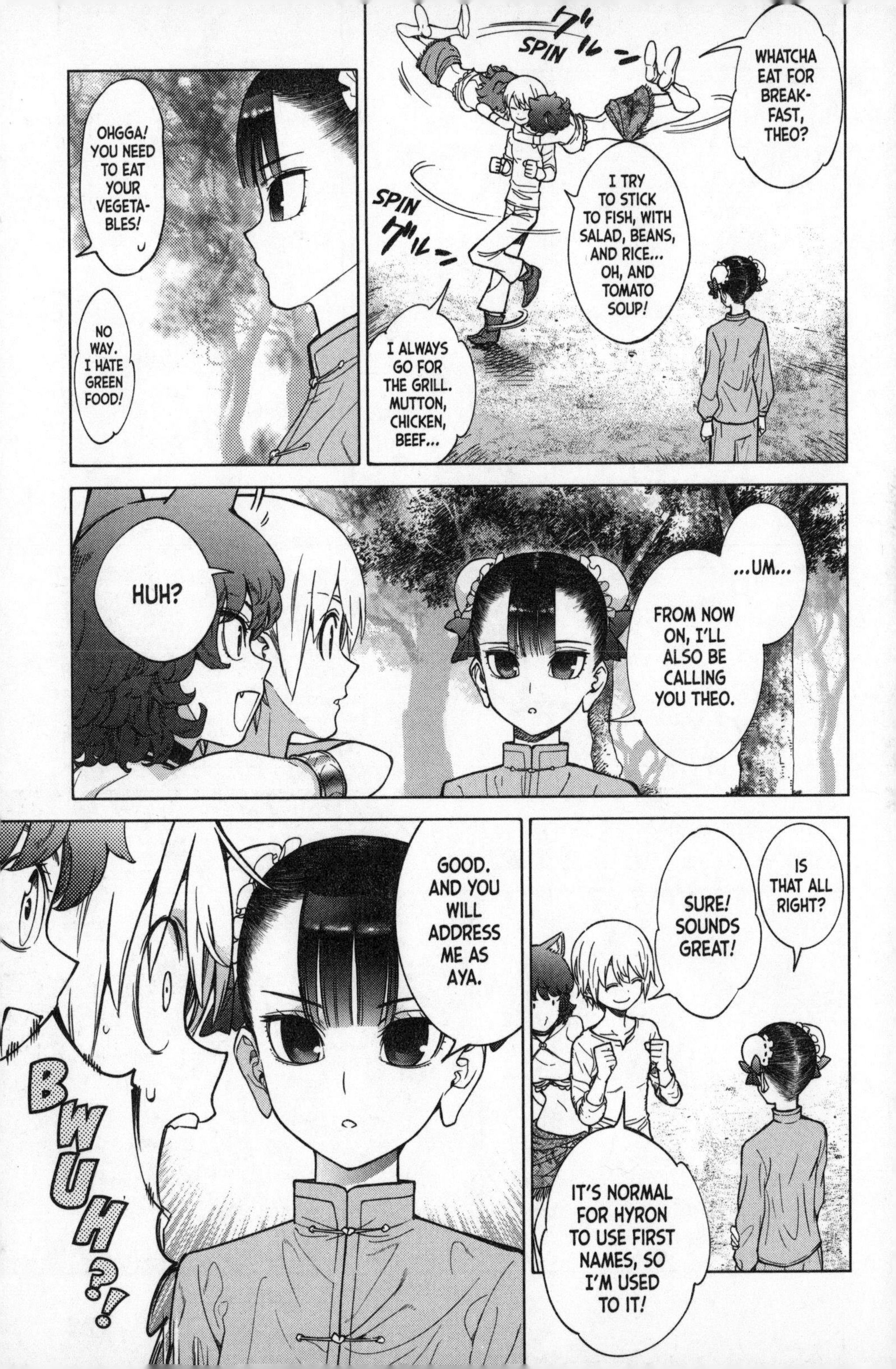
WHATCHA EAT FOR BREAKFAST, THEO?
SPIN グル
I TRY TO STICK TO FISH, WITH SALAD, BEANS, AND RICE... OH, AND TOMATO SOUP!
SPIN グル
I ALWAYS GO FOR THE GRILL. MUTTON, CHICKEN, BEEF...
OHGGA! YOU NEED TO EAT YOUR VEGETABLES!
NO WAY. I HATE GREEN FOOD!
...UM...
FROM NOW ON, I'LL ALSO BE CALLING YOU THEO.
HUH?
IS THAT ALL RIGHT?
SURE! SOUNDS GREAT!
IT'S NORMAL FOR HYRON TO USE FIRST NAMES, SO I'M USED TO IT!
GOOD. AND YOU WILL ADDRESS ME AS AYA.
BWUH?!

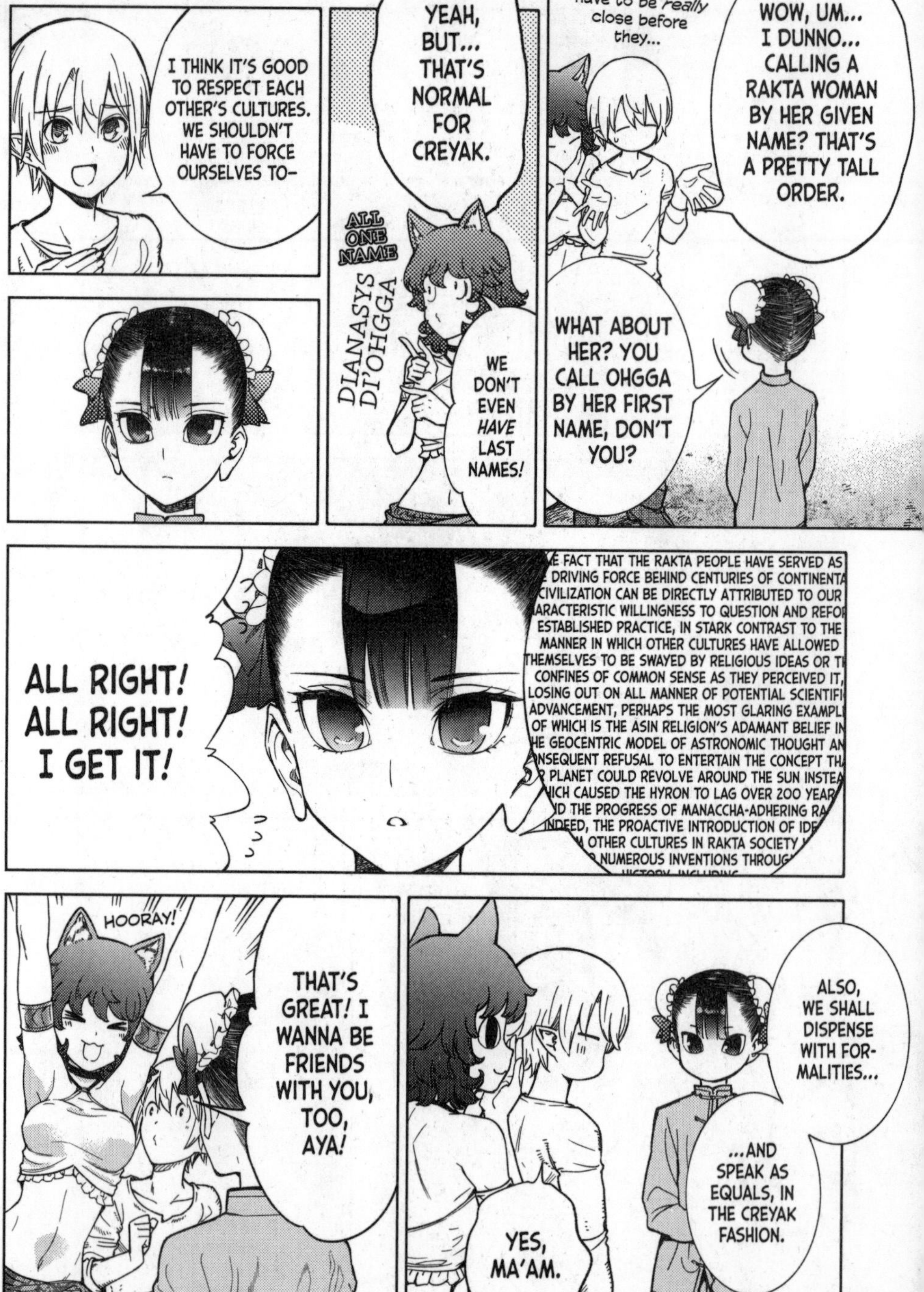
WOW, UM... I DUNNO... CALLING A RAKTA WOMAN BY HER GIVEN NAME? THAT'S A PRETTY TALL ORDER.
Like, Rakta people have to be *really* close before they...
WHAT ABOUT HER? YOU CALL OHGGA BY HER FIRST NAME, DON'T YOU?
YEAH, BUT... THAT'S NORMAL FOR CREYAK.
ALL ONE NAME
DIANASYS DI'OHGGA
WE DON'T EVEN *HAVE* LAST NAMES!
I THINK IT'S GOOD TO RESPECT EACH OTHER'S CULTURES. WE SHOULDN'T HAVE TO FORCE OURSELVES TO-
E FACT THAT THE RAKTA PEOPLE HAVE SERVED AS E DRIVING FORCE BEHIND CENTURIES OF CONTINENTA CIVILIZATION CAN BE DIRECTLY ATTRIBUTED TO OUR ARACTERISTIC WILLINGNESS TO QUESTION AND REFOR ESTABLISHED PRACTICE, IN STARK CONTRAST TO THE MANNER IN WHICH OTHER CULTURES HAVE ALLOWED THEMSELVES TO BE SWAYED BY RELIGIOUS IDEAS OR T CONFINES OF COMMON SENSE AS THEY PERCEIVED IT, LOSING OUT ON ALL MANNER OF POTENTIAL SCIENTIFI ADVANCEMENT, PERHAPS THE MOST GLARING EXAMPL OF WHICH IS THE ASIN RELIGION'S ADAMANT BELIEF IN HE GEOCENTRIC MODEL OF ASTRONOMIC THOUGHT AN NSEQUENT REFUSAL TO ENTERTAIN THE CONCEPT TH R PLANET COULD REVOLVE AROUND THE SUN INSTEA HICH CAUSED THE HYRON TO LAG OVER 200 YEAR D THE PROGRESS OF MANACCHA-ADHERING RA NDEED, THE PROACTIVE INTRODUCTION OF IDE OTHER CULTURES IN RAKTA SOCIETY NUMEROUS INVENTIONS THROUG
ALL RIGHT! ALL RIGHT! I GET IT!
ALSO, WE SHALL DISPENSE WITH FOR-MALITIES...
...AND SPEAK AS EQUALS, IN THE CREYAK FASHION.
YES, MA'AM.
HOORAY!
THAT'S GREAT! I WANNA BE FRIENDS WITH YOU, TOO, AYA!

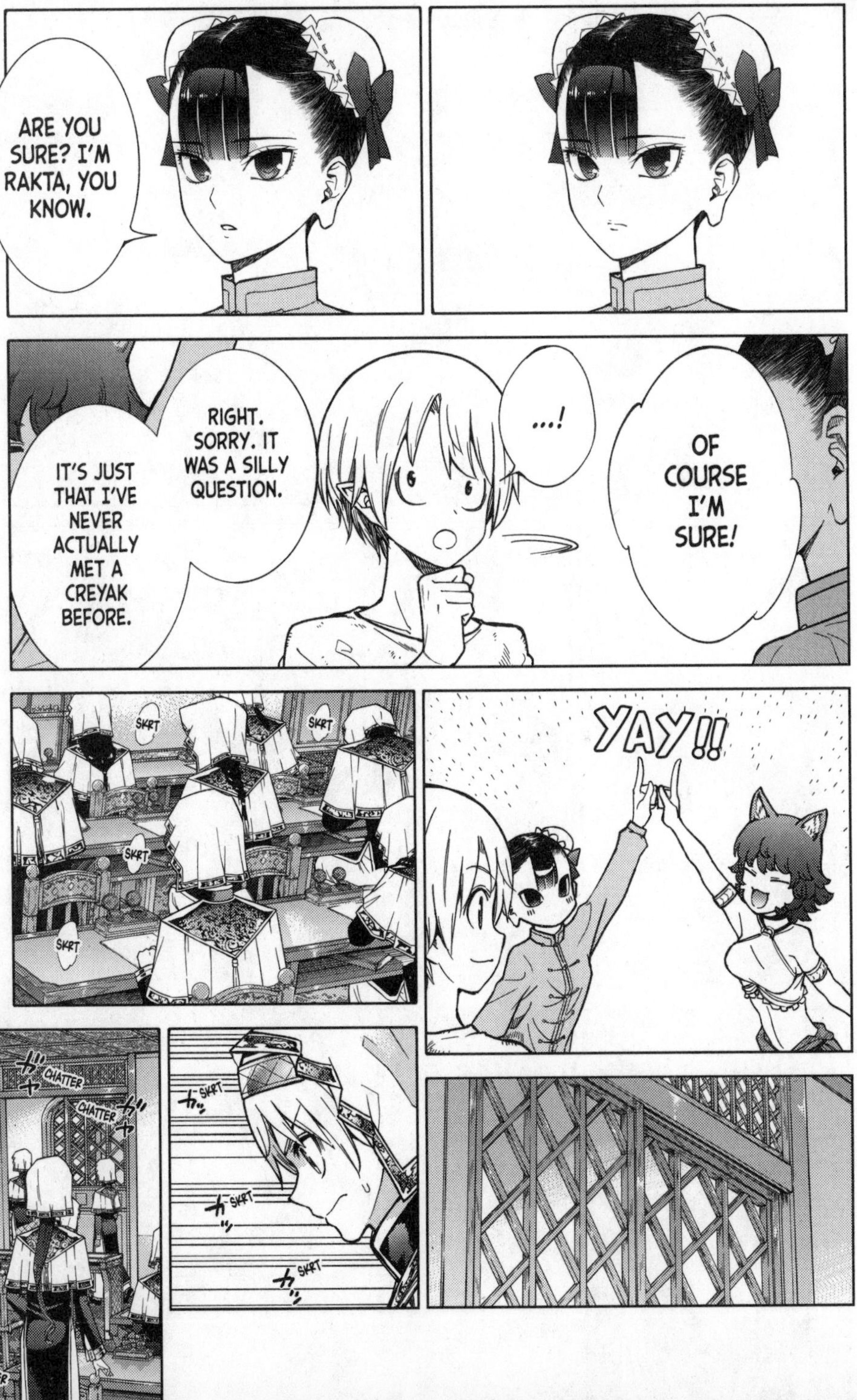
ARE YOU SURE? I'M RAKTA, YOU KNOW.
OF COURSE I'M SURE!
...!
RIGHT. SORRY. IT WAS A SILLY QUESTION.
IT'S JUST THAT I'VE NEVER ACTUALLY MET A CREYAK BEFORE.
YAY!!
SKRT
SKRT
SKRT
SKRT
SKRT
SKRT
SKRT
CHATTER
CHATTER
CHATTER

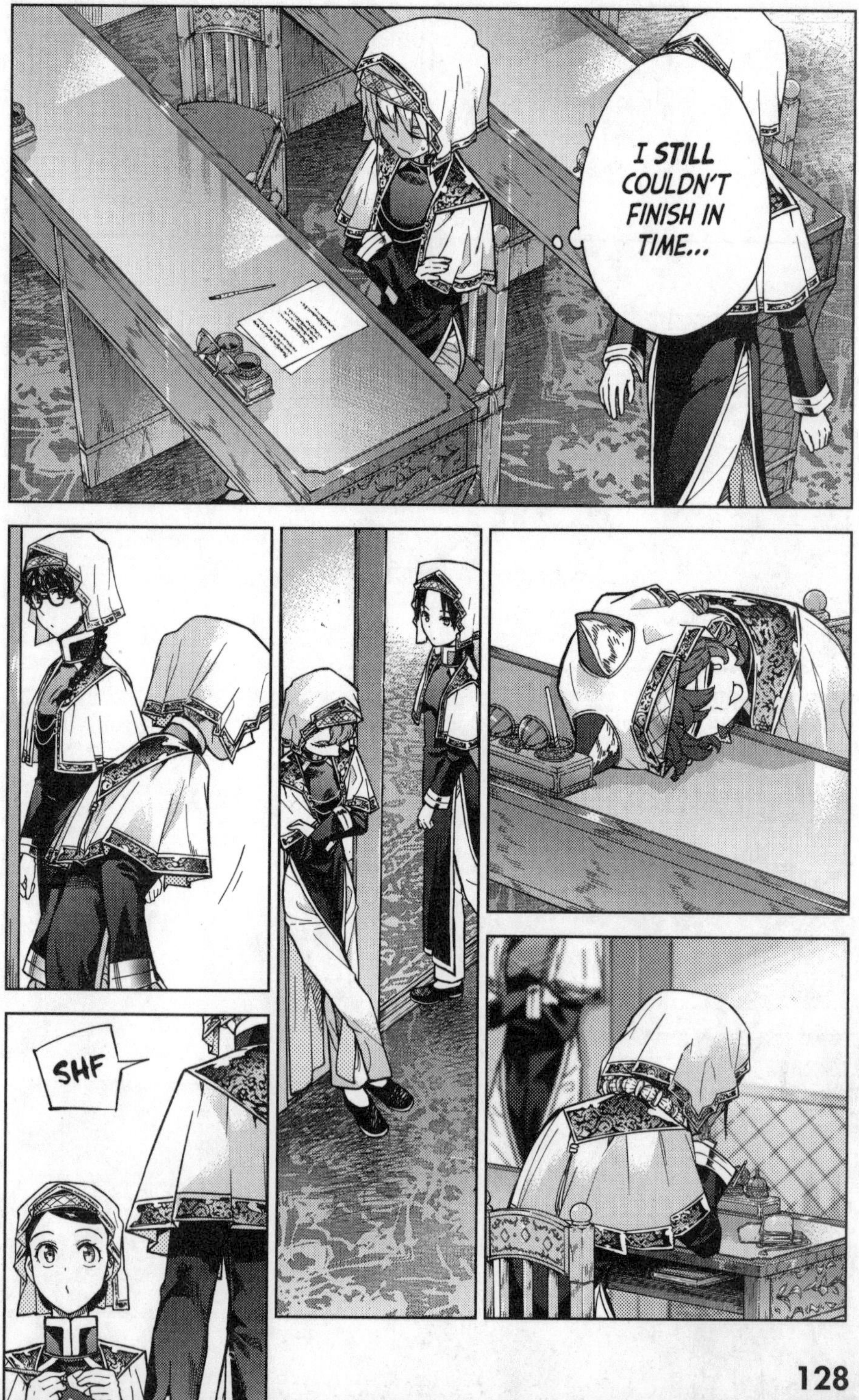

I STILL COULDN'T FINISH IN TIME...
SHF

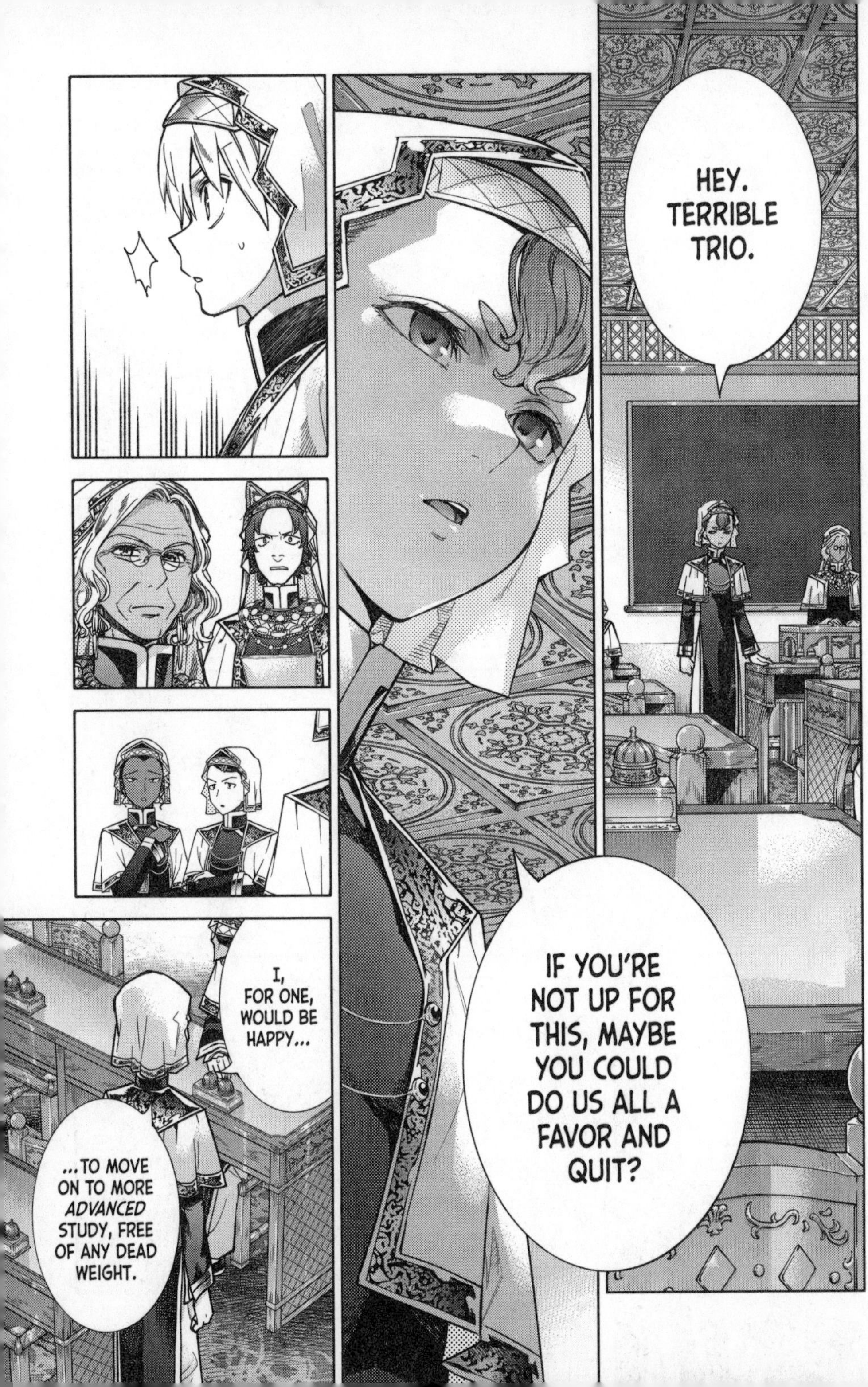
HEY. TERRIBLE TRIO.
IF YOU'RE NOT UP FOR THIS, MAYBE YOU COULD DO US ALL A FAVOR AND QUIT?
I, FOR ONE, WOULD BE HAPPY...
...TO MOVE ON TO MORE *ADVANCED* STUDY, FREE OF ANY DEAD WEIGHT.

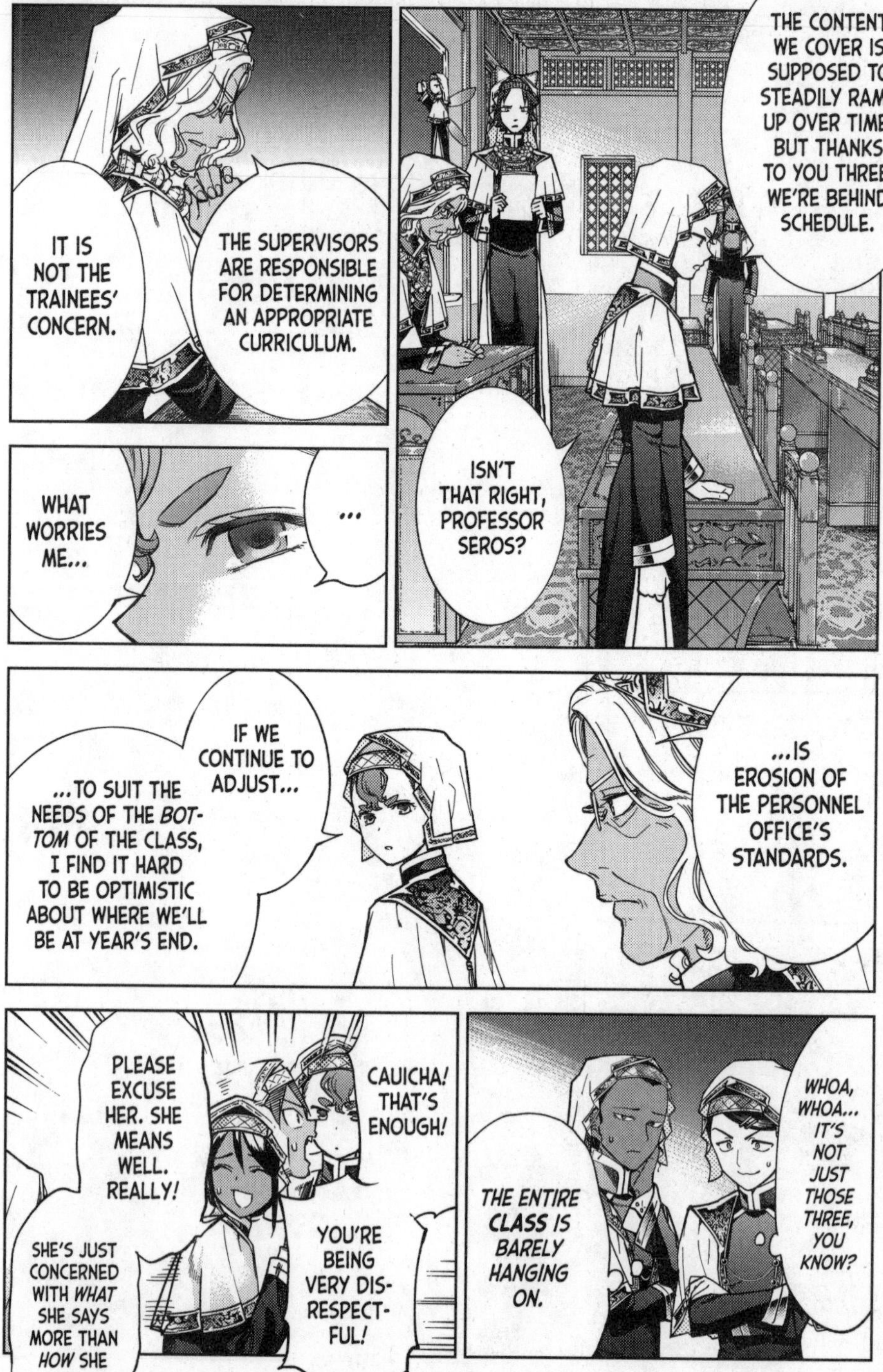
THE CONTENT WE COVER IS SUPPOSED TO STEADILY RAMP UP OVER TIME. BUT THANKS TO YOU THREE, WE'RE BEHIND SCHEDULE.
ISN'T THAT RIGHT, PROFESSOR SEROS?
THE SUPERVISORS ARE RESPONSIBLE FOR DETERMINING AN APPROPRIATE CURRICULUM.
IT IS NOT THE TRAINEES' CONCERN.
...
WHAT WORRIES ME...
...IS EROSION OF THE PERSONNEL OFFICE'S STANDARDS.
IF WE CONTINUE TO ADJUST...
...TO SUIT THE NEEDS OF THE *BOTTOM* OF THE CLASS, I FIND IT HARD TO BE OPTIMISTIC ABOUT WHERE WE'LL BE AT YEAR'S END.
WHOA, WHOA... IT'S NOT JUST THOSE THREE, YOU KNOW?
THE ENTIRE CLASS IS BARELY HANGING ON.
CAUICHA! THAT'S ENOUGH!
PLEASE EXCUSE HER. SHE MEANS WELL. REALLY!
YOU'RE BEING VERY DISRESPECTFUL!
SHE'S JUST CONCERNED WITH *WHAT* SHE SAYS MORE THAN *HOW* SHE SAYS IT!

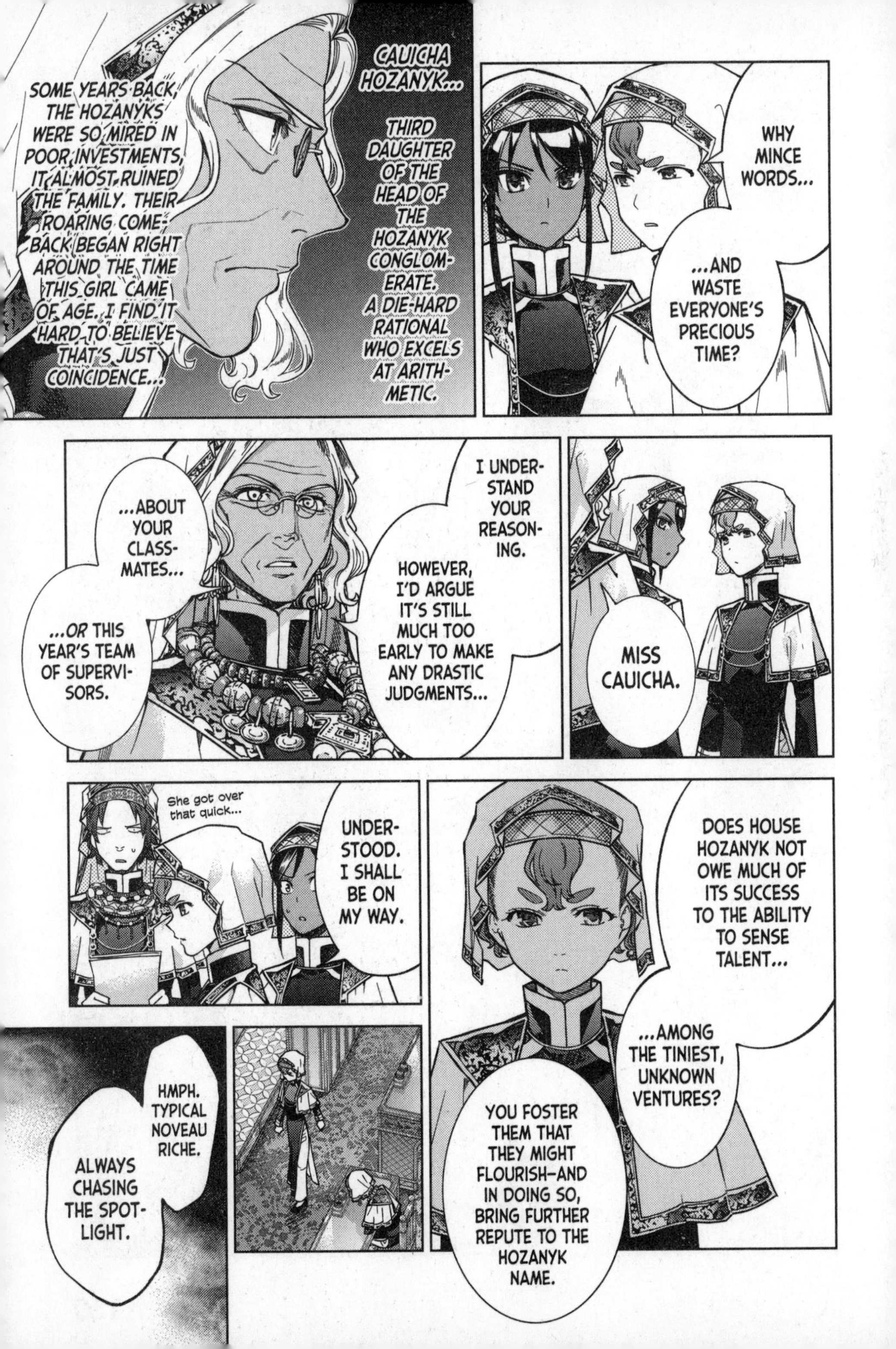
WHY MINCE WORDS...
...AND WASTE EVERYONE'S PRECIOUS TIME?
CAUICHA HOZANYK...
THIRD DAUGHTER OF THE HEAD OF THE HOZANYK CONGLOM-ERATE. A DIE-HARD RATIONAL WHO EXCELS AT ARITH-METIC.
SOME YEARS BACK, THE HOZANYKS WERE SO MIRED IN POOR INVESTMENTS, IT ALMOST RUINED THE FAMILY. THEIR ROARING COME-BACK BEGAN RIGHT AROUND THE TIME THIS GIRL CAME OF AGE. I FIND IT HARD TO BELIEVE THAT'S JUST COINCIDENCE...
MISS CAUICHA.
I UNDER-STAND YOUR REASON-ING.
HOWEVER, I'D ARGUE IT'S STILL MUCH TOO EARLY TO MAKE ANY DRASTIC JUDGMENTS...
...ABOUT YOUR CLASS-MATES...
...OR THIS YEAR'S TEAM OF SUPERVI-SORS.
DOES HOUSE HOZANYK NOT OWE MUCH OF ITS SUCCESS TO THE ABILITY TO SENSE TALENT...
...AMONG THE TINIEST, UNKNOWN VENTURES?
YOU FOSTER THEM THAT THEY MIGHT FLOURISH—AND IN DOING SO, BRING FURTHER REPUTE TO THE HOZANYK NAME.
UNDER-STOOD. I SHALL BE ON MY WAY.
She got over that quick...
HMPH. TYPICAL NOVEAU RICHE.
ALWAYS CHASING THE SPOT-LIGHT.

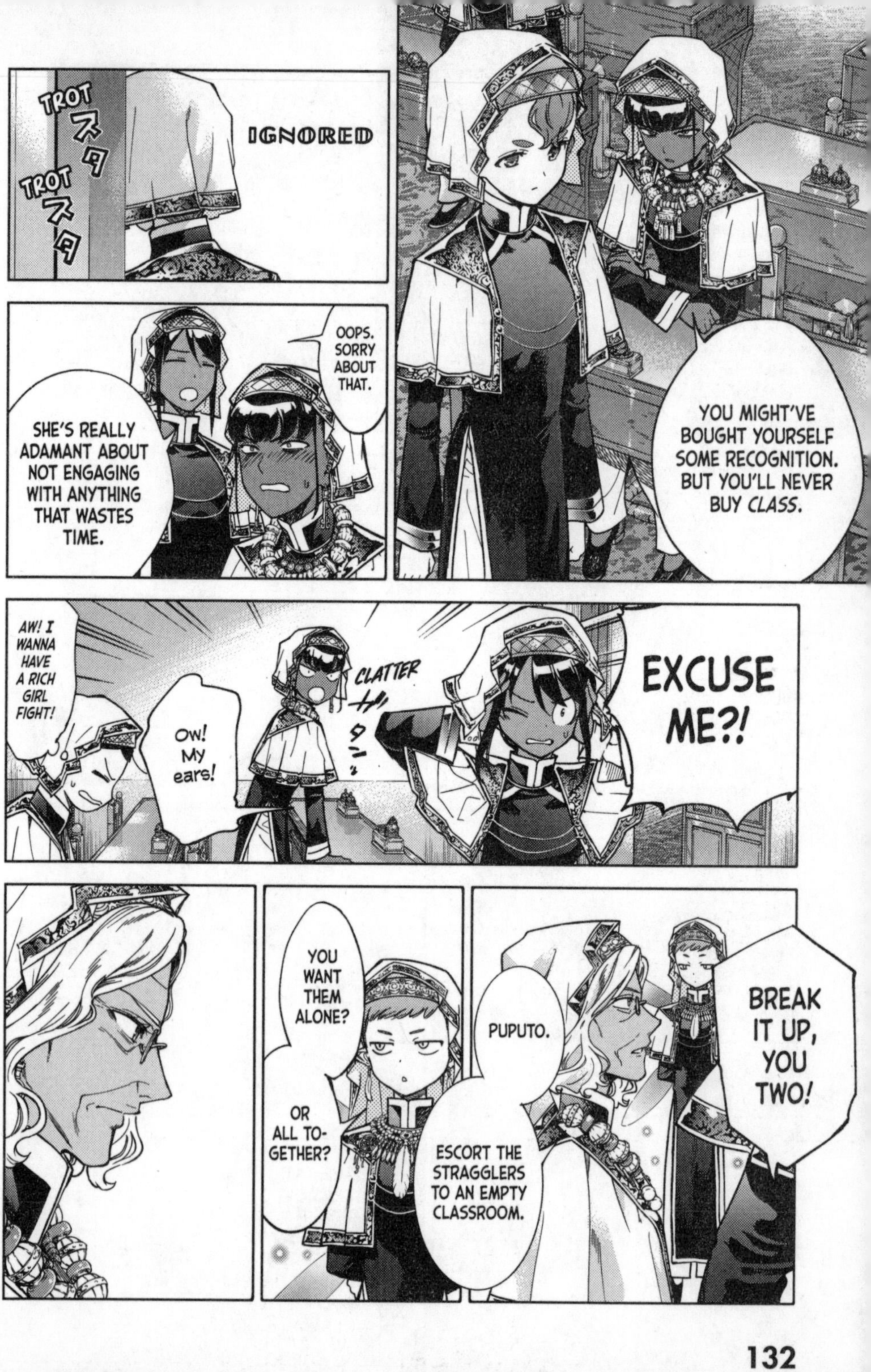

YOU MIGHT'VE BOUGHT YOURSELF SOME RECOGNITION. BUT YOU'LL NEVER BUY *CLASS*.
TROT スタ
TROT スタ
IGNORED
OOPS. SORRY ABOUT THAT.
SHE'S REALLY ADAMANT ABOUT NOT ENGAGING WITH ANYTHING THAT WASTES TIME.
EXCUSE ME?!
CLATTER
Ow! My ears!
AW! I WANNA HAVE A RICH GIRL FIGHT!
BREAK IT UP, YOU TWO!
PUPUTO.
ESCORT THE STRAGGLERS TO AN EMPTY CLASSROOM.
YOU WANT THEM ALONE?
OR ALL TO-GETHER?

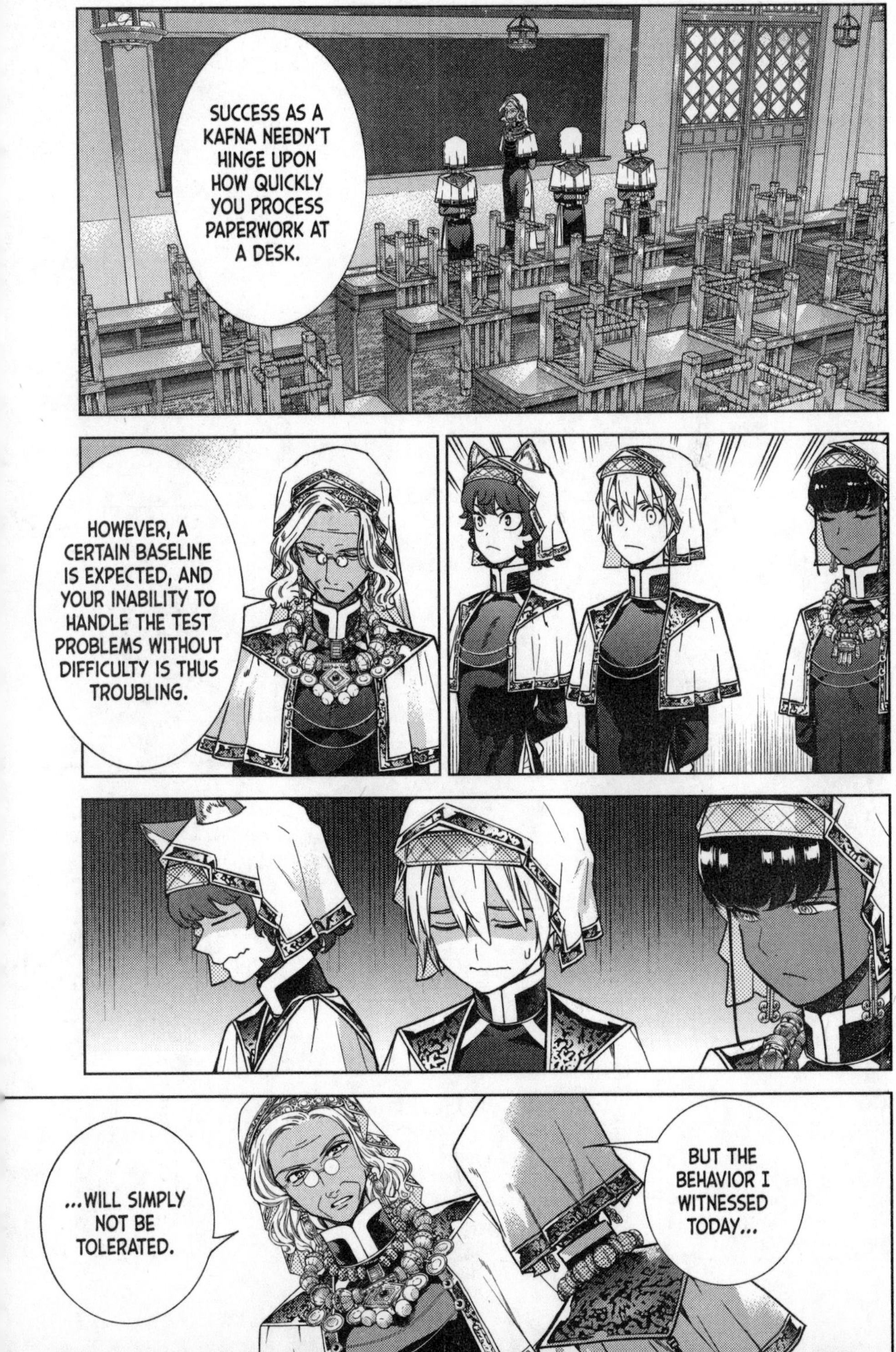
SUCCESS AS A KAFNA NEEDN'T HINGE UPON HOW QUICKLY YOU PROCESS PAPERWORK AT A DESK.
HOWEVER, A CERTAIN BASELINE IS EXPECTED, AND YOUR INABILITY TO HANDLE THE TEST PROBLEMS WITHOUT DIFFICULTY IS THUS TROUBLING.
BUT THE BEHAVIOR I WITNESSED TODAY...
...WILL SIMPLY NOT BE TOLERATED.

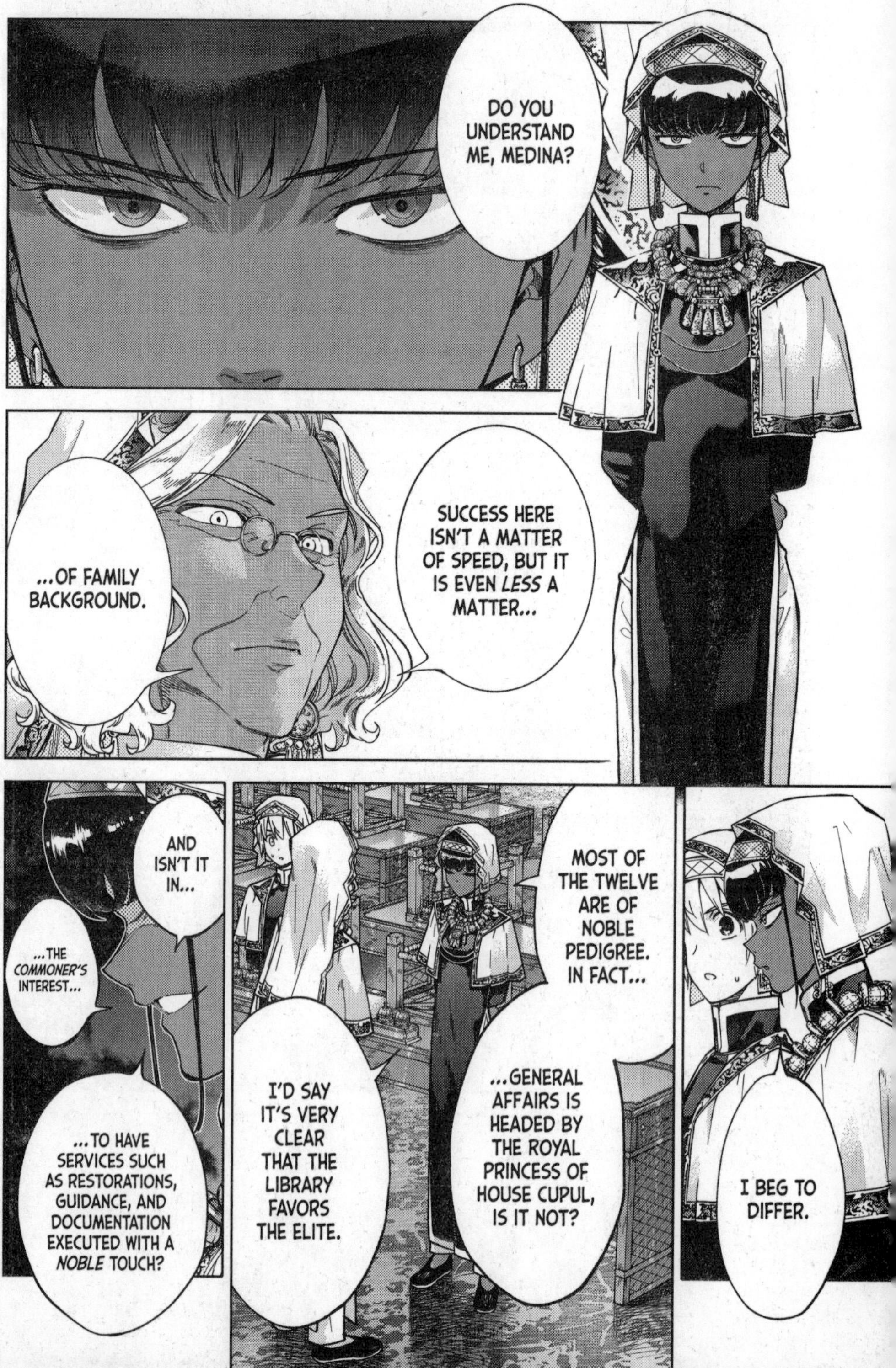
DO YOU UNDERSTAND ME, MEDINA?
SUCCESS HERE ISN'T A MATTER OF SPEED, BUT IT IS EVEN *LESS* A MATTER...
...OF FAMILY BACKGROUND.
I BEG TO DIFFER.
MOST OF THE TWELVE ARE OF NOBLE PEDIGREE. IN FACT...
...GENERAL AFFAIRS IS HEADED BY THE ROYAL PRINCESS OF HOUSE CUPUL, IS IT NOT?
I'D SAY IT'S VERY CLEAR THAT THE LIBRARY FAVORS THE ELITE.
AND ISN'T IT IN...
...THE *COMMONER'S* INTEREST...
...TO HAVE SERVICES SUCH AS RESTORATIONS, GUIDANCE, AND DOCUMENTATION EXECUTED WITH A *NOBLE* TOUCH?

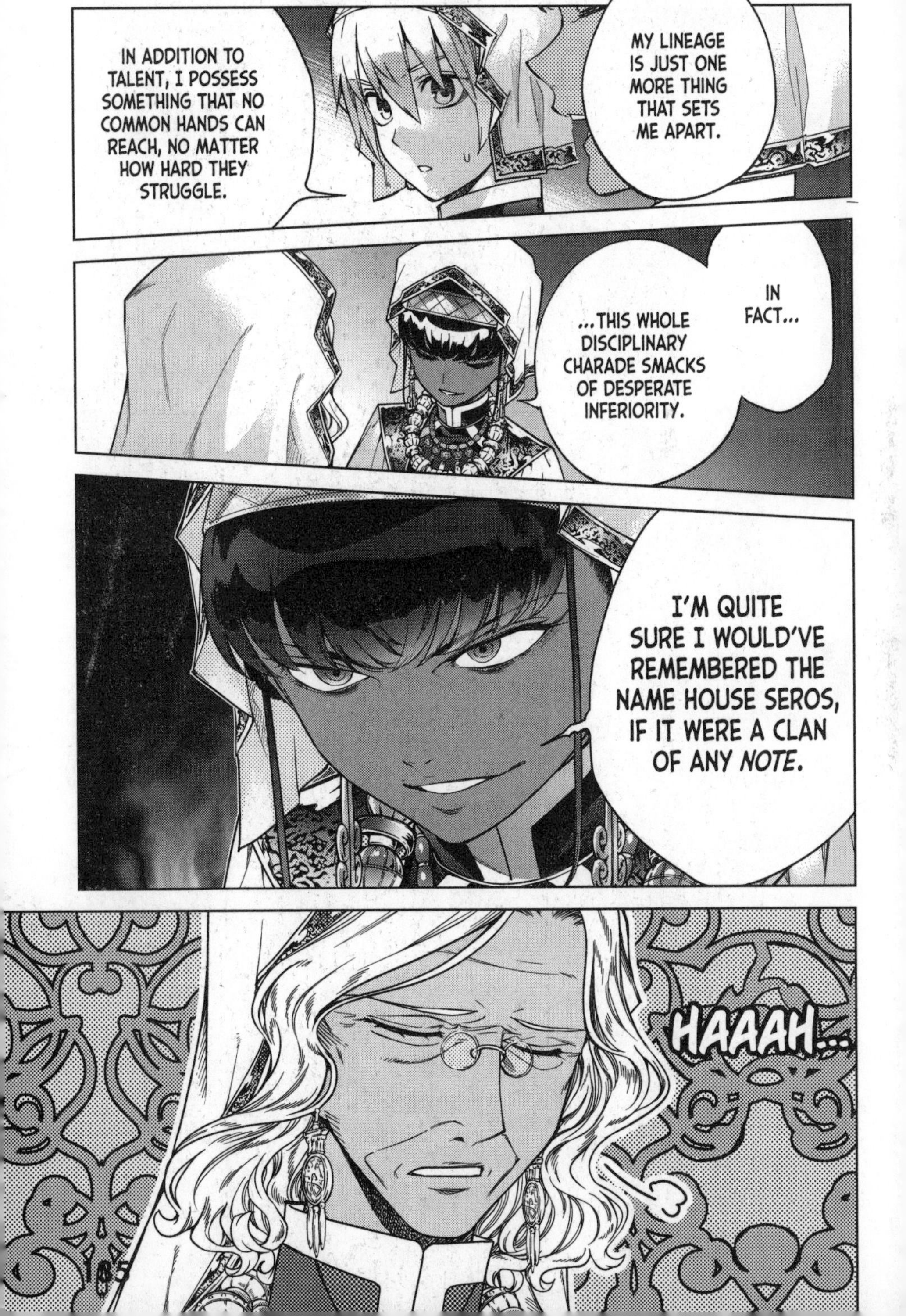
MY LINEAGE IS JUST ONE MORE THING THAT SETS ME APART.
IN ADDITION TO TALENT, I POSSESS SOMETHING THAT NO COMMON HANDS CAN REACH, NO MATTER HOW HARD THEY STRUGGLE.
IN FACT...
...THIS WHOLE DISCIPLINARY CHARADE SMACKS OF DESPERATE INFERIORITY.
I'M QUITE SURE I WOULD'VE REMEMBERED THE NAME HOUSE SEROS, IF IT WERE A CLAN OF ANY *NOTE*.
HAAAH...

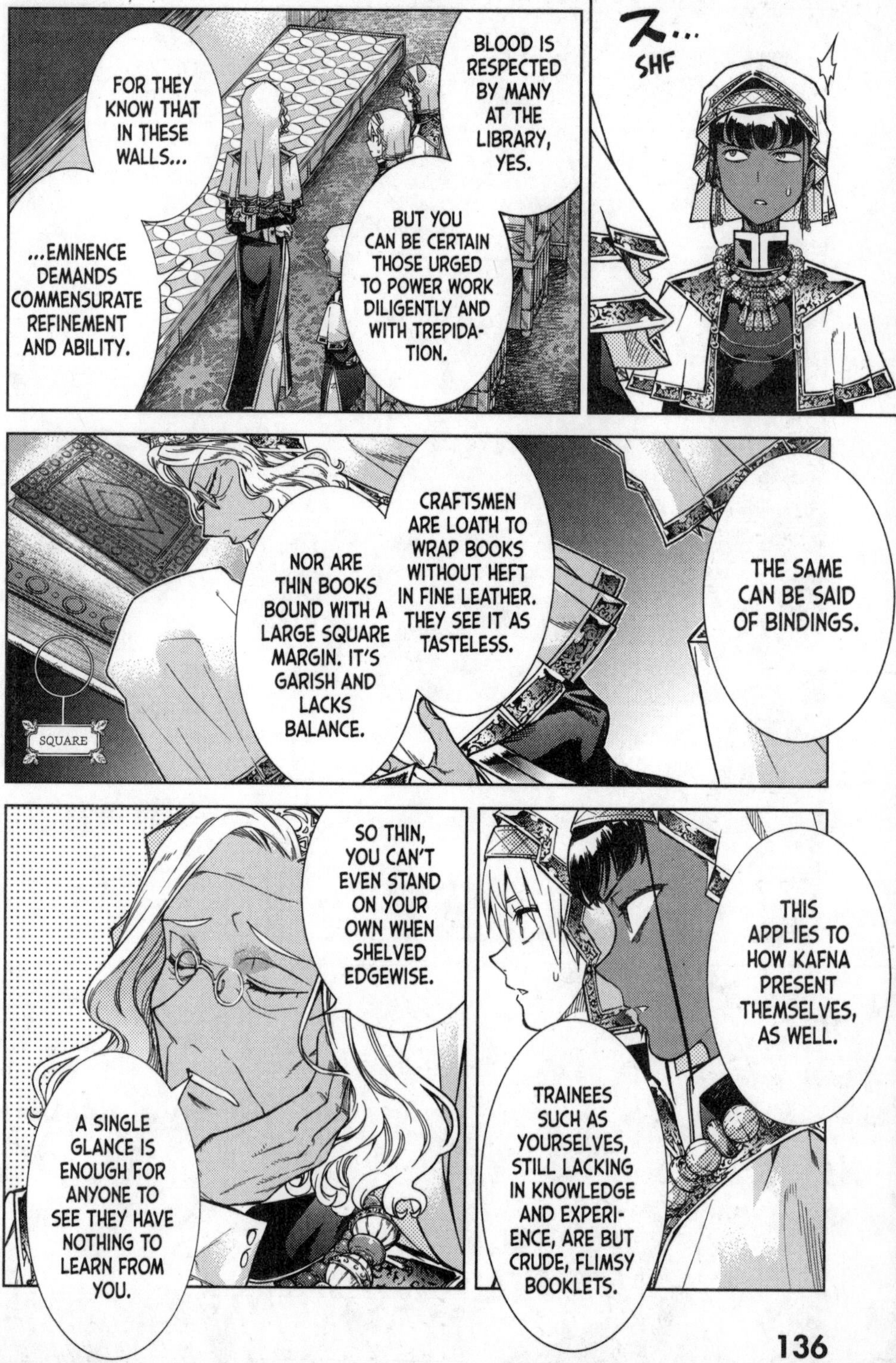

ス...
SHF
BLOOD IS RESPECTED BY MANY AT THE LIBRARY, YES.
BUT YOU CAN BE CERTAIN THOSE URGED TO POWER WORK DILIGENTLY AND WITH TREPIDA-TION.
FOR THEY KNOW THAT IN THESE WALLS...
...EMINENCE DEMANDS COMMENSURATE REFINEMENT AND ABILITY.
THE SAME CAN BE SAID OF BINDINGS.
CRAFTSMEN ARE LOATH TO WRAP BOOKS WITHOUT HEFT IN FINE LEATHER. THEY SEE IT AS TASTELESS.
NOR ARE THIN BOOKS BOUND WITH A LARGE SQUARE MARGIN. IT'S GARISH AND LACKS BALANCE.
SQUARE
THIS APPLIES TO HOW KAFNA PRESENT THEMSELVES, AS WELL.
TRAINEES SUCH AS YOURSELVES, STILL LACKING IN KNOWLEDGE AND EXPERI-ENCE, ARE BUT CRUDE, FLIMSY BOOKLETS.
SO THIN, YOU CAN'T EVEN STAND ON YOUR OWN WHEN SHELVED EDGEWISE.
A SINGLE GLANCE IS ENOUGH FOR ANYONE TO SEE THEY HAVE NOTHING TO LEARN FROM YOU.

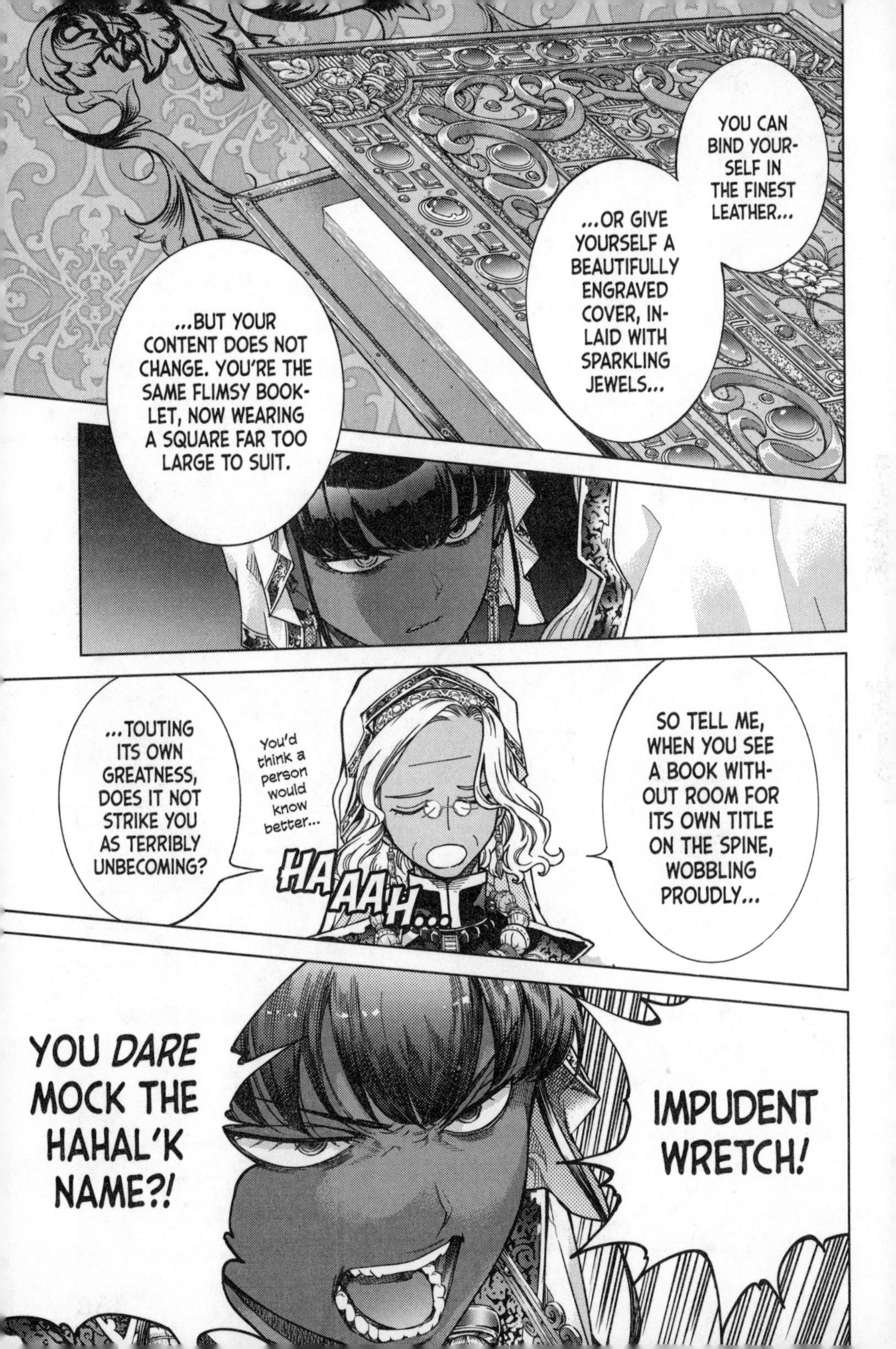
YOU CAN BIND YOURSELF IN THE FINEST LEATHER...
...OR GIVE YOURSELF A BEAUTIFULLY ENGRAVED COVER, INLAID WITH SPARKLING JEWELS...
...BUT YOUR CONTENT DOES NOT CHANGE. YOU'RE THE SAME FLIMSY BOOKLET, NOW WEARING A SQUARE FAR TOO LARGE TO SUIT.
SO TELL ME, WHEN YOU SEE A BOOK WITHOUT ROOM FOR ITS OWN TITLE ON THE SPINE, WOBBLING PROUDLY...
HAAAH...
You'd think a person would know better...
...TOUTING ITS OWN GREATNESS, DOES IT NOT STRIKE YOU AS TERRIBLY UNBECOMING?
IMPUDENT WRETCH!
YOU *DARE* MOCK THE HAHAL'K NAME?!

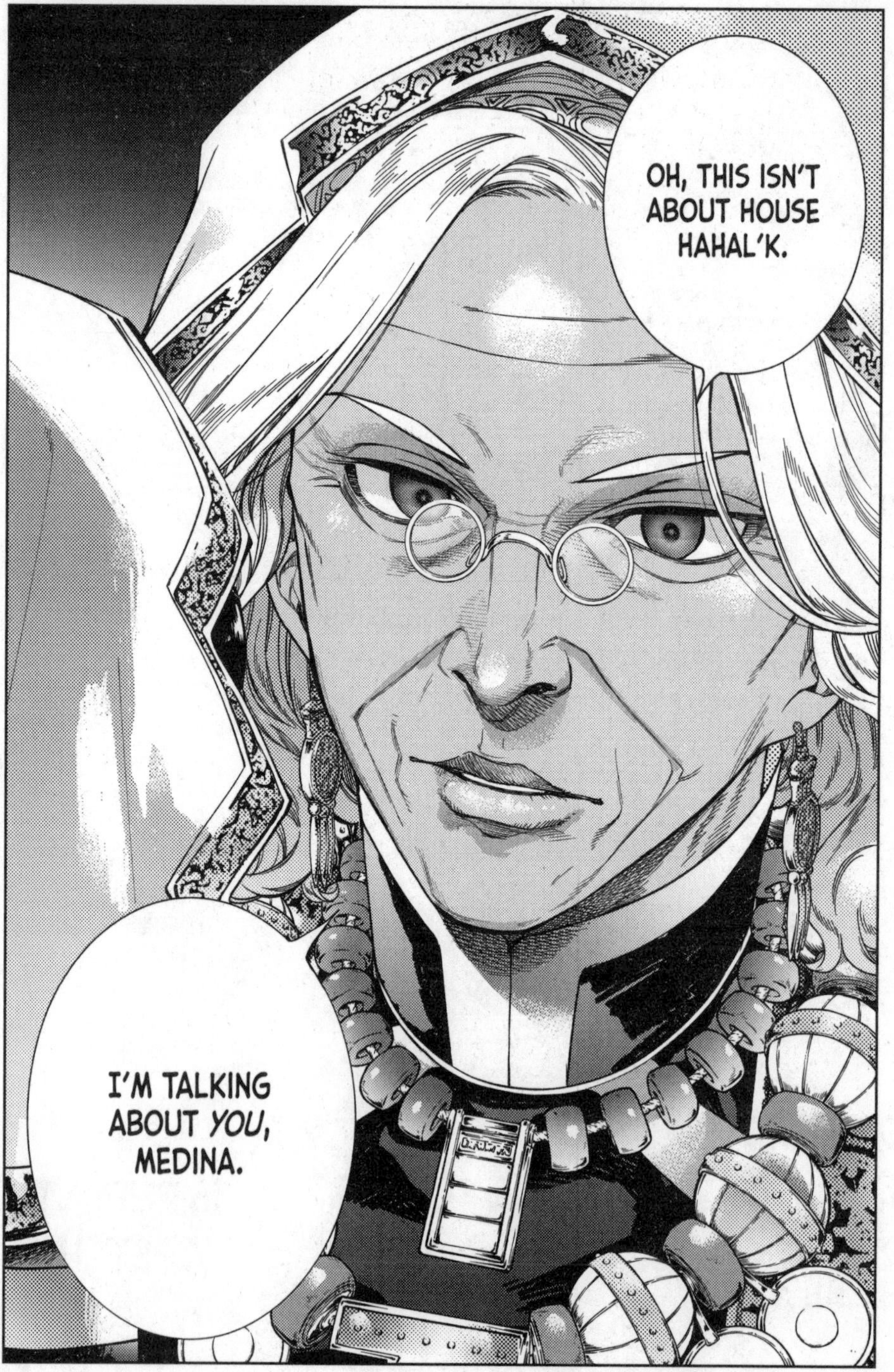
OH, THIS ISN'T ABOUT HOUSE HAHAL'K.
I'M TALKING ABOUT *YOU*, MEDINA.

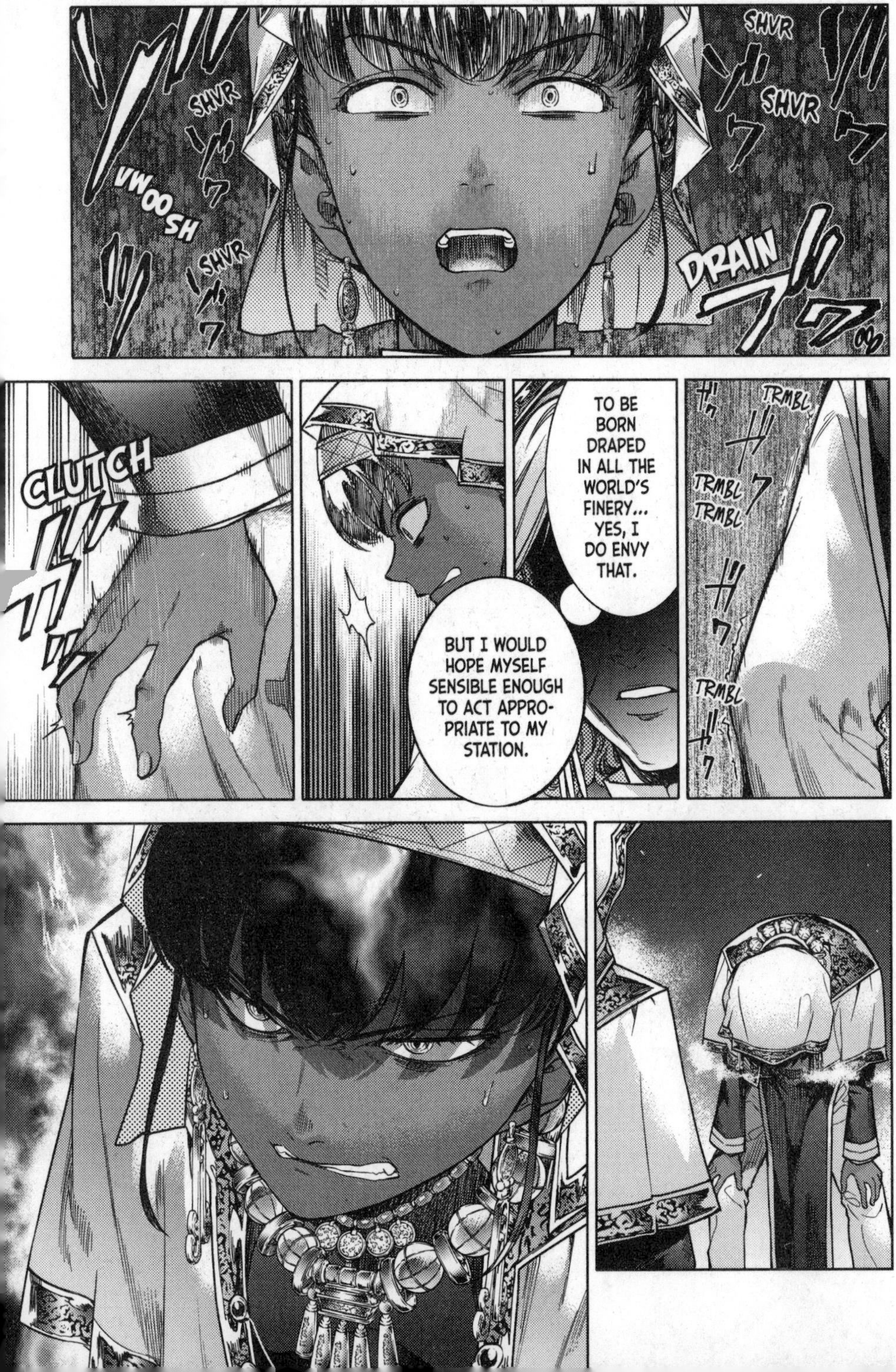

SHVR
SHVR
DRAIN
SHVR
VWOOSH
SHVR
TRMBL
TRMBL
TRMBL
TRMBL
TO BE BORN DRAPED IN ALL THE WORLD'S FINERY... YES, I DO ENVY THAT.
BUT I WOULD HOPE MYSELF SENSIBLE ENOUGH TO ACT APPROPRIATE TO MY STATION.
CLUTCH

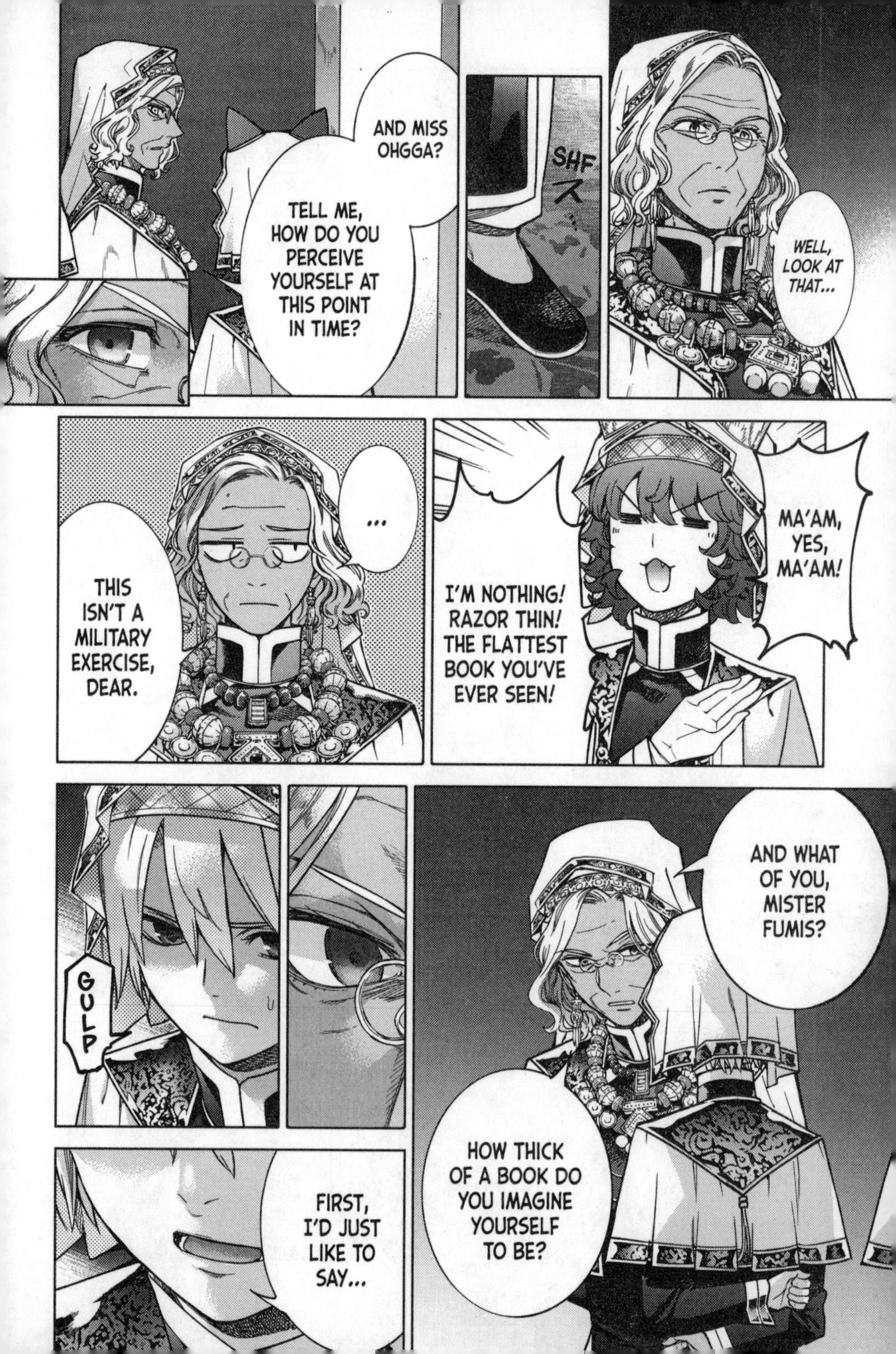
WELL, LOOK AT THAT...
SHF
ス
AND MISS OHGGA?
TELL ME, HOW DO YOU PERCEIVE YOURSELF AT THIS POINT IN TIME?
MA'AM, YES, MA'AM!
I'M NOTHING! RAZOR THIN! THE FLATTEST BOOK YOU'VE EVER SEEN!
...
THIS ISN'T A MILITARY EXERCISE, DEAR.
AND WHAT OF YOU, MISTER FUMIS?
HOW THICK OF A BOOK DO YOU IMAGINE YOURSELF TO BE?
GULP
FIRST, I'D JUST LIKE TO SAY...

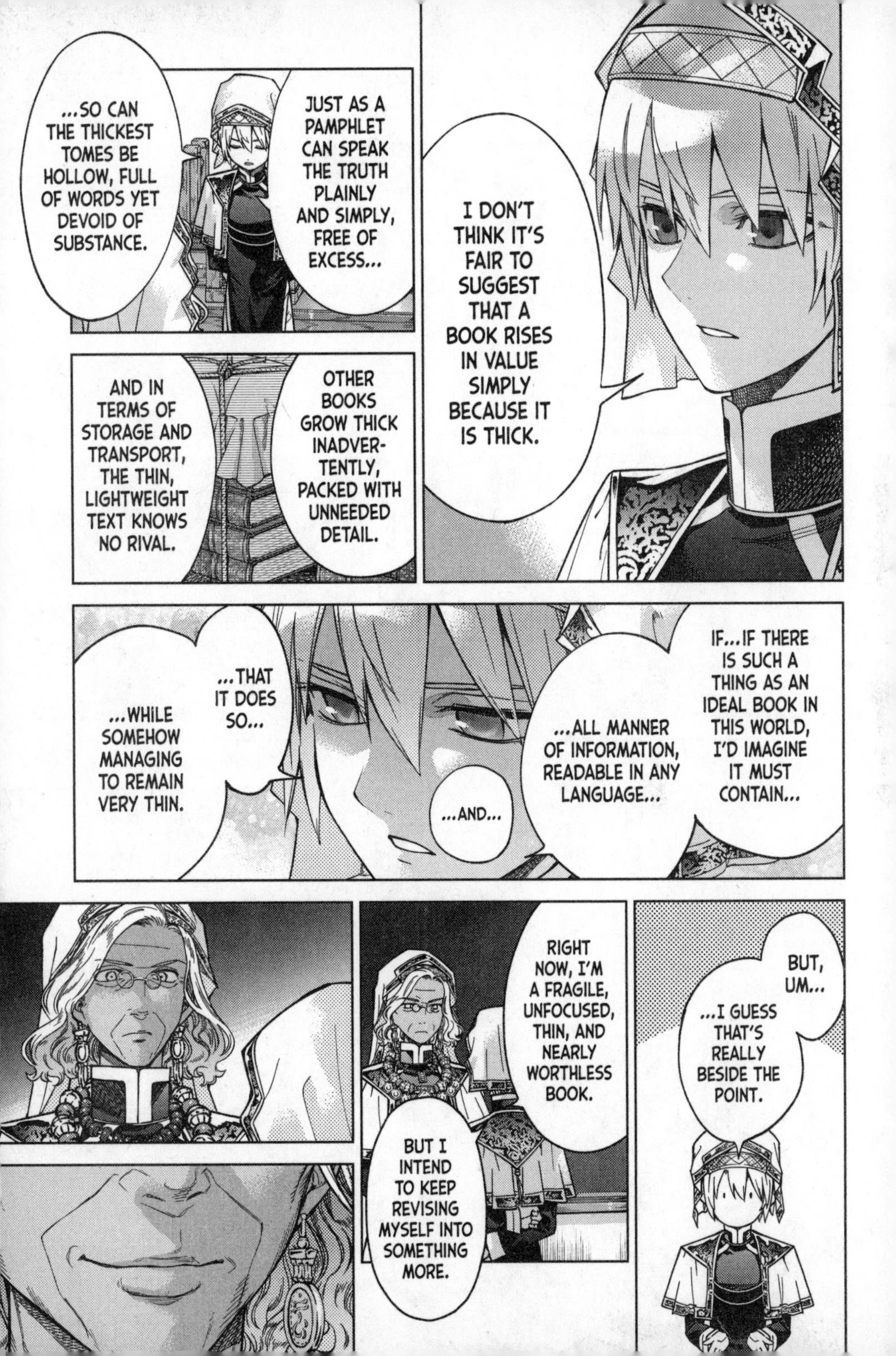
I DON'T THINK IT'S FAIR TO SUGGEST THAT A BOOK RISES IN VALUE SIMPLY BECAUSE IT IS THICK.
JUST AS A PAMPHLET CAN SPEAK THE TRUTH PLAINLY AND SIMPLY, FREE OF EXCESS...
...SO CAN THE THICKEST TOMES BE HOLLOW, FULL OF WORDS YET DEVOID OF SUBSTANCE.
OTHER BOOKS GROW THICK INADVER-TENTLY, PACKED WITH UNNEEDED DETAIL.
AND IN TERMS OF STORAGE AND TRANSPORT, THE THIN, LIGHTWEIGHT TEXT KNOWS NO RIVAL.
IF...IF THERE IS SUCH A THING AS AN IDEAL BOOK IN THIS WORLD, I'D IMAGINE IT MUST CONTAIN...
...ALL MANNER OF INFORMATION, READABLE IN ANY LANGUAGE...
...AND...
...THAT IT DOES SO...
...WHILE SOMEHOW MANAGING TO REMAIN VERY THIN.
BUT, UM...
...I GUESS THAT'S REALLY BESIDE THE POINT.
RIGHT NOW, I'M A FRAGILE, UNFOCUSED, THIN, AND NEARLY WORTHLESS BOOK.
BUT I INTEND TO KEEP REVISING MYSELF INTO SOMETHING MORE.

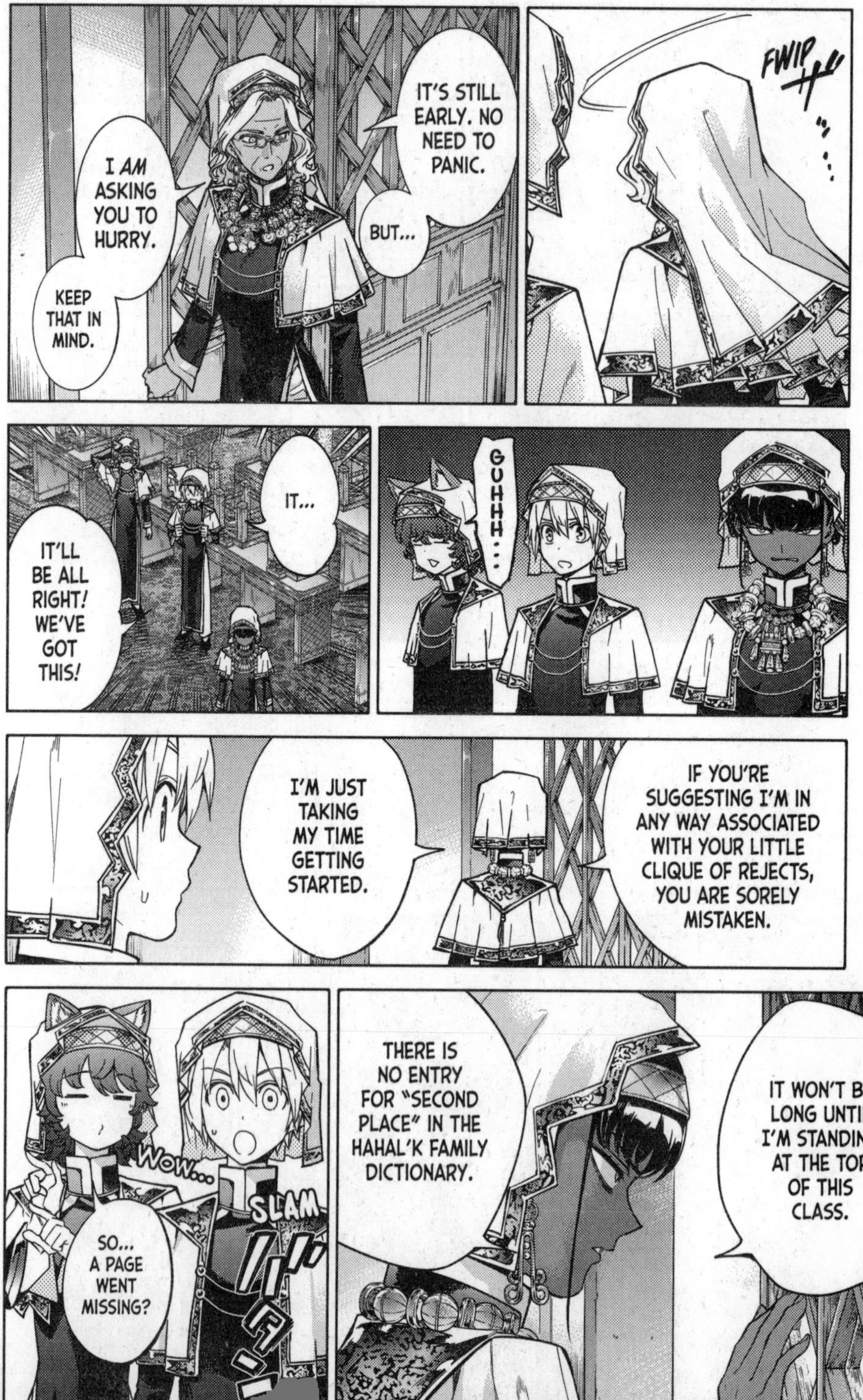

FWIP
...
IT'S STILL EARLY. NO NEED TO PANIC.
BUT...
I *AM* ASKING YOU TO HURRY.
KEEP THAT IN MIND.
GUHHH...
IT...
IT'LL BE ALL RIGHT! WE'VE GOT THIS!
IF YOU'RE SUGGESTING I'M IN ANY WAY ASSOCIATED WITH YOUR LITTLE CLIQUE OF REJECTS, YOU ARE SORELY MISTAKEN.
I'M JUST TAKING MY TIME GETTING STARTED.
IT WON'T BE LONG UNTIL I'M STANDING AT THE TOP OF THIS CLASS.
THERE IS NO ENTRY FOR "SECOND PLACE" IN THE HAHAL'K FAMILY DICTIONARY.
SLAM
WOW...
SO... A PAGE WENT MISSING?

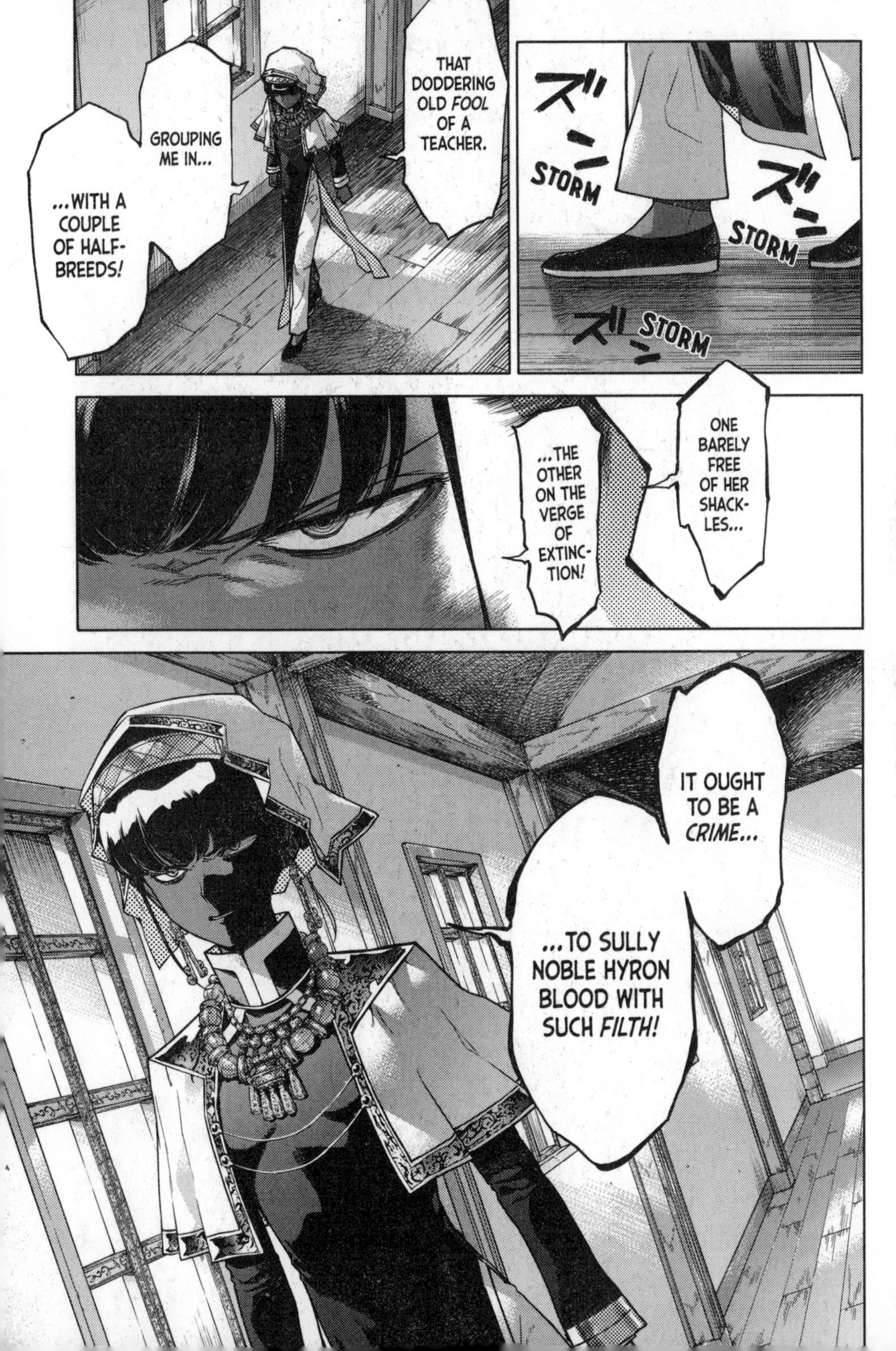
ズン STORM
ズン STORM
ズン STORM
THAT DODDERING OLD *FOOL* OF A TEACHER.
GROUPING ME IN...
...WITH A COUPLE OF HALF-BREEDS!
ONE BARELY FREE OF HER SHACKLES...
...THE OTHER ON THE VERGE OF EXTINCTION!
IT OUGHT TO BE A *CRIME*...
...TO SULLY NOBLE HYRON BLOOD WITH SUCH *FILTH*!

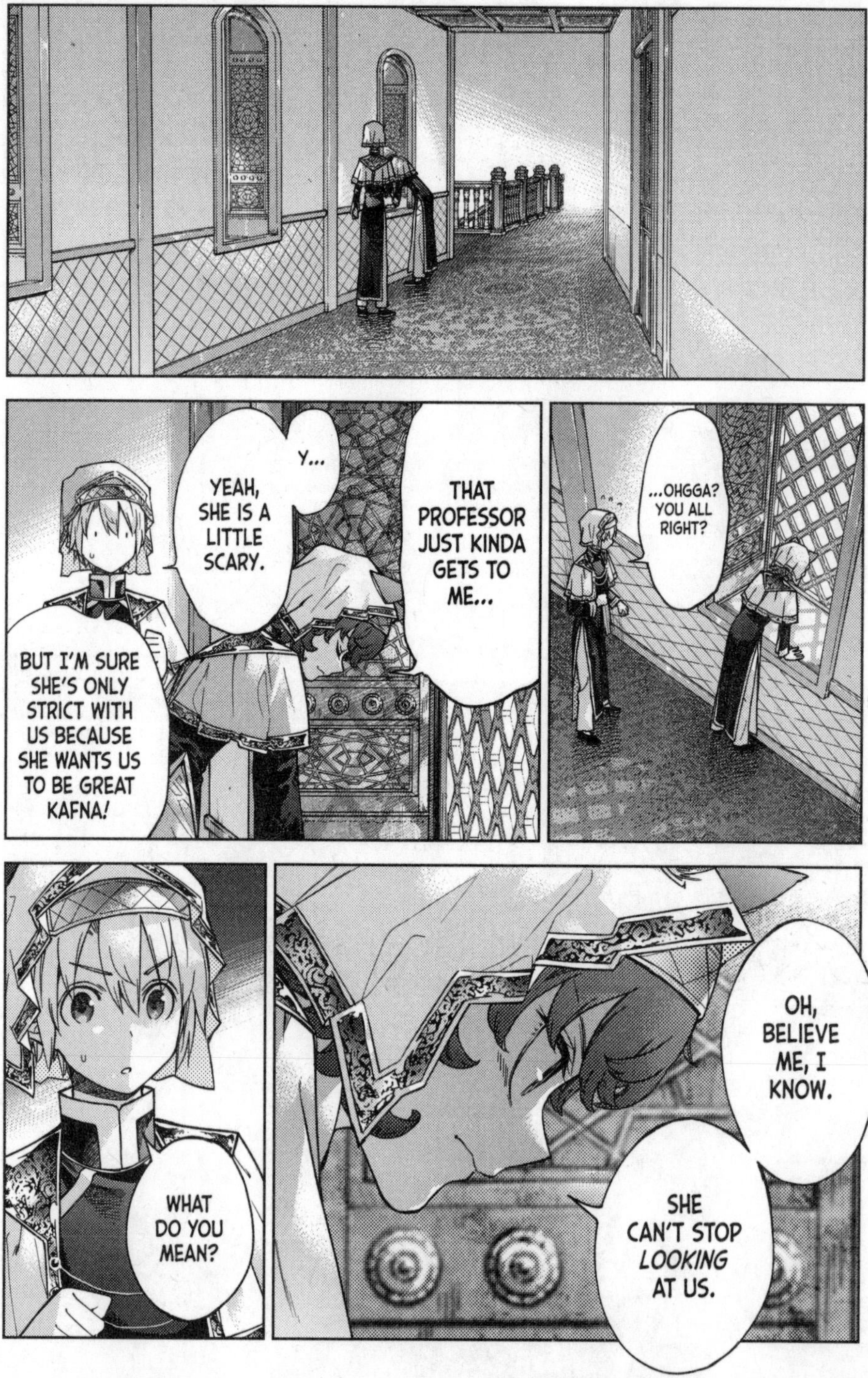
...OHGGA? YOU ALL RIGHT?
THAT PROFESSOR JUST KINDA GETS TO ME...
Y...
YEAH, SHE IS A LITTLE SCARY.
BUT I'M SURE SHE'S ONLY STRICT WITH US BECAUSE SHE WANTS US TO BE GREAT KAFNA!
OH, BELIEVE ME, I KNOW.
SHE CAN'T STOP *LOOKING* AT US.
WHAT DO YOU MEAN?

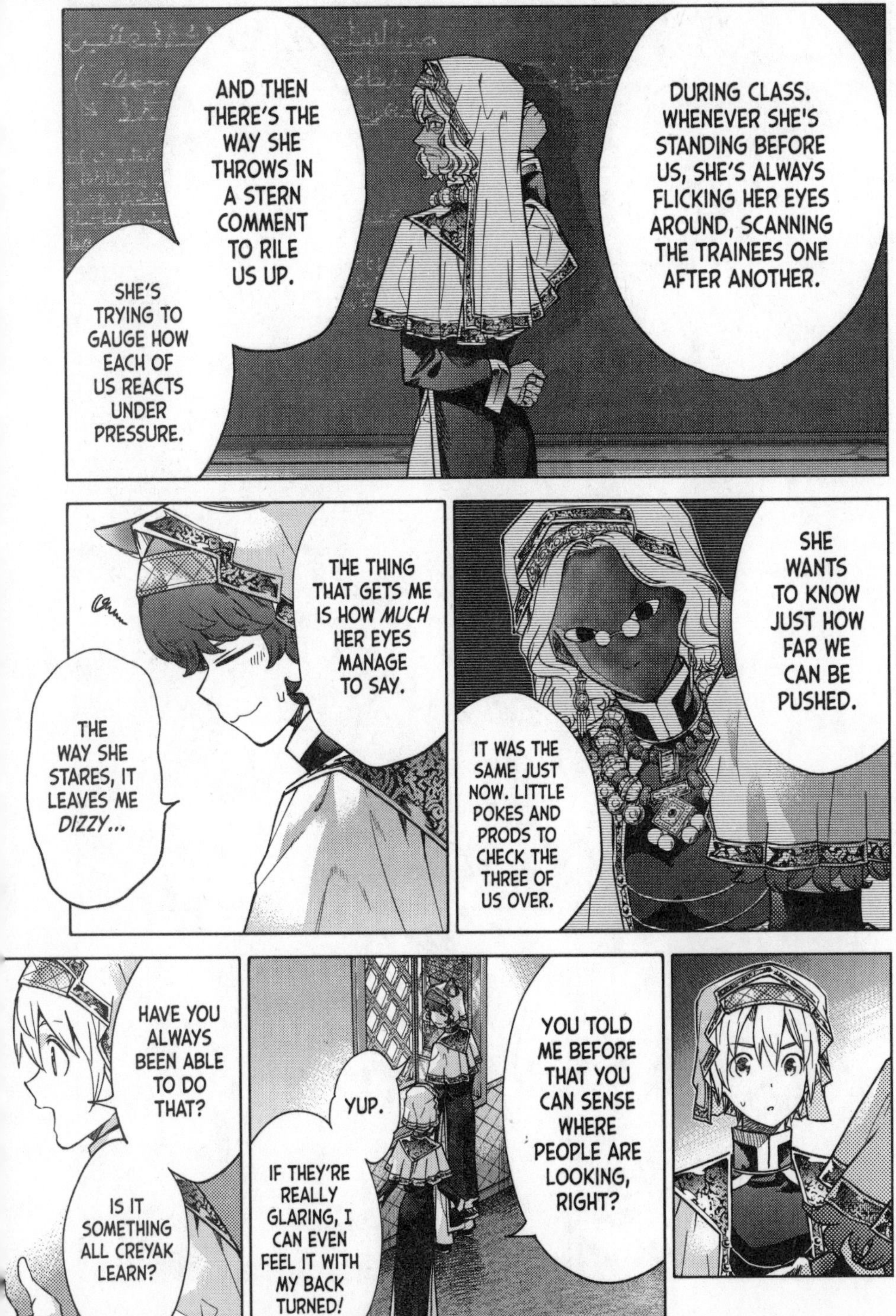
DURING CLASS. WHENEVER SHE'S STANDING BEFORE US, SHE'S ALWAYS FLICKING HER EYES AROUND, SCANNING THE TRAINEES ONE AFTER ANOTHER.
AND THEN THERE'S THE WAY SHE THROWS IN A STERN COMMENT TO RILE US UP.
SHE'S TRYING TO GAUGE HOW EACH OF US REACTS UNDER PRESSURE.
SHE WANTS TO KNOW JUST HOW FAR WE CAN BE PUSHED.
IT WAS THE SAME JUST NOW. LITTLE POKES AND PRODS TO CHECK THE THREE OF US OVER.
THE THING THAT GETS ME IS HOW *MUCH* HER EYES MANAGE TO SAY.
THE WAY SHE STARES, IT LEAVES ME *DIZZY*...
YOU TOLD ME BEFORE THAT YOU CAN SENSE WHERE PEOPLE ARE LOOKING, RIGHT?
YUP.
IF THEY'RE REALLY GLARING, I CAN EVEN FEEL IT WITH MY BACK TURNED*!*
HAVE YOU ALWAYS BEEN ABLE TO DO THAT?
IS IT SOMETHING ALL CREYAK LEARN?

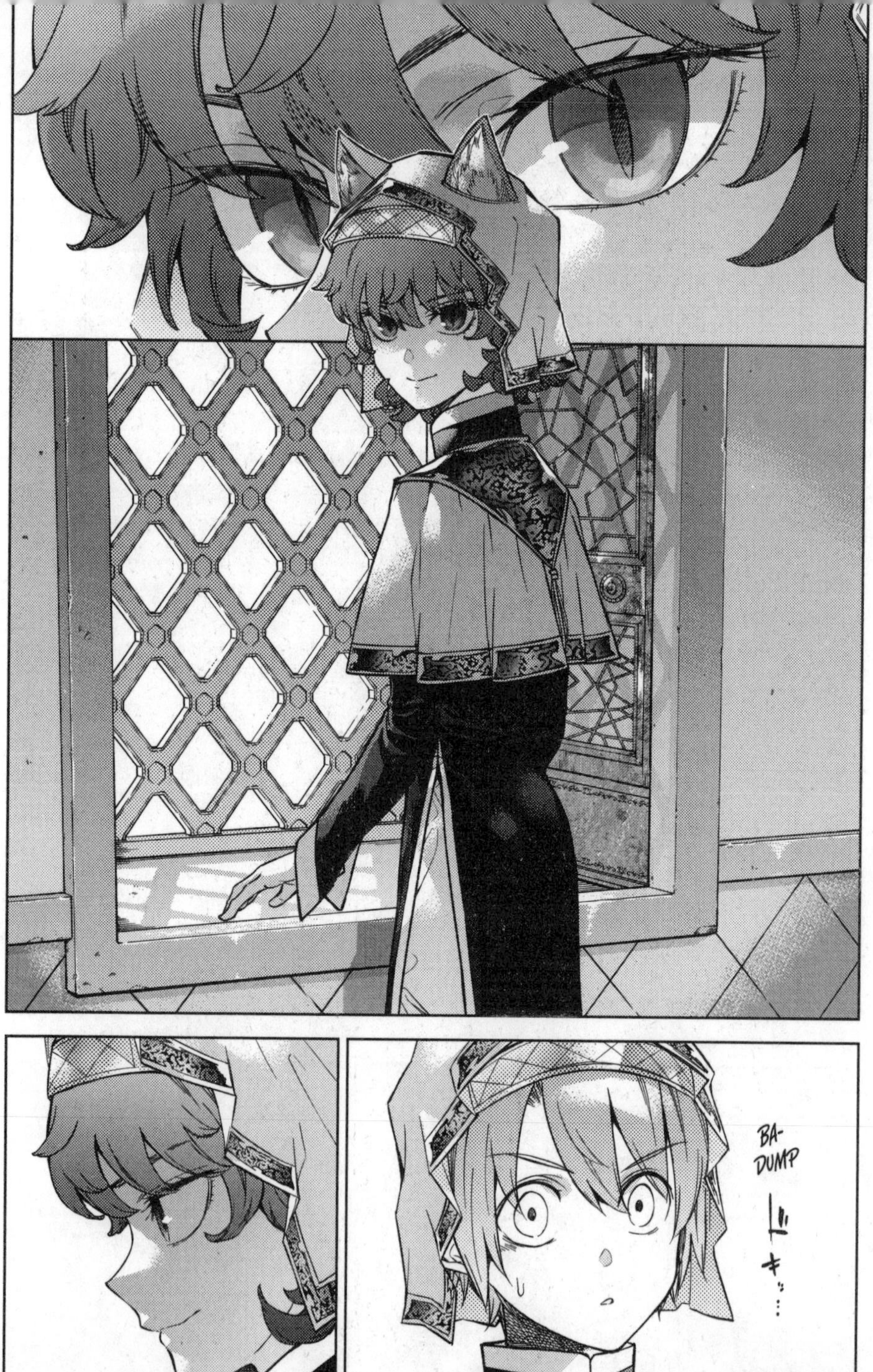
BA-
DUMP
ドキッ…

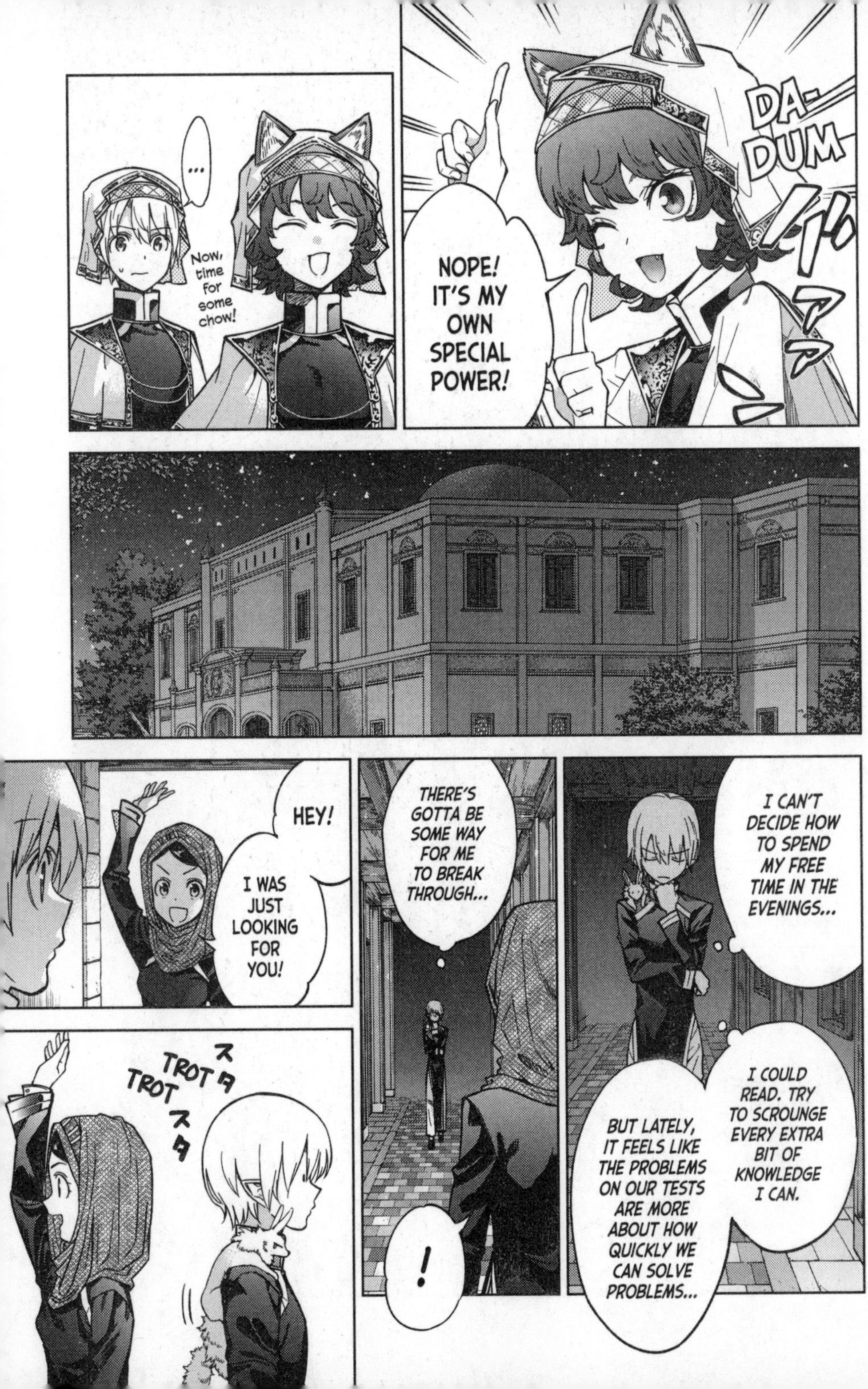
NOPE! IT'S MY OWN SPECIAL POWER!
DA-DUM
...
Now, time for some chow!
I CAN'T DECIDE HOW TO SPEND MY FREE TIME IN THE EVENINGS...
I COULD READ. TRY TO SCROUNGE EVERY EXTRA BIT OF KNOWLEDGE I CAN.
BUT LATELY, IT FEELS LIKE THE PROBLEMS ON OUR TESTS ARE MORE ABOUT HOW QUICKLY WE CAN SOLVE PROBLEMS...
THERE'S GOTTA BE SOME WAY FOR ME TO BREAK THROUGH...
!
HEY!
I WAS JUST LOOKING FOR YOU!
TROT スタ
TROT スタ

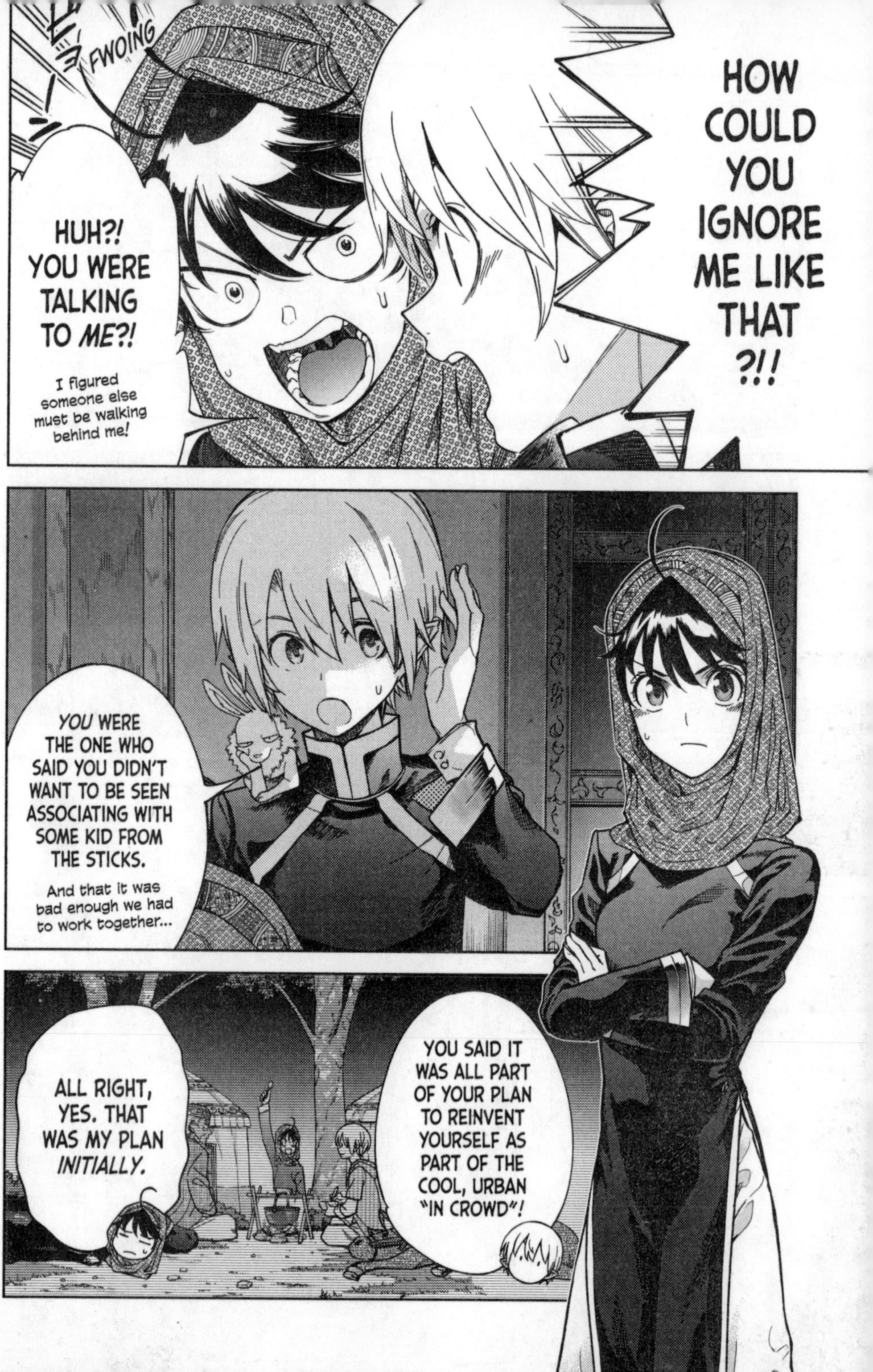
HOW COULD YOU IGNORE ME LIKE THAT?!!
FWOING
HUH?! YOU WERE TALKING TO ME?!
I figured someone else must be walking behind me!
YOU WERE THE ONE WHO SAID YOU DIDN'T WANT TO BE SEEN ASSOCIATING WITH SOME KID FROM THE STICKS.
And that it was bad enough we had to work together...
YOU SAID IT WAS ALL PART OF YOUR PLAN TO REINVENT YOURSELF AS PART OF THE COOL, URBAN "IN CROWD"!
ALL RIGHT, YES. THAT WAS MY PLAN INITIALLY.

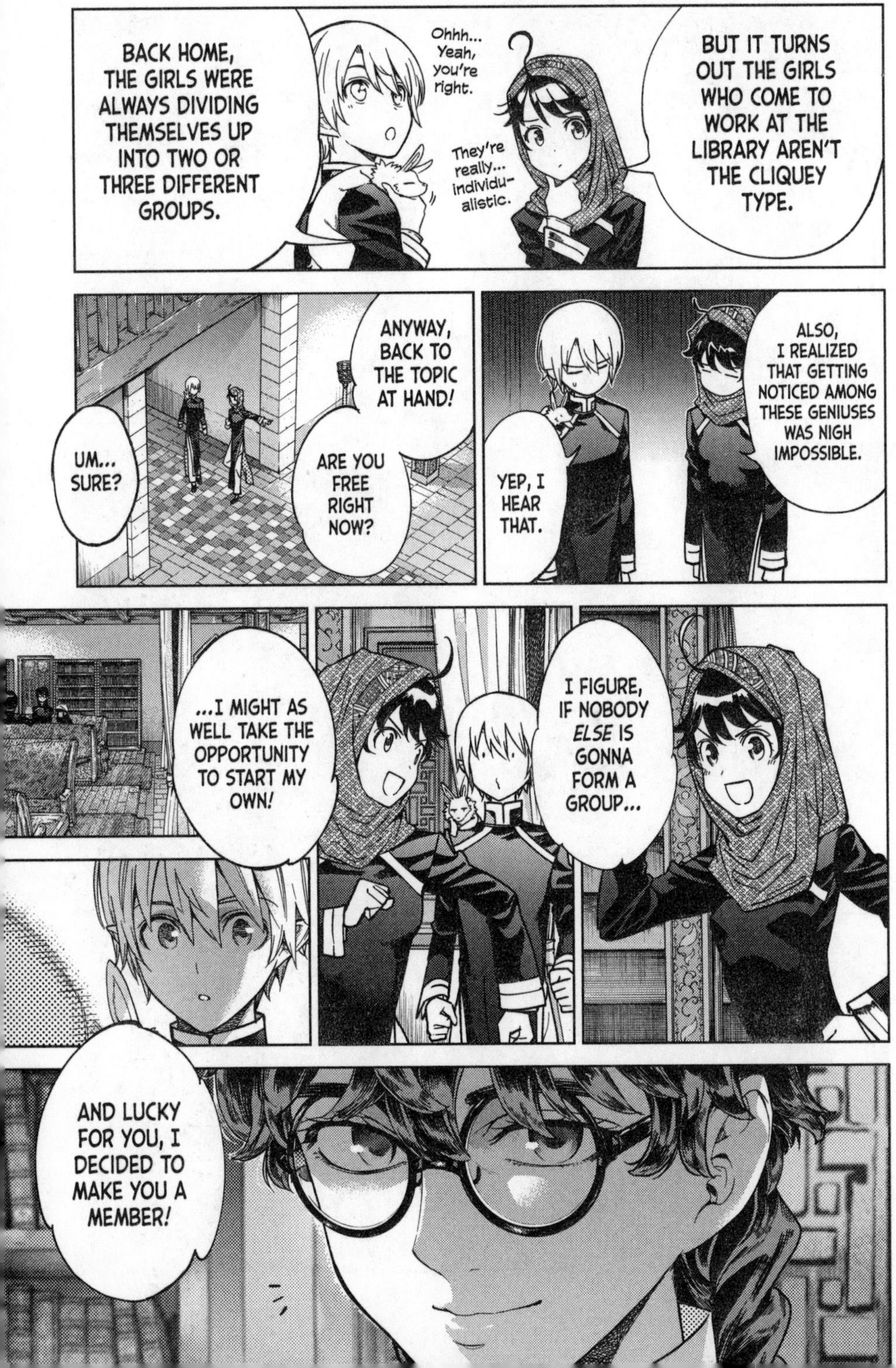
BUT IT TURNS OUT THE GIRLS WHO COME TO WORK AT THE LIBRARY AREN'T THE CLIQUEY TYPE.
They're really... individualistic.
Ohhh... Yeah, you're right.
BACK HOME, THE GIRLS WERE ALWAYS DIVIDING THEMSELVES UP INTO TWO OR THREE DIFFERENT GROUPS.
ALSO, I REALIZED THAT GETTING NOTICED AMONG THESE GENIUSES WAS NIGH IMPOSSIBLE.
YEP, I HEAR THAT.
ANYWAY, BACK TO THE TOPIC AT HAND!
ARE YOU FREE RIGHT NOW?
UM... SURE?
I FIGURE, IF NOBODY *ELSE* IS GONNA FORM A GROUP...
...I MIGHT AS WELL TAKE THE OPPORTUNITY TO START MY OWN!
AND LUCKY FOR YOU, I DECIDED TO MAKE YOU A MEMBER!

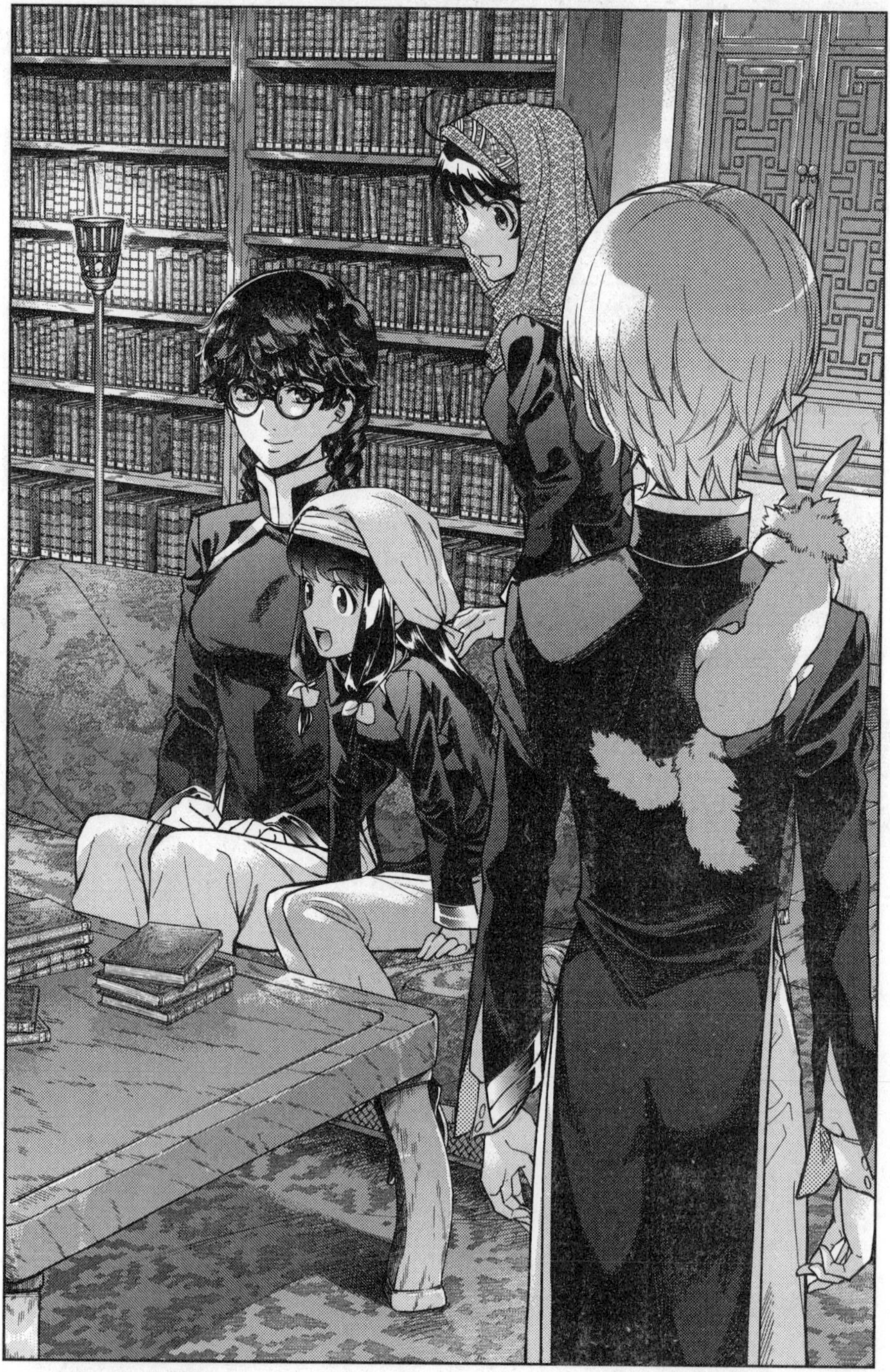

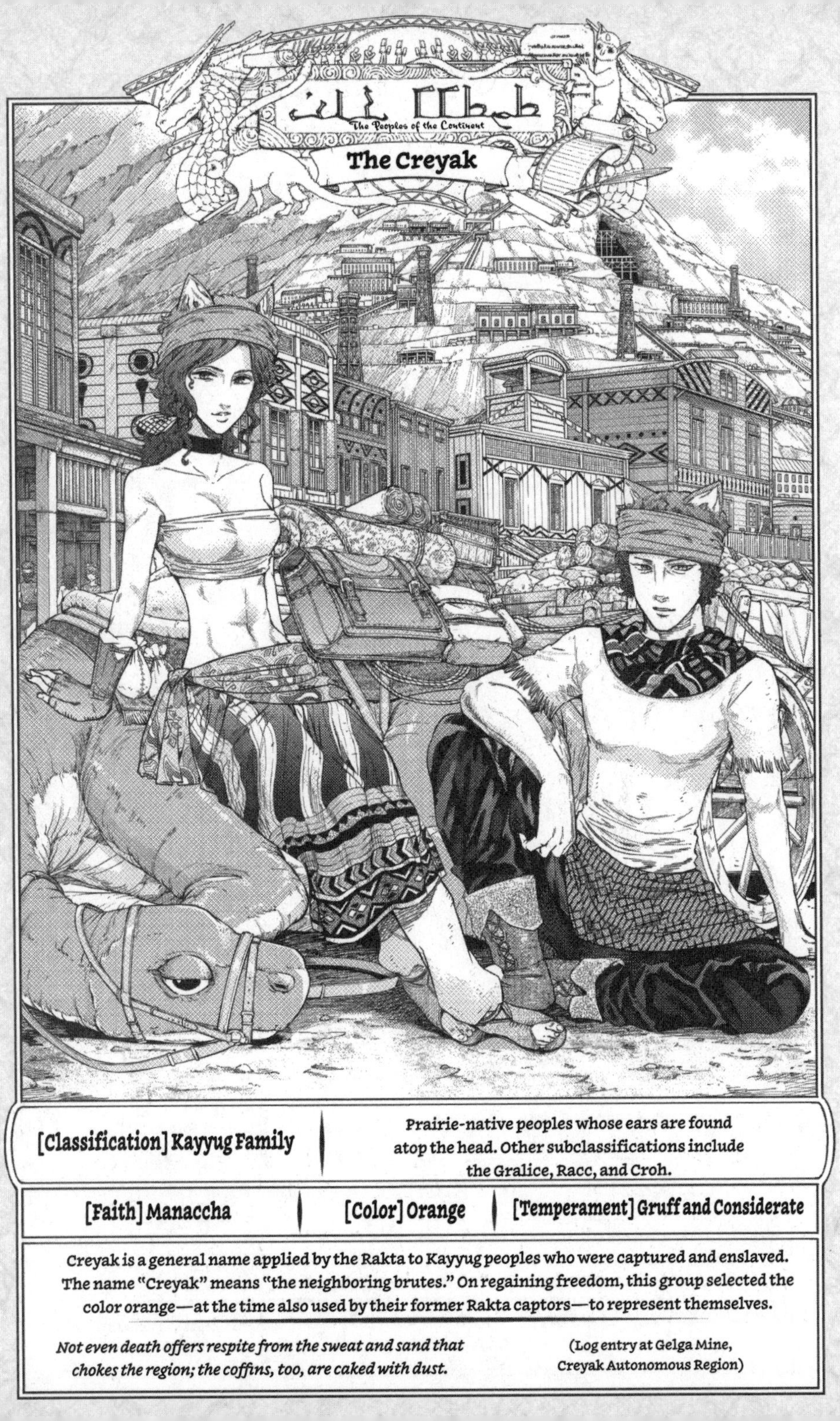
The Peoples of the Continent
The Creyak

[Classification] Kayyug Family

Prairie-native peoples whose ears are found atop the head. Other subclassifications include the Gralice, Racc, and Croh.

[Faith] Manaccha | **[Color] Orange** | **[Temperament] Gruff and Considerate**

Creyak is a general name applied by the Rakta to Kayyug peoples who were captured and enslaved. The name "Creyak" means "the neighboring brutes." On regaining freedom, this group selected the color orange—at the time also used by their former Rakta captors—to represent themselves.

Not even death offers respite from the sweat and sand that chokes the region; the coffins, too, are caked with dust.

(Log entry at Gelga Mine, Creyak Autonomous Region)

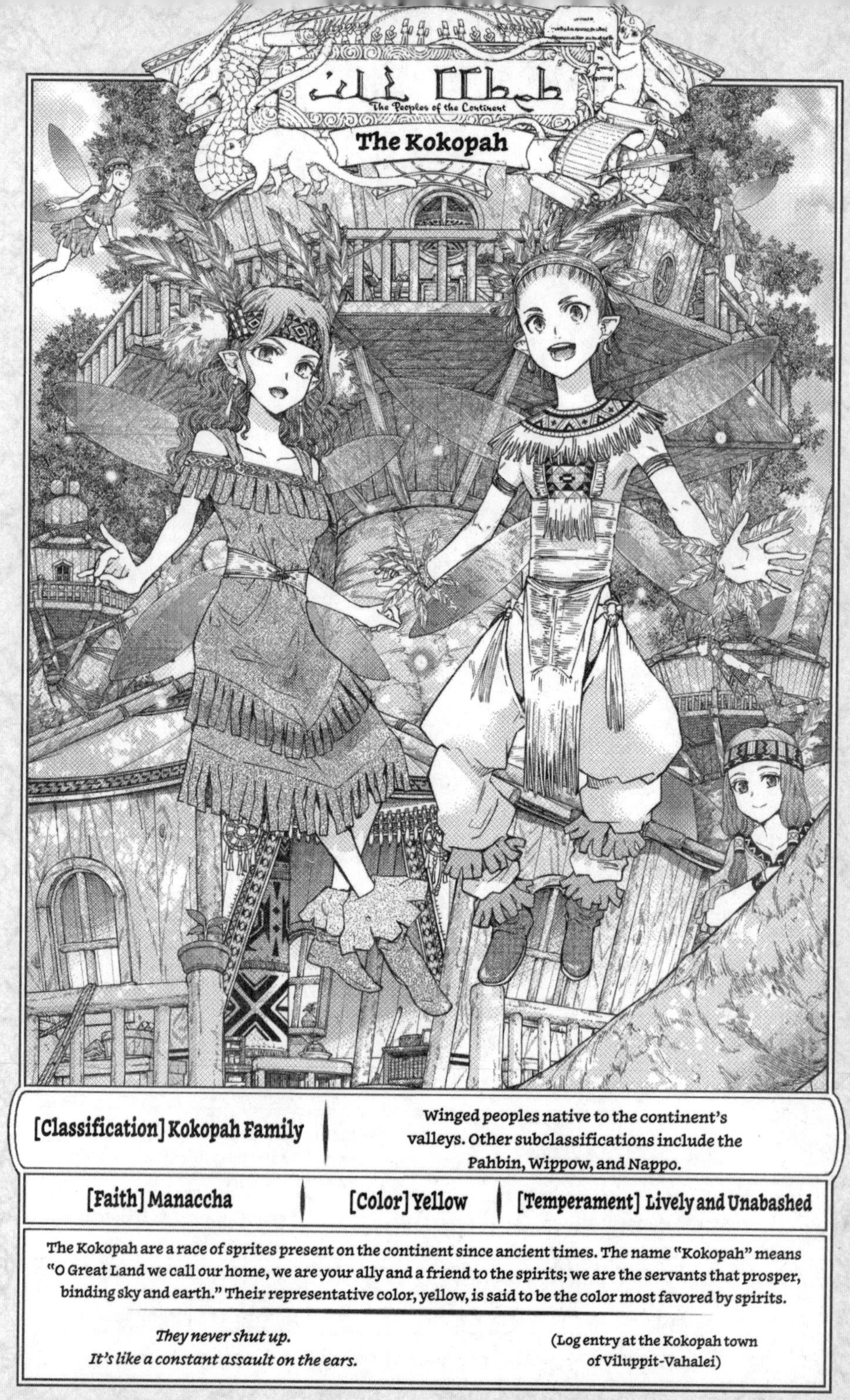
The Peoples of the Continent
The Kokopah

[Classification] Kokopah Family	Winged peoples native to the continent's valleys. Other subclassifications include the Pahbin, Wippow, and Nappo.

[Faith] Manaccha	[Color] Yellow	[Temperament] Lively and Unabashed

The Kokopah are a race of sprites present on the continent since ancient times. The name "Kokopah" means "O Great Land we call our home, we are your ally and a friend to the spirits; we are the servants that prosper, binding sky and earth." Their representative color, yellow, is said to be the color most favored by spirits.

They never shut up.
It's like a constant assault on the ears.

(Log entry at the Kokopah town of Viluppit-Vahalei)

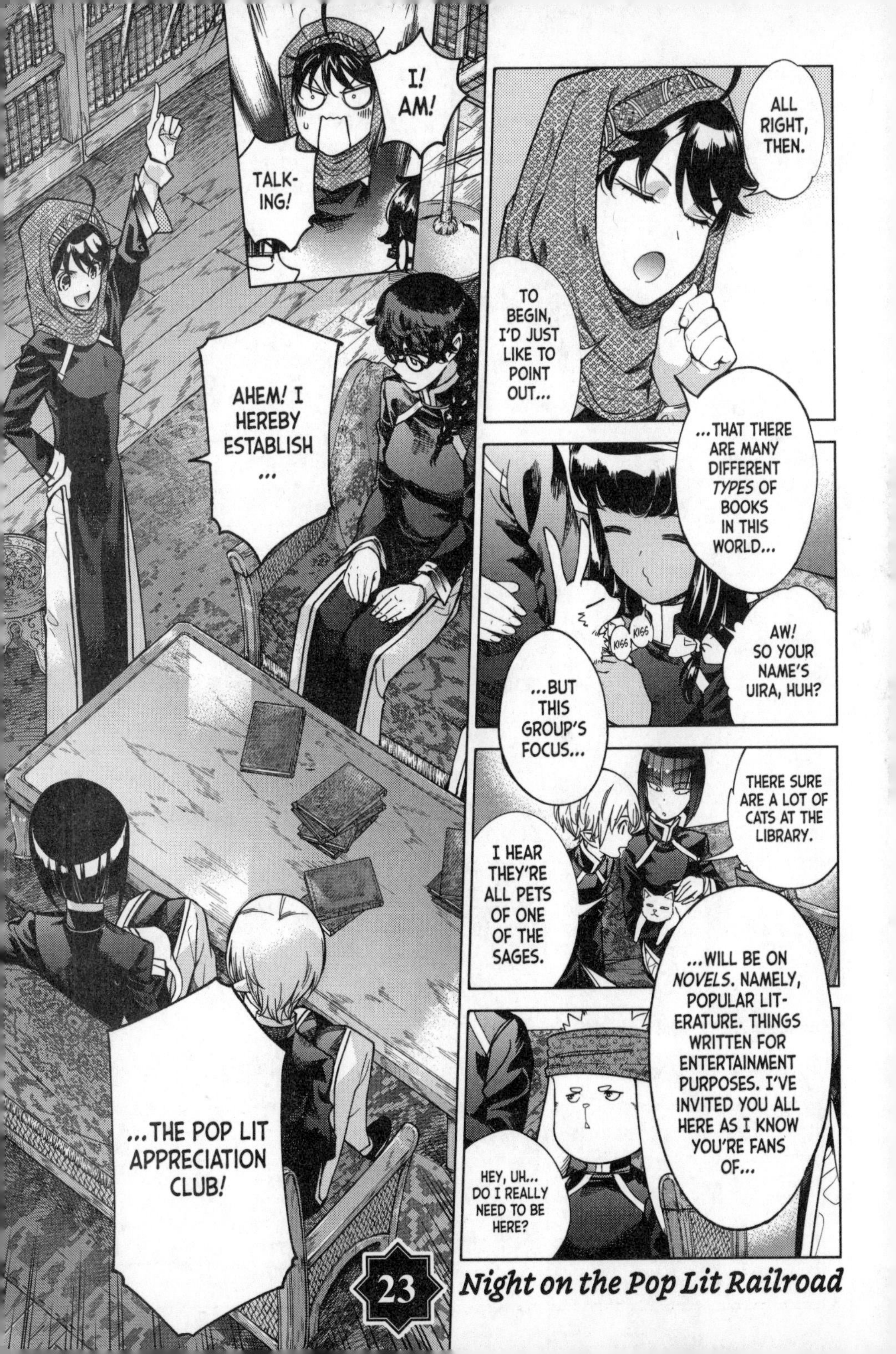
ALL RIGHT, THEN.
TO BEGIN, I'D JUST LIKE TO POINT OUT...
...THAT THERE ARE MANY DIFFERENT *TYPES* OF BOOKS IN THIS WORLD...
AW! SO YOUR NAME'S UIRA, HUH?
KISS
KISS
...BUT THIS GROUP'S FOCUS...
THERE SURE ARE A LOT OF CATS AT THE LIBRARY.
I HEAR THEY'RE ALL PETS OF ONE OF THE SAGES.
...WILL BE ON *NOVELS*. NAMELY, POPULAR LIT-ERATURE. THINGS WRITTEN FOR ENTERTAINMENT PURPOSES. I'VE INVITED YOU ALL HERE AS I KNOW YOU'RE FANS OF...
HEY, UH... DO I REALLY NEED TO BE HERE?
I! AM! TALKING!
AHEM! I HEREBY ESTABLISH ...
...THE POP LIT APPRECIATION CLUB!

23 *Night on the Pop Lit Railroad*

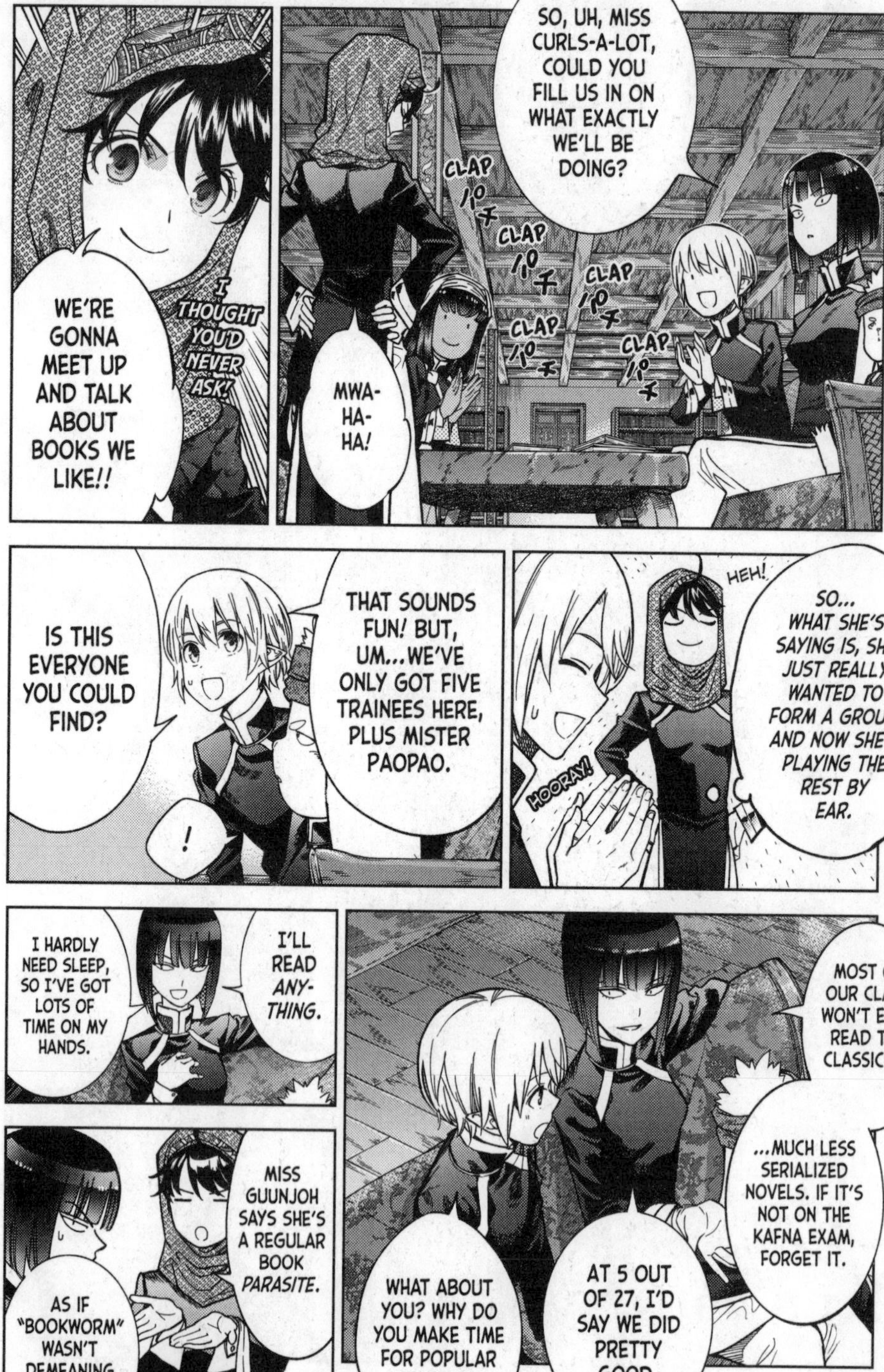
SO, UH, MISS CURLS-A-LOT, COULD YOU FILL US IN ON WHAT EXACTLY WE'LL BE DOING?
CLAP パチ
CLAP パチ
CLAP パチ
CLAP パチ
CLAP パチ
MWA-HA-HA!
I THOUGHT YOU'D NEVER ASK!
WE'RE GONNA MEET UP AND TALK ABOUT BOOKS WE LIKE!!
HEH!
SO... WHAT SHE'S SAYING IS, SHE JUST REALLY WANTED TO FORM A GROUP, AND NOW SHE'S PLAYING THE REST BY EAR.
HOORAY!
THAT SOUNDS FUN! BUT, UM...WE'VE ONLY GOT FIVE TRAINEES HERE, PLUS MISTER PAOPAO.
IS THIS EVERYONE YOU COULD FIND?
!
MOST OF OUR CLASS WON'T EVEN READ THE CLASSICS...
...MUCH LESS SERIALIZED NOVELS. IF IT'S NOT ON THE KAFNA EXAM, FORGET IT.
AT 5 OUT OF 27, I'D SAY WE DID PRETTY GOOD.
WHAT ABOUT YOU? WHY DO YOU MAKE TIME FOR POPULAR FICTION?
I'LL READ ANY-THING.
I HARDLY NEED SLEEP, SO I'VE GOT LOTS OF TIME ON MY HANDS.
MISS GUUNJOH SAYS SHE'S A REGULAR BOOK PARASITE.
AS IF "BOOKWORM" WASN'T DEMEANING ENOUGH...

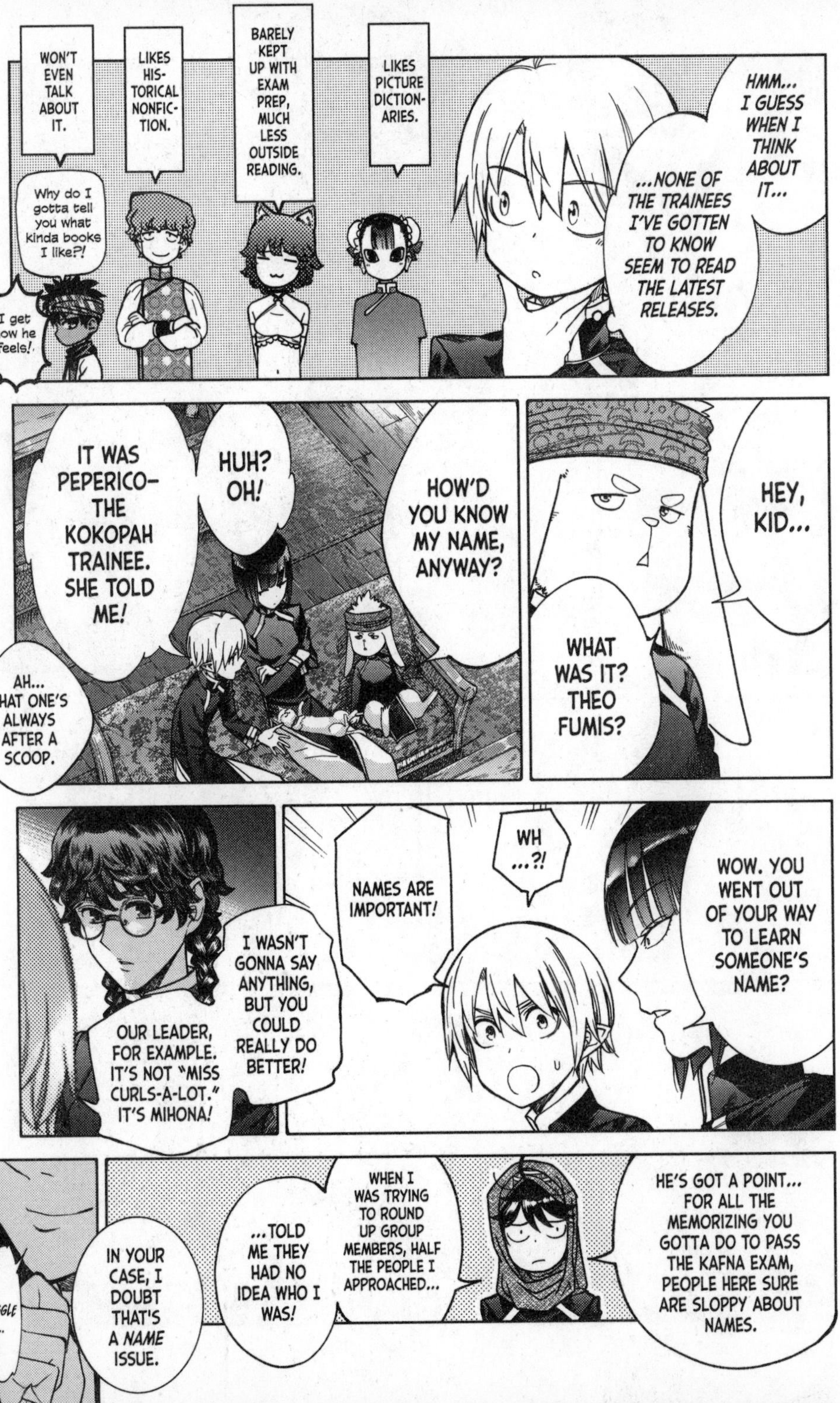
HMM... I GUESS WHEN I THINK ABOUT IT...
...NONE OF THE TRAINEES I'VE GOTTEN TO KNOW SEEM TO READ THE LATEST RELEASES.
LIKES PICTURE DICTIONARIES.
BARELY KEPT UP WITH EXAM PREP, MUCH LESS OUTSIDE READING.
LIKES HISTORICAL NONFICTION.
WON'T EVEN TALK ABOUT IT.
Why do I gotta tell you what kinda books I like?!
I get how he feels!
HEY, KID...
WHAT WAS IT? THEO FUMIS?
HOW'D YOU KNOW MY NAME, ANYWAY?
HUH? OH!
IT WAS PEPERICO— THE KOKOPAH TRAINEE. SHE TOLD ME!
AH... THAT ONE'S ALWAYS AFTER A SCOOP.
WOW. YOU WENT OUT OF YOUR WAY TO LEARN SOMEONE'S NAME?
WH...?!
NAMES ARE IMPORTANT!
I WASN'T GONNA SAY ANYTHING, BUT YOU COULD REALLY DO BETTER!
OUR LEADER, FOR EXAMPLE. IT'S NOT "MISS CURLS-A-LOT." IT'S MIHONA!
HE'S GOT A POINT... FOR ALL THE MEMORIZING YOU GOTTA DO TO PASS THE KAFNA EXAM, PEOPLE HERE SURE ARE SLOPPY ABOUT NAMES.
WHEN I WAS TRYING TO ROUND UP GROUP MEMBERS, HALF THE PEOPLE I APPROACHED...
...TOLD ME THEY HAD NO IDEA WHO I WAS!
IN YOUR CASE, I DOUBT THAT'S A *NAME* ISSUE.
GIGGLE...

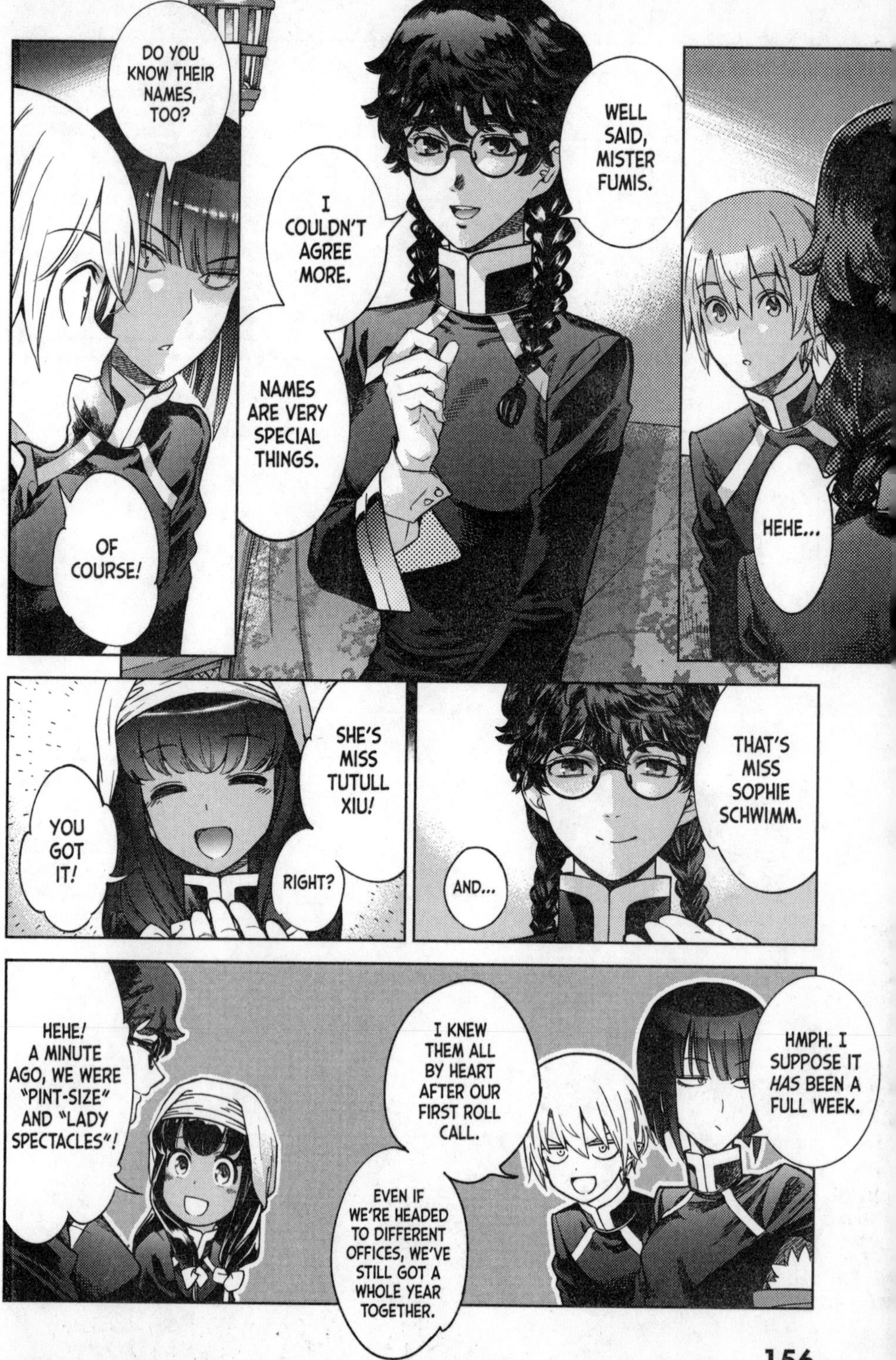
WELL SAID, MISTER FUMIS.
I COULDN'T AGREE MORE.
NAMES ARE VERY SPECIAL THINGS.
HEHE...
DO YOU KNOW THEIR NAMES, TOO?
OF COURSE!
THAT'S MISS SOPHIE SCHWIMM.
AND...
SHE'S MISS TUTULL XIU!
RIGHT?
YOU GOT IT!
HMPH. I SUPPOSE IT *HAS* BEEN A FULL WEEK.
I KNEW THEM ALL BY HEART AFTER OUR FIRST ROLL CALL.
EVEN IF WE'RE HEADED TO DIFFERENT OFFICES, WE'VE STILL GOT A WHOLE YEAR TOGETHER.
HEHE! A MINUTE AGO, WE WERE "PINT-SIZE" AND "LADY SPECTACLES"!

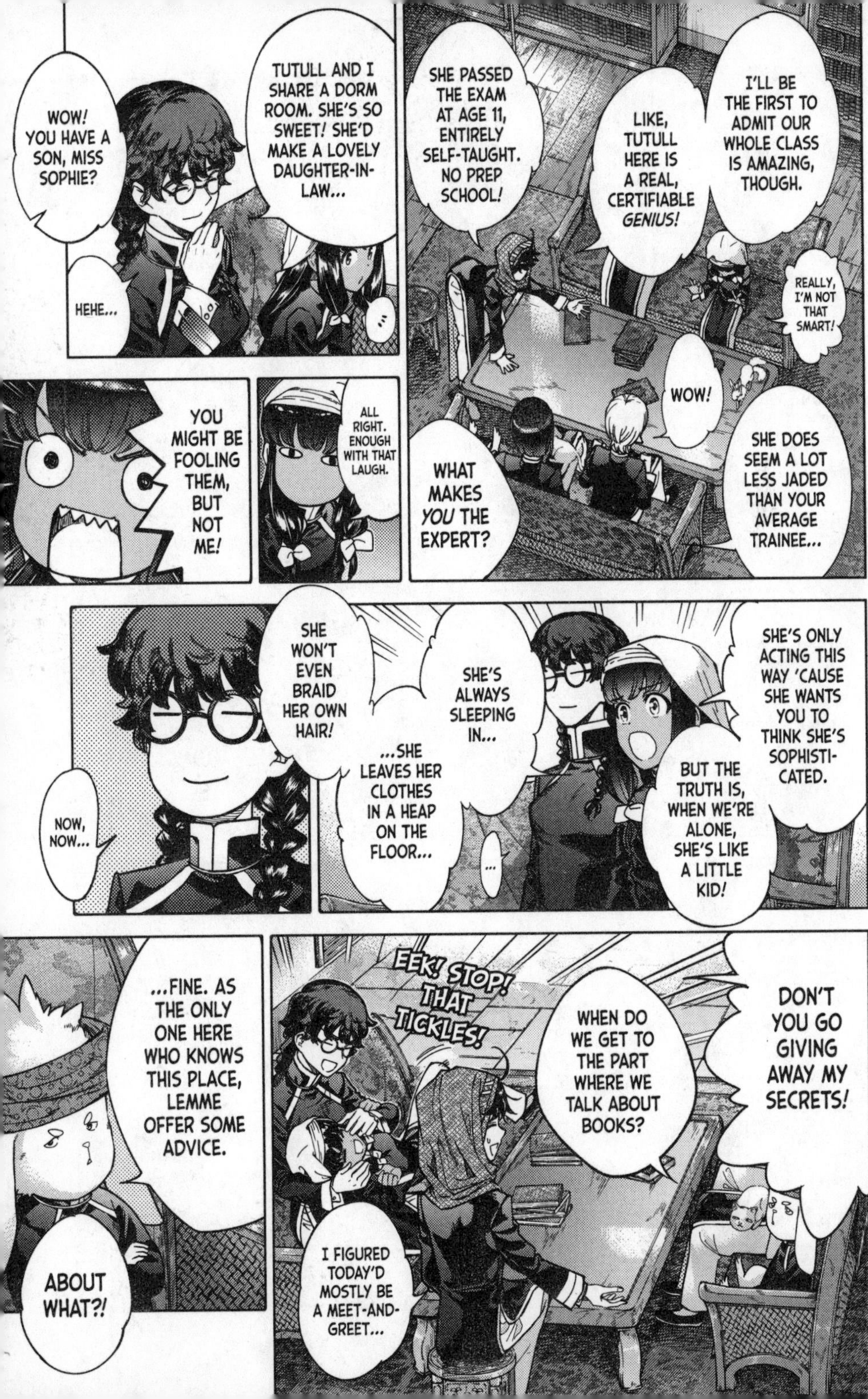
I'LL BE THE FIRST TO ADMIT OUR WHOLE CLASS IS AMAZING, THOUGH.
LIKE, TUTULL HERE IS A REAL, CERTIFIABLE *GENIUS!*
SHE PASSED THE EXAM AT AGE 11, ENTIRELY SELF-TAUGHT. NO PREP SCHOOL!
REALLY, I'M NOT THAT SMART!
WOW!
SHE DOES SEEM A LOT LESS JADED THAN YOUR AVERAGE TRAINEE...
WHAT MAKES *YOU* THE EXPERT?
TUTULL AND I SHARE A DORM ROOM. SHE'S SO SWEET! SHE'D MAKE A LOVELY DAUGHTER-IN-LAW...
WOW! YOU HAVE A SON, MISS SOPHIE?
...!
HEHE...
ALL RIGHT. ENOUGH WITH THAT LAUGH.
YOU MIGHT BE FOOLING THEM, BUT NOT ME!
SHE'S ONLY ACTING THIS WAY 'CAUSE SHE WANTS YOU TO THINK SHE'S SOPHISTICATED.
BUT THE TRUTH IS, WHEN WE'RE ALONE, SHE'S LIKE A LITTLE KID!
SHE'S ALWAYS SLEEPING IN...
SHE WON'T EVEN BRAID HER OWN HAIR!
...SHE LEAVES HER CLOTHES IN A HEAP ON THE FLOOR...
...
NOW, NOW...
DON'T YOU GO GIVING AWAY MY SECRETS!
EEK! STOP! THAT TICKLES!
WHEN DO WE GET TO THE PART WHERE WE TALK ABOUT BOOKS?
I FIGURED TODAY'D MOSTLY BE A MEET-AND-GREET...
...FINE. AS THE ONLY ONE HERE WHO KNOWS THIS PLACE, LEMME OFFER SOME ADVICE.
ABOUT WHAT?!

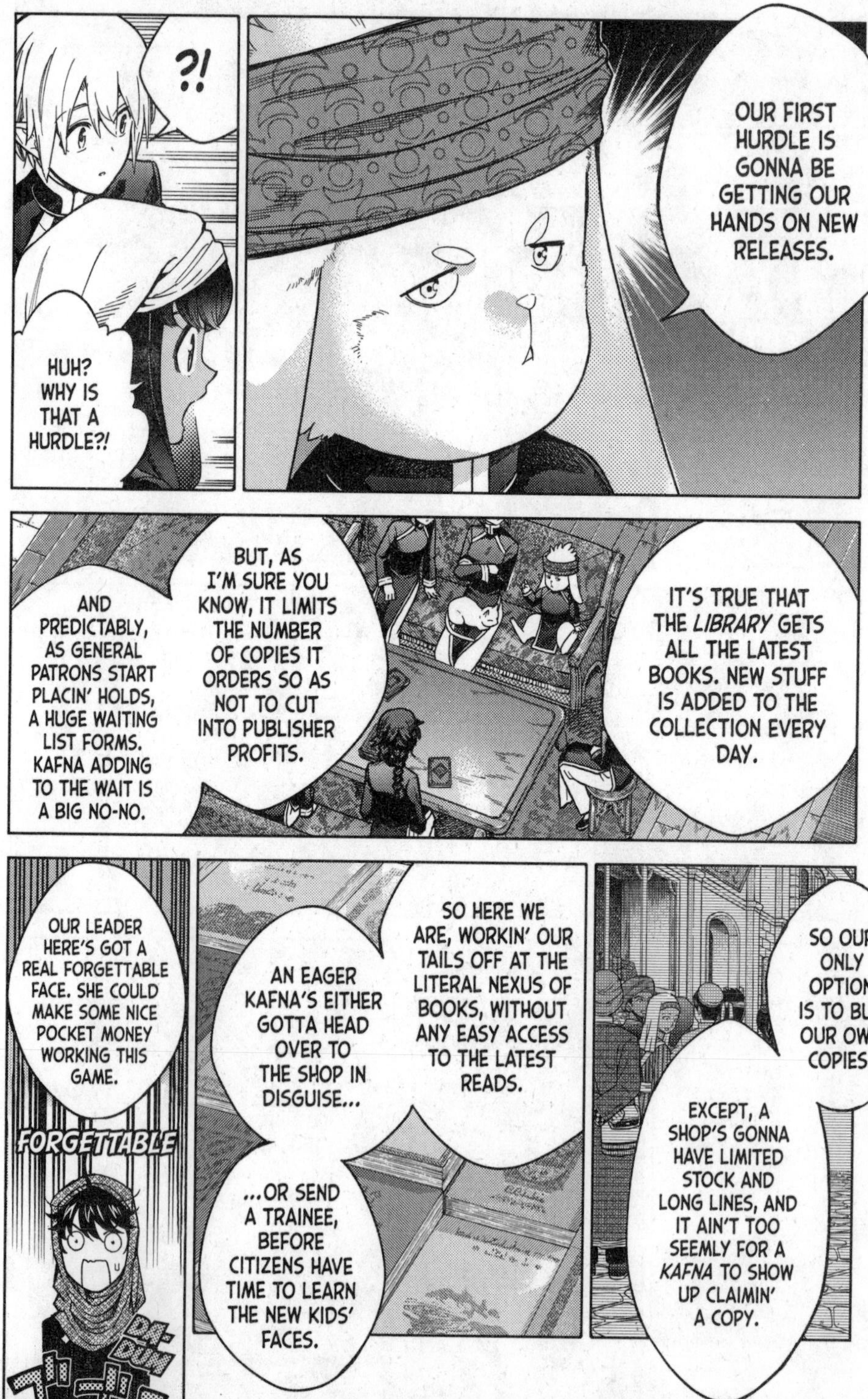
OUR FIRST HURDLE IS GONNA BE GETTING OUR HANDS ON NEW RELEASES.
?!
HUH? WHY IS THAT A HURDLE?!
IT'S TRUE THAT THE *LIBRARY* GETS ALL THE LATEST BOOKS. NEW STUFF IS ADDED TO THE COLLECTION EVERY DAY.
BUT, AS I'M SURE YOU KNOW, IT LIMITS THE NUMBER OF COPIES IT ORDERS SO AS NOT TO CUT INTO PUBLISHER PROFITS.
AND PREDICTABLY, AS GENERAL PATRONS START PLACIN' HOLDS, A HUGE WAITING LIST FORMS. KAFNA ADDING TO THE WAIT IS A BIG NO-NO.
SO OUR ONLY OPTION IS TO BUY OUR OWN COPIES.
EXCEPT, A SHOP'S GONNA HAVE LIMITED STOCK AND LONG LINES, AND IT AIN'T TOO SEEMLY FOR A *KAFNA* TO SHOW UP CLAIMIN' A COPY.
SO HERE WE ARE, WORKIN' OUR TAILS OFF AT THE LITERAL NEXUS OF BOOKS, WITHOUT ANY EASY ACCESS TO THE LATEST READS.
AN EAGER KAFNA'S EITHER GOTTA HEAD OVER TO THE SHOP IN DISGUISE...
...OR SEND A TRAINEE, BEFORE CITIZENS HAVE TIME TO LEARN THE NEW KIDS' FACES.
OUR LEADER HERE'S GOT A REAL FORGETTABLE FACE. SHE COULD MAKE SOME NICE POCKET MONEY WORKING THIS GAME.
FORGETTABLE
DA-DUM

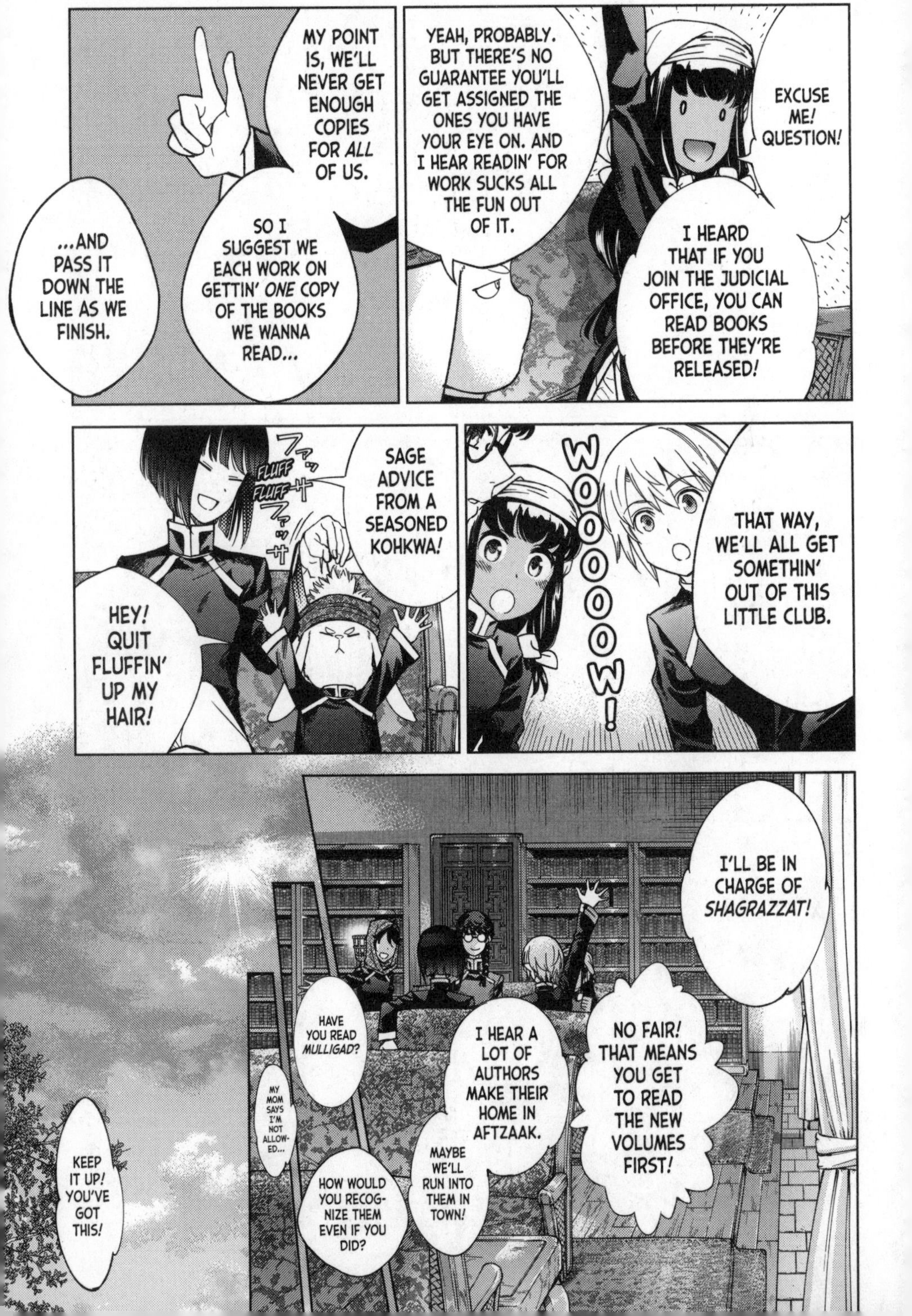
EXCUSE ME! QUESTION!
I HEARD THAT IF YOU JOIN THE JUDICIAL OFFICE, YOU CAN READ BOOKS BEFORE THEY'RE RELEASED!
YEAH, PROBABLY. BUT THERE'S NO GUARANTEE YOU'LL GET ASSIGNED THE ONES YOU HAVE YOUR EYE ON. AND I HEAR READIN' FOR WORK SUCKS ALL THE FUN OUT OF IT.
MY POINT IS, WE'LL NEVER GET ENOUGH COPIES FOR ALL OF US.
SO I SUGGEST WE EACH WORK ON GETTIN' ONE COPY OF THE BOOKS WE WANNA READ...
...AND PASS IT DOWN THE LINE AS WE FINISH.
THAT WAY, WE'LL ALL GET SOMETHIN' OUT OF THIS LITTLE CLUB.
WOOOOOOW!
SAGE ADVICE FROM A SEASONED KOHKWA!
FLUFF
FLUFF
HEY! QUIT FLUFFIN' UP MY HAIR!
I'LL BE IN CHARGE OF SHAGRAZZAT!
NO FAIR! THAT MEANS YOU GET TO READ THE NEW VOLUMES FIRST!
I HEAR A LOT OF AUTHORS MAKE THEIR HOME IN AFTZAAK.
MAYBE WE'LL RUN INTO THEM IN TOWN!
HAVE YOU READ MULLIGAD?
MY MOM SAYS I'M NOT ALLOWED...
HOW WOULD YOU RECOGNIZE THEM EVEN IF YOU DID?
KEEP IT UP! YOU'VE GOT THIS!

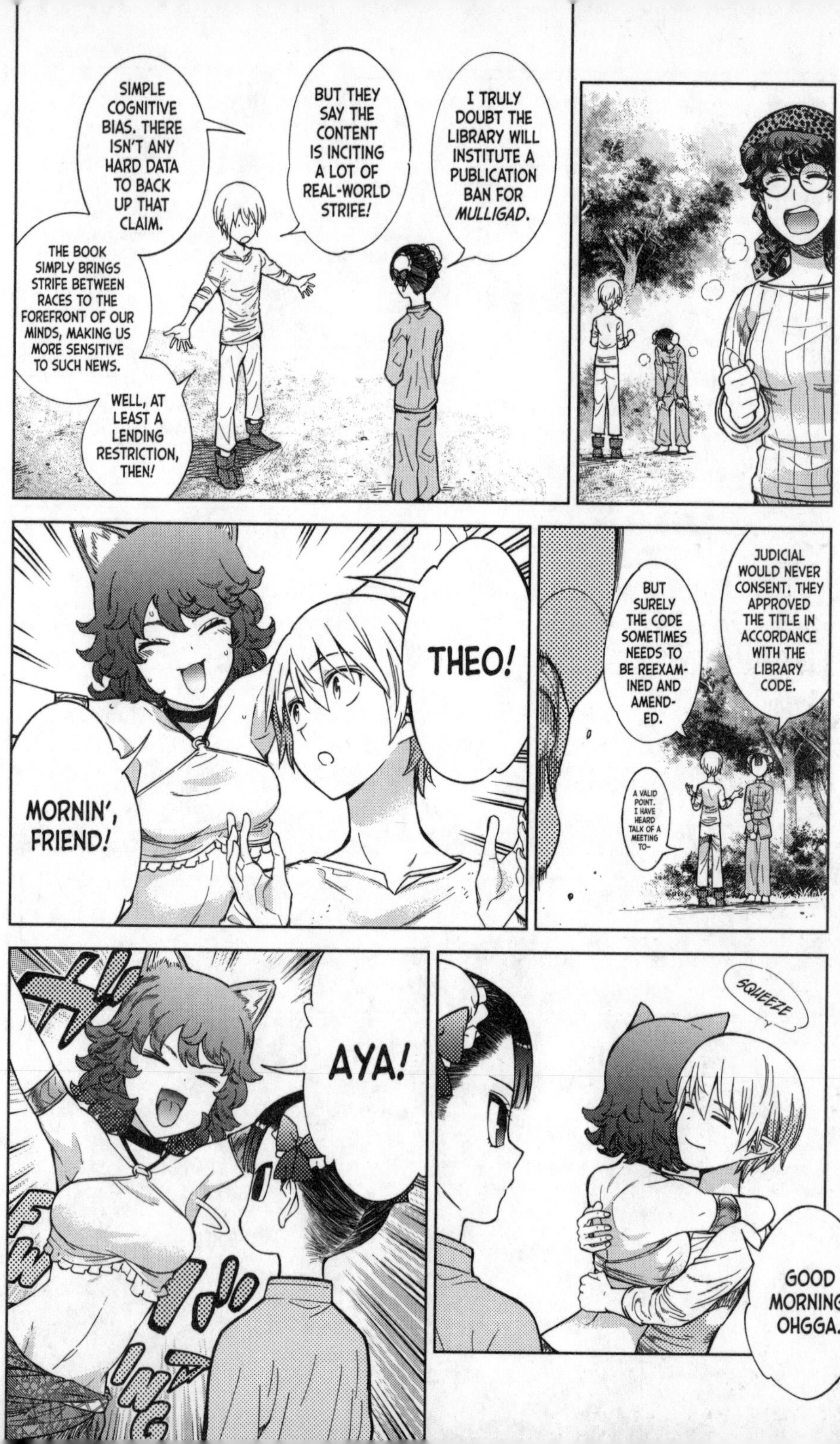
I TRULY DOUBT THE LIBRARY WILL INSTITUTE A PUBLICATION BAN FOR *MULLIGAD*.
BUT THEY SAY THE CONTENT IS INCITING A LOT OF REAL-WORLD STRIFE!
SIMPLE COGNITIVE BIAS. THERE ISN'T ANY HARD DATA TO BACK UP THAT CLAIM.
THE BOOK SIMPLY BRINGS STRIFE BETWEEN RACES TO THE FOREFRONT OF OUR MINDS, MAKING US MORE SENSITIVE TO SUCH NEWS.
WELL, AT LEAST A LENDING RESTRICTION, THEN!
JUDICIAL WOULD NEVER CONSENT. THEY APPROVED THE TITLE IN ACCORDANCE WITH THE LIBRARY CODE.
BUT SURELY THE CODE SOMETIMES NEEDS TO BE REEXAMINED AND AMENDED.
A VALID POINT. I HAVE HEARD TALK OF A MEETING TO—
THEO!
MORNIN', FRIEND!
SQUEEZE
GOOD MORNING, OHGGA.
AYA!

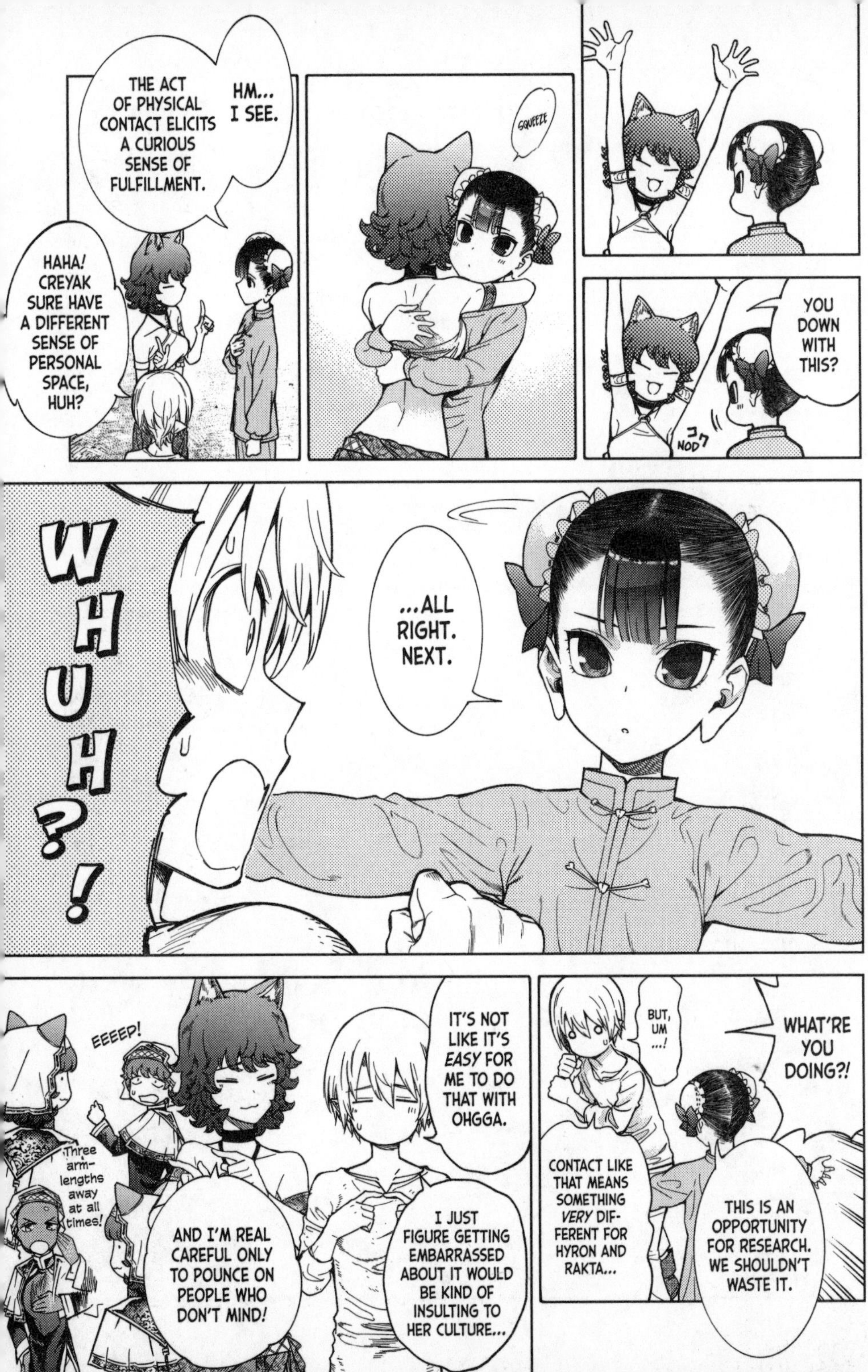

YOU DOWN WITH THIS?
コク NOD
SQUEEZE
HM... I SEE.
THE ACT OF PHYSICAL CONTACT ELICITS A CURIOUS SENSE OF FULFILLMENT.
HAHA! CREYAK SURE HAVE A DIFFERENT SENSE OF PERSONAL SPACE, HUH?
...ALL RIGHT. NEXT.
WHUH?!
WHAT'RE YOU DOING?!
BUT, UM ...!
THIS IS AN OPPORTUNITY FOR RESEARCH. WE SHOULDN'T WASTE IT.
CONTACT LIKE THAT MEANS SOMETHING *VERY* DIFFERENT FOR HYRON AND RAKTA...
IT'S NOT LIKE IT'S *EASY* FOR ME TO DO THAT WITH OHGGA.
I JUST FIGURE GETTING EMBARRASSED ABOUT IT WOULD BE KIND OF INSULTING TO HER CULTURE...
EEEEP!
AND I'M REAL CAREFUL ONLY TO POUNCE ON PEOPLE WHO DON'T MIND!
Three arm-lengths away at all times!

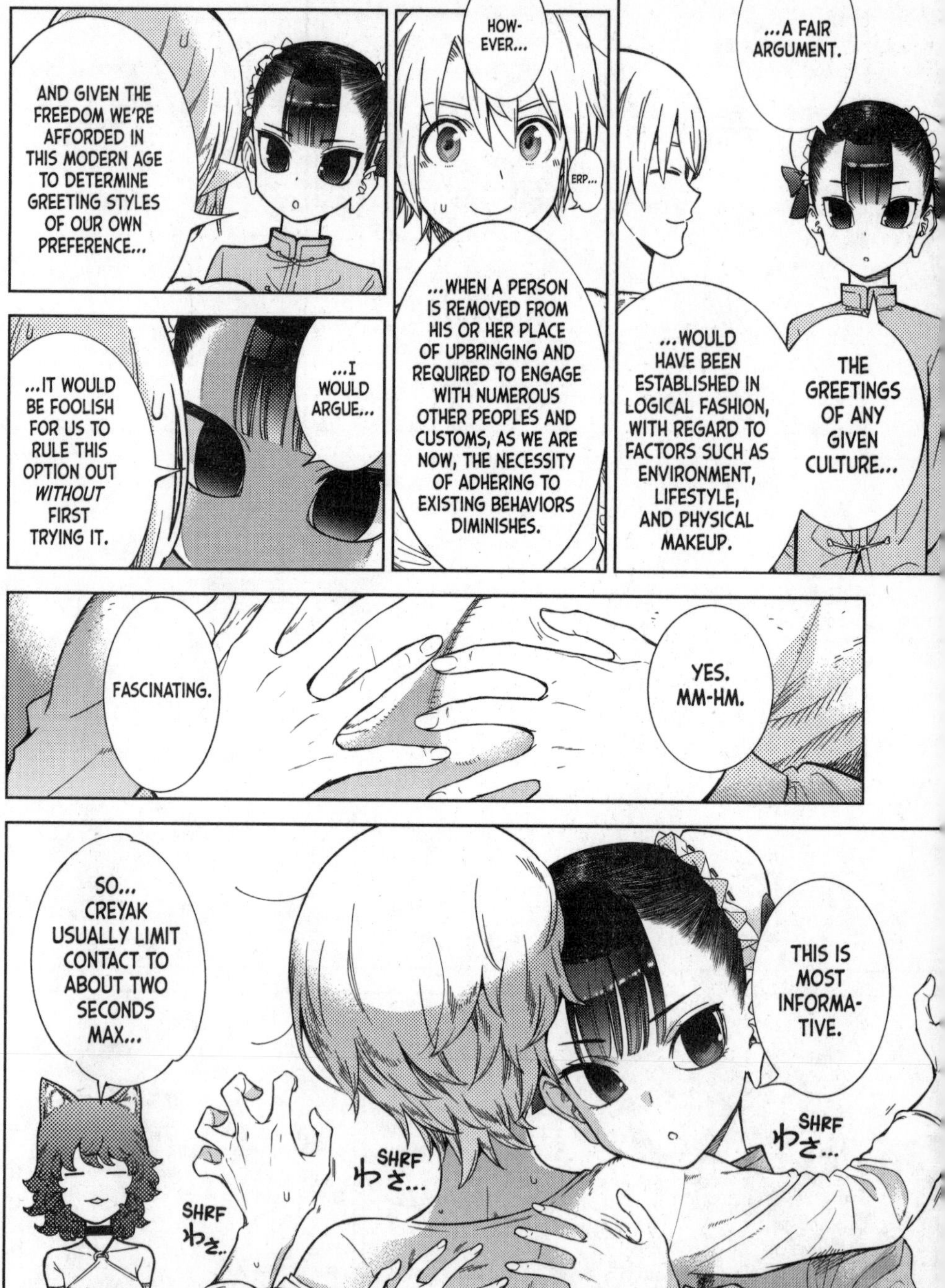
...A FAIR ARGUMENT.
THE GREETINGS OF ANY GIVEN CULTURE...
...WOULD HAVE BEEN ESTABLISHED IN LOGICAL FASHION, WITH REGARD TO FACTORS SUCH AS ENVIRONMENT, LIFESTYLE, AND PHYSICAL MAKEUP.
HOW-EVER...
ERP...
...WHEN A PERSON IS REMOVED FROM HIS OR HER PLACE OF UPBRINGING AND REQUIRED TO ENGAGE WITH NUMEROUS OTHER PEOPLES AND CUSTOMS, AS WE ARE NOW, THE NECESSITY OF ADHERING TO EXISTING BEHAVIORS DIMINISHES.
AND GIVEN THE FREEDOM WE'RE AFFORDED IN THIS MODERN AGE TO DETERMINE GREETING STYLES OF OUR OWN PREFERENCE...
...I WOULD ARGUE...
...IT WOULD BE FOOLISH FOR US TO RULE THIS OPTION OUT *WITHOUT* FIRST TRYING IT.
YES. MM-HM.
FASCINATING.
THIS IS MOST INFORMA-TIVE.
SHRF わさ...
SHRF わさ...
SO... CREYAK USUALLY LIMIT CONTACT TO ABOUT TWO SECONDS MAX...
SHRF わさ..

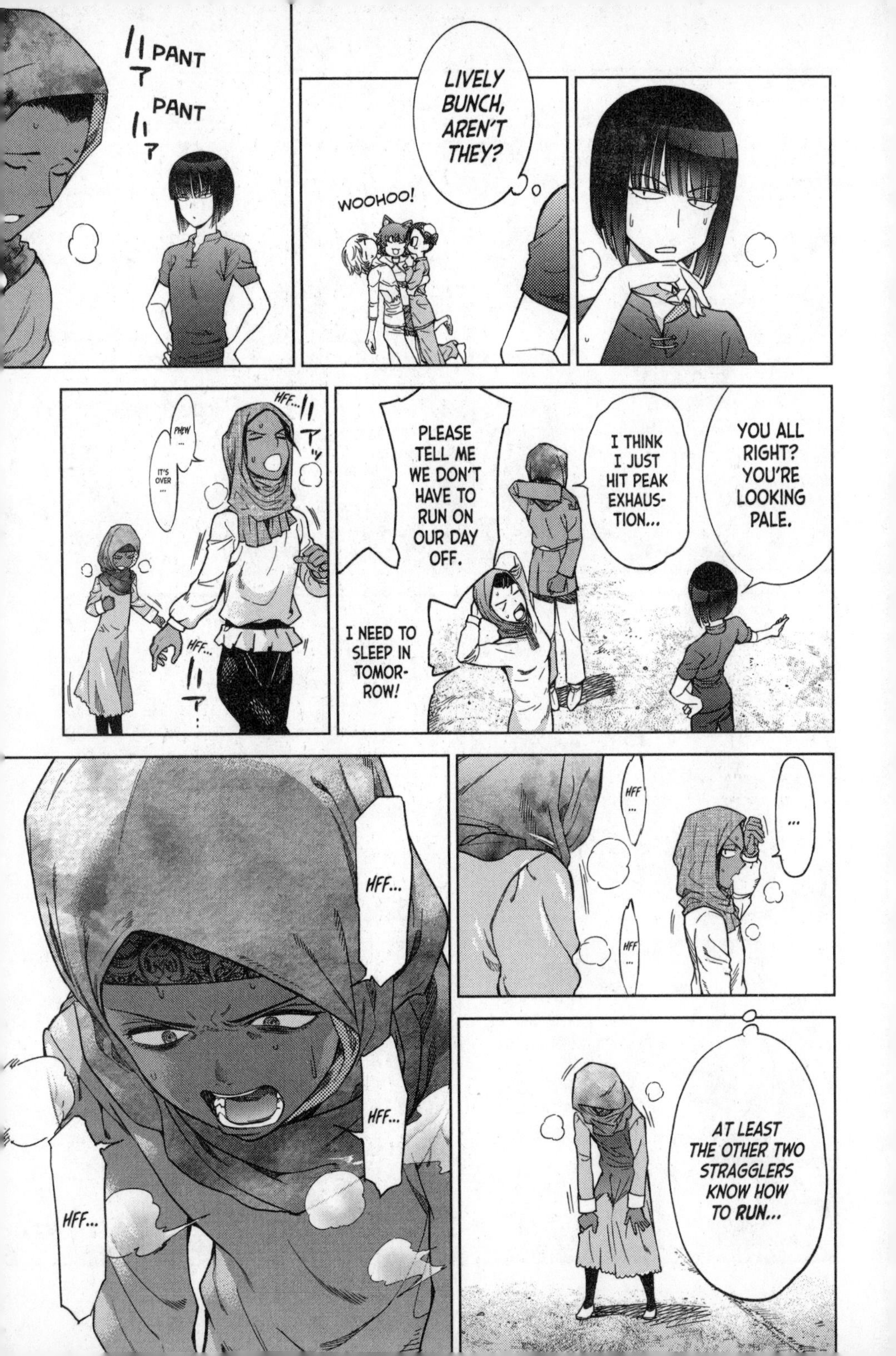
LIVELY BUNCH, AREN'T THEY?
WOOHOO!
PANT
PANT
YOU ALL RIGHT? YOU'RE LOOKING PALE.
I THINK I JUST HIT PEAK EXHAUS-TION...
PLEASE TELL ME WE DON'T HAVE TO RUN ON OUR DAY OFF.
I NEED TO SLEEP IN TOMOR-ROW!
HFF...
PHEW...
IT'S OVER...
HFF...
...
HFF...
HFF...
AT LEAST THE OTHER TWO STRAGGLERS KNOW HOW TO RUN...
HFF...
HFF...
HFF...

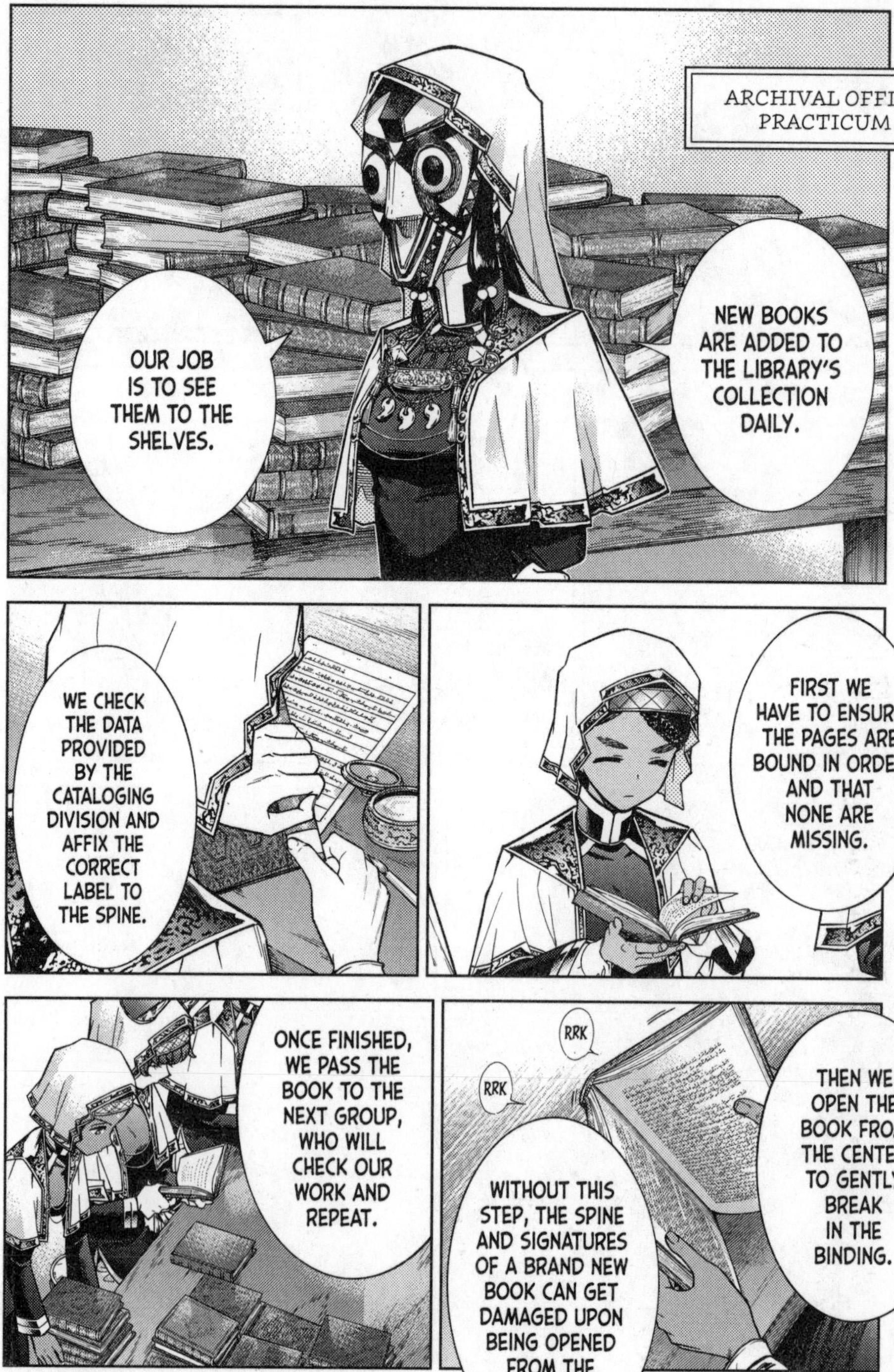
ARCHIVAL OFFICE PRACTICUM
NEW BOOKS ARE ADDED TO THE LIBRARY'S COLLECTION DAILY.
OUR JOB IS TO SEE THEM TO THE SHELVES.
FIRST WE HAVE TO ENSURE THE PAGES ARE BOUND IN ORDER AND THAT NONE ARE MISSING.
WE CHECK THE DATA PROVIDED BY THE CATALOGING DIVISION AND AFFIX THE CORRECT LABEL TO THE SPINE.
RRK
RRK
THEN WE OPEN THE BOOK FROM THE CENTER TO GENTLY BREAK IN THE BINDING.
WITHOUT THIS STEP, THE SPINE AND SIGNATURES OF A BRAND NEW BOOK CAN GET DAMAGED UPON BEING OPENED FROM THE FRONT.
ONCE FINISHED, WE PASS THE BOOK TO THE NEXT GROUP, WHO WILL CHECK OUR WORK AND REPEAT.

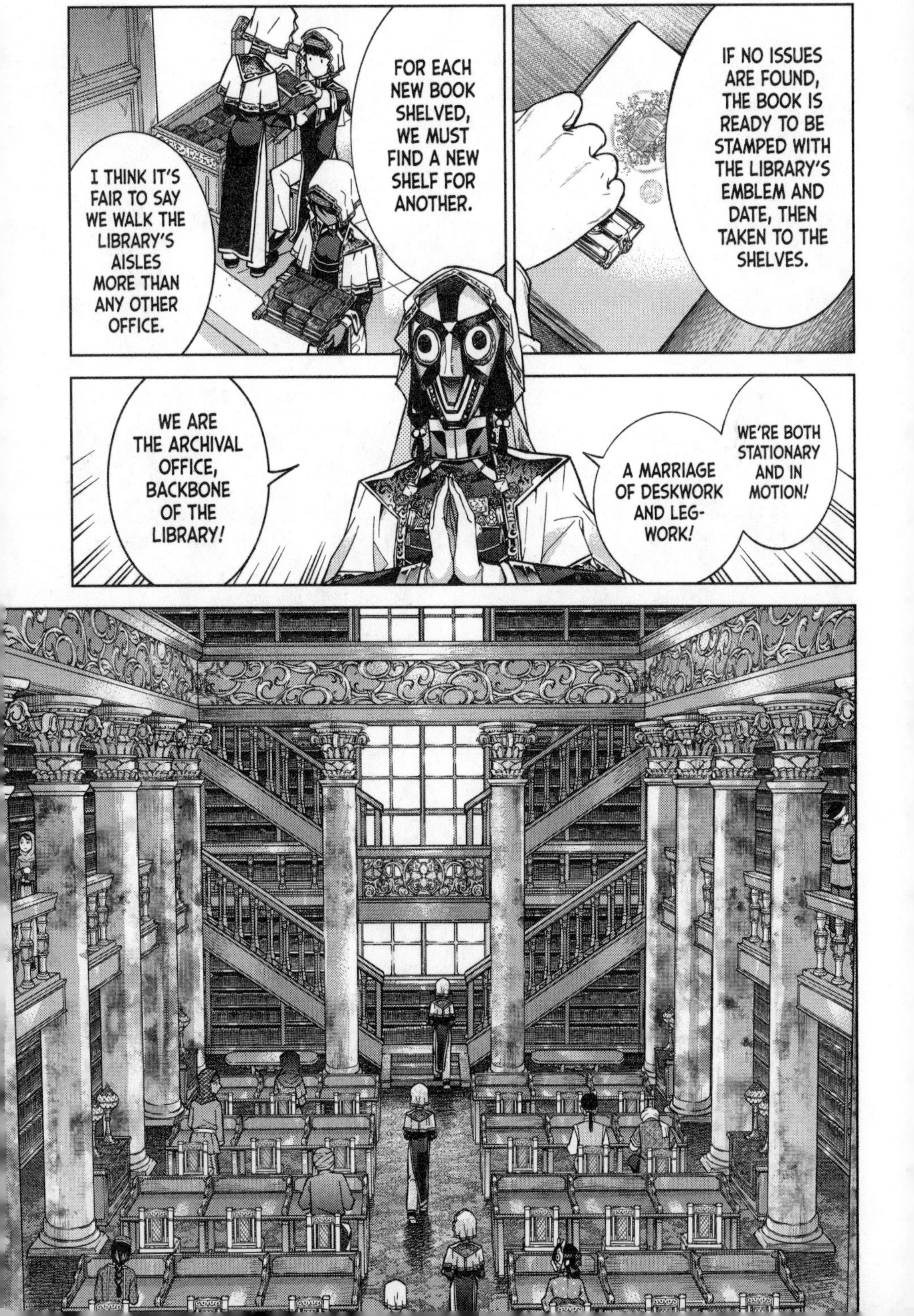
IF NO ISSUES ARE FOUND, THE BOOK IS READY TO BE STAMPED WITH THE LIBRARY'S EMBLEM AND DATE, THEN TAKEN TO THE SHELVES.
FOR EACH NEW BOOK SHELVED, WE MUST FIND A NEW SHELF FOR ANOTHER.
I THINK IT'S FAIR TO SAY WE WALK THE LIBRARY'S AISLES MORE THAN ANY OTHER OFFICE.
WE'RE BOTH STATIONARY AND IN MOTION!
A MARRIAGE OF DESKWORK AND LEG-WORK!
WE ARE THE ARCHIVAL OFFICE, BACKBONE OF THE LIBRARY!

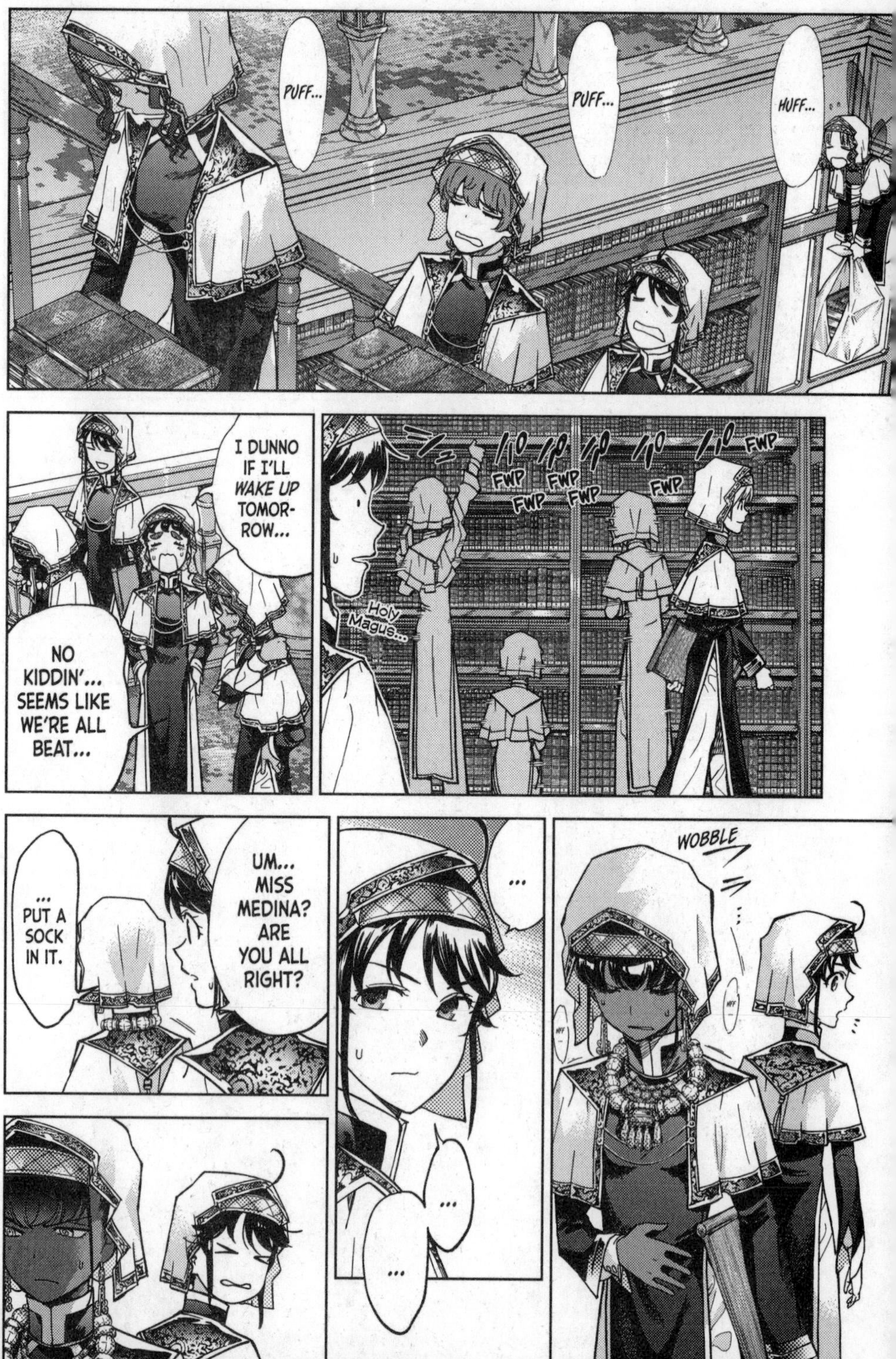

HUFF...
PUFF...
PUFF...
FWP FWP FWP FWP FWP FWP
Holy Magus...
I DUNNO IF I'LL *WAKE UP* TOMORROW...
NO KIDDIN'... SEEMS LIKE WE'RE ALL BEAT...
WOBBLE
...
...
...
UM... MISS MEDINA? ARE YOU ALL RIGHT?
... PUT A SOCK IN IT.

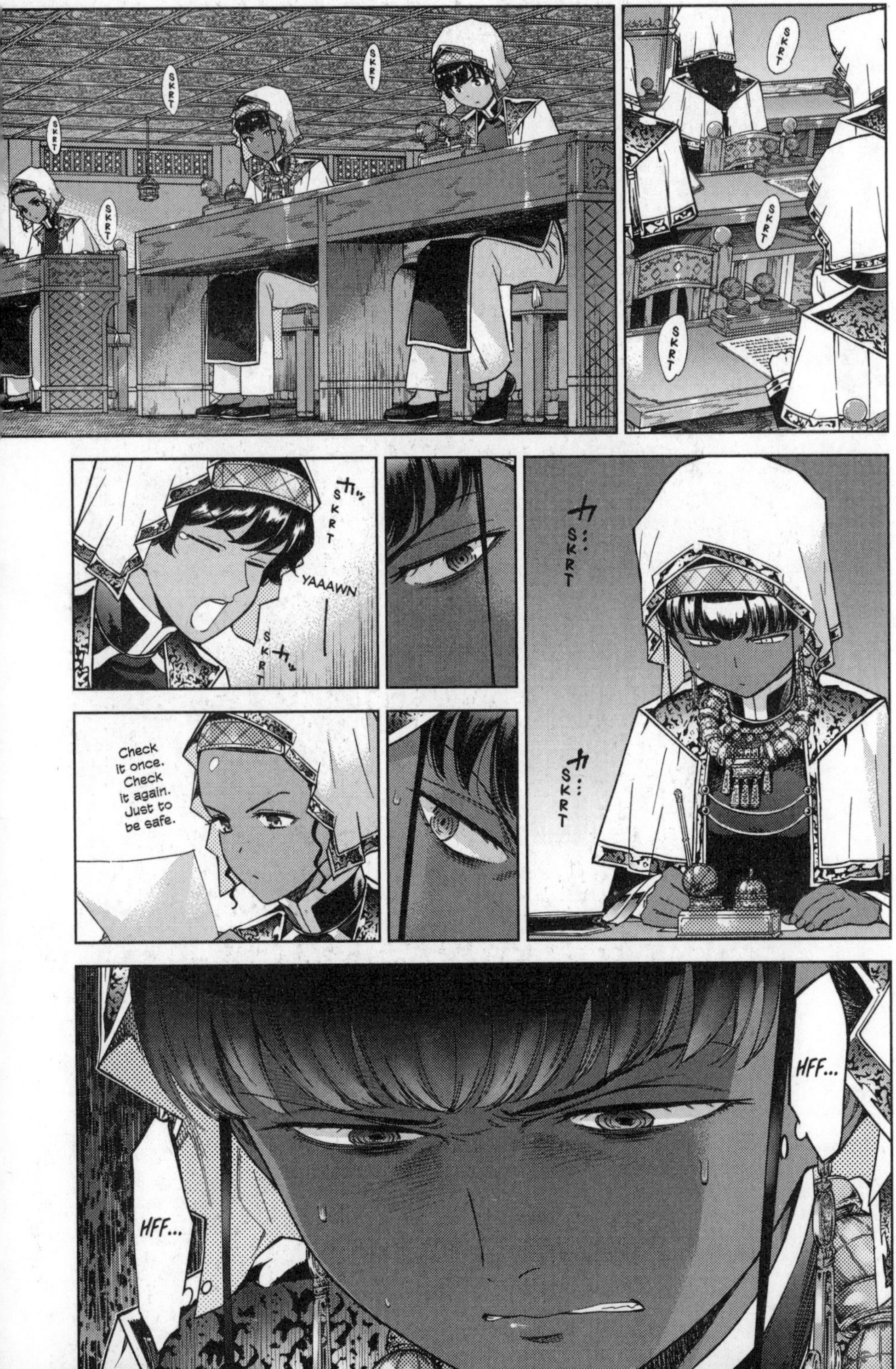

SKRT
SKRT
SKRT
SKRT
SKRT
SKRT
SKRT
SKRT
SKRT
SKRT
YAAAWN
SKRT
Check it once. Check it again. Just to be safe.
HFF...
HFF...

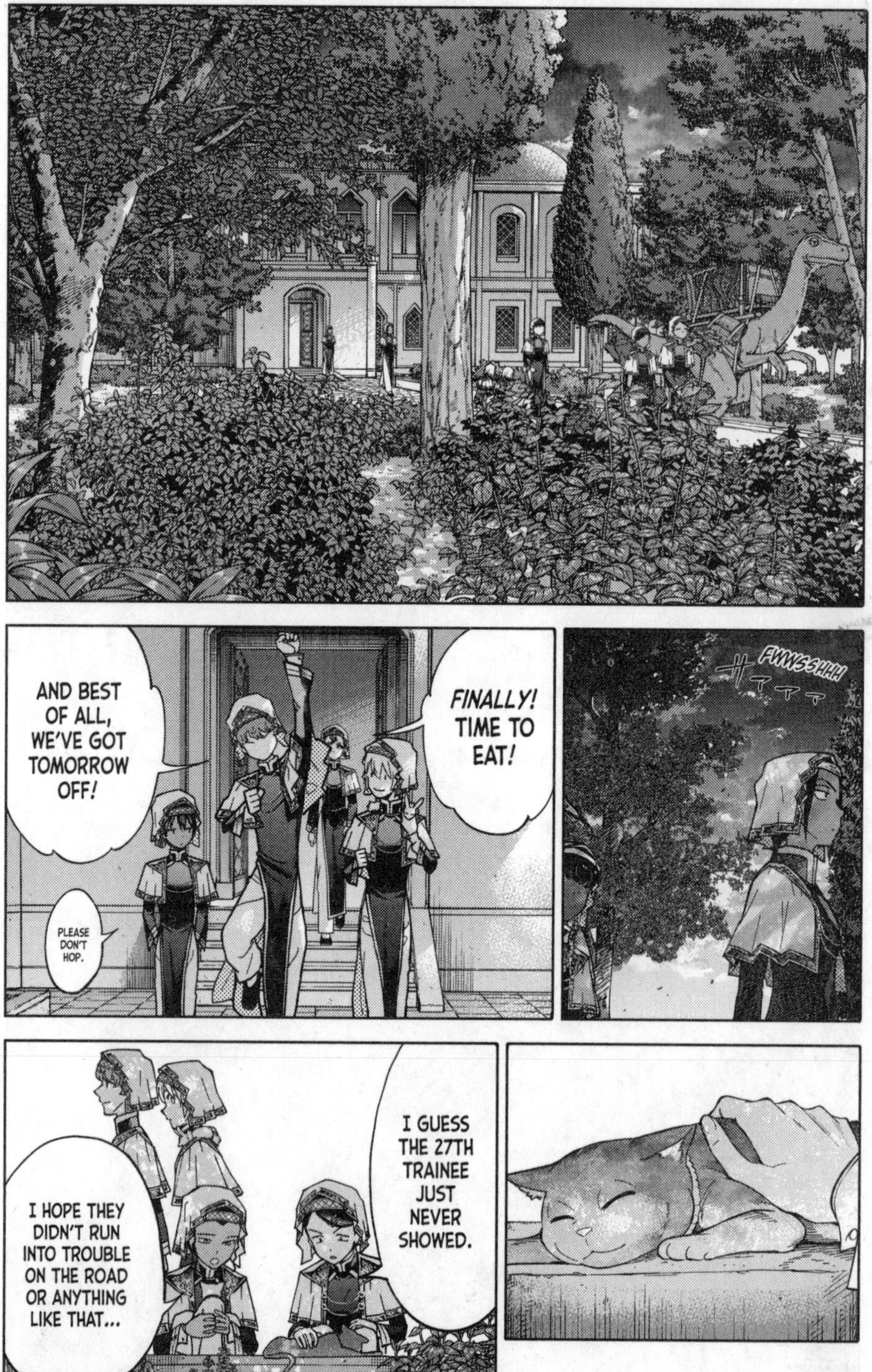
FWWSSHHH
FINALLY! TIME TO EAT!
AND BEST OF ALL, WE'VE GOT TOMORROW OFF!
PLEASE DON'T HOP.
I GUESS THE 27TH TRAINEE JUST NEVER SHOWED.
I HOPE THEY DIDN'T RUN INTO TROUBLE ON THE ROAD OR ANYTHING LIKE THAT...

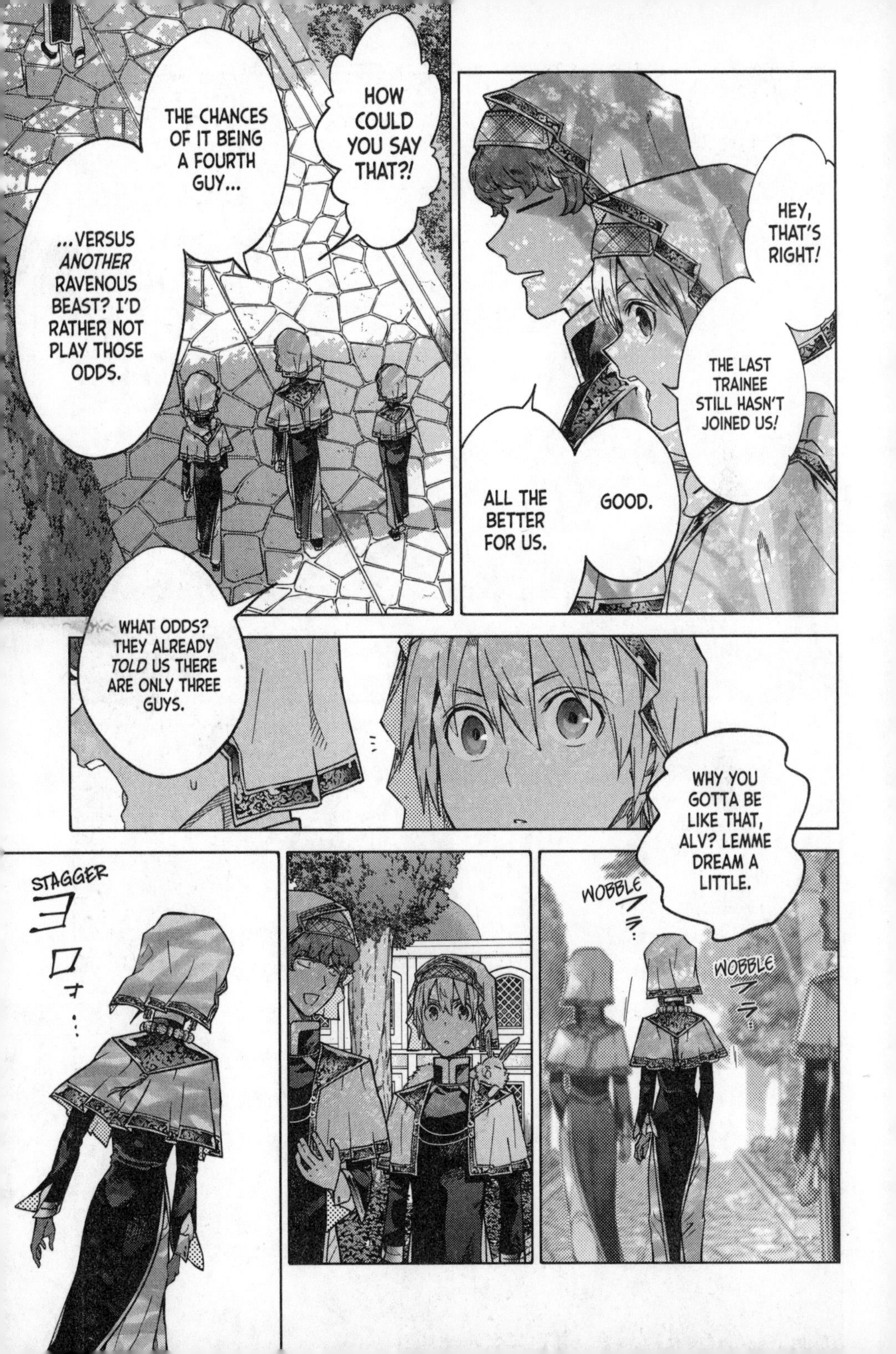
HEY, THAT'S RIGHT!
THE LAST TRAINEE STILL HASN'T JOINED US!
GOOD.
ALL THE BETTER FOR US.
HOW COULD YOU SAY THAT?!
THE CHANCES OF IT BEING A FOURTH GUY...
...VERSUS *ANOTHER* RAVENOUS BEAST? I'D RATHER NOT PLAY THOSE ODDS.
WHAT ODDS? THEY ALREADY *TOLD* US THERE ARE ONLY THREE GUYS.
WHY YOU GOTTA BE LIKE THAT, ALV? LEMME DREAM A LITTLE.
WOBBLE
WOBBLE
STAGGER

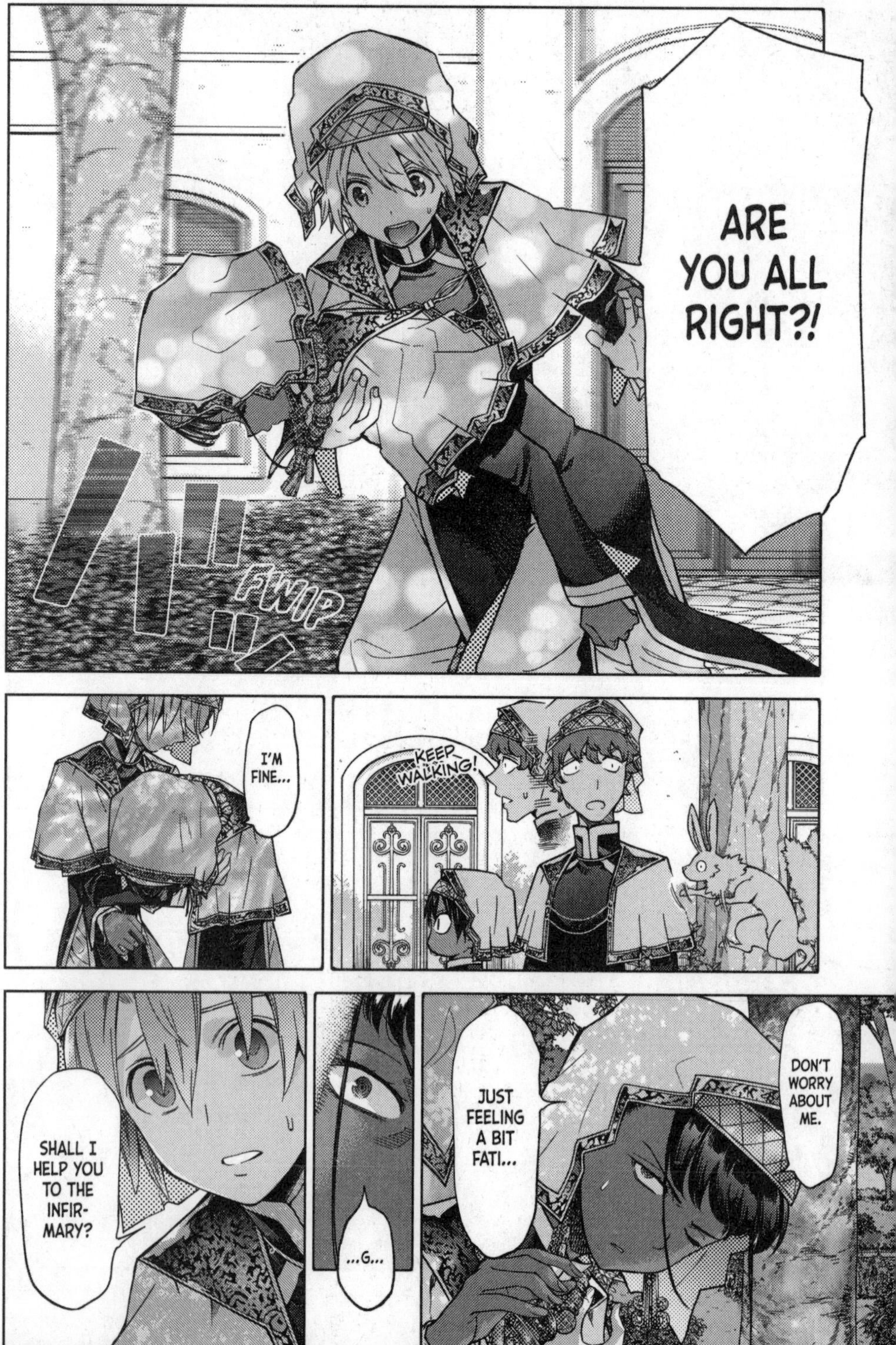
ARE YOU ALL RIGHT?!
FWIP
KEEP WALKING!
I'M FINE...
DON'T WORRY ABOUT ME.
JUST FEELING A BIT FATI...
...G...
SHALL I HELP YOU TO THE INFIRMARY?

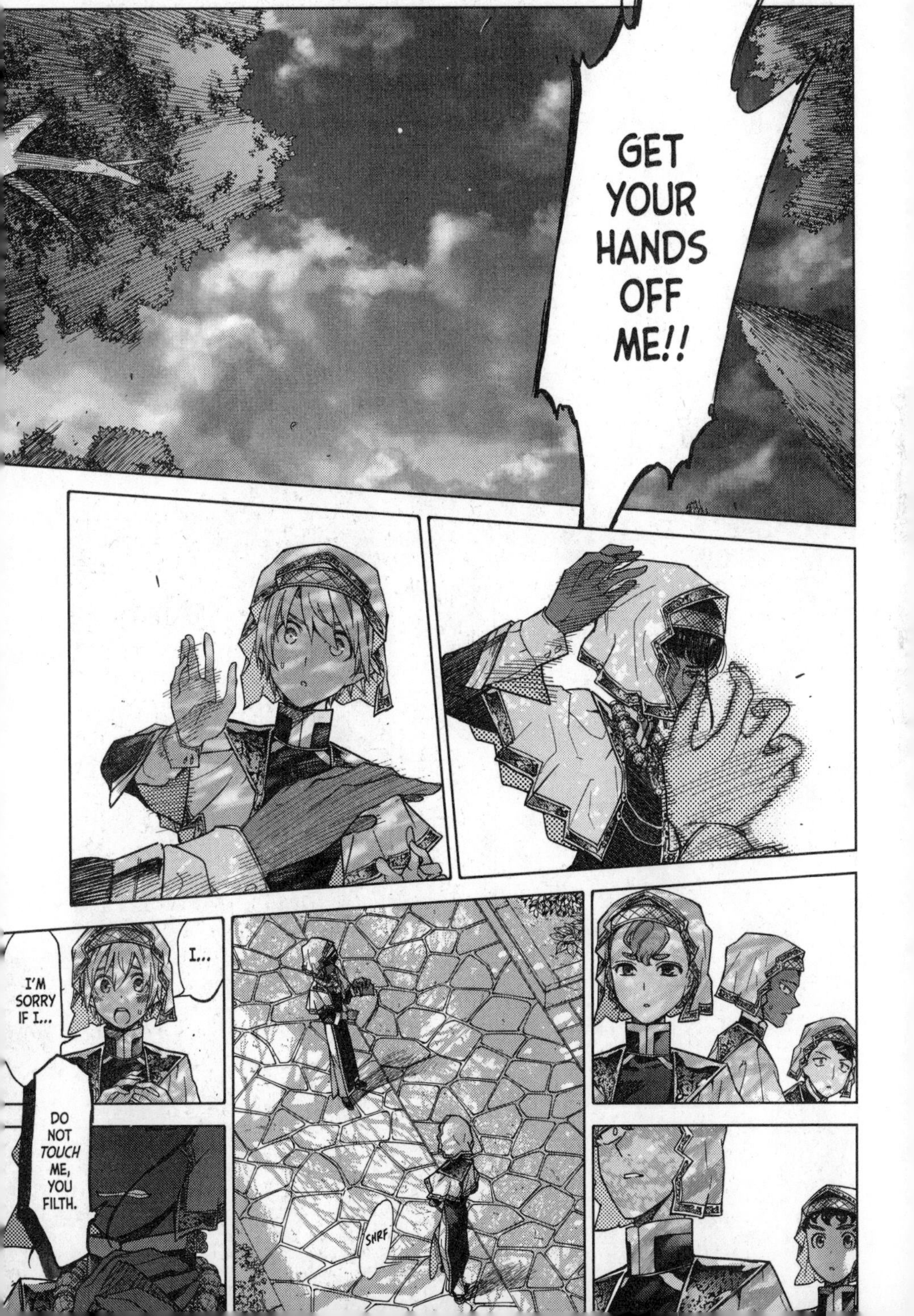
GET YOUR HANDS OFF ME!!
SHRF
I...
I'M SORRY IF I...
DO NOT *TOUCH* ME, YOU FILTH.

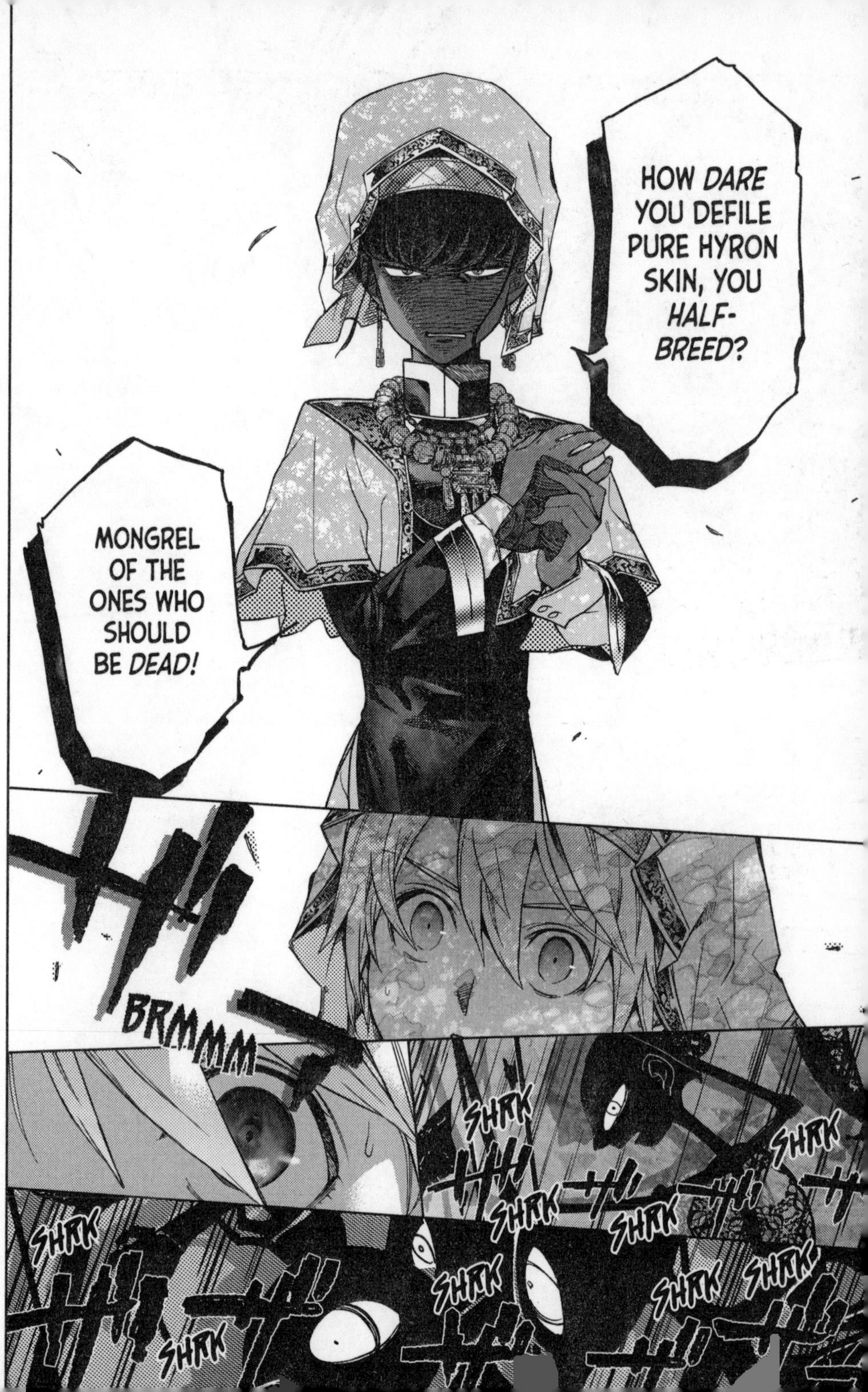
HOW *DARE* YOU DEFILE PURE HYRON SKIN, YOU *HALF-BREED?*
MONGREL OF THE ONES WHO SHOULD BE *DEAD!*
BRMMMM
SHRK
SHRK
SHRK
SHRK
SHRK
SHRK
SHRK
SHRK
SHRK

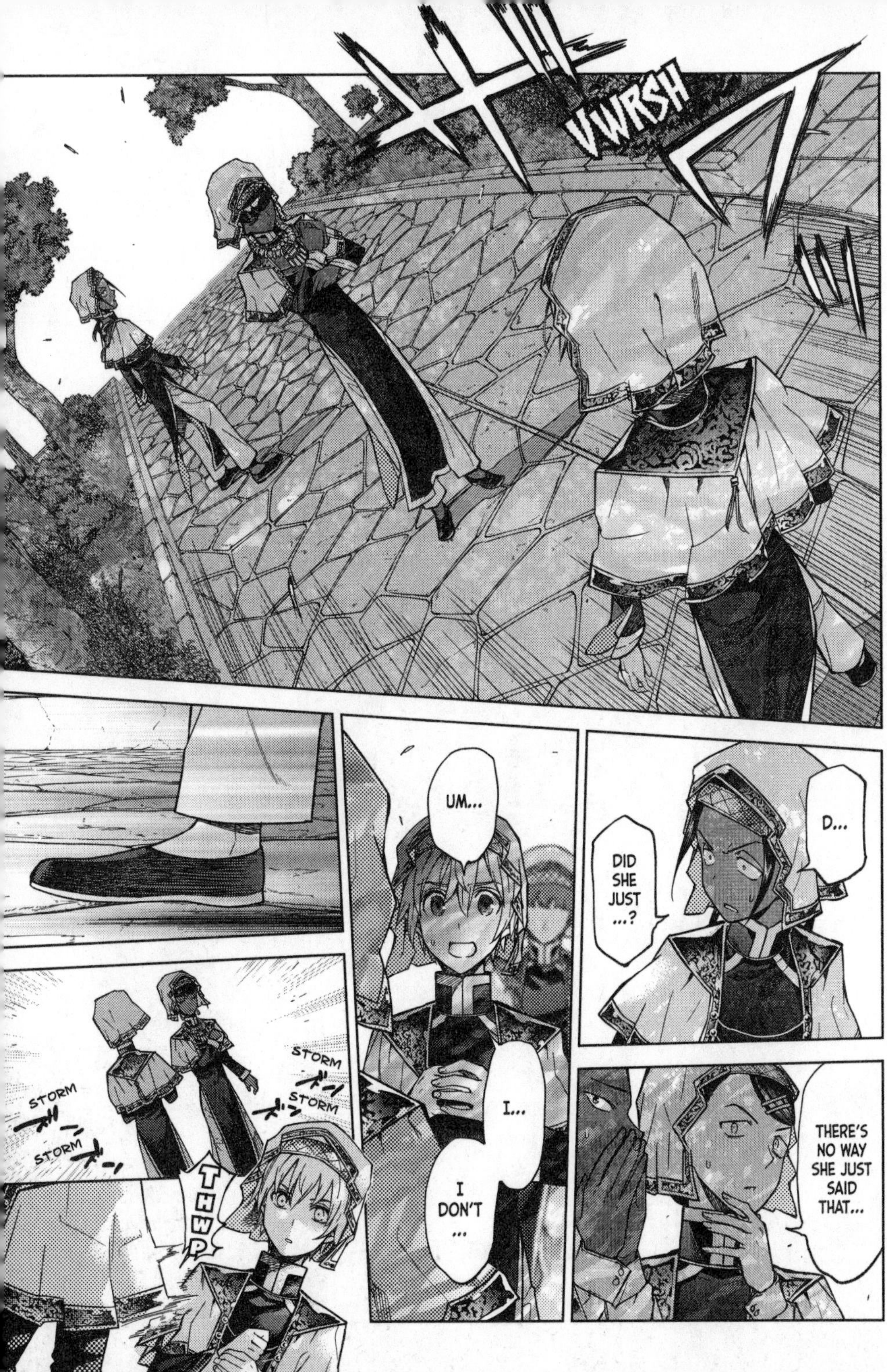
VWRSH
D...
DID SHE JUST ...?
THERE'S NO WAY SHE JUST SAID THAT...
UM...
I...
I DON'T ...
STORM
STORM
STORM
STORM
THWP

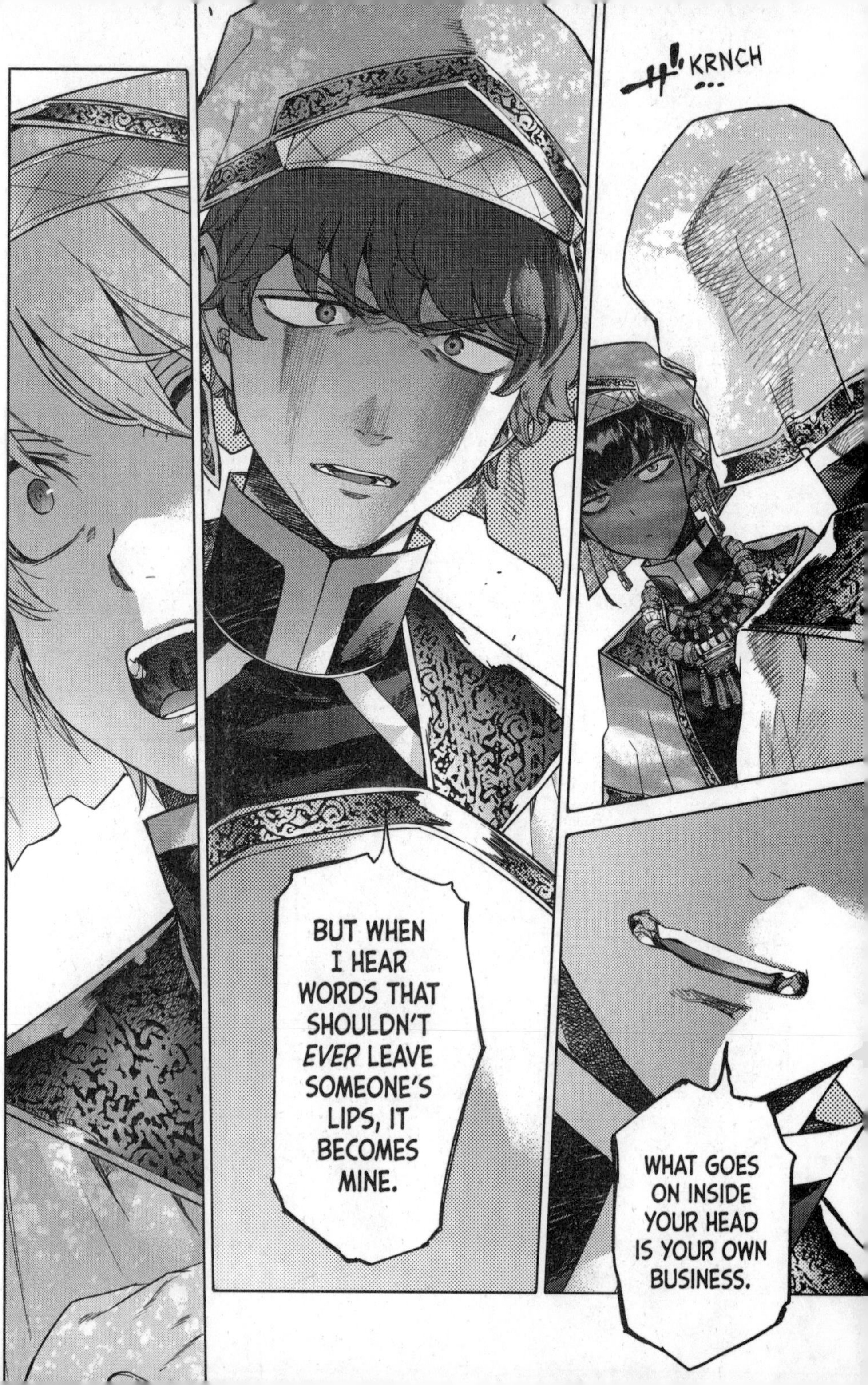
KRNCH
WHAT GOES ON INSIDE YOUR HEAD IS YOUR OWN BUSINESS.
BUT WHEN I HEAR WORDS THAT SHOULDN'T *EVER* LEAVE SOMEONE'S LIPS, IT BECOMES MINE.

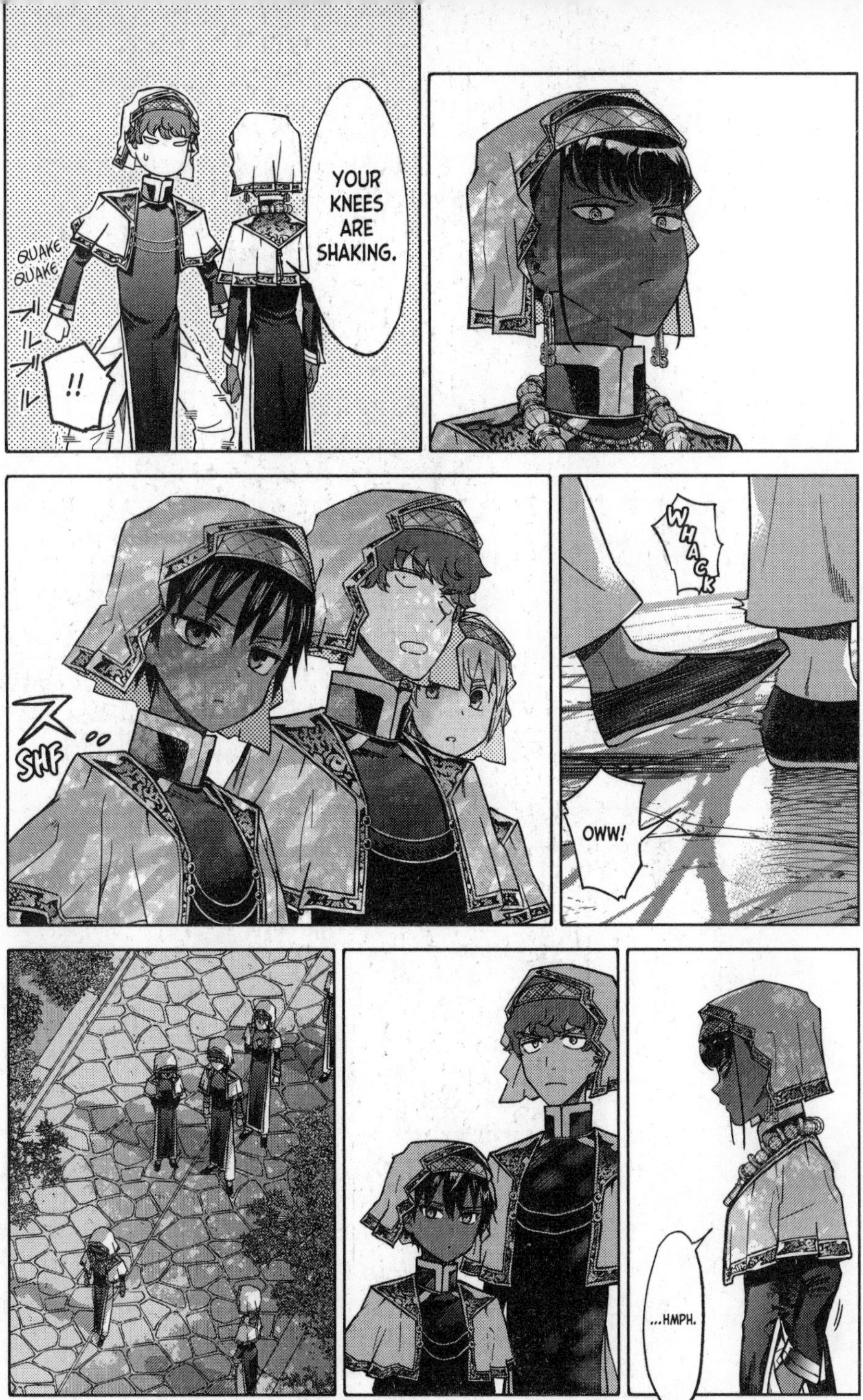
YOUR KNEES ARE SHAKING.
QUAKE QUAKE
!!
WHACK
OWW!
SHF
...HMPH.

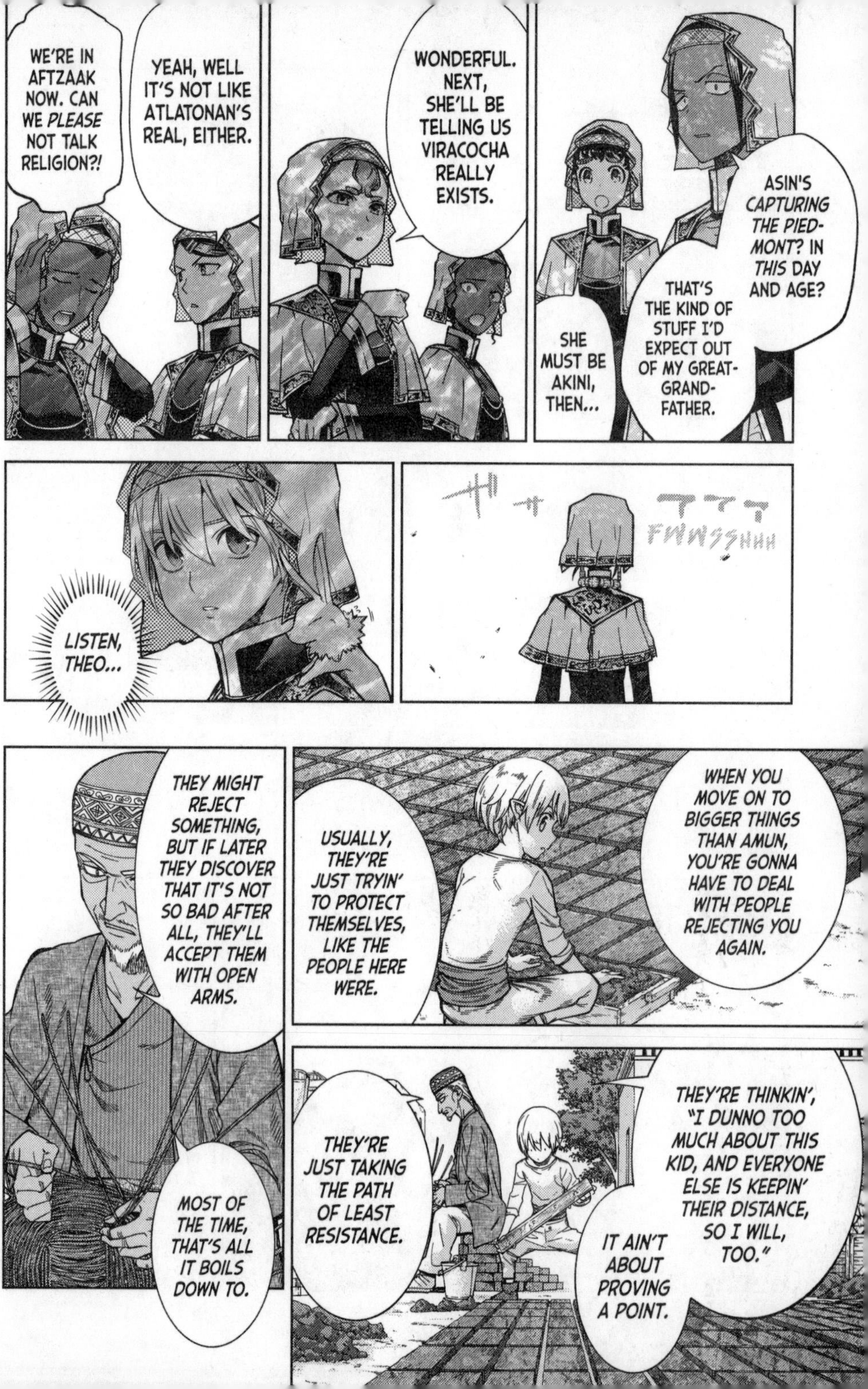
ASIN'S CAPTURING THE PIEDMONT? IN THIS DAY AND AGE?
THAT'S THE KIND OF STUFF I'D EXPECT OUT OF MY GREAT-GRANDFATHER.
SHE MUST BE AKINI, THEN...
WONDERFUL. NEXT, SHE'LL BE TELLING US VIRACOCHA REALLY EXISTS.
YEAH, WELL IT'S NOT LIKE ATLATONAN'S REAL, EITHER.
WE'RE IN AFTZAAK NOW. CAN WE *PLEASE* NOT TALK RELIGION?!
FWWSSHHH
LISTEN, THEO...
WHEN YOU MOVE ON TO BIGGER THINGS THAN AMUN, YOU'RE GONNA HAVE TO DEAL WITH PEOPLE REJECTING YOU AGAIN.
USUALLY, THEY'RE JUST TRYIN' TO PROTECT THEMSELVES, LIKE THE PEOPLE HERE WERE.
THEY'RE THINKIN', "I DUNNO TOO MUCH ABOUT THIS KID, AND EVERYONE ELSE IS KEEPIN' THEIR DISTANCE, SO I WILL, TOO."
IT AIN'T ABOUT PROVING A POINT.
THEY'RE JUST TAKING THE PATH OF LEAST RESISTANCE.
THEY MIGHT REJECT SOMETHING, BUT IF LATER THEY DISCOVER THAT IT'S NOT SO BAD AFTER ALL, THEY'LL ACCEPT THEM WITH OPEN ARMS.
MOST OF THE TIME, THAT'S ALL IT BOILS DOWN TO.

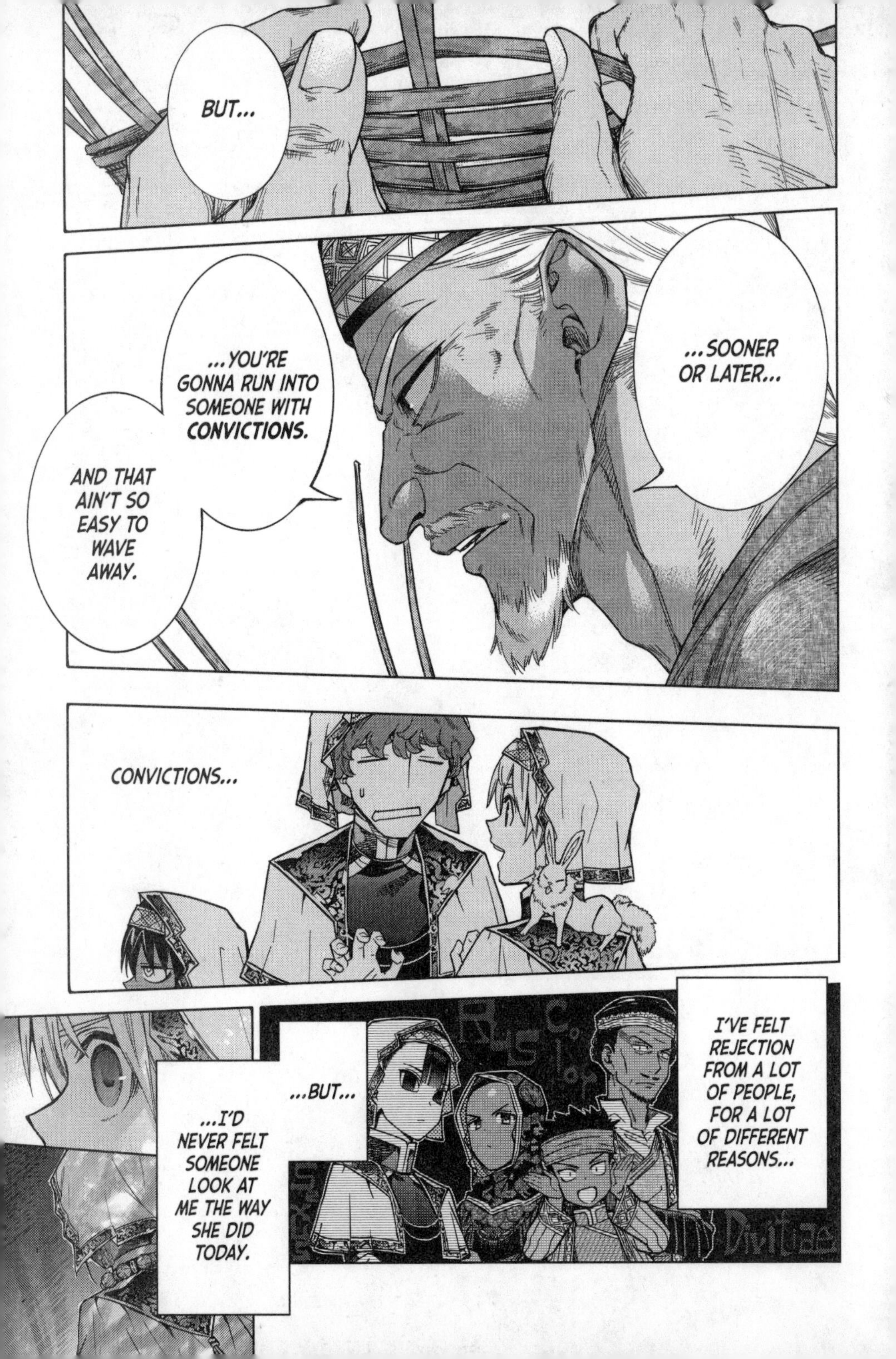
BUT...
...SOONER OR LATER...
...YOU'RE GONNA RUN INTO SOMEONE WITH CONVICTIONS.
AND THAT AIN'T SO EASY TO WAVE AWAY.
CONVICTIONS...
I'VE FELT REJECTION FROM A LOT OF PEOPLE, FOR A LOT OF DIFFERENT REASONS...
...BUT...
...I'D NEVER FELT SOMEONE LOOK AT ME THE WAY SHE DID TODAY.

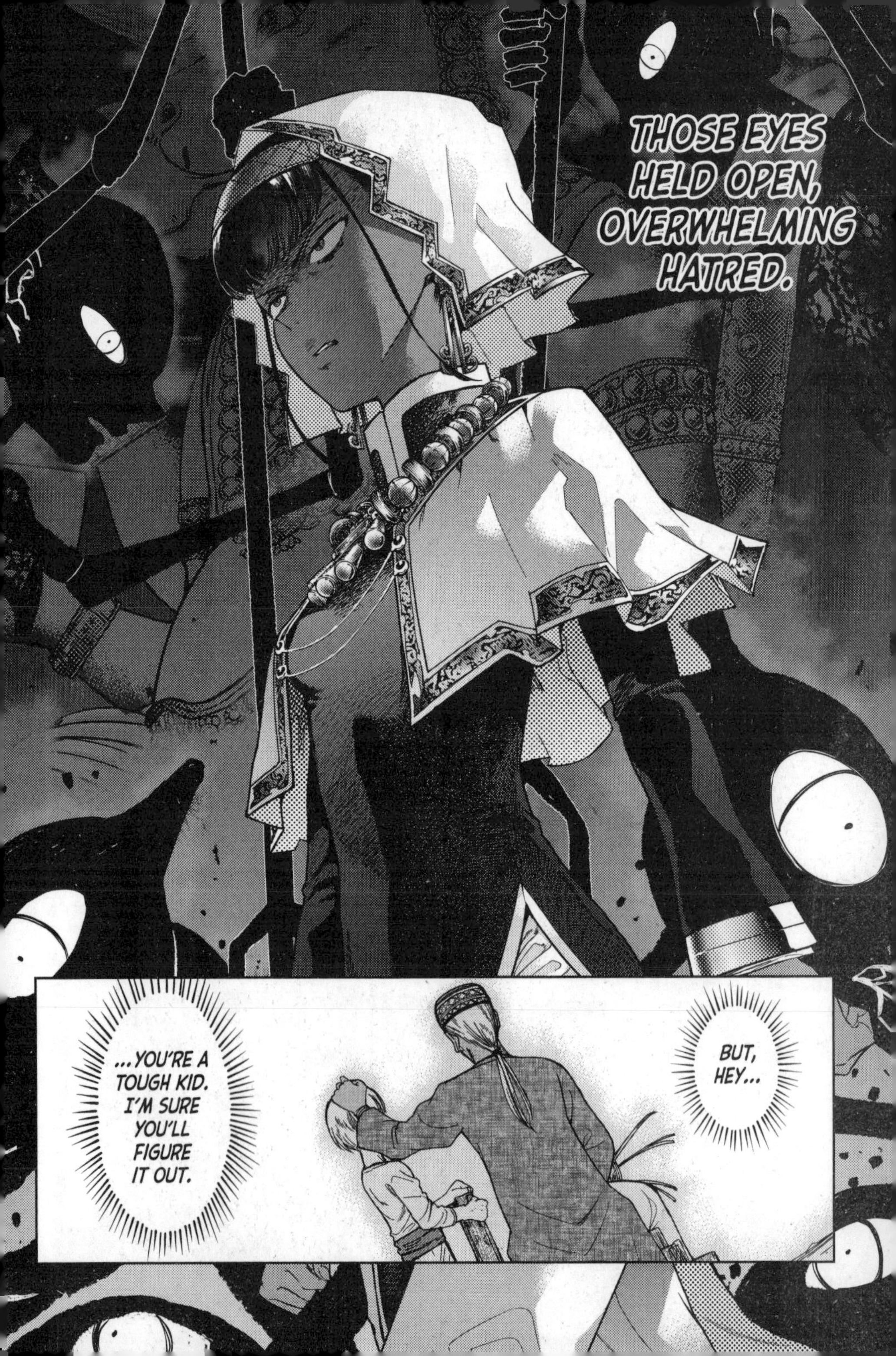
THOSE EYES HELD OPEN, OVERWHELMING HATRED.
BUT, HEY...
...YOU'RE A TOUGH KID. I'M SURE YOU'LL FIGURE IT OUT.

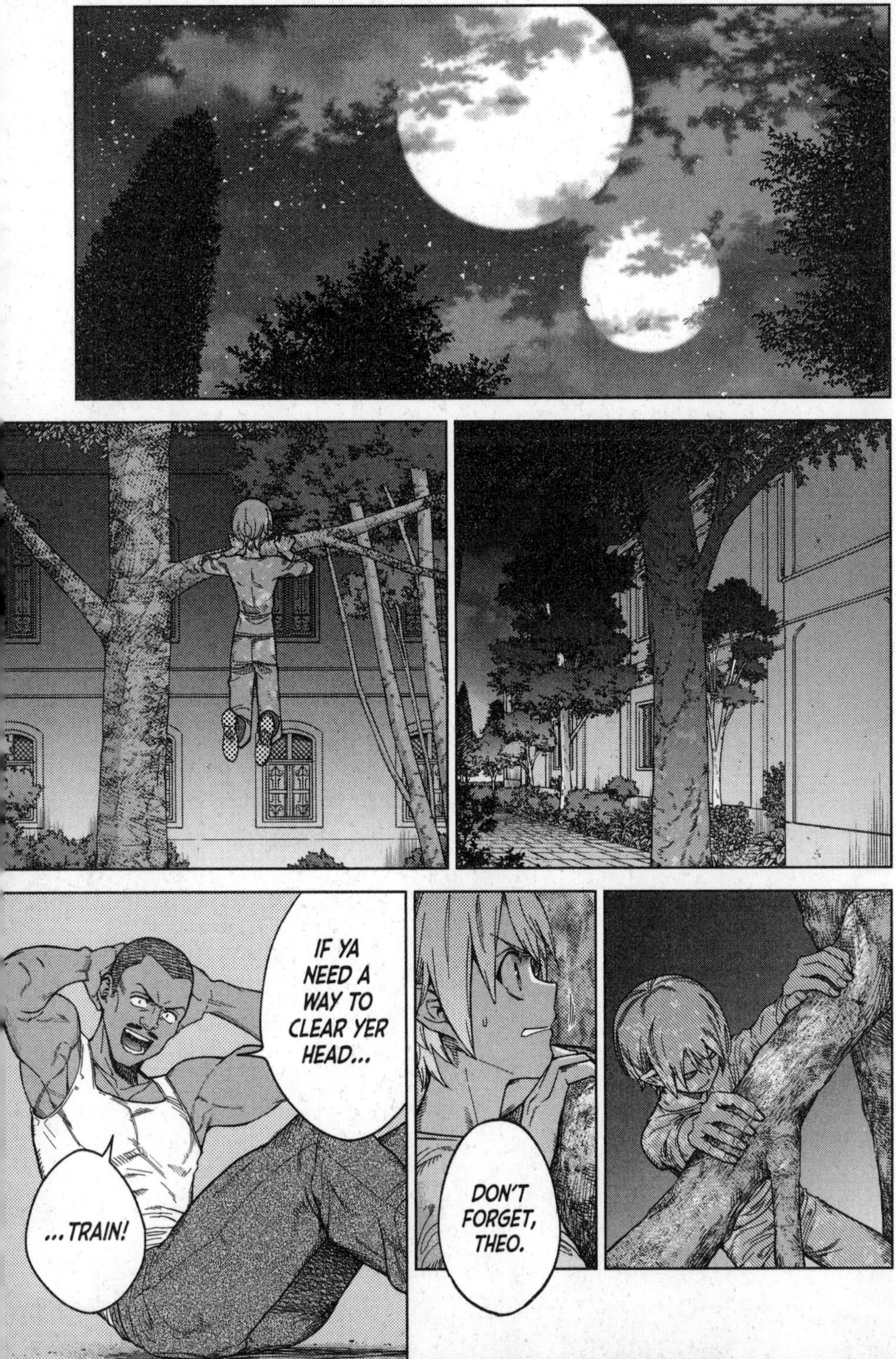
DON'T FORGET, THEO.
IF YA NEED A WAY TO CLEAR YER HEAD...
...TRAIN!

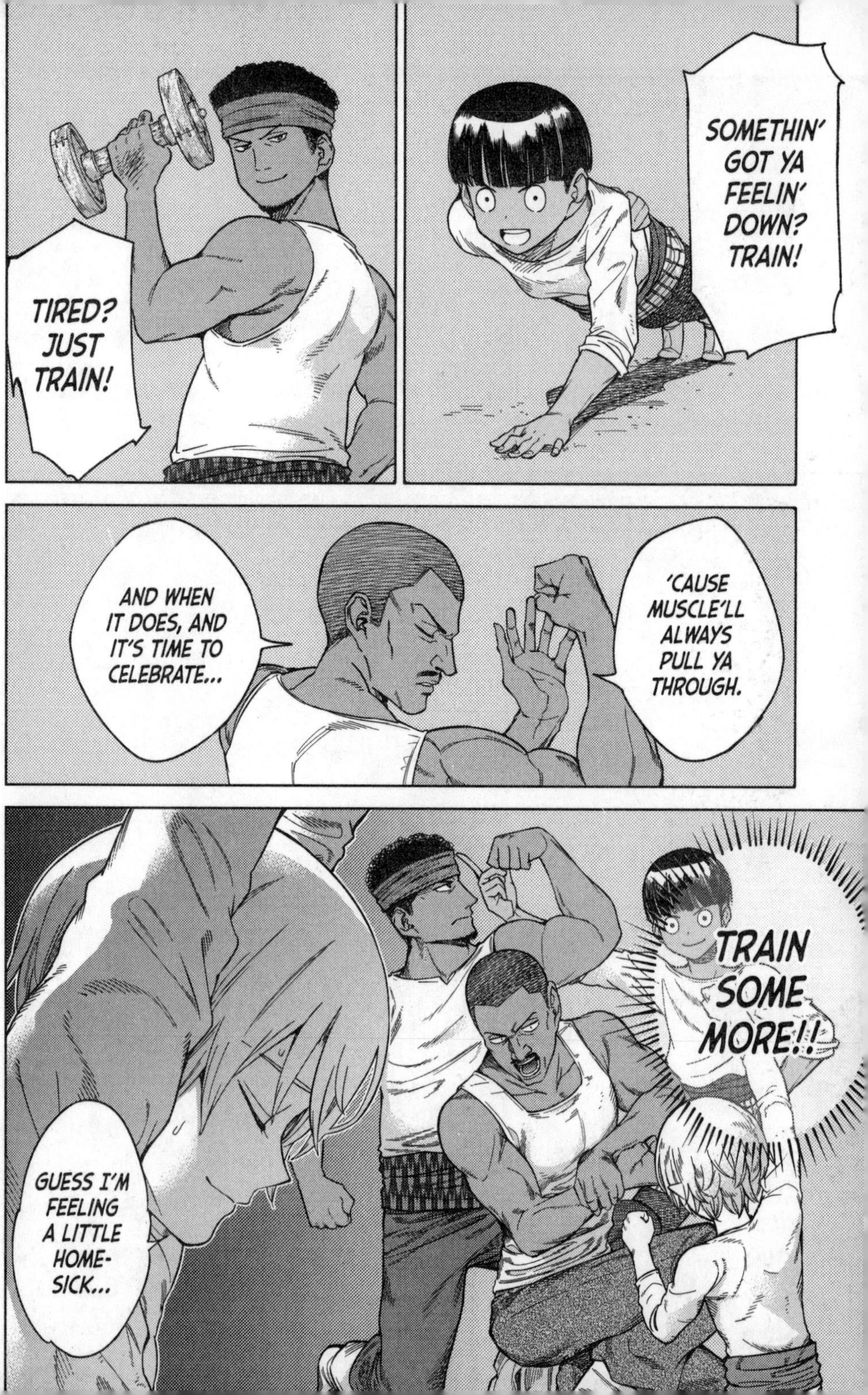
SOMETHIN' GOT YA FEELIN' DOWN? TRAIN!
TIRED? JUST TRAIN!
'CAUSE MUSCLE'LL ALWAYS PULL YA THROUGH.
AND WHEN IT DOES, AND IT'S TIME TO CELEBRATE...
TRAIN SOME MORE!!
GUESS I'M FEELING A LITTLE HOME-SICK...

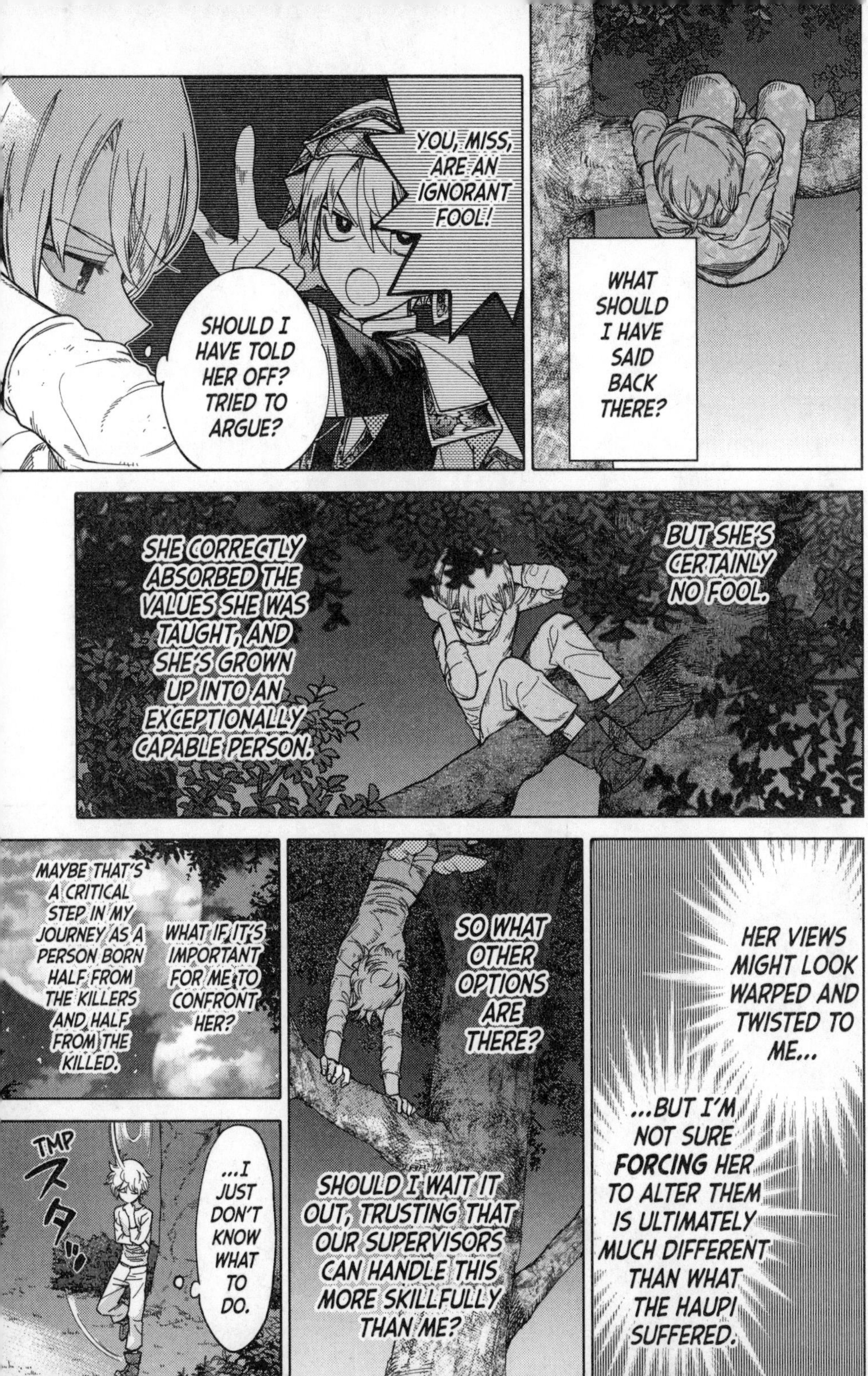
WHAT SHOULD I HAVE SAID BACK THERE?
YOU, MISS, ARE AN IGNORANT FOOL!
SHOULD I HAVE TOLD HER OFF? TRIED TO ARGUE?
BUT SHE'S CERTAINLY NO FOOL.
SHE CORRECTLY ABSORBED THE VALUES SHE WAS TAUGHT, AND SHE'S GROWN UP INTO AN EXCEPTIONALLY CAPABLE PERSON.
HER VIEWS MIGHT LOOK WARPED AND TWISTED TO ME...
...BUT I'M NOT SURE FORCING HER TO ALTER THEM IS ULTIMATELY MUCH DIFFERENT THAN WHAT THE HAUPI SUFFERED.
SO WHAT OTHER OPTIONS ARE THERE?
SHOULD I WAIT IT OUT, TRUSTING THAT OUR SUPERVISORS CAN HANDLE THIS MORE SKILLFULLY THAN ME?
WHAT IF IT'S IMPORTANT FOR ME TO CONFRONT HER?
MAYBE THAT'S A CRITICAL STEP IN MY JOURNEY AS A PERSON BORN HALF FROM THE KILLERS AND HALF FROM THE KILLED.
...I JUST DON'T KNOW WHAT TO DO.
TMP
スタッ

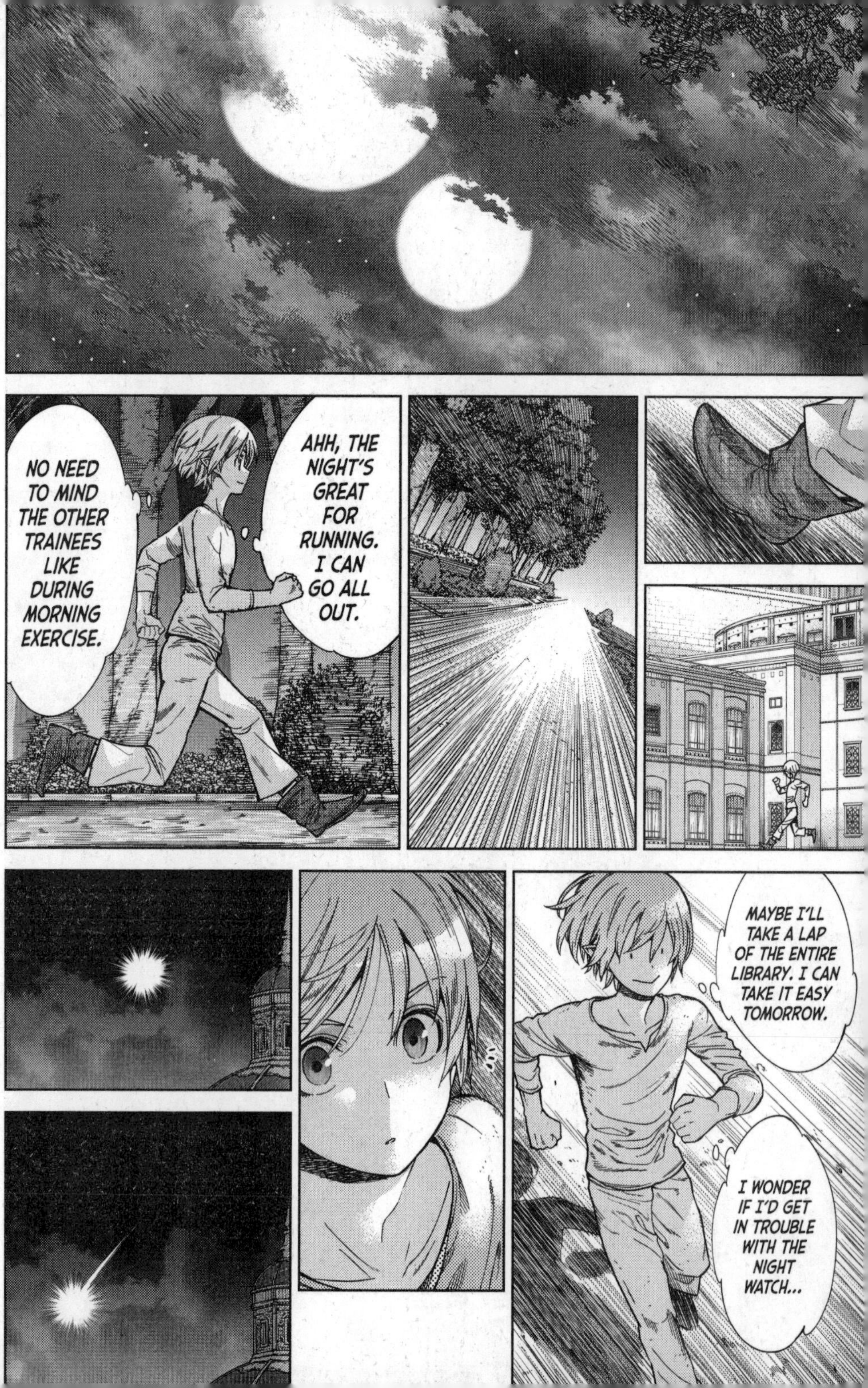
AHH, THE NIGHT'S GREAT FOR RUNNING. I CAN GO ALL OUT.
NO NEED TO MIND THE OTHER TRAINEES LIKE DURING MORNING EXERCISE.
MAYBE I'LL TAKE A LAP OF THE ENTIRE LIBRARY. I CAN TAKE IT EASY TOMORROW.
I WONDER IF I'D GET IN TROUBLE WITH THE NIGHT WATCH...

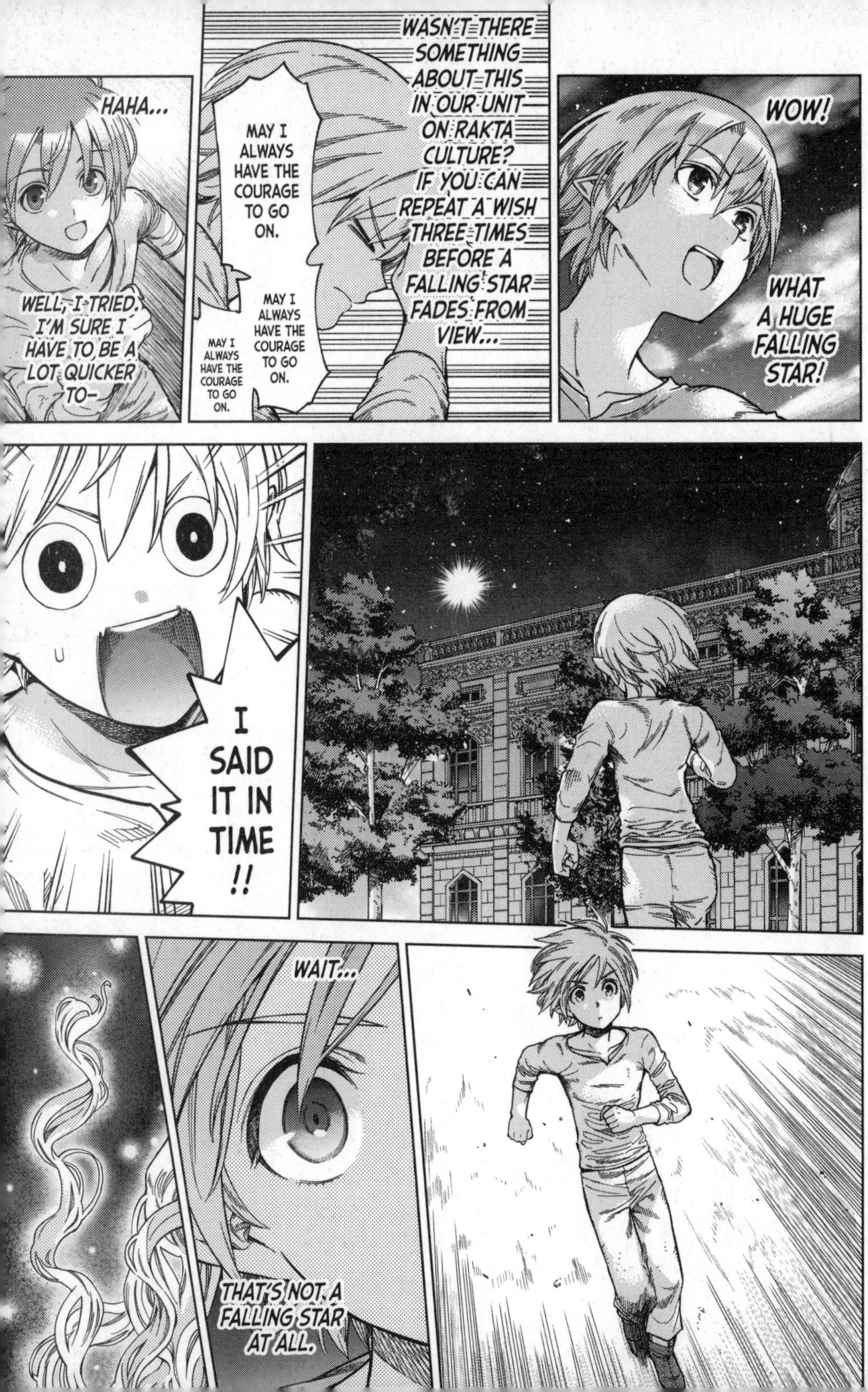
WOW!
WHAT A HUGE FALLING STAR!
WASN'T THERE SOMETHING ABOUT THIS IN OUR UNIT ON RAKTA CULTURE? IF YOU CAN REPEAT A WISH THREE TIMES BEFORE A FALLING STAR FADES FROM VIEW...
MAY I ALWAYS HAVE THE COURAGE TO GO ON.
MAY I ALWAYS HAVE THE COURAGE TO GO ON.
MAY I ALWAYS HAVE THE COURAGE TO GO ON.
HAHA...
WELL, I TRIED. I'M SURE I HAVE TO BE A LOT QUICKER TO-
I SAID IT IN TIME!!
WAIT...
THAT'S NOT A FALLING STAR AT ALL.

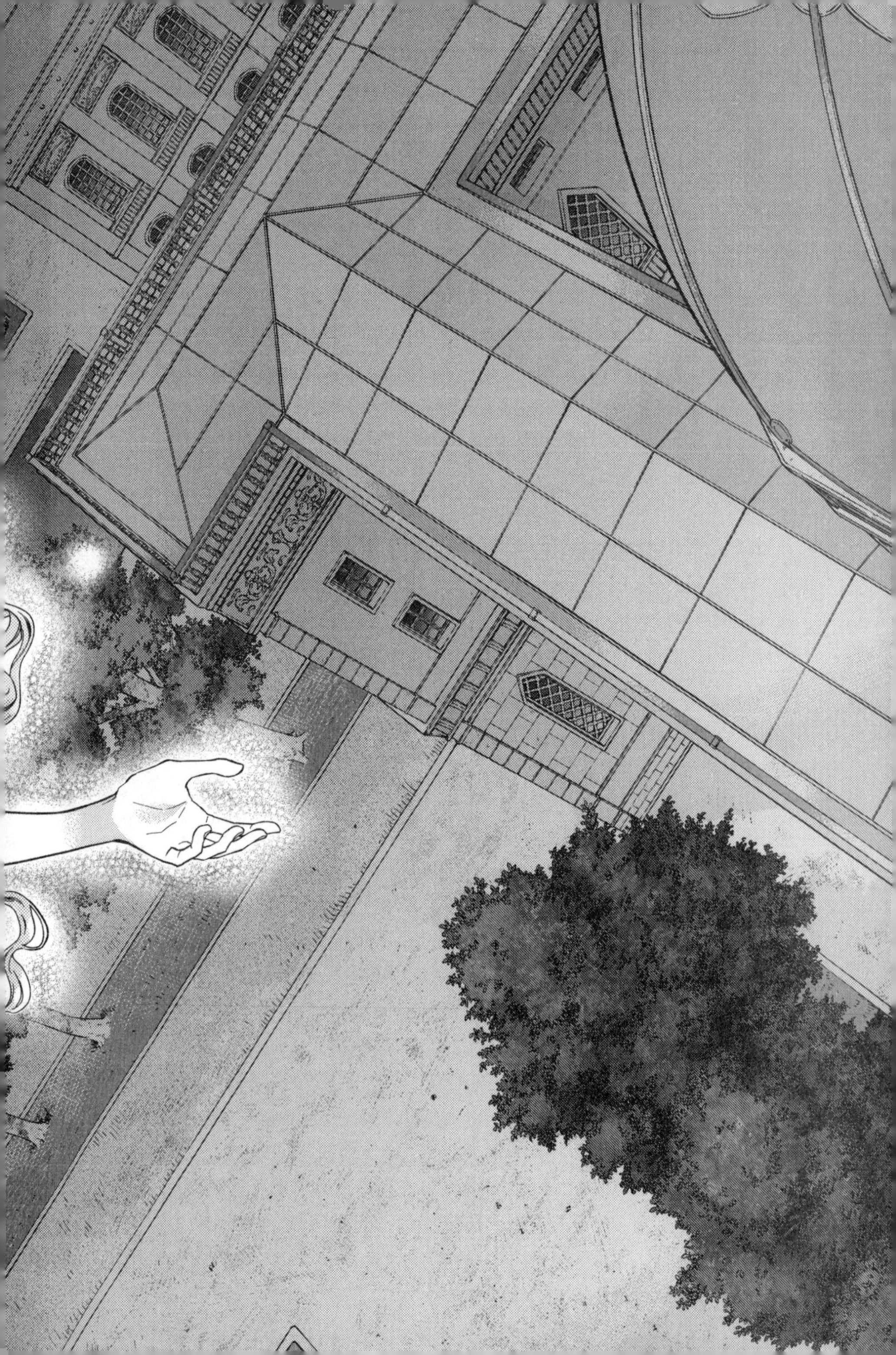

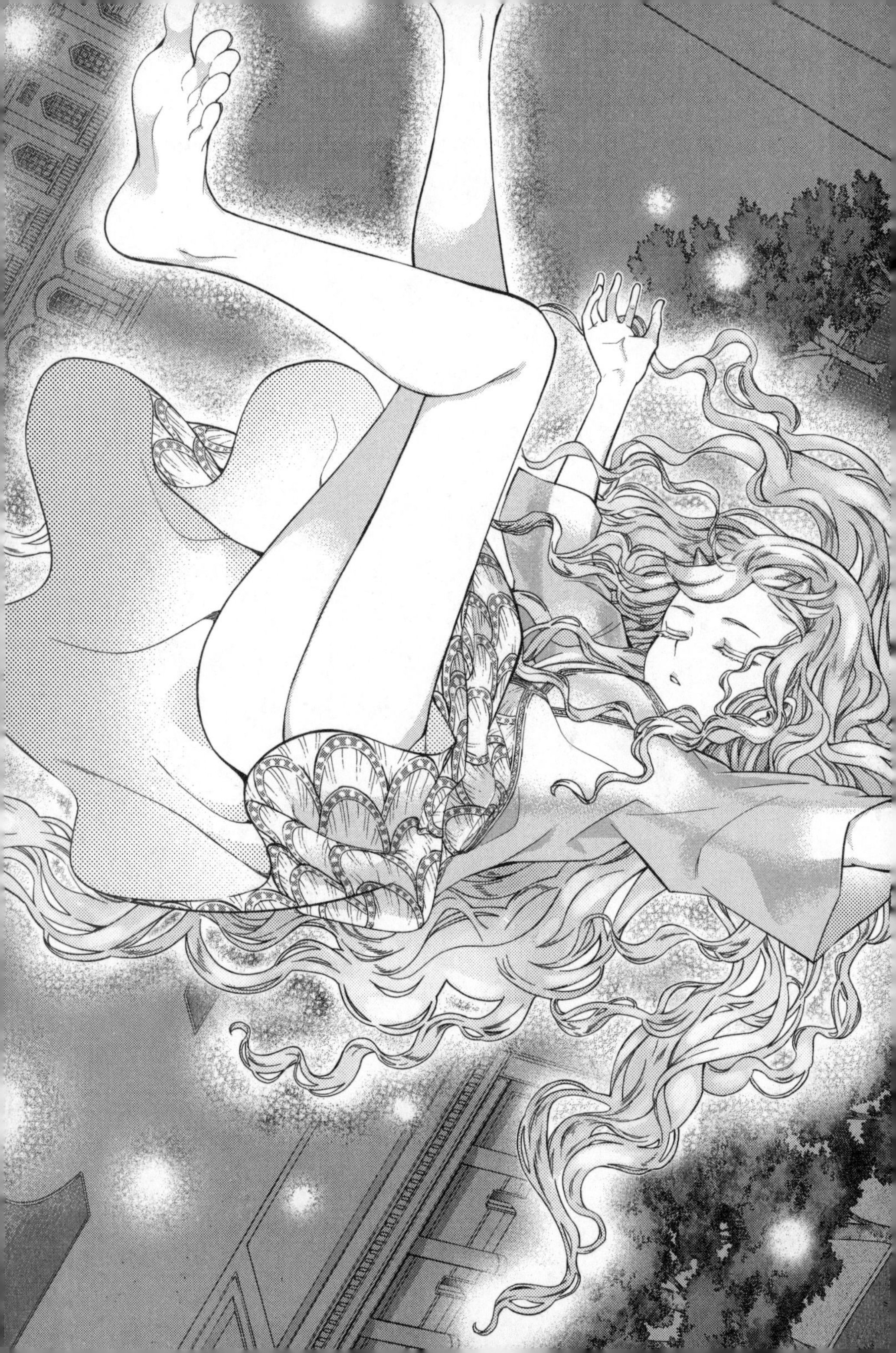

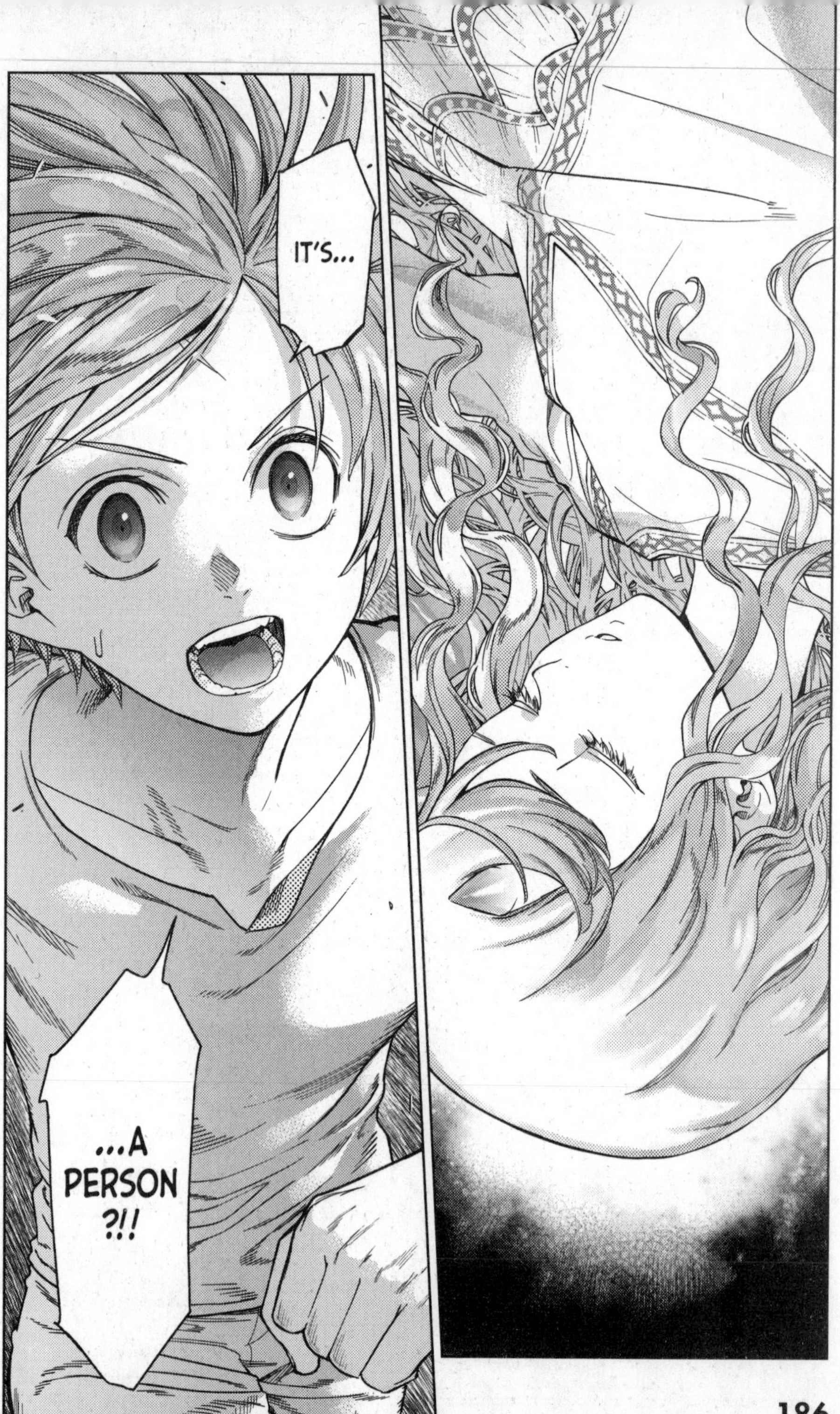
IT'S...
...A PERSON ?!!

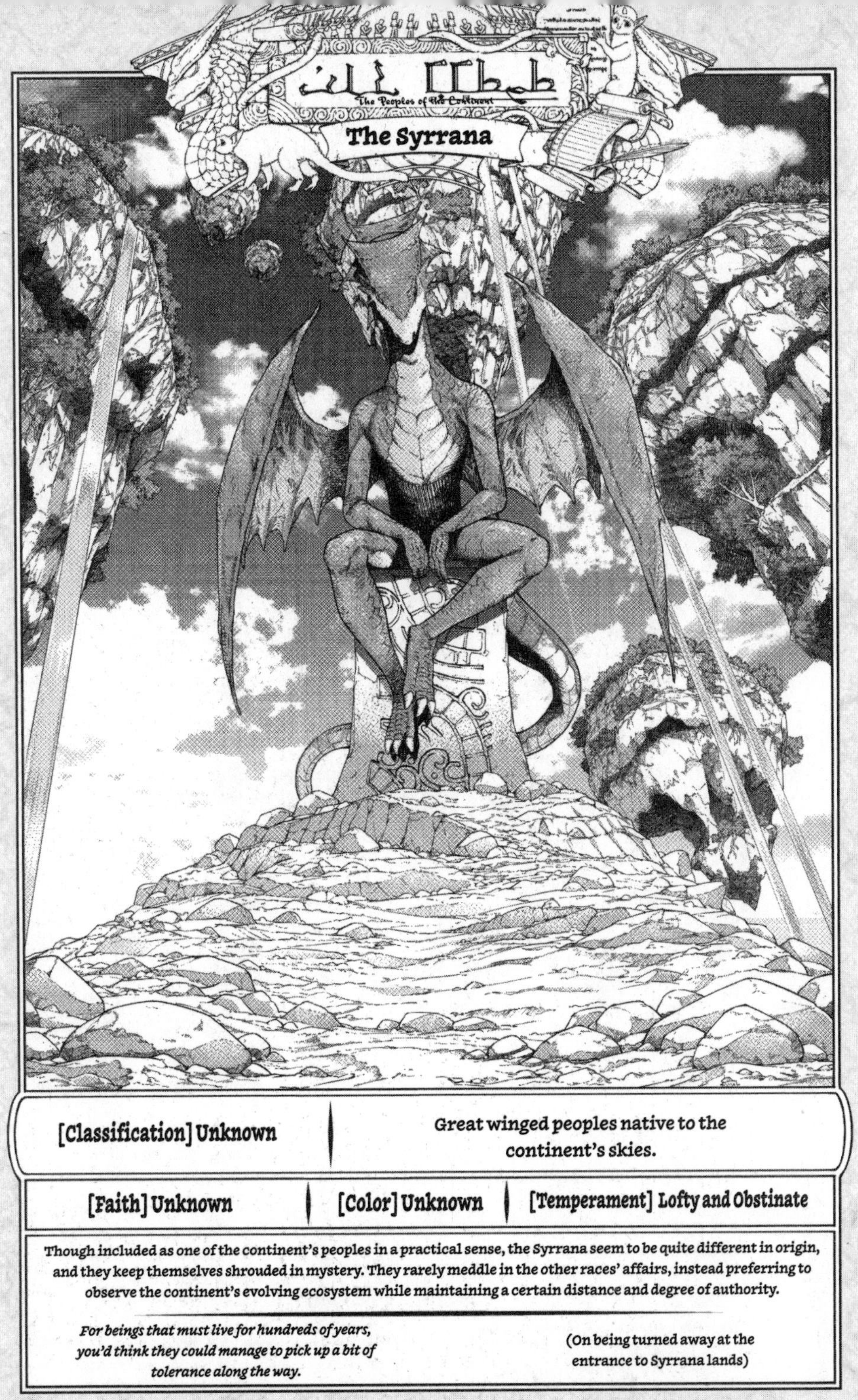
The Peoples of the Continent
The Syrrana

[Classification] Unknown | Great winged peoples native to the continent's skies.

[Faith] Unknown | **[Color] Unknown** | **[Temperament] Lofty and Obstinate**

Though included as one of the continent's peoples in a practical sense, the Syrrana seem to be quite different in origin, and they keep themselves shrouded in mystery. They rarely meddle in the other races' affairs, instead preferring to observe the continent's evolving ecosystem while maintaining a certain distance and degree of authority.

For beings that must live for hundreds of years, you'd think they could manage to pick up a bit of tolerance along the way.

(On being turned away at the entrance to Syrrana lands)

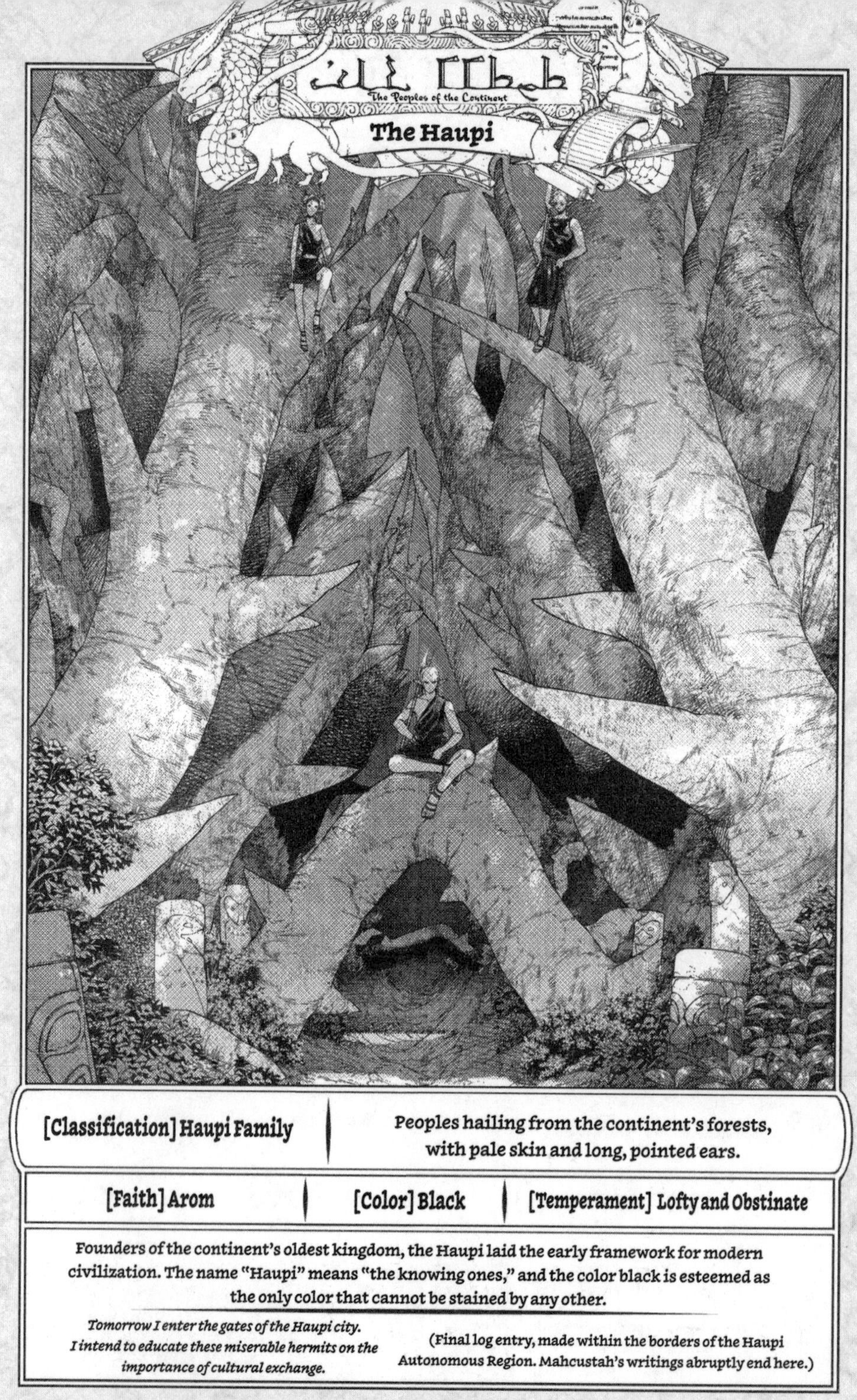
The Peoples of the Continent
The Haupi

[Classification] Haupi Family	Peoples hailing from the continent's forests, with pale skin and long, pointed ears.

[Faith] Arom	[Color] Black	[Temperament] Lofty and Obstinate

Founders of the continent's oldest kingdom, the Haupi laid the early framework for modern civilization. The name "Haupi" means "the knowing ones," and the color black is esteemed as the only color that cannot be stained by any other.

Tomorrow I enter the gates of the Haupi city. I intend to educate these miserable hermits on the importance of cultural exchange.

(Final log entry, made within the borders of the Haupi Autonomous Region. Mahcustah's writings abruptly end here.)

24 The Lights in the Falling Stars Are Mana

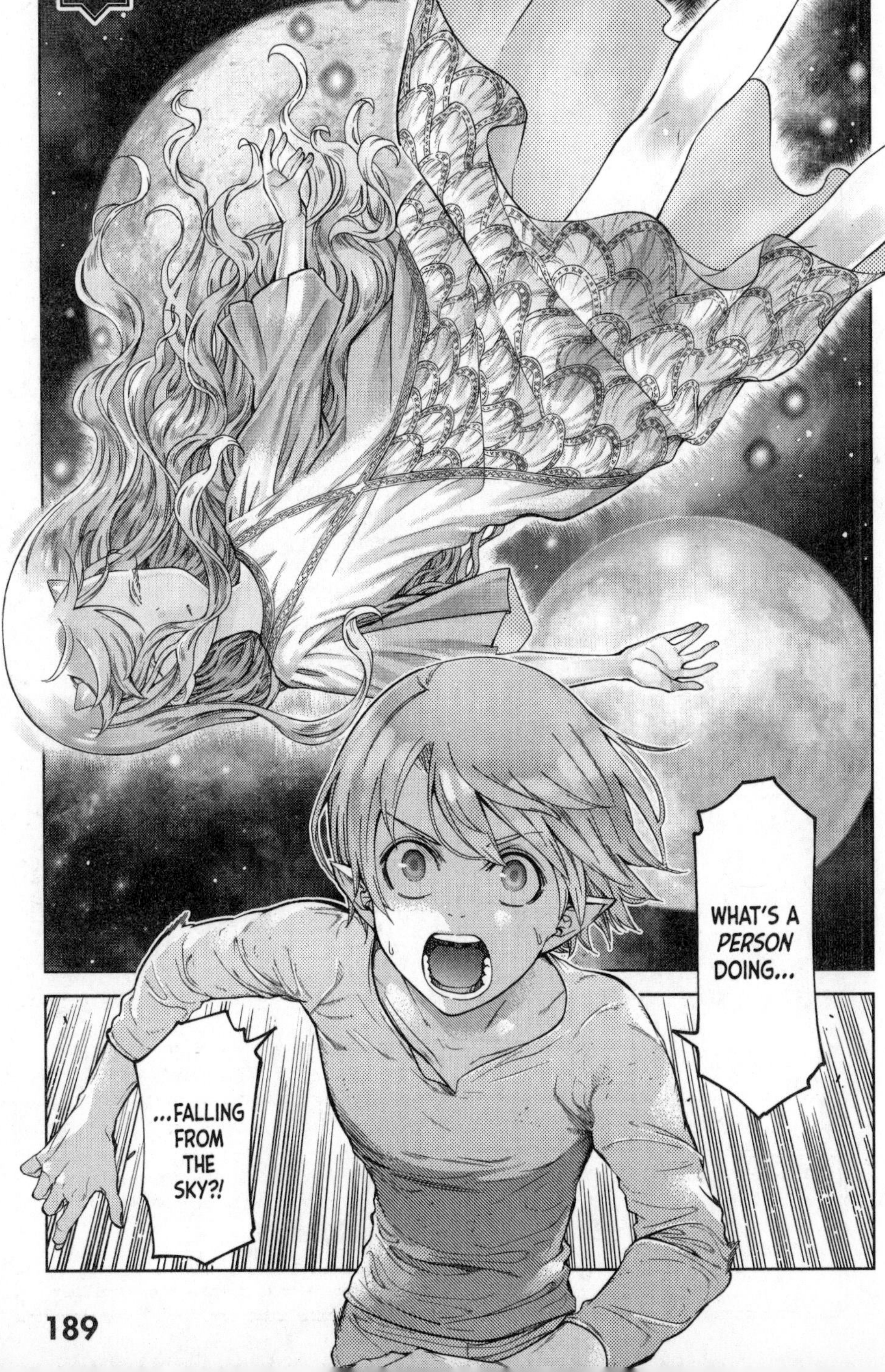
WHAT'S A PERSON DOING...
...FALLING FROM THE SKY?!

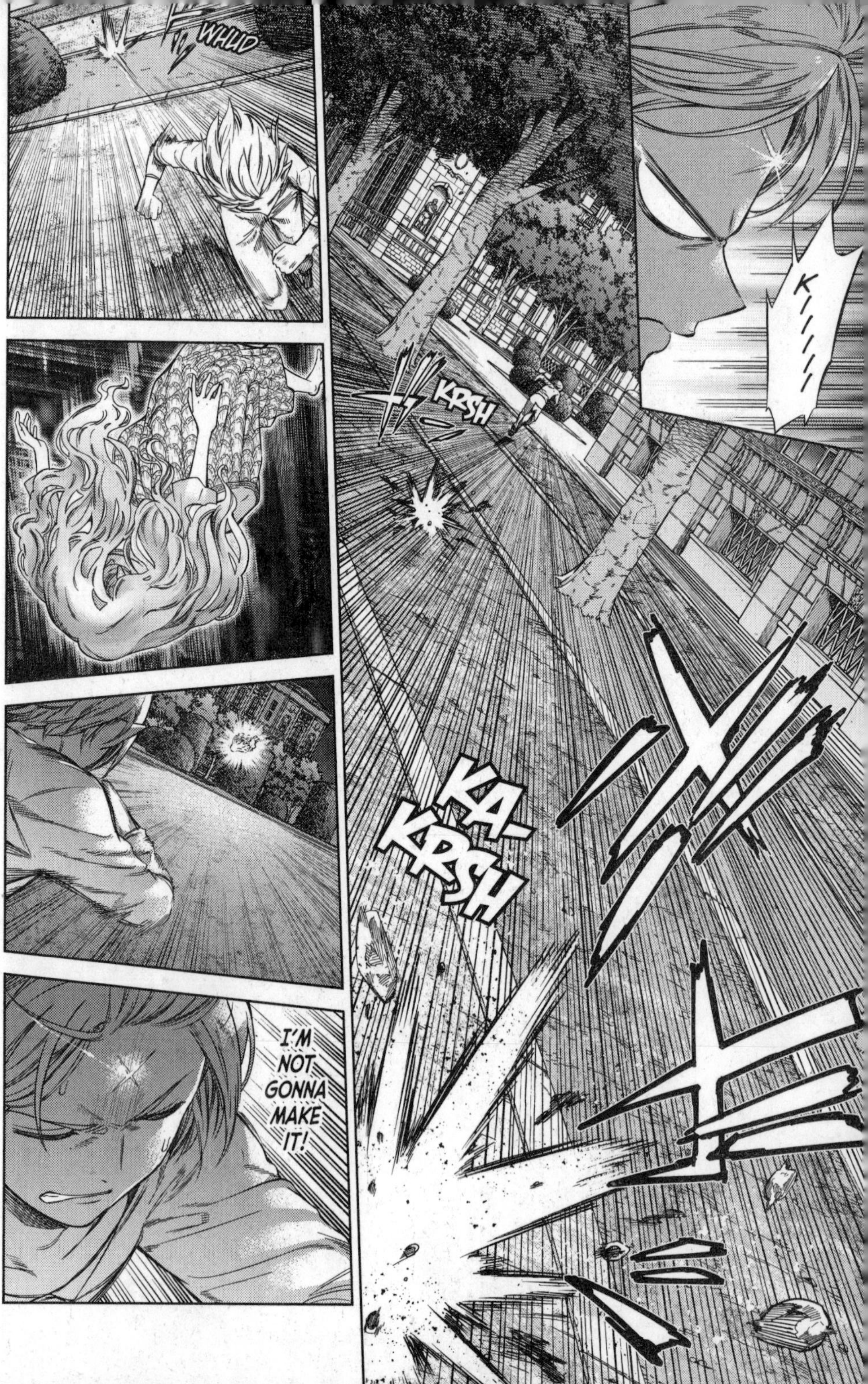
KIIIII
KRSH
KA-KRSH
WHUD
I'M NOT GONNA MAKE IT!

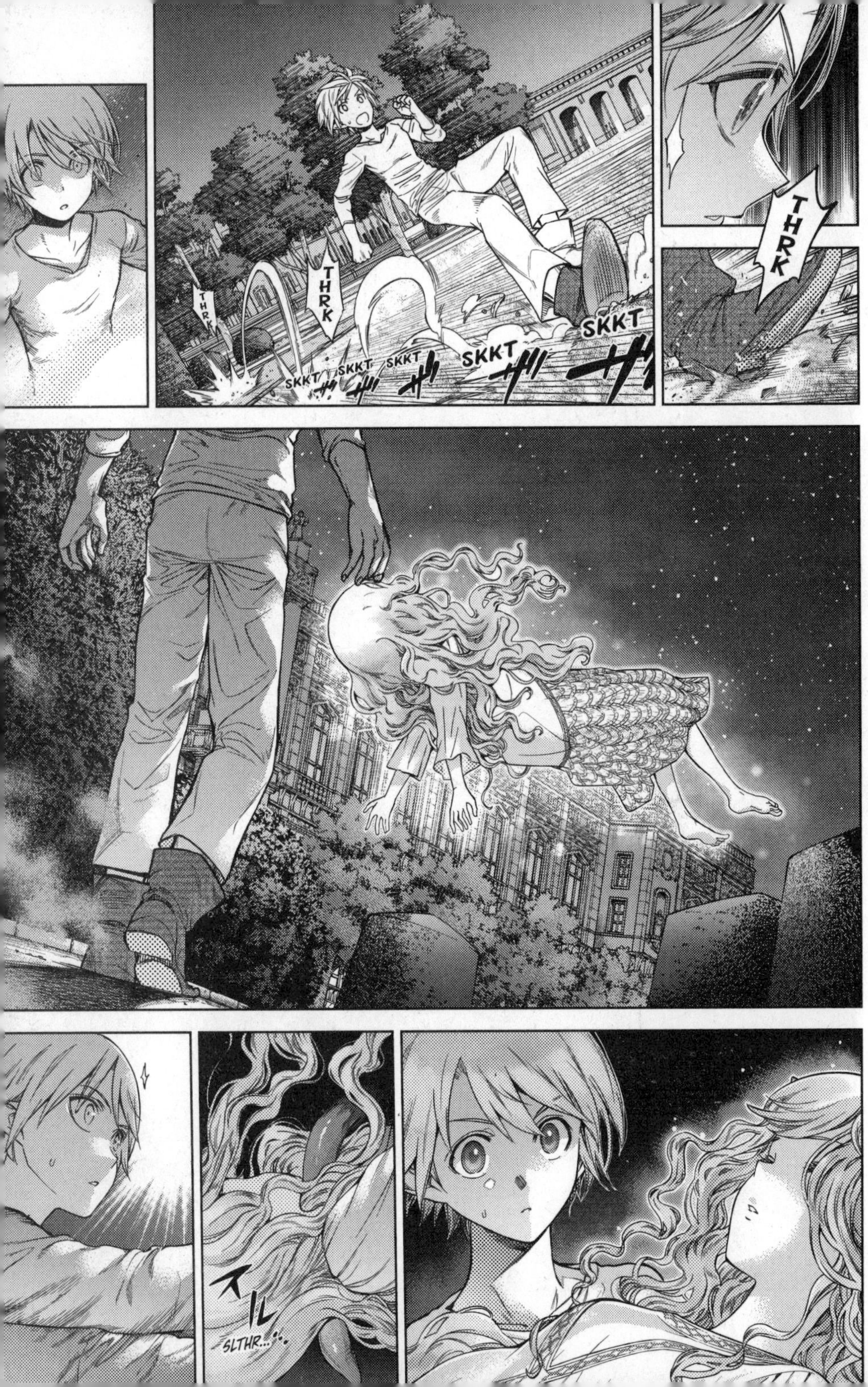

THRK
SKKT
THRK
SKKT
SKKT
SKKT
THRK
SKKT
SLTHR...

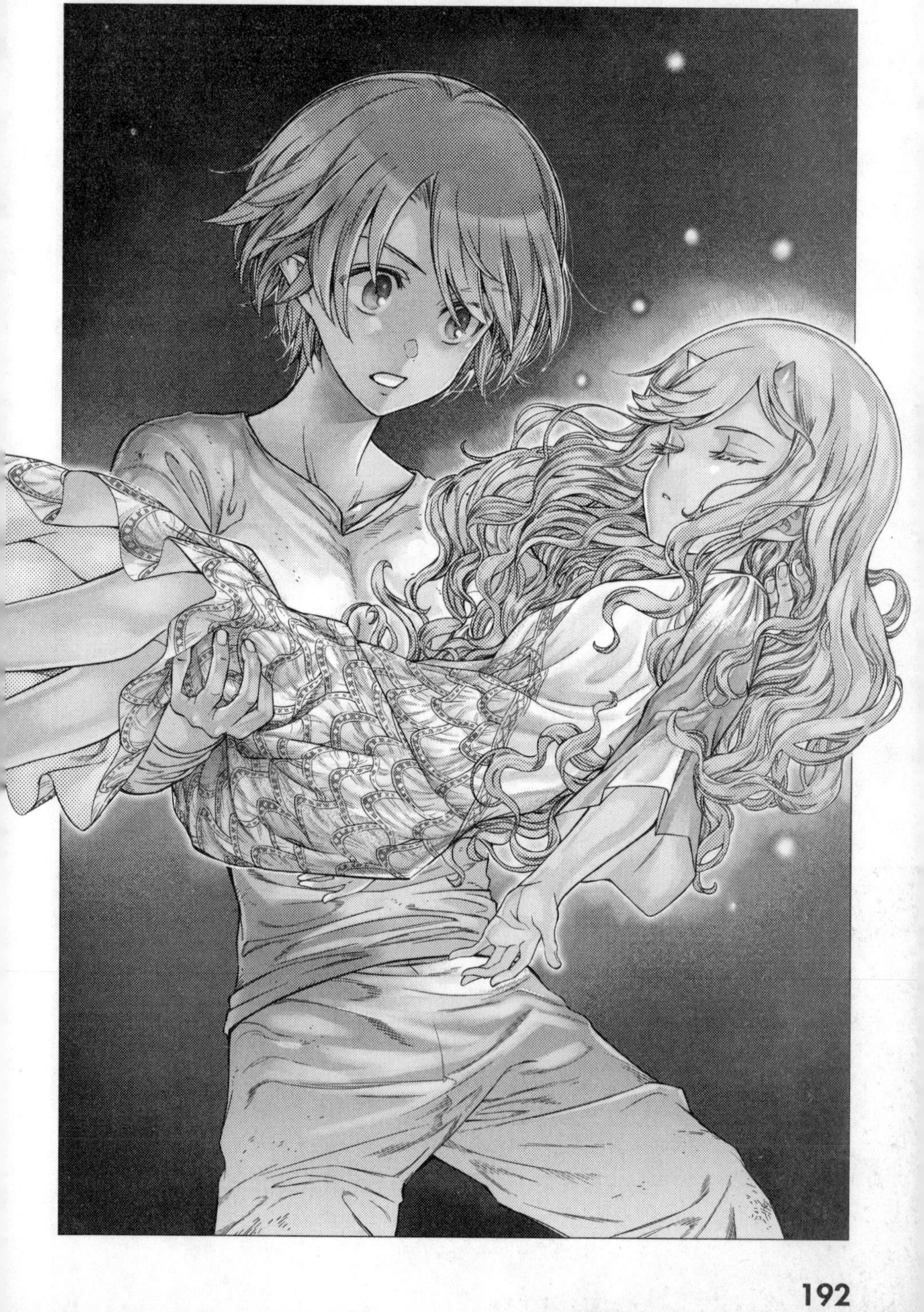

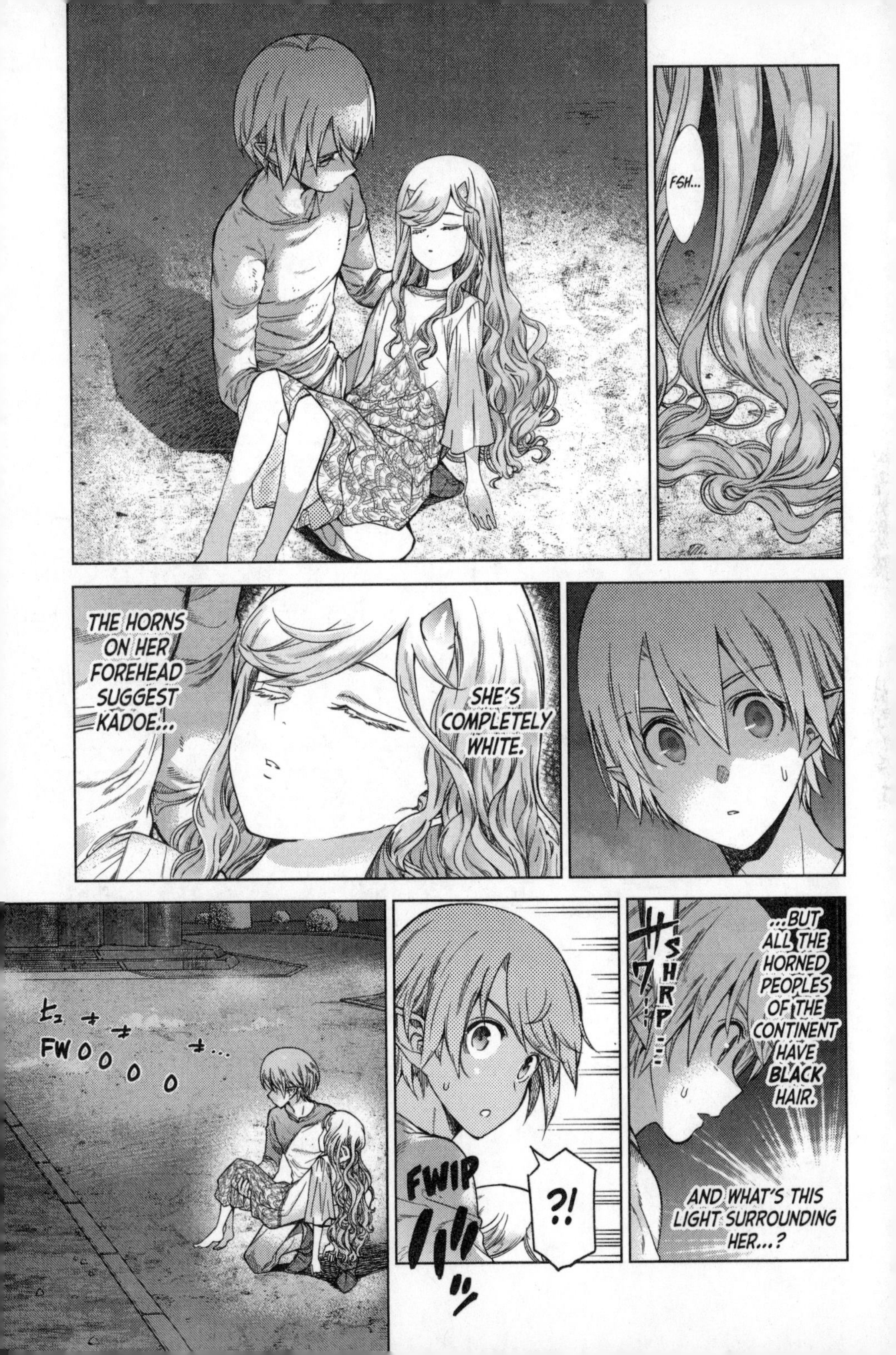
FSH...
SHE'S COMPLETELY WHITE.
THE HORNS ON HER FOREHEAD SUGGEST KADOE...
SHRP...
...BUT ALL THE HORNED PEOPLES OF THE CONTINENT HAVE BLACK HAIR.
AND WHAT'S THIS LIGHT SURROUNDING HER...?
FWIP
?!
FWOOOOO...

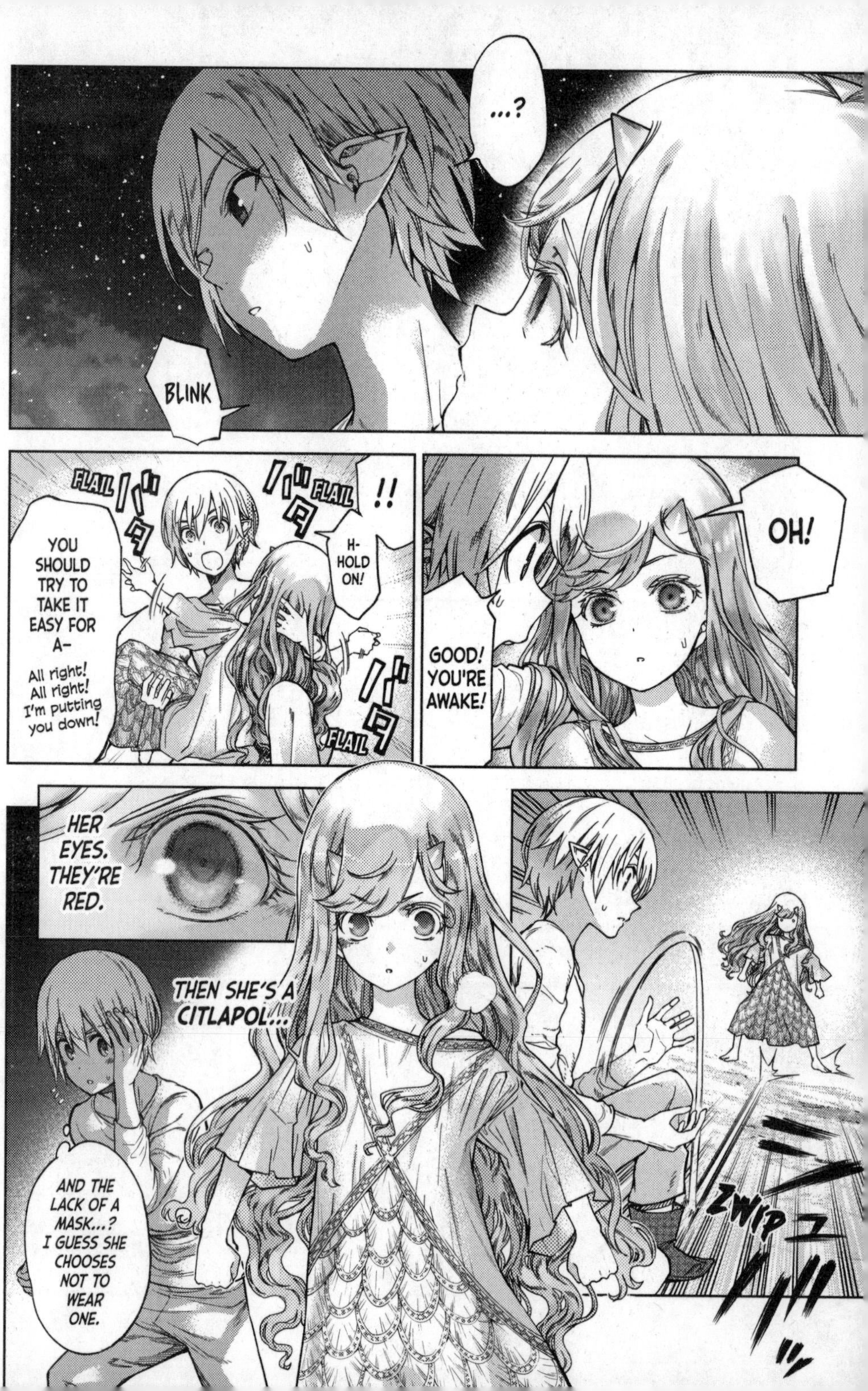
...?
BLINK
OH!
GOOD! YOU'RE AWAKE!
!!
H-HOLD ON!
FLAIL
FLAIL
FLAIL
YOU SHOULD TRY TO TAKE IT EASY FOR A-
All right! All right! I'm putting you down!
ZWIP
HER EYES. THEY'RE RED.
THEN SHE'S A CITLAPOL...
AND THE LACK OF A MASK...? I GUESS SHE CHOOSES NOT TO WEAR ONE.

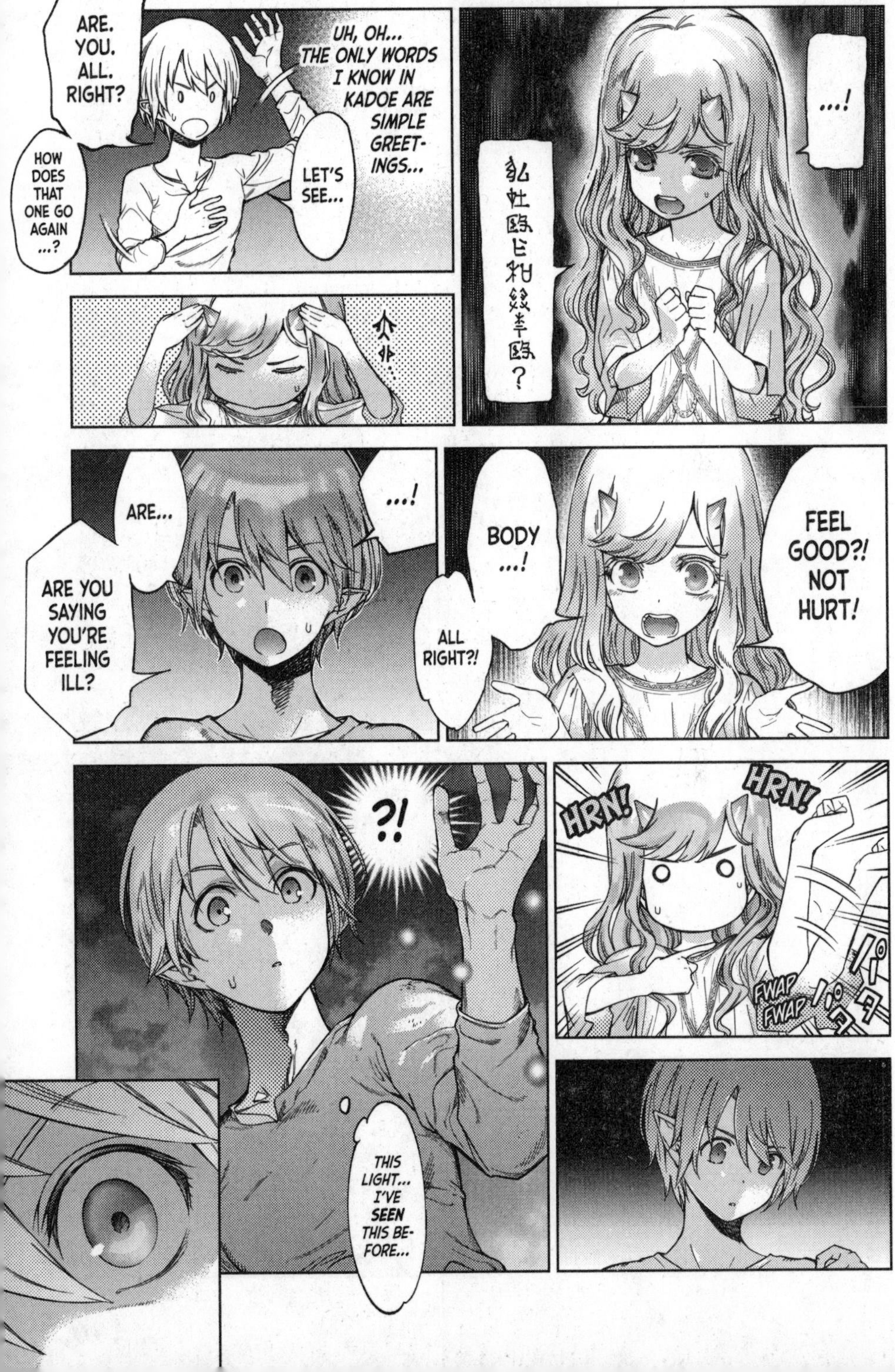
...!
UH, OH... THE ONLY WORDS I KNOW IN KADOE ARE SIMPLE GREET-INGS...
LET'S SEE...
ARE. YOU. ALL. RIGHT?
HOW DOES THAT ONE GO AGAIN ...?
FEEL GOOD?! NOT HURT!
BODY ...!
ALL RIGHT?!
...!
ARE...
ARE YOU SAYING YOU'RE FEELING ILL?
HRN!
HRN!
FWAP FWAP
パタパタ
?!
THIS LIGHT... I'VE SEEN THIS BE-FORE...

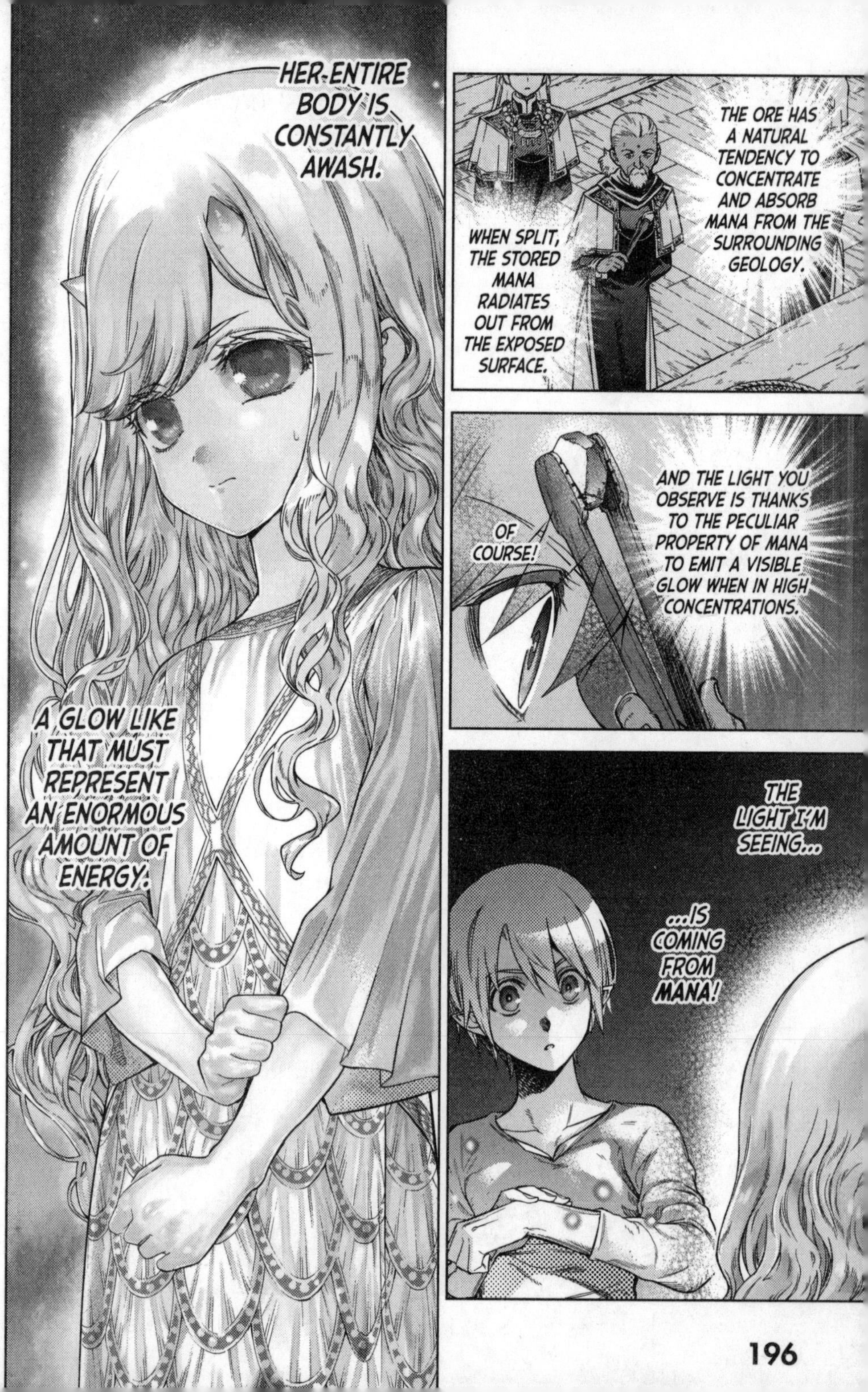

THE ORE HAS A NATURAL TENDENCY TO CONCENTRATE AND ABSORB MANA FROM THE SURROUNDING GEOLOGY.
WHEN SPLIT, THE STORED MANA RADIATES OUT FROM THE EXPOSED SURFACE.
AND THE LIGHT YOU OBSERVE IS THANKS TO THE PECULIAR PROPERTY OF MANA TO EMIT A VISIBLE GLOW WHEN IN HIGH CONCENTRATIONS.
OF COURSE!
THE LIGHT I'M SEEING...
...IS COMING FROM MANA!
HER ENTIRE BODY IS CONSTANTLY AWASH.
A GLOW LIKE THAT MUST REPRESENT AN ENORMOUS AMOUNT OF ENERGY.

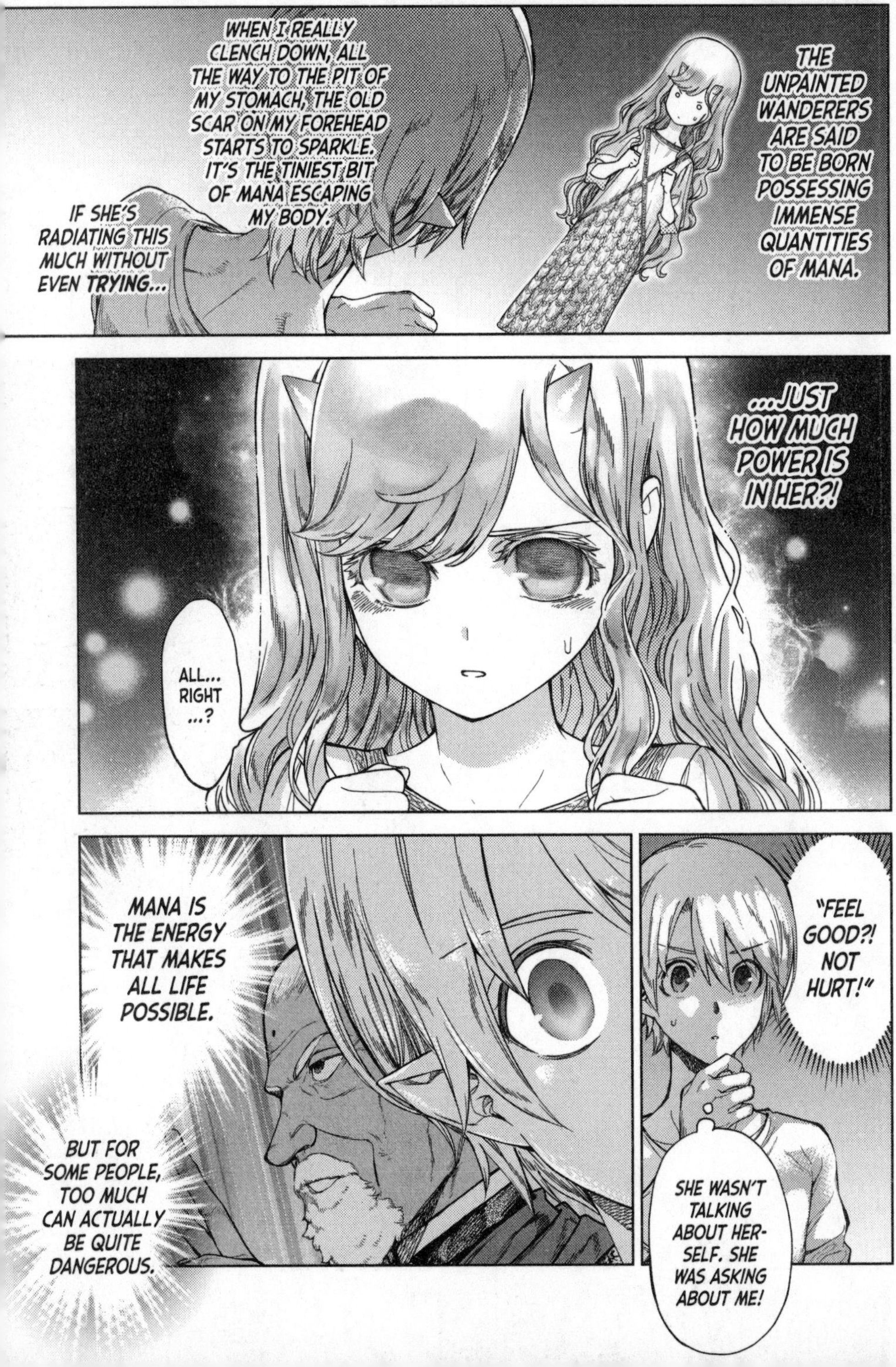
THE UNPAINTED WANDERERS ARE SAID TO BE BORN POSSESSING IMMENSE QUANTITIES OF MANA.
WHEN I REALLY CLENCH DOWN, ALL THE WAY TO THE PIT OF MY STOMACH, THE OLD SCAR ON MY FOREHEAD STARTS TO SPARKLE. IT'S THE TINIEST BIT OF MANA ESCAPING MY BODY.
IF SHE'S RADIATING THIS MUCH WITHOUT EVEN TRYING...
...JUST HOW MUCH POWER IS IN HER?!
ALL... RIGHT ...?
"FEEL GOOD?! NOT HURT!"
SHE WASN'T TALKING ABOUT HER-SELF. SHE WAS ASKING ABOUT ME!
MANA IS THE ENERGY THAT MAKES ALL LIFE POSSIBLE.
BUT FOR SOME PEOPLE, TOO MUCH CAN ACTUALLY BE QUITE DANGEROUS.

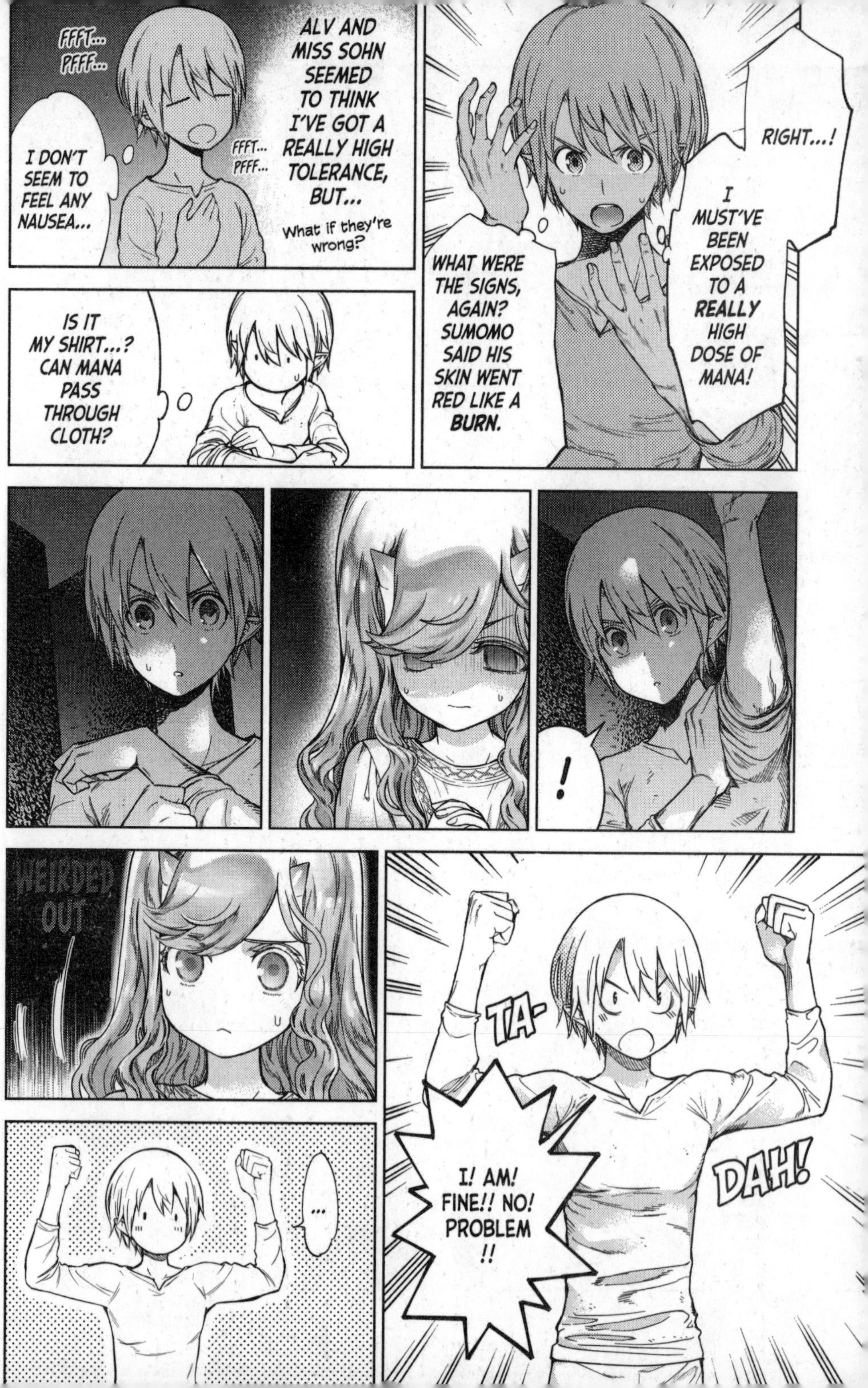
RIGHT...!
I MUST'VE BEEN EXPOSED TO A REALLY HIGH DOSE OF MANA!
WHAT WERE THE SIGNS, AGAIN? SUMOMO SAID HIS SKIN WENT RED LIKE A BURN.
ALV AND MISS SOHN SEEMED TO THINK I'VE GOT A REALLY HIGH TOLERANCE, BUT...
What if they're wrong?
FFFT... PFFF...
FFFT... PFFF...
I DON'T SEEM TO FEEL ANY NAUSEA...
IS IT MY SHIRT...? CAN MANA PASS THROUGH CLOTH?
!
TA-
DAH!
I! AM! FINE!! NO! PROBLEM !!
WEIRDED OUT
...

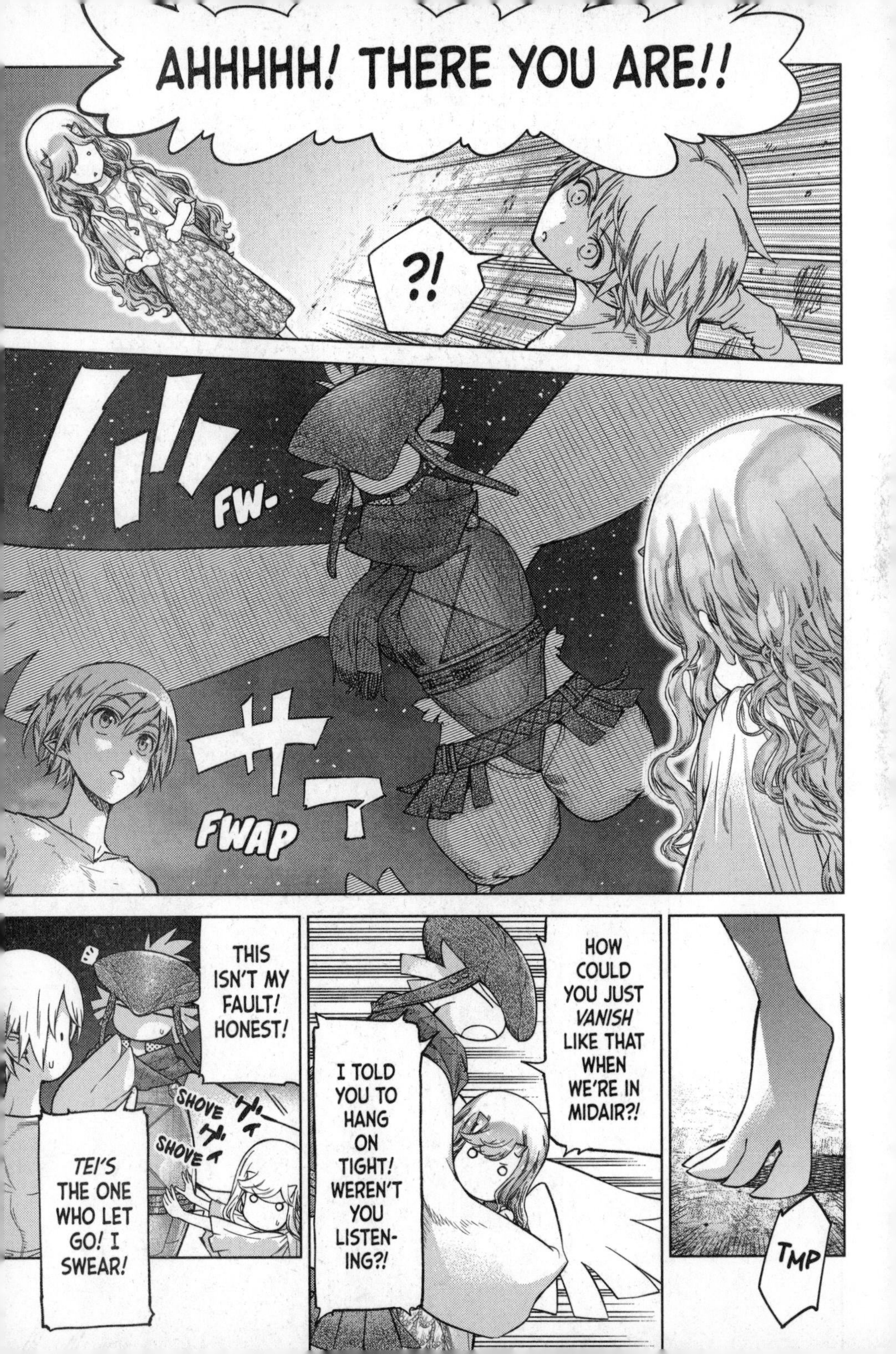
AHHHHH! THERE YOU ARE!!
?!
FW-
FWAP
TMP
HOW COULD YOU JUST *VANISH* LIKE THAT WHEN WE'RE IN MIDAIR?!
I TOLD YOU TO HANG ON TIGHT! WEREN'T YOU LISTENING?!
THIS ISN'T MY FAULT! HONEST!
SHOVE
SHOVE
TEI'S THE ONE WHO LET GO! I SWEAR!

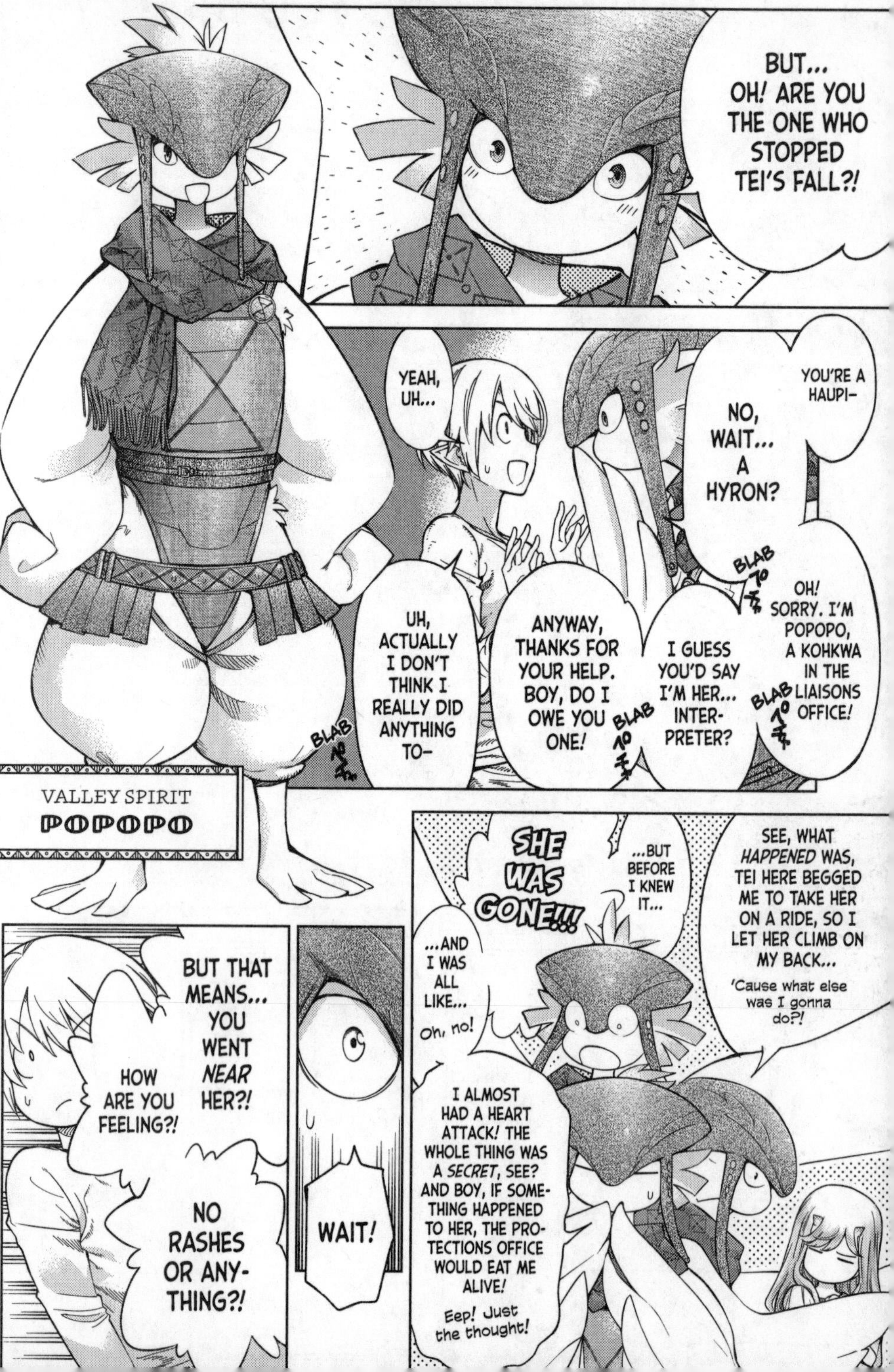
BUT... OH! ARE YOU THE ONE WHO STOPPED TEI'S FALL?!
YOU'RE A HAUPI—
NO, WAIT... A HYRON?
YEAH, UH...
BLAB
OH! SORRY. I'M POPOPO, A KOHKWA IN THE LIAISONS OFFICE!
BLAB
I GUESS YOU'D SAY I'M HER... INTERPRETER?
BLAB
ANYWAY, THANKS FOR YOUR HELP. BOY, DO I OWE YOU ONE!
BLAB
UH, ACTUALLY I DON'T THINK I REALLY DID ANYTHING TO—
VALLEY SPIRIT
POPOPO
SEE, WHAT *HAPPENED* WAS, TEI HERE BEGGED ME TO TAKE HER ON A RIDE, SO I LET HER CLIMB ON MY BACK...
'Cause what else was I gonna do?!
...BUT BEFORE I KNEW IT...
SHE WAS GONE!!!
...AND I WAS ALL LIKE...
Oh, no!
I ALMOST HAD A HEART ATTACK! THE WHOLE THING WAS A *SECRET*, SEE? AND BOY, IF SOMETHING HAPPENED TO HER, THE PROTECTIONS OFFICE WOULD EAT ME ALIVE!
Eep! Just the thought!
WAIT!
BUT THAT MEANS... YOU WENT *NEAR* HER?!
HOW ARE YOU FEELING?!
NO RASHES OR ANYTHING?!

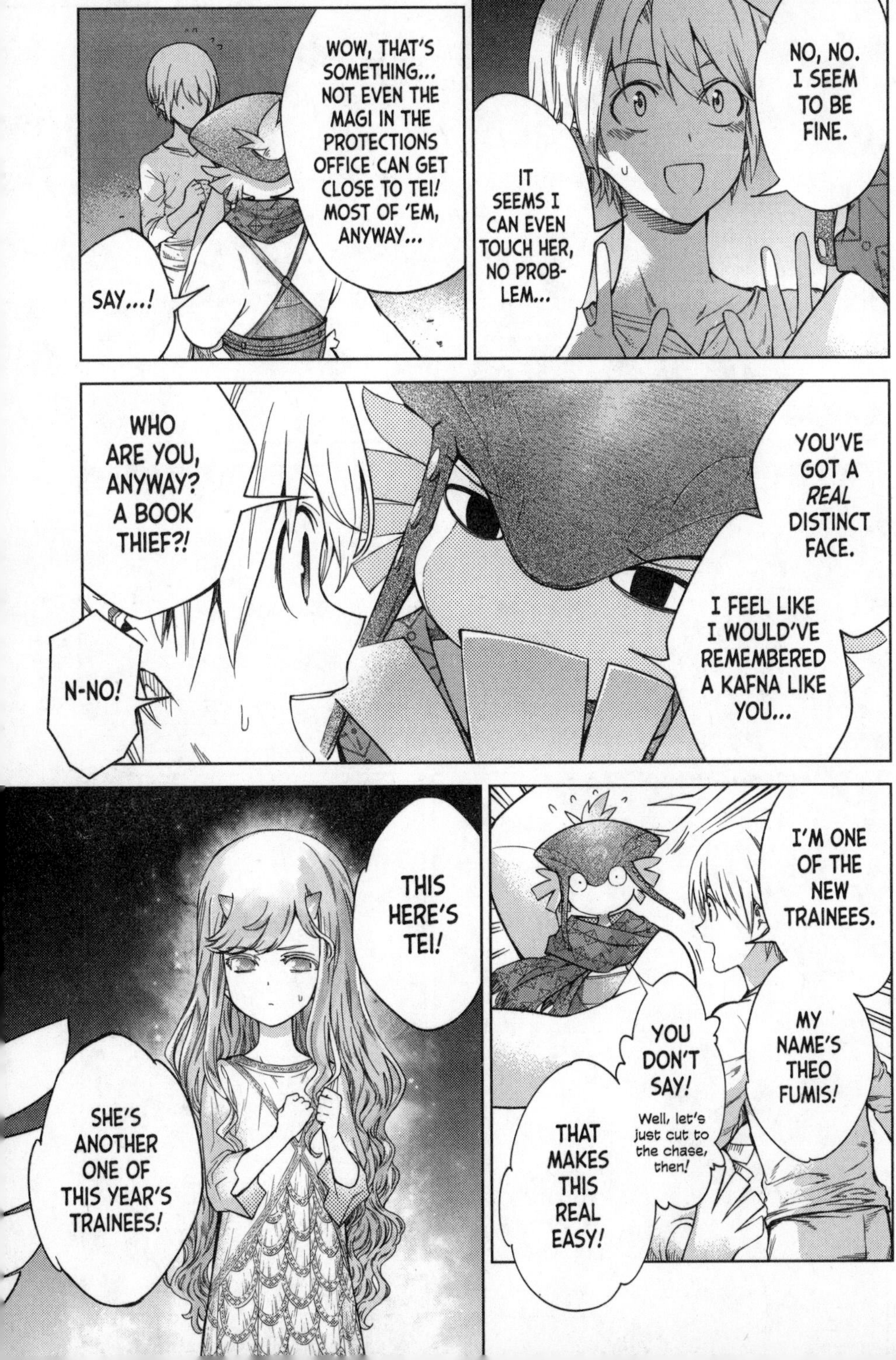
NO, NO. I SEEM TO BE FINE.
IT SEEMS I CAN EVEN TOUCH HER, NO PROB-LEM...
WOW, THAT'S SOMETHING... NOT EVEN THE MAGI IN THE PROTECTIONS OFFICE CAN GET CLOSE TO TEI! MOST OF 'EM, ANYWAY...
SAY...!
YOU'VE GOT A *REAL* DISTINCT FACE.
I FEEL LIKE I WOULD'VE REMEMBERED A KAFNA LIKE YOU...
WHO ARE YOU, ANYWAY? A BOOK THIEF?!
N-NO!
I'M ONE OF THE NEW TRAINEES.
MY NAME'S THEO FUMIS!
YOU DON'T SAY!
Well, let's just cut to the chase, then!
THAT MAKES THIS REAL EASY!
THIS HERE'S TEI!
SHE'S ANOTHER ONE OF THIS YEAR'S TRAINEES!

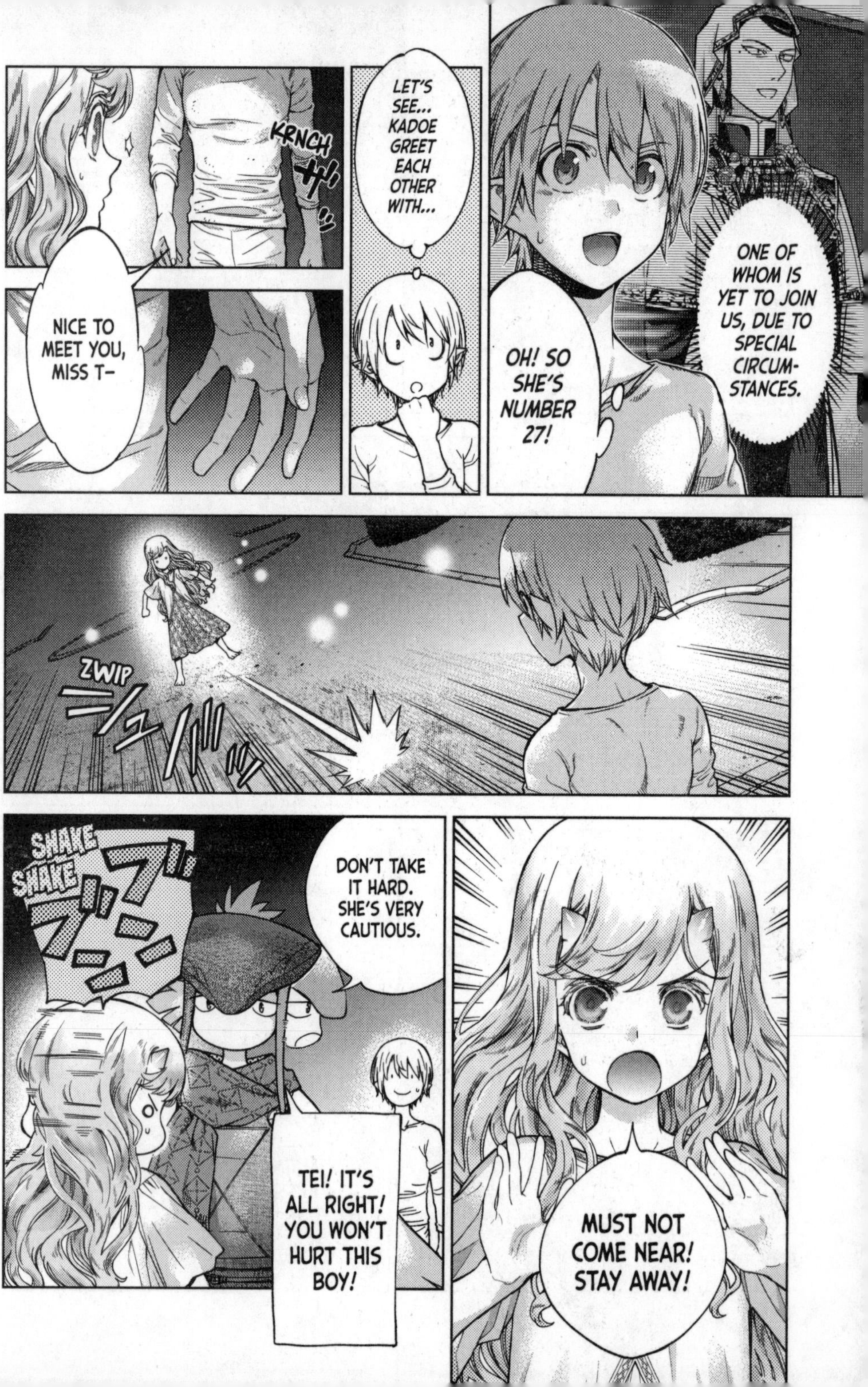
ONE OF WHOM IS YET TO JOIN US, DUE TO SPECIAL CIRCUM-STANCES.
OH! SO SHE'S NUMBER 27!
LET'S SEE... KADOE GREET EACH OTHER WITH...
KRNCH
NICE TO MEET YOU, MISS T-
ZWIP
MUST NOT COME NEAR! STAY AWAY!
DON'T TAKE IT HARD. SHE'S VERY CAUTIOUS.
SHAKE SHAKE
TEI! IT'S ALL RIGHT! YOU WON'T HURT THIS BOY!

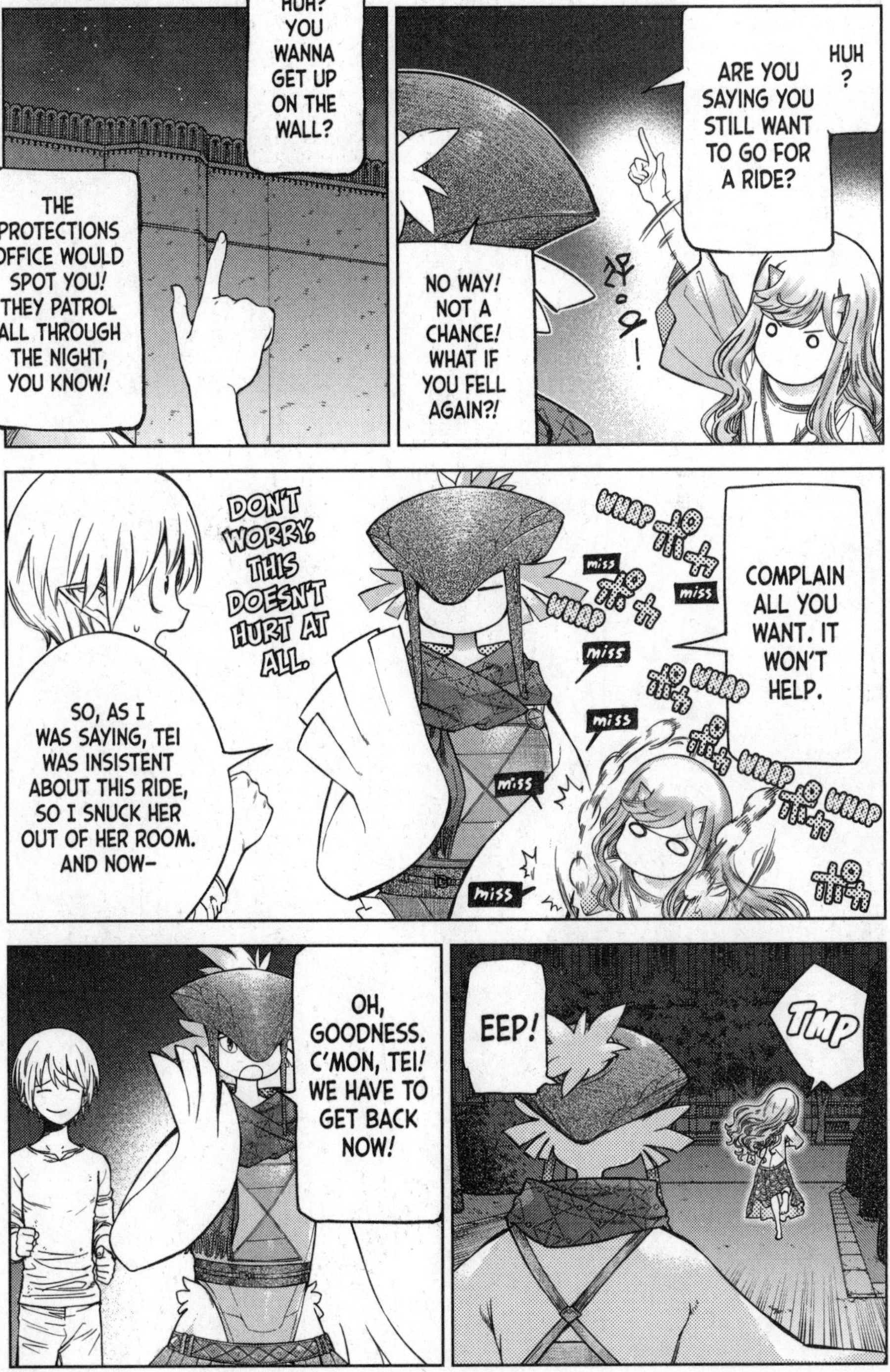
HUH?
ARE YOU SAYING YOU STILL WANT TO GO FOR A RIDE?
NO WAY! NOT A CHANCE! WHAT IF YOU FELL AGAIN?!
HUH? YOU WANNA GET UP ON THE WALL?
THE PROTECTIONS OFFICE WOULD SPOT YOU! THEY PATROL ALL THROUGH THE NIGHT, YOU KNOW!
COMPLAIN ALL YOU WANT. IT WON'T HELP.
WHAP
WHAP
WHAP
WHAP
WHAP
miss
miss
miss
miss
miss
miss
DON'T WORRY. THIS DOESN'T HURT AT ALL.
SO, AS I WAS SAYING, TEI WAS INSISTENT ABOUT THIS RIDE, SO I SNUCK HER OUT OF HER ROOM. AND NOW–
TMP
EEP!
OH, GOODNESS. C'MON, TEI! WE HAVE TO GET BACK NOW!

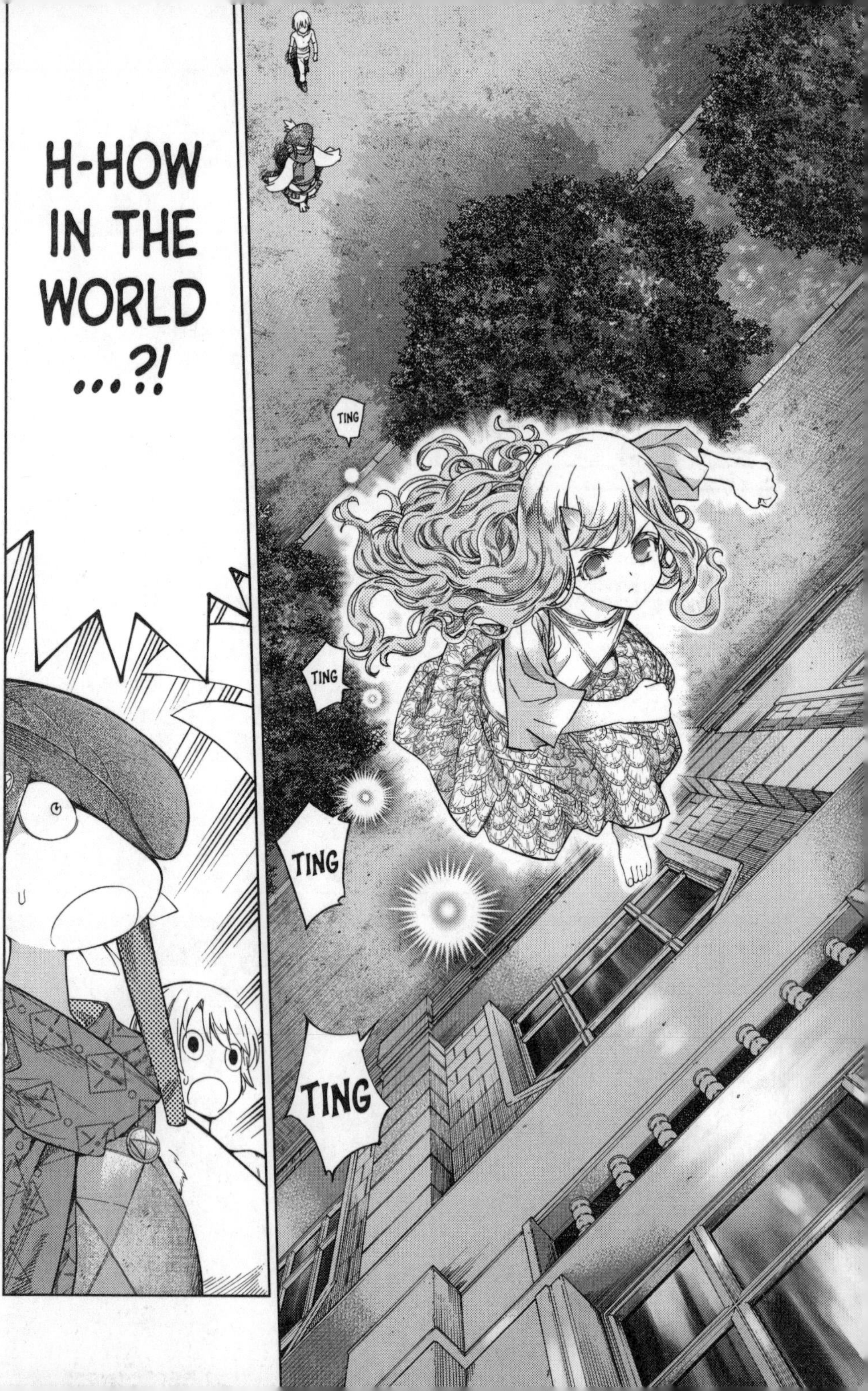
TING
TING
TING
TING
H-HOW IN THE WORLD ...?!

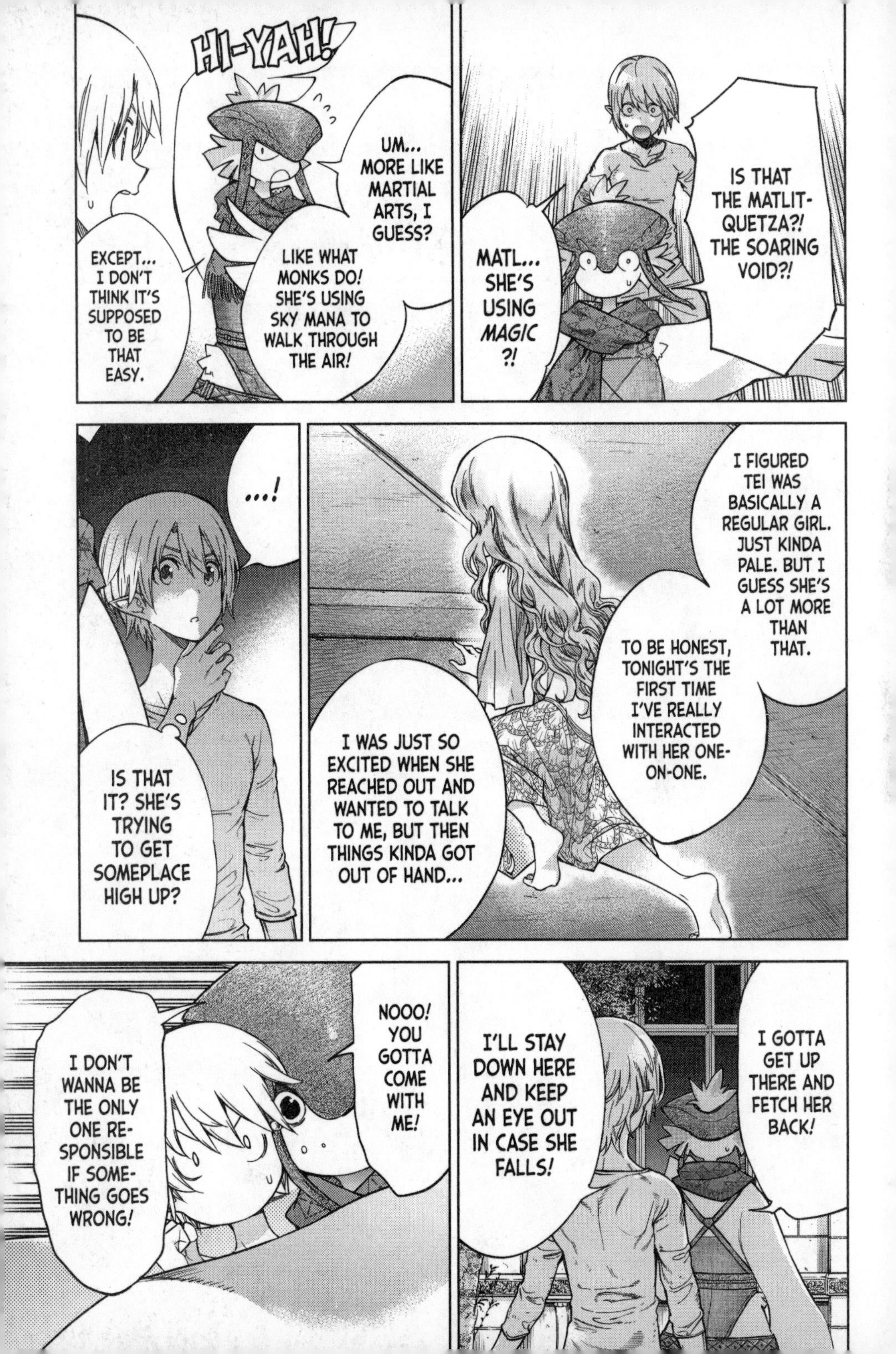
IS THAT THE MATLIT-QUETZA?! THE SOARING VOID?!
MATL... SHE'S USING *MAGIC* ?!
HI-YAH!
UM... MORE LIKE MARTIAL ARTS, I GUESS?
LIKE WHAT MONKS DO! SHE'S USING SKY MANA TO WALK THROUGH THE AIR!
EXCEPT... I DON'T THINK IT'S SUPPOSED TO BE THAT EASY.
I FIGURED TEI WAS BASICALLY A REGULAR GIRL. JUST KINDA PALE. BUT I GUESS SHE'S A LOT MORE THAN THAT.
TO BE HONEST, TONIGHT'S THE FIRST TIME I'VE REALLY INTERACTED WITH HER ONE-ON-ONE.
I WAS JUST SO EXCITED WHEN SHE REACHED OUT AND WANTED TO TALK TO ME, BUT THEN THINGS KINDA GOT OUT OF HAND...
...!
IS THAT IT? SHE'S TRYING TO GET SOMEPLACE HIGH UP?
I GOTTA GET UP THERE AND FETCH HER BACK!
I'LL STAY DOWN HERE AND KEEP AN EYE OUT IN CASE SHE FALLS!
NOOO! YOU GOTTA COME WITH ME!
I DON'T WANNA BE THE ONLY ONE RE-SPONSIBLE IF SOME-THING GOES WRONG!

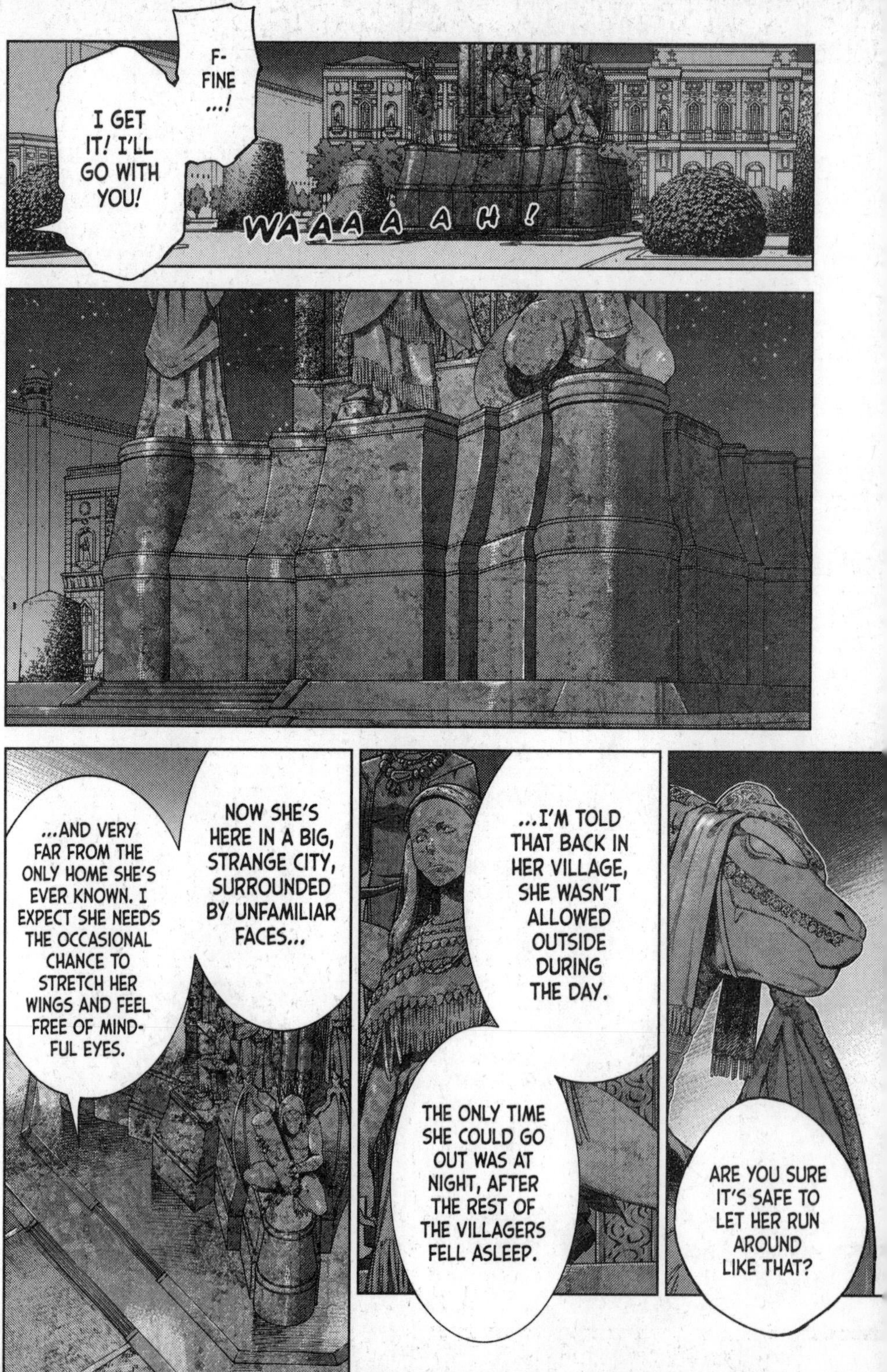
F-FINE ...!
I GET IT! I'LL GO WITH YOU!
WAAAAAH!
ARE YOU SURE IT'S SAFE TO LET HER RUN AROUND LIKE THAT?
...I'M TOLD THAT BACK IN HER VILLAGE, SHE WASN'T ALLOWED OUTSIDE DURING THE DAY.
THE ONLY TIME SHE COULD GO OUT WAS AT NIGHT, AFTER THE REST OF THE VILLAGERS FELL ASLEEP.
NOW SHE'S HERE IN A BIG, STRANGE CITY, SURROUNDED BY UNFAMILIAR FACES...
...AND VERY FAR FROM THE ONLY HOME SHE'S EVER KNOWN. I EXPECT SHE NEEDS THE OCCASIONAL CHANCE TO STRETCH HER WINGS AND FEEL FREE OF MIND-FUL EYES.

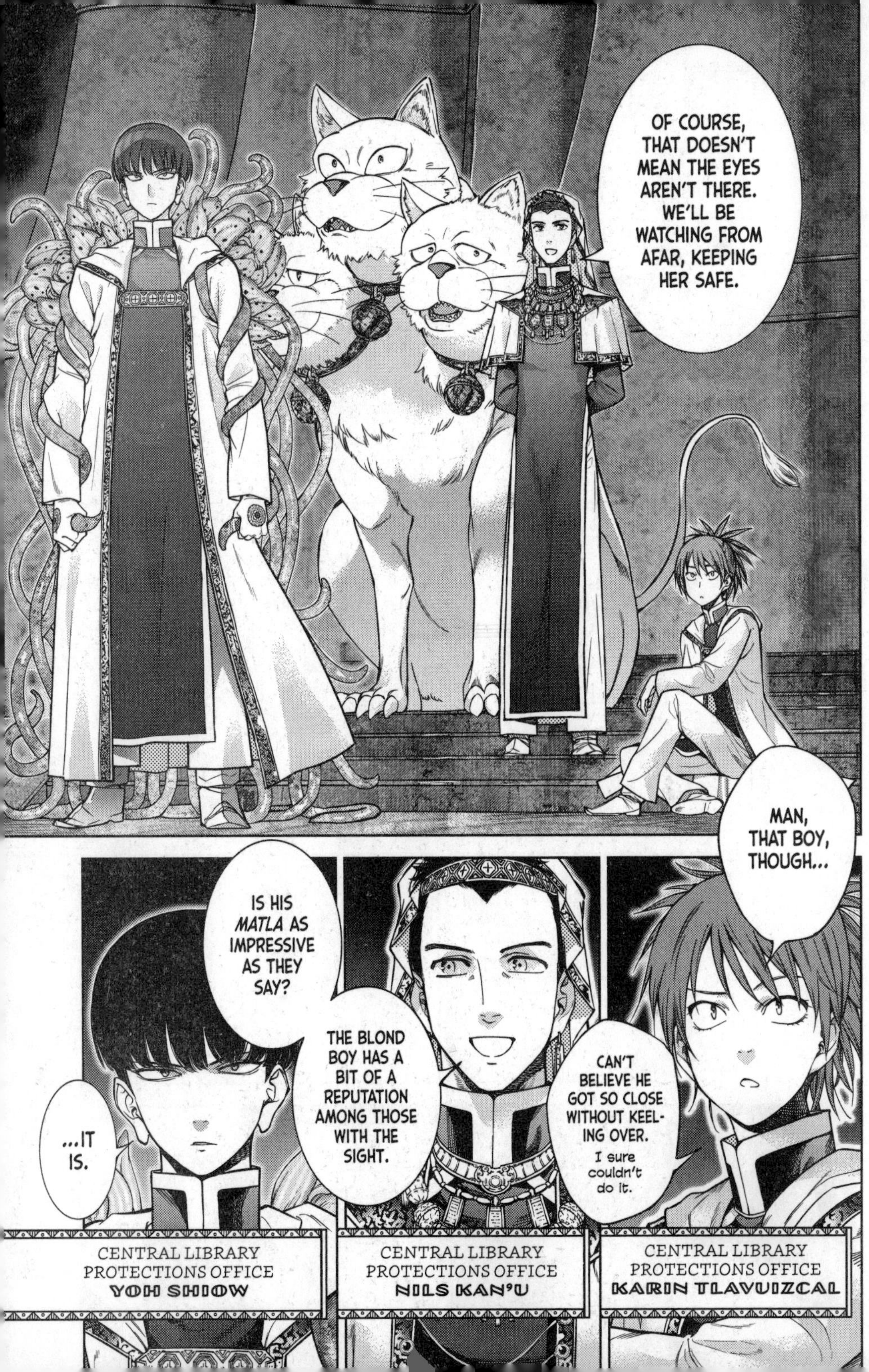
OF COURSE, THAT DOESN'T MEAN THE EYES AREN'T THERE. WE'LL BE WATCHING FROM AFAR, KEEPING HER SAFE.
MAN, THAT BOY, THOUGH...
CAN'T BELIEVE HE GOT SO CLOSE WITHOUT KEEL-ING OVER.
I sure couldn't do it.
CENTRAL LIBRARY PROTECTIONS OFFICE KARIN TLAVUIZCAL
IS HIS *MATLA* AS IMPRESSIVE AS THEY SAY?
THE BLOND BOY HAS A BIT OF A REPUTATION AMONG THOSE WITH THE SIGHT.
CENTRAL LIBRARY PROTECTIONS OFFICE NILS KAN'U
...IT IS.
CENTRAL LIBRARY PROTECTIONS OFFICE YOH SHIOW

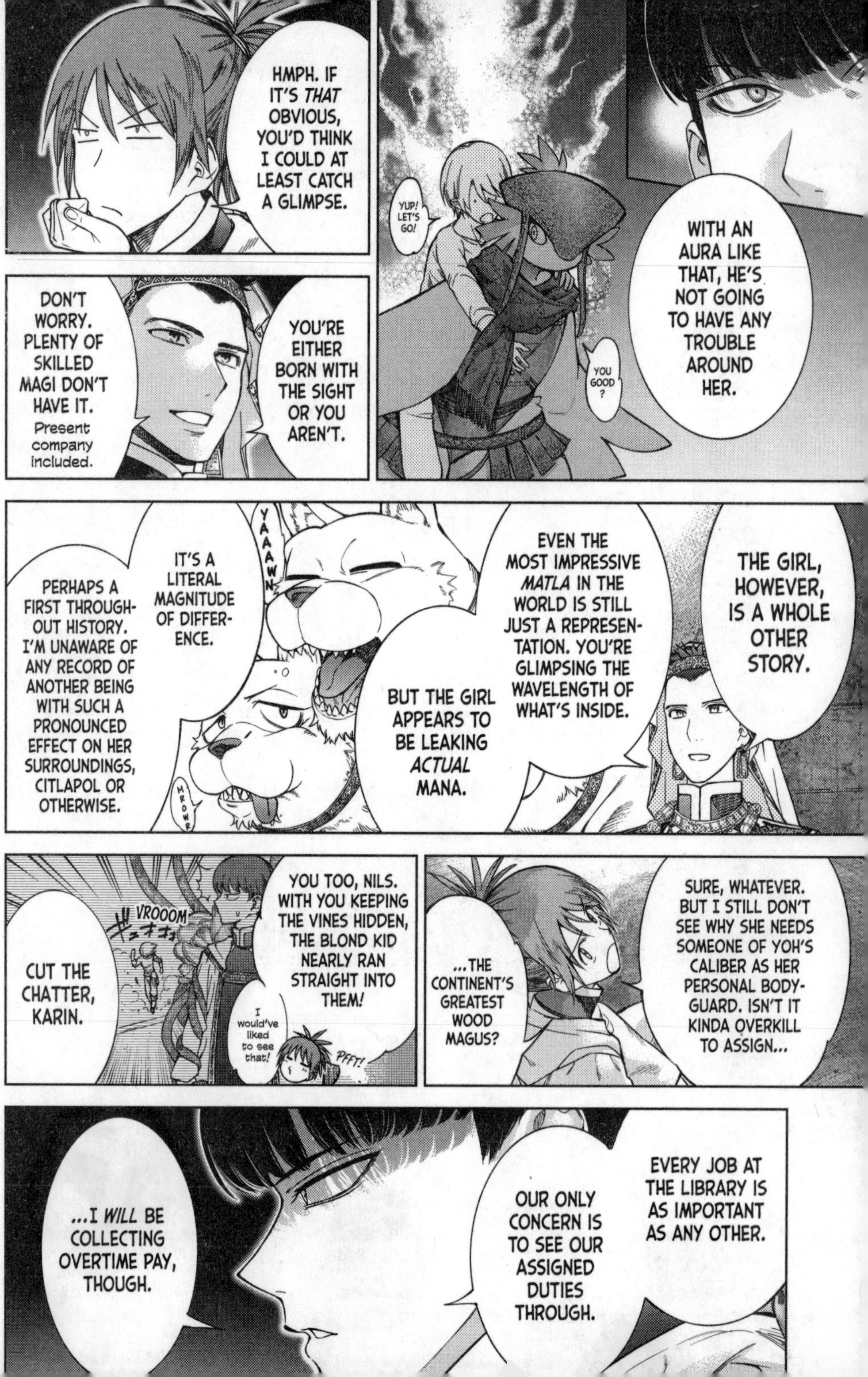
WITH AN AURA LIKE THAT, HE'S NOT GOING TO HAVE ANY TROUBLE AROUND HER.
YUP! LET'S GO!
YOU GOOD?
HMPH. IF IT'S *THAT* OBVIOUS, YOU'D THINK I COULD AT LEAST CATCH A GLIMPSE.
YOU'RE EITHER BORN WITH THE SIGHT OR YOU AREN'T.
DON'T WORRY. PLENTY OF SKILLED MAGI DON'T HAVE IT.
Present company included.
THE GIRL, HOWEVER, IS A WHOLE OTHER STORY.
EVEN THE MOST IMPRESSIVE *MATLA* IN THE WORLD IS STILL JUST A REPRESENTATION. YOU'RE GLIMPSING THE WAVELENGTH OF WHAT'S INSIDE.
BUT THE GIRL APPEARS TO BE LEAKING *ACTUAL* MANA.
YAAAAWN
IT'S A LITERAL MAGNITUDE OF DIFFERENCE.
PERHAPS A FIRST THROUGHOUT HISTORY. I'M UNAWARE OF ANY RECORD OF ANOTHER BEING WITH SUCH A PRONOUNCED EFFECT ON HER SURROUNDINGS, CITLAPOL OR OTHERWISE.
MROWR
SURE, WHATEVER. BUT I STILL DON'T SEE WHY SHE NEEDS SOMEONE OF YOH'S CALIBER AS HER PERSONAL BODYGUARD. ISN'T IT KINDA OVERKILL TO ASSIGN...
...THE CONTINENT'S GREATEST WOOD MAGUS?
YOU TOO, NILS. WITH YOU KEEPING THE VINES HIDDEN, THE BLOND KID NEARLY RAN STRAIGHT INTO THEM!
VROOOM
CUT THE CHATTER, KARIN.
I would've liked to see that!
PFFT!
EVERY JOB AT THE LIBRARY IS AS IMPORTANT AS ANY OTHER.
OUR ONLY CONCERN IS TO SEE OUR ASSIGNED DUTIES THROUGH.
...I *WILL* BE COLLECTING OVERTIME PAY, THOUGH.

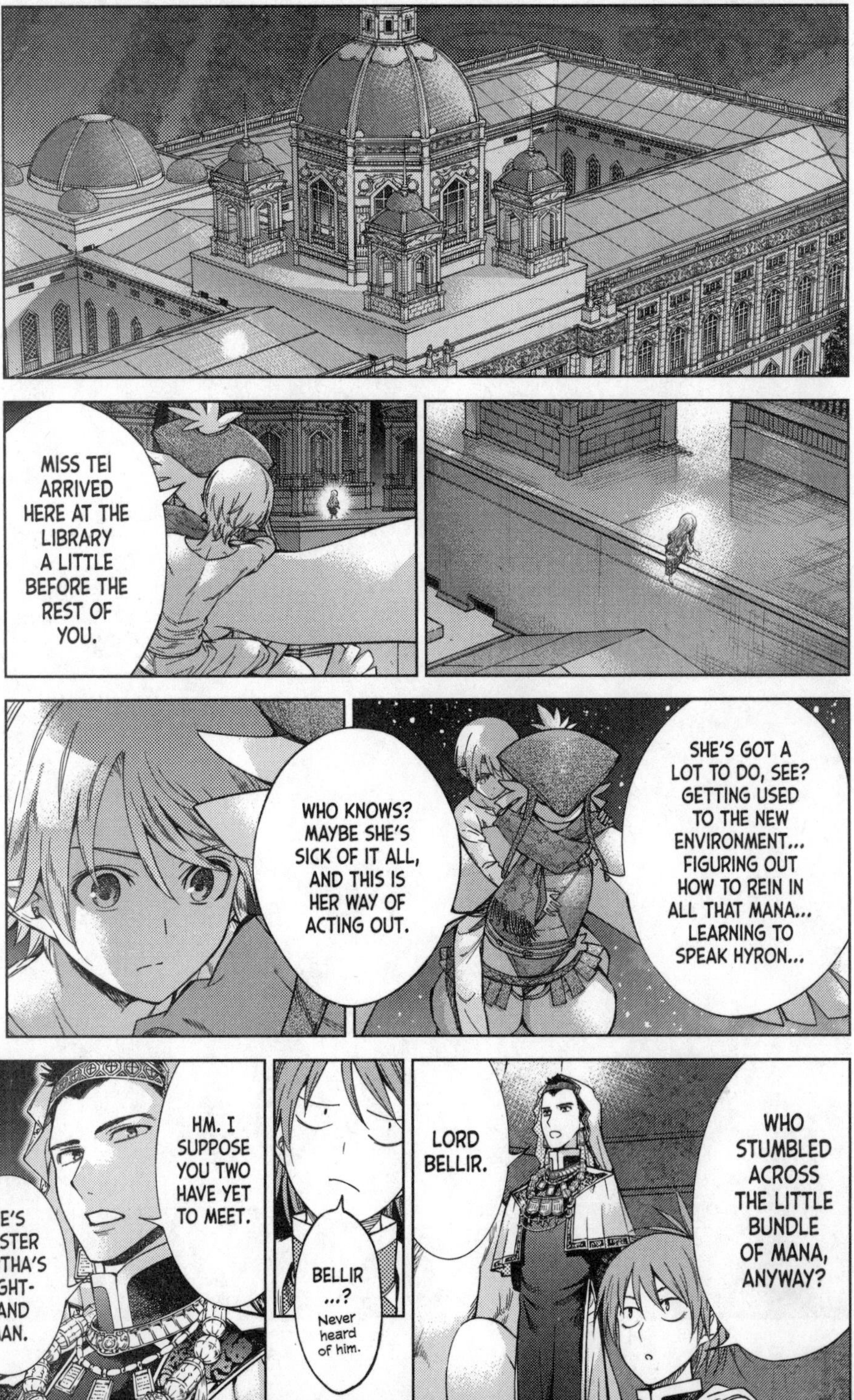
MISS TEI ARRIVED HERE AT THE LIBRARY A LITTLE BEFORE THE REST OF YOU.
SHE'S GOT A LOT TO DO, SEE? GETTING USED TO THE NEW ENVIRONMENT... FIGURING OUT HOW TO REIN IN ALL THAT MANA... LEARNING TO SPEAK HYRON...
WHO KNOWS? MAYBE SHE'S SICK OF IT ALL, AND THIS IS HER WAY OF ACTING OUT.
WHO STUMBLED ACROSS THE LITTLE BUNDLE OF MANA, ANYWAY?
LORD BELLIR.
BELLIR ...?
Never heard of him.
HM. I SUPPOSE YOU TWO HAVE YET TO MEET.
HE'S MASTER PARTHA'S RIGHT-HAND MAN.

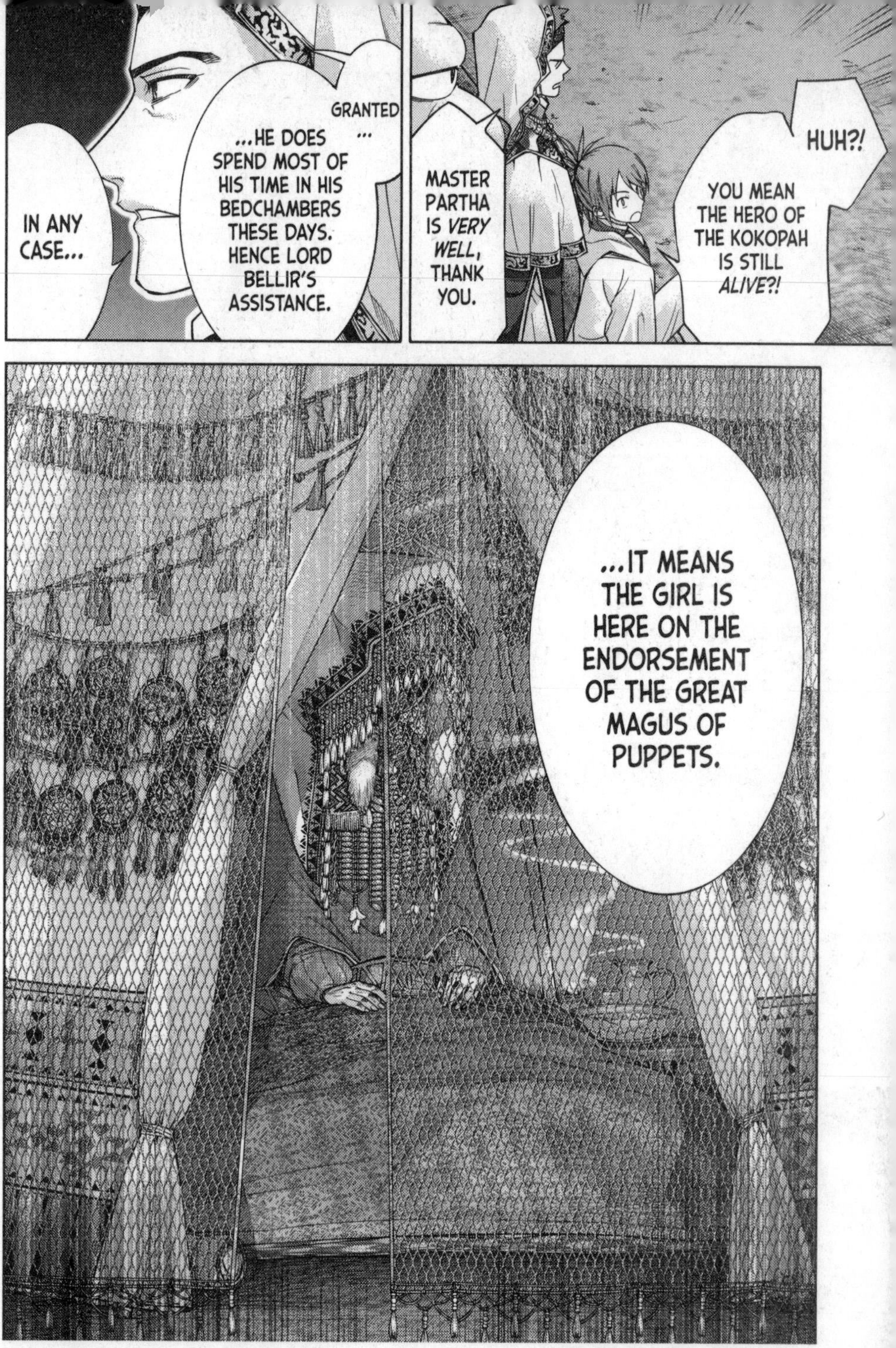
HUH?!
YOU MEAN THE HERO OF THE KOKOPAH IS STILL *ALIVE*?!
MASTER PARTHA IS *VERY WELL*, THANK YOU.
GRANTED...
...HE DOES SPEND MOST OF HIS TIME IN HIS BEDCHAMBERS THESE DAYS. HENCE LORD BELLIR'S ASSISTANCE.
IN ANY CASE...
...IT MEANS THE GIRL IS HERE ON THE ENDORSEMENT OF THE GREAT MAGUS OF PUPPETS.

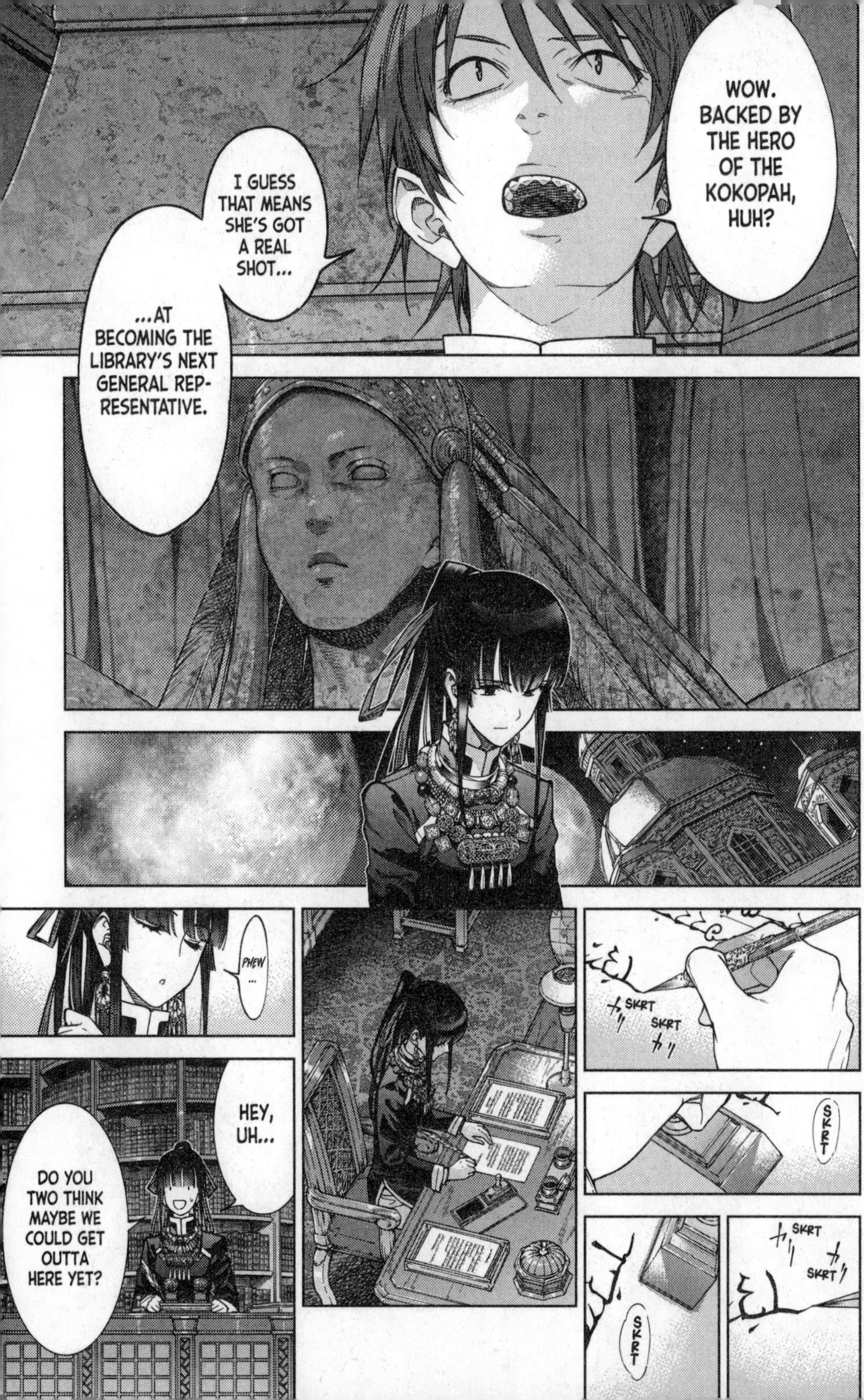
WOW. BACKED BY THE HERO OF THE KOKOPAH, HUH?
I GUESS THAT MEANS SHE'S GOT A REAL SHOT...
...AT BECOMING THE LIBRARY'S NEXT GENERAL REPRESENTATIVE.
SKRT
SKRT
SKRT
SKRT
SKRT
SKRT
PHEW...
HEY, UH...
DO YOU TWO THINK MAYBE WE COULD GET OUTTA HERE YET?

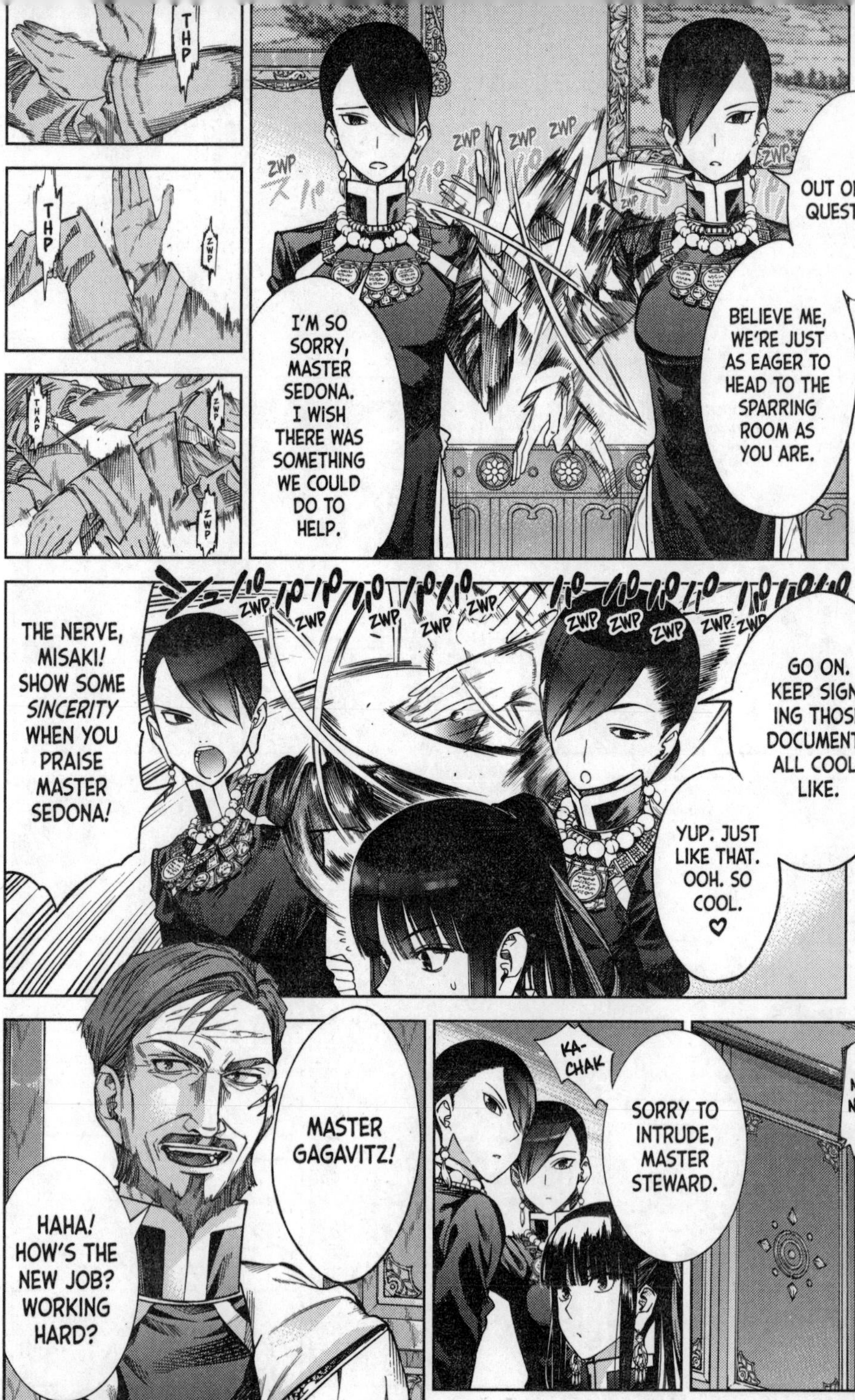
ZWP ZWP ZWP
ZWP
ZWP
OUT OF THE QUESTION.
BELIEVE ME, WE'RE JUST AS EAGER TO HEAD TO THE SPARRING ROOM AS YOU ARE.
I'M SO SORRY, MASTER SEDONA. I WISH THERE WAS SOMETHING WE COULD DO TO HELP.
THP
THP
ZWP
THAP
ZWP
ZWP
ZWP ZWP ZWP ZWP ZWP
ZWP ZWP ZWP ZWP ZWP ZWP
GO ON. KEEP SIGN-ING THOSE DOCUMENTS ALL COOL-LIKE.
YUP. JUST LIKE THAT. OOH. SO COOL. ♡
THE NERVE, MISAKI! SHOW SOME *SINCERITY* WHEN YOU PRAISE MASTER SEDONA!
NOK NOK
KA-CHAK
SORRY TO INTRUDE, MASTER STEWARD.
MASTER GAGAVITZ!
HAHA! HOW'S THE NEW JOB? WORKING HARD?

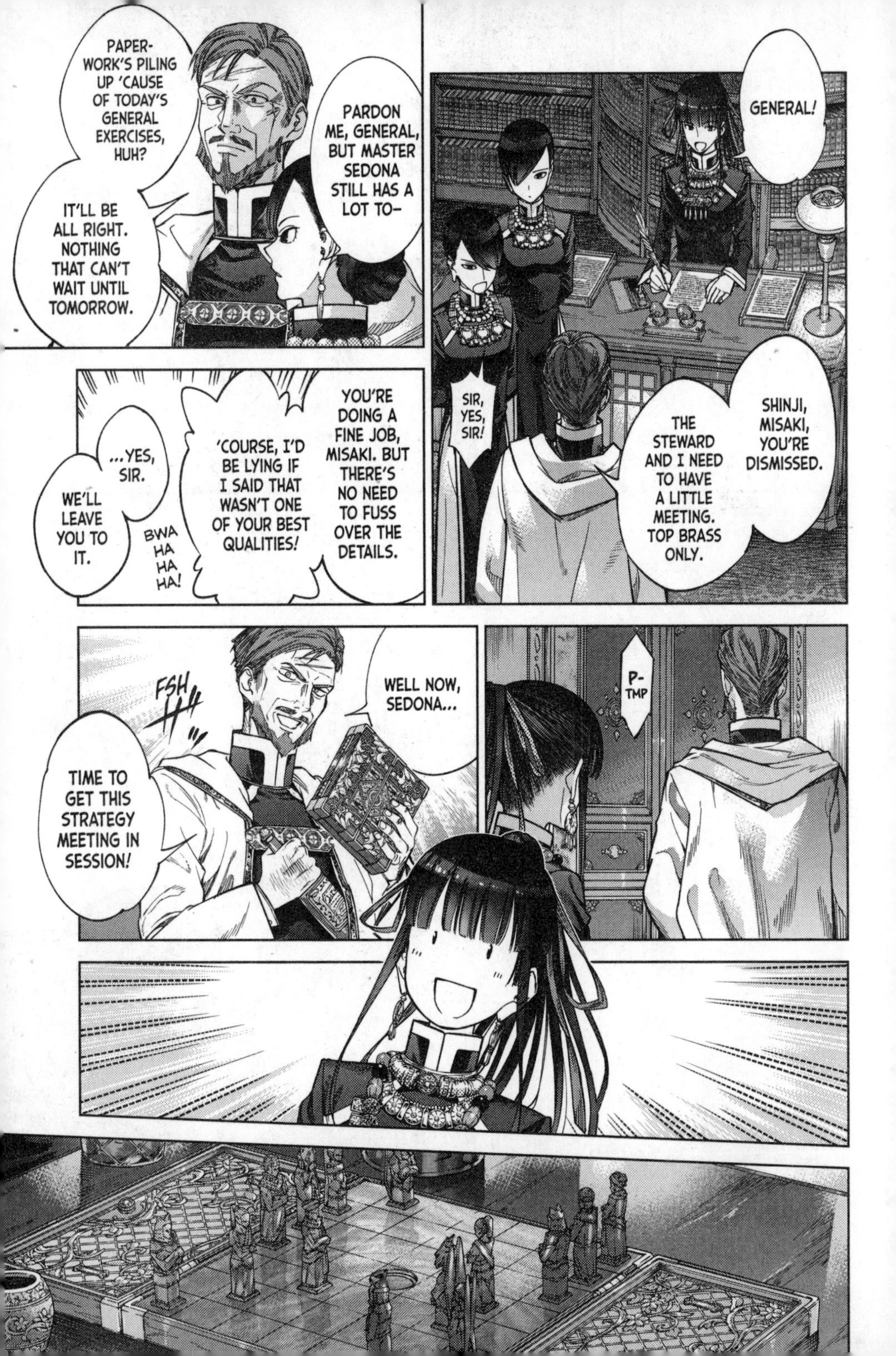
GENERAL!
SHINJI, MISAKI, YOU'RE DISMISSED.
THE STEWARD AND I NEED TO HAVE A LITTLE MEETING. TOP BRASS ONLY.
SIR, YES, SIR!
PAPER-WORK'S PILING UP 'CAUSE OF TODAY'S GENERAL EXERCISES, HUH?
PARDON ME, GENERAL, BUT MASTER SEDONA STILL HAS A LOT TO–
IT'LL BE ALL RIGHT. NOTHING THAT CAN'T WAIT UNTIL TOMORROW.
YOU'RE DOING A FINE JOB, MISAKI. BUT THERE'S NO NEED TO FUSS OVER THE DETAILS.
'COURSE, I'D BE LYING IF I SAID THAT WASN'T ONE OF YOUR BEST QUALITIES!
BWA HA HA HA!
...YES, SIR.
WE'LL LEAVE YOU TO IT.
P-TMP
WELL NOW, SEDONA...
FSH
TIME TO GET THIS STRATEGY MEETING IN SESSION!

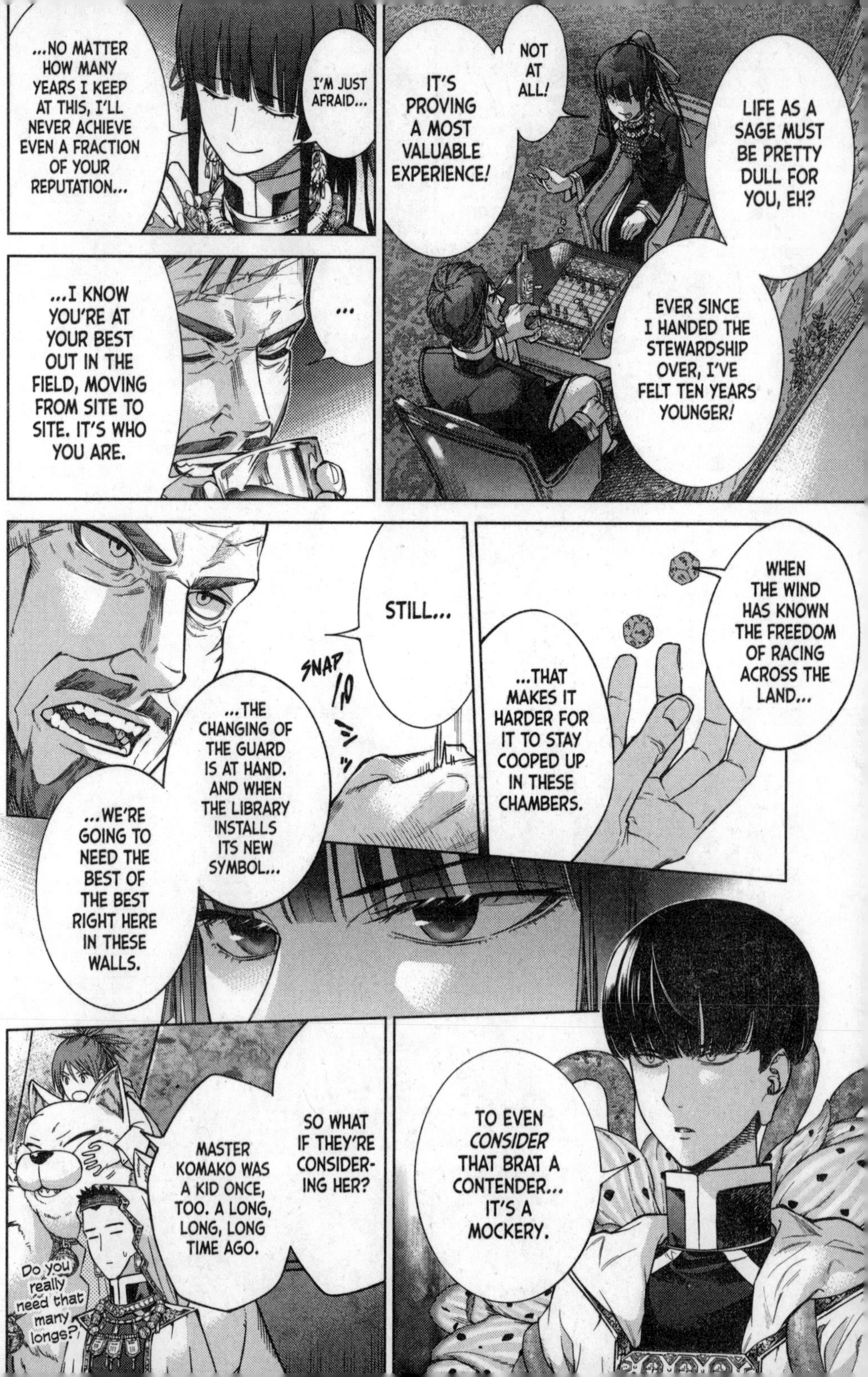
LIFE AS A SAGE MUST BE PRETTY DULL FOR YOU, EH?
EVER SINCE I HANDED THE STEWARDSHIP OVER, I'VE FELT TEN YEARS YOUNGER!
NOT AT ALL!
IT'S PROVING A MOST VALUABLE EXPERIENCE!
I'M JUST AFRAID...
...NO MATTER HOW MANY YEARS I KEEP AT THIS, I'LL NEVER ACHIEVE EVEN A FRACTION OF YOUR REPUTATION...
...
...I KNOW YOU'RE AT YOUR BEST OUT IN THE FIELD, MOVING FROM SITE TO SITE. IT'S WHO YOU ARE.
WHEN THE WIND HAS KNOWN THE FREEDOM OF RACING ACROSS THE LAND...
...THAT MAKES IT HARDER FOR IT TO STAY COOPED UP IN THESE CHAMBERS.
STILL...
SNAP
...THE CHANGING OF THE GUARD IS AT HAND. AND WHEN THE LIBRARY INSTALLS ITS NEW SYMBOL...
...WE'RE GOING TO NEED THE BEST OF THE BEST RIGHT HERE IN THESE WALLS.
TO EVEN *CONSIDER* THAT BRAT A CONTENDER... IT'S A MOCKERY.
SO WHAT IF THEY'RE CONSIDERING HER?
MASTER KOMAKO WAS A KID ONCE, TOO. A LONG, LONG, LONG TIME AGO.
Do you really need that many longs?

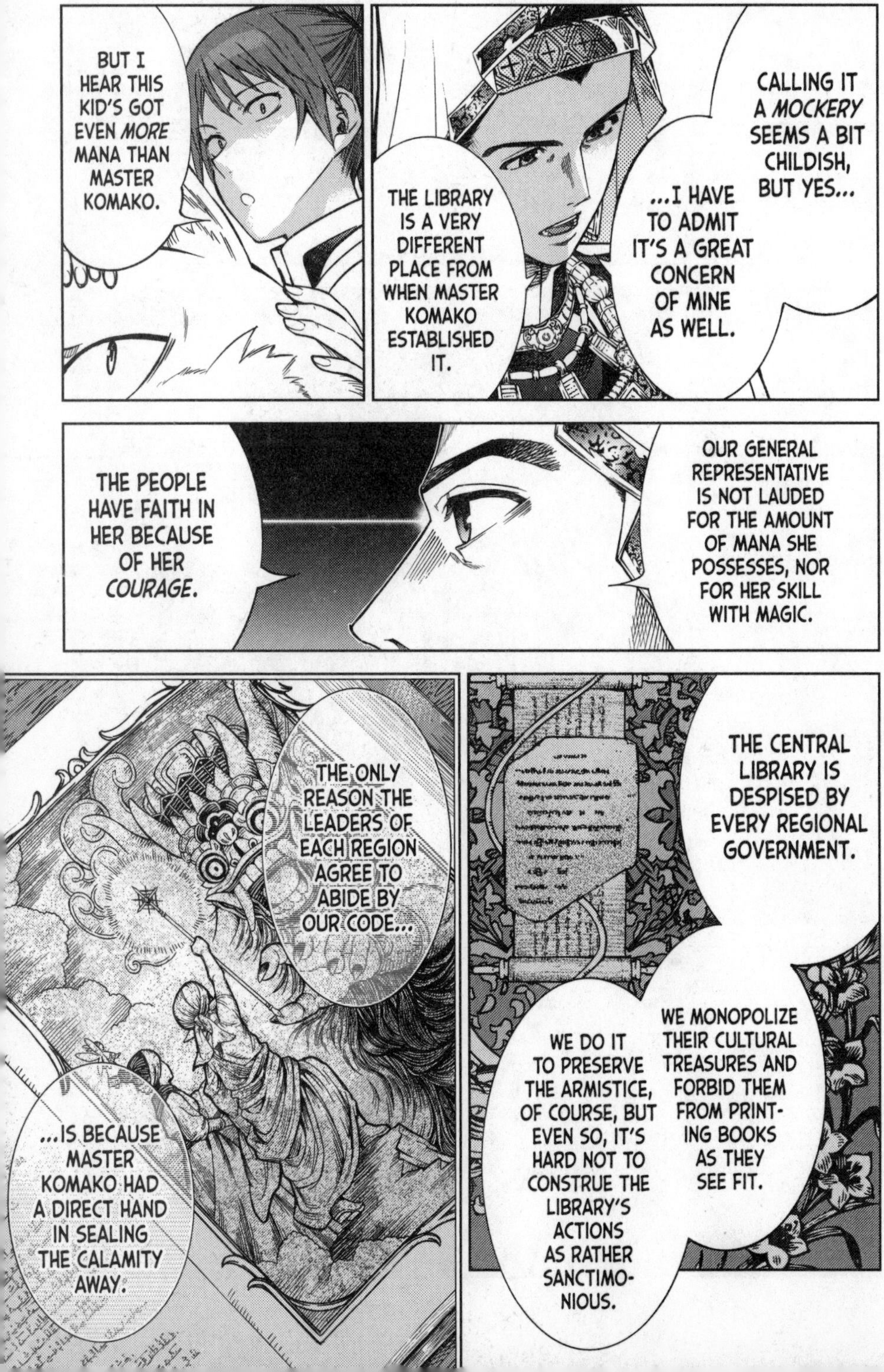
CALLING IT A *MOCKERY* SEEMS A BIT CHILDISH, BUT YES...
...I HAVE TO ADMIT IT'S A GREAT CONCERN OF MINE AS WELL.
THE LIBRARY IS A VERY DIFFERENT PLACE FROM WHEN MASTER KOMAKO ESTABLISHED IT.
BUT I HEAR THIS KID'S GOT EVEN *MORE* MANA THAN MASTER KOMAKO.
OUR GENERAL REPRESENTATIVE IS NOT LAUDED FOR THE AMOUNT OF MANA SHE POSSESSES, NOR FOR HER SKILL WITH MAGIC.
THE PEOPLE HAVE FAITH IN HER BECAUSE OF HER *COURAGE*.
THE CENTRAL LIBRARY IS DESPISED BY EVERY REGIONAL GOVERNMENT.
WE MONOPOLIZE THEIR CULTURAL TREASURES AND FORBID THEM FROM PRINT-ING BOOKS AS THEY SEE FIT.
WE DO IT TO PRESERVE THE ARMISTICE, OF COURSE, BUT EVEN SO, IT'S HARD NOT TO CONSTRUE THE LIBRARY'S ACTIONS AS RATHER SANCTIMO-NIOUS.
THE ONLY REASON THE LEADERS OF EACH REGION AGREE TO ABIDE BY OUR CODE...
...IS BECAUSE MASTER KOMAKO HAD A DIRECT HAND IN SEALING THE CALAMITY AWAY.

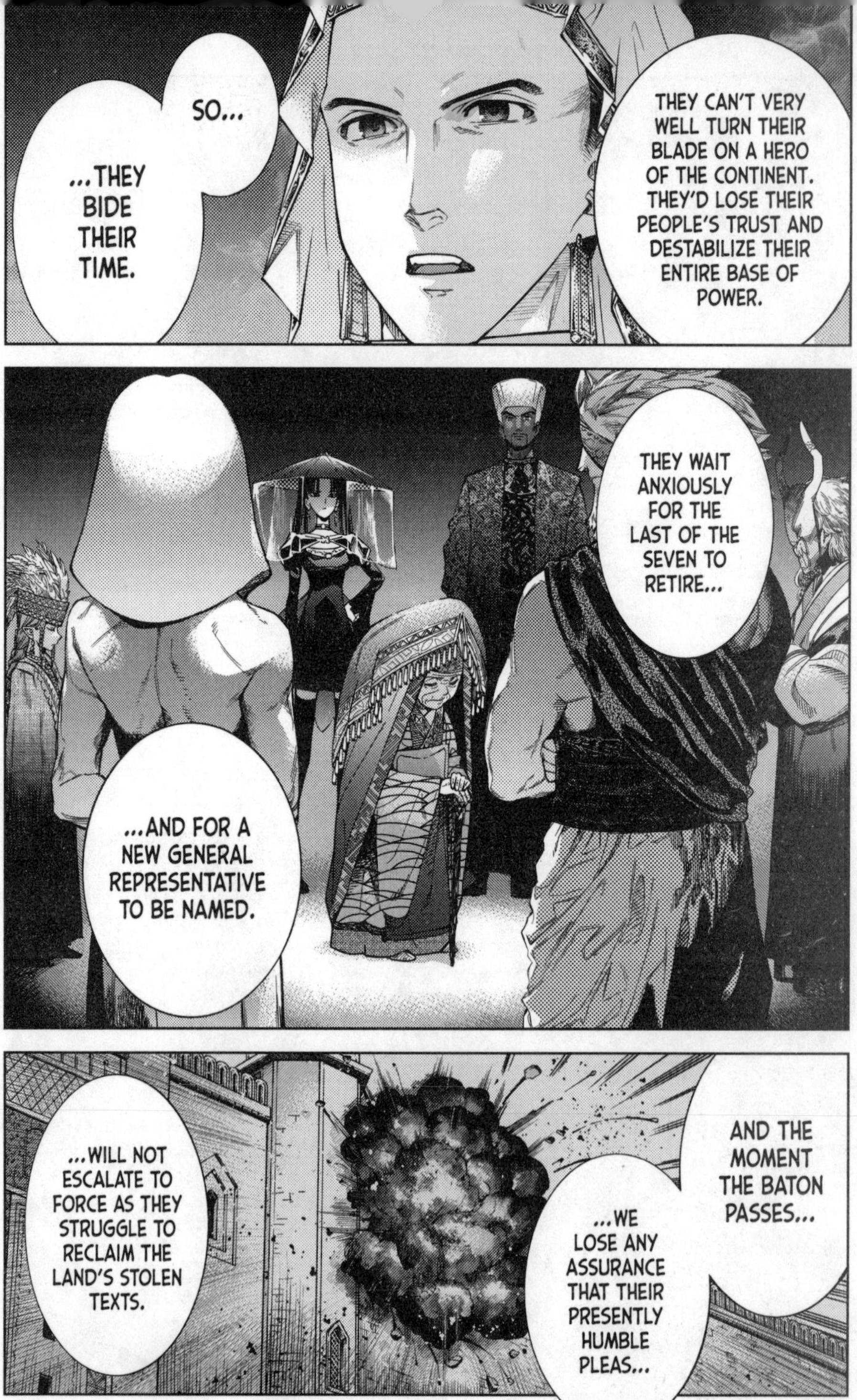
THEY CAN'T VERY WELL TURN THEIR BLADE ON A HERO OF THE CONTINENT. THEY'D LOSE THEIR PEOPLE'S TRUST AND DESTABILIZE THEIR ENTIRE BASE OF POWER.
SO...
...THEY BIDE THEIR TIME.
THEY WAIT ANXIOUSLY FOR THE LAST OF THE SEVEN TO RETIRE...
...AND FOR A NEW GENERAL REPRESENTATIVE TO BE NAMED.
AND THE MOMENT THE BATON PASSES...
...WE LOSE ANY ASSURANCE THAT THEIR PRESENTLY HUMBLE PLEAS...
...WILL NOT ESCALATE TO FORCE AS THEY STRUGGLE TO RECLAIM THE LAND'S STOLEN TEXTS.

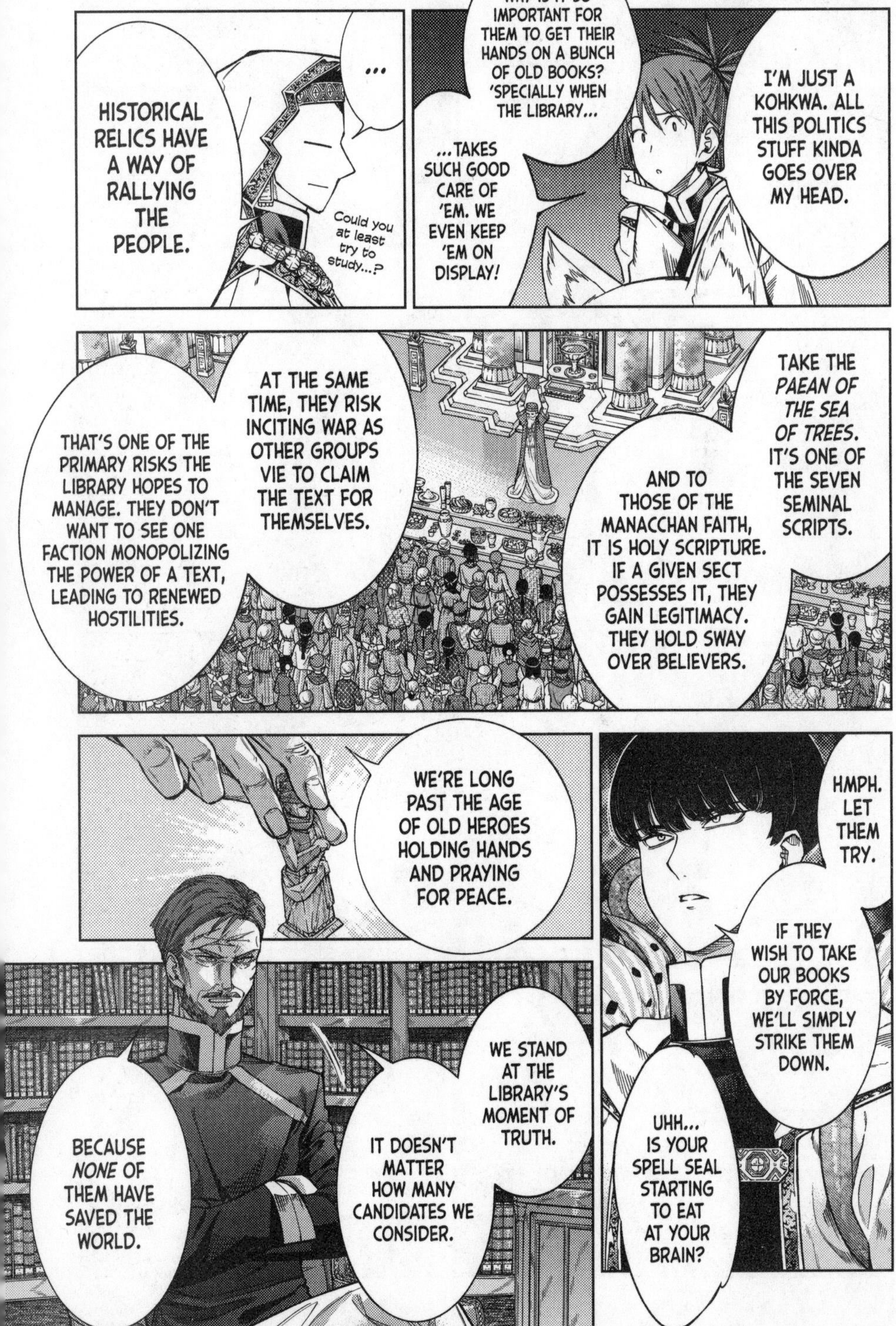
I'M JUST A KOHKWA. ALL THIS POLITICS STUFF KINDA GOES OVER MY HEAD.
WHY IS IT SO IMPORTANT FOR THEM TO GET THEIR HANDS ON A BUNCH OF OLD BOOKS? 'SPECIALLY WHEN THE LIBRARY...
...TAKES SUCH GOOD CARE OF 'EM. WE EVEN KEEP 'EM ON DISPLAY!
...
HISTORICAL RELICS HAVE A WAY OF RALLYING THE PEOPLE.
Could you at least try to study...?
TAKE THE *PAEAN OF THE SEA OF TREES*. IT'S ONE OF THE SEVEN SEMINAL SCRIPTS.
AND TO THOSE OF THE MANACCHAN FAITH, IT IS HOLY SCRIPTURE. IF A GIVEN SECT POSSESSES IT, THEY GAIN LEGITIMACY. THEY HOLD SWAY OVER BELIEVERS.
AT THE SAME TIME, THEY RISK INCITING WAR AS OTHER GROUPS VIE TO CLAIM THE TEXT FOR THEMSELVES.
THAT'S ONE OF THE PRIMARY RISKS THE LIBRARY HOPES TO MANAGE. THEY DON'T WANT TO SEE ONE FACTION MONOPOLIZING THE POWER OF A TEXT, LEADING TO RENEWED HOSTILITIES.
HMPH. LET THEM TRY.
IF THEY WISH TO TAKE OUR BOOKS BY FORCE, WE'LL SIMPLY STRIKE THEM DOWN.
UHH... IS YOUR SPELL SEAL STARTING TO EAT AT YOUR BRAIN?
WE'RE LONG PAST THE AGE OF OLD HEROES HOLDING HANDS AND PRAYING FOR PEACE.
WE STAND AT THE LIBRARY'S MOMENT OF TRUTH.
IT DOESN'T MATTER HOW MANY CANDIDATES WE CONSIDER.
BECAUSE *NONE* OF THEM HAVE SAVED THE WORLD.

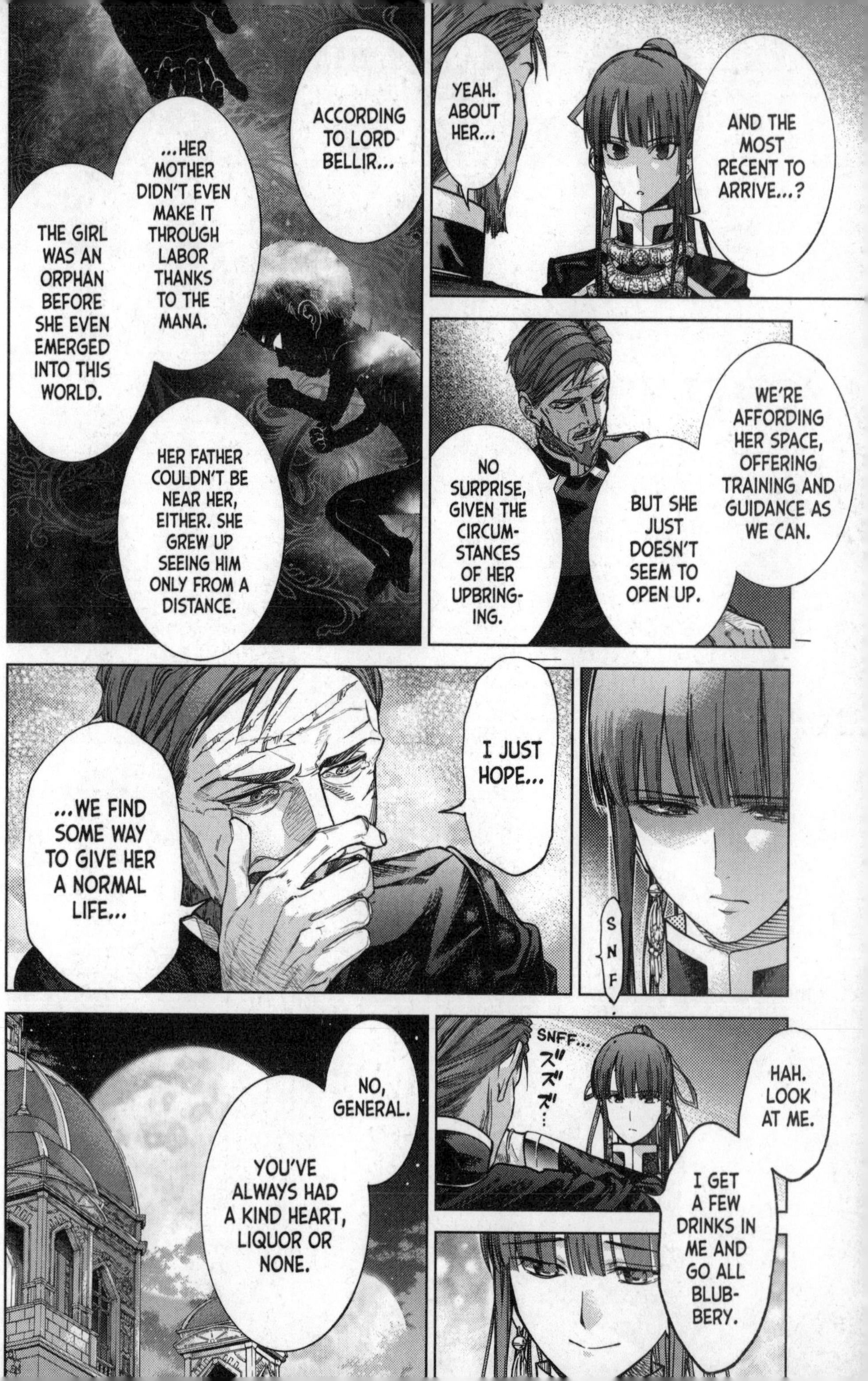
AND THE MOST RECENT TO ARRIVE...?
YEAH. ABOUT HER...
WE'RE AFFORDING HER SPACE, OFFERING TRAINING AND GUIDANCE AS WE CAN.
BUT SHE JUST DOESN'T SEEM TO OPEN UP.
NO SURPRISE, GIVEN THE CIRCUM-STANCES OF HER UPBRING-ING.
ACCORDING TO LORD BELLIR...
...HER MOTHER DIDN'T EVEN MAKE IT THROUGH LABOR THANKS TO THE MANA.
THE GIRL WAS AN ORPHAN BEFORE SHE EVEN EMERGED INTO THIS WORLD.
HER FATHER COULDN'T BE NEAR HER, EITHER. SHE GREW UP SEEING HIM ONLY FROM A DISTANCE.
SNF
I JUST HOPE...
...WE FIND SOME WAY TO GIVE HER A NORMAL LIFE...
HAH. LOOK AT ME.
SNFF...
ズズズ...
I GET A FEW DRINKS IN ME AND GO ALL BLUB-BERY.
NO, GENERAL.
YOU'VE ALWAYS HAD A KIND HEART, LIQUOR OR NONE.

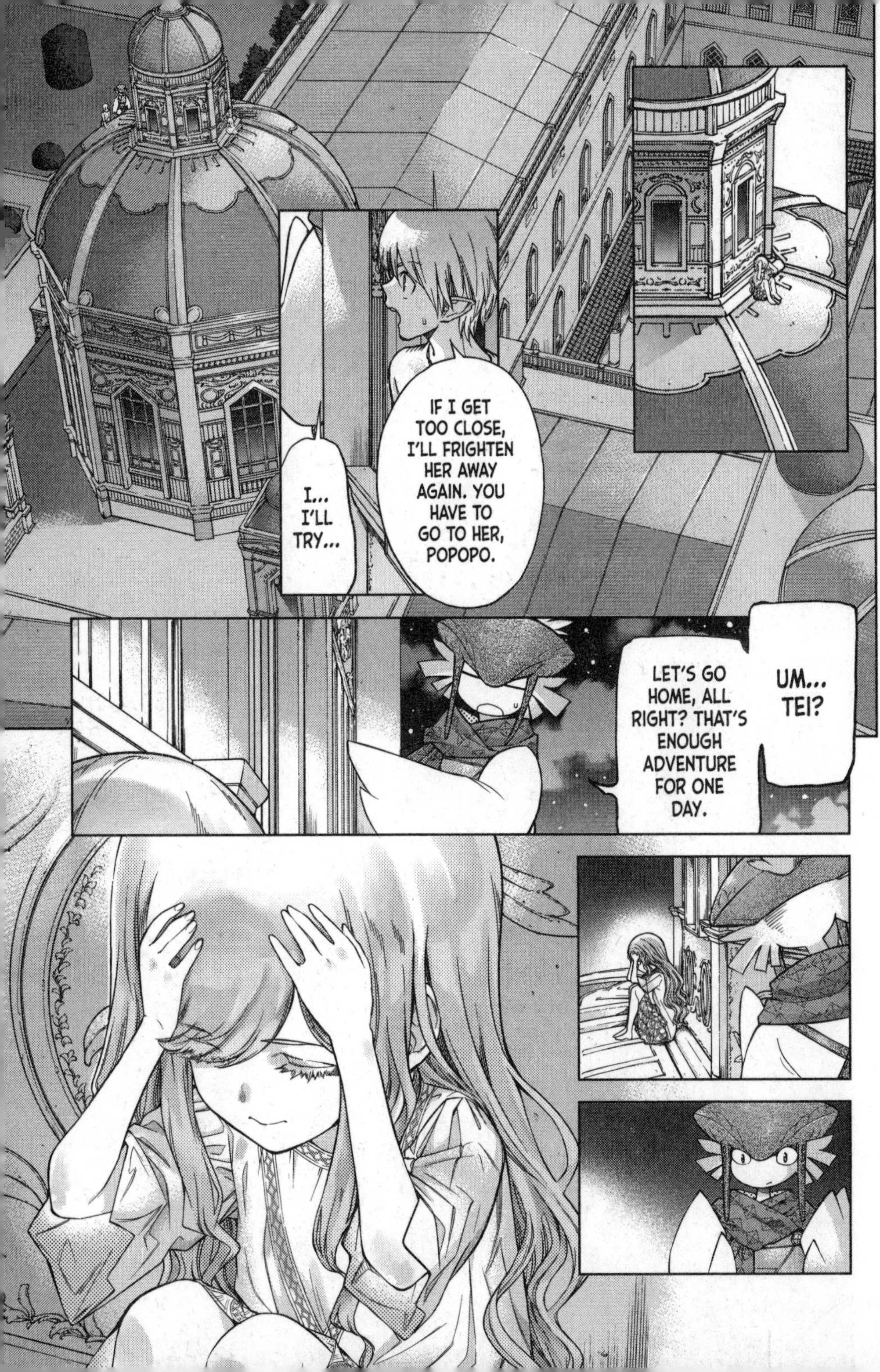
IF I GET TOO CLOSE, I'LL FRIGHTEN HER AWAY AGAIN. YOU HAVE TO GO TO HER, POPOPO.
I... I'LL TRY...
UM... TEI?
LET'S GO HOME, ALL RIGHT? THAT'S ENOUGH ADVENTURE FOR ONE DAY.

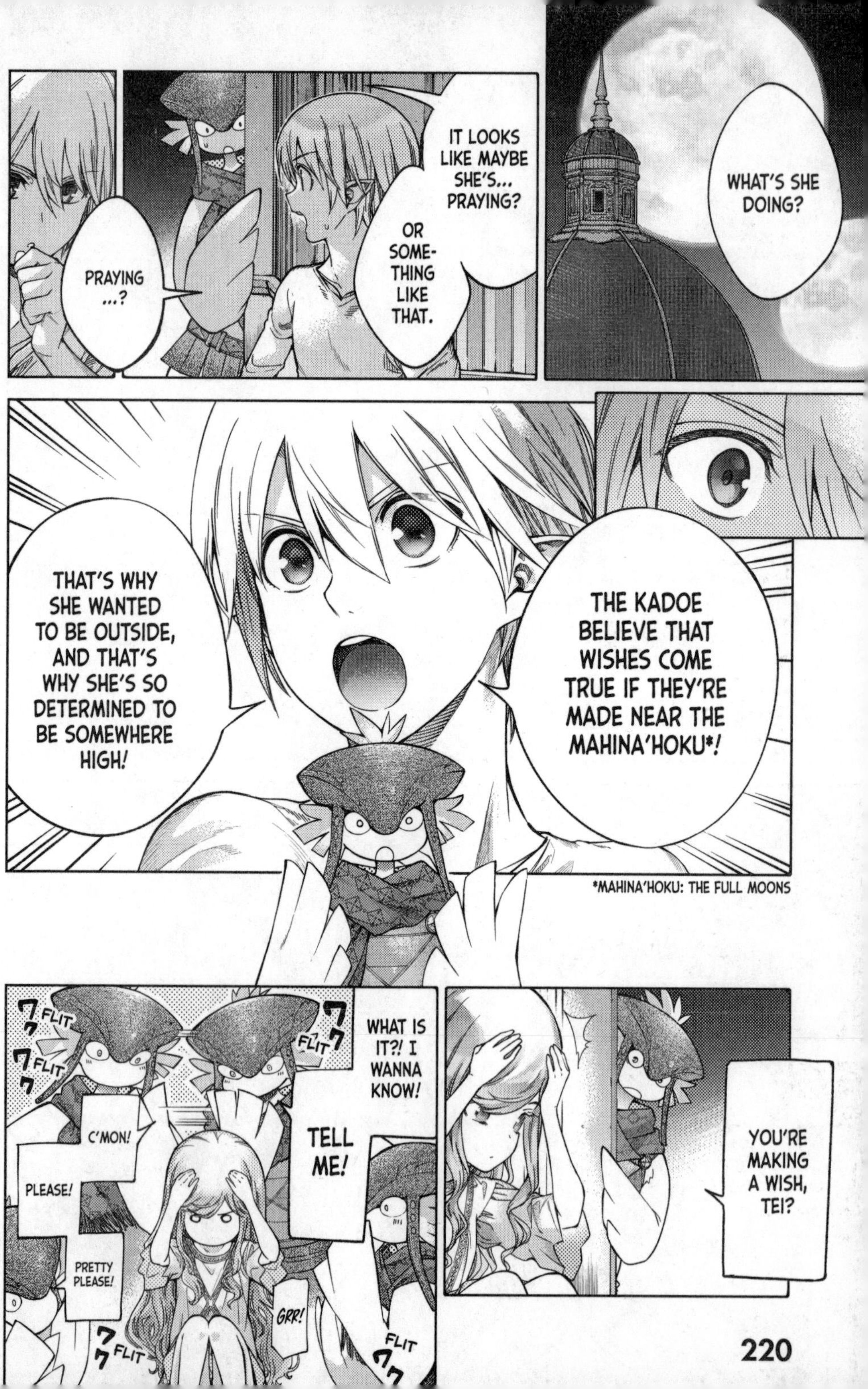
WHAT'S SHE DOING?
IT LOOKS LIKE MAYBE SHE'S... PRAYING?
OR SOME-THING LIKE THAT.
PRAYING ...?
THE KADOE BELIEVE THAT WISHES COME TRUE IF THEY'RE MADE NEAR THE MAHINA'HOKU*!
THAT'S WHY SHE WANTED TO BE OUTSIDE, AND THAT'S WHY SHE'S SO DETERMINED TO BE SOMEWHERE HIGH!
*MAHINA'HOKU: THE FULL MOONS
YOU'RE MAKING A WISH, TEI?
FLIT
FLIT
FLIT
WHAT IS IT?! I WANNA KNOW!
TELL ME!
C'MON!
PLEASE!
PRETTY PLEASE!
GRR!
FLIT
FLIT

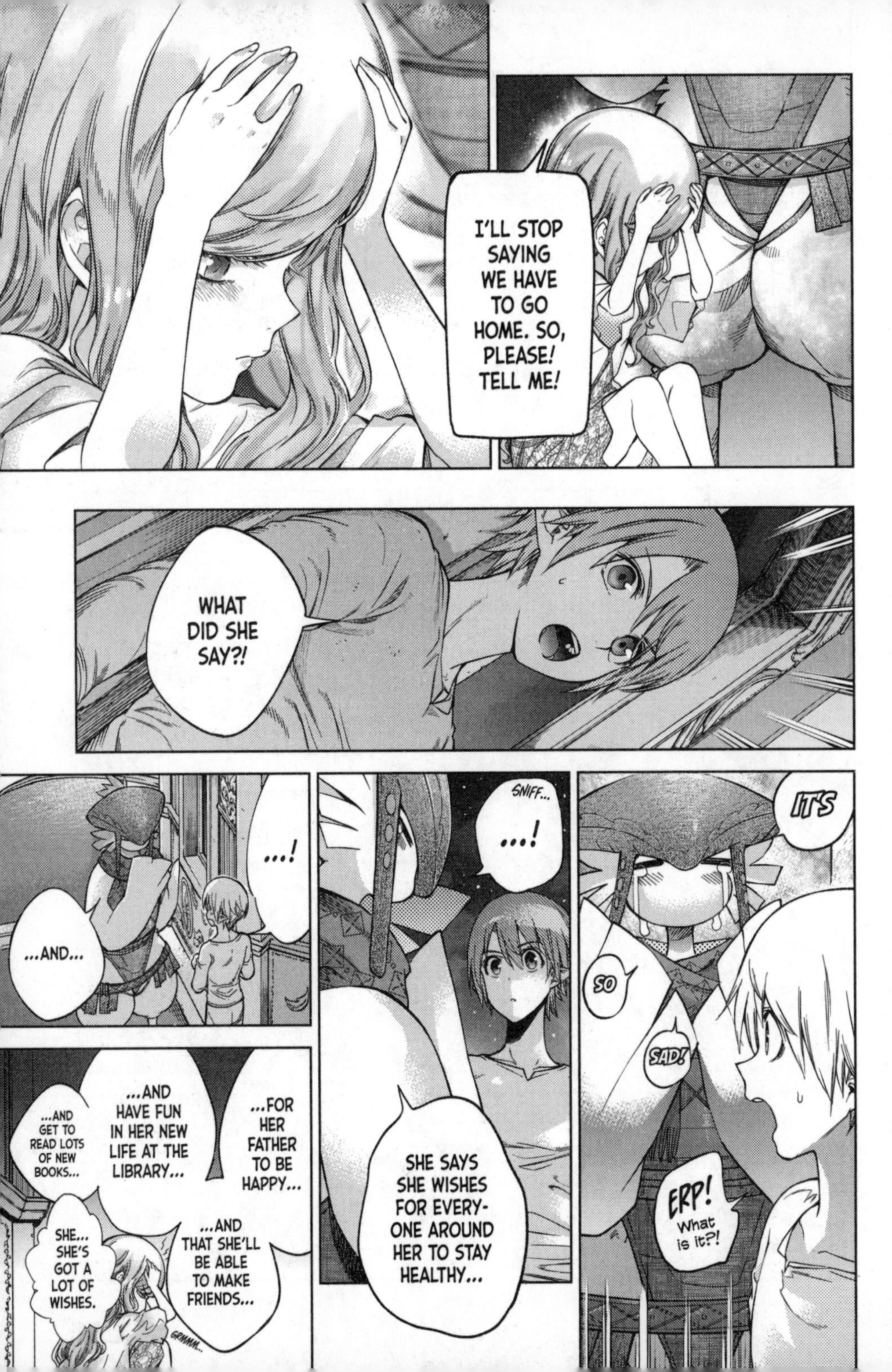
I'LL STOP SAYING WE HAVE TO GO HOME. SO, PLEASE! TELL ME!
WHAT DID SHE SAY?!
IT'S
SO
SAD!
ERP! What is it?!
SNIFF...
...!
SHE SAYS SHE WISHES FOR EVERY-ONE AROUND HER TO STAY HEALTHY...
...!
...AND...
...FOR HER FATHER TO BE HAPPY...
...AND HAVE FUN IN HER NEW LIFE AT THE LIBRARY...
...AND GET TO READ LOTS OF NEW BOOKS...
...AND THAT SHE'LL BE ABLE TO MAKE FRIENDS...
SHE... SHE'S GOT A LOT OF WISHES.
GRMMM..

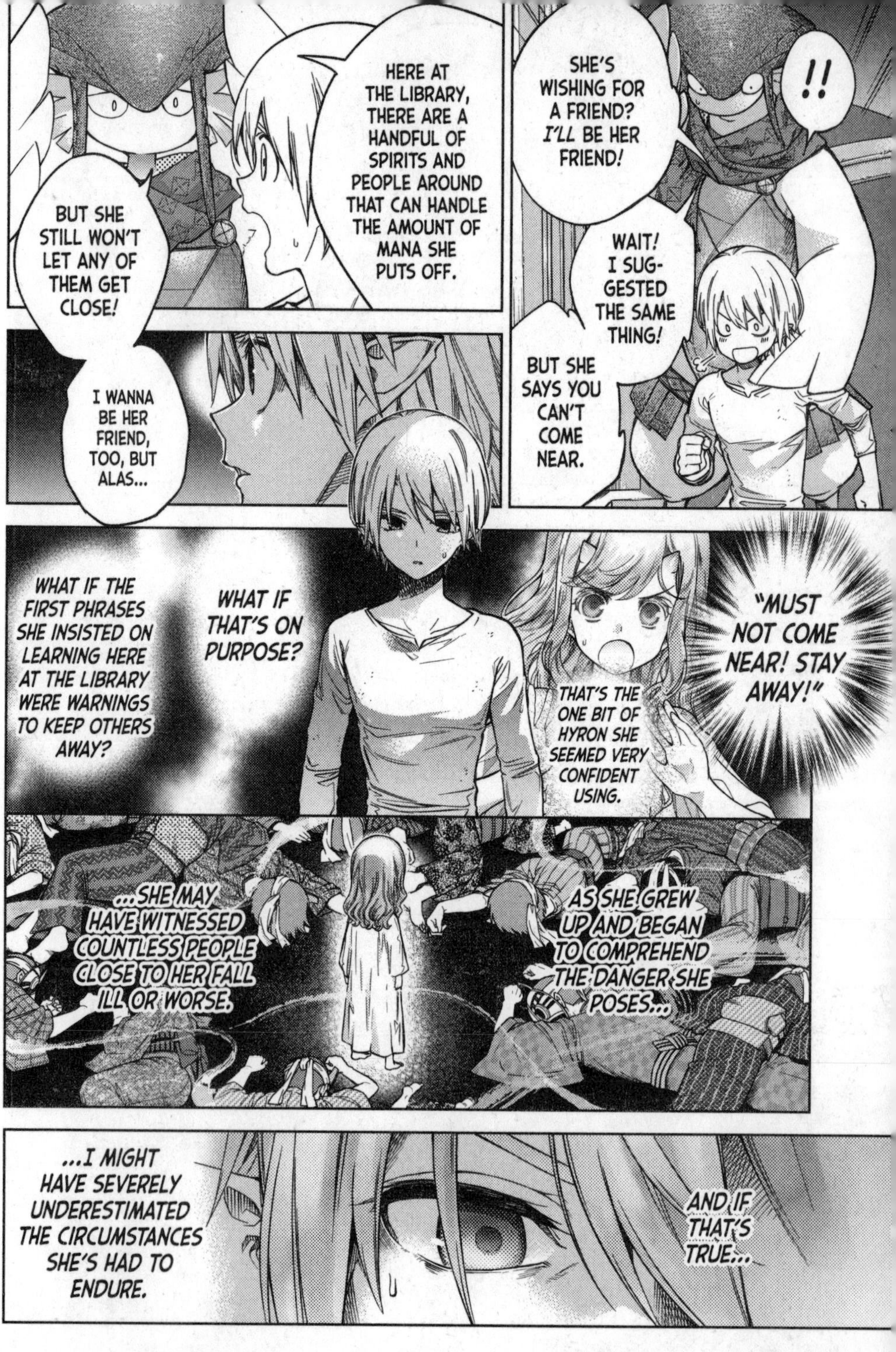
SHE'S WISHING FOR A FRIEND? *I'LL* BE HER FRIEND!
!!
WAIT! I SUGGESTED THE SAME THING!
BUT SHE SAYS YOU CAN'T COME NEAR.
HERE AT THE LIBRARY, THERE ARE A HANDFUL OF SPIRITS AND PEOPLE AROUND THAT CAN HANDLE THE AMOUNT OF MANA SHE PUTS OFF.
BUT SHE STILL WON'T LET ANY OF THEM GET CLOSE!
I WANNA BE HER FRIEND, TOO, BUT ALAS...
"MUST NOT COME NEAR! STAY AWAY!"
THAT'S THE ONE BIT OF HYRON SHE SEEMED VERY CONFIDENT USING.
WHAT IF THAT'S ON PURPOSE?
WHAT IF THE FIRST PHRASES SHE INSISTED ON LEARNING HERE AT THE LIBRARY WERE WARNINGS TO KEEP OTHERS AWAY?
AS SHE GREW UP AND BEGAN TO COMPREHEND THE DANGER SHE POSES...
...SHE MAY HAVE WITNESSED COUNTLESS PEOPLE CLOSE TO HER FALL ILL OR WORSE.
AND IF THAT'S TRUE...
...I MIGHT HAVE SEVERELY UNDERESTIMATED THE CIRCUMSTANCES SHE'S HAD TO ENDURE.

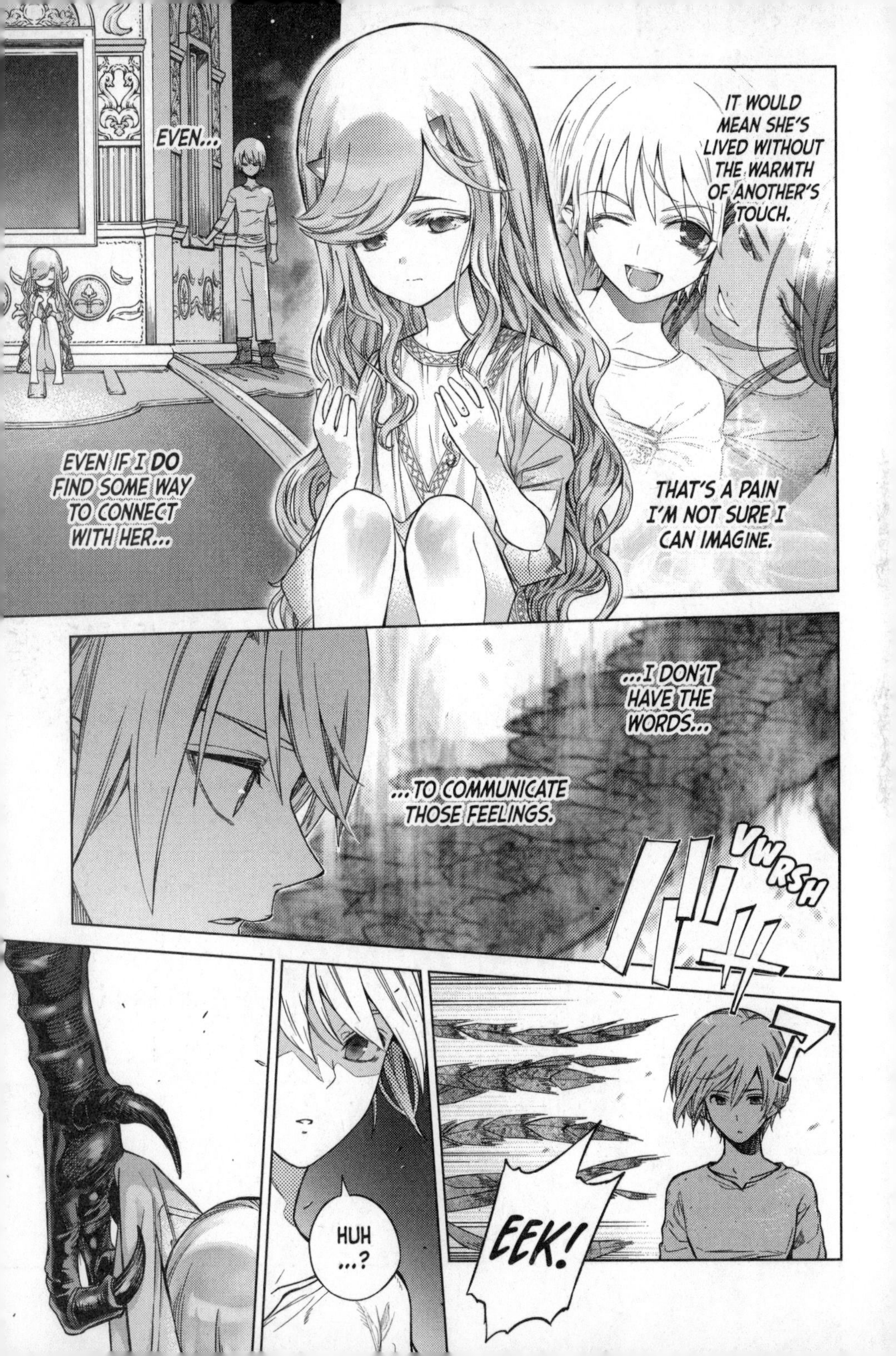
IT WOULD MEAN SHE'S LIVED WITHOUT THE WARMTH OF ANOTHER'S TOUCH.
THAT'S A PAIN I'M NOT SURE I CAN IMAGINE.
EVEN...
EVEN IF I DO FIND SOME WAY TO CONNECT WITH HER...
...I DON'T HAVE THE WORDS...
...TO COMMUNICATE THOSE FEELINGS.
VWRSH
EEK!
HUH ...?

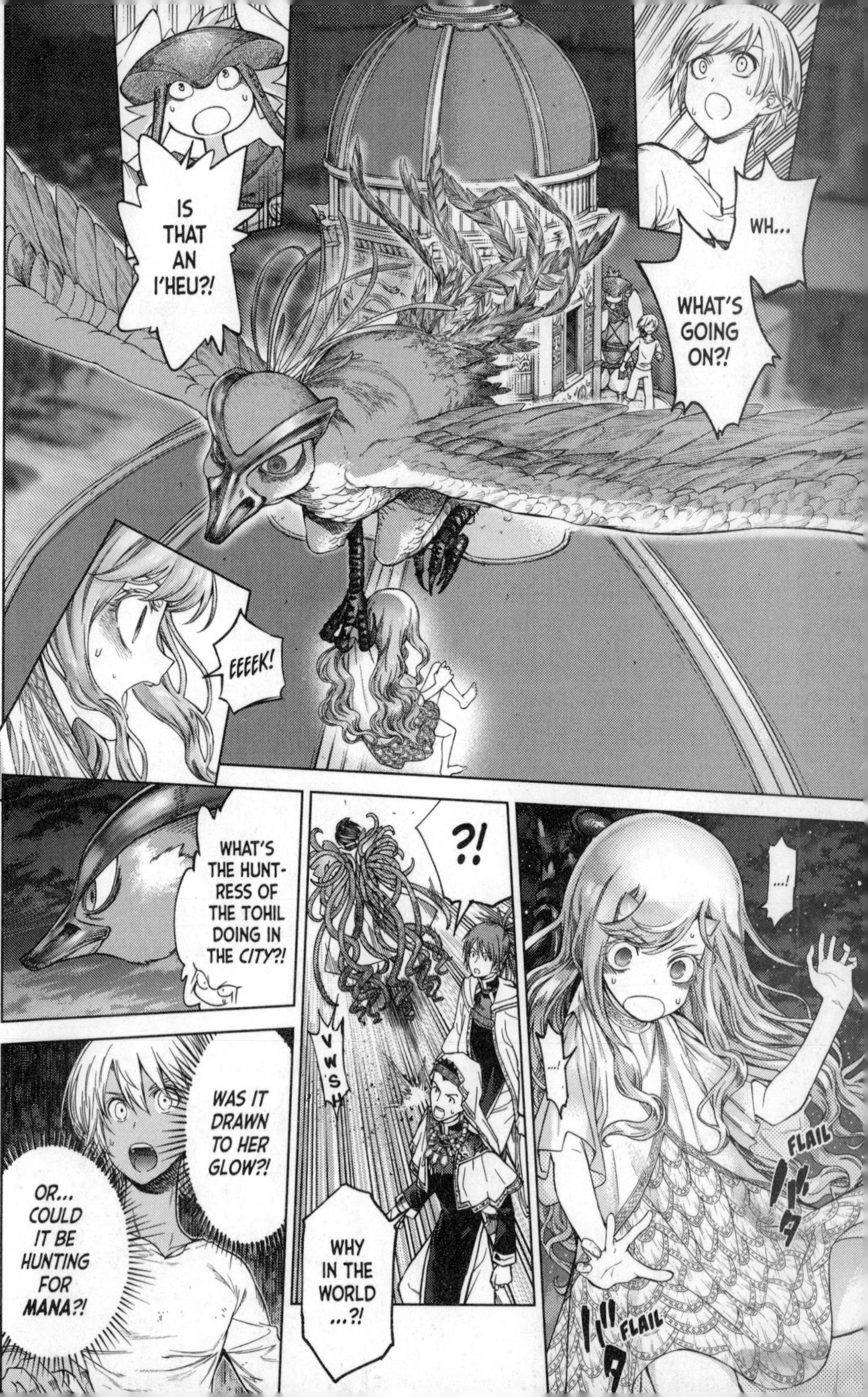
WH...
WHAT'S GOING ON?!
IS THAT AN I'HEU?!
EEEEK!
...!
...!
FLAIL
FLAIL
?!
VWSH
WHY IN THE WORLD ...?!
WHAT'S THE HUNTRESS OF THE TOHIL DOING IN THE CITY?!
WAS IT DRAWN TO HER GLOW?!
OR... COULD IT BE HUNTING FOR MANA?!

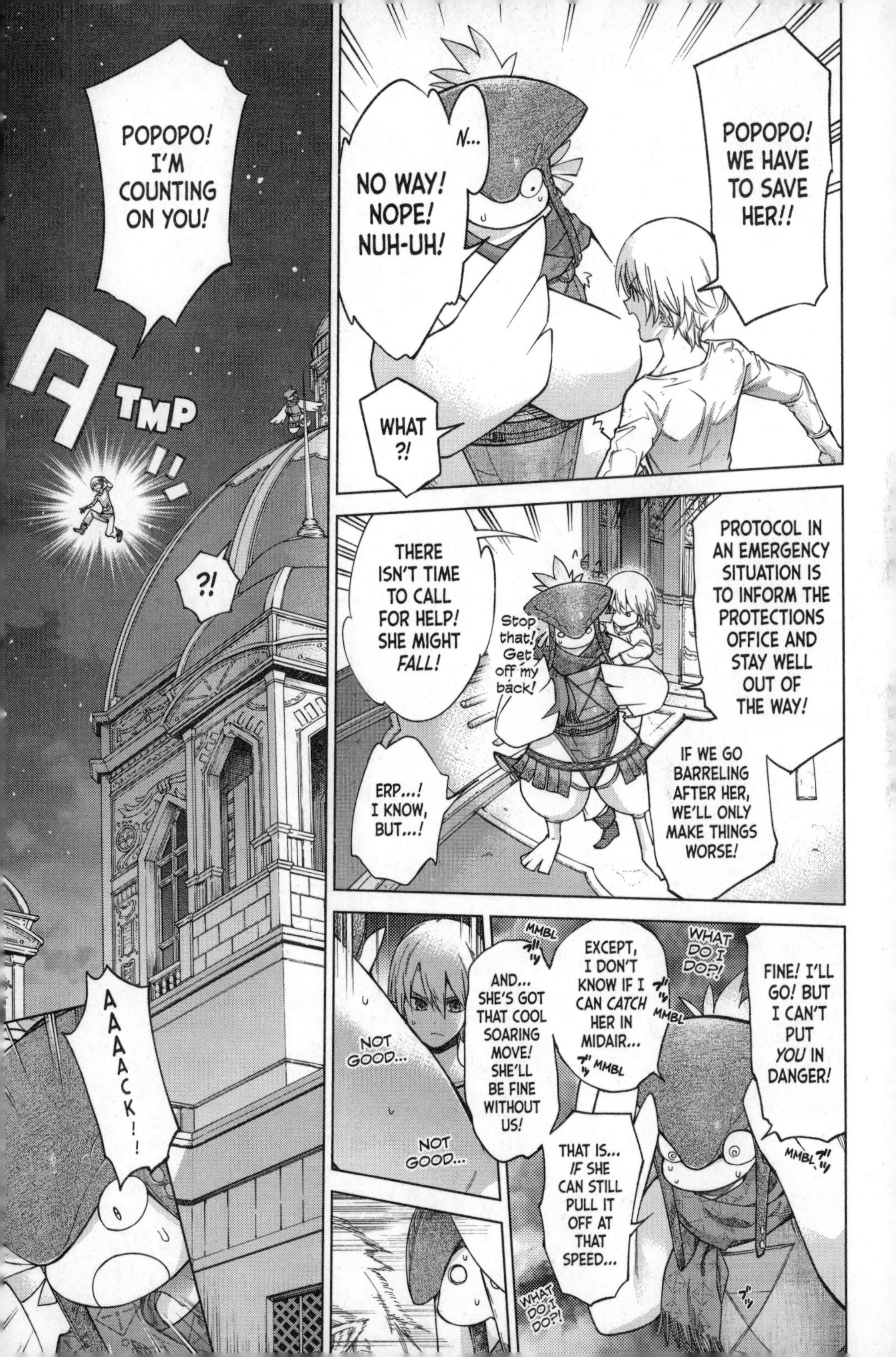
POPOPO! WE HAVE TO SAVE HER!!
N...
NO WAY! NOPE! NUH-UH!
WHAT ?!
PROTOCOL IN AN EMERGENCY SITUATION IS TO INFORM THE PROTECTIONS OFFICE AND STAY WELL OUT OF THE WAY!
THERE ISN'T TIME TO CALL FOR HELP! SHE MIGHT *FALL*!
Stop that! Get off my back!
IF WE GO BARRELING AFTER HER, WE'LL ONLY MAKE THINGS WORSE!
ERP...! I KNOW, BUT...!
FINE! I'LL GO! BUT I CAN'T PUT *YOU* IN DANGER!
WHAT DO I DO?!
EXCEPT, I DON'T KNOW IF I CAN *CATCH* HER IN MIDAIR...
MMBL
MMBL
MMBL
AND... SHE'S GOT THAT COOL SOARING MOVE! SHE'LL BE FINE WITHOUT US!
NOT GOOD...
MMBL
THAT IS... *IF* SHE CAN STILL PULL IT OFF AT THAT SPEED...
NOT GOOD...
WHAT DO I DO?!
POPOPO! I'M COUNTING ON YOU!
TMP!!
?!
AAAACK!!

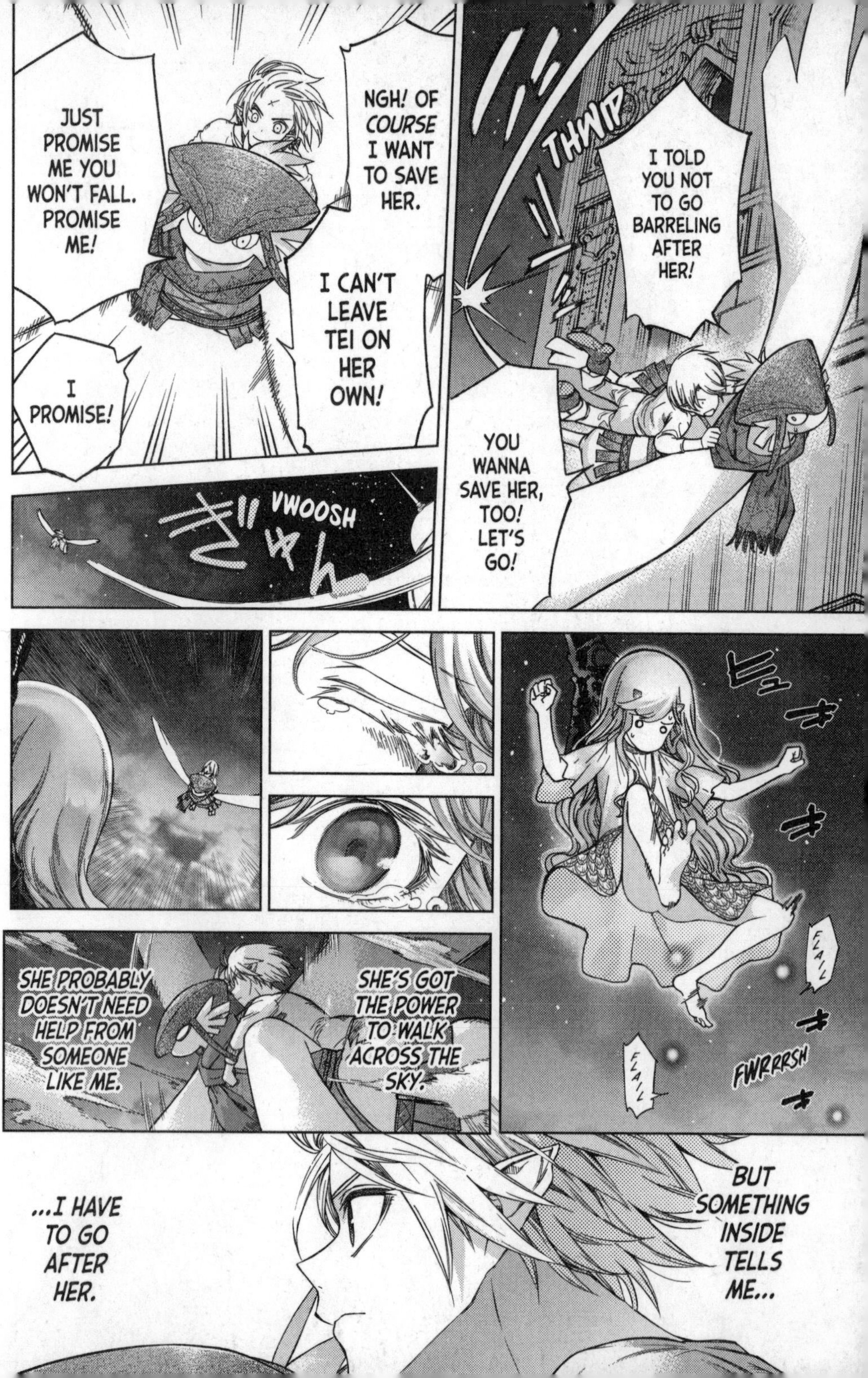
THWIP
I TOLD YOU NOT TO GO BARRELING AFTER HER!
YOU WANNA SAVE HER, TOO! LET'S GO!
NGH! OF COURSE I WANT TO SAVE HER.
JUST PROMISE ME YOU WON'T FALL. PROMISE ME!
I CAN'T LEAVE TEI ON HER OWN!
I PROMISE!
ぎゅん
VWOOSH
FLAIL
FLAIL
FWRRRSH
SHE'S GOT THE POWER TO WALK ACROSS THE SKY.
SHE PROBABLY DOESN'T NEED HELP FROM SOMEONE LIKE ME.
BUT SOMETHING INSIDE TELLS ME...
...I HAVE TO GO AFTER HER.

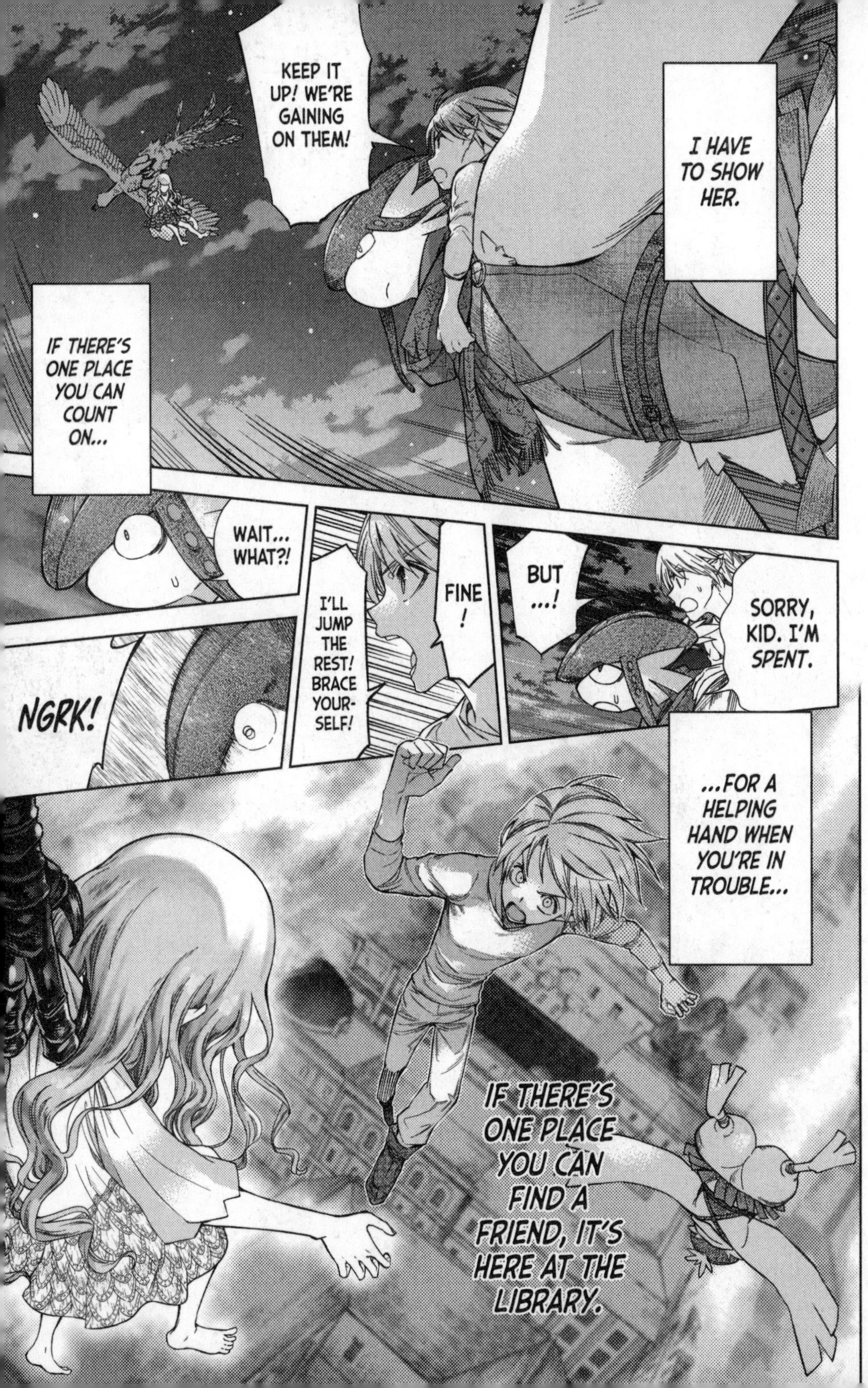
I HAVE TO SHOW HER.
KEEP IT UP! WE'RE GAINING ON THEM!
IF THERE'S ONE PLACE YOU CAN COUNT ON...
SORRY, KID. I'M SPENT.
BUT ...!
FINE!
I'LL JUMP THE REST! BRACE YOURSELF!
WAIT... WHAT?!
NGRK!
...FOR A HELPING HAND WHEN YOU'RE IN TROUBLE...
IF THERE'S ONE PLACE YOU CAN FIND A FRIEND, IT'S HERE AT THE LIBRARY.

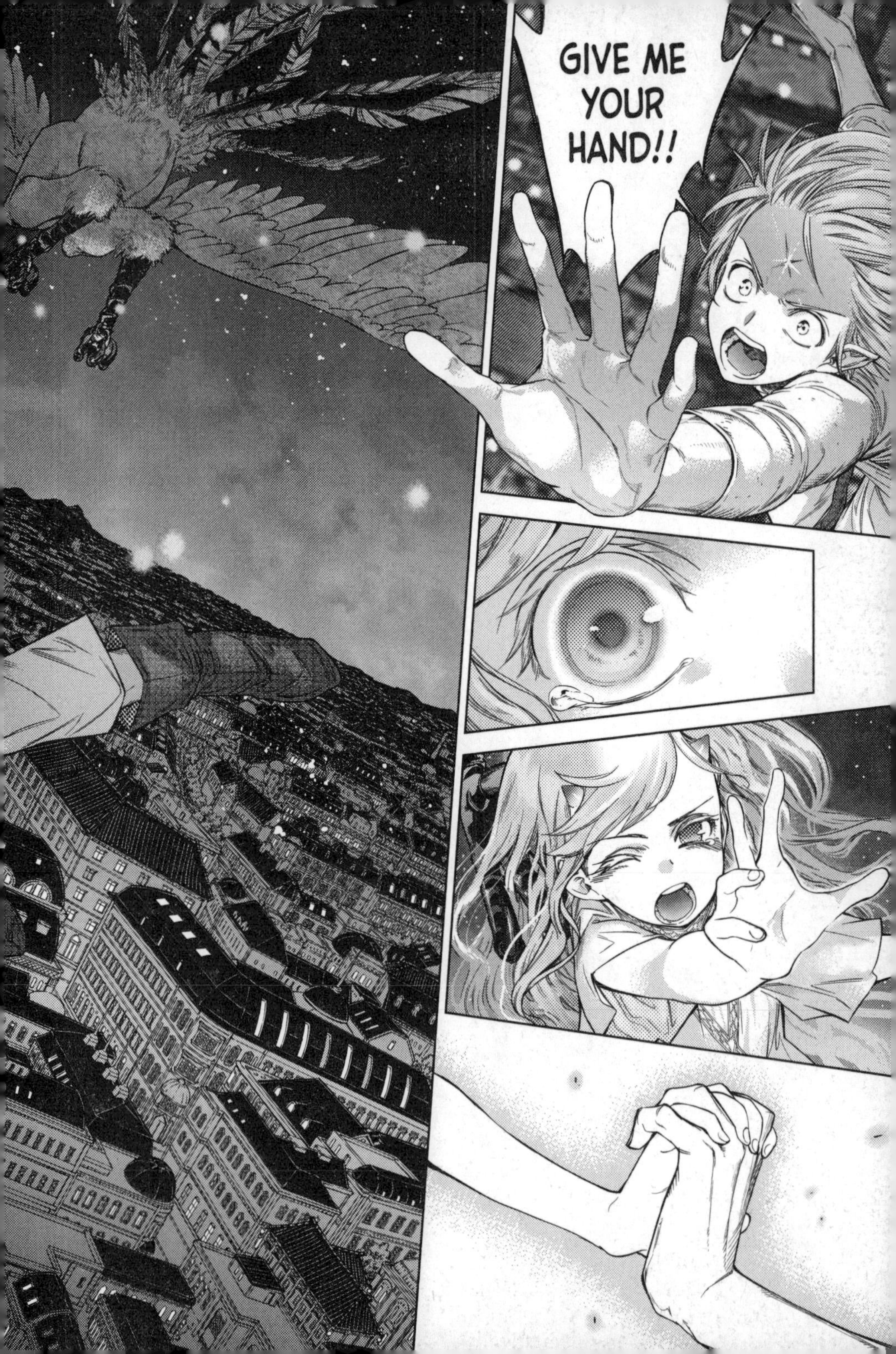
GIVE ME YOUR HAND!!

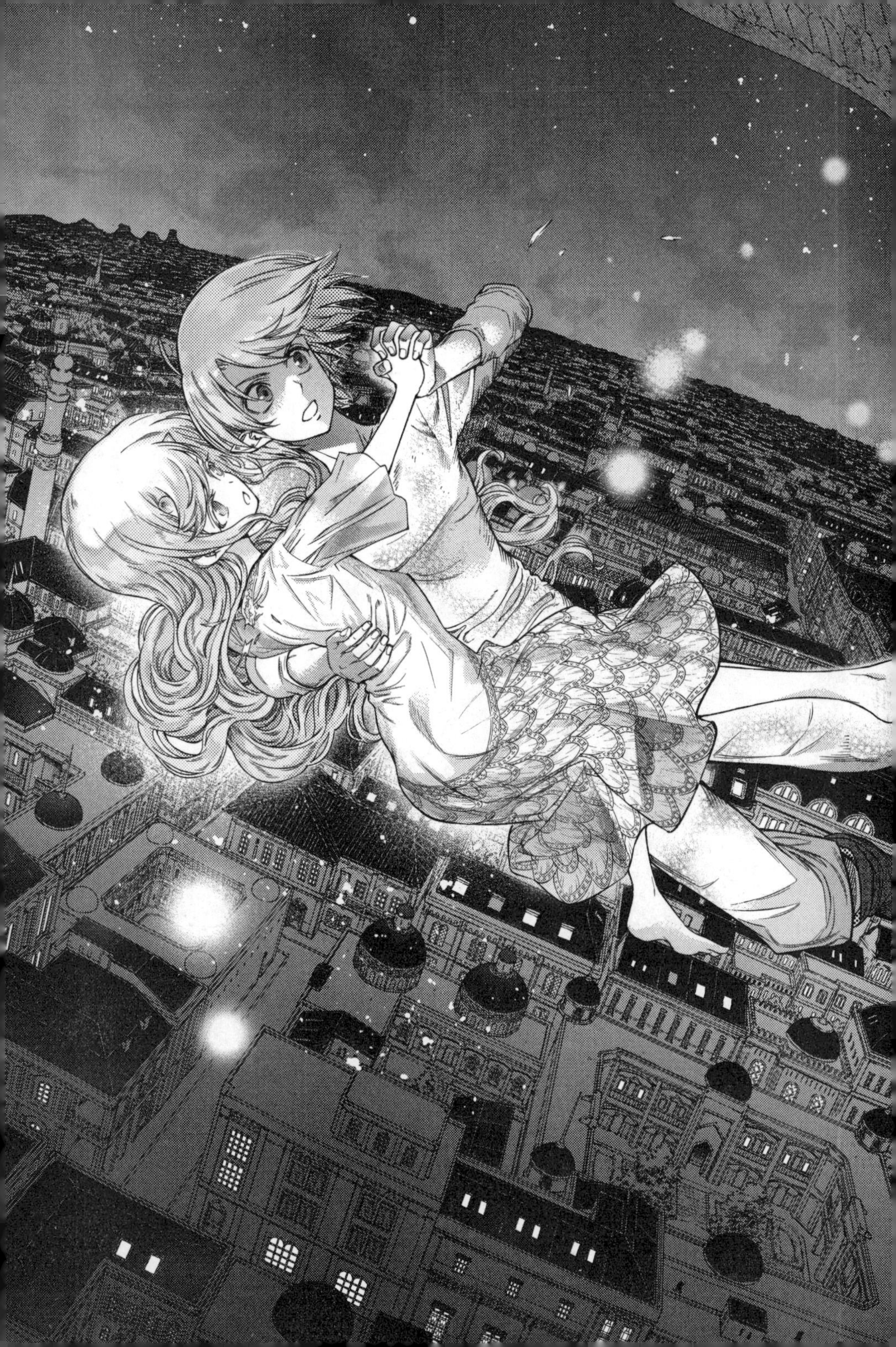

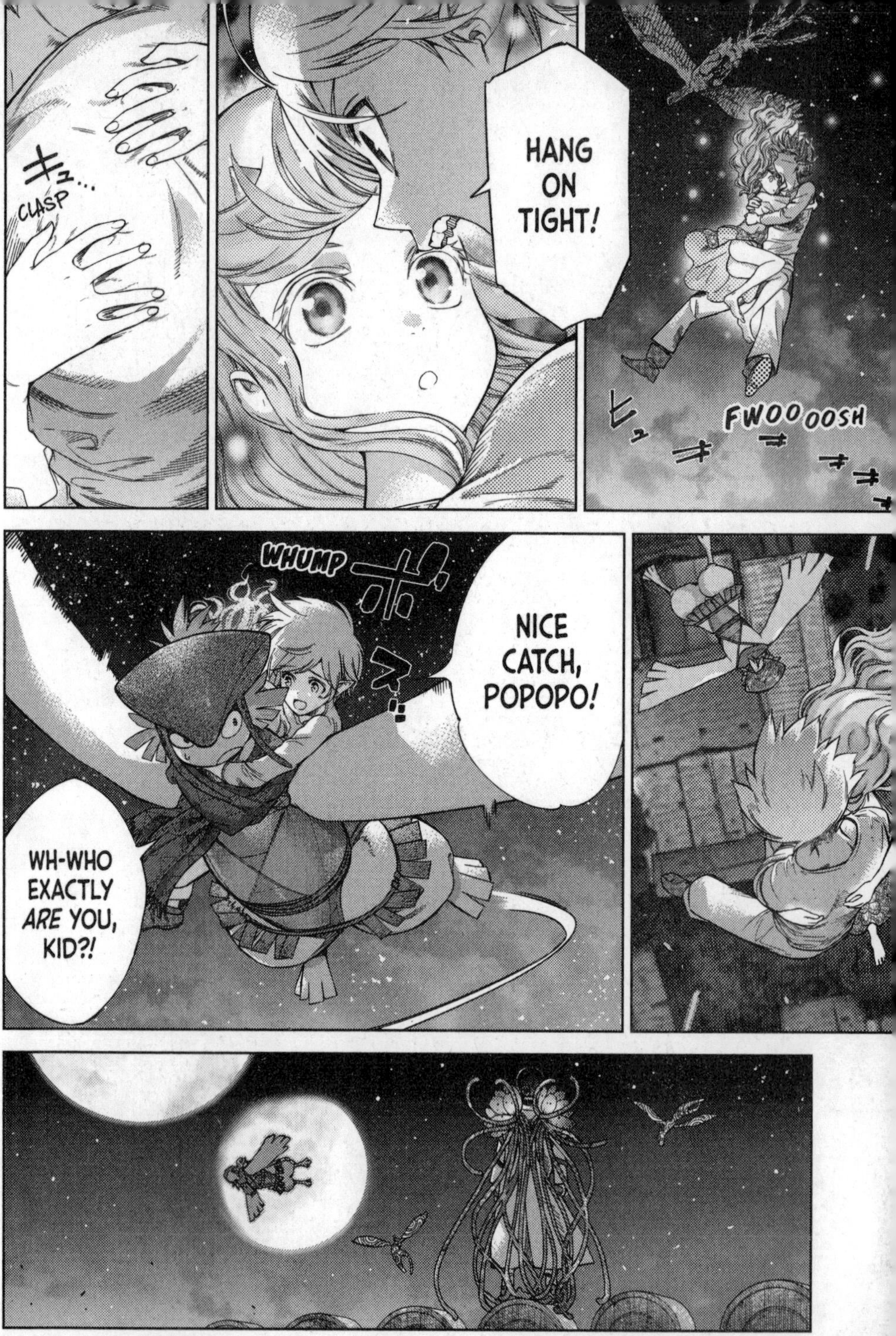
FWOOOOOSH
HANG ON TIGHT!
キュ…
CLASP
WHUMP
NICE CATCH, POPOPO!
WH-WHO EXACTLY *ARE* YOU, KID?!

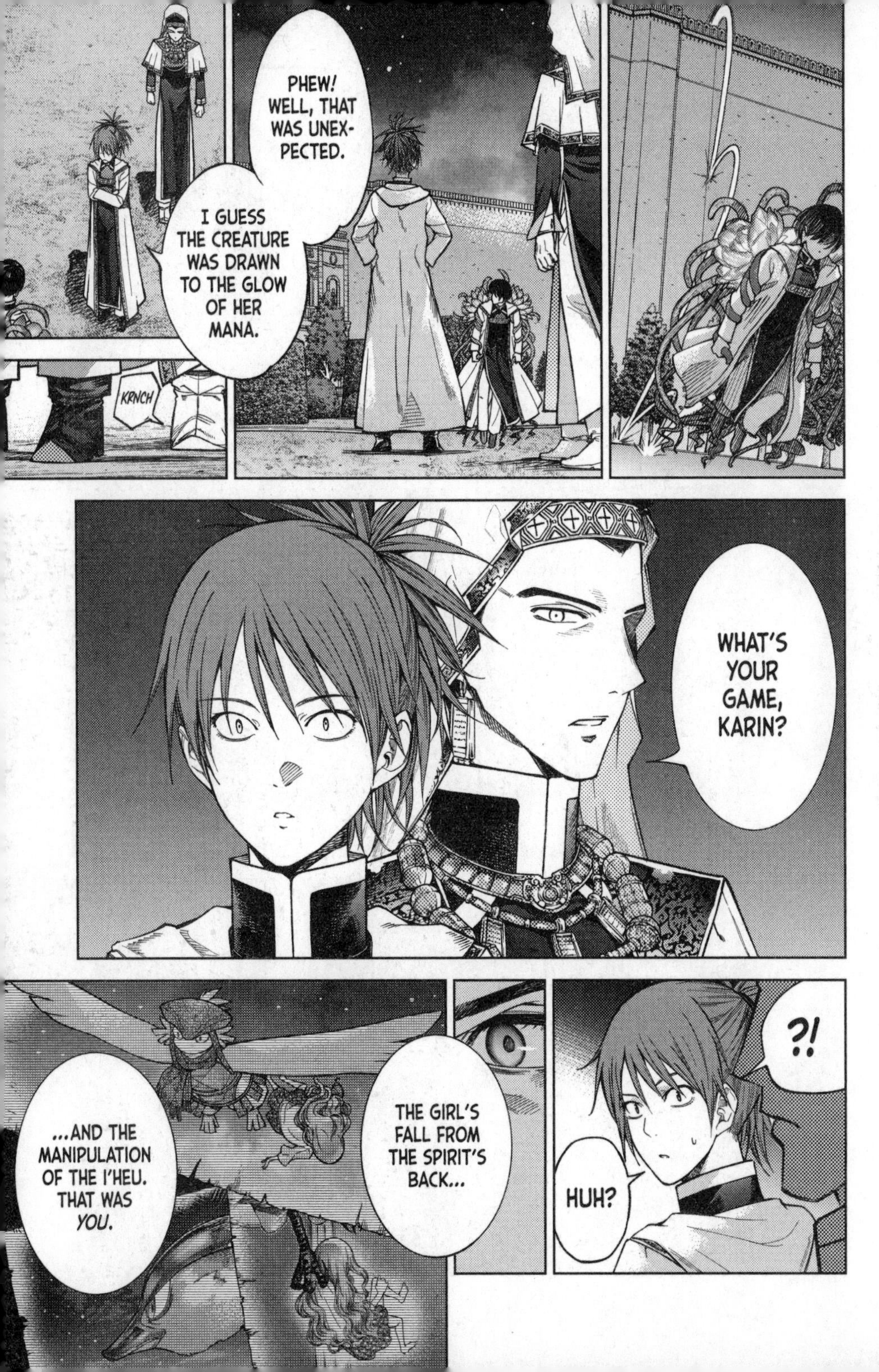
PHEW! WELL, THAT WAS UNEXPECTED.
I GUESS THE CREATURE WAS DRAWN TO THE GLOW OF HER MANA.
KRNCH
WHAT'S YOUR GAME, KARIN?
?!
HUH?
THE GIRL'S FALL FROM THE SPIRIT'S BACK...
...AND THE MANIPULATION OF THE I'HEU. THAT WAS *YOU*.

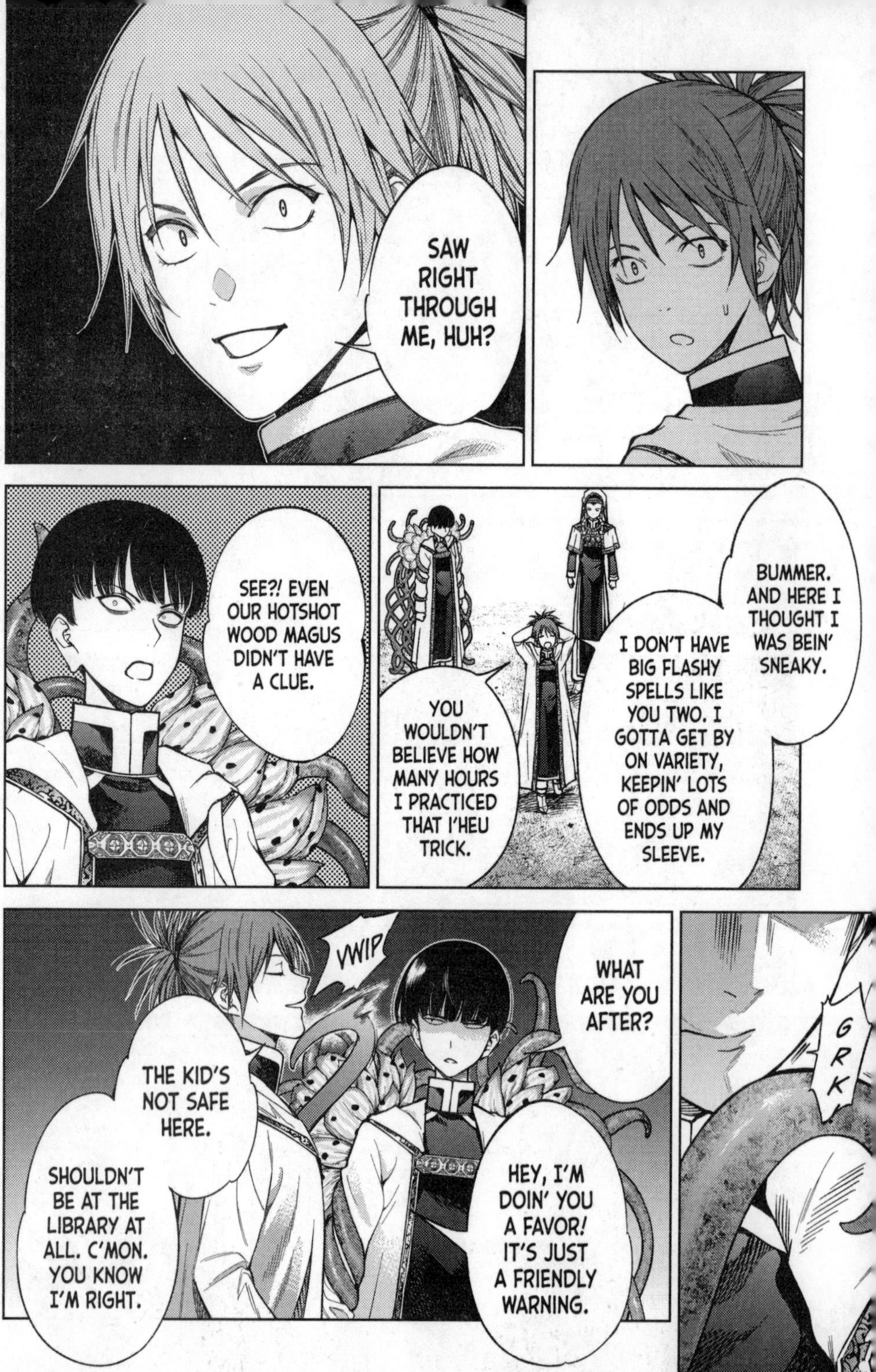
SAW RIGHT THROUGH ME, HUH?
BUMMER. AND HERE I THOUGHT I WAS BEIN' SNEAKY.
I DON'T HAVE BIG FLASHY SPELLS LIKE YOU TWO. I GOTTA GET BY ON VARIETY, KEEPIN' LOTS OF ODDS AND ENDS UP MY SLEEVE.
YOU WOULDN'T BELIEVE HOW MANY HOURS I PRACTICED THAT I'HEU TRICK.
SEE?! EVEN OUR HOTSHOT WOOD MAGUS DIDN'T HAVE A CLUE.
GRK
WHAT ARE YOU AFTER?
VWIP
THE KID'S NOT SAFE HERE.
HEY, I'M DOIN' YOU A FAVOR! IT'S JUST A FRIENDLY WARNING.
SHOULDN'T BE AT THE LIBRARY AT ALL. C'MON. YOU KNOW I'M RIGHT.

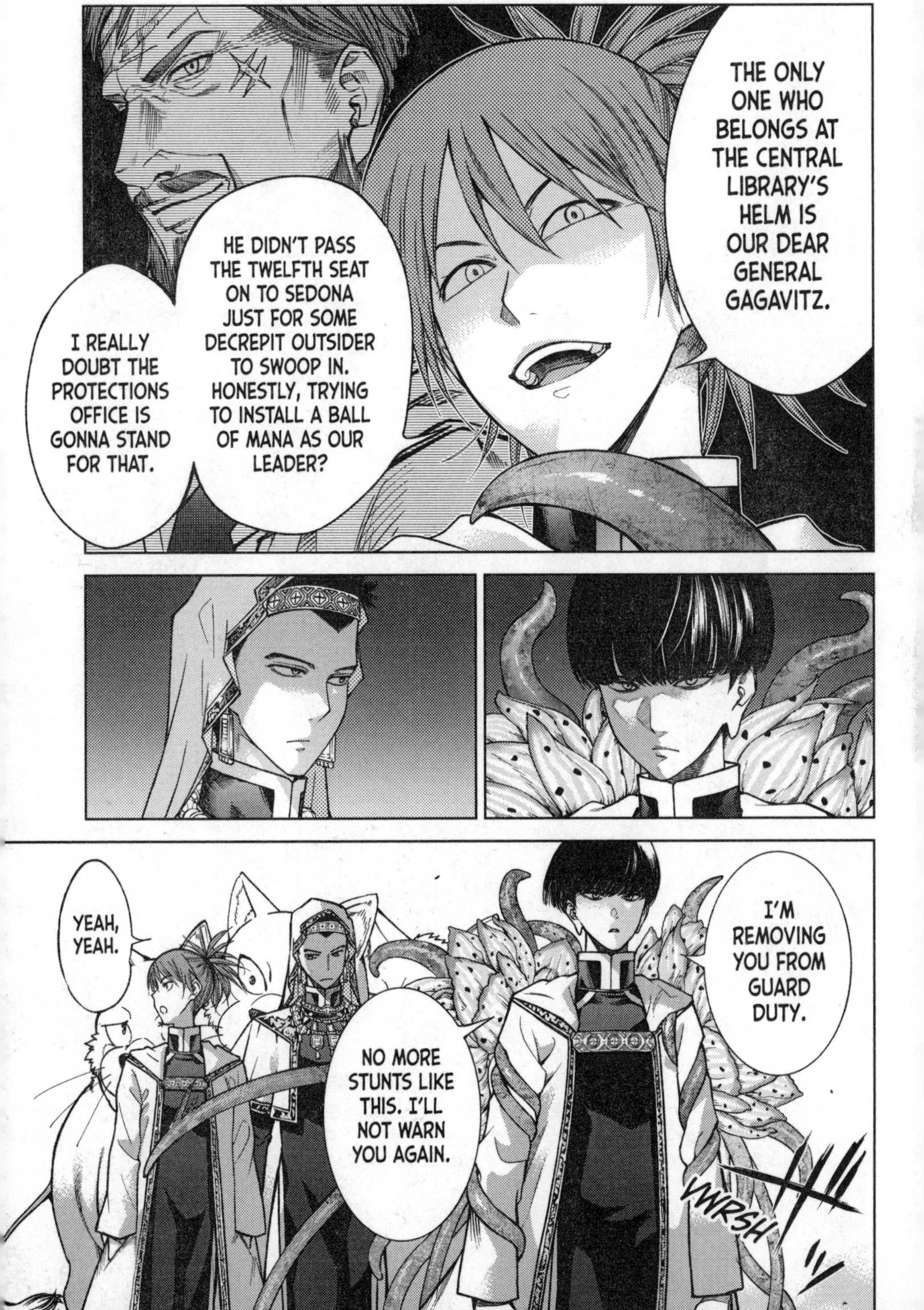
THE ONLY ONE WHO BELONGS AT THE CENTRAL LIBRARY'S HELM IS OUR DEAR GENERAL GAGAVITZ.
HE DIDN'T PASS THE TWELFTH SEAT ON TO SEDONA JUST FOR SOME DECREPIT OUTSIDER TO SWOOP IN. HONESTLY, TRYING TO INSTALL A BALL OF MANA AS OUR LEADER?
I REALLY DOUBT THE PROTECTIONS OFFICE IS GONNA STAND FOR THAT.
I'M REMOVING YOU FROM GUARD DUTY.
VWRSH
NO MORE STUNTS LIKE THIS. I'LL NOT WARN YOU AGAIN.
YEAH, YEAH.

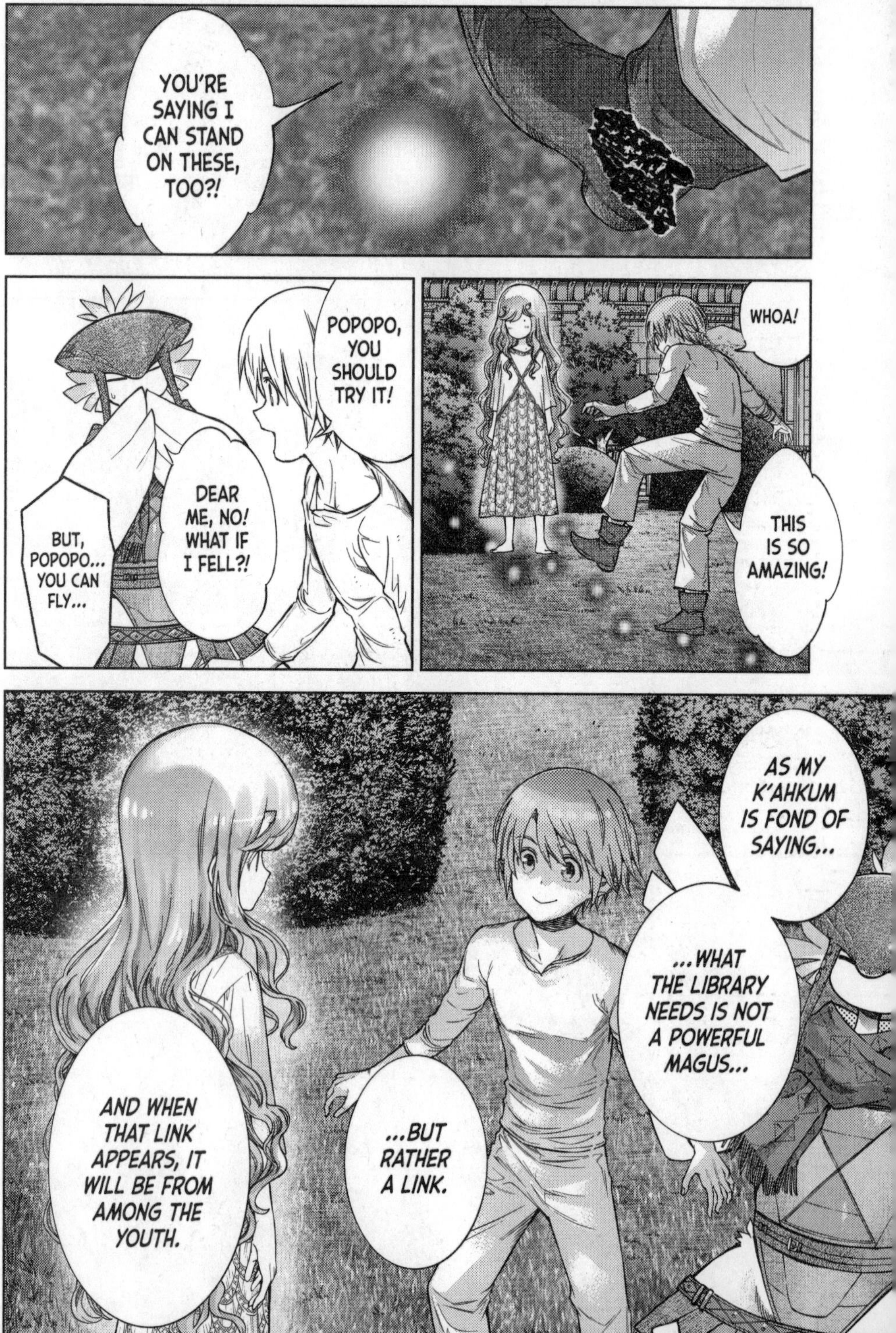
YOU'RE SAYING I CAN STAND ON THESE, TOO?!
WHOA!
THIS IS SO AMAZING!
POPOPO, YOU SHOULD TRY IT!
DEAR ME, NO! WHAT IF I FELL?!
BUT, POPOPO... YOU CAN FLY...
AS MY K'AHKUM IS FOND OF SAYING...
...WHAT THE LIBRARY NEEDS IS NOT A POWERFUL MAGUS...
...BUT RATHER A LINK.
AND WHEN THAT LINK APPEARS, IT WILL BE FROM AMONG THE YOUTH.

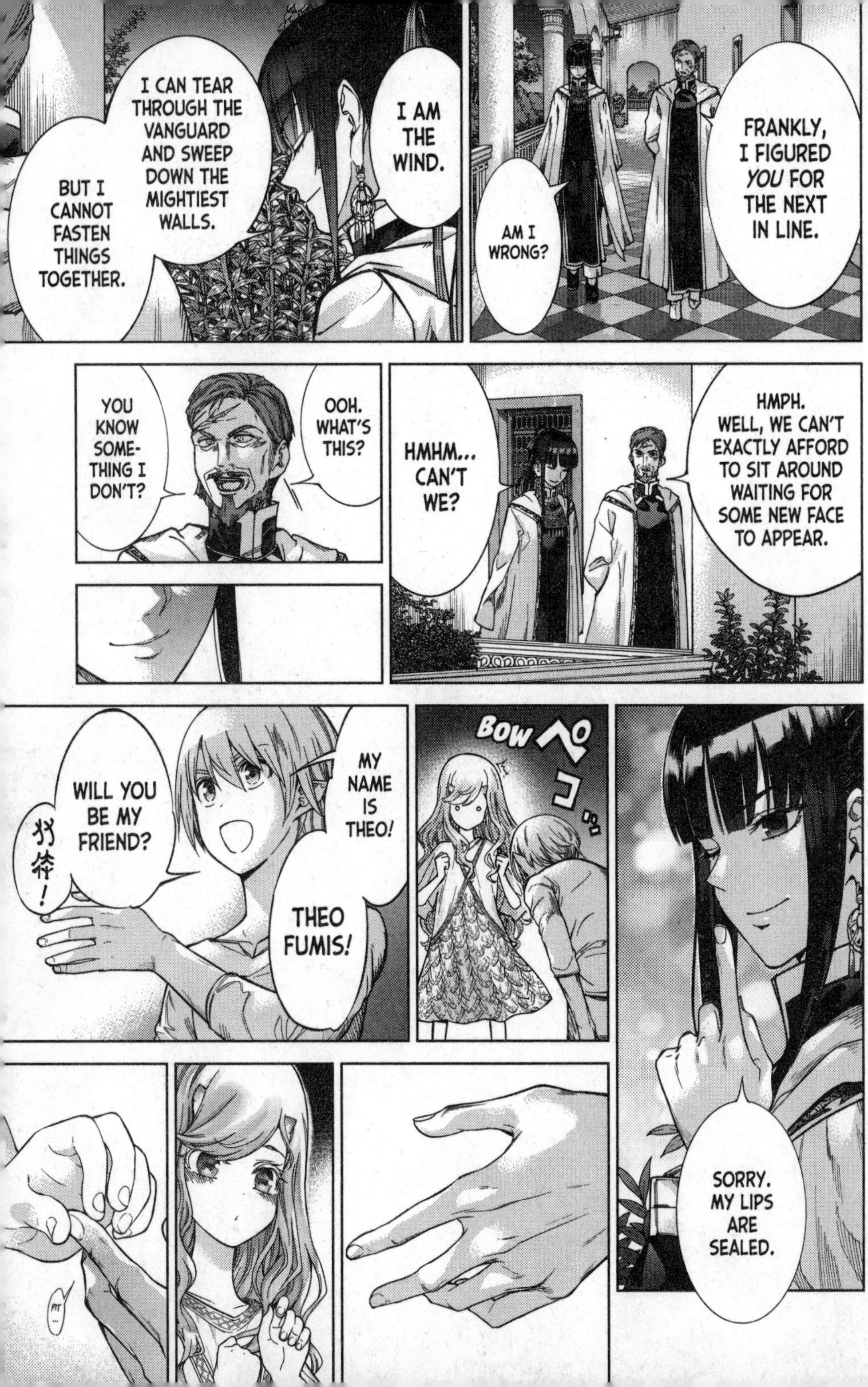
FRANKLY, I FIGURED *YOU* FOR THE NEXT IN LINE.
AM I WRONG?
I AM THE WIND.
I CAN TEAR THROUGH THE VANGUARD AND SWEEP DOWN THE MIGHTIEST WALLS.
BUT I CANNOT FASTEN THINGS TOGETHER.
HMPH. WELL, WE CAN'T EXACTLY AFFORD TO SIT AROUND WAITING FOR SOME NEW FACE TO APPEAR.
HMHM... CAN'T WE?
OOH. WHAT'S THIS?
YOU KNOW SOME-THING I DON'T?
SORRY. MY LIPS ARE SEALED.
BOW
ペコ
MY NAME IS THEO!
THEO FUMIS!
WILL YOU BE MY FRIEND?
PIT...

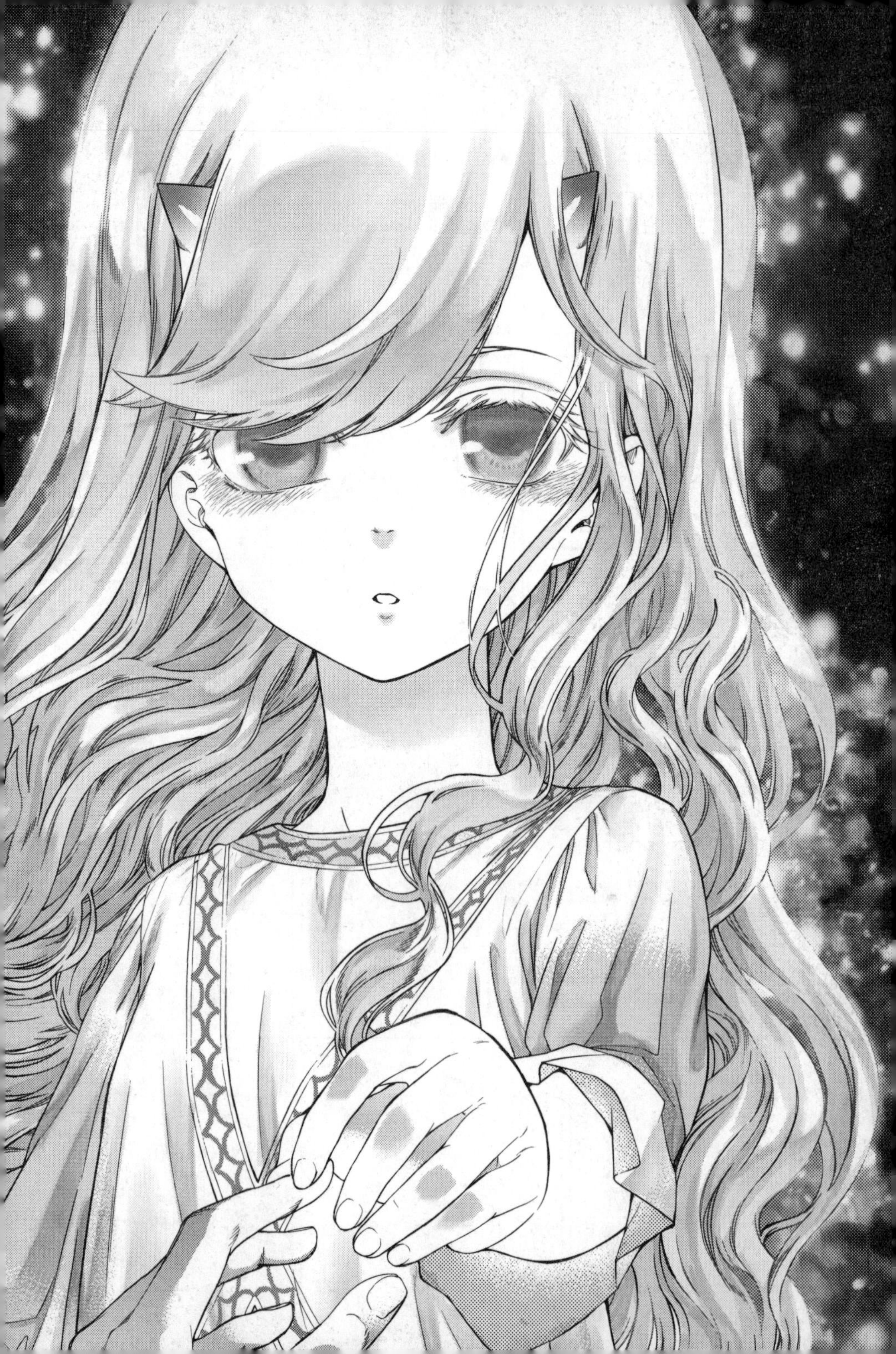

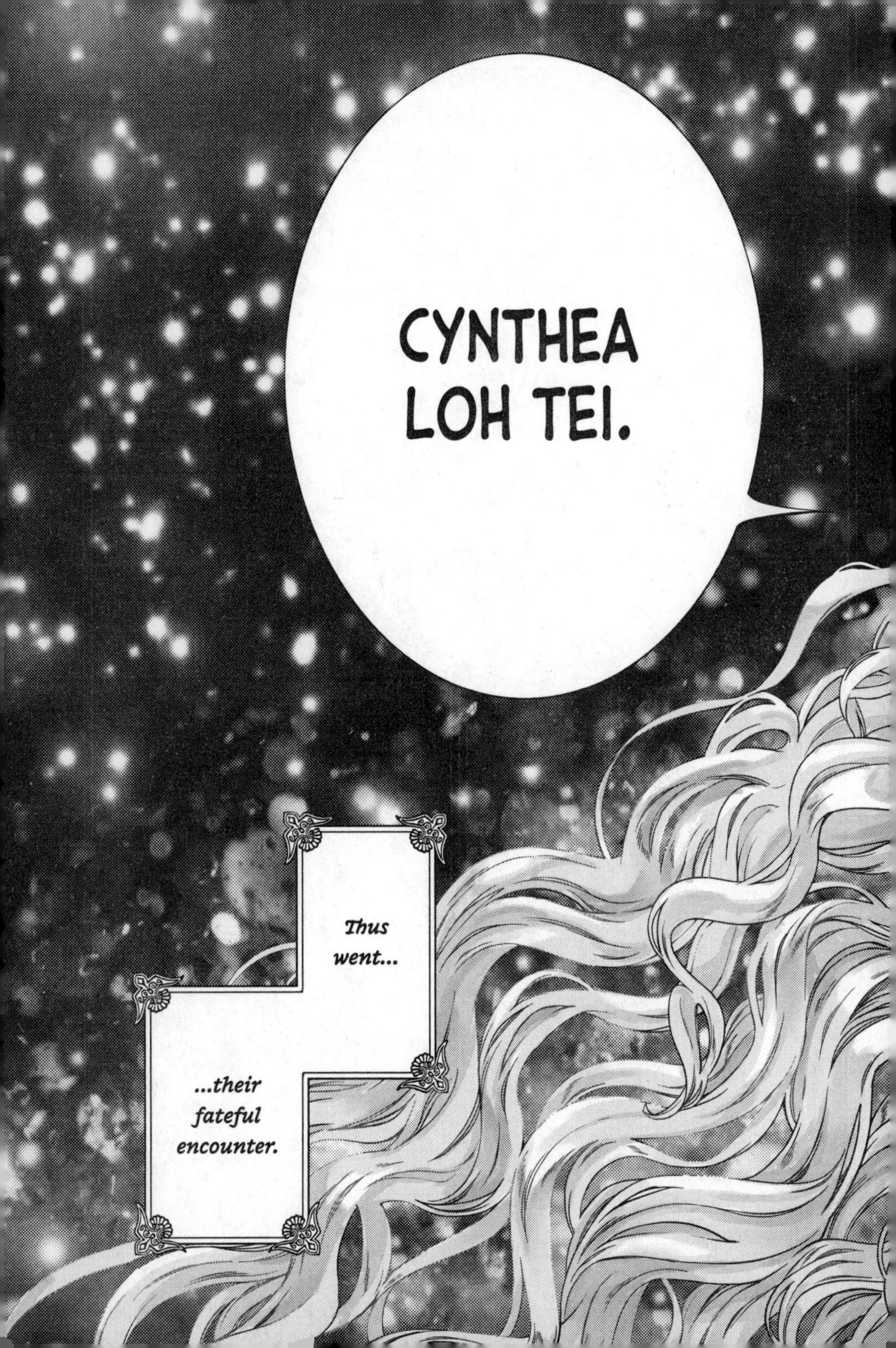
CYNTHEA LOH TEI.
Thus went...
...their fateful encounter.

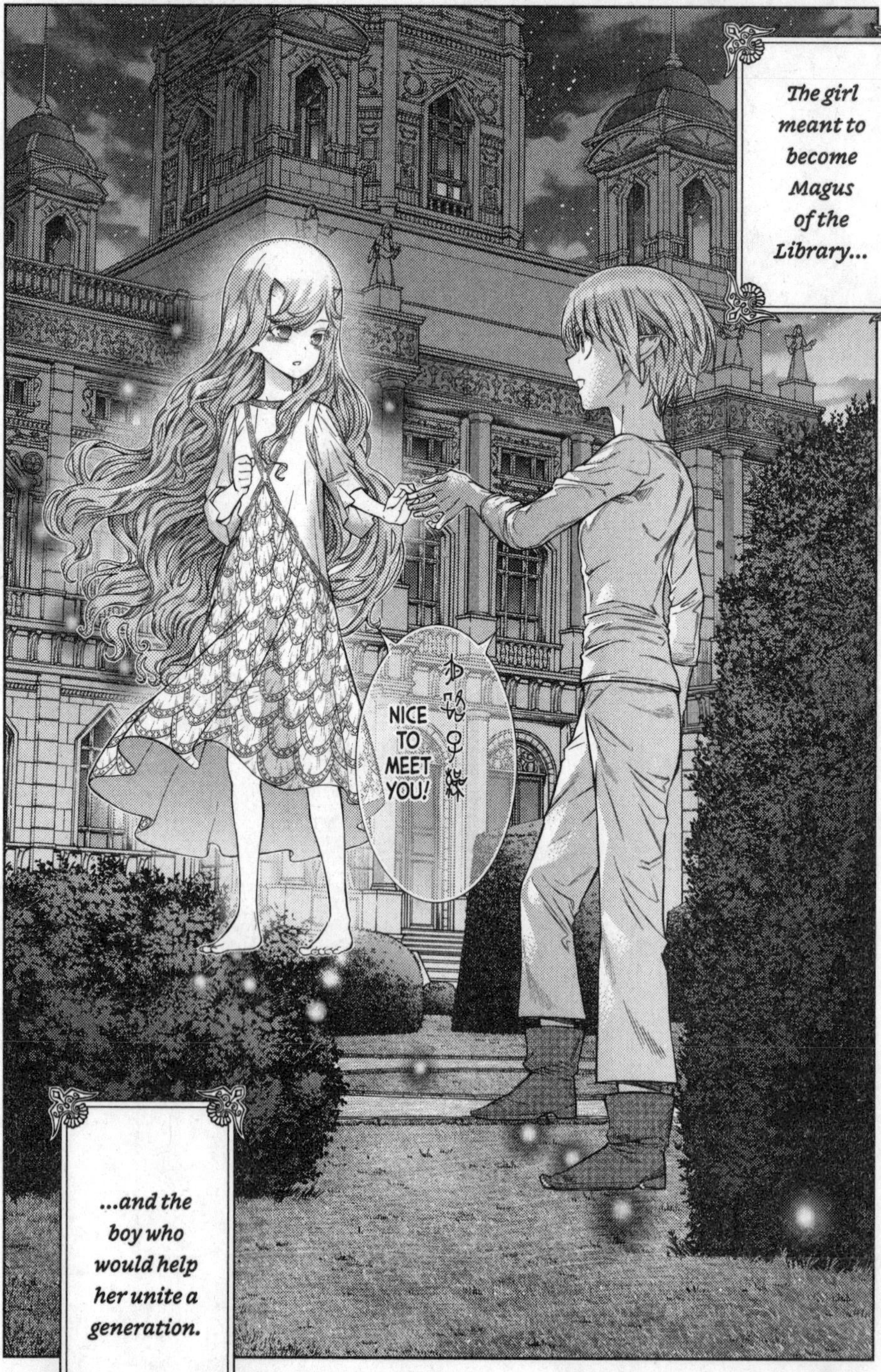
The girl meant to become Magus of the Library...
NICE TO MEET YOU!
...and the boy who would help her unite a generation.

PAT
さす
さす
PAT

To be continued.

◆──●──Magus of the Library──●──◆

Magus of the Library 5 is a work of fiction. Names, characters, places, and incidents are the products of the author's imagination or are used fictitiously. Any resemblance to actual events, locales, or persons, living or dead, is entirely coincidental.

A Kodansha Comics Trade Paperback Original

Published in the United States by Kodansha Comics, an imprint of Kodansha USA Publishing, LLC, New York.

Publication rights for this English edition arranged through Kodansha Ltd., Tokyo.

First published in Japan in 2021 by Kodansha Ltd., Tokyo as *Toshokan no daimajutsushi*, volume 5.

ISBN 978-1-64651-213-3

Printed in the United States of America.

www.kodansha.us
1st Printing

Translation: Stephen Kohler
Lettering: Paige Pumphrey
Editing: Ryan Holmberg
Kodansha Comics edition cover design by Phil Balsman

KC
KODANSHA COMICS

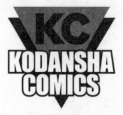

Publisher: Kiichiro Sugawara

Director of publishing services: Ben Applegate
Associate director of operations: Stephen Pakula
Publishing services managing editorial: Madison Salters, Alanna Ruse
Production managers: Emi Lotto, Angela Zurlo